CANADIAN LAW AND INDIGENOUS SELF-DETERMINATION

A Naturalist Analysis

Gordon Christie

For centuries, Canadian sovereignty has existed uneasily alongside forms of Indigenous legal and political authority. *Canadian Law and Indigenous Self-Determination* demonstrates how, over the last few decades, Canadian law has attempted to remove Indigenous sovereignty from the Canadian legal and social landscape. Adopting a naturalist analysis, Gordon Christie responds to questions about how to theorize this legal phenomenon and how the study of law should accommodate the presence of diverse perspectives. Exploring the socially constructed nature of Canadian law, Christie reveals how legal meaning – understood to be the outcome of a specific society – is being reworked to devalue the capacities of Indigenous societies.

Addressing liberal positivism and critical postcolonial theory, *Canadian Law and Indigenous Self-Determination* considers how Canadian jurists, working in a world circumscribed by liberal thought, have deployed the law in such a way as to attempt to remove Indigenous meaning-generating capacity from the Canadian legal landscape.

GORDON CHRISTIE is professor in the Peter A. Allard School of Law at the University of British Columbia.

GORDON CHRISTIE

Canadian Law and Indigenous Self-Determination

A Naturalist Analysis

UNIVERSITY OF TORONTO PRESS
Toronto Buffalo London

Toronto Buffalo London
utorontopress.com

ISBN 978-1-4426-3751-1 (cloth) ISBN 978-1-4426-2899-1 (paper)

Library and Archives Canada Cataloguing in Publication

Title: Canadian law and indigenous self-determination : a naturalist analysis / Gordon Christie.
Names: Christie, Gordon (LL. B.), author.
Description: Includes bibliographical references and index.
Identifiers: Canadiana 20190115521 | ISBN 9781442628991 (paper) | ISBN 9781442637511 (cloth)
Subjects: LCSH: Indians of North America – Civil rights – Canada. | LCSH: Indians of North America – Legal status, laws, etc. – Canada. | LCSH: Sociological jurisprudence – Canada.
Classification: LCC KE7722.C5 .C57 2019 | LCC KF8205 .C57 2019 kfmod | DDC 342.7108/72—dc23

This book has been published with the help of a grant from the Federation for the Humanities and Social Sciences, through the Awards to Scholarly Publications Programme, using funds provided by the Social Sciences and Humanities Research Council of Canada.

University of Toronto Press acknowledges the financial assistance to its publishing programme of the Canada Council for the Arts and the Ontario Arts Council, an agency of the Government of Ontario.

Canada Council for the Arts Conseil des Arts du Canada

Funded by the Government of Canada | Financé par le gouvernement du Canada | Canada

Contents

CANADIAN LAW AND INDIGENOUS SELF-DETERMINATION

A Naturalist Analysis

Introduction: A Journey in Making Sense

This text tracks my quest to make sense of Aboriginal law in Canada, with a focus on Aboriginal rights. "Aboriginal law in Canada" refers to Canadian law as it applies to the situations and lives of Aboriginal people and communities.[1] As a field of domestic Canadian law, it emanates from legislative and judicial bodies of Canada[2] and is the law that courts of Canada work with when making determinations about the respective rights and obligations of Aboriginal and non-Aboriginal peoples and governments. It is the kind of law the vast bulk of law students study, should they have an interest in (or need to learn about) "Aboriginal issues."[3]

This text does not, however, provide a simple unpacking of Aboriginal law. My quest has been intellectually arduous, and this work records a difficult journey. It is a journey made difficult by labyrinthine jurisprudence presenting a deeply puzzling face and the presence of strong disagreement from observers as to what the law seems to express and the nature of impacts it has had on lives

1 I distinguish in this work between "Aboriginal peoples" and "Indigenous peoples." "Aboriginal peoples" refers to three groups identified by – and indeed arguably defined by – Canadian constitutional law, as "Indians, Inuit, and Métis" who are identified as "Aboriginal peoples" with rights under section 35 of the *Constitution Act, 1982*, being Schedule B to the *Canada Act 1982* (UK), 1982, c 11 [*Constitution Act, 1982*]. "Indigenous peoples," on the other hand, I use to refer to peoples with histories that predate European contact in North America, peoples whose identities are fixed internally – that is, from *within* these communities.

2 In select contexts, like that of treaty making, the executive branch can "make law" through such instruments as negotiated agreements, though these agreements are subject to ratification by legislation.

3 Amongst other matters, Aboriginal law (a) serves to define who counts as an "Aboriginal" person, (b) determines the manner by which many Aboriginal communities are structured and managed (via such instruments as the *Indian Act*, RSC 1985, c I-5), (c) sets out what counts as a treaty and what such legal/constitutional instruments mean and entail, and (d) determines the nature and extent of Aboriginal rights and title.

and peoples. Equally challenging are quagmires produced by inefficacious legal theory. Not only do mainstream and critical theories move off in completely different directions, but they seem to do so as a result of grounding in fundamentally different presumptions about human nature and the nature of reality itself. Working out how to theorize about Aboriginal law turned out to be one of the more daunting hurdles to overcome before sense could be made of what Canadian courts and legislators have been up in to the last few decades.

A moment's reflection on the situation before us casts light on key reasons why making sense of Aboriginal law should be so challenging. Chronicling the development of Aboriginal law is not a simple matter of tracing efforts by domestic courts to deal with a challenging domestic matter – rather, courts of the Canadian state have been constructing law meant to regulate the lives of *Indigenous* peoples, peoples related to but also distinct from the "Aboriginal peoples" whose rights are now "recognized and affirmed" in Canada's constitution. Indigenous communities have histories stretching out to times *before* the Canadian state (and its European predecessors) asserted legislative and judicial control over what is now the territorial extent of this liberal democracy. The phenomena to be explored have specific and troubling characteristics, as they implicate the imposition of Crown sovereignty upon peoples with prior intimate ties to this one land, upon peoples with continuing claims to be self-determining, upon peoples with independent legal and political authority. How is one to make sense of law that washes over other self-determining entities – indeed, of law that seems implicated in efforts to remove these competing authorities?

When one sees that Canadian law does not even entertain questions about these fundamentally troubling matters – when one sees it begins with and is grounded upon the *presumption* of Crown sovereignty over Indigenous territories and peoples – the strangeness of this landscape opens up. This text begins from a distinct, different starting point – the fact of independent Indigenous legal and political authority – and attempts to make sense of the emergence of the doctrine of Aboriginal rights in light of that fact. In response to the failure of theory to provide a way to make reasonable sense of the entirety of the situation before us, a major component of this work is taken up with the construction of a theoretical framework within which sense can be made of what we witness when the laws of one society reach out over other legal and political systems, in this instance attempting to enfold within one non-Indigenous "reality" Indigenous peoples exercising independent authority.

The Complications of Theory

Societies build forms of social reality within which they live. Social roles and interactive structures emerge in varied forms in different societies, where each society gives these roles and structures meaning. Independent Indigenous societies, exercising legal and political authority, have their authority inextricably tied to their independent ways of generating meaning. So, for example, any particular Indigenous legal order exists as an aspect of the social world built by a specific Indigenous society according to meanings generated by this collective. This extends down to basic levels of social reality. What is "law" for any specific Indigenous community? It is what this collective vests with meaning, such that if called upon to translate it would say, "This is what we understand 'law' to be in our social world."[4]

These points apply as well to non-Indigenous societies – in particular to social worlds built and lived within by Canadian society. The Canadian legal system is itself a manifestation of meaning in the world – meaning generated by the society within which this social institution exists. When we trace the history of interaction between what becomes the Canadian Crown and Indigenous peoples over the last few centuries, we see the rise and dominance of forms of colonial dispossession, oppression, and destruction. Lands are taken and peoples are beaten down. But we also witness struggles over other forms of Indigenous self-determination, and in this work I focus on the interaction of Crown and independent Indigenous authority, when both are viewed as essentially being exercised in ways that reflect their groundings in separate meaning-generating social spheres.

The story told is of contemporary efforts, through development and deployment of the doctrine of Aboriginal rights, to remove the last vestiges of Indigenous self-determination from the Canadian landscape. The attempt is to pull Indigenous peoples fully and completely into worlds built according to non-Indigenous ways of thinking of such things as sovereignty, law, and authority. Once the independent meaning-generating abilities of Indigenous peoples are subsumed within the one system of meaning developed by

---

4 As with all these matters of translation, great care has to be exercised, as knowledge-holders from an Indigenous community are likely to be conscious of two distinct aspects of their social reality that might translate into "law" within non-Indigenous conceptions: those aspects that correspond, to some degree, with aspects of social life tightly controlled, and those aspects that correspond to how the group manages itself so as to flourish, with life-ways intimately tied to a place. So, for example, Mohawk scholar Patricia Monture-Angus speaks of the "Great Law of Peace," *Kaienerekowa*, which is translated by Mohawk knowledge-holder Tom Porter as "the way to live most nicely together," while Mariano Aupilaarjuk, an Inuit elder from the Eastern Arctic, describes an analogue to Western law in traditional Inuit belief systems: "*Tirigusungniit* are the rules relating to *pittailiniq*, things one should refrain from" (what one might think of as "taboos" in the language of anthropology). See Patricia Monture-Angus, *Journeying Forward: Dreaming First Nations' Independence* (Halifax: Fernwood, 1999) at 41; Mariano Aupilaarjuk, "Tirigusuusit and Maligait" in Jarich Oosten et al, eds, *Interviewing Inuit Elders: Perspectives on Traditional Law* (Iqaluit: Nunavut Arctic College, 1999), vol 2 at 16 [emphasis in original].

Canadian governments and courts, Indigenous self-determination fades from the landscape.

I present this ultimately not as a picture presented from an Indigenous perspective, but as the outcome of a naturalist examination into phenomena there for all to observe and study. What the text focuses on are ways in which different social worlds exist and interact in the one natural world before us. All independent societies exercise meaning-generating capacities in order to generate aspects of the social worlds they then inhabit, but we narrow our investigation to *one* form of *one* social world – the legal apparatus of Canadian society – and examine its attempts to apply itself to independently developed social worlds, those of Indigenous peoples.

Approached in this way, many aspects of the world before us that might otherwise appear confusing or irreconcilable now appear sensible. Puzzles about the doctrine of Aboriginal rights (that strike Indigenous peoples as profoundly perplexing) are made sensible as efforts by Canadian authorities to subvert Indigenous self-determination, lack of common understanding about what is happening in the Canadian legal landscape is revealed (at least partially) to be the result of differences in perspectives grounded in different worlds of meaning, and the incoherent array of available theories of Aboriginal law is shown to be the result of these theories often being directed not towards making sense of Aboriginal law but to the tasks of feeding into, maintaining, and strengthening efforts of Canadian society to subvert and destroy Indigenous self-determination.

The presence of deeply troubling puzzles within the jurisprudence, the lack of common understanding about what is transpiring, radical divergence within theoretical efforts at making sense, the lack of any attempt by legal scholars to pull accounts together along some defensible path, and the fact that key theories seem implicated in the construction of troubling aspects of the social reality being strongly impressed upon Indigenous peoples all call for the sort of inquiry with which I engage in the middle chapters of this work. I argue that while one must delve into theoretical accounts to begin to develop explanations that push past detailing *how* the law has developed to *why* we see what we do, ultimately even the business of theorizing has to be explored carefully if we are to arrive at sufficiently rich, insightful, and defensible accounts. The fact is, I argue, theoretical accounts of Aboriginal law themselves tend to express particular perspectives, and this fact needs to be properly analysed in order for Aboriginal law to be explained in a way that promises a measure of objectivity.

Grounding analysis in facts and processes in the natural world in this manner joins the political with the cultural, placing both in a frame that permits their study in an objective manner, and opens the door to questions about how one can go about making sense of the domestic law of the state meant to remove the perspectives – the forms of meaning – generated by Indigenous peoples. Indeed, it is in asking questions about how law is generated, the role perspectives play in the creation of aspects of social reality, and about how law can be aimed at the destruction of meaning-generating communities that we are led into an investigation into roles that theories of the law may themselves play as manifestations of the generation of meaning in the social world.

Including theories grounded in sociocultural communities in the larger category of "perspectives," I argue that, for their proper examination, *perspectives themselves* must be situated in the natural world. This naturalistic examination then focuses on how perspectives (including certain theoretical accounts) function in relation to the jurisprudence on Aboriginal rights. Given that this is an unusual approach to the business of making sense of an aspect of the law of a liberal democracy, this text contains some weighty discourse on what this approach entails, why it is best suited for the task at hand, and how it functions to make sense of the intersection of law and perspectives on law.

The application of this approach to the jurisprudence on Aboriginal rights leads to the conclusion that a liberal theoretical model of the case law does indeed "make sense" of much of what we witness, but at the cost of being shown not to be a *theory* (in certain common sense articulations of such a notion), but rather nothing more than a recording of how Canadian courts have been attempting to construct an institution that can subsume within it the separate lives and understandings of Indigenous communities. This does not leave critical theories the sole viable alternative, for they, too – by their very constitution – do not aim at *explaining* phenomena in the world.[5] However, aspects of critical theory – placed in the cast of naturalist understandings of how we come to make sense of phenomena – can be recast so they come to provide the best explanation we currently have of the true nature of Aboriginal rights jurisprudence. This exercise in exploring a component of Canadian constitutional law through the application of methodological naturalism reaches its conclusion in the last chapter, then, with some thoughts about how discourse and power are inextricably linked in the workings of the courts of Canada.

In the next few sections of this Introduction, I reconstruct portions of my quest to "make sense" of Aboriginal law. This is presented as a personal journey, not as a stylistic choice, but to reinforce the point that how one is positioned in the world and how one thinks of the world are connected in complex ways to what one thinks of social institutions like the law. Contained in this personal tale is an account of problems all researchers face (whether they are aware of this or willing to admit it) once they decide to try to make sense of Canadian

5 This work builds on thoughts and arguments woven into Gordon Christie, "Critical Theory and Aboriginal Rights" in Sandra Tomsons & Lorraine Mayer, eds, *Philosophy and Aboriginal Rights: Critical Dialogues* (Don Mills, ON: Oxford University Press Canada, 2013) 123.

law as it applies to peoples whose lives, histories, and identities exist independent of Crown sovereignty and its intended effects in the world. I then expand upon arguments touched on above, those that implicate the business of theorizing in the construction of forms of social reality meant to remove Indigenous self-determination, so the text can be properly framed. The very particular way that I approach what it is to attempt to "make sense" must be kept in mind as chapters unfold, as arguments made and conclusions reached must be understood in light of this method. This Introduction then ends with something of a roadmap, setting out how specific chapters work us towards a detailed picture of the nature of Aboriginal rights.

Making Sense as a Personal Quest

"Learning the Law"

Working to attempt to make sense of Aboriginal law has been at the core of my academic life since I entered law school several decades ago as a naive student, one foot planted in the southern *Qallunaat* world,[6] the other tenuously reaching out to my mother's families' Inuvialuit and Inupiat world. Much of my time during the first few years of my quest was spent following the same path of inquiry tread by most law students and young academics – I wanted to know how the law functioned, what rules and tests applied in which situations, and how the law was developing.

This was an exciting time to be new to the law. In 1982 Canada took its final step out from under the wing of the United Kingdom and patriated its constitution, taking that opportunity to craft a new *Constitution Act.*[7] As a result of a long and difficult struggle, Aboriginal and treaty rights were "recognized and affirmed" in section 35 of that new constitutional document: "The existing aboriginal and treaty rights of the aboriginal peoples of Canada are hereby recognized and affirmed."[8]

---

6 *Qallunaat* refers to non-Inuit, those from the south.

7 *Constitution Act, 1982, supra* note 1. After a long political struggle, Canada "repatriated" the Constitution in 1982 – until then, Canada's constitution was in fact legislatively tied to the British Parliament. Prime Minister Pierre Trudeau had made it something of a personal quest to have the constitution severed from its British roots and reinvigorated with a new *Canadian Charter of Rights and Freedoms*, Part I of the *Constitution Act, 1982*, being Schedule B to the *Canada Act 1982* (UK), c 11.

8 *Constitution Act, 1982, supra* note 1; *Constitution Act, 1867* (UK), 30 & 31 Vict, c 3, reprinted in RSC 1985, App II, No 5 [*Constitution Act, 1867*]. For the history of the struggle to have section 35 included in the new *Constitution Act*, see Ardith Walkem & Halie Bruce, eds,

I entered law school a few short years after the first major decision about these newly constitutionally protected Aboriginal rights came down from the Supreme Court of Canada (*R v Sparrow*),[9] I was still a student when a phalanx of landmark cases on Aboriginal and treaty rights emerged (including *R v Van der Peet, R v Gladstone, R v Adams,* and *R v Badger*),[10] and it was just months after I graduated that the first landmark case on Aboriginal title was handed down from the high court (*Delgamuukw v British Columbia (AG)*).[11]

Confusion and Frustrations

While I found it an exciting time, it was quite confusing, and, frankly, frustrating (eventually rising to the point of intolerability). The confusion was not difficult to trace to its source. My impression was that judicial decisions seemingly came down out of nowhere – I could not fathom *why* the Supreme Court would say the things it ended up saying. Up through to around the late 1990s I found I could not at all anticipate what the Court was going to say next about the nature of Aboriginal and treaty rights.

The sense of frustration bordering on intolerability was a bit harder to trace to its source – the feeling of deep frustration was clearly connected to the seeming arbitrariness of the Court's rulings, but also seemed to have something to do with its flip side, a sense I had of what *should* be going on, given what I understood about the history of the relationship between

---

Box of Treasures or Empty Box? Twenty Years of Section 35 (Penticton, BC: Theytus Press, 2003); Arthur Manuel & Ronald Derrickson, *Unsettling Canada: A National Wake-Up Call* (Toronto: Between the Lines, 2015).

9 *R v Sparrow*, [1990] 1 SCR 1075, 70 DLR (4th) 385 [*Sparrow*].

10 *R v Van der Peet*, [1996] 2 SCR 507, 137 DLR (4th) 289 [*Van der Peet*]; *R v Gladstone*, [1996] 2 SCR 723, 137 DLR (4th) 648 [*Gladstone*]; *R v Adams*, [1996] 3 SCR 101, 138 DLR (4th) 657 [*Adams*]; *R v Badger*, [1996] 1 SCR 771, 133 DLR (4th) 324. For other important cases decided in this period, see also *R v Côté*, [1996] 3 SCR 139, 138 DLR (4th) 385 [*Côté*]; *R v NTC Smokehouse*, [1996] 2 SCR 672, 137 DLR (4th) 528; *R v Marshall*, [1999] 3 SCR 533, 179 DLR (4th) 193.

11 *Delgamuukw v British Columbia (Attorney-General)*, [1997] 3 SCR 1010, 153 DLR (4th) 193 [*Delgamuukw*]. Interestingly, in the early stages of writing this book, the second landmark case on Aboriginal title passed through the Supreme Court. That it took seventeen years for a second case to emerge from the courts – with no actual finding of Aboriginal title for any nation in the intervening years, with no Aboriginal title existing in Canada until 2014 – says something about the contentious nature of Aboriginal rights. See *Tsilhqot'in Nation v British Columbia*, 2014 SCC 44 [*Tsilhqot'in Nation*]. That it took the Tsilhqot'in Nation well over twenty years – and millions of dollars in costs – for their claim to actually wind its way through the courts says something about the efficacy of the litigative approach to dealing with Crown-Aboriginal relations. On top of all that, the impact of *Tsilhqot'in Nation* will likely become clear only over the next few decades.

Canada and the Indigenous peoples of Canada. During this time my own historical consciousness was undergoing considerable expansion, and at each moment of expansion my frustration magnified – "How could this be what Aboriginal rights amount to?," given what I increasingly came to imagine they surely *must* be meant to respond to. The feeling of intolerability emerged most forcefully upon closer rereadings of the landmark cases, as I searched for some sense that could be made of all this and found – with growing incredulity – that the Court apparently felt it was developing jurisprudence intended to move Canadian society towards justice and a process of reconciliation. My own sense was that this was most certainly not what the Court was working towards!

Consider, briefly, *Sparrow*,[12] a case lying at the foundations of Canadian jurisprudence on section 35. While *Sparrow* concerned specific rights-claims of the Musqueam, it set out general frameworks for understanding and working with this new constitutional instrument.

The Musqueam, "people of the river grass," are Coast Salish people with territory in what is now commonly known as the lower mainland of British Columbia. In 1984 Ronald Sparrow (of the Musqueam Indian Band) had been fishing at one mouth of the Fraser River in British Columbia with a net that, according to a food-fishing licence issued under the federal *Fisheries Act*, was too long. Mr Sparrow's argument was that he was fishing according to an Aboriginal right the Musqueam enjoyed under section 35. After characterizing the claim as a right to fish for food or social and ceremonial purposes, and finding that such a right existed, the Supreme Court turned to what it saw as the core issue presented in this scenario – the question of how to manage the intersection of an Aboriginal right and a particular piece of Canadian law. How, the Court wondered, were Aboriginal rights to be fit into the Canadian legal landscape?[13]

The Court decided the key to this puzzle lay in imagining that the intent of constitutionalizing these rights was to signal that the previously unfettered power of the federal government now had to be "tempered" in relation to Aboriginal claims.[14] The Court made much of the move from (a) the model of

---

12 *Supra* note 9.

13 *Ibid* at 1101.

14 The Court felt that these rights already existed in Canadian law before their constitutionalization, though the jurisprudence through this earlier era heavily tilted towards treaty rights, with only the very occasional case recognizing stand-alone Aboriginal rights (considered to have continued within the common law under the doctrine of continuity). See e.g. *Casimel v Insurance Corporation of British Columbia* (1993), 106 DLR (4th) 720, [1994] 2 CNLR 22 (BCCA); *Connolly v Woolrich* (1867), 11 LCJ 197, 17 RJRQ 75 (regarding the doctrine of continuity). A form of Aboriginal title was also recognized before section 35 came into being. See e.g. *St Catharine's Milling and Lumber Co v The Queen*, [1887] 13 SCR 577, 14 AC 46 (JCPC) [*St Catharine's Milling*]; *Calder v British Columbia (AG)*, [1973] SCR 313, 34 DLR (3d) 145 [*Calder*].

parliamentary supremacy under which the Canadian system had functioned prior to 1982, to (b) a model of constitutional supremacy after patriation.[15] As Aboriginal claims rest in factual matters predating the emergence of the Canadian state itself (a point acknowledged years earlier in *Calder v British Columbia*),[16] rights acknowledged under section 35 called upon the high court to conceive of some sort of balancing act that might be struck between federal power and federal responsibility. While the federal government maintained its ability to make decisions about activities that would affect the exercise of Aboriginal rights, in doing so according to the law (acting under the rule of law) it would have to consider its legal responsibilities (spelled out in some passages in *Sparrow* in terms of fiduciary doctrine)[17] and act accordingly.

Educated as I had been in constitutional law, this made some sense. But its sensibility could extend only to a very definite point, past which all sense fell away. I imagined if the ends sought were *justice*, inevitably the Court would have to come to see this sort of fundamental matter within the larger historical context within which this entire situation unfolded – that of colonialism. The Musqueam, for example, have been living in and around the mouths of the Fraser River for thousands of years. They never signed (and still have never signed) a treaty with the Crown, and so continue to live on ancestral lands they never surrendered or ceded. Regardless of the lack of a treaty, from around the mid-1800s onward, the provincial government (at times in accord with, and at times in some opposition to, the wishes of the federal government)[18] dispossessed the Musqueam of most of their traditional lands, placed them on

---

15 Under the model of parliamentary supremacy, the judiciary had had to acknowledge that within their respective spheres of jurisdiction, Canadian legislative bodies could act with "absolute power," while under a model of constitutional supremacy, constitutionalized Aboriginal and treaty rights could cut into that hitherto absolute power. The new *Constitution Act*, *supra* note 1, contains a supremacy clause at s 52(1): "The Constitution of Canada is the supreme law of Canada, and any law that is inconsistent with the provisions of the Constitution is, to the extent of the inconsistency, of no force or effect."

16 *Calder*, *supra* note 14.

17 In *Sparrow*, *supra* note 9 at 1110, the Supreme Court held that:

> [W]e find that the words "recognition and affirmation" incorporate the fiduciary relationship referred to earlier and so import some restraint on the exercise of sovereign power. Rights that are recognized and affirmed are not absolute. Federal legislative powers continue, including, of course, the right to legislate with respect to Indians pursuant to s. 91(24) of the Constitution Act, 1867. These powers must, however, now be read together with s. 35(1). In other words, federal power must be reconciled with federal duty and the best way to achieve that reconciliation is to demand the justification of any government regulation that infringes upon or denies aboriginal rights.

18 From 1849 to 1871 (for Vancouver Island) and 1858 to 1871 (for much of the southern mainland), what became the province of British Columbia was made up of British colonies. The two colonies merged in 1866 to form the single colony of British Columbia. On joining

a small reserve,[19] and generally made the maintenance of traditional ways of living very difficult.

If the Court, then, were really pursuing "justice," it seemed to me, it would have to be driven to question such matters as the very legitimacy of the power it felt had to be "tempered." The Court, however, did the opposite, stating explicitly in *Sparrow* that the sovereignty of the Crown over Aboriginal lands has never been questioned (strongly implying that it was in no position to do so now).[20]

This stance indicated the presence of some sort of barrier (at least in the minds of the judges) beyond which Canadian law apparently could not venture – its imagination could not reach out to the task of questioning matters of state legitimacy.[21] Furthermore, this seemed linked to a deep reluctance on the part of the judiciary to examine historical and political context, reflected in its narrow approach to matters of Crown-Aboriginal relations. Striking to me as well was the fact the Court did not acknowledge its own position of immense power, vis-à-vis not only the Musqueam, but all Aboriginal peoples in Canada.

While numerous commentators (of a range of backgrounds and persuasions) saw promise in *Sparrow*,[22] my reaction at the time was that whatever positive

---

Confederation in 1871, this new province agreed to a reserve creation policy (in Article 13 of the Terms of Union) that had the federal government apply to have lands transferred from the Local Government (the new province). With the federal government having, however, no real power to affect this reserve-creation, the matter sat unresolved for generations. The outcome lingers on, with very small and unilaterally established reserves sprinkled across the province. See Paul Tennant, *Aboriginal Peoples and Politics: The Indian Land Question in British Columbia, 1849–1989* (Vancouver: UBC Press, 1990); Cole Harris, *Making Native Space: Colonialism, Resistance, and Reserves in British Columbia* (Vancouver: UBC Press, 2002). For the role government, law, and policy played in restricting Aboriginal economies, see Doug Harris, *Fish, Law, and Colonialism: The Legal Capture of Salmon in British Columbia* (Toronto: University of Toronto Press, 2001).

19 The Musqueam have several pieces of reserve land, but their community rests on Musqueam Indian Reserve #2.

20 *Sparrow, supra* note 9 at 1104:

> It is worth recalling that while British policy towards the native population was based on respect for their right to occupy their traditional lands, a proposition to which the Royal Proclamation of 1763 bears witness, there was from the outset never any doubt that sovereignty and legislative power, and indeed the underlying title, to such lands vested in the Crown[.]

21 This thought was captured well by Michael Asch and Patrick Macklem in their analysis of *Sparrow*. See Michael Asch & Patrick Macklem, "Aboriginal Rights and Canadian Sovereignty: An Essay on *R. v. Sparrow*" (1991) 29 Alta L Rev 498 [Asch & Macklem]. John Borrows recently argued that nothing prevents Canadian courts from engaging in this kind of questioning of state action. See John Borrows, *Canada's Indigenous Constitution* (Toronto: University of Toronto Press, 2010) [Borrows, *Canada's Indigenous Constitution*]. I suspect quite different conceptions of "Indigenous sovereignty" are at play here.

22 See e.g. Brian Slattery, "Aboriginal Sovereignty and Imperial Claims" (1991) 29 Osgoode Hall LJ 681 at 703, n 27 (characterizing the then-recent *Sparrow* decision as providing a "broad

force it possessed was primarily in relation to how much more poorly things might have otherwise turned out.[23] For example, the Court could have simply dismissed key claims advanced in *Sparrow*, or found that the claimed right did not continue to exist in Canada, or that the state continued to enjoy relatively unfettered power to control or regulate such rights if they did still persist.

I was faced with more moments of confusion and frustration just a few years later, when in *Van der Peet* the Supreme Court took upon itself the task of identifying the nature of, and setting out the tests for establishing, Aboriginal rights.[24] Dorothy Van der Peet (of the Stó:lō nation in British Columbia) was charged with selling ten fish caught under a food-fishing (hence non-commercial) licence. Her defence was that she was exercising a right enjoyed by the Stó:lō.

Rather than consider the historical colonial relationship that plays a fundamental role in determining the contemporary situation of Aboriginal peoples and communities, the Court focused on notions of "Aboriginality" and culture, and found that the purpose of the constitutionalization of Aboriginal rights was to protect certain traditional ways of living (those deemed "integral" to the culture of the Aboriginal community making the claim of an Aboriginal right).[25] This focus on pre-contact culture (on "traditional" ways) shifted attention away from the devastating effects of colonial law and policy, and fit seamlessly with the Court's earlier distancing from any suggestion that Crown sovereignty might itself be challenged by the presence of pre-existing Indigenous political and social structures ranging over Indigenous territories.[26]

In the years just after *Van der Peet* (and its companion decision, *R v Gladstone*) came out – as I read and reread the emerging case law (together with close

---

interpretation" of Aboriginal rights under section 35). Andrea Bowker, in looking at how *Sparrow* was being put to use in subsequent cases in British Columbia, characterized the decision as containing great promise. See Andrea Bowker, "Sparrow's Promise: Aboriginal Rights in the B.C. Court of Appeal" (1995) 53 UT Fac L Rev 1. I should note as well, though, that a few commentators – again, from across a range of backgrounds – saw essential flaws in *Sparrow*. See e.g. Monture-Angus, *supra* note 4; Asch & Macklem, *supra* note 21.

23 McHugh holds that "[i]n the end ... section 35's measurable achievement might have been no more than prophylactic, to have saved Aboriginal and treaty rights and entitlements from executive, implied, or unjustified infringement": Paul McHugh, "A Common Law Biography of Section 35" in Patrick Macklem & Douglas Sanderson, eds, *From Recognition to Reconciliation: Essays on the Constitutional Entrenchment of Aboriginal and Treaty Rights* (Toronto: University of Toronto Press, 2016) 137 at 163 [Macklem & Sanderson].

24 *Van der Peet*, *supra* note 10.

25 All the cases mentioned in this overview are extensively discussed in future chapters of this work. See chapters 2, 6, 7. The Court's discussion of the test for Aboriginal rights can be found in *Van der Peet*. See *supra* note 10 at paras 26–75.

26 At least as troubling as the direction taken in *Van der Peet* were remarks the Supreme Court made in a companion decision, *Gladstone*, released on the same day in 1996. In 1988

readings of troubling arguments concerning justifiable infringement of Aboriginal title in *Delgamuukw v British Columbia*)[27] – my confusion began to dissipate, though levels of frustration advanced, growing right up to the point of intolerability. I could now begin to see, I believed, just how judges on the Court were thinking. I now had a glimpse, it seemed, into the sort of "justice" and "reconciliation" they were imagining.

Aboriginal people were on notice that all their claims had to fit a specific form – they all must be characterized as contemporary attempts to maintain "traditional" practices, practices somehow determined to be essentially "Aboriginal." To the extent an Aboriginal people were thereby claiming a right that had little or no impact on established non-Aboriginal interests, Canadian governments were on notice that they should be acting to seriously uphold and protect the Aboriginal interests at stake. Should an Aboriginal people make a claim, however, with potential impact on non-Aboriginal interests, this claim could be justifiably treated as nothing more than a call on Canadian governments to act in non-discriminatory ways – in essence, to treat Aboriginal claimants as full-fledged members of Canadian society. In most contexts this would amount to an injunction to carry out a weighted balancing of all interests at stake, to treat Aboriginal claims proportionately, measured in relation to the presence of the Aboriginal people in the contemporary demographic sea within which they and their claims might arise.[28]

Donald and William Gladstone (of the Heiltsuk of the British Columbia coast) attempted to sell several thousand pounds of herring spawn on kelp, contrary to several pieces of federal legislation. Their defence rested on the argument that the Heiltsuk enjoy an Aboriginal right to trade things they gather from the sea. In returning to the framework established in *Sparrow* for deciding how the Canadian government might "justifiably infringe" upon this right, the Court noted that the earlier *Sparrow* ruling had not contemplated this sort of claimed right – that is, a right lacking an "internal limit." The right claimed in *Sparrow* was characterized in *Gladstone* (looking back from this later vantage point) as having just such an internal limit – as a right to fish *for food or ceremonial purposes*; it would be exhausted once these ends were met. A right to fish *in order to trade*, however, would be exhausted only once external factors played out – either the market would have to be saturated or the fish all caught. With this sort of right, the Court went on to say, the *Sparrow* framework had to be modified. See *Gladstone, supra* note 10 at paras 39, 54 (discussing infringement and how the Crown might go about justifying infringement).

27 *Delgamuukw, supra* note 11.

28 *Gladstone, supra* note 10 at paras 62–4. In paragraph 64, the Court held that questions to be asked in determining whether appropriate "priority" has been granted the Aboriginal rights at issue would include

> whether the government has accommodated the exercise of the aboriginal right to participate in the fishery (through reduced licence fees, for example), whether the government's objectives in enacting a particular regulatory scheme reflect the need to take into account the priority of aboriginal rights holders, the extent of the participation in the fishery of aboriginal rights holders

However, this does little (or nothing) over and above trying to move Canadian governments into treating Aboriginal peoples in non-discriminatory ways.[29] While Aboriginal peoples clearly benefit from being treated non-discriminatorily (indeed, treating Indigenous peoples in discriminatory ways was one common – indeed, arguably defining – action of Canadian governments during earlier overtly colonial eras), it struck me that this entire approach avoided putting any meaningful substance into Aboriginal rights.[30] Contemporary Canadian governments *should* be acting in non-discriminatory fashion, regardless of the existence of section 35, so I took it as obvious that one had to wonder what, under this interpretation, this section of the *Constitution* might add to the Canadian legal landscape. Once again, routes not taken struck me; rather than even glimpse into the dark colonial history enveloping and defining Crown-Aboriginal relations, the Supreme Court rendered that history an ineffectual echo within the realm of judicial discourse.

I felt I could now begin to see *how* the judiciary was approaching Aboriginal claims, but this just led to more questions. *Why* was the highest court only pressing for non-discriminatory action on the part of the Crown when Aboriginal interests threaten to collide with non-Aboriginal interests? *Why* was it focused on protecting nothing more than "Aboriginal" cultural practices? *Why* was the focus not on lost lands and territories?[31] *Why* not focus *principally* on loss of Indigenous self-determination, on the ability of Aboriginal communities

---

relative to their percentage of the population, how the government has accommodated different aboriginal rights in a particular fishery (food versus commercial rights, for example), how important the fishery is to the economic and material well-being of the band in question, and the criteria taken into account by the government in, for example, allocating commercial licences amongst different users.

29 That is, the jurisprudence does not seem to require any more than this when the rights in question potentially intersect with the interests of non-Aboriginal Canadians. When that is not the case, Aboriginal law requires "traditional practices" be accorded significant respect (though that does not mean they cannot be "justifiably infringed" by the Crown).

30 Indeed, McLachlin J, as she then was, made much the same point in her dissent in *Van der Peet*. See e.g. *supra* note 10 at para 306, McLachlin J, dissenting [emphasis added]:

> *The extension of the concept of compelling objective* to matters like economic and regional fairness and the interests of non-aboriginal fishers ... *would negate the very aboriginal right to fish itself*, on the ground that this is required for the reconciliation of aboriginal rights and other interests and the consequent good of the community as a whole. This is not limitation required for the responsible exercise of the right, but rather limitation on the basis of the economic demands of non-aboriginals.

31 In *Tsilhqot'in Nation*, the Supreme Court found the Tsilhqot'in Nation had Aboriginal title to about 40 per cent of the land they had claimed in this action (title being found, then, over about 5 per cent of their total overall traditional territory). See *Tsilhqot'in Nation*, *supra* note 11. The entire structure around Aboriginal title claims seems skewed, however, as Aboriginal peoples must claim against the Crown, as if they are the parties with weaker claims to

to chart their own collective futures according to their own understandings of law and responsibilities?

Could I Be Wrong?

But perhaps all this was frustration misdirected. Perhaps my persistent feeling that the judiciary was laying down law that failed to address key historical issues was ungrounded. Perhaps my visceral reaction was more emotional than rational or principled.

Is it not the case, after all, that "we are all here to stay" (as was said in the last line of the majority decision in *Delgamuukw*)?[32] If so, is it not reasonable to position the Supreme Court as tasked with working out how groups of people with varied interests can be fit into a satisfactory legal matrix? And is it not the fact that in some clearly visible respects the landscape around Canadian-Indigenous relations has improved dramatically over the last half-century, with Aboriginal law playing a major part in this apparently progressive development?

There were no courses on Aboriginal law for Canadian law students to take in the 1960s, and if there had been such courses, there would have been little content. At that time "historical" treaties were routinely ignored, there was no thought given to the negotiation of further treaties, the lives of many Aboriginal peoples were controlled within a heavily paternalistic system (dominated by the *Indian Act*),[33] most Aboriginal communities were dispiritingly poor (with many families struggling to provide basics of food and shelter), and one (seriously considered) government "solution" for the entire "Indian problem" at

---

land interests. As the *original* settlers and occupiers of the lands in question it would seem, however, that they would have a form of Indigenous title to all the lands they considered traditional territories, while the Crown would have to (somehow) justify its subsequent claims. For arguments to this effect made from within the common law, see Kent McNeil, "The Onus of Proof of Aboriginal Title" in Kent McNeil, *Emerging Justice? Essays on Indigenous Rights in Canada and Australia* (Saskatoon, SK: Native Law Centre, 2001) 136 [McNeil, *Emerging Justice?*]. McNeil canvasses possible reasons Canadian courts put the onus on Aboriginal claimants and finds certain "pragmatic and legal reasons" for this state of affairs, reasons that do not satisfactorily account for the "evident unfairness of presuming the title of the Crown": *ibid* at 141.

32 *Delgamuukw*, *supra* note 11 at para 186.

33 Non-status and Metis, on the other hand, have long suffered from government neglect – with both provinces and the federal government refusing to accept jurisdictional responsibility for these peoples, services most non-Aboriginal Canadians could fairly easily rely upon were often not available. Only in recent years have courts turned to these matters. See *Daniels v Canada (Minister of Indian Affairs and Northern Development)*, 2014 FCA 101. On the question of legislative jurisdiction, the Supreme Court agreed with the trial judge, that for the

the time centred on thorough assimilation of Indigenous peoples into the body politic and social milieu.[34]

The intervening years have seen tremendous change. Historical treaties and the obligations they generate have come back into the consciousness of the Canadian state, new treaties and agreements have been and continue to be negotiated across Canada, "existing Aboriginal and treaty rights" have been constitutionally entrenched in section 35 of the new *Constitution Act, 1982*,[35] and the *Indian Act* has become the focus of ongoing efforts at reform (arguably with an eye to its eventual replacement with other instruments).[36] With the 2014 decision in *Tsilhqot'in Nation v British Columbia*,[37] Aboriginal peoples have come to have land interests over significant portions of their traditional territories elevated to a legal status akin to that of private property.

The sense I had developed was that contemporary Canadian law as applied to Aboriginal peoples was repressive. Perhaps, however, it is in fact progressive. Surveying changes over the last half century, how could one imagine it has been anything but progressive? While Canadian law had historically played a critical role in articulating and implementing colonial policies of dispossession, oppression, and repression, is it not the case we now live in a new era of reconciliation? To think otherwise, one might suggest, reveals an ideological bias, to suggest little more than the expression of an unreasoned perspective, one

---

purposes of section 91(24) of the *Constitution Act, 1867*, *supra* note 8, the Metis are a federal responsibility. See *Daniels v Canada (Indian Affairs and Northern Development)*, 2016 SCC 12 [*Daniels*, SCC].

34 In 1969 Prime Minister Trudeau unveiled the White Paper, a federal government policy paper that proposed removing all legal and constitutional differences between Aboriginal and non Aboriginal people in Canada. See Canada, Indian and Northern Affairs, *Statement of the Government of Canada on Indian Policy* (Ottawa: Department of Indian and Northern Affairs, 1969), online: <aadnc-aandc.gc.ca/DAM/DAM-INTER-HQ/STAGING/texte-text/cp1969_1100100010190_eng.pdf>.

35 *Supra* note 1.

36 *Indian Act*, *supra* note 3. From 2016 onward the federal government reinvigorated activities of the last decade to reconfigure the relationship between "Indian bands" (those communities defined by and falling under the *Indian Act*) and the federal government. Some of the discussion has been about the possibility of replacing the *Indian Act* entirely. See e.g. *First Nations Financial Transparency Act*, SC 2013, c 7; *First Nations Elections Act*, SC 2014, c 5; *First Nations Fiscal Management Act*, SC 2005, c 9; *First Nations Oil and Gas Moneys Management Act*, SC 2005, c 48; *First Nations Commercial and Industrial Development Act*, SC 2005, c 53. Recently there have also been attempts at putting in place a *First Nations Property Ownership Act* and a *First Nations Control of First Nations Education Act*. Other discussions concern reconfiguring the very nature of the *Indian Act* band system. See Jorge Barrera, "Justice Minister Wilson-Raybould Tells AFN to Prepare for Future beyond the Indian Act," *APTN National News* (25 July 2017), online: <aptnnews.ca/2017/07/25/justice-minister-wilson-raybould-tells-afn-to-prepare-for-future-beyond-the-indian-act/>.

37 *Tsilhqot'in Nation*, *supra* note 11.

tainted perhaps by emotion and narrow "nationalist" or "sovereigntist" leanings (and not the *truth* about the matter).

"Bias" and "Perspective"

I seemed left with two troubling possibilities that intertwine and build on each other: first, that my frustration and confusion were simply products of a biased position; and second, that I was expressing simply (and inappropriately) nothing but a perspective.[38] However much merit any model of Aboriginal law I developed might have, I had to face the possibility such a model might be – or might be *perceived* to be – either the product of a biased position (and thus dismissed) or the result of a sociocultural construct (and thus set aside as a novelty). Others might argue, for example, that to the extent I was confused and frustrated it was because I – being an Indigenous scholar – was unable to properly – "objectively" – imagine how to measure such things as progress and justice.

Some might brush aside such concerns and get on to the business of analysing Aboriginal law. I, however, could not begin to systematize my thoughts and speculations without first attempting to take these concerns seriously. Other than excessive caution on my side, one might wonder, though, why I have devoted time and energy to worrying about possible biases and perspectives. Reasons for this go to the heart of the nature of the work carried out in the core of this text.

This does not emerge from doubt I may entertain about my own integrity and abilities (doubt that might seep in if I were to struggle with the fact that I come to the study of Aboriginal law as not just a scholar, but as an Indigenous scholar).[39] Rather, it comes from the fact I take seriously the notion that

---

38 These are not precisely the same; to assert I am *biased* in my views on Canadian law speaks to the possibility that I fail to appreciate the need to be even-handed in assessing what is going on in the legal-political realm (more precisely, it makes the claim that my assessments are *skewed* as a result of what I pre-reflectively *believe*), while to assert I present nothing more than a *perspective* on matters is to argue that there exist conceptual filters through which I make sense of the world, that these "interpretative" tools generate a picture of the world for me that I have trouble correcting (with more appropriate, more inclusive models of reality). While both charges would lead to the claim that I hold a distorted view of the way things are, the first points to a belief-set I (apparently) cannot easily shake (that I use to skew data and evidence to fit), while the second points to interpretative devices I employ that likewise generate a model of reality, which I have trouble seeing is simply "my" model of how things are.

39 Over the years, some have tried to have me doubt myself, insidiously suggesting that as an Indigenous person I may not quite "get it," that my bona fides may not be that bona fide, that I am too emotionally vested in my studies. I have done my best not to respond to this pressure, which would have had me defending myself overly vigorously in a non-Indigenous intellectual milieu.

all legal researchers should be – indeed must be – cognizant of their place as theorists and willing to wonder at whether their sociocultural embeddedness affects their scholarship. Is bias an ineliminable feature of legal theorizing? Is all legal theory infected by the presence of perspective? These are questions about which all legal researchers should spend some time thinking carefully, *especially when investigating the intersection of varied legal systems, understood as expressions of meaning.*

Such concerns cannot be limited through the expediency of pushing them all into realms of evaluation. Even if we presuppose answers to questions of moral or political valuation, problems in addressing possible roles played by perspectives continue to arise. Leaving aside questions of moral or political grounding of the law, given simply a legal system in the process of being constructed, arguably we can ask what it should look like in the next stage of construction; in this context this question is intimately tied to what lawmakers are responding to, which requires a specific take on what counts as harms to be remedied. These are theory-laden matters, and legal theorists will be inevitably caught up in matters connected to this ongoing construction of a social institution, an institution at the heart of sociocultural worlds they inhabit. Given this structure, can legal theorists blithely ignore concerns about bias and perspectives?

Theorists can certainly attempt to ignore such matters, but only if they are willing to ignore roles *they* may play in matters of construction, roles that arguably connect to perspectives they bring to the tasks of theorizing. Theories of human nature and of self-society interactions lie at the heart of the business of constructing all legal institutions, and legal theorists inevitably play a critical role in developing and promoting these theories. Can they be in such positions and yet simultaneously manage to theorize about the law in ways that simply "make sense"?

All these concerns are heightened in the context of the study of intersecting legal systems or orders. The personal journey sketched out over the last few pages *should* be just one articulation of distinct journeys embarked upon by *all* who turn their attention to Aboriginal law, where somewhere along each path the traveller noticed the odd character of divergent legal analyses. A cursory glance at the literature on Aboriginal rights reveals positions argued at the extremes of possibility – who could fail to notice such stark divergences in position on the nature of Aboriginal rights? Who could fail to wonder at what this hints at in relation to the whole practice of legal analysis? Who – as an individual legal researcher – could fail to eventually question his own "neutral" position, a position arguably tightly connected to his initial non-critical opinion that how he sees the world of law and policy is bounded by nothing but "sense" and "right"? While it is natural for me to wonder at possible connections between perspective, the law, and knowledge, how could these deep problems not inform the work of *all* who turn their minds to trying to "make sense" of Aboriginal law?[40]

This is a pivot around which much of the rest of the analysis in this text spins. How do we get around, or at least manage, these problems? Concerns about bias seem manageable through careful reflection, coupled with insistent and persistent efforts to set aside personal prejudgments about the nature of Aboriginal law. Much more difficult challenges come from the possibility that my knowledge – indeed, the knowledges of all who examine Aboriginal law – is nothing but "perspectival." These challenges seem to rest essentially on the role of perspective in developing understandings of law and its place in our world. Much of the rest of this work details efforts to grapple with this question about the (apparent) role of perspective in trying to "make sense" of Aboriginal law. I spend considerable time in upcoming chapters digging ever deeper into this issue, though along the way I also try to refine it in ways that make the ensuing analysis manageable.

Behind the Rules: Principles and Forces at Play

Let me return to my tale of a personal journey. I have said a few things about how one's evaluative stance and the legal theory with which one comes to the task of making sense may themselves affect the project of "making sense" of Aboriginal law. The narrative continues, so I might weave into this introductory chapter more reasons why we need to look deeply and carefully into matters of theorizing and perspective.

---

40 The fact that I am not alone in the particular frustration I feel with the development of Aboriginal law would seem to indicate nothing more than that my personal perspective is shared, that many Indigenous people (and their allies) cannot help but impose their perspective onto a complex situation.

When I turn my focus inward rather than outward, I notice as well the problem of perspective can be found in one and the same consciousness, as I can at times see "progress" within the field of Aboriginal law and policy, while at other times I cannot help but feel frustration at the direction towards which Aboriginal law is pushing. Indeed, this internal bifurcated vision itself seemed shared by many. Arguably this is the product of the interstices within which Indigenous peoples find themselves in contemporary society, as communities and individuals exist in between spaces (one set of sociocultural threads woven back into ancestral ways of thinking and living, while another set is now entwined with "modern" or Western sensibilities). My experience has been that many Indigenous people find it possible to see Aboriginal law as progressive when looked at one way, while when they look at this same field of law *as Indigenous people*, it appears to be playing a key role in channelling generations of dissent and resistance down dead ends (with tremendous resources dedicated to completion of a deeply troubling program of assimilation, well over a century after this became an over-arching goal of the Canadian state).

In the closing years of the last millennium my sense was that I could now begin to see *how* the Supreme Court was thinking its way through the development of Aboriginal law. At that point of my journey, however, I was just becoming aware of the need to think carefully about problems posed by position and "perspective." This growing sense of what was really happening sat uncomfortably with the possibility that I could be simply wrong, that in fact Canadian law was essentially progressive.

What were the alternatives? Could it be that Canadian law is, in some sense, both progressive and repressive (or, in an "objective" sense, neither)? My sense was that the Supreme Court was focused on eliminating the possibility that Indigenous self-determination might continue to inform decisions made by communities about their futures and their relations with lands and waters lying within their traditional territories. Others either ignored such a possibility or argued that in fact the Supreme Court was on a path that would soon eventuate into a world built around "reconciliation," justice, and fairness. Might it be that I am neither biased nor un-biased, that Aboriginal law is simply one thing when viewed from one perspective, but something else when seen from another? If sense could be made of the last possibility, how could one go about showing such a thing, so that some sense could be made of Aboriginal law (sense that anyone could see, no matter her specific location in the world)?

As the new millennium unfolded, as I read and reread leading cases, trying to figure out why the Supreme Court chose the routes it did in navigating these very difficult waters, as I wondered about questions of perspective and evaluation, I found my interests in Aboriginal law shifting to two deeply related matters. A layer of confusion had been pulled back – I could now begin to see clearly (it seemed to me) *how* the high court was thinking – but below that lay deeper levels of mystery: *why* would the Court think in these ways? Could I investigate these questions in ways that illuminate the nature of Aboriginal law, ways distanced from concerns that I would be merely exercising evaluative tools that reflected my stance as an Indigenous scholar? On the one hand there were clearly well-formed questions to ask, while on the other there were concerns about how to go about trying to answer these questions.

I wanted to know what might be responsible for the rules, tests, and procedures making up the law – I wanted to know what might lie below or behind the surface of the jurisprudence, what deeper or external mechanisms and forces, lying behind the development of the law, could account for legislation and jurisprudence itself – and I wanted to know how best to work towards *knowledge* about these matters. I became interested in larger issues – both theoretical and methodological – touching on this question of "making sense."

Why would the Court in *Sparrow* find "there was ... never any doubt ... sovereignty ... vested in the Crown"?[41] Why would this Court continue over the next few decades to build its entire jurisprudence in this area upon this one central point? Hypotheses are not hard to come by – one might suspect, for example, that the Court is singularly ignorant of the history of Crown-Indigenous relations, or that it is ideologically responsive, or one could imagine that the *position* in the world occupied by the Supreme Court – as the highest court in the *Canadian* judicial system – has had primary impact upon how it approaches these matters.[42] Alternatively, however, one might also suspect the Court has been working all along under a theory of justice, that it has had in mind since *Sparrow* what it considers to be a *proper* and *justifiable* approach to this complex matter handed to it in 1982. How are these possibilities to be approached? How is a researcher to work towards a defensible picture of why jurisprudence has developed as it has?

It seemed natural to begin the task of digging below the level of legal tests and rules by asking questions about how concepts like "justice," "fairness," and "reconciliation" fit into how the Court was operating. One would begin, then, with an investigation into how the Court understands itself, its role, and its proper procedures. Where I perceived fundamental shortcomings in the jurisprudence, the Supreme Court framed its approaches to these matters with the language of justice and reconciliation. Recall this was one of the central puzzles I faced once I began to get a sense of how the Court was thinking through how to develop Aboriginal rights – how could sense be made of injustice I *perceived* and *felt* when the jurisprudence itself contained extensive rhetoric built upon notions of "fairness," "reconciliation," and "justice," high-level concepts tied to principles that seemed to animate rules and tests the Court developed? Early attempts to get past personal frustration, to grapple with questions of perspective, to find means by which sense might be made of Aboriginal law, had me engage with these concepts and their relationships with and within the field of Aboriginal law. What kind of relationship exists between Aboriginal law and justice or fairness? How were these concepts being used in this context?

---

41 *Sparrow, supra* note 9 at 1103.

42 Indeed, one might wonder how Aboriginal law could not be essentially a matter of politics, given that it emanates from (a) a government that historically sought either absorption of or separation from Aboriginal polities, and (b) the legal system of this state. Furthermore, besides "natural" unwillingness of Canadian courts to fundamentally question the legitimacy of which they compose one arm, there are also matters that come up around the impact of those political forces to which these courts might feel allegiances, and questions that arise about the effects of jurists existing within the sorts of social, economic, and political strata they inhabit (and by and large continue to inhabit).

Again, however, fairly stark and seemingly opposed possibilities seemed to present themselves. Do these concepts point to transcendent notions to which the law aspires? This reading would again present the distinct possibility *my* readings of Aboriginal law – perhaps being essentially sociopolitically biased – were mistaken. Perhaps I did not understand what justice and fairness *required* in this context, and lacking that understanding I did not see how Canadian courts were indeed working towards reconciliation on terms befitting high aspirational ideals.

On the other hand, however, it might well be, I imagined, that the meanings these concepts possess in this context were determined *within* this particular cultural and social setting (with meaning essentially emanating from an arm of the nation state). What was I to make of the nagging feeling that the more I understood about what "justice" and "fairness" referred to within mainstream political and legal theory, and the more I contemplated how these meanings functioned in the context of Aboriginal law, the more *the whole matter* seemed to be socioculturally determined?[43] If this is the case, would everything not then come down to power and politics?

Turning to Theoretical Inquiry

Where was I to turn for insight? Stepping back from details of its structure and operations, how is one to make sense of the law concerning Aboriginal rights? Concerns turn back to the central matter introduced a few pages ago: do processes of thinking about this field depend, in some important and ineliminable manner, on who is conducting the investigation, and the world view he brings to the task?

My focus naturally fell on legal theory – or on what might be termed "theoretically driven" accounts of Aboriginal law. Here I imagined I would find serious attempts to truly make sense of the law, to get down below the level of what judges happened to say to what is really going on – indeed, to engage with the role of concepts in determining the content of a legal system. I thought I might find, for example, scholars looking into the efficacy of certain legal realist positions in this context, as it seemed obvious to me that most people moving into the legal world see or intuit very early in their studies some connection between the natures and backgrounds of judges and the

43 It might be tempting to slide from the notion that meaning is culturally determined (at least in this context) to the idea that meaning is purposefully developed to advance certain interests. We should keep these two suggestions separate, however, if only for the purposes of analysis. It is sufficient as a first point to acknowledge the possibility that sociocultural setting could determine meaning.

outcomes of cases.[44] Clearly as well, intersections between politics and the law in the field of Aboriginal law are there to see for anyone willing to reflect upon legal developments.[45] Indeed, I found in my explorations that commentators often make gestures at making sense of Aboriginal law that appeal on some level to this notion that law and politics are here joined at the hip. I found as well others commenting on the development of Aboriginal law who acknowledge the presence of political machinations or personal and systemic bias in the jurisprudence but who believe some "principled approach" will ultimately carry

44 The common adage that "we are all legal realists" – that all jurists today accept that the law is not capable of being understood as though it functions as an autonomous quasi-logical science, with judges simply working through syllogisms as they make judgments – rings as true in the Canadian context as elsewhere. This cliché, however, likely makes sense only to the degree that it expresses the truism that understandings of the law have moved beyond forms dominant before the 1920s, when many jurists were captured by simplistic formalist (and early positivist) models. In what sense, one might wonder, do contemporary jurists actually work within a world view structured by the insights of the school of legal realists? For an overview of its emergence in the United States and reactions to – including its role as precedent for – many "critical" movements of the later twentieth century, see Brian Bix, "American Legal Realism" in Brian Bix, *Jurisprudence: Theory and Context*, 2nd ed (London: Sweet & Maxwell, 1999) 165. Bix does not discuss the Scandinavian variant of legal realism.

Leiter argues that the legacy of legal realism is muted in the context of legal theory, but he hopes to resurrect certain strands of the movement in his articulation of a project of "naturalizing" jurisprudence. My project in this work touches on Leiter's work, but we overlap only in certain common base understandings – our projects are fairly distinct; he is concerned principally with the question of how one might go about justifying decisions judges arrive at, the thesis being that only a naturalized approach to questions of justifications can make sense of this matter, much as Quine's move to naturalize epistemology makes sense of how we actually go about determining the justification of our scientific knowledge. See Brian Leiter, *Naturalizing Jurisprudence: Essays on American Legal Realism and Naturalism in Legal Philosophy* (Oxford: Oxford University Press, 2007).

45 See Kent McNeil, "The Vulnerability of Indigenous Land Rights in Australia and Canada" (2004) 42 Osgoode Hall LJ 271 at 272–3. It was revealing, for example, to have McNeil remark at pages 272–3:

> [T]he decisions in *Mabo* [the leading Australian case on "native title"] and *Delgamuukw* [the leading Canadian case on "Aboriginal title"] share a common theme: the vulnerability of Indigenous land rights to the creation of third party interests by the Crown. This article will ... suggest that the explicit explanations for this vulnerability given by the High Court and Supreme Court do not tell the whole story. Lurking behind the decisions, in my opinion, are other explanations that relate more to political stability and economic priorities than to legal principle and precedent.

I imagine it is a common experience amongst legal scholars working in this field to be led to "other explanations," reaching behind legal principle and precedent. Beginning from the starting point that the law is the law – perhaps a bit biased and in need of reform, but basically just a system working towards resolution of difficult challenges – the scholar gradually comes to see that the bias is more than can be accounted for in terms of residual racism or colonialism, that there seems to still be some deep strand of "politics" unfortunately colouring the law in this field.

the day, promising a real measure of "justice" or "fairness."[46] Surely, I thought, these sorts of questions about how judges actually reason and about what roles politics might play in shaping how the jurisprudence develops would be at the forefront of analyses of Aboriginal law. Given these varied articulations of what the law is about, I expected to find debate and discussion between these different positions.

I was encouraged to see attempts at explaining the law that seemed to reflect some of my own sense of what was happening below the surface of the case law. For example, a few of the critical approaches (inheriting aspects of the classical legal realist movement) seemed to illuminate what I took to be forces that had driven, and continue to drive, development within this field of domestic law. I was also excited to see that contrary positions abound, as this promised an enlightened avenue for debate, hopefully initiating some steps on the way to making sense of Aboriginal law.

Unfortunately, however, the cycle continued of looking for solid ground and finding what I came across to be shifting and uneven. While I could find *some* aspects of *some* legal theories seemingly enlightening, once again I was quickly struck by how little they actually helped to resolve deeper matters that demand attention.

Let me begin wrapping up this Introduction by sketching out how legal theory revealed itself to be not only not helpful, but in fact the source of yet more questions that demand attention. In middle chapters I explore in some depth a range of questions that emerge about current understandings of theorizing – here I focus on a specific sort of problem, one that both helps explain why I engage so deeply with theoretical and methodological concerns and that leads into an introductory discussion of how the concerns I tackle are approached.

Grappling with Theories

Let me now shift attention to questions that I argue should engage any theorist trying to make sense of any legal phenomena. Over the last decade or so, as I looked into theories that seemed directed towards making sense of the

46 See e.g. John Borrows, *Recovering Canada: The Resurgence of Indigenous Law* (Toronto: University of Toronto Press, 2002) [Borrows, *Recovering Canada*]. For a transition from an analysis of Aboriginal rights to a prescriptive analysis of treaty rights, see Michael Asch, *On Being Here to Stay: Treaties and Aboriginal Rights in Canada* (Toronto: University of Toronto Press, 2014) at 68–72 [Asch, *On Being Here to Stay*]. The second half of this text rests on a conclusion he reaches along the way that "[while it is] impossible to imagine that our Supreme Court ... would ever declare on its own – in the absence of pressure from the larger society – that 'the right of colonial peoples to exercise their right to self-determination by breaking away from the "imperial" power is now undisputed,'" treaty relations, if properly understood and implemented (and the rights they might generate), could lead to a just outcome: *ibid* at 72.

jurisprudence, I came across those that purported to explain why the Court would use the concepts it did in the ways it did.[47] Liberal theory, in particular, seemed to help explain the thinking that went into the development of senses of justice and fairness that the Supreme Court deployed as it articulated what Aboriginal rights would look like and how they would fit into the established Canadian legal-political landscape.[48] I also found theories that seemed to

---

47 For general overviews of Aboriginal law (or significant aspects of Aboriginal law), see e.g. Kerry Wilkins, *Essentials of Canadian Aboriginal Law* (Toronto: Carswell, 2018); Sebastien Grammond, *Terms of Coexistence: Indigenous Peoples and Canadian Law* (Toronto: Carswell, 2013); Thomas Isaac, *Aboriginal Law: Commentary and Analysis*, 4th ed (Saskatoon, SK: Purich, 2012); Jim Reynolds, *Aboriginal Peoples and the Law: A Critical Introduction* (Vancouver: UBC Press, 2018); JR Miller, *Compact, Contract, Covenant: Aboriginal Treaty-Making in Canada* (Toronto: University of Toronto Press, 2009); Asch, *On Being Here to Stay*, *supra* note 46; Maria Morellato, ed, *Aboriginal Law since Delgamuukw* (Aurora, ON: Canada Law Book, 2009).

For analyses of aspects of Aboriginal law, see e.g. Brian Slattery, "Understanding Aboriginal Rights" (1987) 66 Can Bar Rev 727; Brian Slattery, "The Legal Basis of Aboriginal Title" in Frank Cassidy, ed, *Aboriginal Title in British Columbia: Delgamuukw v. The Queen* (Fernie, BC: Oolichan Books, 1992) 113; Brian Slattery, "Making Sense of Aboriginal and Treaty Rights" (2000) 79 Can Bar Rev 196; Brian Slattery, "The Metamorphosis of Aboriginal Title" (2006) 85 Can Bar Rev 255; Macklem & Sanderson, *supra* note 23; Dwight Newman, *Revisiting the Duty to Consult Aboriginal Peoples* (Saskatoon, SK: Purich, 2014).

For general analyses, see e.g. Borrows, *Recovering Canada*, *supra* note 46; Patrick Macklem, *Indigenous Difference and the Constitution of Canada* (Toronto: University of Toronto Press, 2001) [Macklem, *Indigenous Difference*]; Monture-Angus, *supra* note 4; Thomas Flanagan, *First Nations? Second Thoughts* (Montreal & Kingston: McGill-Queen's University Press, 2000); Mary Ellen Turpel, "Aboriginal Peoples and the Canadian Charter: Interpretive Monopolies, Cultural Differences" (1989–90) 1989 Can Hum Rts YB 3; McNeil, *Emerging Justice?*, *supra* note 31.

For general commentary on Crown-Aboriginal relations, see e.g. Ovide Mercredi & Mary Ellen Turpel, *In the Rapids: Navigating the Future of First Nations* (Toronto: Penguin Books, 1994); Howard Adams, *Prison of Grass: Canada from a Native Point of View* (Saskatoon, SK: Fifth House, 1989); Paul McHugh, *Aboriginal Societies and the Common Law: A History of Sovereignty, Status, and Self-Determination* (Oxford: Oxford University Press, 2004); Borrows, *Canada's Indigenous Constitution*, *supra* note 21; Michael Asch, John Borrows & James Tully, eds, *Resurgence and Reconciliation: Indigenous-Settler Relations and Earth Teachings* (Toronto: University of Toronto Press, 2018). For a discussion of a number of the works that present theoretical analyses, see "Academic Understandings" in chapter 3.

48 This is, of course, completely unsurprising, given that the Court exists within a liberal democracy. While works such as Patrick Macklem's *Indigenous Difference* rest firmly on a liberal theoretic foundation, it was in Will Kymlicka's corpus that I had to dig around in order to find an articulation of liberal thought that might apply to "multicultural" settings. See Macklem, *Indigenous Difference*, *supra* note 47; Will Kymlicka, *Liberalism, Community and Culture* (Oxford: Oxford University Press, 1989); Will Kymlicka, *Multicultural Citizenship: A Liberal Theory of Minority Rights* (Oxford: Oxford University Press, 1995); Will Kymlicka, *Multicultural Odysseys: Navigating the New International Politics of Diversity* (Oxford: Oxford University Press, 2007).

plausibly explain what goes on behind this process – helping to explain why, for example, issues of Indigenous self-determination are ignored, and why fundamental questions of land dispossession (as these relate to decision-making authority) are transformed into matters of private property and economic development.[49] Specifically, various forms of critical analysis speak to the disappearance of Indigenous forms of understanding, and to the control over discourse visible in how the Supreme Court exercises its immense power over the lives of Indigenous peoples.

Troublingly, however, these different sorts of theories offer radically incommensurable accounts of the nature of Aboriginal law. Equally troubling, they seem to emerge as manifestations of perspectives on the phenomena to be explored and explained. Varied theoretical accounts are not at all compatible, and in fact they leave one in the same bind of being faced with conflicting fundamental positions, a bind bedevilling other attempts to work out what is going on in Aboriginal law. This is a fact all working in this field must face: varied theoretical underpinnings point in radically dissimilar directions. In addition, there is no hint offered on any front about how convergence towards truth or explanation might be forthcoming.

At some point, then, anyone seeking to make sense of Aboriginal law must look for *ways to decide between theoretical paths (or whether a new pathway must be forged)*. If a theorist coming to the phenomena of radically differing theoretical accounts adheres to a fundamental concern with understanding and explaining Aboriginal law, a difficult question arises: How does one *properly* approach theories and the role of theorizing?

It is not sufficient to simply note that radically diverse theories seem to reflect scholars' perspectives (that is, reflect their seeming embeddedness in specific sociocultural settings). Could it not be that while different theorists tend to *see* Canadian law differently, there is still a single *proper* way to understand its nature? To put this another way, what exactly follows from pointing to this diversity of points of view? Perhaps some theorists are not sufficiently attuned to the possibility they might be building models of Aboriginal law with elements drawn unreflectively from their own lives and experiences. Perhaps some even mask their actual intentions and actions in engaging in activity that they present as "theorizing" but is actually politics in disguise. Does any of this *require* that we find a way to theorize about Aboriginal law that accommodates perspectives?

49 Above all else this is the signal sent through the *Tsilhqot'in Nation* decision. See *Tsilhqot'in Nation*, *supra* note 11. Though it has to be teased out of the mass of theory, these notions tend to arise within strands woven into the fabric of postcolonial studies.

To see the necessity to do so, we need to think more carefully about how perspectives are embedded in the nature of theorizing about the law. This entanglement goes beyond simply the possibility that a scholar's point of view *may* influence how she theorizes about the law.

A wide and diverse spectrum of theories is available to choose from when thinking about how to theorize Aboriginal law. At a deep level this range runs parallel to the variety to be found more generally in the field of legal theory. Divergent theories all fit neatly into one of two broad camps – those we could characterize as "grand theories" and those we find eschewing grand narratives for localized, historicized accounts.

In the field of Aboriginal law grand theories rest on (generally unreflective) acceptance of principles of justice and fairness. This leads to two possible levels of discourse. On the one hand, we find theorists who accept that there is *some* answer to what principles and ideals should underscore the development of the law and who exert time and energy debating what these may be. On the other hand, we find theorists who simply accept or presume that *their* position on the nature of the right principles and ideals is correct and who debate how this should play out in the development of the law. The key point is that grand theories posit or presume a realm of moral or political matters that provide the proper content for those worried about how to build legal systems. Rather than worry about how all that is supposed to work, let us shift attention to another specific attribute of grand theories – namely, their disdain for the notion that perspectives play an ineliminable role in the production of knowledge. In this camp "Justice" (however defined) *is what it is*, as difficult as it may be for scholars to agree on what that might be.

Alternatively, critical theories aim to produce accounts of how things *appear* to be, accounts that consciously reflect the positionality of their generators. For those in this camp, all theorizing is determined by sociocultural/historical position, there being no "view from nowhere."[50] Critical theorists do not simply accept that perspectives may play a role in the knowledge of production; they place perspectives at the core of knowledge itself.

We find ourselves faced with essentially two types of theories, resting on two theories (or in the case of many, two sets of presumptions) about the business of theorizing. On the one hand, some theorists set their work in an intellectual space framed by understandings of knowledge as something emptied of subjectivity, while on the other hand we find those who understand their own work – as with that of all others – as systematizations of the sociocultural milieu

50 Thomas Nagel contrasts views from the inside (our individual subjective experiences) with the "view from nowhere," that point of view that would exist independent of particular perspectives. See Thomas Nagel, *The View from Nowhere* (Oxford: Oxford University Press, 1986).

within which they live and work. The one camp eschews any intermingling of knowledge-production and perspectives, while the other finds that knowledge fits directly overtop perspectives. Being faced with such a stark and strongly divergent set of choices is troubling enough, but we are not yet at the core reason why we must develop a way to satisfactorily address the intersection of theorizing and perspectives.

First, consider the former, "grand theory," camp. We need to grapple with reasons and causes that might account for the position these theorists take vis-à-vis perspectives, as (a) we cannot just accept this position, given its potential impact on Indigenous ways of knowing and being, and (b) it is arguably the manifestation of a perspective on the world, human nature, and the creation of social institutions.

All well and good, but now turn to the camp occupied by critical theorists. There we find as well that we are forced to grapple with reasons and causes that might account for their position vis-à-vis perspectives, as once again (a) we cannot simply accept their position, given its potential impact on Indigenous ways of knowing and being (placing all this, as critical theorists must, into the world of power and politics), while (b) it is not just that critical theories situate positionality in a central role, because such theories cannot escape consuming themselves, as the general critical position is itself (something critical theorists must admit) the product of a Western intellectual tradition, one that may not sit well with Indigenous understandings and histories. We see, then, an injunction arise, a requirement that we carefully explore the nature of theory and theorizing. Whether grappling with a grand theory or a localized/historicized account, we have larger background concerns that drive us into questioning how theories of the law function in the world.

How processes around the development and promulgation of theories of law might work, whether this is all done with some purpose in mind (*other* than explaining what is happening in the world), what the intent might be if this is so, what this might imply for not only our understanding of Aboriginal law but also for what we are to do in this situation, is all – I feel – essentially important to Indigenous communities and nations. How are we to know we are doing what we must for generations to come if we do not delve into these matters?

It may be that results of work on these questions may ultimately amount to little in Indigenous communities and lives. I believe, however, it should lead to realizations about what really count as some of the great challenges facing Indigenous peoples, realizations that are important as Indigenous peoples map out collective strategies for future generations. Given the work that went into putting together this text, it should not be surprising I think so.

These hints in hand about what is to come in the text, the rest of the Introduction sketches out the approach taken to working with legal theory and ultimately making sense of Aboriginal rights, and it says something about how this approach then unfolds into an analysis of Aboriginal rights in the second half of this text. The Introduction concludes with something of a roadmap, setting out how pieces of this work fit together.

The Journey Depersonalized: How the Text Unfolds

One can try to understand jurisprudence on Aboriginal rights by attempting to see how individual elements within the law function and how they fit with each other (or not) – one might begin, that is, with "doctrinal analysis."[51] The first step beyond such "black letter" analysis would naturally be to the level of principles, substrata of the law sitting in the background, arguably serving as architectural elements of emerging jurisprudence. Here we expect to find elements of the law that speak to *why* it is as it is, what *reasons* (in the minds of the judiciary) account for developments we witness.[52]

In this study, however, we need to maintain focus on the larger picture: these principles structure relations between a sovereign entity – the Canadian state – and Indigenous peoples with separate and independent legal and political orders. Complicating matters – especially when we suspect the content of these principles may come from the sociocultural world within which the Canadian state and its courts sit – is that these principles are not objects to be simply picked up and examined from different angles. Rather, principles are anchored in the world as *beliefs* held by individuals (initially, and most importantly in this context, by judges and legislators).

We earlier noted two possibilities concerning how these principles might manifest in the world. On the one hand, these principles might seem to capture in language things that reach out past our lives as social animals (a "principle of justice," for example, might be something that can be put into words, but is understood [at least by some] to point to a further transcendent "thing" – *justice* – meant to determine or fix the content of beliefs about it). When conceived of in this manner, one might then wonder how our awareness of these transcendent entities is possible. Following down this path, we seem to need to posit unusual sensory or intellectual capacities. On the other

51 Kerry Wilkins provides a careful, detailed doctrinal survey of Aboriginal law. See Wilkins, *Essentials of Canadian Aboriginal Law*, *supra* note 47. See also Isaac, *Aboriginal Law*, 4th ed, *supra* note 47.

52 A handful of texts purport to provide analyses of the law on Aboriginal rights that attempt to put the jurisprudence onto a principled level. See e.g. Reynolds, *supra* note 47; Borrows, *Recovering Canada*, *supra* note 46. Works that attempt to advance beyond doctrinal analysis in this area of jurisprudence never do explore how to think about roles that principles, values, and ideals may play in the generation of the law of a state as it applies to independent peoples.

hand, these principles might seem to be *entirely* constructed, in which case a different set of questions arises around where their content comes from, who determines this content, what functions these instruments are meant to be put towards, etc.

To make sense of how these principles are supposed to be understood, we must then press onward, digging down to the level of theoretical inquiry. We need to explore the *nature* of principles, how they enter our social lives, how they act to structure rule-making enterprises, how they function within social institutions, and so forth. We need to work out *how to study* these difficult creatures so as to determine how complex worlds of social institutions are formed and function.

Over the last few pages, however, we detailed difficulties in looking for fixed and objective sense once we turn to theories and models of the law – rather than help us gain insight into Aboriginal law, theories only seem to muddy the waters. Where can we turn if the quest is to make sense of Aboriginal rights, but the project seems beset by powerful and fundamental challenges?

The difficulty of our quest is heightened when we dig into key cases. There we find that *puzzles* populate the jurisprudence, many of which both (a) emerge from consideration of Indigenous perspectives on law and history, and (b) seem to themselves reflect the fact that understanding law itself is arguably a matter of perspective. It turns out not to be so much that theories of law and Aboriginal law fail to respond to these puzzles, but that they entirely ignore key background issues concerning the intersection of law and perspectives. Unfortunately, we find in established legal theory simply more conflict and confusion.

The first step through this thicket requires that we appreciate the nature of the socio-legal matter under investigation. What does it mean to try to "make sense" when the phenomena inextricably relate to existing sociocultural worlds and related perspectives? What might it mean to think of a legal order as an expression of perspectivally grounded sets of beliefs (about such things as values and ideals)? We can begin addressing these matters by noting that in the situation under examination we can think of one legal order – the liberal democratic state – as a manifestation *in the world* of a set of beliefs about liberal values and ideals, while when we then turn our minds to Indigenous legal orders we see these likewise constitute manifestations *in the world* of other sets of beliefs about varied Indigenous values and ideals. The situation we are examining is then visible in the world and we can formulate a hypothesis: we witness the legal order of the state put to use in an attempt to control and regulate Indigenous communities, and we consider the possibility that we can adequately explore the way this takes place in the world so as to explain what we observe.

My suggestion is simple at its heart. Let us consider what we can witness and explore in the world before us and around us: the generation of legal meaning by meaning-generating communities, and the attempt by one meaning-generating community to have its meanings inform a system of rules that would regulate not just the lives, but also the meanings that infuse the lives of other meaning-generating communities. Now, if all this were to be carefully examined as phenomena *in the world*, we can begin to make sense of Aboriginal law.

My argument is that this approach provides not just another perspective on Aboriginal law, but an explanation for what we all witness that contains some *truth* about the matter. Much of the constellation of concerns and considerations detailed above seemingly comes into being as a result of the focus for this inquiry – we hope to probe a very particular set of socio-legal phenomena, the application of aspects of one legal order onto the lives and legal orders of communities possessed of separate legal and political authority – but my position is that the nature of this set of socio-legal phenomena can be studied as part of the world around us.

This approach is adopted in a search for roots to the problem, roots that lie in how legal theory has been challenged by the notion that theorizing could ever provide *grounded* insight into legal phenomena. I carefully pick apart arguments that all legal theories are either (a) essentially culturally bounded, and/or (b) entirely merely interpretive. Either possibility questions whether we could ever hope to explain Aboriginal law, as all attempts – all theories or models – would be open to the charge that they are no more than perspectives on phenomena (and not "objective"). I develop and apply an approach that meets these challenges head-on.

To resolve how one makes progress, I begin by spending considerable time picking apart the nature of problems that arise in theorizing about the law. I begin with the presumption that theories *in general* should be approachable as efforts to make sense of phenomena and look to see how they fare when we begin with the general business of broadly theorizing about phenomena. My reason for starting from such a ground-floor level is straightforward – it provides an opportunity to explore broad and difficult problems that emerge at a fundamental level, which then persist as core challenges to the business of theorizing about the law. It is at this base floor, as well, that we can identify ways to address apparent problems with theorizing, the adoption of which carry us through the tangle of problems peculiar to the business of theorizing about the law and about Aboriginal law.

The way to address these problems is to adopt a specific approach to understanding theorizing – that of methodological naturalism. This approach is introduced over the rest of this Introduction, put into the context of an overview of how I move through the middle chapters of this text into the analysis of Aboriginal law. We conclude with a few words about how the rest of the text then unfolds.

Methodological Naturalism Introduced

Thinking about the general business of theorizing about phenomena leads into challenges around how we might ever *know* we are making progress, and whether we are moving towards more *truthful* accounts. These challenges have bedevilled intellectual thought in the West from early stages of the Enlightenment.[53] While a prominent articulation of a form of these challenges can be read out of such early works as Descartes' *Meditations*,[54] they rose to a new level of prominence in the middle of the twentieth century. Questions around truth and progress towards truth came to a head in the middle of that century, as challenges mounted against the edifice of the scientific enterprise. I follow the lead of naturalist thinkers in arguing there are ways these challenges can be tempered, preserving sense in the notion that theories can be understood as attempts to work towards *better* accounts of the *way things are*.[55] I argue one can (a) accept the conclusions of key arguments developed in these struggles over understanding how truth and progress fit within the scientific enterprise (the conclusion, for example, that it is fruitless to attempt to validate scientific knowledge by use of a priori concepts or processes) and yet (b) still salvage a reputable understanding of knowledge production.

I focus on one identifiable sensible response to the concern about establishing the absolute validity of claims to truth or knowledge: to shift focus to how truth and knowledge actually function *within the human-social world*. In particular, one can sensibly decide that rather than worry about metaphysical challenges arising out of centuries of philosophical debate over how we can *know* scientific accounts *progress*, we can leave questions about how science works to the *practice of science*, so questions about "truth" and "progress" – to the extent such questions arise within scientific discourse – are left to standards and practices *within* the ongoing business of doing science, all of which is understood to be an *activity* of exploration into the natural world that *occurs within the natural world*. This is understood to signal the "naturalization" of epistemology – seemingly intractable problems about the ultimate grounding of truth-claims are left behind, replaced by inquiries into what truth and progress might mean in the natural world (the very same world being opened up to scientific, naturalist inquiry).

---

53 Similar questions also plagued intellectual life in early Greek and Roman eras.

54 René Descartes, *Meditations on First Philosophy*, vol 2, translated by Elizabeth Haldane & GRT Ross (Cambridge, UK: Cambridge University Press, 1911).

55 See e.g. Jack Ritchie, *Understanding Naturalism* (Stocksfield, UK: Acumen Press, 2008); Peter Godfrey-Smith, *Theory and Reality: An Introduction to the Philosophy of Science* (Chicago: University of Chicago Press, 2003).

This is one pillar to the form of methodological naturalism worked with in this text – the notion that questions about theorizing (indeed, how to think about theorizing) should all be approached as matters to be explored within the natural world. While this might seem a bland and harmless grounding for theorizing, it actually captures a revolution in how scholars in the West think about what it is to explore the world of phenomena. The dominant approach up to the mid-twentieth century, clearly underlying the world view built up through and around the Enlightenment and practically unquestioned through centuries of Western thought, imagines one can develop theories about theorizing – about how we attain truth and work towards knowledge – simply by *thinking* about such matters. Approaches thereby developed – *all* making use of either a priori concepts, principles, or methods – run us up into seemingly irresolvable confusion.

A key section in chapter 4 ("General Challenges to the Common Sense Model") details some of the seemingly intractable problems generated.[56] The appeal of a naturalized approach to theory-production and evaluation is at that point more fully introduced, as it provides a path away from these sources of confusion. It is argued to be far better to accede to the idea (even if only provisionally in the exercise in this text, within *methodological* naturalism) that everything develops within (or initially should be studied as part of) the natural world. Indeed – and crucially – it is better that we accede to the simple notion that *we*, as researchers, are simply components of this larger natural world. This, I argue, leads the way to a resolution, not just to problems with the notion of perspectival knowledge, but also to questions about *our* place in all this, as positionally placed researchers looking into the law.

Serious challenges seem to remain, however, as *legal theory* is about an aspect of the world – a complex social institution – that arguably cannot be studied adequately using tools and techniques appropriate to the study of the natural world. Questions come up about both (a) the possibility that there are aspects of the social-normative realm that cannot be adequately studied as one would the natural world, and (b) the possibility that what humans build cannot be adequately understood naturalistically.

My response is to allow for these possibilities, but to argue we can still work our way towards sensible accounts of the law when our focus is on precisely the sort of phenomena to be accounted for in this study – the attempted

56 Even the great debate through the Enlightenment years – between empiricists and rationalists – was waged within this frame of reference. Empiricists also developed "armchair" theories of theorizing, adhering to the sense that *externally devised* standards of knowledge production could be used to adjudicate between their accounts and those of the rationalists. The process of naturalizing epistemology pulls these standards into a field determined by the practitioners of knowledge-production.

application of the Canadian legal system to the lives and worlds of Indigenous peoples (with separate and independent meaning-generating capacities). As noted above, behind the notion that all theorizing is to be approached as taking place in the natural world is the sense that all human existence is contained within the larger natural world. The study is undertaken, then, with the presumption that social worlds that humans construct and inhabit emerge in the natural world.[57] This generates the presumption that much of what we observe in the human-social realm (including processes that encompass the generation of meaning, processes that account for the fact that words come to carry meaning with them) is susceptible to naturalistic analysis.

On top of all that, as we look particularly at attempts to pull Indigenous peoples into a world built in and through the generation of meaning carried by judicial pronouncements of Canadian courts, we find that not only must we take jurisprudence as an element of the social world to be naturalistically studied, but also that some theories about that jurisprudence must be understood to function *not* to *describe* a legal world, but to assist in its creation, maintenance, and strengthening (and in this context, its imposition on Indigenous peoples).[58] To summarize: we end up taking *all* this material (the jurisprudence, the beliefs and attitudes of juristic actors, and theories about the law) as material to be studied and worked with, as *all* constituting things we can observe and study in the natural world. This study as a whole fits generally under the umbrella of naturalistic analysis.

Should one periodically return when necessary to the core vision (of humans as sociolinguistic tool-users, as social animals emerging within the natural world), this is not a difficult form of analysis to understand. At the core of the approach is the presumption that we must focus on parts of the world around us that we can observe and study. We presume that rules, tests, principles, and theories are elements of the natural world around us, and we see where this leads (following basic processes of study, those appropriate to the study of the natural world). The flipside – the place where concern enters the picture from some quarters – is that we do our best to begin analysis with no link to a priori principles, concepts, theories, or models.

This might seem to put me down on one side of a disputed point I brought up earlier – whether concepts like "justice" and "fairness" are grounded in

57 I lean heavily on Searle's work in this regard, though I move a fair distance beyond his model, given its narrow focus on explaining the nature of relatively self-contained social worlds. See John Searle, *Making the Social World: The Structure of Human Civilization* (Oxford: Oxford University Press, 2010).

58 I discuss examples of this in a section in chapter 7, where I look at representative contemporary Aboriginal rights scholars. See "Liberal Theory and Liberal Theorists in the Natural World" in chapter 7.

sociocultural worlds or whether they can reach out to and be grounded by transcendent objects. But the approach employed in this text avoids the horns of this dilemma. First, under naturalism we can safely accept the idea that meaning is generated in sociocultural settings. Indeed, the idea of separate, independent meaning-generating communities is important when we turn to what we witness with Canadian law (as we witness attempts by one meaning-generating community to impose its social reality onto other meaning-generating communities). Second, in looking at all this from the perspective of examinations of the natural world, we distance ourselves from the notion that all meaning is simply perspectival, that all is ultimately grounded in nothing more than sociocultural settings.

Further, I work within a form of *methodological* naturalism (in contrast to substantive, material, or ontological naturalism). This is understood in this work to mean that while it is productive to study what is observable in the world around us, no hard and fast assumptions are made about what exists or might be found to exist. There is no a priori denial, then, of the possibility that referents such as "justice" and "fairness" *may* indeed reach out to realms not experienced through the usual senses.[59] Such possibilities, however, are kept to one side and not deployed in the analysis that follows. I focus on how *beliefs* in such concepts *function* in the world, about the *impacts* they have, for example, on the lives of Indigenous peoples. I do my best to avoid potentially endless debates about what such concepts purportedly "ultimately" might mean, what they might point to, and their value, soundness, or justification.

The analysis is meant to unfold in the general form of an exercise – in the form of an experiment; we begin with naturalist presumptions and ask if, from them, we can make progress towards making sense of Aboriginal rights in a way that can be defended as reasonable and – in some acceptable sense – objective.

How the Chapters Unfold

Over the rest of this text I explore means by which one might make sense of Aboriginal rights and the sense developed through such means. Before focusing on this central task, however, a significant amount of stage-setting is required. The work begins with a chapter introducing the Indigenous/Aboriginal peoples of what is now Canada, one that focuses on the disjunction between self-understandings of the many peoples who can now be gathered under these

59 For a discussion of access to non-natural realms, among other serious issues, see Michael Ridge, "Moral Non-Naturalism," *Stanford Encyclopedia of Philosophy* (Fall 2014), Edward N Zalta, ed, online: <plato.stanford.edu/archives/fall2014/entries/moral-non-naturalism>.

broad terms, and constructed understandings that emerge from Canadian history (and Canadian law and policy). While I do not have the opportunity to say nearly enough about the lived experiences and histories of Indigenous people and communities, hopefully the reader can begin to appreciate some of the complex narratives behind such innocuous-sounding expressions as "the Aboriginal and treaty rights of the Aboriginal peoples of Canada."[60]

A sense in place of who the Indigenous peoples are with whom the Canadian state interacts, a few words are necessary on the history of Indigenous resistance weaving its way through the dark history of colonialism in Canada. Following that, the first chapter wraps up with two sections that prepare the way for a detailed examination of the jurisprudence on Aboriginal rights. First, some further historical context is required, as we quickly trace the development of Canadian law and policy concerning Indigenous people. To keep this brief, the focus is on one sliver of this tale: the treatment of gender in law and legislation and its effects on self-identity. Second, we need to dig a bit more deeply into perspectives (and the interaction of perspectives and analyses of the law). We need to look not just at what "Indigenous perspectives" might mean in this context, but at how perspectives complicate any attempt to say something substantive about any field identified as "law." This discussion closes chapter 1.

The second chapter provides an overview of Aboriginal law in Canada, with focus shifting quickly to the constitutionalization of Aboriginal rights under section 35 of the *Constitution Act, 1982*.[61] In mapping out the jurisprudence around Aboriginal rights, I introduce puzzles engendered by this case law. Puzzles are generally presented as matters in particular need of explication and explanation. While some puzzles simply call for clarification of the case law, others seem akin to apparent anomalies in data that a scientist might face when trying to make sense of phenomena through the lens of some theory. These latter puzzles are of particular interest in this study, as they challenge our ability to make sense of Aboriginal law through the lens of (liberal) legal theory.

Chapter 3 begins with a look into differing evaluations of the law on Aboriginal rights. The end-product is a further sense of puzzlement, as theoretical attempts to make sense of Aboriginal rights themselves present divergent views of the jurisprudential landscape, with no apparent attempt to work towards convergence on important matters. I end this look into the jurisprudence and its attendant puzzles with the suggestion in the second half of chapter 3 that the application of the form of methodological naturalism sketched out above might help make sense of the package of law, puzzles, and theories. The form of naturalism I intend to experiment with is introduced in more detail at that

60 *Constitution Act, 1982*, *supra* note 1, s 35 (recognizing and affirming those rights).
61 *Supra* note 1.

point – though it should also be appreciated that as the last third of the text is taken up with its application to the mass of legal phenomena under examination, along the way its nature is constantly revealed and tested in yet more detail.

This sets up the middle section of this text, a discussion of the landscape of theorizing. This text has been put together so readers need not necessarily traverse this difficult terrain. Those interested principally in just how sense can be made of Aboriginal rights can jump ahead to chapter 6. Those curious about the larger historical-intellectual context, and those interested in seeing how debates in the West about knowledge-production and progress seemed to create roadblocks for those working out how the law of the Canadian state is laid over the lives and understandings of Indigenous peoples, will likely profit from working through the middle of this text. I do return later, in chapter 6, to retrace a few key points uncovered and dissected. Further, how the approach of methodological naturalism actually functions is illustrated in the last few chapters, and it is likely sufficient for the reader to see how the experiment unfolds, to assess its success as they decide whether insight is provided into the nature of Canadian courts' pronouncements on Aboriginal rights.

The discussion in the middle "theory" chapters advances from a most general level (about theorizing in general, about any phenomena), to theorizing in relation to human activity, to theorizing about the law. As the discussion progresses through these stages, I introduce specific problems that seem to rise up around the business of theorizing at these different levels, at junctures along the way arguing that a form of methodological naturalism defuses concerns.

Stage-setting complete, the last three substantive chapters contain the promised analysis, as I turn directly to the question of how one might make sense of Aboriginal rights. My focus is on striving to do so in a manner that tackles perspective, while keeping a distance from the easy slide into what is essentially political or ideological discourse. One concern driving analysis in the last part of this text is that *all* analysis of Aboriginal rights is susceptible to a quick judgment – that it is all perspectival *and thereby* "political." Indeed, no matter what article or book I pick up to find out about the nature of Aboriginal rights, I find it next to impossible not to see before me work suffused with presuppositions and buried premises that render the analysis suspect. If my goal is to make sense of Aboriginal rights, a path forward must be charted that holds out some realizable promise that I am not taking that common route set down by both defenders of the status quo and deep critics – *both parties* are open to charges of being political (as no one in either camp provides a sense of how he can present his analyses as truly making sense of this field of Canadian law).[62]

62 Indeed, many of these scholars exhibit bias, as they often seem remarkably unconcerned with the possibility that what they say begins from a coloured view of matters before them. Little to no effort seems to go into thinking about, acknowledging, or attempting to manage bias.

In chapters 6 and 7, liberal doctrine is revealed to be a good way to explain most contemporary developments in Aboriginal rights jurisprudence, but it is also shown to have a blind spot in relation to the very sorts of historical events that most concern Indigenous communities and individuals. The inability of this doctrine to explain key aspects of Aboriginal rights jurisprudence is explored, and there is an examination into how liberal theorists function in "theorizing" Aboriginal rights.

Attention then shifts in the last substantive chapter to the ability of critical (postcolonial) thought to make sense of these matters. The conclusion is that a "sanitized" form of postcolonial thought can very well explain not just what liberal theory illuminates (as it subsumes these liberal explanations within its own framework of analysis), but also areas of contemporary jurisprudence otherwise left mysterious.

As noted earlier, my project is essentially an exercise in the application of methodological naturalism to this investigation into the field of Aboriginal law. The analysis of the ability of liberal theory to make sense of much of the jurisprudence and its attendant puzzles is carried out by treating both the jurisprudence and this form of legal theory as sociolinguistic systems put into play in our complex social worlds, while the ability of a (sanitized) critical theory to make sense of this process of liberalizing Indigenous societies is presented as a better explanation only insofar as the theory is divested of non-naturalist underpinnings. The reader is left, at the end of the exercise, to judge the success of this attempt to make sense of Aboriginal rights.

1 Setting the Stage

Indigenous Peoples, Aboriginal People, and Canada

Serious challenges attend attempts to provide a reasonable background discussion to the sort of analysis I intend to provide in this text. While most of the analysis is focused on "the law," on Canadian law, and on how domestic Canadian law intersects with the lives of Indigenous people, behind this lies a mass of stories coming from the experiences of Indigenous/Aboriginal peoples in Canada. These stories bring in the lives of individuals, families, clans, communities, and nations, and they are as varied as one can imagine. In a few pages I turn to Aboriginal law, providing a description of that "thing" to be analysed in this work. But just behind this field of domestic law we find Indigenous cultures, languages, histories, and worlds. For the reader unaware of the general social, political, and legal histories of Indigenous peoples in Canada, I must try to say something adequate, something that can provide enough background to make the analysis sensible and meaningful. But what is adequate?

I am not able to devote more than a few pages to the task of grounding analysis in the lived experiences of communities and individuals. Rather than attempt an impossible task, I have decided, then, to aim for a more reasonable goal. What follows relies to some extent on the generation of perceptions or impressions rather than anything like a detailed account – but more importantly it says something about the lives, histories, and worlds of Indigenous peoples in such a way as to begin to build up themes and arguments advanced in the rest of the text.[1]

---

1 In a few chapters, when we analyse how to make sense of Aboriginal law, we necessarily return to the business of providing some historical and political context, as the present state of Aboriginal law cannot be described without that tracing. That hardly suffices, however, to fill this lacuna. For those coming fairly fresh to the history of Crown-Indigenous relations, and left puzzled at complexities hinted at, my hope is that research energies can be turned

Before beginning this overview, let me note that some measure of responsibility falls on you, the reader. You should ask yourself, in a moment of self-reflection, about the state of your education in this matter. If a sense of concern floats up, please consider broadening your education into historical, social, cultural, and economic interactions between Indigenous/Aboriginal peoples and both Canadian society and the Canadian state. If you are Canadian and feel lost in a strange landscape of history and politics, this is more an imperative than a request – narratives around these interactions directly relate to fundamental events, forces, and narratives eventuating in the dominion we inhabit and share.

Here I can do no more than wave at the complex and rich set of histories that lead to our contemporary scene. The overview is structured to focus attention on particular threads, chosen for the material support they provide later when, in going through stages of analysis, I attempt to weave arguments around the nature of the current relationship. My focus is on actions by the respective Crowns signalling deployment of linguistic-symbolic tools to further fairly well-defined goals. The historical overview, then, says little about the lives and struggles of peoples or communities – detail about lives and experiences must be read into and around these remarks, and if the need or opportunity arises, be investigated by the reader.

After saying a bit about self-identity and the imposition of constructed identities by the state, the chapter concludes with a brief overview of the Crown's more overtly legal manoeuvres during the last century and more, and a few prefatory words about how contemporary Canadian Aboriginal law may look from the perspectives of peoples whose communal and individual lives have been affected by passage through long colonial histories.

Brief Histories Told through Forms of Language

There are numerous legal and political matters that complicate even the most simple attempts to describe the historical and social context of Aboriginal peoples in Canada. Several can be introduced by focusing on the terminology that constrains discourse. For example, on a most general level we speak of "Canada," and we speak of "Aboriginal peoples" in their relationships to this modern nation state. Both referential terms carry a lot of historical weight – they mean what they do today as a result of the gradual development of certain legal, political, and social forms over the last few centuries.

Let me focus discussion on the expression "Aboriginal peoples," reaching out past this as the discussion develops. I noted earlier that I distinguish between

---

to materials noted in the footnotes. My notes are far from exhaustive, but they can serve at the very least as openings to accounts that provide the sorts of histories necessary for a fuller understanding of the current situation of Aboriginal peoples in Canada.

this term and "Indigenous Peoples," a term I use to denote peoples whose identities have been and continue to be essentially matters of self-identification. The term "Aboriginal peoples," in contrast, has a specific constitutional/legal meaning within Canada, the result of the inclusion of section 35 in the *Constitution Act, 1982*.[2] The core of that provision reads:

> 35 (1) The existing aboriginal and treaty rights of the aboriginal peoples of Canada are hereby recognized and affirmed.
>
> (2) In this Act, "aboriginal peoples of Canada" includes the Indian, Inuit and Métis peoples of Canada.[3]

"Aboriginal peoples," then, is a term *within Canadian law* with three separate referent sub-bodies – Indian, Inuit, and Metis. Each term carries along its own history, sociocultural context, and legal milieu.

"Indian"

Besides (apparently) mischaracterizing most of the original inhabitants of North America through mistaken denotation linked to a population on the other side of the world, the expression "Indian" has a long and difficult history, beginning in the first few decades of contact and interaction with European powers. When used in general discourse to point to the "Indian" peoples living in contemporary Canada, it points to the many and varied original societies (speaking within ten larger language groupings, broken up into approximately sixty-five regional cultural-linguistic polities)[4] inhabiting present-day Canada, except for areas in the Far North (for thousands of years occupied by the Inuit).

Each of these communities – comprising self-determining peoples – has an identity emergent out of its own history, language, and culture. The Cree, for example, designate themselves as such in the contemporary world, but also call themselves the Nēhilawē, and only fairly recently have come to be gathered into the larger classificatory scheme, the larger body of "the Indians of Canada." As Nēhilawē they have a history all their own, reaching back thousands of years. This is the sort of history often skipped over or abbreviated in opening sections of texts on the history of Canada. Given the enormous geographic reach of this ethno-linguistic community – from present-day northeastern British Columbia to present-day Labrador – multiple sub-histories need to be told to capture

2 *Constitution Act, 1982*, being Schedule B to the *Canada Act 1982* (UK), 1982, c 11) [*Constitution Act, 1982*].

3 *Ibid*, s 35.

4 Pamela Williamson & John Roberts, *First Nations Peoples*, 2nd ed (Toronto: Edmond Montgomery Publications, 2004) at 46–51.

this rich tapestry. There are many such Indigenous histories, all grounded in the long existences of Indigenous peoples in North America.

I use the term "Indigenous people" to point to self-designated peoples with long histories long before the arrival of Europeans. This level of generality is itself new in lexicons of Indigenous peoples – they seldom group themselves naturally into such pan-identified structures, but rather use such particularized identifiers as Musqueam, Innu, Cree (Nēhilawē), Maliseet, Mohawk, and many others.

Many of these peoples (I here refer to them as peoples, borrowing from the meaning now attached to this term in international law)[5] have been articulating their own histories in written or expressive form over the last few generations, and much of this can be found online.[6] I cannot do more here than note this quickly growing body of material. The reader is asked to explore if she is not already doing so.

What is most troubling in the histories of "Indian" peoples in Canada is the emergence of legal manoeuvres, beginning in the middle of the nineteenth century, meant to undercut Indian control of Indian lives on both individual and collective levels. Narratives around political machinations of the Crown are troubling enough – of particular import in this stage-setting overview, however, is that we note the way *legal* developments coincided with growing efforts to control the political lives of Indian communities.

There was a fascinating period of interaction between newly arrived Europeans and Indigenous polities in the first few centuries of contact on the east coast of North America.[7] European countries consistently fought amongst themselves for advantage in this "New World," in the process forming trade and military alliances with the "several nations" they encountered along the seaboard.[8] Even towards the end of this period, as the British Crown consolidated power over

---

5 This meaning is well captured in the *United Nations Declaration on the Rights of Indigenous Peoples*. See UNGA, *United Nations Declaration on the Rights of Indigenous Peoples*, UNGAOR, 61st Sess, Supp No 49, UN Doc A/RES/61/295 (13 September 2007).

6 A useful first window (when used with appropriate caution!) into contemporary work on self-definition and self-understanding is Wikipedia. Searching for the entry on the Innu, for example, takes one to an overview of Innu history, culture, and current situations and challenges. More importantly, however, this page provides a connection under "external links" to, for example, the website of the Innu Nation of Labrador. See Innu Nation, online: <innu.ca>.

7 For a discussion of the stages of historical interaction, see e.g. Canada, Royal Commission on Aboriginal Peoples, "Stage Two: Contact and Co-operation" in *Report of the Royal Commission on Aboriginal Peoples*, vol 1 (Ottawa: Minister of Supply and Services, 1996) 94 [*RCAP Report*]. In a somewhat different way – and arguably to a lesser extent – this form of interaction can be witnessed in the north and west of the continent, and along the northwest coast.

8 See e.g. *RCAP Report*, *supra* note 7 at 114–20; Arthur Ray, "Welcoming the Newcomers" in Arthur Ray *I Have Lived Here since the World Began: An Illustrated History of Canada's Native People* (Toronto: Key Porter Books, 1996) 46; Arthur Ray, "New Friends and Foes" in *ibid* at 60.

northeastern North America, the notion of dealing with Indigenous peoples as constituting self-organized political units was not uncommon. We see this reflected in policy and action – consider, for example, the wording of a section of the *Royal Proclamation of 1763*[9] (which generally set out in broad terms an overview of concerns, policy, and future considerations for the British Crown, as it consolidated its victory in North America over French forces and strove to work out how to maintain good relations with both its Indian military allies and those who had allied with the French):

> And whereas it is just and reasonable, and essential to our Interest, and the Security of our Colonies, that the several Nations or Tribes of Indians with whom We are connected, and who live under our Protection, should not be molested or disturbed in the Possession of such Parts of Our Dominions and Territories as, not having been ceded to or purchased by Us, are reserved to them or any of them, as their Hunting Grounds – We do therefore ... declare it to be our Royal Will and Pleasure that no Governor or Commander in Chief ... do presume, upon any Pretence whatever, to grant Warrants of Survey, or pass any Patents for Lands beyond the Bounds of their respective Governments.[10]

We see similar notions in the decisions of Chief Justice Marshall of the United States Supreme Court in the first half of the nineteenth century, where we observe language recognizing a degree of Indian or tribal sovereignty, considered within American law to be "domesticated" and "dependent" within the

9 *George R, Proclamation*, 7 October 1763 (3 Geo III), reprinted RSC 1985, App II, No 1 [Proclamation] [emphasis added].

10 The proclamation continues:

> And We do further declare it to be Our Royal Will and Pleasure, for the present as aforesaid, to reserve under our Sovereignty, Protection, and Dominion, for the use of the said Indians, all the Lands and Territories not included within the Limits of Our said Three new Governments, or within the Limits of the Territory granted to the Hudson's Bay Company, as also all the Lands and Territories lying to the Westward of the Sources of the Rivers which fall into the Sea from the West and North West as aforesaid....
>
> And whereas great Frauds and Abuses have been committed in purchasing Lands of the Indians, to the great Prejudice of our Interests and to the great Dissatisfaction of the said Indians: In order, therefore, to prevent such Irregularities for the future, and to the end that the Indians may be convinced of our Justice and determined Resolution to remove all reasonable Cause of Discontent, We do ... strictly enjoin and require that ... if at any Time any of the Said Indians should be inclined to dispose of the said Lands, the same shall be Purchased only for Us, in our Name, at some public Meeting or Assembly of the said Indians, to be held for that Purpose by the Governor or Commander in Chief of our Colony respectively within which they shall lie.... And we do ... declare and enjoin, that the Trade with the said Indians shall be free and open to all our Subjects whatever provided that every Person who may incline to Trade with the said Indians do take out a Licence for carrying on such Trade from the Governor or Commander in Chief of any of our Colonies respectively where such Person shall reside.

new Republic.[11] Indian communities were knit together into larger political-cultural-linguistic entities, and as late as the middle of the nineteenth century we witness their being treated by British/American authorities sometimes as akin in some ways to constituted "nations."[12]

In Canada, however, by the middle of the nineteenth century the forces at play had shifted. Indian polities had suffered in many ways (through, amongst other things, the introduction of new diseases, settler force and fraud, Crown deceit, and economic deprivations). With Indigenous populations decimated, British authorities began to vacillate between two policy objectives, aggressively pursuing one or the other (and sometimes, oddly, both simultaneously).[13] In concert with a powerful drive to acquire (unencumbered, if possible) as much Indigenous land as possible, the British Crown began to interfere with the lives

---

11 See *Cherokee Nation v Georgia* (1831) 30 US 1 at 17, Marshall CJ:

> It may well be doubted whether those tribes shall reside within the acknowledged boundaries of the United States can, with strict accuracy, be denominated foreign nations. They may more correctly, perhaps, be denominated domestic dependent nations. They occupy a territory to which we assert a title independent of their will, which must take effect in point of possession when their right of possession ceases; meanwhile, they are in a state of pupilage. Their relations to the United States resemble that of a ward to his guardian. They look to our Government for protection, rely upon its kindness and its power, appeal to it for relief to their wants, and address the President as their Great Father.

12 This is not to suggest parity or synonymy in relation to most characteristics – either internal or external – that typically mark such sociopolitical creatures. As Taiaiake Alfred notes, his community – that of the Mohawk – would not see itself as in any way akin to a European nation state. Its own sense of itself would not translate into a notion that could be mapped onto the kinds of sociopolitical units that emerged from the period after the Treaty of Westphalia. See Taiaiake Alfred, *Peace, Power, Righteousness: An Indigenous Manifesto* (Don Mills, ON: Oxford University Press, 1999) [Alfred, *Peace, Power, Righteousness*]; Taiaiake Alfred, *Wasáse: Indigenous Pathways of Action and Freedom* (Peterborough, ON: Broadview Press, 2005) [Alfred, *Wasáse*]. Nevertheless, in a very general sense we can reasonably say the sociopolitical Indigenous communities along the east coast (indeed, many if not all those within North America) were, and often continue to be, self-directing political communities, bound by language, story, and culture. How these elements of narrative and culture play out into how any such community sees itself when it gazes within, or how it thinks of itself when it considers itself in its relations to other communities with which it interacts, was, and can still be, rich and varied. Meanwhile, as the Supreme Court noted in *R v Sioui*, during much of the period of early interaction with the French and British, it was good policy for the European powers to treat Indian peoples as though they were nations. See *R v Sioui*, [1990] 1 SCR 1025, 70 DLR (4th) 427.

13 Some do not see any confusion in this, finding instead a comprehensive plan to deal with the "Indian problem," first in the short term with separation and isolation, and then in the longer term with assimilation. See e.g. John Tobias, "Protection, Civilization, Assimilation: An Outline History of Canada's Indian Policy" in JR Miller, ed, *Sweet Promises: A Reader on Indian-White Relations in Canada* (Toronto: University of Toronto Press, 1991) 127 [Miller, *Sweet Promises*].

of Indigenous communities. On the one hand, authorities in some places at some times stepped up the aim of assimilation (now directed and facilitated by law and policy), while on the other hand they also seemed attracted principally to the goal of separation and removal.[14]

These objectives, of course, could not be pursued without enfolding Indian populations under the authority and control of colonial governments. How this happened is rather mysterious. We can see records for *how* this happened, with some clear traces persisting to this day. But mystery attends any search into plausible accounts of *sources of legitimacy* for moves that transpired. Indians who were gathered into political-linguistic-cultural units – akin to "nations" – were simply pulled into the orbit of the Crown. Mysteriously, these Indian polities now "unquestionably" found themselves ruled over (de facto, if not de jure) by what had been, until just recently, foreign states.[15]

We saw hints of this on the horizon in the passage above, from the *Royal Proclamation*. On the one hand, it spoke of "several nations" and of ensuring that Indians would not be molested in the use of their lands. On the other hand, however, it also contained language suggesting the British Crown had *already* attained sovereignty over Indian nations and tribes – even those it had never seen or contacted in the north and west of the continent no European had yet explored!

Nevertheless (and none too surprisingly), the difference is relatively sharp between the language of the *Royal Proclamation*, and several decades later, the intrusion of British (and soon Canadian) governments into the lives of Indian peoples. While in the late 1700s the Crown may have spoken *as if* it were sovereign over large tracts of land it claimed (but had little or no presence), this can

---

14 In the 1830s, a proposal was made to follow the American program of settling all Indians from east of the Appalachians in one "Indian territory" (what came to be known as Oklahoma). Manitoulin Island was to be the site of this new "Indian territory" in what was to become Canada, and several groups of people from Southern Ontario were indeed settled there. For a letter from Sir Francis Bond Head (then the lieutenant governor of the colony of Upper Canada) to Lord Glenelg (then secretary of state for war and the colonies) in late summer of 1836, detailing his plans, see "Sir Francis Bond Head to Lord Glenelg" (20 August 1836) in *Report on the Indians of Upper Canada by a Sub-Committee of The Aborigines Protection Society* (London: William Ball, Arnold, & Co, 1839), online: <eco.canadiana.ca/view/oocihm.35802/19?r=0&s=1> at 17. For the reply of Lord Glenelg, see "Lord Glenelg to Sir F.B. Head" (5 October 1836) in *Report on the Indians of Upper Canada by a Sub-Committee of The Aborigines Protection Society* (London: William Ball, Arnold, & Co, 1839), online: <eco.canadiana.ca/view/oocihm.35802/20?r=0&s=1> at 18.

15 The expression "ruled over by" is essential, as it is difficult to see exactly how these polities could come to be "governed by." The British Crown, on the other hand, undertook to see itself as governing these peoples.

only have been talk at that point.[16] By the 1840s, however, British colonies were passing legislation that authorized action and had most definite results in the lives of Indian peoples.

It was around this time that the British Crown also began a systematic program of entering into land-cession treaty negotiations with Indian political-cultural-linguistic groups.[17] The treaty-making era is a truly remarkable period of time, as it marks out a transitional shift from the last vestiges of recognition by the Crown that Indian peoples constitute separate political groups (otherwise, what sense is there to the act of treaty-making?)[18] to the present landscape, one defined largely in terms of small, isolated subunits of Indigenous populations.

From the midpoint of the nineteenth century into the first few decades of the twentieth, large-scale treaties were signed across a vast swath of the mid-section of what would become Canada.[19] While each treaty was signed with peoples constituting large-scale political bodies (Treaty 3, for example, was negotiated with the Anishnawbe – or Ojibway – of what is now northwestern Ontario and parts of eastern Manitoba),[20] the result of each treaty was uniformly a major step towards dissolution of larger Indigenous polities into reserve communities (known today as "First Nations"). As small tracts of the vast lands covered by these treaties were "set aside" as reserves for Indian communities, the federal government came to recognize only the isolated communities living on these reserves as "political" units (as the defined units of organization, managed by chiefs and councils who were, for the most part, put in place by the federal government). Given that band councils and chiefs enjoyed (and continue to enjoy) minimal authority (and for most of the last 130 years that authority has been understood to be delegated from the federal Canadian government), the enormity of the transition should be clear.

---

16 This could be no more efficacious, one would think, than if Canadian officials were to today boldly proclaim that Canada, in the interests of the people living in the forty-ninth state, would, as the self-proclaimed sovereign authority in that region, forthwith protect the interests of Alaskans by assuming control over that territory.

17 For a good discussion of the breadth of treaty making in Canada, see JR Miller, *Compact, Contract, Covenant: Aboriginal Treaty-Making in Canada* (Toronto: University of Toronto Press, 2009) [Miller, *Compact, Contract, Covenant*].

18 For remarks to this effect, see e.g. *Calder v British Columbia (AG)*, [1973] SCR 313, 34 DLR (3d) 145, Judson J, Hall J.

19 The federal ministry responsible for interacting with Aboriginal peoples (Crown-Indigenous Relations and Northern Affairs Canada) maintains web materials relevant to all treaties and agreements, both historic and modern. For archives dealing with the historical treaties, see Canada, Crown-Indigenous Relations and Northern Affairs Canada, "Treaties, Agreements and Negotiations," online: <rcaanc-cirnac.gc.ca/eng/1100100028568/1529354090684>.

20 For a first-hand recount of the treaty negotiations from the perspective of the representative of the Crown, see Alexander Morris, *The Treaties of Canada with the Indians of Manitoba and the North-West Territories, Including the Negotiations on Which They Were Based, and*

The result of such events was fairly uniform across Canada (remarkable, given that in some large areas of the country there were no treaties negotiated akin to the numbered treaties, as is the case for most of present-day British Columbia, the Maritimes, and Quebec).[21] By the early/mid-part of the twentieth century, Indian peoples across the new confederation lived for the most part on reserves, captured by law and policy directives of the federal government, oppressed in ways that typically startle those unaware of this part of the history of Canada, should they ever come to learn about this multi-generational, deeply troubling chapter.

Young children were taken (often forcibly) from their families to attend residential schools (religiously run institutions, with strict rules and policies meant to "civilize" and Christianize the young).[22] Divisions were introduced that further splintered even the small Indian communities now understood to fall under federal authority, as laws and regulations led to some Indians being legally recognized while others would not be considered "Indian(s)" for purposes of Canadian law.[23] This splitting between "status" and "non-status" could occur on both individual (and family) and communal levels. Things like travel, education, and employment were strongly regulated (for example, one would lose "status" as an Indian should a university or college degree be obtained).[24] Ceremonies and practices were outlawed (sometimes with an eye to their "pagan" roots, but also at times with an eye to the role they played in

---

Other Information Relating Thereto (Toronto: Belfords, Clarke & Co, 1880). For an interesting examination of the intent in the minds of the Crown negotiators in relation to early treaty negotiations, see Michael Asch, *On Being Here to Stay: Treaties and Aboriginal Rights in Canada* (Toronto: University of Toronto Press, 2014) [Asch, *On Being Here to Stay*]. For a good example of the view of treaty-making from the perspective of Indian peoples on the prairies, see Treaty 7 Elders et al, *The True Spirit and Original Intent of Treaty 7*, ed by Walter Hildebrandt (Montreal & Kingston: McGill-Queen's University Press, 1996) [*True Spirit and Original Intent of Treaty 7*].

21 Within treaty areas, as well, it is not uncommon to find Indigenous communities that were not party to the treaties. Such was the case, for example, with the Lubicon Cree of northern Alberta, and is still the case for Algonquin communities in eastern Ontario and western Quebec.

22 For a comprehensive accounting of this episode in Canadian policy, see Truth and Reconciliation Commission of Canada, online: <https://nctr.ca/reports2.php>.

23 *Indian Act*, RSC 1985, c I-5. For a historical overview of the early development of the Indian Act, see John Tobias, "Protection, Civilization, Assimilation: An Outline History of Canada's Indian Policy" in Miller, *Sweet Promises, supra* note 13 at 127.

24 *Indian Act, supra* note 23. John Milloy traces the development of the *Indian Act* and discusses early policy that informed enfranchisement provisions. See John Milloy, "The Early Indian Acts: Developmental Strategy and Constitutional Change" in Miller, *Sweet Promises, supra* note 13 at 145. Miller discusses some of the "silly" and "ironic" sections of the *Indian Act* as it evolved – it is clear, for example, looking back, that few non-status Indians (i.e., British/

the cultural, political, and economic life of the community, as with the potlatch of West Coast peoples).[25]

Canadian laws, policies, and regulations were numerous, broad, and most often draconian. The reader is invited to explore the literature, with an eye to accounts from Aboriginal peoples.[26] More will be said about some of the details of this powerful web of legal control when our attention turns more directly to "Aboriginal law."

Inuit

Until the early/middle stages of the twentieth century, the Inuit were left alone, for the most part, by the federal government. The socio-economic lives of the Inuit – especially in the western and eastern reaches of the Arctic – had been powerfully disrupted by contact from the late nineteenth century onward as whaling opened the door to new economic paradigms.[27] Within a few decades hunting, trapping, and trading were common across large areas of the north. Along with this activity came sparsely scattered police outposts, but the presence of the Canadian government remained largely unobtrusive. It was only with the new strategic interest the southern government began to take

---

Canadian settlers) would have met the general conditions that determined enfranchisement (educated, debt-free, and of good moral character): JR Miller, "Reserves, Residential Schools, and the Threat of Assimilation" in JR Miller, *Skyscrapers Hide the Heavens: A History of Indian-White Relations in Canada*, 3rd ed (Toronto: University of Toronto Press, 2000) 125 [Miller, *Skyscrapers Hide the Heavens*].

25 *Indian Act*, *supra* note 23. For discussion of the impact of this provision (though set obliquely, in a text that focuses on the papers that developed around the banning of this central event in the lives of northwest coast peoples), see Christopher Bracken, *The Potlatch Papers: A Colonial Case History* (Chicago: University of Chicago Press, 1997). For a brief discussion of the particular response amongst the First Nations of the British Columbia coast to the banning of their central institution, see Robin Fisher, *Contact and Conflict: Indian-European Relations in British Columbia, 1774–1890* (Vancouver: University of British Columbia Press, 1977).

26 See e.g. "Post-Treaty Life of Treaty 7 Nations" in *True Spirit and Original Intent of Treaty 7*, *supra* note 20 at 146. See also *RCAP Report*, *supra* note 7. The *RCAP Report* is an excellent resource in this regard, as behind the actual five-volume, 4000+ page–report lie not just related commission publications, but also a CD containing transcripts of the hearings themselves. This contains the "voices" of many hundreds of Aboriginal peoples, talking about the many varied topics relating to their own histories, particularly in connection to Crown law and policy.

27 For a chronicle of the incursion of whalers into the eastern Arctic, see Dorothy Harley Eber, *When the Whalers Were Up North: Inuit Memories from the Eastern Arctic* (Montreal & Kingston: McGill-Queen's University Press, 1989). For an exploration of the history of whaling in the western region, see John Bockstoce, *Whales, Ice, and Men: The History of Whaling in the Western Arctic* (Seattle: University of Washington Press, 1986).

in the midst of the Second World War, vastly heightened as the world moved into a Cold War, that significant bureaucratic and governmental intrusions occurred.

As with "Indians," behind this recent history of settler-Inuit relations lay many centuries of life connected to the land (and water), countless generations lived according to Inuit belief-structures.[28] While the timeframe encompassing contact and government intrusion is much shorter, the same devastating effects of colonialism are felt across the Far North.

While the reserve system was not implemented above the sixtieth parallel, policies and techniques deployed in the second half of the twentieth century (at times aggressively) pulled families and groups off the land and into a small number of permanent communities. In that setting, "civilizing" quickly led to centralized schooling, competing religious institutions, a mix of "country" (traditional) and "southern" foods, high unemployment, high rates of addictions, and other signs of psychological and social dysfunction, and generally low socio-economic indicators.[29]

Over the last few decades, as real and potential resource-based opportunities have emerged, a strong push has led to local and regional political empowerment. Modern treaties have now been reached across the full extent of the north, ranging from a "public government" model defining the new territory of Nunavut (carved out of the Northwest Territories as result of an agreement with the Inuit of the eastern Arctic),[30] to more land- and resource-focused agreements in the northwest corner of the Northwest Territories and the northern extent of Quebec (the *Inuvialuit Final Agreement*, which resulted in a corporation-model of local Inuit governance,[31] the *James Bay Cree and Northern Quebec Agreement*,[32]

---

28 See e.g. Jarich Oosten et al, eds, *Interviewing Inuit Elders* (Iqaluit: Nunavut Arctic College, 1999). This five-volume collection details different aspects of traditional Inuit life in the Eastern Arctic. For a good initial source covering the Western Arctic, see Bob Simpson et al, eds, *Taimani: At That Time* (Inuvik, NWT: Inuvialuit Regional Corporation, 2011); online: <issuu.com/itvg/docs/taimani>.

29 For results of the 2006 census with a focus on the Inuit population, see e.g. Statistics Canada, *Inuit in Canada: Selected Findings of the 2006 Census* (Ottawa, Statistics Canada, 2008) online: <statcan.gc.ca/pub/11-008-x/2008002/article/10712-eng.htm>. See also Statistics Canada, "2006 Census: Aboriginal Peoples in Canada in 2006: Inuit, Metis and First Nations, 2006" (Ottawa: Statistics Canada, 2008), online: <www12.statcan.ca/census-recensement/2006/as-sa/97-558/index-eng.cfm?CFID=363213&CFTOKEN=81818789>.

30 *Nunavut Act*, SC 1993, c 28.

31 *The Inuvialuit Final Agreement as Amended*, 2005, online: <irc.inuvialuit.com/sites/default/files/Inuvialuit%20Final%20Agreement%202005.pdf>.

32 *James Bay and Northern Québec Agreement and Complementary Agreements*, 1998, online: <epe.lac-bac.gc.ca/003/008/099/003008-disclaimer.html?orig=/100/200/301/inac-ainc/james_bay-e/jbnq_e.pdf>.

and *Nunavik Inuit Land Claim Agreement*),[33] to the most recent agreement in Labrador.[34]

This is a particularly challenging time for Inuit across the Arctic regions. Climate change has already had a highly pronounced effect north of the sixtieth parallel, and signs are these changes are accelerating. In what some might take to be a perverse development, the sharp warming of the far north is seen by northern nations (and industry) as an economic opportunity, as many parties now eye the possibility of opening up large regions of the north to such things as oil and gas exploration. The very fossil fuels that in being burnt have generated immense challenges facing the Inuit now both draw more southern forces into their territory and hold out economic promise in the form of partnerships and new agreements. Choices to be made are stark and extremely challenging.

Metis

The Metis were accorded constitutional status in 1982 as one of the three peoples recognized with Aboriginal rights under section 35. Their histories go back many generations, to periods of interaction between European traders, trappers, and voyageurs and (typically) Indian women in different regions of what is now a wide area of central and western Canada. While their legal identity continues to be the subject of intense court activity, their own identities focus on the emergence of distinct political and social cultures. The *Report of the Royal Commission on Aboriginal Peoples* details some of this history, noting that after early generations of children of mixed parentage followed the ways of (most typically) their mothers,

> gradually ... distinct Métis cultures emerged, combining European and First Nations or Inuit heritages in unique ways. Economics played a major role in this process. The special qualities and skills of the Métis population made them indispensable members of Aboriginal/non-Aboriginal economic partnerships, and that association contributed to the shaping of their cultures. Using their knowledge of European and Aboriginal languages, their family connections and their wilderness skills, they helped to extend non-Aboriginal contacts deep into the North American interior. As interpreters, diplomats, guides, couriers, freighters, traders and suppliers, the early Métis people contributed massively to European penetration of North America.[35]

---

33 *Nunavik Inuit Land Claims Agreement*, 2006, online: <aadnc-aandc.gc.ca/DAM/DAM-INTER-HQ/STAGING/texte-text/ldc_ccl_fagr_nk_lca_1309284365020_eng.pdf>.

34 *Land Claims Agreement between the Inuit of Labrador and Her Majesty the Queen in Right of Newfoundland and Labrador and Her Majesty the Queen in Right of Canada*, 2005, online: <https://www.aadnc-aandc.gc.ca/eng/1293647179208/1293647660333>.

35 "Métis Perspectives" in *RCAP Report*, *supra* note 7, vol 4, 186 at 186.

It is not uncommon in the early stages of the twenty-first century to find commentators focused primarily on the notion of a large "Metis nation," encompassing lands stretching from north-central Ontario, up over the top of Lake Superior, through northwestern Ontario, and in an ever-expanding triangle across the prairies (and southern Northwest Territories), to the north-eastern corner of British Columbia.[36]

In the decades leading up to the constitutionalization of Aboriginal rights (and in the early stages of "land claim" negotiations in the 1970s), other areas of Canada were said, however, to contain separate Metis communities – most notably an area in Labrador, the home of what was, until recently, peoples who referred to themselves as the "Labrador Inuit-Metis." This community, originally a mix of Inuit and British traders, referred to itself through the nineteenth century as made up of "settlers" or "livyers." In the decades after Newfoundland and Labrador joined Confederation (in 1949) it was split in two, as northern mixed peoples were amalgamated into Inuit communities, while the southern group was deemed too far removed from traditional Inuit lands. By the first decade of the twenty-first century, however, the southern community had shifted away from use of the term "Metis," and they now enjoy a political structure representing all excluded Aboriginal peoples in southern Labrador (known as NunatuKavut Community Council). The former Labrador Inuit-Metis now refer to themselves as "southern Inuit."[37]

It seems less common now to find talk of two separate forms of Metis identity – that of a single "Metis *nation*" (described above, centred on the fur trade and the traditional buffalo hunt, and on a land-mass encompassing much of the Canadian prairies and lands just to the north and east) and that of discrete Metis *peoples* across Canada (including, for example, the Labrador Inuit-Metis). This is visible in contemporary writings on Metis identity, as the focus seems to have shifted to different sources of confusion.[38]

Metis lawyer and scholar Jean Teillet, for example, highlights two remaining ways in which the term "Metis" can still cause difficulty (especially, it would seem, in the minds of some Canadian judges). On the one hand,

> the term "Métis" is often used to describe two distinct groups. Until the 1960s, references to the Métis were generally references to the historic Métis of the Northwest – the people in the Northwest part of Canada usually associated with

---

36 See e.g. Chris Andersen, *"Métis": Race, Recognition, and the Struggle for Indigenous Peoplehood* (Vancouver: UBC Press, 2014); Jean Teillet, *Métis Law in Canada* (Vancouver: Pape Salter Teillet, 2013), online: <pstlaw.ca/publications.html>.

37 For this history, as well as for reasons for recent developments, see *NunatuKavut: Our Ancient Land*, online: <nunatukavut.ca/home>.

38 See e.g. Andersen, *supra* note 36; Teillet, *supra* note 36.

> the buffalo hunt, the fur trade and Louis Riel. However, in the 1960s the common usage of the term expanded significantly to include all persons of mixed aboriginal and non-aboriginal ancestry.[39]

On a group level, then, confusion remains around the extent of the range of the term Metis, seen by some as one that includes individuals (and families) who historically had *some* intermixing of lineage (without necessarily any link to the larger politically grounded Metis nation). On the other hand,

> another source of the confusion with respect to Métis identity arises from the close kinship between Indians and Métis. Intermarriage between Indians and Métis has been a constant and continuing fact of history. Because of this intermarriage some individuals may be Métis (from one ancestor) and Indian (status or non-status from another ancestor). Such an individual might self-identify as Métis or Indian.[40]
>
> Again, confusion centres on the range of the term "Metis," with some seeing the term encompassing many individuals who otherwise have Indian status.

Both sorts of confusion are present in recent judicial pronouncements. In 2013, for example, Phelan J, of the Federal Court, was tasked with determining whether the Metis are "Indians" for the purposes of section 91(24) of the *Constitution Act, 1867.*[41] If they were to be considered Indians for this purpose, they would fall under federal jurisdictional authority (which would require, for example, that the federal government then step up to fill service lacunas, as Metis are traditionally the Aboriginal group most often prone to slipping between federal and provincial systems). The case dealt not just with the Metis, but also non-status Indians (those Indians who, for a variety of possible reasons, may never have had, or lost, Indian status in Canadian law). The judge, naturally enough, seemed to want to work out how to treat these two groups together for the purposes of engaging in constitutional analysis. His attempt to define the Metis should be seen in this light.[42] The Metis are, he says, "a group of native people who maintained a strong affinity for their Indian heritage without possessing Indian status. Their 'Indianness' was based on self-identification and group recognition."[43]

The Federal Court of Appeal addressed the apparent confusion in this definition, noting that if one were to interpret "Indian heritage" and "Indianness" in the wrong way, this is not in accord with the common understandings of Metis

39 Teillet, *supra* note 36 at 1–6.

40 *Ibid* at 1–6.

41 *Daniels v Canada (Minister of Foreign Affairs and Northern Development)*, 2013 FC 6.

42 *Ibid* at para 117.

43 *Ibid.*

identity currently at play in Canada. It would seem to suggest being Metis was essentially a matter of having Indian genetic heritage. These two terms (the Federal Court of Appeal rather generously went on to say) should actually be taken by the reader to refer to "Aboriginality," which all three groups under section 35 share; the term does not comprise a single cultural identity, but rather the aspect of their identity that places them within this group of three distinct "pre-existing" peoples.[44] As the Federal Court of Appeal went on to note, the notion of Metis identity has been relatively settled in Canadian law since the *R v Powley* decision of the Supreme Court in 2003: "The Métis have their own language, culture, kinship connections and territory. It is these factors that make the Métis one of the Aboriginal peoples of Canada."[45]

The Supreme Court weighed in on this matter by substantially upholding the trial judge's ruling.[46] A division was maintained between questions of Metis identity in relation to section 91(24) and questions around identity in relation to section 35: for the purposes of legislative jurisdiction a person (or family) may be "Metis" without being recognized by an established Metis community, while for the purposes of determining proper Metis rights-holders the *Powley* framework (with community recognition being one element) applies.[47]

It should be clear, however, that although the high court may have intended to help those often most ignored (to address the legislative gap into which Metis and non-status have so often fallen), its approach leaves identity as confusing as ever. There are now clearly two groups of "Metis" within Canadian law, where the one group (those who, for many reasons – many of which likely trace directly to the effects of colonization and oppression – do not enjoy community recognition) can now consider themselves "Metis" within Canadian law, however much the second group might disagree.[48] The second group, note,

---

44 *Daniels v Canada (Minister of Foreign Affairs and Northern Development)*, 2014 FCA 101 at paras 88–109 [*Daniels, FCA*].

45 *R v Powley*, 2003 SCC 43 [*Powley*]; *Daniels*, FCA, *supra* note 44.

46 *Daniels v Canada (Minister of Indian Affairs and Northern Development)*, 2016 SCC 12 [*Daniels*, SCC].

47 As a result of this outcome, and that in *Manitoba Metis Federation v Canada (AG)*, 2013 SCC 14 (finding that a provision of the *Manitoba Act, 1870* constituted a "constitutional promise" to the Metis that went substantially unfulfilled, generating persisting legal obligations on the Crown), a special ministerial representative on reconciliation with the Metis was established. See Thomas Isaac, Indigenous and Northern Affairs Canada, "A Matter of National and Constitutional Import: Report of the Minister's Special Representative on Reconciliation with Métis: Section 35 Métis Rights and the *Manitoba Métis Federation Decision*" (Ottawa: Ministry of Indigenous and Northern Affairs, 2016), online: <publications.gc.ca/collections/collection_2016/aanc-inac/R5-123-2016-eng.pdf>.

48 I use the term "group" in both contexts advisedly. The first group is composed mostly of discrete individuals (and families). For the second "group" there may or may not be a core Metis nation (or several Metis nations), and this is not an issue with which I would engage.

often argues for recognition as rights-bearing as much on political grounds as cultural grounds, but on this matter of self-determination, matters are clearly out of their hands.

As with the other "Aboriginal peoples" of Canada, it is essential to bear in mind that behind these debates over identity lay countless stories of people, families, and communities. There are stories well told, and reasonably well known, within contemporary Canada of the initial development of Metis communities along trading routes (and in areas that supplied traders), of the emergence of the Red River Metis, of the struggles of the Metis in what is now Manitoba and Saskatchewan in the period from the 1810s to the 1880s, of the Riel Rebellion, of negotiations with the Canadian government that led to provisions within the *Manitoba Act, 1870* meant to protect key Metis interests, and of subsequent hardship and deprivation (as the Canadian government failed to live up to its promises).[49] Within these larger stories, however, cannot be forgotten the embedded stories, and the stories of the many thousands of descendants of original Metis sociopolitical collectives.

Struggles to Be Heard and Understood

These, then, are the "Aboriginal peoples" of Canada, rights-holders under section 35 of the *Constitution Act, 1982*. While intimately related to the Indigenous peoples whose polities predate the presence of the Crown, not only do definitions of who they are but indeed their very lives inextricably intertwine with Canadian law. Contemporary narratives from Indian, Metis, and Inuit perspectives avoid the notion that identity formation as a function of self-determination is a thing of the past, but it is impossible not to acknowledge how much the histories and stories of contemporary Indigenous peoples contain unavoidable linkages to the oppressive actions of Canadian governments and courts.

Consider one group of people who struggle to access section 35 rights – non-status Indians. These are people who, as the Federal Court of Appeal noted in *Daniels*, have suffered tremendously as a result of "buck-passing" between provincial and federal Crowns:

The federal government acknowledged:

> The Métis and non-status Indian people, lacking even the protection of the Department of Indian Affairs and Northern Development, are far more exposed

49 For a fairly concise but detailed narrative, see "Métis Perspectives" in *RCAP Report*, *supra* note 7, vol 4, 186.

> to discrimination and other social disabilities. It is true to say that in the absence of Federal initiative in this field they are the most disadvantaged of all Canadian citizens.[50]

There are hundreds of thousands of non-status people across Canada – people who are not strictly legally speaking "Indians" (at least for the purposes of section 91(24), *within Canadian law*). The key argument accepted by the Federal Court of Appeal in support of their conclusion that non-status are not "Indians" for the purposes of section 91(24) is that they *do* already fall under this provision – they just happen to be those Canadians (with Aboriginal heritage – indeed, many with strong cultural and community links to Aboriginal communities) who find themselves unable to meet legal requirements within Canadian law for gaining status under the statutory regime.

Essentially the same fact, however, was deployed by the Supreme Court to find that the non-status *should* fall under section 91(24). The Court sees one operation of federal power under section 91(24) being to decide who is and is not status, where determinations of non-status are made in relation to individuals who, then, cannot thereby fall entirely out of the scope of this constitutional provision. Not only does confusion abound, but it continues to affect daily the lives of thousands across Canada. We find people then who, if you try to track the byzantine pathways of imposed definition laid out by the Canadian state and its courts, both are and are not "Indian," who may or may not be "Aboriginal." As difficult as this can be for families struggling to make sense of all this, it carries over to acts of self-definition, as Indigenous communities struggle to maintain forms of self-definition in face of these outside forces.

This too brief snapshot has been focused on the role Canadian law and policy continues to play in structuring identity. It is remarkable how forcefully, through the overtly colonial era, law and policy were attempting to undercut Indigenous senses of self-identity. When one looks at the history of residential schools, it can be shocking to learn of the naked racism and brutality of many who worked in the system. Equally troubling, however, is to see in the thoughts and actions of those orchestrating this apocryphal regime similar combinations of racism and brutality, side-by-side with the beliefs of some that they were doing "the right thing" to so devastatingly disrupt the political-legal-social lives of Indigenous peoples.

But resistance to Indian residential schools was constant,[51] as was resistance to all Crown efforts to destroy the meaning-generating and meaning-transmission

50 *Daniels*, FCA, *supra* note 44 at para 70.

51 The varied histories of the residential school system are laid out in the Truth and Reconciliation Commission's writings. See *supra* note 2. Notably, some Indigenous communities asked that schools be established and their children educated in non-Indigenous

mechanisms of Indigenous collectives. Two matters were inextricably connected through the overtly colonial era – the stripping away of lands, authority, and livelihoods, and a constant effort to change how peoples thought of themselves and their relations to their lands and waters. Throughout all this period, Indigenous peoples struggled to maintain physical connections to their lands, waters, and livelihoods, but their struggles were often futile in the face of overwhelming exercises of Crown power. However, they also struggled to maintain understandings of who they were, of what meanings they projected into the world around them. That form of resistance also ran up against the relentless application of force, but in dealing with personal and collective identity, they continued on, while all about them the colonial state was facilitating the exploitation of – and devastating – their lands and waters.

Much of the contemporary literature from Indigenous authors carries a thread of this resistance, capturing the ways their communities *historically* resisted efforts by Canadian governments to assimilate and eliminate, and articulating how these struggles to *continue* as Mohawk, Cree, and Dene (and others) are being waged today.[52]

Much of the rest of this text is about that contemporary struggle, though the effort in this text is to understand the nature and parameters of current Canadian law, so the forces at play can be appreciated – so continued essential resistance can be best formed and channelled.

General Remarks about Aboriginal Law

In saying "Aboriginal law" is the law of Canada as it applies to Aboriginal peoples in Canada, we distinguish this legal realm from the laws or legal systems of Indigenous peoples (hereinafter referred to as *Indigenous legal systems* or *legal orders*). Before we say anything substantive about Aboriginal law, it is essential to note this clear divide. My focus is not so much on the *content* of Indigenous

---

ways – they did not, however, request the kinds of community-destroying systems the Crown put in place in concert with religious orders. Commissioner Clifton noted that in leading up to Treaty No. 8, the assembled Indigenous peoples "seemed desirous of securing educational advantages for their children, but stipulated that in the matter of schools there should be no interference with their religious beliefs": *Treaty No. 8 Made June 21, 1899 and Adhesions, Reports, Etc.*, online: <canadiancrown.com/uploads/3/8/4/1/3841927/treaty_8.pdf> at 5.

52 See e.g. Leanne Betasamosake Simpson, *Dancing on Our Turtle's Back: Stories of Nishnaabeg Re-Creation, Resurgence and a New Emergence* (Winnipeg: Arbeiter Ring Publishing, 2011); Alfred, *Wasáse*, *supra* note 12; Audra Simpson, *Mohawk Interruptus: Political Life across the Borders of Settler States* (Durham, NC: Duke University Press, 2014); Andersen, *supra* note 36; Glen Sean Coulthard, *Red Skin, White Mask: Rejecting the Colonial Politics of Recognition* (Minneapolis: University of Minnesota Press, 2014).

versus state legal orders (though they will often differ, and on levels of content), but concentrated on the *source* of systems or orders in the world. I am not speaking here of "sources of law," as this expression is often used in legal discourse, but of the fact that Indigenous collectives produce meaning. What they produce may borrow from non-Indigenous worlds, but such acts of borrowing will be *theirs*, for to generate content mirroring of systems encircling them *they* must decide to do so.[53]

One matter that comes up when the presence of Indigenous legal systems is acknowledged concerns possible interplay between these systems and Canadian-Aboriginal law. For example, whether Aboriginal law contains within it rules, principles, institutions, or mechanisms with roots in Indigenous communities is touched on in our discussion, in later chapters.

A further matter (more pressing in our study) concerns the impact of Indigenous legal and political orders on legal theorizing. When we look into the social and political reality within which Aboriginal law is situated, we see that the presence of distinct Indigenous legal and political orders seriously complicates the picture of theorizing in this context. As we acknowledge the presence of Indigenous legal systems and orders within the territory claimed by the Canadian state, we are led into theories about Aboriginal law that refocus the lens of analysis away from forms that purport to adopt a "neutral" stance to those that can accommodate positions occupied by Indigenous peoples, while simultaneously positioning Canadian law as the product of a meaning-generating community. This forms one pillar of support for the naturalistic approach to both law and legal theory adopted in this work.

Aboriginal law has a long and complex history in Canada. In this text, given time and space constraints, we focus on the current status of just a few key components. Even in restricting ourselves in this manner, substantial historical exegesis is required, as is sensitivity to differences between Indigenous communities (and their histories). Components to be explored cover the long history of Crown-Aboriginal relations, but they do not exhaust the nature of this history or this relationship. A relatively complete discussion of the nature of Aboriginal law in Canada would require several volumes delving into history, economics, politics, and policy.[54] I propose to focus on a key contemporary

53 "They decide" is problematic on its face in this context. I do not presume a collective mind, or even any sort of obvious decision-making process easily identifiable. Rather, I simply suggest what I think is clearly there – some mechanism(s) by which a self-defined group generates its own way of ordering itself, making group decisions, and generally charting its own future.

54 For a good historical overview, see *RCAP Report*, *supra* note 7, vol 1. For fairly rich and inclusive historical, political, and economic accounts, see e.g. Olive Dickason & David McNab, *Canada's First Nations: A History of Founding Peoples from Earliest Times*, 4th ed (Don Mills, ON: Oxford University Press, 2009); Ray, *supra* note 8.

component, which permits substantial analysis of the project of this text and plays a large role in the lives of Indigenous peoples in Canada – Aboriginal rights (which within Aboriginal law subsumes Aboriginal title and, arguably, Aboriginal rights to governance).

At these early stage-setting points, the intent is to provide an overview that evades interpretive, normative, or theoretical overlays as much as possible. In an upcoming section – when aspects of the law are presented in some detail married to certain puzzles – an attempt is made to keep the puzzles and law separate, so the reader can get a reasonably unadulterated sense of key components. In the next section, while the discussion is necessarily about history, in introducing aspects of Aboriginal law, it is hoped that historiographic concerns do not excessively intrude.[55] As much as possible the following overview discusses background aspects of Aboriginal law without substantively interacting with larger questions about different meanings or imports of laws, systems, or events.

General History and Context

The story of Aboriginal law begins at the point of contact between Indigenous communities and European powers. Elements of this story – other stories linked to this particularly Canadian story, about Indigenous systems of law and politics – have much deeper roots in time and narrative, and in the course of this text we see the prominence of these other linked stories. Keeping our focus on Aboriginal law, we see its own tale of genesis pointing to initial interaction between Indigenous communities and the British/Canadian (and French) Crown.

The first chapters in this story of contact are about the meetings of Indigenous sociopolitical communities and French and British explorers and early settlers. As the French and British expanded their physical presence in the "New World,"

For other informative texts, see Sebastien Grammond, *Terms of Coexistence: Indigenous Peoples and Canadian Law* (Toronto: Carswell, 2013); Asch, *On Being Here to Stay*, *supra* note 20; John Borrows, *Canada's Indigenous Constitution* (Toronto: University of Toronto Press, 2010); Miller, *Sweet Promises*, *supra* note 13; Miller, *Skyscrapers Hide the Heavens*, *supra* note 24; Miller, *Compact, Contract, Covenant*, *supra* note 17; Patrick Macklem, *Indigenous Difference and the Constitution of Canada* (Toronto: University of Toronto Press, 2001); Ovide Mercredi & Mary Ellen Turpel, *In the Rapids: Navigating the Future of First Nations* (Toronto: Penguin Books, 1994); Kent McNeil, *Emerging Justice? Essays on Indigenous Rights in Canada and Australia* (Saskatoon, SK: Native Law Centre, 2001); Alfred, *Peace, Power, Righteousness*, *supra* note 12; Patricia Monture-Angus, *Journeying Forward: Dreaming First Nations' Independence* (Halifax: Fernwood, 1999).

55 These are the sorts of questions briefly mentioned in the Introduction, *supra* – questions around how one might *understand* or *interpret* historical events marking the interaction between Indigenous communities and Canadian society and the Canadian state.

they strengthened their political presence, necessitating political negotiations (and, inevitably, conflict) with Indigenous communities. The results were numerous and varied agreements, directed towards trade and commerce, the creation of military alliances, and the more general aim of the establishment of "peace and friendship."[56] As binding instruments, these become the earliest "legal" components of Aboriginal law (though they become firmly recognized as being legal – within the law in Canada – only in the middle of the twentieth century. Before then, they were most often viewed as political instruments, subject to the vagaries of Canadian political moods and interests).

By the second half of the eighteenth century – on the eastern edges of what would become Canada, through the early to middle parts of the nineteenth century in the colonies of Upper and Lower Canada, Nova Scotia, New Brunswick, Prince Edward Island, and Newfoundland, and by the middle of the nineteenth century in the lower southwest corner of what would become British Columbia – a British political presence had asserted itself. Interestingly, it also asserted itself in a projective fashion, claiming sovereign authority over large parts of the "northwest," through the *Royal Proclamation of 1763* or broad interpretations of this policy instrument (these lands being Rupert's Land, the watersheds of Hudson's Bay, and the North-Western Territory, lying to the north and west of Rupert's Land, much of it yet to be explored and settled by the British, much of it – according to British understandings – held or administered under Charter).[57]

At its moment of constitutional formation, in the *British North America Act, 1867*, the new confederation of Canada (with a federal structure dividing jurisdictional authority between a central government and the provinces) determined that "Indians and Lands Reserved for Indians" would be subject to federal jurisdictional authority.[58] Connected to this bifurcation of jurisdictional authority was a continuation of a Westminster model of governance, with the respective Crowns in right of the federal and provincial governments referring to both executive and legislative branches of both levels of government. Some

---

56 *RCAP Report, supra* note 7; *R v Simon*, [1985] 2 SCR 387, 24 DLR (4th) 390; *R v Marshall*, [1999] 3 SCR 456, 177 DLR (4th) 513.

57 See *Proclamation, supra* note 9. John Borrows has argued convincingly that it is possible to see this proclamation as grounding a process of treaty-making that brought together a very large number of Indigenous communities from the Great Lakes region in and around 1763–4. See John Borrows, "Wampum at Niagara: The Royal Proclamation, Canadian Legal History, and Self-Government" in Michael Asch, ed, *Aboriginal and Treaty Rights in Canada: Essays on Law, Equality, and Respect for Difference* (Vancouver: UBC Press, 1998) 155.

58 *British North America Act, 1867*, now referred to as the *Constitution Act, 1867* (UK), 30 & 31 Vict, c 3, reprinted in RSC 1985, App II, No 5 [*Constitution Act*, 1867]. Section 91(24) sets out federal power over "Indians and Lands Reserved for Indians."

might argue that only the legislative branch of the Crown in right of the federal government enjoys jurisdictional authority over "Indians and Lands Reserved for Indians," but practically speaking, the "Crown" that assumed responsibility for Indians and Lands reserved for Indians was clearly the federal government as a whole.[59]

Some of the colonies that came to form the new country had been legislating in relation to "Indians" since the 1840s, and the new federal government continued to do so in the decade after confederation. In 1876 the slate of federal legislation directed at Indians was collected into one federal statute, the *Indian Act, 1876*.[60] Over the last 140 years or so, the *Indian Act* has been substantially revised on several occasions,[61] but today it remains generally similar to that early instantiation. It is a remarkably broad piece of legislation, dealing with membership in a First Nations community (and classification as a "registered" Indian), rules on elections on reserves, the capacities of band councils and chiefs, requirements for the development of wills and estates, and the nature of land holdings on reserves.

The *Indian Act* continues to form a legislative scheme within Canada with enormous impact on Aboriginal peoples (particularly those of "status,"[62] as the Inuit and Metis feel the impact of this legislative regime indirectly, and the non-status by exclusion). Other government policies and legislative

59 As we will see when we get into discussion of section 35, actions of the federal government that affect Aboriginal peoples – and that are then often challenged – can emanate from either legislative or executive branches. Aboriginal peoples, then, certainly do not see or feel some significant divide generated through the Westminster model.

60 *Indian Act, supra* note 23.

61 The major changes after the Second World War occurred in 1951 and 1985. The changes in 1985 were focused principally on gender-membership issues. An attempt at a large-scale transformation failed in the aftermath of the introduction of a federal White Paper policy statement in 1969 (due to a powerful response from an emergent First Nations political front). See Canada, Indian and Northern Affairs, *Statement of the Government of Canada on Indian Policy* (Ottawa: Department of Indian and Northern Affairs, 1969), online: <aadnc-aandc.gc.ca/DAM/DAM-INTER-HQ/STAGING/texte-text/cp1969_1100100010190_eng.pdf>. See also Harold Cardinal, *The Unjust Society: The Tragedy of Canada's Indians* (Vancouver: Douglas & McIntyre, 1999). Similarly, an attempt at significant legislative changes in the early years of this new millennium stalled in the face of strong opposition from within First Nations communities (much of this opposition being best described as "grass-roots").

62 Since the nineteenth century, the federal government has maintained in Ottawa a master list, containing the names of all those "Indians" determined thereby to have "status" (the Inuit – and the Metis – do not fall under the *Indian Act, supra* note 22). One effect of this list (and the complex rules around how one could be on – or off – the list) has been to create a division in Canada between "status" and "non-status" Indians. Some of the rules were such as to have the line between these categories run through families, between parents and children, brothers and sisters.

enactments intersected with the lives of Aboriginal peoples in Canada.[63] Before the dramatic rise of "Aboriginal law" in the 1970s, few other legislative instruments directly affected the lives of Aboriginal peoples. Many indirectly affected communities and individuals, insofar as (a) they ignored Aboriginal peoples (as with, for example, "jurisdictional gaps" between federal and provincial oversight over such matters as health provision), or (b) they reserved powers and interests to non-Aboriginal parties (as, for example, fisheries were nearly entirely restricted to non-Aboriginal fishers on both coasts through stretches of the twentieth century). The decades since the 1970s have seen an explosion of legislative enactments that either relate directly to Aboriginal communities, or that begin to respond to legislative gaps, or that slowly undo hitherto restrictive regimes (around primarily natural resource access and utilization). In the first few decades of the twenty-first century, rarely does a month go by without the appearance of a significant provincial or federal legislative enterprise.

This text, however, does not explore this aspect of Aboriginal law in detail, because (a) that would vastly increase the phenomena to be analysed, but also (and more importantly), (b) to a significant degree the new legislative atmosphere results from the inclusion of section 35 in the *Constitution*. For the most part, new legislative regimes result from developments in the jurisprudence around section 35.[64]

Still, a few words are in order. To get a flavour of legislative treatment of Aboriginal peoples over the last 150 years, consider one chapter in the

---

There are several narratives and sub-stories about these status rules, from varied attempts at either enticing or forcing individuals away from having status (for example, through different ways an individual could be "enfranchised" – being university educated being an interesting example), to mechanisms that strongly tended to privilege male membership (and control) over female membership.

63 The Supreme Court determined many years ago that Inuit fall under subsection 91(24), being then subjects of federal responsibility. See *Reference as to whether "Indians" includes in s 91 (24) of the BNA Act includes Eskimo in habitants of the Province of Quebec*, [1939] SCR 104, [1939] 2 DLR 417. The Federal Court of Appeal more recently made a similar finding for Metis, though interestingly they declined to make a similar declaration in respect of non-status Indians, finding rather that they must wage individual battles around inclusion under section 91(24), as "non-status" constitutes those who have been deemed not to meet the requirements for status. See *Daniels*, FCA, *supra* note 44. The SCC reversed the finding concerning non-status Indians but upheld the finding for the Metis. See *Daniels*, SCC, *supra* note 46.

64 Of course, this postulates a cause–effect relationship that is considerably more complicated than here suggested. As an example of the interplay, as this text is being put together, a relatively new federal government is beginning to follow through on a campaign promise to "implement" the *United Nations Declaration on the Rights of Indigenous Peoples*, UNGAOR, 61st Sess, Supp No 49, UN Doc A/RES/61/295 (13 September 2007) [UNDRIP]. It announced in May 2016, however, that any such implementation must be carried out within

creation and development of the *Indian Act*, the story of the treatment of gender under "status" (from its early days the *Indian Act* set out criteria for being designated "Indian," and those who met these criteria were registered as such and had "status").

Beginning in the latter part of the nineteenth century, membership rules stipulated that when a status female Indian married a non-status individual (either a non-Indian, or a non-status Indian), she was stripped of her status (as were all her descendants). Conversely, when a status male Indian married a non-status individual (either a non-Indian, or a non-status Indian) this conferred status upon that female spouse, a status transmitted to all descendants (so long as female descendants did not themselves "marry out").

In 1960 the federal government passed a *Canadian Bill of Rights*.[65] In the 1970s an attempt was made to use rights enumerated in this statute to challenge the discriminatory effect of the marrying-out provisions of the *Indian Act*. In *Canada (AG) v Lavell*,[66] the Supreme Court held that the *Bill of Rights* could not simply invalidate legislation, with four of the judges holding that the marrying-out provision did not violate "equality before the law" protected within the bill. All Canadian women were being treated "equally," the Court maintained, insofar as they were all equally subject to the law.

It was only in 1985 that the offending provisions were transformed, ostensibly the result of challenges launched through the use of international law.[67] The new provisions allowed for the reinstatement of thousands of "married out" women

---

the limits of Canadian constitutional law, and specifically its position is that what UNDRIP can do is inform the continued development of section 35. In an address to the Assembly of First Nations, Attorney-General Wilson-Raybould announced, "Ultimately, the UNDRIP will be articulated through the constitutional framework of section 35": Jody Wilson-Raybould, "Notes for an Address by the Honourable Jody Wilson-Raybould, PC, QC, MP, Minister of Justice and Attorney General of Canada" (speech, Niagara Falls, ON, 12 July 2016), online: <drive.google.com/file/d/0B_bPXJbq-wgWenpoa2NIRmgwT2NlWkx3enNSWXJELTFSSzc4/view>.

65 *Canadian Bill of Rights*, SC 1960, c 44. This legislation is in still in effect, though for the most part it is effective today only in relation to rights it recognizes that are not in the *Charter of Rights and Freedoms* (principally around property).

66 *Canada (AG) v Lavell* (1973), [1974] SCR 1349, 38 DLR (3d) 481.

67 See *Sandra Lovelace v Canada*, Communication No R.6/24, UN Doc Supp No 40 (A/36/40) at 166 (1981). The UN Human Rights Committee focused attention on Article 27 of the *International Covenant on Civil and Political Rights, which* provides that persons "shall not be denied the right, in community with the other members of their [ethnic, religious, or linguistic] group, to enjoy their own culture, to profess and practice their own religion, or to use their own language": *International Covenant on Civil and Political Rights*, 19 December 1966, 999 UNTS 171, Can TS 1976 No 47 (entered into force 23 March 1976) art 27. Since one effect of losing status was losing the right to reside on reserve, and the committee agreed that life on reserve was critical in maintaining cultural ties, it found that the marrying-out provisions ran counter to Article 27.

and their children (noticeably, without provision for reasonable increases in funding for the reserve communities that now faced the prospects of sudden significant increases in population in already over-crowded situations).

The complex new rules, however, still led to the loss of status should a reinstated child marry a non-status individual. This "second generation" cut-off was subsequently challenged, principally as being opposed to rights protected under the Canadian *Charter of Rights and Freedoms*. In the *McIvor* case, the British Columbia Court of Appeal found discrimination within the current framework, but (a) characterized the problem as "enhancement" of the rights of male status Indians who married before 1985, and (b) disagreed with a lower court judgment that sought to invalidate the 1985 provisions.[68] The BCCA felt that the federal government would be the proper body to consider how to remedy the situation, one possibility being to change the legislative scheme to ensure that *all* "second-generation" children are denied status (in line with the notion that the problem is that males were granted "extra" rights). Refusing to grant an appeal, the Supreme Court of Canada seemingly sent the message that this is an acceptable ruling on the matter.[69]

The federal government responded to this litigation with the *Gender Equity in Indian Registration Act*,[70] but it was immediately apparent that this effort was not meant to address all the discriminatory possibilities embedded in how women's status is treated under the *Indian Act*. Three women of the Abénakis of Odanak First Nation launched a challenge to the newly updated processes of registration in 2011 in the Superior Court of Quebec, and the decision in that case came down in 2015.[71] Responding to this decision, the federal government announced it will engage in a two-stage process meant to finally, (relatively) completely address discrimination that arises from the status-provisions of the *Indian Act*.[72] The outcome has been the coming into force in December of 2017

---

68 *McIvor v Canada (Registrar of Indian and Northern Affairs)*, 2009 BCCA 153.

69 *McIvor v Canada (Registrar of Indian and Northern Affairs)*, 2009 BCCA 153, leave to appeal to SCC refused, 33201 (5 November 2009). In 2011 the federal government enacted the *Gender Equity in Indian Registration Act*, SC 2010, c 18. This altered the offending provision, section 6(2), to allow (for example) the children of Sharon McIvor to register (as second-generation children). But left untouched within the new section 6(2) was the inability of those now falling within 6(2) to transfer status to their children if they marry a non-status individual. It is left, then, for others to continue the struggle. See *Matson et al v Indian and Northern Affairs Canada*, 2013 CHRT 13. The reader might wonder why the federal government would respond to a clear legal signal sent by the courts with a piece of legislation that maintains a key element generating the original challenge.

70 *Gender Equity in Indian Registration Act*, SC 2010, c 18.

71 *Descheneaux v Canada (Procureur général)*, 2015 QCCS 3555.

72 See Canada, Crown-Indigenous Relations and Northern Affairs Canada, "The Government of Canada's Response to the Descheneaux Decision" (2016), online: <aadnc-aandc.gc.ca/eng/

of *An Act to Amend the Indian Act in Response to the Superior Court of Quebec Decision in Descheneaux c Canada (Procureur général)*,[73] an Act that is singularly confusing and confounding.

Our story does not end there. While we will not come back to this matter of "marrying out" and status, this chapter in Canadian law helps set the stage for introducing a central focus of this text. Our primary interest lies in the constitutionalization of Aboriginal and treaty rights in section 35 of the newly patriated *Constitution Act, 1982*.[74] While focusing on such rights might seem to divert our attention from many aspects of Canadian law that affect – and indeed strive to structure – the lives of Aboriginal peoples,[75] the stated intent in "recognizing and affirming" Aboriginal and treaty rights was purportedly to address fundamental forms of injustice that had pervaded the legal and

---

1467227680166/1467227697623>. In 2018, as this work entered its last stages of composition, uncertainty surrounded the government's response. Bill s-3 (which became the *Act* noted in the next sentence) had received royal assent, but the government had indicated on occasion it wished to *fully* address gender discrimination present within the current registration procedures, while in the two-stage process set out in the *Act* it is not clear this will be the end result. Through the summer of 2018, consultation began over how the *Act* would be implemented (in particular, the second-stage provisions, sections 2.1, 3.1, 3.2, and 10.1). Yet the sections themselves already have content, and so it is unclear what precisely consultations are to be directed towards. With such a confusing and cumbersome process unfolding, it seemed likely the registration system as a whole would be suspended while court struggles unfolded. Meanwhile, in an analysis of the current status of legislative efforts to address gender discrimination within the *Indian Act*, the Indigenous Bar Association recommended that "[i]t is only within the context of Indigenous self-determination that sex inequality must be addressed": Indigenous Bar Association, "Bill S-3 *An Act to Amend the Indian Act (Elimination of Sex-Based Inequities in Registration*" (24 April 2017), online: <indigenousbar.ca/pdf/ibc_bill_S-3.pdf> at 29.

73 SC 2017, c 25.

74 *Constitution Act, 1982*, *supra* note 2, stating, "The existing [A]boriginal and treaty rights of the [A]boriginal peoples of Canada are hereby recognized and affirmed," s 35(1)). Up until the patriation of the Constitution in 1982, the acknowledged constitution for Canada was actually an Act of the British Parliament, *The British North America Act, 1867*, *supra* note 58. With the patriation of the Constitution, this older piece of British legislation was renamed the *Constitution Act, 1867*.

75 Over the last few generations the criminal law system in Canada has come to have an ever-increasing impact on the lives of thousands of Aboriginal people. Incarceration rates are shocking in comparison to non-Aboriginal peoples. As of February 2013, Aboriginal peoples made up approximately 4 per cent of the Canadian population, but 23.2 per cent of the federal prison population. Similar – or more shocking – statistics exist across the board (for example, in relation to provincial and territorial incarceration rates, and in relation to such ratios as those between Aboriginal and non-Aboriginal youth offenders, and between Aboriginal and non-Aboriginal women). See Canada, Office of the Correctional Investigator, "Backgrounder: Aboriginal Offenders – A Critical Situation" (2013), online: <oci-bec.gc.ca/cnt/rpt/oth-aut/oth-aut20121022info-eng.aspx>.

constitutional landscape of Canada for many generations. For better or worse, these new constitutional-legal instruments have come to be seen as the primary interface between the Canadian state and Aboriginal peoples. To some extent, for example, they are even seen as instruments to address such failings as the old discriminatory provisions of the *Indian Act*.[76] To make sense of Aboriginal law in Canada today is to make sense of the nature and place of Aboriginal and treaty rights in the lives of Aboriginal communities and individuals.

Indigenous Perspectives

We are about to embark on a look into the law as it has developed concerning section 35. In doing so, certain puzzles are introduced, many of which call out for explication should we wish to fully understand the nature of contemporary Aboriginal law. Embedded as these puzzles are in this discussion of key components of the law around Aboriginal rights, a few words are in order about "Indigenous perspectives" – which are key to much of the analysis that follows. Some forms of puzzlement about to be presented are best felt from, or require an appreciation of, Indigenous points of view. In the context, however, of the matter under exploration – the nature of Aboriginal law (*Canadian law as it applies to Aboriginal peoples*) – the relevant notion of such points of view, what makes them all possible, and their importance to analyses tendered are not what one might initially expect.

I do not attempt to detail what the term "Indigenous perspectives" might refer to or entail, nor do I defend a particular set of Indigenous understandings. Rather, my aim is to present a fairly non-contentious and non-complicated picture of what it might mean to have and employ an Indigenous perspective, one that speaks to general aspects of the notion of "perspectives." I do not need to go so far, for example, as to argue – in this context – that perspectives create (in some sense) entirely separate and different worlds of experience.[77] Less powerful and more general claims about the nature of perspectives suffice in this context.

---

76 Aboriginal communities can attempt to establish the rights to determine and manage their own membership. This, though, seems to create the potential for other problems to emerge. For example, discriminatory practices might be put in place through new membership codes. How such problems arise as a result of the structure of Aboriginal law in the context of a larger liberal setting is a matter that could be profitably explored in relation to the general analysis of Aboriginal rights carried out in the later chapters of this text. I leave it to the reader, however, to carry out this exercise.

77 Such notions are not uncommon in the literature. For the early work of Sapir and Whorf, and in particular Whorf's work on Hopi notions of time, see e.g. Benjamin Whorf, "An American Indian Model of the Universe (*circa* 1936)" in John B Carroll, ed, *Language, Thought, and*

Let me begin by recounting something important about the exercise in this text. We are restricting ourselves to the study of a very particular sort of social-cultural-political situation,[78] that of the application of the law of a liberal democracy to Indigenous communities – to communities with collective histories, identities, and social mechanisms predating the emergence of the Canadian legal system. Given this restriction, we need only focus on the question of perspectives as they may influence experiences of such things as history, law, and social reality.

More importantly, however, we can also narrow our focus just to the notion that Indigenous perspectives mark different ways of experiencing and thinking about events that happen between and amongst humans as social creatures. Besides making clearer just what sort of commitments are necessary to consider the impacts of Indigenous perspectives on understanding puzzles that arise within Aboriginal law, this provides an opportunity to reintroduce a key notion in the theoretical analysis that follows, the notion that different sociocultural communities can be seen – from a naturalist point of view – as elements of

---

Reality: Selected Writings of Benjamin Lee Whorf (Cambridge, MA: MIT Press, 1956) 57. An implication of Whorf's work is that Hopi experience the world of time and space differently as a result of their having different categories of experience (to borrow a phrase from Kant, though for Whorf these were linguistic in nature and not transcendental). Whorf's work was strongly criticized, with Malotki's text, for example, challenging the truth of many of Whorf's basic claims. See Ekkehart Malotki, *Hopi Time: A Linguistic Analysis of the Temporal Concepts in the Hopi Language* (Berlin: Mouton, 1983).

While strong versions of the notions of linguistic relativity (to the effect that linguistic structures *determine* thought) are no longer commonly accepted (or studied), weaker versions (seeing connections between certain linguistic structures and elements and the concepts a linguistic community may use) seem to have enjoyed a renaissance in such fields as linguistics, philosophy, and cultural studies, in large part the result of different forms of an "interpretive turn" in these and other fields. So, for example, Geertz champions an anthropological approach that positions the anthropologist as an interpreter of signs, where the signs themselves are manifestations of meanings generated by communities. Within such an approach there is no set of "facts" to be explored, only signs and symbols (explored through the *understanding*, not in terms of any form of causal network, as the anthropologist herself will be carrying out her interpretive investigations from a position within her own world of signs and symbols). See Clifford Geertz, *Local Knowledge: Further Essays in Interpretive Anthropology* (New York: Basic Books, 1983). For more critical examinations of "linguistic relativism," see John J Gumperz & Stephen Levinson, eds, *Rethinking Linguistic Relativity: Studies in the Foundation of Language* (Cambridge, UK: Cambridge University Press, 1996).

78 It would be common to find this characterized as a political situation as well, but that would add more descriptive layering than required. Here I am trying to make the point that what we *sense* in the situation before us is the attempt to apply a set of rules and institutions developed within *one* community to the members of various *other* communities – an effort at a very basic level of description is sociocultural. Nevertheless, it can assuredly be described as political, that is to say something more than required in the context of the current discussion.

the natural world that generate meaning. I make extensive use of what I term "meaning-generating communities" in the larger discourse that follows.

It is not uncommon in the literature to find talk of perspectives sliding into talk of ways of thinking of the world. It is not uncommon to discuss perspectives through the language of "world views,"[79] global all-encompassing sets of conceptual filters that purportedly function to make sense of the "raw experience" of human interaction. One can run with this notion to different lengths, with varying results.

One might argue for a strong sense of what a "world view" might signify, holding that an individual within a given society matures and develops (is acculturated) so as to "cut up" and reassemble the world of raw experience in a unique fashion into a world now made sensible *only* from *within* this sphere of meanings. Under this strong sense of world view, the creation of meaning can be seen making intercultural understanding difficult (if not impossible). Meaning itself is argued to be entirely context-dependent. Not only, however, does this make intercultural communication challenging (it certainly counts as a problem from this view), but it also calls into question the project of making sense of what any particular person *means* from a perspective outside that person's sociocultural setting. Accepting such a strong sense can lead to the position that you are doomed to failure should you attempt to understand how any particular person understands the world from vantage points *outside* her socioculturally determined world view.

Note, though, that it is not just the fact the person or group we might be trying to study is somehow removed from our ability to conceive of how they experience the world that poses fundamental problems in understanding, but that this model of "world views" is presented as a global view of human existence, so *we*, the observers, must *also* be seen "cutting up" the world according to *our own* socioculturally determined modes. Meaningful notions of objectivity become hard to come by.

Alternatively, however, one might hold there is a weaker notion of what a "world view" might signify, one that does not raise deep issues of intercultural (or acultural) communication and understanding. Within this weaker sense we still say an individual within a given society finds herself in a social setting wherein the social forms and institutions she lives and thinks through are unique and her own, but argue this simply signals the fact that communities of humans generate meaning around, and experience their social lives through, their particular communally generated webs of meaning. Here we consider still the notion that meaning is generated by social groups, that different social

79 See e.g. Nelson Goodman, *Ways of Worldmaking* (Indianapolis: Hackett, 1978); Betty Bastien, *Blackfoot Ways of Knowing: The Worldview of the Siksikaitsitapi* (Calgary: University of Calgary Press, 2004).

groups can come to vest elements of the world, and actions and relationships in the world, with different meanings and understandings, but imagine all this can be made sense of within a larger framework within which we imagine it is possible to study groups of humans as meaning-generating animal-collectives.

It should be apparent we can easily find ourselves tangled within copses of theory around the nature and role of perspectives in how people come to perceive and "know" the reality around them (realities some might argue they create).[80] These are the sorts of thicket we slide by in narrowing our focus to the sociocultural political situation before us – attempts by those within the legal order of Canada to have their legal system apply to peoples with separate and independent systems of meaning-generation. Our studies being limited to this specific phenomenon, it is not necessary to work out whether one can "get inside" the perspective of a people, or what the world looks like from within this structured reality. The key aspect of the social reality before us is that different meaning-generating systems – different social groups – are interacting. We need not rely upon appeals to the notion of separate worlds created through strong forms of "perspective" as we consider the nature of puzzles about to be presented.[81]

---

80 In the sciences, stronger senses of "world view" have been largely ignored or discredited, with only weak forms of the Sapir-Whorf hypothesis considered worthy of investigation. Weak forms posit the ability of language to influence thought, so that, for example, how one categorizes certain stimuli might influence how one thinks about the world. There seems to be little empirical work undertaken even in relation to this weaker form, perhaps because (a) researchers seem to have agreed that there was little empirical support for any such hypothesis to begin with, and (b) once empirical work has been carried out it has seemed to clearly indicate that how one uses language does not have an impact on how one thinks of the world around. One classic case of the latter sort of work is that of Berlin and Kay dealing with the categorization of colour. See Brent Berlin & Paul Kay, *Basic Color Terms: Their Universality and Evolution* (Berkeley: University of California Press, 1969). Not much work seems to have been done, however, on structural elements of language (as opposed to the Berlin-Kay work, on aspects of vocabulary).

In other disciplines, however, we find sharp divisions, so that within some fields we find – in contrast to those who espouse empirical approaches to the generation of knowledge – scholars arguing that "perspectival-knowledge" is all knowledge possible, that how one perceives the world (determined, for example, through one's placement in certain linguistic-cultural settings) determines what the world is, as known ("known" for that person, though without any non-perspectival knowledge acknowledged what the world is-as-known for a perceiver is what the world is). For a clear example of the internal struggles evident in many social science disciplines, see James Lett, *Science, Reason, and Anthropology: The Principles of Rational Inquiry* (Lanham, MD: Rowman & Littlefield, 1997). Lett's work is meant to answer the challenge of "interpretive anthropology," which regards "cultures as texts to be read and interpreted, just as a critic reads and interprets works of literature": *ibid* at 6.

81 I know I touch on complicated matters here, as a central pillar of my argument in this text is that Indigenous peoples have capacities to generate meaning in social settings, a capacity that plays out into forms of social reality. My point here is two-fold: (a) that this does not

And so, while I make substantial use of the general notion of a world view in this text, the reader must bear in mind I take it to capture the weaker idea that independent social groups develop their own forms of meaning, as is clear to any who are familiar with social settings outside their own. In this sense, we would speak generally of *many* Indigenous perspectives, as there are many and varied Indigenous peoples, each with its own systems of social ordering (indeed, and most importantly, each with its own system or traditions of law). This notion of such particularized Indigenous perspectives is of ways of seeing the world of social interaction (positional modes of perceiving and understanding social worlds), each tied to a particular people's particular history and collective existence.

Only this thin notion of a world view need be acknowledged in order to understand and appreciate puzzles about Canadian law. Grasping the sense of these puzzles relies only on seeing how they involve or revolve around the *fact* of peoples' differing situations, and the fact of peoples' differing perceptions of how the world of human interaction might look, given the fact of their collective history and experience.

With this narrowing in hand, let me introduce, then, two senses of Indigenous perspective required to see and understand puzzles about to be sketched out. On the one hand, there are the perspectives of peoples who have *experienced* particular histories – those who were subject to (and arguably continue to be subject to) colonial laws and policies. In such circumstances, with no more than a suitably rich appreciation for the history of colonialism itself, the reader should be in a position to see and understand certain of the puzzles about to be presented. All required is a reasonably robust sense of the history of colonialism in what is now Canada, and the ability and willingness to see that a complete accounting of history requires looking at events from multiple points of view. A robust grasp of history contains stories from the lives of Indigenous individuals and communities, stories of their struggles – and modes of resistance – under heavy and overt colonial laws and policies they have lived under for generations.

On the other hand, there are the sorts of perspectives alluded to just a few paragraphs ago: Indigenous perspectives on social reality can present different understandings of such things as "law," and those elements that might go

---

necessarily lead conceptually to separate and isolated social worlds, worlds inaccessible to more general forms of understanding, and (b) more importantly, that we need focus only on the fact of the existence of this capacity to generate meaning (and not the content of meaning thereby generated). The naturalist picture I sketch is just one of different meaning-generating communities using cultural-linguistic tools to make forms of relationships, thereby creating their own forms of social reality.

into the architecture of legal understandings, instruments, or institutions.[82] For example, someone deeply embedded in a liberal world view may have initial trouble seeing any other way to think of social problems than as matters affecting individuals, where, as a result, perceived solutions envisioned can only work on and affect individuals.[83] Someone else living within an Indigenous community still structured around understandings handed down as "original instructions," however, is likely to see individuals as fundamentally (normatively) socially embedded – society is understood to be primary, likely arranged around extended-family units, and individuals are understood to receive their basic normative form and nature in that context.[84] This sort of difference in basic understandings of basic units of the social world then plays out into different constructions of such things as "law" and "governance." In chapter 6 I come back to this matter of the constructed nature of the concept of the person (and the closely related concept of the self–society relationship) in examining the nature of liberal positivism and the apparent role of liberal thought in structuring Canadian law concerning Indigenous peoples.

Once again, however, it is essential to note the reader need not grasp the lens through which any particular Indigenous community actually sees the social

82 Here we need to be careful with terminology, as within any particular Indigenous community there may be no clear term that translates directly the Canadian notion of "law." In the traditional Inuit world, for example, there are things that must not be done, practices that must be followed, and rules that must be applied to all these matters. Elder Mariano Aupilaarjuk describes an analogue to Western law in traditional Inuit belief systems in Oosten et al, eds, *supra* note 28 at 16:

> *Tirigusungniit* are the rules relating to *pittailiniq*, things one should refrain from. *Maligait* are things that had to be followed. Back then we didn't use the term *maligaq*, but there was a set way of doing things that had to be followed. They are not really the same, but they are related to each other. To obey a *pittailiniq*, we would have to *tirigusuk*, refrain from doing certain things. If I did not follow the *tirigusungniq*, I would be doing something wrong because I would be breaking the *maligaq* relating to the *pittailiniq*. When a woman became pregnant, one *maligaq* she had to follow was putting on her *kamiik*, boots, right away and going out. Her husband had to do the same.

83 For an illustration of this effect while otherwise exploring contemporary political problems in countries with "internal colonies," see Duncan Ivison, *Postcolonial Liberalism* (Cambridge, UK: Cambridge University Press, 2002).

84 See e.g. Leroy Little Bear, "Aboriginal Paradigms: Implications for Relationships to Land and Treaty Making" in Kerry Wilkins, ed, *Advancing Aboriginal Claims: Visions/Strategies/Directions* (Saskatoon, SK: Purich, 2004) 26; Leroy Little Bear, "A Concept of Native Title" (1982) 5 Can Legal Aid Bull 99; Leroy Little Bear, "An Elder Explains Indigenous Philosophy and Indigenous Sovereignty" in Sandra Tomsons & Lorraine Mayer, eds, *Philosophy and Aboriginal Rights: Critical Dialogues* (Don Mills, ON: Oxford University Press, 2013); Monture-Angus, *supra* note 54; Bastien, *supra* note 79. See especially "Eurocentred and Niitsitapi Identity" in *ibid* at 165–72; Kathleen Dean Moore et al, eds, *How It Is: The Native American Philosophy of V.F. Cordova* (Tucson: University of Arizona Press, 2007).

world (in the sense the reader need not actually have to *see* the world through that lens – though having that perspectival knowledge is always a good thing!). In this context, as we examine the relationship between the Canadian state and its legal system and Indigenous peoples and their legal systems, it is sufficient in understanding peculiar matters that emerge in the context of this relationship that the reader simply be aware of the existence of such Indigenous perspectives and of the meaning-generating capacity that lies behind and within each one.

What I ultimately put primary emphasis on as we progress towards the arguments in latter stages of this text are not specific and unique forms of social reality through which Indigenous communities generate and understand their social worlds, but the more important fact that all Indigenous communities are the sorts of cultural-linguistic communities – the sorts of social units – that can *generate* such unique social realities. What is essential to understand and acknowledge is the social fact that any particular Indigenous community in Canada possesses not only its own normative structures (within which may reside structures they could frame as "law"), but also its own *capacities* for building, maintaining, and modifying these structures. It is ultimately *this* element of self-determination that undergirds the puzzles and that leads to the need for the sorts of explanations of Aboriginal law examined in the last stages of this text.

2 Canadian Law and Its Puzzles

For the most part, this study is focused on the development of Aboriginal law since the Aboriginal and treaty rights of the Aboriginal peoples of Canada were "recognized and affirmed" in section 35 of the *Constitution Act, 1982*.[1] How are we to understand Aboriginal law in the early twenty-first century, looking back over developments of the last few decades – what forces and principles account for the evolution of this law, explaining, for example, the trajectory of judicial decisions as they have unfolded before us? In the interests of manageability, the focus is narrowed to the nature of *Aboriginal rights* as this has been revealed in the jurisprudence over the last few decades.

In the Introduction, I began to sketch out concerns driving my studies over the last decade, which I flesh out and address in the next chapter. Once these concerns are laid out I hope the reader can appreciate why the text – ostensibly about an area of Canadian law – dives into discussions of theory and methodology. I argue that a specific methodological approach – that of methodological naturalism – is best suited to working towards understanding the place of Canadian jurisprudence in the lives of Indigenous peoples in Canada.

A first step along the way to building up and applying this approach involves looking more carefully at puzzles that emerge when one tries to make sense of Aboriginal law. Some were touched on in the Introduction, while most are yet to be laid out. They are presented in some order – first are those that arise within points in the jurisprudence, then those that emerge on a more general level or when one turns to what the Supreme Court itself has said about how this jurisprudence is supposed to make sense. The survey concludes with a few words about one particular sort of claimed right – not yet established within the jurisprudence – that of "governance." Much of the puzzlement around how

1 *Constitution Act, 1982*, being Schedule B to the *Canada Act 1982* (UK), c 11 [*Constitution Act, 1982*].

Aboriginal law has developed can be pulled together and captured in thinking about how the notion of Indigenous governance (or claims to Indigenous sovereignty) has been treated by Canadian courts. Finally, we look at puzzles that emerge when we look at matters of evaluation (looking first at general assessments of Aboriginal law and then analyses of academics – where we might otherwise have expected clarity might be found!).

The General Nature of Aboriginal Rights

Aboriginal and treaty rights have their own distinct historical sources and enjoy contemporary status as constitutionally protected rights. Treaty rights emerge out of the many and varied agreements reached over the last few centuries between the British/Canadian Crowns and Indigenous peoples.[2] Aboriginal rights, on the other hand, protect a range of "customs, practices and traditions" engaged in by Aboriginal peoples prior to contact with Europeans.[3] One species of Aboriginal right – Aboriginal title – protects Aboriginal land interests reaching back to the occupancy of traditional territories at the time of the assertion of Crown sovereignty.[4] A second species – Aboriginal rights to governance – may eventuate in powers held by Aboriginal communities to determine aspects of their collective futures.[5]

Following the patriation of the constitution in 1982, and the inclusion of section 35, "recognizing and affirming" the Aboriginal and treaty rights of Aboriginal peoples, these two sets of rights came to have constitutional status. Once a historic agreement is found to have met the criteria to be properly seen as a Crown-Aboriginal treaty, or once a practice, custom, or tradition is

---

2 See *R v White* (1964), 50 DLR (2d) 613, 52 WWR 193 (BCCA), aff'd [1965] SCR vi (note), 52 DLR (2d) 481; *R v Simon*, [1985] 2 SCR 387, 24 DLR (4th) 390; *R v Horseman*, [1990] 1 SCR 901, [1990] 4 WWR 97; *R v Sioui*, [1990] 1 SCR 1025, 70 DLR (4th) 427; *R v Badger*, [1996] 1 SCR 771, 133 DLR (4th) 324; *R v Marshall*, [1999] 3 SCR 456, 177 DLR (4th) 513; [1999] 3 SCR 533, 179 DLR (4th) 193; *Mikisew Cree First Nation v Canada (Minister of Canadian Heritage)*, 2005 SCC 69 [*Mikisew Cree 2005*]; *R v Morris*, 2006 SCC 59; *West Moberly First Nations v British Columbia (Chief Inspector of Mines)*, 2011 BCCA 247, leave to appeal to SCC refused, 34403 (23 August 2011); *Grassy Narrows First Nation v Ontario (MNR)*, 2014 SCC 48.

3 See *R v Van der Peet*, [1996] 2 SCR 507, 137 DLR (4th) 289 [*Van der Peet*].

4 See *Delgamuukw v British Columbia (AG)*, [1997] 3 SCR 1010, 153 DLR (4th) 193 [*Delgamuukw*]; *Tsilhqot'in Nation*.

5 There have been no clear, successful attempts to argue a right of self-government up to the Supreme Court. One significant case led to an unsuccessful outcome, but most likely as a result of very poor facts (around attempts at locally governing gambling on reserves). See *R v Pamajewon*, [1996] 2 SCR 821, 138 DLR (4th) 204. Most agree that section 35 contains such rights, but their nature and extent remain unresolved in Canadian jurisprudence.

found to have been integral to the distinctive culture of the relevant Aboriginal community at contact, or once an Aboriginal community is able to show they exclusively and sufficiently occupied a tract of land at the relevant point in colonial history, a constitutionally protected treaty right, Aboriginal right, or claim to Aboriginal title is well on its way to being made out.

Two cases, *R v Sparrow* and *R v Van der Peet*,[6] lie at the base of Aboriginal rights jurisprudence. In *Sparrow*, a Musqueam fisher (Ronald Sparrow) was charged with fishing with an improperly sized net, and his defence was that, as a member of the Musqueam nation, he enjoyed an Aboriginal right to fish. In *Van der Peet*, a member of the Stó:lō nation (Dorothy Van der Peet) was charged with selling ten fish without a licence, and her defence was that the Stó:lō people enjoy an Aboriginal right to trade in fish and that this right in a contemporary setting translates into a right to sell fish.[7] Our look into the framework of the law concerning Aboriginal rights begins with a look at how Aboriginal rights are defined and established. In the next section we turn to the question of how established rights are to be fit into the Canadian legal landscape.

While *Sparrow* preceded *Van der Peet* by six years, *Van der Peet* is first up in terms of which naturally precedes the other in subject matter. The basic test for the existence of an Aboriginal right is set out in this case – the "integral to the distinctive culture" test: "[I]n order to be an aboriginal right an activity must be an element of a practice, custom or tradition integral to the distinctive culture of the aboriginal group claiming the right."[8] So, for example, to claim a right to hunt for sustenance or social purposes (for food for the community), an Aboriginal people would need to show that, at the time of contact with Europeans, hunting for sustenance (or social purposes) was integral to its distinctive culture.

In introducing this test, the Supreme Court offered a number of factors that a court could consider in its application to a claimed right.[9] I will not go through all them, but I will bring some in as I draw out puzzles swirling around the Court's way of unpacking "Aboriginal rights."

Hopefully the reader first encountering this test was puzzled on her own, at least on this first point: why would a set of constitutionally protected rights be so very narrow in definition and scope and so very hard to show (that is, why focus on cultural practices from many generations ago, with all the attendant

6 *R v Sparrow*, [1990] 1 SCR 1075, 70 DLR (4th) 385 [*Sparrow*]; *Van der Peet*, *supra* note 3; *Gladstone* (touched on in passing).

7 Similarly, two individuals from the Heiltsuk (Donald and William Gladstone) argued their Aboriginal community enjoyed a right to trade herring spawn on kelp (on a commercial scale). See *Gladstone*, *ibid.*

8 *Van der Peet*, *supra* note 3 at para 46.

9 *Ibid* at paras 48–74.

evidentiary problems that would carry along)? It might take a few moments' consideration to see further points of confusion and contention: why would the "rights" in question be *activities, practices, or traditions* (and not defined in such a way as to cover broader forms of social life – would anyone, for example, consider defining freedom of speech as essentially being *nothing more than* protection of *particular* acts of speaking or *particular* forms of speech)? Why, furthermore, would the test force Aboriginal peoples to go so far back into history, to what may seem an *arbitrary* point in time? What could it be about first contact with Europeans that could sensibly determine that *rights* are fixed at that point in time? Why, as well, would the *onus of proof* be on Aboriginal peoples to show all that is required under this test (especially as they – and presumably the grounds for their rights – predate the Crown itself)?

The Court further noted that at the first stage of assessing a rights-claim a court will have to properly characterize the right. This matter of defining the right was originally seen in *Sparrow* inviting in "Aboriginal perspectives,"[10] as it seemed necessary to imagine the Aboriginal claimant having significant input into defining the nature of the right being alleged. In that earlier case the Court also specifically removed the possibility that the claimed right might be defined in relation to government regulation (as this would, the Court at that time found, create a "patchwork" of Aboriginal rights, dependent on particular government regulations with which a claimed practice, custom, or tradition might have interacted).[11]

In *Van der Peet*, however, the Court (a) removed reference to the essential need for an Aboriginal perspective in defining the right,[12] and (b) specified three things a court should consider when engaged in the process of characterization:

> [T]he nature of the action which the applicant is claiming was done pursuant to an aboriginal right, the nature of the governmental regulation, statute or action being impugned, and the tradition, custom or practice being relied upon to establish the right.[13]

---

10 "While it is impossible to give an easy definition of fishing rights, it is possible, and, indeed, crucial, to be sensitive to the aboriginal perspective itself on the meaning of the rights at stake": *Sparrow, supra* note 6 at 1112.

11 "[A]n existing aboriginal right cannot be read so as to incorporate the specific manner in which it was regulated before 1982": *ibid* at 1091.

12 *Van der Peet, supra* note 3 at paras 51–4. The closest the Court comes in these paragraphs to the notion that the Aboriginal claimant might have a say in how the right is defined is in acknowledging that Lambert J at the BC Court of Appeal had invoked the significance of the practice to the Stó:lō in defining the right – an approach that the Supreme Court rejects, holding that the significance of the practice goes to whether it is "integral" to the distinctive culture of the Aboriginal community.

13 *Ibid* at para 53.

Why would courts no longer have to pay specific attention to the understandings of the Aboriginal claimant around what she believes she is claiming as a right? Why, as well, would it now be acceptable to generate a patchwork of rights (dependent on varied "governmental regulation, statute or action")?[14] Stepping back at this point to a broader vantage point, we could also wonder why (perhaps most troublingly as we see this power exercised unilaterally) this is all in the hands of Canadian courts, an arm of the Canadian state.

From Indigenous perspectives, these are all puzzling matters. Indeed, I would suggest these matters should seem puzzling to any observer, neutral or otherwise, whatever her perspective. Let us put that to the side for the moment and continue our journey through the oddities of this area of jurisprudence.

The Court in *Van der Peet* went on to say that while a practice underlying a right may evolve (so that, for example, a right originally practised with bow and arrow may now be practised with a rifle), this is only in relation to the *mode* of *exercising* the right – the right itself cannot change in character (so a right to hunt for food may not transform over time into a right to hunt to sell the meat to buy groceries and pay rent).[15] Why, if these rights were to be (mysteriously) tied to culture, would there not be acknowledgment of cultural change (a feature of all cultures, at all times)?[16]

Besides "evolution in mode of exercise" noted above, there is acknowledgment in *Van der Peet* of one other form of cultural change, but of an odd sort, acknowledged in a way that generates further puzzlement. The Court notes that when an Aboriginal right is asserted, it must be determined if it is "Aboriginal," which means determining whether or not the custom, tradition, or practice

---

14 One might argue the earlier remark in *Sparrow* was restricted to the possibility of defining a right that came to be recognized in 1982 in relation to regulations that might have existed in relation to the practice *up to that point in time*, while the approach taken in *Van der Peet* focused on government regulation from 1982 onward. See *Sparrow*, *supra* note 6; *Van der Peet*, *supra* note 3. But (a) the discussion in *Sparrow* was generally about the undesirability of any "patchwork," regardless of when it might arise, and (b) those concerns now manifest post-*Van der Peet*. From an Indigenous perspective the real question, of course, is how one would even consider that Aboriginal rights would be defined on the basis of how practices, traditions, and customs might have interacted with Crown interference with their exercise.

15 *Van der Peet*, *supra* note 3. One problem with this revolves upon the use of this distinction – it will seldom be clear whether a change is to the manner of exercise of a right or to the right itself.

16 RL Barsh & James Youngblood (Sakej) Henderson, "The Supreme Court's *Van der Peet* Trilogy: Naïve Imperialism and Ropes of Sand" (1997) 42 McGill LJ 993; Michael Asch, "The Judicial Conceptualization of Culture After *Delgamuukw* and *Van der Peet*" (2000) 5 Rev Const Stud 119; Michael Murphy, "Prisons of Culture: Judicial Constructions of Indigenous Rights in Australia, Canada, and New Zealand" (2008) 87 Can Bar Rev 357; Neil Vallance, "The Misuse of 'Culture' by the Supreme Court of Canada" in Avigail Eisenberg, ed, *Diversity and Equality: The Changing Framework of Freedom in Canada* (Vancouver: UBC Press, 2006) 97.

presently engaged in has become over time essentially "European."[17] If the right has become "European" it could not possibly be an Aboriginal right, as it would not be then "Aboriginal." While this unpacking of the test might be thought to fit well with the earlier point we explored (as one might see the transition from an "Aboriginal" practice into a "European" practice as an instance of an Aboriginal right evolving in a way transforming the right into something else), we must wonder what odd notion of "culture" the Court works under. Cultural change and adaptation are acknowledged, but in ways that set off against each other two general worlds of "culture" – that of the West and that of Aboriginal communities.[18]

Finally, while in *Van der Peet* the Court continued to *speak* of placing equal weight on Aboriginal and non-Aboriginal perspectives in working through what rights might exist,[19] on the general question of what role Aboriginal perspectives might play in Aboriginal law, we see the Court pull back from earlier pronouncements and lead the way to further pullbacks.[20] We noted

---

17 *Van der Peet*, *supra* note 3 at para 73.

18 While I do my best in this chapter to avoid exegesis of the development of this test in the text itself, any reader familiar with Said's *Orientalism* (or, reaching back further, Fanon's *Black Skin, White Masks* and *Wretched of the Earth*, or Aimé Césaire's *Discourse on Colonialism*) is probably wondering at this point about how the Supreme Court could – in 1996 – so blithely move in such a direction. See Edward Said, *Orientalism* (New York: Pantheon Books, 1978); Frantz Fanon, *Black Skin, White Masks* (New York: Grove Press, 1952); Frantz Fanon, *The Wretched of the Earth* (New York: Grove Press, 1963); Aimé Césaire, *Discourse on Colonialism*, translated by Joan Pinkham (New York: Monthly Review Press, 2001).

19 *Van der Peet*, *supra* note 3 at para 49: "In assessing a claim for the existence of an aboriginal right, a court must take into account the perspective of the aboriginal people claiming the right. In *Sparrow* [*supra* note 6], Dickson C.J. and La Forest J. held, at p. 1112, that it is 'crucial to be sensitive to the aboriginal perspective itself on the meaning of the rights at stake.'"

20 The Court went on to add (after noting that the law must be sensitive to the Aboriginal perspective), *ibid* at para 49 [emphasis added]:

> It must also be recognized, however, that that perspective must be framed in terms cognizable to the Canadian legal and constitutional structure.... Courts adjudicating aboriginal rights claims ... must also be aware that aboriginal rights exist within the general legal system of Canada. To quote again Walters [Mark Walters, "British Imperial Constitutional Law and Aboriginal Rights: A Comment on *Delgamuukw v. British Columbia*" (1992) 17 Queen's LJ 350 at p. 413]: "[A] morally and politically defensible conception of aboriginal rights will incorporate both [aboriginal and non-aboriginal] legal perspectives." The definition of an aboriginal right must, if it is truly to reconcile the prior occupation of Canadian territory by aboriginal peoples with the assertion of Crown sovereignty over that territory, take into account the aboriginal perspective, *yet do so in terms which are cognizable to the non-aboriginal legal system.*

The Court went on to state in the next paragraph that "the only fair and just reconciliation is ... one which takes into account the aboriginal perspective while at the same time taking into account the perspective of the common law. *True reconciliation will, equally,*

above that in *Sparrow* the Court spoke of equal weight being put on Aboriginal perspectives concerning the matter of *defining* the nature of the right in question and that in *Van der Peet* this no longer holds.[21] In later decisions the Court tightened things up further,[22] holding that (a) while the right may initially be *claimed* in accord with concepts and perspectives of the Aboriginal community, it must ultimately be *defined* in such a way that it fits entirely within the understandings of the common law (fitting within notions of "rights" Canadian courts can recognize), and (b) it may be appropriate to define Aboriginal rights in light of a key purpose of section 35, the reconciliation of Aboriginal peoples to their place within Canada.[23]

While it is odd that the notion of "equal weight" is transformed into a process of forcing one kind of conception of legal interests into forms defined within another legal system, the truly puzzling aspect of all this is how it could be that grounds for rights that *predate* the Crown (and for peoples who suffer the direct impacts of colonialism, wrought by the Crown) come to be treated such that they must fit within the conceptual system of the laws of the state. That these processes of definition are then further confined within a notion of reconciliation, so that an Aboriginal community may find its claim narrowly defined simply because, for example, it involves an interest that might have a commercial aspect that might touch on non-Aboriginal interests, is simply another layer to the puzzles that now surround the process of characterization.

---

place weight on each": *ibid* at para 50 [emphasis added]. At this point in the development of the jurisprudence, it would seem the Court imagines that having the Aboriginal perspective be "cognizable" to the non-Aboriginal system means incorporating a mode of translation that can accommodate the transmission of the essential meaning of the Aboriginal view. This requirement of "cognizability," however, does weaken the notion of equality of perspectives, as it is a requirement falling only on the Aboriginal articulation of their interests.

21 *Sparrow*, *supra* note 6 at 1112.

22 *Mitchell v Minister of National Revenue*, 2001 SCC 33 [*Mitchell v MNR*]; *R v Sappier*; *R v Gray*, 2006 SCC 54 [*Sappier & Gray*].

23 *Lax Kw'alaams Indian Band v Canada (AG)*, 2011 SCC 56 at para 46, Binnie J:

> [I]n the event that an Aboriginal right to trade *commercially* is found to exist, the court, when delineating such a right should have regard to what was said by Chief Justice Lamer in *Gladstone* (albeit in the context of a *Sparrow* justification), as follows:
>
> Although by no means making a definitive statement on this issue, I would suggest that with regards to the distribution of the fisheries resource after conservation goals have been met, objectives such as the pursuit of economic and regional fairness, and the recognition of the historical reliance upon, and participation in, the fishery by non-aboriginal groups, are the type of objectives which can (at least in the right circumstances) satisfy this standard. *In the right circumstances, such* objectives are in the interest of all Canadians and, more importantly, the reconciliation of aboriginal societies with the rest of Canadian society may well depend on their successful attainment. [Emphasis in original; para 75.]

An implication of this determination of the nature of Aboriginal rights was made crystal clear in subsequent decisions: since Aboriginal rights constitute *practices, customs, and traditions*, they are not rights *to* resources (or things). So, for example, in the 2006 decision in *Sappier & Gray*, the Supreme Court made it clear the *Van der Peet* articulation left no possibility an Aboriginal community could present arguments that implied they enjoyed any form of a right *to* a resource as a result of having an Aboriginal right.[24] Charged with illegal cutting of trees for the construction of furniture and housing, the Mi'kmaq and Maliseet defendants in that case were barred from trying to assert they might have an Aboriginal right *to the trees themselves* – the only arguments they could assert within this field of jurisprudence are those that might demonstrate a right to *cut down* and *use* trees.

After living in and on their territories for hundreds of years – in many cases, thousands of years – Indigenous communities apparently acquired (under general Aboriginal rights) no territory-wide property interests (that is, interests in any particular resource lying within the territory as a whole). Only by showing one particular form of right – Aboriginal title – could an Indigenous community enjoy any form of property interest.[25] This should strike the reader as puzzling, as it is to many Aboriginal peoples, who find themselves naturally slipping into arguments about claims to resources when making claims before Canadian courts. Outside successful title-claims, however, no such rights exist within Canadian law.

Before we leave particularities in the development of Canadian law on the nature of Aboriginal rights, we need to say a few words about how the Supreme Court has begun to treat Metis claims. It was only in 2003 that the Court had an opportunity to spell out how it would deal with what was obviously an unresolved situation, as (a) the test in *Van der Peet* was calibrated so an Aboriginal rights claimant had to reach back to contact with Europeans to locate those Aboriginal practices integral to a distinctive culture that could ground current claims, while (b) the Metis only formed *after* European contact. Clearly, at the very least the test was going to have to be recalibrated (unless it turned out the Metis had no rights under section 35).

In *R v Powley* the Court dealt with the claims of two members of a Metis community based near Sault Ste Marie, in central Ontario.[26] The Court

24 "[A]n aboriginal right cannot be characterized as a right to a particular resource because to do so would be to treat it as akin to a common law property right": *Sappier & Gray*, *supra* note 22 at para 21.

25 This matter is discussed in the section on Aboriginal title. It should be noted once again that it was only in 2014 that an Aboriginal community was able to achieve Aboriginal title "on the ground." See *Tsilhqot'in Nation*, *supra* note 4.

26 *R v Powley*, 2003 SCC 43 [*Powley*].

had not only to wonder about how best to modify the *Van der Peet* test to reflect the nature of the Metis, but how the Metis would be identified under 35 (as potential rights-holders). Modes of identification need to function on two levels – there needs to be some way to identify those communities across Canada that can be identified (within Canadian law) as Metis,[27] and there needs to be some way to identify whether some individual is a member of a community so identified. The Court wisely avoided any definitive pronouncements on tests for Metis identity. For the most part it recognized that the matter is best left up to the Metis themselves.[28] It did speak of frameworks, setting out parameters within which it assumed Metis would work out definite modes of self-identification, and it reserved to Canadian courts the role of ultimate arbiter for questions about whether a community that claims Metis status is "actually" Metis.[29]

As to the modification of *Van der Peet*, the Court simply (a) chose a different sort of time frame (looking to periods of time *after* the formation of the distinct Metis community but *before* the Crown had established effective sovereign control over the territory in which the community might be located),[30] and (b) asked for evidence of practices, traditions, and customs at that time that would be integral to the distinctive Metis community.[31]

Puzzles around this adjustment for the Metis touch on the fact this group with rights under section 35 falls under a different time frame (and frankly a much easier one to fulfil). Other important puzzles, however, parallel those we detailed above, in our general examination of the tests and rules around section 35 rights. We will say a bit more about the place of Metis interests under section 35 when we look at larger frameworks the Court has articulated around or behind such rights.

---

27 As of the writing of this text, a dispute within Canadian law continues unresolved as to whether there is a single Metis community (the Metis Nation) or regional Metis communities (Metis nations). See *R v Hirsekorn*, 2013 ABCA 242; *Daniels v Canada (Indian Affairs and Northern Development)*, 2016 SCC 12 [*Daniels*].

28 *Powley*, *supra* note 26 at paras 29–30.

29 There have been numerous attempts, for example, to defend charges in cases in the Maritimes through the assertion of the exercise of Metis rights, all of which have failed on the basis of a failure to establish an historical Metis community. See e.g. *R v Castonguay*, 2012 NBPC 19; *R v Vautour*, 2015 NBQB 94; *R v Babin*, 2013 NSSC 434.

30 *Powley*, *supra* note 26 at paras 36–40.

31 One note of interest is the Court's use of the notion of "when Europeans effectively established political and legal control in a particular area" as an apparent proxy for Crown assertion of sovereignty (the point in time used in the test for establishment of Aboriginal title): *ibid* at para 37. Asserting sovereignty and establishing effective control would likely seem to most observers as often pointing to different points in time.

Crown-Aboriginal Interactions

Justifiable Infringement under Sparrow

In 1984 a member of the Musqueam community, Ronald Sparrow, was charged with several fishing offences under the *Fisheries Act*.[32] Early in the proceedings in *R v Sparrow* at the Supreme Court level it was accepted that it was an integral part of the Musqueam culture to fish for food and ceremonial purposes.[33] Having characterized the claimed right in this fashion, the matter of establishing the right was passed over quite quickly. This (chronologically earlier) decision wound up focusing on the question of the power of the Crown to justifiably infringe upon an established Aboriginal right, which is essentially the question of how Aboriginal rights are to be fit into the contemporary Canadian legal-political landscape. The Supreme Court found that the *effect* of the constitutionalization of Aboriginal rights was to *temper* what had been previously accepted to be absolute Crown power (in this context, an absolute power to extinguish or infringe upon whatever common law rights Aboriginal peoples enjoyed before 1982).[34]

In setting out a vision of Crown power being tempered with Crown obligations, the Court in *Sparrow* set out a basic framework addressing the question of how the Crown could continue to "justifiably infringe" Aboriginal rights now constitutionally protected. Two conditions were set, with Crown action *justifiably* infringing upon an existing Aboriginal right only if both are met. First, the objective of the Crown in acting must be sufficiently "compelling and substantial."[35] Second, in acting, the Crown must appropriately act within its role as a fiduciary in this situation.[36]

To see that language of fiduciary doctrine might be appropriate in this context, consider the history of the relationship between the Crown and the Musqueam. Over the last century or so the Crown took upon itself control over the legal and practical interests of the Musqueam (creating a situation in which the Musqueam are vulnerable to the exercise of Crown power – forced

32 *Sparrow*, *supra* note 6. In particular, under the Food Fishing Licence he held within the federal fishing regulatory scheme, he was restricted in the length of net he might use. The net he was using did not fall within those limits.

33 This determination must be put in context: the Musqueam originally asserted a *right to fish* (*sans* qualifiers) and included in that assertion claims to attendant powers and responsibilities (for example, they held their right to fish included a responsibility to regulate fishing by the community, through use of their own legal structures). This comes out in the trial judgment and is noted in the rulings of the British Columbia Court of Appeal.

34 *Sparrow*, *supra* note 6 at 1109. The Court held that henceforth "federal power must be reconciled with federal duty": *ibid.*

35 *Ibid* at 1113–14.

36 *Ibid* at 1114–19.

in essence to trust in the honour of the Crown).[37] Given these background conditions, one might reasonably imagine a fiduciary relationship arises.[38] Within this relationship the Crown – as fiduciary – would presumably be bound to act in the best interests of the Musqueam as it engages with or acts in relation to their established rights (now constitutionally protected).

In this specific case, where the Crown was attempting through regulations to control and limit the exercise of a Musqueam right to fish for food and ceremonial purposes, the Supreme Court held that such regulatory regimes have to fall under the rule of law, first having to have compelling and substantial objectives, and second having to meet the requirements that flow from the Crown finding itself in the position of fiduciary.[39]

The Court did not provide much guidance on what might constitute sufficiently "compelling and substantial" objectives. In *Sparrow* the suggestion seemed to be that objectives equally benefiting all concerned – that parties all have a strong interest to protect and uphold – could be considered valid. In the case of laws and regulations on fishing activities, conservation would then be an appropriate objective.[40] So long as the Crown regulated the Musqueam

---

37 On the application of fiduciary doctrine in a general sense, see e.g. *Lac Minerals Ltd v International Corona Resources Ltd*, [1989] 2 SCR 574, 61 DLR (4th) 14; *Norberg v Wynrib*, [1992] 2 SCR 226, 92 DLR (4th) 449.

38 In *Manitoba Metis Federation v Canada (AG)*, 2013 SCC 14 at paras 49–50 [*Manitoba Metis Federation*], the Supreme Court seems to have introduced a measure of confusion into matters, stating that:

> In the Aboriginal context, a fiduciary duty may arise as a result of the "Crown [assuming] discretionary control over specific Aboriginal interests": *Haida Nation v. British Columbia (Minister of Forests)*, 2004 SCC 73, [2004] 3 S.C.R. 511, at para. 18. The focus is on the particular interest that is the subject matter of the dispute: *Roberts v. R.*, 2002 SCC 79, [2002] 4 S.C.R. 245 (S.C.C.) [hereinafter *Wewaykum*], at para. 83. The content of the Crown's fiduciary duty towards Aboriginal peoples varies with the nature and importance of the interest sought to be protected: *Wewaykum*, at para. 86.
>
> A fiduciary duty may also arise from an undertaking, if the following conditions are met: (1) an undertaking by the alleged fiduciary to act in the best interests of the alleged beneficiary or beneficiaries; (2) a defined person or class of persons vulnerable to a fiduciary's control (the beneficiary or beneficiaries); and (3) a legal or substantial practical interest of the beneficiary or beneficiaries that stands to be adversely affected by the alleged fiduciary's exercise of discretion or control. (*Elder Advocates of Alberta Society v. Alberta*, 2011 SCC 24, [2011] 2 S.C.R. 261 (S.C.C.), at para. 36)

Given that the *Manitoba Metis Federation* case was specifically about possible Metis interests in land, subsequent courts have taken these passages as signalling that fiduciary duties arise in a sui generis manner in the Aboriginal context when (*and only when*) a particularly "Aboriginal" interest *in land* is at the base of the situation at issue. See e.g. *Nunavut Tunngavik Inc v Canada (AG)*, 2014 NUCJ 31. It remains for later courts to clear up this confusion. It would seem odd, for example, that the use of fiduciary doctrine would then somehow have been inappropriate in *Sparrow*, where the situation did not at all involve Musqueam interests in land. See *Sparrow*, *supra* note 6.

39 *Sparrow*, *supra* note 6 at 1113–19.

40 *Ibid* at 1114.

fishery with this sort of objective in mind, the first hurdle regarding justification of infringement could be crossed. In regard to the second matter, that of acting appropriately as a fiduciary, the Court found that in the circumstances the Crown must establish a hierarchical set of priorities. After legitimate interests were satisfied (such as those around conservation), the Crown would need to prioritize Aboriginal food and ceremonial fishing, ahead of both commercial and recreational or sport fishing.[41]

Beyond the legislative enactment and scheme having to meet these two requirements, the Court also added a non-exhaustive list of additional concerns that may come up (depending on the circumstances):

> [W]hether there has been as little infringement as possible in order to effect the desired result; whether, in a situation of expropriation, fair compensation is available; and, whether the aboriginal group in question has been consulted with respect to the conservation measures being implemented.[42]

As noted in the Introduction, *Sparrow* was the first case to emerge under section 35, and my puzzlement (and concern) with the direction Canadian law was taking arose at that point. In the next section I focus on broader features of the jurisprudence as it emerged, and there some key features of this case will be discussed in some detail. Let me here note two discrete elements of the structure put in place that should strike the reader as quite puzzling (bearing in mind particularly the discussion of Indigenous perspectives a few pages ago).[43]

First, of course, is the overarching power of the Crown. While the Court speaks of tempering federal power (by federal responsibility), this was not meant to question the fact of Crown sovereignty. Before *Sparrow*, Canadian courts understood the Crown to be the sole sovereign authority, vested with absolute power (with the federal government enjoying exclusive legislative power over "Indians and Lands Reserved for Indians" under section 91(24) of the *Constitution Act, 1867*).[44] After *Sparrow*, Canadian courts *continued* to understand the Crown to be the sole sovereign authority, vested with absolute

41 *Ibid* at 1116.

42 *Ibid* at 1119.

43 See *supra* "Indigenous Perspectives" in chapter 1.

44 Whether this meant that the federal government had exclusive jurisdictional authority (and so responsibility) for the Inuit, Metis, and non-status Indians were matters to be worked out within Canadian law. In 1939 the Supreme Court determined that for the purposes of section 91(24), Inuit are considered "Indians." See *Reference as to whether "Indians" includes in s. 91 (24) of the B.N.A. Act includes Eskimo in habitants of the Province of Quebec*, [1939] SCR 104, [1939] 2 DLR 417. Questions about the Metis and non-status Indians (within Canadian law) were answered as this text was being completed. See *Daniels, supra* note 27.

(unchallenged) power (that now must be exercised under the rule of law – Canadian law that is – with aspects of the law spelling out fiduciary responsibilities to Aboriginal peoples).

There are passages in *Sparrow* that suggest the "rules of the game" were to be rewritten, that colonialism itself was to be addressed and pushed past.[45] Yet details of the judgment say otherwise, as Aboriginal peoples find themselves still entirely under the control of legislative (and jurisdictional) authority exercised by the Crown (and its courts). An Indigenous perspective would have suggested that recognition and affirmation of their claims and interests in the newly patriated constitution should speak to the colonial history lying beneath the entire history of Crown-Indigenous relations, but the Supreme Court deftly avoids any substantive move in that direction. A reasonable appreciation of the history of Crown-Indigenous relations should suffice to make evident this source of intense puzzlement.

Second, the heart of colonialism lay in (and arguably continues to lie in) the exercise of colonial-state power to dispossess, disempower, and oppress Indigenous peoples in Canada. For over 150 years the British colonies and later the Canadian state acted in myriad ways to do just these things – to take away the lands and livelihoods of Indigenous peoples, to attempt to destroy their cultures, languages, and social structures,[46] and to generate conditions in which families, clans, and nations were destitute and – ultimately – dependent on economic and political relationships with the state. Given this history, it should strike one as deeply puzzling that the promise of a new "just settlement"[47] played out in *Sparrow* in the foundational use of fiduciary doctrine. How would merely *recognizing* that the Crown has indeed taken control over the legal and practical interests of Indigenous peoples move Canadian law (and policy) *past* this history? Would not the need be (*at a minimum*) to establish a framework for movement towards a world in which the relationship making fiduciary doctrine applicable is no more?

---

45 *Sparrow*, *supra* note 6 at 1105–6:

> Professor Lyon in "An Essay on Constitutional Interpretation" (1988), 26 *Osgoode Hall L.J.* 95, says the following about s 35(1):
>
> > Section 35 calls for a just settlement for aboriginal peoples. It renounces the old rules of the game under which the Crown established courts of law and denied those courts the authority to question sovereign claims made by the Crown.

46 The Report of the Truth and Reconciliation Commission details the history and consequences of the Crown policy of separating children from their families in residential schools from the late 1800s to the 1990s. See Truth and Reconciliation Commission, "Honouring the Truth, Reconciling for the Future" (2015), online: <http://www.nctr.ca/assets/reports/Final%20Reports/Executive_Summary_English_Web.pdf>.

47 *Sparrow*, *supra* note 6 at 1106 (at which point the Court approved of the quote it had taken from an article by Professor Lyon. See *supra* note 45).

Justifiable Infringement under Gladstone

Let us move on to a case in which the basic framework around "justifiable infringement" was modified: *R v Gladstone*.[48] The Heiltsuk of the Central Northwest Coast had argued they enjoy an Aboriginal right not just to harvest and to trade herring spawn on kelp, but to do so in a manner best described today as "commercial." Evidence tendered at trial for two members of the community charged with illegally selling herring spawn on kelp convinced courts up to the Supreme Court that such a right existed. In its decision, however, the Supreme Court focused most of its attention on the question of Crown efforts to justify infringement of rights with a commercial aspect to them.

In the context of this discussion the Court distinguished between two kinds of claimed Aboriginal rights – those with and those without an internal limit.[49] In the particular case of a right that is internally limited (as when the right to fish *for food or ceremonial purposes* would be exhausted once fish sufficient to meet these needs were caught), the framework articulated in *Sparrow* would apply. Where, however, the right lacked such an internal limit (where, for example, the right to fish was commercial in scope, and so could be limited or exhausted only by such external constraints as the supply of fish or the demands of the market), a framework was deemed appropriate that allowed for lesser requirements on the fiduciary.[50]

In explaining what the problem might be with rights-with-no-internal-limits the Court said,

> Where the aboriginal right has no internal limitation, however, what is described in *Sparrow* as an exceptional situation becomes the ordinary: in the circumstance where the aboriginal right has no internal limitation, the notion of priority, as articulated in *Sparrow*, would mean that where an aboriginal right is recognized and affirmed that right would become an exclusive one.[51]

So how might the Crown justify infringements? In relation to the question about how the Crown might show it has acted as a fiduciary the Court determined that on an abstract level the law would be looking to see whether

> [the Crown] has taken account of the existence of aboriginal rights and allocated the resource in a manner *respectful* of the fact that those rights have priority over the exploitation of the fishery by other users.... [A]t the stage of justification the government must demonstrate both that the process by which it allocated the

48 *Gladstone*, *supra* note 6.
49 *Ibid* at para 57.
50 *Ibid* at paras 57–68.
51 *Ibid* at para 59.

> resource and the actual allocation of the resource which results from that process *reflect the prior interest* of aboriginal rights holders in the fishery.
>
> The content of this priority – something less than exclusivity but which nonetheless gives priority to the aboriginal right – *must remain somewhat vague*.... [Priority must] be assessed in each case to determine whether the government has acted in a fashion which *reflects that it has truly taken into account the existence of aboriginal rights*.... [W]here the aboriginal right to be given priority is one without internal limitation, courts should assess the government's actions ... to determine whether the government has *taken into account* the existence and importance of such rights.[52]

The last few sentences are crucial (in generating puzzles). In the next paragraph the Court indicates how "taking into account" Aboriginal rights might be demonstrated on a concrete level. Questions for a court to ask would have to do with

> consultation and compensation, as well as questions such as whether the government has accommodated the exercise of the aboriginal right to participate in the fishery (through reduced licence fees, for example), whether the government's objectives in enacting a particular regulatory scheme reflect the need to take into account the priority of aboriginal rights holders, *the extent of the participation in the fishery of aboriginal rights holders relative to their percentage of the population*, how the government has accommodated different aboriginal rights in a particular fishery (food *versus* commercial rights, for example), how important the fishery is to the economic and material well-being of the band in question, and the criteria taken into account by the government in, for example, allocating commercial licences *amongst different users*.[53]

It is certainly left "vague" as to how a court might measure whether the Crown had met its fiduciary obligations. What does it mean to be "respectful" of the priority of the interests of the Heiltsuk, and to allocate the resource so as to "reflect the prior interest" of the rights holder? While these are drafted as practical questions, they point to deeper layers of puzzlement. Even if it were better determined just what "respect" might amount to in this context, why has the standard of conduct of the Crown been put at this level? How can a *fiduciary* be held to such a low level of responsibility vis-à-vis the interests of beneficiaries?[54]

52 *Ibid* at paras 62–3 [emphasis added].

53 *Ibid* at para 64 [emphasis added].

54 In standard fiduciary doctrine, the fiduciary is held to a strict standard of conduct – that of undivided loyalty, an obligation that "betokens loyalty, good faith and avoidance of a conflict of duty and self-interest": *Canadian Aero Service Ltd v O'Malley* (1973), [1974] SCR 592, 40 DLR (3d) 371 at 606.

The reader might also wonder about the first highlighted portion of this last excerpt. Why would it matter what the population-percentage participation rate of an Aboriginal community might be in the use of a resource? Presumably its use was absolute (in relation to other users) before settlers and the colonial state arrived. Through the effects of colonial law and policy, (a) Aboriginal population levels severely decreased, (b) their ability to access and make use of resources was severely limited, and (c) their resultant ability – as measured against general use of the resource – was severely affected. Why would the Crown *now* be able to infringe upon an Aboriginal communities' use of the resource as a function of its current percentage participation?

Consider as well the second highlighted portion of the last excerpt. Why should it be possible that the Crown meet its fiduciary obligations to Aboriginal rights-holders by balancing the Aboriginal rights at issue (constitutionally protected rights) against non-Aboriginal interests (which are non-constitutionally protected, and presumably in many cases not even "rights" recognized at law)?[55] The oddity of having a form of "reconciliation" come in to inform processes of Crown infringement begins to be laid bare – as we move into the second part of the justification, this oddity becomes yet more pronounced.

Finally, consider what is presumed in the reasoning of the Court as it ponders a situation in which "an exceptional situation becomes the ordinary." The Court imagines that if the Crown did not enjoy an expanded power to infringe upon the right in question, this right would appear on the scene in an "absolute" fashion, potentially pushing aside all other interests. Where in this, however, is the thought that the Heiltsuk have their own modes of regulation, that for thousands of years they have governed the practices of fishing and trading fish? Only if the presumption is that Indigenous forms of governance are entirely absent from the situation potentially unfolding do we arrive at the sense of the narrative being laid out by the Court, of a right becoming such as to thoughtlessly push out all other interests.

Let us turn now to the second modification of the justifiable-infringement structure, dealing with the question of which objectives suffice such that under them Crown acts might be deemed sufficiently compelling and substantial. Beginning, again, with the claim that *Sparrow* had an (understandably) narrow focus – the claim here being that the Court in *Sparrow* did not *explain* why conservation counted as sufficiently compelling and substantial, such that one could then glean how one should go about determining whether any particular

---

55 See e.g. Kent McNeil, "How Can Infringements of the Constitutional Rights of Aboriginal Peoples Be Justified?" in Kent McNeil, *Emerging Justice? Essays on Indigenous Rights in Canada and Australia* (Saskatoon, SK: Native Law Centre, 2001) 281 [McNeil, *Emerging Justice?*]. For a strong critique of this approach to the matter of justifying infringement, see the dissenting judgment of McLachlin J in *Van der Peet*, *supra* note 3.

objective would meet some general test – the Court went on to develop a general principled approach to the question of how to decide whether a Crown objective was "valid."[56] Its analysis built on an approach developed in another area of constitutional law: just as in *Charter* matters (where limitations on *Charter* rights must make sense in relation to the purposes furthered by protection of those rights and freedoms): "[T]he purposes underlying the rights must inform ... the identification of those limits on the rights which are justifiable."[57]

Given the Court had said in *Van der Peet* that purposes behind section 35 have to do with recognition of the pre-existence of distinct Aboriginal societies and reconciliation of these societies with the assertion of Crown sovereignty, this means that

> because ... distinctive aboriginal societies exist within, and are a part of, a broader social, political and economic community, over which the Crown is sovereign, there are circumstances in which, in order to pursue objectives of compelling and substantial importance to that community as a whole (taking into account the fact that aboriginal societies are a part of that community), some limitation of those rights will be justifiable. Aboriginal rights are a necessary part of the reconciliation of aboriginal societies with the broader political community of which they are part; *limits placed on those rights are, where the objectives furthered by those limits are of sufficient importance to the broader community as a whole, equally a necessary part of that reconciliation*.[58]

On a concrete level this spells out so:

> [W]ith regards to the distribution of the fisheries resource after conservation goals have been met, objectives such as the pursuit of economic and regional fairness, and the recognition of the historical reliance upon, and participation in, the fishery by non-aboriginal groups, are the type of objectives which can (at least in the right circumstances) satisfy this standard. *In the right circumstances*, such objectives are in the interest of all Canadians and, more importantly, the reconciliation of aboriginal societies with the rest of Canadian society may well depend on their successful attainment.[59]

In an upcoming section we discuss more fully the place of "reconciliation" in section 35 jurisprudence, when we turn to look at the larger framework the Supreme Court erects around this discourse. We will see that when the Court introduced this notion in *Van der Peet* it spoke of the need to reconcile the fact of the pre-existence of organized Aboriginal societies with the assertion of Crown

56 *Gladstone, supra* note 6 at para 54.
57 *Ibid* at para 71.
58 *Ibid* at para 73 [emphasis added].
59 *Ibid* at para 75 [emphasis in original].

sovereignty. The Court states that the need to reconcile these two matters accounts for one purpose behind the constitutionalization of Aboriginal (and treaty) rights.

In this passage in *Gladstone*, however, the Court puts the notion of "reconciliation" to a very different use. Here we see reconciliation now appearing as a means by which the ability of the Crown to infringe upon Aboriginal rights may be underpinned. While at first blush this may strike the reader as reasonable, consider (a) the things being reconciled are *not* as they were in *Van der Peet* (so, why now do we see that the things to be reconciled are Aboriginal and non-Aboriginal interests, *within* a given larger society?), (b) reconciliation seems to appear here more as an outcome to be worked towards (rather than the *process* it seemed to indicate in *Van der Peet*), and (c) the result of all this is that a *vast range* of objectives is made available to Canadian governments acting to "justifiably infringe" upon constitutionally protected rights. With the history of Crown–Indigenous relationships in mind, all this becomes most puzzling – how can this possibly be a judicial response to many generations of oppressive colonial law and policy?[60]

Obvious puzzles can be quickly summarized: how can constitutionally protected rights be prone to a scheme of justifiable infringement that leaves the rights virtually unprotected, and in this context how can these constitutionally protected Aboriginal rights be balanced and weighed against non-Aboriginal non-constitutionally protected interests?

However, in the background is a puzzle alluded to earlier, one at least as puzzling (especially from an Indigenous perspective): how can all this transpire through a *unilaterally developed discourse* of "reconciliation"? Digging more into this question, what can possibly account for the fact that a court of the one party is assumed to have the "right" to decide the rules for how Indigenous interests will fit into the legal and political landscape of Canada, especially when that very court acknowledges the unique historical situation to which it is responding (marked by the assertion of sovereignty of one party in relation to pre-existing organized societies)?

Aboriginal Title

The Nature and Source of Aboriginal Title

In the years leading up to the landmark case dealing with rights to land – the 1997 decision in *Delgamuukw v AG (British Columbia)* – Crown authorities began to develop arguments around "title" claims aimed at minimizing their impact on the

60 As noted earlier, in two dissenting opinions penned in *Van der Peet*, McLachlin J and L'Heureux-Dube J raised concerns, with McLachlin J particularly focused on how the majorities' approach in *Gladstone* could accord with the constitutional status of the rights being "recognized and affirmed": *Van der Peet*, *supra* note 3. See especially *ibid* at para 306.

legal landscape.[61] The central argument, advanced at trial by the Crown, was that, at most, Aboriginal title amounts to a bundle of rights already present as Aboriginal rights. So, for example, the Gitksan and Wet'suwet'en (the two Indigenous claimants in this case, attempting to establish the nature and extent of their rights to and over their traditional territories)[62] would be said to have *no more* in having title to their lands than what they would have if they had focused on establishing the rights they might enjoy to hunt, fish, and gather over the lands they claim.

The claimants, on the other hand, believed they held under and associated with title full rights of "ownership" and "jurisdiction" over their entire traditional territories. With no treaty between themselves and the Crown, their position was that they enjoyed as powerful a set of rights as one could imagine (within the legal system within which they were forced to advance their claims).

At the end of very long and expensive litigation, the Supreme Court disagreed with both understandings, holding rather that the claimants enjoy a true "right to property" under Aboriginal title, but one limited to those lands over which they could establish exclusive occupation at the time the Crown asserted sovereignty.[63] This *communal* right to the "exclusive use and occupation" of the land in question would include an "inescapable economic component,"[64] allow for any use not incompatible with an "inherent limit" (that the land not be used in such a way as to run entirely counter to the forms of land-use grounding the claim),[65] and necessarily include a right to make decisions on how the land is to be used.[66] The central components of Aboriginal title were noted at paragraph 117:

> [T]he content of aboriginal title can be summarized by two propositions: first, that aboriginal title encompasses the right to exclusive use and occupation of the land

---

61 *Delgamuukw, supra* note 4.

62 It is important to note, however, that these two nations were not the original parties on record for the statement of claim. This action was initiated by the heads of seventy-one houses of these two nations (all the houses of the Wet'suwet'en and all but twelve of the Gitksan), the original political representatives of the peoples living in the territories of the houses, within a house-based system of ownership and governance.

63 It should be noted the claimants did not come out of this case with these rights established, as they still had to pass through the tests for establishing title – the Court sent the entire matter back to trial, essentially on "technical" grounds. To the day of my writing this note, the Gitksan and Wet'suwet'en have not been able to establish in Canadian law their Aboriginal title. Of course, within their own legal systems, their property interests remain as they have for many generations.

64 *Delgamuukw, supra* note 4 at para 166 [emphasis omitted].

65 *Ibid* at paras 111, 125–32. So, for example, the Court held that an Aboriginal title-holder could not expect to pave over title-lands that were found to be title-lands due to their nature as hunting grounds.

66 *Ibid* at paras 166, 168.

> held pursuant to that title for a variety of purposes, which need not be aspects of those aboriginal practices, customs and traditions which are integral to distinctive aboriginal cultures; and second, that those protected uses must not be irreconcilable with the nature of the group's attachment to that land.[67]

One can see in this quote one key way in which Aboriginal title is not just a bundle of Aboriginal rights to use lands and resources – the purposes to which title lands can be put go beyond those demonstrated through the establishment of Aboriginal rights typically found under the *Van der Peet* test. Nevertheless, this form of property right was said to be a species of Aboriginal right, lying on one end of a spectrum of such rights, and as such there was some discussion about how it relates to culture (recalling the general test for Aboriginal rights, that they comprise aspects of customs, traditions, and practices integral to the distinctive culture of the people claiming the right).[68] Holding that land interests are naturally integral to the distinctive culture of the claimants, the Court found that the search for lands that met the test for title would (implicitly) parallel that for activities or practices.

The picture that emerges, then, is of a property right established in contemporary Canadian law, a right shown through connections to aspects of the lives of pre-existing Aboriginal communities but that exists today (largely) removed from those matters that go into showing its roots or groundings in pre-Crown-sovereignty settings. This is an important matter – that the nature of the right today is largely divorced from the source or roots of the right (in connections to lands and territories at the moment of the assertion of Crown sovereignty).

Intriguingly, the Court spoke of two ways the roots of Aboriginal title could be shown. As a contemporary right to the exclusive use and occupation of land contiguous with use and occupation of that same land at the time the Crown asserted sovereignty, it could be shown by demonstrating (at that earlier time) either *physical* use and occupation or *legal* use and occupation.[69] So, for example, an Aboriginal nation attempting to show it enjoys contemporary

---

67 *Ibid* at para 117.

68 *Ibid* at para 145.

69 The Court stated, *ibid* at paragraph 147, that:

> This debate over the proof of occupancy reflects two divergent views of the source of aboriginal title. The respondents argue, in essence, that aboriginal title arises from the physical reality at the time of sovereignty, whereas the Gitksan effectively take the position that aboriginal title arises from and should reflect the pattern of land holdings under aboriginal law. However, as I have explained above, the source of aboriginal title appears to be grounded both in the common law and in the aboriginal perspective on land; the latter includes, but is not limited to, their systems of law. It follows that both should be taken into account in establishing the proof of occupancy.

Aboriginal title over a piece of land could go back to when the Crown asserted sovereignty over that land and show that at that point either (or both) (a) it *physically* occupied that land at that time such that its occupation was exclusive, or (b) it exercised *legal* occupation of that land, such that it was understood (within its legal order and [presumably] those of its neighbours) that it was the legal owner of those lands, in an "exclusive" fashion.

It is important to bear in mind a point made above, that the Court separates questions about how to *show* Aboriginal title from questions about its current *nature* within Canadian law. An "Indigenous perspective" appears with some definite content and force in how an Aboriginal community might try to *show* it enjoyed exclusive use and occupation of law at the point the Crown asserted sovereignty over its territory, but that perspective is not significant in how Aboriginal title manifests in contemporary settings.[70]

While some have argued one can still accommodate a contemporary form of Indigenous law within the legal structure established (holding that Aboriginal title functions like a shell or shield, essentially establishing boundaries around what might happen within the title-lands, where within the title-lands the Aboriginal communities' Indigenous legal understandings of landholdings would continue to structure how land–people relationships are legally understood),[71] the fact remains that as an instrument within Canadian law, Aboriginal title is defined through understandings of the common law.

Tellingly, the Supreme Court in *Delgamuukw* did not actually rule that the Gitskan and Wet'suwet'en held title. The matter was sent back to trial (which never happened) on the basis that pleadings had changed during the advancement of the case up through the courts (to the prejudice of the Crown – the power that had stripped ownership from the original inhabitants).[72]

In the first decade after *Delgamuukw*, no substantive case dealing directly with Aboriginal title emerged. In 2005, in one of the few cases touching on title issues, *R v Marshall; R v Bernard*,[73] the Supreme Court looked into how Aboriginal title might function as a defence to quasi-prosecutions. The defendants – Mi'kmaq from communities in Nova Scotia and New Brunswick, respectively – were charged with

70 *Ibid.* See Kent McNeil, "Aboriginal Rights in Canada: From Title to Land to Territorial Sovereignty" in McNeil, *Emerging Justice?*, *supra* note 55 at 93 [McNeil, "Aboriginal Rights in Canada"].

71 See e.g. McNeil, "Aboriginal Rights in Canada," *ibid* at 93; Kent McNeil, "The Meaning of Aboriginal Title" in Michael Asch, ed, *Aboriginal and Treaty Rights in Canada: Essays on Law, Equality, and Respect for Difference* (Vancouver: UBC Press, 1998) 135.

72 *Delgamuukw*, *supra* note at paras 76–7. The Court felt the amalgamation of the original individual claims of the fifty-one chiefs (representing seventy-one houses) of the Gitskan and Wet'suwet'en into two collective claims – one for each nation – prejudiced the Crown.

73 *R v Marshall; R v Bernard*, 2005 SCC 43 [*Marshall & Bernard*].

offences tied to their cutting down of trees within what they claimed were lands held by Aboriginal title. In that setting, the Court ventured into areas left vague in *Delgamuukw* – in particular, they addressed two key matters left unclear: what *constitutes* "sufficient occupation," and what is required to *show* "exclusive" occupation.

Court analysis began with a summary of what could be gleaned from *Delgamuukw*:

> "Occupation" means "physical occupation." This "may be established in a variety of ways, ranging from the construction of dwellings through cultivation and enclosure of fields to regular use of definite tracts of land for hunting, fishing or otherwise exploiting its resources": *Delgamuukw, per* Lamer C.J., at para. 149.
>
> "Exclusive" occupation flows from the definition of aboriginal title as "the right to *exclusive* use and occupation of land": *Delgamuukw, per* Lamer C.J. at para. 155.... Exclusive occupation means "the intention and capacity to retain exclusive control," and is not negated by occasional acts of trespass or the presence of other aboriginal groups with consent (*Delgamuukw*, at para. 156).[74]

The suggestion is that occupation must be sufficient in the sense that the land must have been regularly and intensively used at the time of the assertion of Crown sovereignty, and the occupation must be "exclusive" in the sense that the Aboriginal community could have exercised control if it had wished.

One might suspect, then, that occupation is a first-up requirement: one cannot claim title to land one did not occupy, and occupation is more a matter of physical fact than legal determination – an Aboriginal community must show how the land they claim under Aboriginal title was physically occupied in a manner that would today satisfy the common law's understanding of "occupation." It would seem to follow, then, that exclusivity is a second-up requirement: that the Aboriginal community must also then show it enjoyed or held the "intention and capacity to retain exclusive control" over lands for which sufficient occupation has been shown.[75]

---

74 *Ibid* at paras 56–7 [emphasis in original].

75 A few paragraphs later in their judgment, at paragraph 70, however, the Court muddied the waters, *ibid*:

> In summary, exclusive possession in the sense of intention and capacity to control is required to establish aboriginal title. Typically, this is established by showing regular occupancy or use of definite tracts of land for hunting, fishing or exploiting resources: *Delgamuukw*, at para 149.

Here they seem to suggest one can show exclusivity through showing sufficient occupation! The resolution to this mini-puzzle seems to lie in an intervening paragraph 64, wherein they mused about how an Aboriginal community might go about showing exclusivity, *ibid*:

> The right to control the land and if necessary to exclude others from using it is basic to the notion of title at common law. In European-based systems, this right is assumed by dint of law. Determining whether it was present in a pre-sovereignty aboriginal society, however, can pose difficulties. Often,

Also emerging from the discussion in *Marshall & Bernard* was the strong suggestion that Aboriginal title may be limited in geographic scope to just those lands over which sufficient occupation and exclusivity can be sufficiently demonstrated. This suggested what came to be known as the "site-specific" theory of Aboriginal title. Those who saw Aboriginal title as having to be based on *territory* (and not discrete pieces of land such that for each piece sufficient occupation and exclusivity has been shown) challenged this suggestion, but it was not until the Supreme Court ruled in 2014 in *Tsilhqot'in Nation* that this matter was settled.[76]

There was certainly reason to be concerned before *Tsilhqot'in Nation* came down, as the Court had indicated in *Marshall & Bernard* that title is more likely to be found over *parts* of territory, with Aboriginal rights (to hunt, fish, etc.) possibly being found over those *other* parts of a community's territory not covered by title.[77] The Court seemed to have adopted a fairly narrow view as far back as *Delgamuukw*, that Aboriginal title is tied to lands *intensively* used (in ways that did not seem to fit well at all with the worlds of nomadic and semi-nomadic peoples).[78] In *Tsilhqot'in Nation*, however, the Supreme Court seemed to accept the trial judge's view of Aboriginal title, finding that the Tsilhqot'in held title to about 40 per cent of the area they claimed in that particular action. This – in 2014 – was the first clear finding of Aboriginal title over any land in Canada.

While it was a major step forward for Aboriginal peoples without treaties,[79] the decision maintained a common pattern in seminal decisions handed down by the Court, as it held out what seemed to be renewed promise of justice and fairness in one part of the judgment while greatly troubling matters appeared in

---

> no right to exclude arises by convention or law. So one must look to evidence. But evidence may be hard to find. The area may have been sparsely populated, with the result that clashes and the need to exclude strangers seldom if ever occurred. Or the people may have been peaceful and have chosen to exercise their control by sharing rather than exclusion. It is therefore critical to view the question of exclusion from the aboriginal perspective. To insist on evidence of overt acts of exclusion in such circumstances may, depending on the circumstances, be unfair.

It would seem, then, that the question of exclusivity *is* distinct from that of sufficient occupation, but given the difficulties a community may have in showing exclusivity, the evidence showing sufficient occupation may itself suffice in showing this other component.

76 *Tsilhqot'in Nation*, *supra* note 4.

77 For the Court picking up on remarks made in *Delgamuukw*, see *Marshall & Bernard*, *supra* note 73 at paras 58–9. These remarks traced back to the earlier decision in *R v Adams*, [1996] 3 SCR 101, 138 DLR (4th) 657 [*Adams*].

78 The key passage spoke of showing sufficient occupation by establishing "regular use of definite tracts of land for hunting, fishing or otherwise exploiting": *Delgamuukw*, *supra* note 4 at para 149. Again, in contrasting the possibility of showing *title* with the alternate possibility (particularly salient for nomadic and semi-nomadic peoples) of showing Aboriginal *rights* (to hunt, fish, etc), the Court was building on remarks made in *Adams*. See *Adams*, *supra* note 77.

79 The *Tsilhqot'in Nation* decision was unquestionably progressive in relation to earlier jurisprudence on Aboriginal title (especially *Marshall & Bernard*). See *Tsilhqot'in Nation*, *supra* note 4; *Marshall & Bernard*, *supra* note 73.

later sections. We end this section with a few words about puzzles around the nature and scope of title, moving on in the next section to equally baffling matters in pronouncements on how Aboriginal title is to be fit into the Canadian legal-political landscape.

Puzzles swirl around the pronouncements on the nature of Aboriginal title.[80] Some we can note and pass by, while others we need to detail more carefully. The link to culture is baffling but understandable, given the Court's concomitant architectural plan, with Aboriginal title being said to be just one form of Aboriginal right. How exactly the link is meant to be understood (and why an "inherent limit" appears in the midst of this) remains, however, mystifying. Likewise, determining the date for the establishment of title to the assertion of Crown sovereignty is perplexing but (somewhat) understandable, given the Court's continuation of earlier jurisprudence, which held that Aboriginal title is a "burden on Crown title."[81] As the Court notes in *Delgamuukw*, for Aboriginal title to be a burden on Crown title, it must arise at the time Crown title arises. Of course, this leaves as a conundrum why the Court chose not to alter that particular element of the jurisprudence in relation to Aboriginal rights in general (given it was willing to exercise its power – as the supreme court of the land – to adjust precedence in other respects).[82] If Aboriginal rights temper Crown power, would we not expect they, too, arise at the time the Crown asserts sovereign authority over the lives and territories of affected Indigenous peoples?

The test for possession (and the application of this test) is also perplexing, as it is more onerous than tests for possession within the common law (which, furthermore, most often apply to claims for *adverse possession*, which does not describe the situation with Aboriginal title).[83] This seems connected

---

80 The number of puzzles that swirl around the "reasoning" in the second half of the *Tsilhqot'in Nation* decision is such that I could not list them here. For the most part there is no reasoning per se evident – it would seem a conclusion was reached (if Aboriginal title is to be expansively defined – geographically speaking – then it must be subject to provincial jurisdictional authority) and the Court threw out as many "reasons" as they could to support this conclusion. Most of the reasons would not count as reasons in most objective accounts of what those are supposed to look like. See *Tsilhqot'in Nation*, *supra* note 4.

81 It had been determined that Aboriginal interests in land constituted burdens on Crown title (so that when these interests were surrendered in a treaty, Crown title was "perfected"). See *St Catharine's Milling & Lumber Co v The Queen*, [1887] 13 SCR 577, 14 AC 46 (JCPC) [*St Catharine's Milling*].

82 The Privy Council had also, for example, found in *St. Catharine's Milling*, *ibid*, that Aboriginal interests in land existed at the pleasure of the Crown and constituted nothing more than "personal and usufructuary" rights. See *ibid* at para 7.

83 For a discussion of the difference between possession-in-law at common law and the standard applied in *Delgamuukw* and *Marshall*, see Nicole Petersen, "Aboriginal Title in Canada: The Standard of Occupation at Issue in *William v. British Columbia*" (2013), online: <papers.ssrn.com/sol3/papers.cfm?abstract_id=2394594>.

to movement by the Court towards a site-specific, discrete-tract model of Aboriginal title (regardless of whether the discrete tracts be "postage stamps" or "territory"), a model that conflicts fundamentally with conceptions of land relationships common amongst Indigenous peoples.

While it might seem this movement was checked somewhat in *Tsilhqot'in Nation*, the notion that title exists only over discrete areas in relation to which particular tests are passed remains, just not in the excessively tight formulation laid out in *Marshall & Bernard*. Not only do Indigenous peoples commonly think of land in terms of responsibilities (that then *might* translate into rights), but they tend to have highly developed ideas about territory, large expanses of land they see themselves related to, as *their* lands.[84] These territories are so extensive they bump right into each other – the edges of Inuit territory, for example, run right against those of the Dene, or Innu, or other southern neighbours. Why would Canadian law not recognize these Indigenous conceptions of content and scope of Aboriginal title?

Further, even with the "win" of *Tsilhqot'in Nation*, we see Aboriginal communities gaining rights over land that look remarkably like those enjoyed by private property owners – within Canadian law the Tsilhqot'in Nation begins to look as though it is the collective owner of a large piece of land, enjoying ownership not that dissimilar in form and content to that enjoyed by, for example, nearby ranch owners. While this might not strike the reader new to this jurisprudence as troubling, consider for a moment the Indigenous perspective: these lands were *not* held as private property within some other state before the assertion of Crown sovereignty – they were simply the lands of the people living there, more akin (if one must try to compare) to lands "held" by a nation state.

As striking as these puzzles might be, at least as odd are other Court determinations about the place of Aboriginal title within Canada, most of which seem directed to effecting an underlying balance of the possible geographic extent of Aboriginal title with continued power of the Crown to legislate.

Aboriginal Title in the Canadian Landscape

Let us turn then to the matter of how the Supreme Court envisioned Aboriginal title fitting within the Canadian legal landscape. As with Aboriginal rights generally, a pressing concern is the continuing power of the Crown to infringe upon any title-claims duly established.

---

84 See e.g. Leroy Little Bear, "Aboriginal Rights and the Canadian Grundnorm" in Rick J Pointing, ed, *Arduous Journey: Canadian Indians and Decolonization* (Toronto: McClelland & Stewart, 1986) 243; Leroy Little Bear, "A Concept of Native Title" (1982) 5 Can Legal Aid Bull 99; Canada, Royal Commission on Aboriginal Peoples, "Lands and Resources" in *Report of the Royal Commission on Aboriginal Peoples*, vol 2 (Ottawa: Minister of Supply and Services, 1996) 415.

As Aboriginal title – the Court determined – generally has no "internal limits,"[85] it was found in *Delgamuukw* to fall under the category that emerged in *Gladstone*, of a kind that demands less scrutiny on Crown action, that falls prey to a broader range of "valid objectives," and that demands less of the Crown as fiduciary.

Indeed, in *Delgamuukw* the Supreme Court listed examples of sufficiently compelling objectives (satisfying the first stage of the *Sparrow/Gladstone* test for justification of infringement)[86] that suggested that nearly any non-corrupt goal the Crown had in mind could be considered valid:

> In my opinion, the development of agriculture, forestry, mining, and hydroelectric power, the general economic development of the interior of British Columbia, protection of the environment or endangered species, the building of infrastructure and the settlement of foreign populations to support those aims, are the kinds of objectives that are consistent with this purpose and, in principle, can justify the infringement of aboriginal title.[87]

The Court arrived at this list by noting it had found in *Gladstone* that generally objectives aimed at reconciliation would be held to be sufficiently compelling and substantial:

> In the wake of *Gladstone*, the range of legislative objectives that can justify the infringement of aboriginal title is fairly broad. Most of these objectives can be traced to the *reconciliation* of the prior occupation of North America by aboriginal peoples with the assertion of Crown sovereignty, which entails the recognition that "distinctive aboriginal societies exist within, and are a part of, a broader social, political and economic community" (at para. 73).[88]

---

85 The thinking seems to be that as a right to the *exclusive* use and occupation of land, it generates the same concern raised by rights without internal limits, namely that it can have an impact upon the rights and interests of others, of non-Aboriginal Canadians.

86 That most of the matters listed would fall under provincial control was noted immediately by observers. While the Court made it clear in *Delgamuukw* that provincial Crowns could not extinguish Aboriginal title, it seemed (at least by implication) to leave it open that such Crowns could infringe upon title. Their only explicit comment on the matter is that "[t]he aboriginal rights recognized and affirmed by s. 35(1), including aboriginal title, are not absolute. Those rights may be infringed, both by the federal (e.g., *Sparrow*) and provincial (e.g., *Côté*) governments": *Delgamuukw*, *supra* note 4 at 160.

How this might be so was, however, left mysterious. Vickers J's trial judgment in *Tsilhqot'in Nation* meticulously worked through the reasoning around the doctrine of inter-jurisdictional immunity and its application to Aboriginal title lands, the conclusion being that this doctrine should preclude provincial legislative authority. See *Tsilhqot'in Nation v British Columbia*, 2007 BCSC 1700.

87 *Delgamuukw*, *supra* note 4 at para 165.

88 *Ibid* at para 165 [emphasis in original].

When turning to the second stage of the *Sparrow/Gladstone* framework, the Court looked to specific features of the right at issue, arguing that these features demanded different questions be asked of the Crown, the fiduciary. First is the question of what sort of "priority" Aboriginal title should enjoy in relation to other rights and interests:

> The exclusive nature of aboriginal title is relevant to the degree of scrutiny of the infringing measure or action. For example, if the Crown's fiduciary duty requires that aboriginal title be given priority, then it is the altered approach to priority that I laid down in *Gladstone* which should apply. What is required is that the government demonstrate [*citations omitted*] "both that the process by which it allocated the resource and the actual allocation of the resource which results from that process reflect the prior interest" of the holders of aboriginal title in the land.
>
> By analogy with *Gladstone*, this might entail, for example, that governments accommodate the participation of aboriginal peoples in the development of the resources of British Columbia, that the conferral of fee simples for agriculture, and of leases and licences for forestry and mining reflect the prior occupation of aboriginal title lands, that economic barriers to aboriginal uses of their lands (e.g., licencing fees) be somewhat reduced. This list is illustrative and not exhaustive. This is an issue that may involve an assessment of the various interests at stake in the resources in question.[89]

The Court then went on to note other features of Aboriginal title leading into other forms by which the Crown can legitimately justify infringing upon these constitutionally protected rights:

> [A]boriginal title encompasses within it a right to choose to what ends a piece of land can be put.... This aspect of aboriginal title suggests that the fiduciary relationship between the Crown and aboriginal peoples may be satisfied by the involvement of aboriginal peoples in decisions taken with respect to their lands. There is always a duty of consultation....
>
> [A]boriginal title ... has an inescapably economic aspect, particularly when one takes into account the modern uses to which lands held pursuant to aboriginal title can be put. The economic aspect of aboriginal title suggests that compensation is relevant to the question of justification as well.[90]

89 *Ibid* at para 167.

90 *Ibid* at para 168. The Court's first substantive discussion of the duty to consult emerges in this paragraph. For a mention of the duty to consult in passing, see *Sparrow*, *supra* note 6. In the landmark 2004 decision *Haida Nation v British Columbia (Minister of Forests)*, the Court greatly expanded upon the notion of a duty on the Crown to consult with Aboriginal rights

All this was left substantially unchanged after the Supreme Court revisited Aboriginal title in *Tsilhqot'in Nation*.[91] The Court added language to the test for justification that suggested the Crown should now also be concerned to ensure there are proper connections between objectives and means used to achieve objectives, as the Court employed language testing such connections used to evaluate infringement of a *Charter* right.[92] The Court also added language suggesting the Crown should seek consent of an Aboriginal titleholder before authorizing actions that would substantially damage these property interests.[93] The addition of *Charter* language, however, is untested (and may turn out to have a minimal effect on requirements established in *Delgamuukw*), and the question of consent is put as a *procedural* matter (the Crown seems required to *try to seek* consent before it then goes about meeting its other requirements for justifying infringement, suggesting consent is not actually a substantive requirement).

What did substantially alter in *Tsilhqot'in Nation* was the Court's treatment of division of powers analysis in this context. Until now, questions and analysis of "division of powers" (constitutional law questions about the jurisdictional powers and authorities of the federal versus the provincial governments) occupied a role essentially in line with those one would expect in other legal

---

holders (even when the rights have not yet been established either in Canadian courts or through negotiation). See 2004 SCC 73 [*Haida Nation*]. In paragraph 168 of *Delgamuukw*, *supra* note 4, the Court when on to say:

> The nature and scope of the duty of consultation will vary with the circumstances. In occasional cases, when the breach is less serious or relatively minor, it will be no more than a duty to discuss important decisions that will be taken with respect to lands held pursuant to aboriginal title. Of course, even in these rare cases when the minimum acceptable standard is consultation, this consultation must be in good faith, and with the intention of substantially addressing the concerns of the aboriginal peoples whose lands are at issue. In most cases, it will be significantly deeper than mere consultation. Some cases may even require the full consent of an aboriginal nation, particularly when provinces enact hunting and fishing regulations in relation to aboriginal lands.

91 *Tsilhqot'in Nation*, *supra* note 4.

92 *Ibid* at para 87:

> Implicit in the Crown's fiduciary duty to the Aboriginal group is the requirement that the incursion is necessary to achieve the government's goal (rational connection); that the government go no further than necessary to achieve it (minimal impairment); and that the benefits that may be expected to flow from that goal are not outweighed by adverse effects on the Aboriginal interest (proportionality of impact).

93 See e.g. *ibid* at para 76:

> The right to control the land conferred by Aboriginal title means that governments and others seeking to use the land must obtain the consent of the Aboriginal title holders. If the Aboriginal group does not consent to the use, the government's only recourse is to establish that the proposed incursion on the land is justified under s. 35 of the *Constitution Act, 1982*.

For the same point made in different ways, see *ibid* at paras 2, 88, 90, 91, 97.

contexts. In this most recent decision, however, the Supreme Court carved out an area of exception for Aboriginal title.[94] Arguing that the tension in this context has always been between Canadian governments and Aboriginal peoples, the Court found the legal outcome should be that any tension *within* the levels of Canadian government should be put aside.

The doctrine of interjurisdictional immunity would have been expected to normally apply in this kind of situation. One might have supposed this component of division-of-powers doctrine would prevent provincial law from applying to Aboriginal title lands, as one would expect these lands *should* be subject only to federal power (supposing they would fall within *exclusive* federal authority under section 91(24) of the *Constitution Act, 1867*: "Indians and Lands Reserved for Indians"). Of note, Justice Vickers (in obiter, at the trial level) had followed this seemingly reasonable line of thought, holding that should his finding of title stand, provincial law would then be inapplicable to the lands in question due to the application of this doctrine.[95]

Under interjurisdictional immunity, "since federal and provincial legislative powers under ss. 91 and 92 of the *Constitution Act, 1867* are exclusive, each level of government enjoys a basic unassailable core of power on which the other level may not intrude."[96] Vickers J argued that Aboriginal title lands would naturally fall within the scope of section 91(24) of the *Constitution Act, 1867*, and so fall under the exclusive jurisdiction of the federal government. Vickers J's application of this doctrine followed fairly standard principles of constitutional law in Canada, but it implied in this context that substantial portions of Crown land lying within a province might fall outside the jurisdictional authority of the province in question.

The Supreme Court's response was essentially to remove the doctrine of interjurisdictional immunity from playing any substantive role in the context of section 35 jurisprudence. The Court's reasoning is odd, to say the least. It held that:

> The doctrine of interjurisdictional immunity is directed to ensuring that the two levels of government are able to operate without interference in their core areas of exclusive jurisdiction. This goal is not implicated in cases such as this. Aboriginal rights are a limit on both federal and provincial jurisdiction.[97]

---

94 While the Court argued that, generally speaking, concerns over division of powers have been lessening in Canadian jurisprudence over the last decade or so, the radical shift effected in this narrower context (to essentially remove any substantive analysis of these matters) was still startling.

95 *Tsilhqot'in Nation v British Columbia*, 2007 BCSC 1700, *supra* note 86 at paras 1001–49.

96 *Tsilhqot'in Nation*, *supra* note 4 at para 131.

97 *Ibid* at para 141.

This is a clear example of begging the question (as this expression was once used). That is, the conclusion is contained in the premises, and so the reasoning is remarkably circular. The real question (of course) should be *whether* Aboriginal rights are a limit on both federal and provincial jurisdiction – to say that Aboriginal rights are a limit on both jurisdictions, that therefore the doctrine does not apply, and therefore Aboriginal rights are a limit on both jurisdictions, is to simply move from conclusion to premise to conclusion.

So we are led into yet more oddities tied to the jurisprudence on Aboriginal title. After more than a century of jurisprudence that often fixated on questions about which level of Canadian government enjoyed which degree of deference to power, a new world is opened up, one wherein *either* Crown can "justifiably" act in relation to Aboriginal land interests.[98] This, though, is just one puzzle amongst several circling the jurisprudence detailing how title is to be fit within the contemporary Canadian legal and political landscape,[99] puzzles that deepen when proper attention is paid to Indigenous perspectives, and to possibilities concerning different Indigenous conceptions of power, responsibility, and land use.

One fairly obvious puzzle is the fact legislative acts that can be justified within this framework are those that were historically simply acts of colonial dispossession. How can it be that Aboriginal interests in land, now constitutionally recognized and protected, are no more protected from legislative taking than they were in the overtly colonial period?[100]

This speaks to a primary puzzle – how can it be that, post-1982, ultimately the power of decision-making about Aboriginal lands continues to rest with the Crown, the very power that dispossessed Indigenous peoples of their territories? Why (as we noted earlier) does the general response to the constitutional protection of interests formerly unjustly denied or taken away through the power of the Crown *begin* with – and indeed seem to

---

98 It should be noted the Court left untouched (as it must be) the doctrine of paramountcy. Should the federal government *act* in relation to section 91(24) of the *Constitution Act, 1867*, the province in question could not then similarly legislate in such a way as to interfere with the federal regime. Sections 91 and 92 still function to set out exclusive spheres of jurisdiction when the respective Crown actually legislates. See *supra* note 1. The doctrine of interjurisdictional immunity was meant to function, for example, when a province acted in relation to an area of federal jurisdiction concerning a subject about which the federal government had not yet directly acted.

99 There are puzzles, for example, about why an "inherent limit" was introduced to Aboriginal title.

100 See e.g. Kent McNeil, "Aboriginal Title as a Constitutionally Protected Property Right" in McNeil, *Emerging Justice?*, *supra* note 55 at 292 [McNeil, "Aboriginal Title as a Constitutionally Protected Property Right"].

end with – simple acknowledgment of that power (through, once again, fiduciary doctrine)?[101]

A second key puzzle – one that later centres much of the analysis – concerns requirements of the Crown should it seek to make decisions about the use of Aboriginal title lands: in order to justify infringement the Crown should "accommodate the participation of Aboriginal peoples in the development of the resources of British Columbia."[102] What if – as has been the record across Canada and across generations – Aboriginal peoples are generally wary of resource-development, or (as is indeed often the case with major extractive projects) they see it as antithetical to their interests? How is a particular vision of "progress" – defined along lines of resource development – presumed to be in the interests of Aboriginal title-holders (so that "allowing them to participate" in this exploitation will suffice to justify infringing upon their title interests)? In what sense are Aboriginal title-holders being *involved* in decision-making when they have only an opportunity to agree with projects the Crown has in mind?

Let us leave this section with a few words about a related matter we touched on earlier and that cannot but strike the observer as perverse. On many occasions in *Tsilhqot'in Nation* the Court states the Crown "must" seek consent before infringing established Aboriginal title.[103] This is a very odd use of the word "must," however, as this notion is always put together with the idea that the Crown can get around failure to obtain consent by meeting the other usual conditions under the *Sparrow/Gladstone/Delgamuukw* framework for justifying infringement.

The suggestion seems to be that the Crown should always *begin* by trying to obtain consent. Then this would be principally a procedural matter. It might turn out that if the Crown tries to simply skip over this step (and just plunge right into trying to ensure it can justify infringement, with a "sufficiently compelling and substantial objective," and measures to meet its fiduciary obligations) a court might say after the fact it should not have done that, that *first* (as a matter of *process*) it should have at least tried to get consent. What can

101 As something of an aside, one further puzzle emerging out of *Tsilhqot'in Nation* is the continued application of fiduciary doctrine in relation to Aboriginal title. See *supra* note 4. The Court was clear that title confers *full* beneficial interests in the lands in question – why, then, would trust doctrine not be where one turned for enlightenment? It was only because the Aboriginal land interests at issue in *Guerin v The Queen*, [1984] 2 SCR 335, 13 DLR (4th) 321 [*Guerin*], were found not to clearly include (or constitute) something more than some indefinite set of mere beneficial interests that the Supreme Court turned away from trust doctrine, settling instead on fiduciary doctrine.

102 *Delgamuukw, supra* note 4 at para 167.

103 *Tsilhqot'in Nation, supra* note 4 at paras 2, 76, 80, 90–2, 97.

"consent" possibly mean, however, when it is rendered a matter of process and not substance?[104]

Broader Features and Principles

We are now prepared to look behind or below the level of test, rule, and basic structure, to explore elements of the jurisprudence that function on a more general level (serving as both underlying forms of justification and as general structural elements, holding the rest of the jurisprudence together).

We begin by noting that besides providing the approach Canadian courts should take to Crown infringement of Aboriginal rights, the Court in *Sparrow* set out a larger framework for the approach courts should take to the general matter of a claim to an Aboriginal right (in face of continuing Crown sovereignty).[105] There are four stages to analysis in such matters: first, the Aboriginal claimant must establish the nature and existence of the right claimed; second, the Crown may attempt to demonstrate that before this claimed right was recognized and affirmed in section 35 it was extinguished; third, if the right continues as unextinguished (an "existing" right under section 35), the Aboriginal claimant must then demonstrate prima facie infringement; and finally, should the right appear to be infringed by Crown action, the Crown may attempt to demonstrate that the infringement is justifiable.[106]

Of particular note within this structure is the matter of extinguishment, as it signals clearly the Court's reluctance to use section 35 to address the fact of colonialism in Canada's treatment of Indigenous peoples. Once we note the nature of the Court's pronouncements and the puzzles this engenders, we then turn to background framing that the Court has constructed and used as

---

104 One obvious response would be to see this as proxy for something like "the Crown should begin with negotiations on such things as permanent solutions (a modern treaty) or interim solutions (with such things as Impact Benefit Agreements), in attempts to negotiate consensual arrangements. Failing success in such endeavours, the Crown can then proceed to attempt to justify its infringement."

105 *Sparrow*, *supra* note 6 at 1092–111.

106 In *Lax Kw'alaams Indian Band v Canada (AG)*, the Supreme Court seemed to suggest a different framework, but (a) one would expect it would do so only explicitly, referencing *Sparrow* in doing so, and regardless (b) the "new" framework on examination appears to be a loose rendition of key steps laid out in *Sparrow* (those most appropriate to the sort of case being argued in *Lax Kw'alaams*). Of note, the matter of characterizing the right (a key contentious issue in *Lax Kw'alaams*, as it is in so many Aboriginal rights cases) is put up front, as the first matter for a court to examine. See 2011 SCC 56 at para 46:

> [A] court dealing with a s. 35(1) claim would appropriately proceed as follows:
>
> 1. First, at the characterization stage, identify the precise nature of the First Nation's claim to an Aboriginal right based on the pleadings. If necessary, in light of the evidence, refine the characterization of the right claimed on terms that are fair to all parties.

it builds the larger structures of law it has erected for Aboriginal rights – the notions of "reconciliation" and "the honour of the Crown."

Extinguishment

For this overview the important component in the larger *Sparrow* framework is extinguishment.[107] All Aboriginal interests – whether simply "rights" (which in this context, recall, are simply *activities*, or abilities to do certain clearly defined things) or at the level of title – are understood to have been subject to the exercise of unlimited federal Crown power before they were recognized and affirmed in 1982. So, for example, as with Aboriginal rights generally, an Aboriginal community seeking to establish title must be concerned with the possibility its property rights had been extinguished before the time they were constitutionally protected. The Supreme Court understood the inclusion of the word "existing" in section 35 to signal that the *Constitution* took notice of the supreme power held by the Crown under the system of parliamentary supremacy (before 1982) to unilaterally eliminate Aboriginal interests. The Court held that such a power existed solely in the hands of the federal government and could have been exercised only when there was demonstrated a sufficiently clear and plain intent to have the right(s) in question extinguished.[108]

Again we are faced with a multitude of puzzling matters, and again our focus narrows to those matters most bewildering from an Indigenous perspective. The notion of extinguishment runs up against the notion of reconciliation, that fundamental underlying process that the Court repeatedly asserts informs all aspects of the development of contemporary Aboriginal law. If reconciliation is the overarching objective, how can we begin with the notion that all that happened before 1982 to unilaterally eliminate Indigenous interests (so long as there was the requisite "clear and plain intent") is water under the bridge? For most of the colonial era, the clear general intent of the federal government was to eliminate Indigenous interests of any sort (that is when it turned its mind to such matters – most often the Crown simply ignored the possibility Indigenous interests existed in any form that required attention). The legal requirement placed on the Crown in the new constitutional environment, should it wish to argue that an Aboriginal claimant's position rests on non-existent Indigenous interests, is that it must show these *particular* interests were eliminated in an earlier point in Canada's colonial past in a manner that demonstrated that its mind was directed towards this process of elimination. All this does is (once again) acknowledge the power of the Crown and ask that it have been exercised clearly and plainly when the issue was the elimination of Aboriginal interests.

107 *Sparrow*, *supra* note 6 at 1099–100.

108 See e.g. *Delgamuukw*, *supra* note 4 at para 180.

Before we leave this central puzzle, note how deep it runs, a point that becomes clearly visible once we place this in the context of other elements of the jurisprudential package being assembled. Recall that section 35 is said to "recognize and affirm" Aboriginal rights, which is to say (as the Supreme Court acknowledges) that these rights did not come into being in 1982. Indeed, as we noted earlier, the Court set out in *Van der Peet* that Aboriginal rights held by any specific community generally came into existence at contact with Europeans, while in *Delgamuukw* it held that Aboriginal title in any specific territory came into being at the time of the assertion of Crown sovereignty at that location. This means that these rights existed through the generations during which they were being systematically ignored (or under attack). What this suggests, when we turn to extinguishment, is that the response in *Sparrow* is to allow for the elimination of these rights by the Crown through these years, so long as legislative authorities simply turned their mind to doing so. There would now, looking back, be no retrospective legal requirement that the Crown ever have attempted to accommodate into the Canadian landscape these interests *that existed then as rights and title.*

"Aboriginality" and Understandings of Reconciliation

Having noted the important role that reconciliation has come to play in the jurisprudence, we should take the time to explore how this underlying concept came to occupy the position it does, and how it has come to mean different things, and function in different ways in different contexts. Along our way through this discussion, we note how the Court came to develop its general approach to Aboriginal rights, one that centres on the notion of "Aboriginality."

We begin by returning to *Van der Peet*, looking at a few key paragraphs in that decision, those just preceding its introduction of the test for the existence of an Aboriginal right. We then return to passages in *Gladstone* we touched on earlier, where reconciliation came to take on an entirely different character. In key paragraphs in *Van der Peet* the Court laid out some important groundwork, saying a few things about the general nature of constitutionally protected Aboriginal rights (and what a "purposive" approach to these rights required). As we work our way through these general (quasi-philosophical) remarks, we come up to a general vision concerning the place of Aboriginal rights in the contemporary Canadian landscape.

The Court began by saying, "Section 35(1), it is true, recognizes and affirms existing aboriginal *rights*, but it must not be forgotten that the rights it recognizes and affirms are *aboriginal*."[109] This posed a problem, the Court held, as it conflicts with the normal sense of what constitutes a "right" in law:

109 *Van der Peet, supra* note 3 at para 17 [emphasis in original].

> In the liberal enlightenment view, reflected in the American Bill of Rights and, more indirectly, in the *Charter*, rights are held by all people in society because each person is entitled to dignity and respect. Rights are general and universal; they are the way in which the "inherent dignity" of each individual in society is respected[.][110]

Given this characterization of rights, how are Aboriginal rights to be approached? The first point is straightforward:

> Aboriginal rights cannot, however, be defined on the basis of the philosophical precepts of the liberal enlightenment. Although equal in importance and significance to the rights enshrined in the *Charter*, aboriginal rights must be viewed differently from *Charter* rights because they are rights held only by aboriginal members of Canadian society.[111]

They are stand-alone rights, defined as lying outside or alongside the normal sense given rights in a liberal democracy. They have a unique status, one that strives to incorporate conceptual tenets relating to rights, but in such a way as to acknowledge this stand-alone nature:

> They arise from the fact that aboriginal people are *aboriginal*.... The Court must neither lose sight of the generalized constitutional status of what s. 35(1) protects, nor can it ignore the necessary specificity which comes from granting special constitutional protection to one part of Canadian society. The Court must define the scope of s. 35(1) in a way which captures *both* the aboriginal and the rights in aboriginal rights.[112]

We should pause for a moment to ponder the leap in reasoning that occurs in the last few sentences of this passage. Why, precisely, do Aboriginal rights eventually end up tied down to questions of identity? Why must they be seen as essentially *Aboriginal* rights (where the nature of the rights themselves is tied to "Aboriginality," so the rights end up having a cultural core)? That is, why could Aboriginal rights have not been distinctly *defined* in a way appropriate to the context of their grounding and development, and then only happen to be *held* (because of this context) by Aboriginal peoples? As it is, the Court slides from the fact Aboriginal rights are going to be held exclusively by Aboriginal peoples to the conclusion that thereby Aboriginal rights must be linked to "Aboriginality."

---

110 *Ibid* at para 18.

111 *Ibid* at para 19 [emphasis in original].

112 *Ibid* at paras 19–20 [emphasis in original].

Why, alternatively, was it not the case that the nature of Aboriginal rights emerged out of careful consideration of the history of colonial relations between British/Canadian Crowns and Indigenous peoples, being then rights that reflected the history of these interactions?[113] Following this path, they could have come to be either rights tied to powers and "things" unjustly appropriated (rights that – out of this historical interaction – were held by those unjustly treated), or rights that somehow came to reflect the fact peoples treated to colonizing force were indeed pre-existing self-determining peoples.

The Court, however, rather mysteriously sets out on a very different path from this point onward. In tying Aboriginal rights to "Aboriginality," it creates a situation it now needs to make sense of. It now must struggle with setting out what Aboriginal rights might amount to, given the first (puzzling) step it has taken. Given this preliminary stage setting, the Court went on to find – following a "purposive" analysis, required by the constitutional status of the rights in question – that

> the doctrine of aboriginal rights exists, and is recognized and affirmed by s. 35(1), because of one simple fact: when Europeans arrived in North America, aboriginal peoples *were already here*, living in communities on the land, and participating in distinctive cultures, as they had done for centuries.[114]

Temporal priority enters the picture, then, to ground the existence of the rights in question. Interestingly, the Court ties this priority not to the simple existence of Aboriginal communities on the land prior to the arrival of Europeans, but to their living on the land in "communities," "in distinctive cultures." The Court goes on in the next sentence to point out that this fact can be seen as separating out the claims of Aboriginal peoples from those of other minority groups in Canada: "It is this fact, and this fact above all others, which separates aboriginal peoples from all other minority groups in Canadian society and which mandates their special legal, and now constitutional, status."[115]

---

113 Alternate grounding for rights-talk was not unknown in nineteenth-century Canada. Heaman notes that at that time there "existed a vibrant tradition of conservative rights talk in Canada" and that "not infrequently conservatives took the part of people marginalized by liberal hegemony, including native people and the dependent poor, and tried to find ways of supporting them that were outside the liberal order." Furthermore, the rights talk of conservatives was of "collective, social or historical rights, rights that were actually incompatible with hegemonic liberalism and that made the work of abstract and individualistic liberalism all the more difficult": EA Heaman, "Rights Talk and the Liberal Order Framework" in Jean-Francois Constant & Michel Ducharme, eds, *Liberalism and Hegemony: Debating the Canadian Liberal Revolution* (Toronto: University of Toronto Press, 2009) 147 at 154–5.

114 *Van der Peet*, *supra* note 3 at para 30 [emphasis in original].

115 *Ibid.*

The suggestion, then, is that some minority groups in Canada might also enjoy legal (if not constitutional) rights,[116] but that whatever these might be they do not enjoy the same nature and status as those held as Aboriginal rights. The next two sentences are often quoted, as they bring together this fact of pre-existence (spelled out in interesting language) with the notion of reconciliation:

> More specifically, what s. 35(1) does is provide the constitutional framework through which the fact that aboriginals lived on the land in distinctive societies, with their own practices, traditions and cultures, is acknowledged and reconciled with the sovereignty of the Crown. The substantive rights which fall within the provision must be defined in light of this purpose; the aboriginal rights recognized and affirmed by s. 35(1) must be directed towards the reconciliation of the pre-existence of aboriginal societies with the sovereignty of the Crown.[117]

This conclusion to the line of reasoning establishes the ultimate ground for the existence of Aboriginal rights – lying in acknowledgment of the pre-existence of Aboriginal societies, connected to the need to reconcile this with the sovereignty of the Crown. After canvassing case law from several jurisdictions in support of this line of reasoning, the Court restates this conclusion at the end of its discussion of how to make sense of Aboriginal rights:

> [T]he aboriginal rights recognized and affirmed by s. 35(1) are best understood as, first, the means by which the Constitution recognizes the fact that prior to the arrival of Europeans in North America the land was already occupied by distinctive aboriginal societies, and as, second, the means by which that prior occupation is reconciled with the assertion of Crown sovereignty over Canadian territory. The content of aboriginal rights must be directed at fulfilling both of these purposes.[118]

This introduces one foundational understanding of "reconciliation" we see in the jurisprudence, but one that – mysteriously – seems to speak more to the idea of a weaker party having to reconcile to a stronger, as when, for example, the person who slips on ice must accept that certain matters – the effects of gravity and hardness of the surface – are simply fixed, and so she must "reconcile"

116 We could, of course, understand francophone rights (as these are expressed within both the *Constitution Act, 1867* and the *Constitution Act, 1982*) as "minority rights." See *supra* note 1. This would not be received particularly well by many. The Court is likely mindful of other culturally/ethnically grounded rights, such as rights to language.

117 *Van der Peet*, *supra* note at para 31.

118 *Ibid* at para 43.

herself to that situation.[119] Crown sovereignty appears in this context as it did in *Sparrow* – not as something to be examined but as something given, never to be questioned.

In *Gladstone* the Supreme Court put reconciliation to a quite different use. There the Court held that reconciliation can justify certain kinds of Crown actions and behaviour – the Crown can justify the infringement of Aboriginal (and treaty) rights so long as "reconciliation" animates its decisions. On one hand, this aligns with the use of reconciliation in *Van der Peet* – one could think that an aspect of the reconciliation of pre-existing Aboriginal societies with Crown sovereignty is that when the Crown acts it is exercising its unquestioned sovereign power, and Aboriginal rights must be reconciled to it. But on the other hand we see in *Gladstone* a level at which reconciliation functions that implies a different thing at work. When justifying activity, the Crown can turn its mind towards reconciliation between Aboriginal peoples and Canadian society.

This is quite puzzling. No matter what one's understanding of reconciliation may be in this context (where we are looking at damaged relations between a colonizing force and Indigenous peoples adversely affected by colonial laws and policies), it is difficult to see how it can be a matter of "reconciliation" that the colonizing power gets to justify *further* adversely affecting the now constitutionally protected rights of Aboriginal peoples on the basis that – without dialogue between the two sides – the Crown's actions somehow further reconciliation between two parts of society writ large.

When we examined the decision in *Sparrow* we found a general framework established for how Canadian law would approach the interaction of the Crown and Aboriginal societies. One might suggest this framework was established in its most general architectural form with the invocation of "unquestioned" Crown sovereignty. While Crown power must be tempered, that very power is not challenged or examined. One fundamental puzzle we come upon in the larger framework is the fact we find the very purpose of the constitutionalization of Aboriginal rights is to have pre-existing Aboriginal societies reconciled to this unquestioned sovereignty.

We have seen, however, that if we look more carefully into how reconciliation functions within the decision-making apparatus of the state, yet other puzzles emerge. The jurisprudential response to the mystery we focused on above would be to point to the need to reconcile those things the Crown was weighing and balancing – the interests of non-Aboriginal Canadians with rights under section 35. This, however, just opens the door to a multitude of riddles. How did reconciliation

119 For consideration of different possible meanings of "reconciliation," see Mark D Walters, "The Jurisprudence of Reconciliation: Aboriginal Rights in Canada" in Will Kymlicka & Bashir Bashir, eds, *The Politics of Reconciliation in Multicultural Societies* (Oxford: Oxford University Press, 2008) 165.

transform from something that transpires between the power of the Crown (as sovereign) and Aboriginal peoples to a weighing and balancing of interests *within* Canadian society? How did Aboriginal people suddenly find themselves holding only what must now be seen to be essentially interests (to be balanced with what have always been essentially interests of non-Aboriginal Canadians)? What purpose is served by section 35 when one would assume that without section 35, if Aboriginal peoples are already contained with Canadian society (as the Court seems to assume), one would expect their interests would be equitably weighed against those of other Canadians? Why, when this purported balancing takes place, are constitutionally protected rights weighed against interests?[120]

The Honour of the Crown

At the turn of the millennium the Supreme Court began to systemize, revitalize, and expand upon its discussions of "the honour of the Crown."[121] Most recently, in the *Mikisew Cree* case (of 2018), the waters were muddied as a split Court said a number of puzzling things about the nature of the honour of the Crown and how it fits with the duty to consult.[122] The best one can speculate at this point is that the Court is struggling to determine where to take the notion of the honour of the Crown, with some jurists worried it is being developed in directions that are unsupportable and potentially unwise.

This notion first appeared in Canadian jurisprudence in the mid-twentieth century, informing a principle of treaty interpretation essentially precluding findings of "sharp dealings" by the Crown during treaty negotiations.[123] In the first few decades of the twenty-first century, however, it has come to take on a much more substantive set of roles and understandings.

---

120 Many of these questions and concerns – though not worded in quite this way – were expressed by McLachlin J in her dissent in *Van der Peet*, *supra* note 3 (which came out the same day as *Gladstone*, *supra* note 6, and in which she spoke as much about *Gladstone* as about *Van der Peet*).

121 Recent systemization and expansion occurred in *Manitoba Metis Federation*, *supra* note 39.

122 *Mikisew Cree First Nation v Canada (Governor General in Council)*, 2018 SCC 40 [*Mikisew Cree 2018*]

123 See e.g. *R v Taylor* (1981), [1981] 3 CNLR 114, 34 OR (2d) 360. Earlier incantations of the honour of the Crown exist in case law, but arguably the notion played no substantive role in how Crown-Aboriginal relations were defined and enforced by courts. In *Ontario v Dominion of Canada* (1895), 25 SCR 434, 1895 CarswellNat 46, the Supreme Court held at paragraph 40 that "the terms and conditions expressed in those [treaty] instruments as to be performed by or on behalf of the Crown, have always been regarded as involving a trust graciously assumed by the Crown to the fulfilment of which with the Indians the fate and Honour of the Crown is pledged."

This, however, was understood by courts to be the articulation of a political trust, not a legal trust of any sort.

Its transformation began in 1999, still in the treaty context. In *R v Marshall*, Binnie J transformed this principle of treaty interpretation into a legal tool with substantially more weight and impact.[124] He invoked the honour of the Crown to arrive at an interpretation of a treaty reached between the British and the Mi'kmaq in 1760, an interpretation few observers would have anticipated coming from the Supreme Court. The Court found that a promise by the Crown to provide a system of "truck houses" (trading posts tailored specifically to facilitate exclusive British-Mi'kmaq trade) must be seen – if it to be understood in light of a presumption of the honour of the Crown – to include by implication a right to gather things from the sea to trade (for "necessaries").[125]

Seemingly building on that unexpected elevation of the notion came a new use in 2004, in *Haida Nation v British Columbia (Minister of Forests)*.[126] This case arose principally as a result of continued Crown inertia or inaction in the face of well over a decade of Court pronouncements on Aboriginal rights. From the release of *Sparrow* right up to the handing down of this judgment, governments across Canada had consistently ignored obligations suggested by what courts had said about the nature of Aboriginal (and treaty) rights.[127] Canadian governments argued during this period that until such Aboriginal rights were *established* (either by court determination or negotiated outcome), they did not exist in Canadian law. In *Haida Nation* the Court reached over to the notion of the honour of the Crown and lifted it out of the context of treaty interpretation. The honour of the Crown required, the Court found, that whenever the Crown contemplates action that might substantially infringe upon *asserted rights*, the Crown must consult with those asserting these not-yet-established Aboriginal rights (so long as the claim is known to the Crown and the Crown can assess its strength).[128] In the years since *Haida Nation*, one practical result has been

---

124 *R v Marshall*, supra note 2.

125 The key part of the truck-house clause of the treaty simply stated: "And I do further engage that we will not traffick, barter or Exchange any Commodities in any manner but with such persons or the managers of such Truck houses as shall be appointed or Established by His Majesty's Governor at Lunenbourg or Elsewhere in Nova Scotia or Accadia": *ibid* at paras 123–26 [emphasis omitted]. Binnie J noted that during negotiations leading up to the treaty "the aboriginal leaders ... asked for truckhouses 'for the furnishing them with necessaries, in Exchange for their Peltry'": *ibid* at para 19.

126 *Haida Nation, supra* note 90.

127 In a judgment released the next year, *Mikisew Cree, supra* note 2, the Supreme Court extended the notion of a duty to consult to the context of treaty implementation, finding that when the Crown contemplates action that might have substantial impact upon a treaty right (even when it is acting within the terms of the treaty), it must consult with the affected Indigenous treaty nation.

128 The Crown can also fall under a duty if it *ought* to have known of the asserted right. The Court was well aware that the Crown might close its eyes and cover its ears, then claim it did not know that its decisions might affect Aboriginal claims.

a momentous shift in the focus of litigation, as now much of the discussion of Aboriginal rights concerns claims involving alleged failures by the Crown to adequately consult.[129]

In 2013 the Supreme Court added a further chapter to this saga. In *Manitoba Metis Federation Inc v Canada (AG)* the Court held that while a provision in the *Manitoba Act* of 1870 had promised 1.4 million acres of land on the prairies would be deeded to the children of Metis families, this could not be construed as an element of a treaty or as something capable of grounding fiduciary duties on the Crown.[130] Nevertheless, the Court went on to find that the honour of the Crown required of the Crown that it have acted to diligently fulfil this "constitutional promise." In light of the historical record, indicating the Crown did a very poor job transferring much land at all to the children of the Metis, the Court granted the sought-after declaration (that "the federal Crown failed to implement the *Manitoba Act* in a manner consistent with the honour of the Crown"), effectively putting the Metis into a hitherto unavailable negotiating position.

We see the honour of the Crown arise, then, in essentially two contexts – as a means of arriving at what the Court takes to be better interpretations of understandings between the Crown and Indigenous peoples (both the *Marshall* and *Manitoba Metis Federation* situations), and as a means of imagining obligations that might fall on the Crown even when the Aboriginal claims at issue have not been established within either litigation or negotiation (the *Haida Nation* situation).

Why might the honour of the Crown be needed as a legal instrument? Two possibilities arise, one grounded in the jurisprudence and the other speculative. Given the aim in this chapter – to provide an overview of the jurisprudence that is as non-exegetical as possible, and to tie to that puzzles that emerge – the second speculative possibility (that the Court has been forced over the last few decades to search for increasingly inventive ways to get the Crown to act, to understand that it has binding legal obligations)[131] will not be explored at this

129 One reason for this is that Aboriginal peoples seldom have the resources to actually establish their rights in Canadian courts, and south of the sixtieth parallel the modern treaty process has been fraught with challenges and shortcomings.

130 *Manitoba Metis Federation*, *supra* note 38; *Manitoba Act, 1870* (UK), 33 Vict, c 3, reprinted in RSC 1985, App II, No 8.

131 A second speculative possibility is that the Supreme Court aims to *replace* fiduciary doctrine (as the fundamental way of understanding Crown-Aboriginal relations) with the doctrine of the honour of the Crown. While this may be so, there is no sign of this in the current jurisprudence: while the Court does speak in *Haida Nation*, *supra* note 90, and *Manitoba Metis Federation*, *supra* note 38, of the honour of the Crown underscoring fiduciary obligations, this does not signal a new conceptual underpinning for Aboriginal law, as the notion of honour they deploy speaks only to the same sort of understanding of the power dynamic – that marked essentially by a sole sovereign power with control over the lives and lands of Indigenous/Aboriginal peoples.

point. The non-speculative point comes up within the case law, though to see why the honour of the Crown is required along this line of reasoning one has to go back a bit into the history of the jurisprudence around Crown-Aboriginal relations.

In *Guerin v The Queen* the Supreme Court was faced with a situation that seemed to demand a just resolution – in the 1950s the Musqueam had surrendered to the Crown a portion of their (small) reserve in order to facilitate economic development.[132] They had to surrender the land in this manner, as at that time this was the only way to activate the value of the land and to make it available for development. On receiving the land on the basis of certain assurances to the Musqueam, Crown representatives, however, got into a differently worded agreement with a golf course developer that heavily favoured that other party's interests. The Musqueam found out details about this only by chance in the late 1960s. It then took fifteen years to find a lawyer to argue the case and for Canadian courts to address the problem.

At the Supreme Court, the court split on whether it could apply trust law or not to this sort of situation. In a concurring opinion, three judges were willing to find that the Musqueam had an actual legal beneficial interest in the lands they had surrendered, an interest that, when transferred to the Crown, would generate a trust-like relationship.[133] The majority held that the Musqueam held something *more* than a mere "personal and usufructuary" interest, but still an interest that constituted little more than a burden on Crown title, something that once surrendered simply disappeared (Crown title then being "perfected").[134] Since under either view of the matter *no property right per se* was there to be transferred, no trust *simpliciter* could be generated. And so it was that the notion of fiduciary doctrine came to be introduced into Aboriginal law in Canada, as the Court then reached into this area of the law of equity to arrive at something approaching a just outcome for the Musqueam.

---

132 *Guerin, supra* note 101.

133 *Ibid.* Speaking for three, Wilson J said at 349 that section 18 of the *Indian Act*, RSC 1985, c I-5, which spelled out how reserve land could be surrendered to the Crown: it

> acknowledg[ed] a historic reality, namely that Indian Bands have a beneficial interest in their reserves and that the Crown has a responsibility to protect that interest and make sure that any purpose to which reserve land is put will not interfere with it. This is not to say that the Crown either historically or by s. 18 holds the land in trust for the Bands. The Bands do not have the fee in the lands; their interest is a limited one.

134 *Guerin, supra* note 101. Speaking for four, Dickson J held at 382 that:

> Indians have a legal right to occupy and possess certain lands, the ultimate title to which is in the Crown. While their interest does not, strictly speaking, amount to beneficial ownership, neither is its nature completely exhausted by the concept of a personal right. It is true that the *sui generis* interest which the Indians have in the land is personal in the sense that it cannot be transferred to a grantee, but it is also true ... that the interest gives rise upon surrender to a distinctive fiduciary obligation on the part of the Crown to deal with the land for the benefit of the surrendering Indians.

Fiduciary obligations, however, still require that *some* identifiable "legal or practical" interest of the beneficiary be in the hands of the fiduciary (in the case of the Musqueam in *Guerin* it was the "personal and usufructuary" interest this First Nation held in its reserve lands). So while it is true that there is a general fiduciary relationship between the Crown and Aboriginal peoples (the result in *Sparrow* of transplantation of the *Guerin* discourse into section 35 discourse), particular fiduciary obligations arise only *on the facts*, when it can be shown that the Crown has – within the situation under examination – control over some *legally recognized interest* sufficient to impose fiduciary obligations. The lack of any interest of this sort when either (a) an Aboriginal community merely *asserts* it has Aboriginal rights, or (b) a *promise* is made to transfer lands in individual allotments (where the land to be transferred is not dependent on or tied to pre-existing Aboriginal land interests) leads to situations wherein fiduciary doctrine cannot step in to resolve a difficult matter. The honour of the Crown, then, is required as a legal instrument in just those situations wherein fiduciary doctrine falls short, when appeal to it will not suffice to generate legal obligations on the Crown.

Seen in this light, puzzles considered earlier re-emerge, while new forms crystallize. Focus falls on the impact of *Haida Nation*, as (a) the role *Manitoba Metis Federation* may play in the development of Aboriginal law is still unclear, and, more pressingly, (b) from the language in *Manitoba Metis Federation*, it seems clear it will be difficult to make substantive further use of the way the honour of the Crown was employed in that special context.[135]

First is the recurring matter of Crown sovereignty. Why is Crown sovereignty fixed and unquestioned, while "merely asserted" Indigenous rights – grounded in matters *predating* Crown sovereignty – are deemed too inchoate to ground *substantive* legal obligations? Several puzzling matters touched on can be linked at this point. One is the fact that section 35 speaks of "recognition and affirmation," and yet the rights in question are taken by the Crown not to exist until proven in Canadian courts (according to tests set out by these non-Indigenous bodies). A second builds on this, bringing up the question of onus of proof: why does the jurisprudence not start with the presumption that Aboriginal rights are robust and extensive (since they point to the nature of the legal landscape before the Crown asserted itself over Indigenous lands), so that the starting point for disputes under section 35 would be that

135 *Manitoba Metis Federation*, *supra* note 38. The Court held that "the honour of the Crown is engaged by constitutional obligations to Aboriginal groups": *ibid* at para 91. They seemed to view this kind of situation as akin to those generating treaty obligations on the Crown, stating that "it may be helpful to consider [section 31's] treaty-like history and character," the proviso being that "[s]ection 31, though, is not a treaty": *ibid* at paras 92–3. How many other instances will arise wherein a document contains "constitutional obligations" but is not considered a treaty?

the rights in question exist unless the Crown can demonstrate either they do not exist or that they are of lesser form than that argued by the Aboriginal peoples asserting them?[136]

With these fundamental matters put aside for a moment, why, as a result of all this action by the Court, do Aboriginal peoples find themselves with what is essentially a procedural right? Why, furthermore, is this "consultation" presented as though Aboriginal peoples have a meaningful role in decision-making? In light of the tremendous focus put on "duties to consult and accommodate" in litigation since 2004, these internal puzzles should be carefully unpacked.

Consider a hypothetical First Nation in British Columbia with rights they assert but that have not yet been established in Canadian law. Let us narrow this down to an asserted right to hunt in a specific locale within their territory. The duty to consult (and potentially accommodate) arises when the Crown contemplates action – in this case imagine the Crown is contemplating authorizing an open pit mine in one of the last prime hunting territories of this people. We *begin*, then, with a decision made or about to be made, arising out of the exercise of Crown sovereignty. If it is known (or if the Crown should know) that the contemplated action might have a substantial effect on the right being asserted by the First Nation (once established), a legal obligation falls on the Crown to consult with this affected Aboriginal community. If the projected impact is severe and the interests at stake are serious, the duty may include a requirement of the Crown to contemplate altering the action in an attempt to accommodate the Aboriginal interests at stake.

We see here how this is essentially a procedural right (what it generates is almost always nothing more than an obligation on the Crown to engage in

136 Through the spring and summer of 2018 (as this work was being finalized) the federal government engaged in consultation on a proposed "rights recognition" framework, to be established in statutory form. It is something of a puzzle (at least to Indigenous peoples) why such a framework should be necessary when section 35 already speaks of "recognition and affirmation," but one key purported outcome – removing the presumption that asserted rights do not exist until proven in a Canadian court or established in a modern treaty – nevertheless might be helpful to Aboriginal communities trying to make use of their constitutionally protected rights. It should be noted, however, that (a) this is not the first time there has been apparent movement towards a new framework, and past efforts did not bear fruit (there was movement in that direction during the tenure of the Campbell government in British Columbia in the earlier 2000s, with grounding in a rights-recognition foundation, but that grounding did not come to pass), and (b) this most recent movement has been strongly criticized. For example, Indigenous academics Joyce Green and Gina Starblanket describe the package as "a cage, containing Indigenous nations and governments within a legal apparatus that assumes all sovereignty and jurisdiction belong to the federal and provincial governments": Joyce Green & Gina Starblanket, "Op-Ed: Recognition of Rights or Termination of Rights Framework?" APTN National News (2 August 2018), online: <aptnnews.ca/2018/08/02/op-ed-recognition-of-rights-or-termination-of-rights-framework/>.

dialogue with the potentially affected Aboriginal community)[137] *and* how it presents only a veneer of decision-making power for Aboriginal communities. Decision-making power is fundamentally in the hands of the Crown – the Aboriginal community enjoys at best the ability to have a say in how a decision already made (to contemplate authorizing the mine) may be modified. So we arrive back at fundamental puzzles, all deeply connected to Indigenous perspectives.

In *Mikisew Cree 2018* this already confusing picture became more muddled, not simply because the jurisprudence leading up to the case was fairly amorphous (though it certainly was and remains so) but as factions within the Court argued about different directions in which the doctrine of the honour of the Crown might be developed. We can divide the three-three-two-one-split-Court into two groups – five who see the need to continue expansion along certain lines and four who strongly oppose any further reach for the doctrine.[138]

This debate takes place in what is all, essentially, obiter, as the Court unanimously agreed that the federal court that heard this case lacked jurisdiction in the matter before it. The case itself concerned two pieces of federal legislation passed in 2012, which together acted to redefine a legislative regime (environmental assessment) and eviscerate protections under others (relating to fisheries, navigable waters, and species at risk). The Mikisew Cree First Nation hoped to challenge these omnibus bills on the basis that their effects would be drastic in relation to the ongoing protection of their treaty rights. All judges of the Supreme Court agreed that the mandate of the federal court did not cover such challenges.

In all four separate judgments that split the Court we find, nevertheless, further remarks about the nature of the duty to consult and its relationship to the honour of the Crown. Recall that in *Haida Nation* the Court reached over to the honour of the Crown as grounding for the duty to consult doctrine developed in that case, holding that fiduciary doctrine would not function when the rights were merely claimed (as they were, then, determined to be inchoate within Canadian law). In *Mikisew Cree 2018* five of the judges centred their attention on a supplementary account, one focused on the *nature* of the honour of the Crown and not simply its reason for being brought into the mix.

---

137 And, on those rare occasions when the Crown must seek to accommodate the Aboriginal interest, the decision to move ahead is not affected – indeed, the Court was clear in its finding that nothing coming out of *Haida Nation* suggests that an affected Aboriginal nation has a veto in relation to decisions made by the Crown. See *Haida Nation*, *supra* note 90 at paras 42, 48.

138 *Mikisew Cree*, *supra* note 122. Karakatsanis J wrote for Wagner CJ, and Gascon J and Abella J wrote for Martin J (the five), while Rowe J wrote for Moldaver and Côté JJ, and Brown J wrote his own opinion (the four).

Three of this group, led by Karakatsanis J, decided the honour of the Crown can underscore yet further forms of obligation, making it possible that in future cases Aboriginal peoples might be able to challenge legislation, *once it is in place*, on the basis that the development and/or enactment of the legislation failed to demonstrate actions by the Crown that were suitably honourable (with the measure for this being whether the effects of the legislation *adversely affected* rights of Aboriginal peoples). The other two jurists, led by Abella J, felt that the honour of the Crown functioned in the context of the doctrine of the duty to consult to enable Aboriginal peoples potentially *adversely affected* by legislation to argue they were not sufficiently consulted *in the processes of the development and/or enactment of legislation.*

The other four judges reacted strongly against the notion the honour of the Crown might come to underscore these new actions (whether it be a perceived expansion of the duty to consult into the realm of legislative processes or the creation of entirely new legal instruments that might function once legislation exists). Much of the back-and-forth between the two camps revolved around the respective functions of and weights accorded to constitutional principles involved in this challenge, the constitutional protection of Aboriginal and treaty rights being set up against doctrines of the separation of powers and parliamentary supremacy.[139]

The four opposed to expansion held that the separation of powers and parliamentary supremacy preclude both direct and indirect challenges to the legislative process (the indirect challenge comes from the fact that if the new legal instruments hinted at by Karakatsanis J were in place, while as a matter of process challenges could come about only once the legislation was operable, it would nevertheless be wise for legislatures developing legislation to try to

---

139 *Mikisew Cree 2018, supra* note 122 at para 35 Karakatsanis J noted that the doctrine of the separation of powers:

> recognizes that each branch of government "will be unable to fulfill its role if it is unduly interfered with by the others" ... It dictates that "the courts and Parliament strive to respect each other's role in the conduct of public affairs"; as such, there is no doubt that Parliament's legislative activities should "proceed unimpeded by any external body or institution, including the courts."

In the next paragraph she goes on to describe the doctrine of parliamentary supremacy:

> Parliamentary sovereignty mandates that the legislature can make or unmake any law it wishes, within the confines of its constitutional authority. While the adoption of the *Canadian Charter of Rights and Freedoms* transformed the Canadian system of government "to a significant extent from a system of Parliamentary supremacy to one of constitutional supremacy" ... democracy remains one of the unwritten principles of the Constitution.... Recognizing that the elected legislature has specific consultation obligations may constrain it in pursuing its mandate and therefore undermine its ability to act as the voice of the electorate.

It is eye-opening that Karakatsanis J accepts the transformation signalled by the introduction of a *Charter of Rights and Freedoms* but does not accept that this might also have been the effect of introducing section 35 into the landscape.

avoid complications by considering Aboriginal interests at the time they were engaged in the legislative process).

The five proposing new developments in the law, on the other hand, see a process of reconciliation operating in this sort of situation, with a need to *balance* doctrines of separation of powers and parliamentary supremacy against the constitutional protection of Aboriginal and treaty rights. While on its face this appears quite progressive, the progressive tone turns out to be misleading. Karakatsanis J suggests a path already laid out in another context, noting that "*declaratory relief* may be an appropriate remedy even in situations where other forms of relief would be inconsistent with the separation of powers."[140] While choosing to make use of the duty to consult in relation to the legislative process, Abella J reaches a similar conclusion, noting first that the duty to consult differs from case to case, depending on the circumstances, and then suggesting circumstances in this sort of case – where the challenge of the Mikisew Cree First Nation must be weighed against powerful doctrines of the separation of powers and parliamentary supremacy – lead to the conclusion that "[w]ithout ruling out the possibility that in certain cases legislation enacted in breach of a duty to consult could be struck down by the reviewing court, *a declaration will generally be the appropriate remedy*."[141] Of what use, to an Aboriginal community expending time and resources at very short supply, would a declaration be? Presumably the next stage, if a declaration could be obtained, would be negotiations, a second costly and time-consuming process (one that the Crown may, furthermore, simply choose to avoid).

It should be noted as well that behind variations in the judgments we can find some commonalities, one in particular that brings back to the surface the key puzzle noted earlier. While the five see a need to balance the protection of Aboriginal and treaty rights with the doctrines of separation of powers and parliamentary supremacy, the four hold these other two constitutional principles inviolate and would have the flexibility built into section 35 jurisprudence do all the work necessary to resolve this sort of challenge to the Crown's law-making processes. It should be noted all nine signal strong deference to the Crown's law-making process, the only question being whether Aboriginal peoples' *voices*, as they express concerns about their constitutionally protected rights, should be given a place within this process. Crown sovereignty is under no challenge here, as the progressive group's advancement is only in relation to consideration of Aboriginal peoples' concerns about impacts on their rights. One might ask, If the views of the five were to be adopted in a future case, to what extent would Canadian law advance beyond *Sparrow*?

140 *Ibid*, at para 47 (referencing *Canada (Prime Minister) v Khadr*, 2010 SCC 3.

141 *Ibid*, at para 97.

Indeed, one might fairly ask whether the law would regress or progress if the honour of the Crown were to play one of the more expansive roles envisioned by Karakatsanis J or Abella J. Recall that the Court in *Sparrow* held that section 35 called for the old rules of the game to be put aside – those rules that prevented the judiciary from questioning what had been the absolute power of the Crown to that point – and held that, as a result, not only could the rights of the Musqueam require consultation about legislation that would affect the preferred exercise of these rights, but also that in developing legislation that might do so, the Crown was obligated to prioritize those rights. The situation is different in *Mikisew Cree 2018*, but arguably not so different as to imagine a drastically different manner by which conflict between the Crown and Aboriginal peoples would be managed. Would it not be better to focus on *Sparrow* and put *Mikisew Cree 2018* – even its "progressive" elements – to one side?[142]

Let us return to a puzzle introduced earlier in other contexts, beginning with the "fact" of Crown sovereignty. In *Manitoba Metis Federation* the Supreme Court equates the honour of the Crown with the history of Crown-Aboriginal relations, which begins with the assertion of Crown sovereignty over Indigenous communities.[143] At the moment when the Crown asserts sovereignty over a particular Indigenous people, its honour is engaged (and a process of reconciling Crown sovereignty to this pre-existing Aboriginal society begins).

But while one can see (and feel, as it were) the presence of Crown sovereignty from moment to moment through the history of colonial activity by the Crown, why must that reconciliation be between this grounding fact of colonialism and the pre-existence of Aboriginal societies? Putting in place a presumption (not meant to reflect reality) that the Crown always had honourable intentions may generate legal obligations (at least today, if not in the past when its actions were almost always marked by dishonour),[144] but all this rests, still, on the *given* of

---

142 The one area where a possible gap is identified that might warrant further attention is the possibility a legislative body in Canada could use the fact that no legal challenge can be made to legislative processes to pass laws that then significantly undermine protections to Aboriginal and/or treaty rights. But, as members of the Court point out, this is a kind of situation seemingly captured by the law set out in *Sparrow*.

143 *Manitoba Metis Federation*, *supra* note 38 at para 70 (here the Court quotes from *Haida Nation:* "In all its dealings with Aboriginal peoples, from the assertion of sovereignty to the resolution of claims and the implementation of treaties, the Crown must act honourably"). See *Haida Nation*, *supra* note 90 at para 17. The discussion in *Manitoba Metis Federation* on this passage is, however, much more detailed than that found in the earlier duty to consult context. See *Manitoba Metis Federation, supra* note 38 at paras 65–83.

144 This is not an exegetical remark, as, for example, the Supreme Court itself noted in *Sparrow*, *supra* note 6 at 1103 that:

> [T]here can be no doubt that over the years the rights of the Indians were often honoured in the breach.... As MacDonald J. stated in *Pasco v. C.N.R.*, 69 B.C.L.R 76, [1986] 1 C.N.L.R. 35 at 37 (S.C.): "We cannot recount with much pride the treatment accorded to the native people of this country."

Crown sovereignty. We witness once again the foundation of the Canadian law of Aboriginal rights – the Crown's place as sole sovereign authority is "unquestioned," its power over Aboriginal peoples simply a given around which all else must revolve.

An Indigenous history of colonial Crown-Aboriginal relations would not begin with Crown sovereignty as either given or unquestionable. Indeed, from an Indigenous perspective one would expect a legal response to the history of Crown-Indigenous interaction to be directed principally towards the *question* of Crown sovereignty.[145] This, I suggest, lies close to the core of Indigenous puzzlement over the basic treatment of Aboriginal rights in Canadian law.

Aboriginal Rights to Governance

Bearing in mind, then, this fundamental puzzle about the emergence of jurisprudence in this area of Canadian law, consider a question intimately related to the matter of "unquestioned" Crown sovereignty – the status of "Indigenous sovereignty" in Canadian law.

We need to begin with an important caveat. Canadian courts do not tackle the question of "Indigenous sovereignty," if by that we mean to imagine they might have directly considered and addressed the fact of Indigenous politically constituted bodies having occupied all of what is now Canada before the arrival of European powers and settlers. By "Indigenous sovereignty" I refer to the fact that before French/British/Canadian Crowns achieved (what some accept as) sovereign status in what is now Canada, Indigenous peoples existed in distinct legal-political bodies, governing all matters relating to their traditional territories.

I deliberately cast the notion of Indigenous sovereignty at a high level of abstraction, as the *particular* ways in which distinct Indigenous communities constituted "nations," with legal-political "institutions," "governing" matters relating to their traditional territories are widely variant across both time and

---

McHugh notes the oddity of structuring Aboriginal law so that current pronouncements on the nature of Crown obligations reach back to essentially rewrite legal history. See Paul McHugh, "A Common Law Biography of Section 35" in Patrick Macklem & Douglas Sanderson, eds, *From Recognition to Reconciliation: Essays on the Constitutional Entrenchment of Aboriginal and Treaty Rights* (Toronto: University of Toronto Press, 2016) 137.

145 The first section of Macklem & Sanderson's *From Recognition to Reconciliation* contains analysis by several legal scholars on various issues tied to the assertion of Crown sovereignty, though little is said that intersects directly with Indigenous perspectives on sovereign authority. See Patrick Macklem & Douglas Sanderson, eds, *From Recognition to Reconciliation: Essays on the Constitutional Entrenchment of Aboriginal and Treaty Rights* (Toronto: University of Toronto Press, 2016).

place. Not only should one expect to see great variance between Indigenous and European forms of governance, but as well between different Indigenous collectives. Equally important, one should note that beyond recognition of wide variance between Indigenous *forms* of governance should be recognition that *concepts* and *understandings* of such things as "sovereignty," "governance," "nationhood," and "territory" are unique and peculiar to Indigenous understandings (and widely variant across time and place).[146]

None of this is hinted at in the jurisprudence of Canadian courts as they tackle "Aboriginal governance." The attention of Canadian courts is directed solely to the question of the space they might open up *within* the Canadian legal and political landscape for powers of Aboriginal communities to exercise *rights to self-government* (rights to manage matters that are, essentially, internal to the community).

In the early decades of the twenty-first century, thoughts of Aboriginal rights to self-government naturally gravitate to section 35. As we have seen, however, the wording in section 35 is quite sparse. The need to fill up section 35 was clear from the beginning, and through the 1980s a number of mandated constitutional conferences were held to flesh out this provision, with particular attention to governance rights of Aboriginal peoples.[147]

While these conferences led to the inclusion of a few subsections to section 35,[148] they failed to make substantive headway on matters of governance. Clearly the high-water mark of all this activity occurred in 1992, when a national referendum was held on the issue of restructuring constitutional arrangements in Canada (the *Charlottetown Accord*).[149] For better or worse, the referendum failed to gain sufficient support.[150] This accord would have

---

146 See e.g. Taiaiake Alfred, *Peace, Power, Righteousness: An Indigenous Manifesto* (Don Mills, ON: Oxford University Press, 1999).

147 For a discussion of these conferences, see Roy Romanow, John Whyte & Howard Leeson, *Canada ... Notwithstanding: The Making of the Constitution 1976–1982* (Toronto: Carswell, 1984); Ardith Walkem & Halie Bruce, eds, *Box of Treasures or Empty Box? Twenty Years of Section 35* (Penticton, BC: Theytus Press, 2003).

148 *Constitution Act, 1982*, *supra* note 1. See *ibid*, ss 35(3), 35(4):

> (3) For greater certainty, in subsection (1) "treaty rights" includes rights that now exist by way of land claims agreements or may be so acquired.
>
> (4) Notwithstanding any other provision of this Act, the aboriginal and treaty rights referred to in subsection (1) are guaranteed equally to male and female persons.

149 For an insider perspective on the lead up to the referendum on the accord and the reaction to its failure (articulated by a key figure in the First Nation's political arena at the time, Ovide Mercredi, then national chief of the Assembly of First Nations), see Ovide Mercredi & Mary Ellen Turpel, *In the Rapids: Navigating the Future of First Nations* (Toronto: Penguin Books, 1994) at 207–28.

150 An assessment of "unfortunately" would not be likely to run into many disagreeing voices today within the larger Indigenous community. At the time – not fully aware yet of the bleak future and the Herculean task of fleshing out governance matters for Aboriginal peoples by other means – many were not terribly distraught at the failure.

entrenched Aboriginal governments as a third order of government in Canada (alongside federal and provincial bodies), though in a form that was yet to be determined. With these failures, many have naturally come to see the challenge as one of locating rights around governance under the general umbrella of section 35 itself.

Some have argued that there is a form of governance right within Aboriginal title.[151] Since a finding of Aboriginal title over a tract of land would place in the hands of the title-holders a *communal* right to decide how the land should be put to use, holding such title would seem to entail enjoying a communal right to govern (in relation to land-use matters) within the boundaries of that property.[152]

But what is the status and strength of this governance power? Imagine an Aboriginal community with Aboriginal title established. According to the understanding of Aboriginal title articulated in both *Delgamuukw* and *Tsilhqot'in Nation*, this community thereby enjoys the right to make collective decisions about land use in relation to this land. While this goes beyond the "bundle of rights" conception advanced by the Crown, how far would this community actually *control* land use on this part of its territory?[153]

---

151 See e.g. McNeil, "Aboriginal Title as a Constitutionally Protected Property Right," *supra* note 100. For an acceptance of this form of argument, see *Campbell v British Columbia (AG)*, 2001 BCSC 1400, Williamson J.

152 See Kent McNeil, *Defining Aboriginal Title in the 90's: Has the Supreme Court Finally Got It Right?* (Toronto: Robarts Centre for Canadian Studies, 1998) (pointing this out shortly after *Delgamuukw* came down from the high court). It has become a commonly accepted position, though the Supreme Court has not pronounced on this interpretation. In *Tsilhqot'in Nation*, *supra* note 4, for example, they only said at paragraphs 75–6 that:

> Aboriginal title post-sovereignty reflects the fact of Aboriginal occupancy pre-sovereignty, with all the pre-sovereignty incidents of use and enjoyment that were part of the collective title enjoyed by the ancestors of the claimant group – most notably the right to control how the land is used. However, these uses are not confined to the uses and customs of pre-sovereignty times; like other land-owners, Aboriginal title holders of modern times can use their land in modern ways, if that is their choice.
>
> The right to control the land conferred by Aboriginal title means that governments and others seeking to use the land must obtain the consent of the Aboriginal title holders. If the Aboriginal group does not consent to the use, the government's only recourse is to establish that the proposed incursion on the land is justified under s. 35 of the *Constitution Act, 1982.*

153 See Gordon Christie, "Who Makes Decisions over Aboriginal Title Lands?" (2015) 48 UBC L Rev 743. See also John Borrows, "Aboriginal Title in Tsilhqot'in v. British Columbia [2014] SCC 44" (Aug 2014) Maori L Rev, online: <maorilawreview.co.nz/2014/08/aboriginal-title-in-tsilhqotin-v-british-columbia-2014-scc-44/>:

> [T]he Supreme Court of Canada assumed away Indigenous peoples' underlying title and overarching governance powers in the *Tsilhqot'in* decision. While a future decision might recognize Indigenous governance power there is now a new obstacle for future actions to address: the presumptive application of provincial laws of general application to Indigenous lands. This obstacle is present courtesy of the application of a troublingly modified terra nullius assumption.

Besides the fact it would most likely have to abide by usual restrictions that attach to any property within Canadian property regimes,[154] this community's interests would be subject to federal and (from *Tsilhqot'in Nation*) provincial exercise of power. Imagine, for example, that this particular community felt very strongly, as a collective, that its title lands should be mostly free of intrusive resource-exploitation activities. Imagine as well that exploratory work has already indicated that there are significant mineral deposits under the surface of this land, and that regional and national economies would receive substantial boosts through further exploration and mine development. Could this community *prevent* this sort of activity from being authorized through Crown infringement? Almost certainly not, should the Crown act to meet its fiduciary obligations in matters like consultation and compensation.[155]

We noted earlier the odd use of the term "consent" in the *Tsilhqot'in Nation* judgment. In that decision the Court said, "The right to control the land conferred by Aboriginal title means that governments and others seeking to use the land must obtain the consent of the Aboriginal title holders."[156] This seemingly strong statement about the power Aboriginal title vested in title-holders was followed immediately, however, by this sentence: "If the Aboriginal group does not consent to the use, the government's only recourse is to establish that the proposed incursion on the land is justified under s. 35 of the *Constitution Act, 1982*."[157] The result of this strange set of statements seems to be that no Aboriginal title-holder could complain after activity had been authorized by the Crown on its title-lands if, as a matter of process, its consent had in fact been *sought* beforehand (*not* that it had been *given*).

And so we turn to section 35 itself, to see how current Canadian jurisprudence has generally approached Aboriginal rights to govern. Broader or more substantial rights to govern are not easily pulled out of the apparatus assembled by *Van der Peet* around Aboriginal rights. One might wonder, indeed, how to pull out what are essentially *powers* from a test meant to narrowly define culturally based rights (especially when these "rights" are just activities).

---

154 The Supreme Court noted in *Delgamuukw* that Aboriginal title runs parallel in nature to land interests on reserves, and that it is a form of property interest within Canadian law. See *supra* note 4. It would seem that it would be, then, subject to federal power to regulate *as property* (which would run outside matters of infringement).

155 This would likely be the case outside pieces of land held pursuant to particularly important cultural interests, such as burial grounds. Consent might be required in certain narrowly defined circumstances, and "[s]ome cases may even require the full consent of an aboriginal nation, particularly when provinces enact hunting and fishing regulations in relation to aboriginal lands": *Delgamuukw*, *supra* note 4 at para 168.

156 *Tsilhqot'in Nation*, *supra* note 4 at para 76.

157 *Ibid* at para 76.

In one of the very few cases in this area, *R v Pamajewon*,[158] the Supreme Court held to the basic strictures laid out in the earlier *Van der Peet* judgment, requiring that the rights-claimant argue for a narrowly defined right, one that could be shown is tied to a "practice, custom or tradition" integral to the culture of this Aboriginal community at the time of contact with Europeans. The Shawanaga First Nation and Eagle Lake First Nation had run afoul of provincial law in operating bingo halls without provincial licences. They argued the operations were authorized under by-laws they had passed under the authority of their rights to self-govern. The court-run process of characterization, however, narrowed their claim to a right to "regulate high-stakes gambling," and at that point on the outcome was not at issue, as it was not surprising the Aboriginal nations could not establish its existence.

The obvious conundrum circles back to core puzzles articulated earlier in other contexts: why should it be presumed that Indigenous governance capacities must meet narrow tests set out in *Van der Peet*? Tied to this are mysteries about what became of Indigenous self-determination through the long history of Crown-Indigenous interaction. Not only does discussion begin with the presumption of overarching Crown sovereignty, but connected to it seems to be the thought that whatever forms Indigenous sovereignty might retain, they all exist *within* this larger sovereign structure.[159] We arrive, once again, at a core sense of puzzlement about Aboriginal rights.

Initial Thoughts on Puzzles

We now have in hand an overview of jurisprudence on Aboriginal rights, one tied to an articulation of puzzles that emerge from the case law, particularly those that connect to Indigenous perspectives on history, society, identity, and law. One response to the puzzles might be to suggest that they express misunderstandings about what Canadian law is responding to, or unsupported evaluations dependent on peculiar senses of what ought to have transpired over the last thirty years and more.

The fact is Canadian courts function to develop and implement, within the confines of the Canadian legal order, an approach to Crown-Indigenous relations that emanates from a specific set of understandings of justice and fairness. This can be pulled apart into two distinct, though interwoven, concerns. First, *all* this happens *within* the judicial system of one of the two interacting bodies, with independent Indigenous legal and political authority playing no role in

158 *R v Pamajewon*, [1996] 2 SCR 821, 138 DLR (4th) 204.

159 For a presentation of a model of this, see *Mitchell v MNR*, *supra* note 22 at 111–73, Binnie J, concurring.

how all this jurisprudence is being developed and implemented. Second, the specific set of understandings of justice and fairness at play in this Canadian jurisprudence are themselves products of this one side of the equation, and their content does not reflect understandings of justice and fairness that animate independent Indigenous legal and political orders.

It is essential that both components of this troubling and puzzling model are fully appreciated. On the one hand there is only one system of legal authority at play in the development of this jurisprudence, and on the other hand there is only one understanding of what the nature of the situation might be like that is animating this authority as it builds law to govern the lives of Indigenous peoples (who become Aboriginal peoples through this activity). At the heart of all this are two distinct perspectives on the world around us: *that of the Crown and its courts* – that Indigenous peoples are *already* subsumed within the nation state of Canada, the only details being how this subsumption will be finalized in a new "just and fair" arrangement – and *that of Indigenous peoples* – that the project of colonialism is not complete, and that before an internal "just and fair" arrangement can be imagined, first the matter of the existence of *continuing* multiple independent legal and political authorities must be acknowledged and addressed.

One might wonder why these perspectives exist and how one could justify the holding of either, but while I inject a few words about this, these are not meant to signal the start of a journey down such an investigative route. Rather, I offer a few words just to highlight the challenges that perspectives play in trying to make sense of the law on Aboriginal rights.

There are, of course, "realist" arguments lying at the core of the Crown's perspective – the notion that the Crown believes the power of the state has overwhelmed Indigenous communities. These arguments are likely allied with notions of capitalism and neoliberalism emergent out of centuries of history of dispossession and alienation. But these suggestions lead into just the sorts of arguments best left to later investigations, building on the work in this text. Before we get to such arguments, we find ourselves with arguments meant to operate on the level of principle.

In a series of papers, Jeremy Waldron argues that, as time passes, what was formerly unjust comes to be fairly judged just (or at least not unjust).[160] Within the "supersession of historic injustice" argument, it is not simply the passing of time that creates this change in evaluation – rather, as *circumstances* change, some may bring to bear "morally relevant" changes, of the sort that evaluations

160 Jeremy Waldron, "Superseding Historic Injustice" (1992) 103(1) Ethics 4; Jeremy Waldron, "Redressing Historic Injustice" (2002) 52 UTLJ 135; Jeremy Waldron, "Supersession and Sovereignty" (2006) New York University Public Law and Legal Theory Working Papers, paper 406.

today of what might have been unjust in the past should alter. One might think, for example, that odious acts of colonialism need to be addressed in today's world, but Waldron argues the supersession argument reveals the mistake in this thinking, pointing the way to the proper approach to addressing the place of Aboriginal peoples in modern liberal democracies, an approach that is necessarily "forward-thinking." One might think (or hope) the High Court of Australia had in mind such an argument when they spoke in *Mabo* of the "tide of history" washing over Aboriginal peoples and their historic claims (I am assuming most would think it better they had a supersession argument in mind rather than the notion that just the passage of time simpliciter could have such effects).[161]

However, a moment's thought about the structure of this argument should give one pause.[162] Notions of both "justice" and "morally relevant" changes are simply presumed to have content – which is conveniently provided within the world view of the non-Indigenous scholar. Can these presumptions build new forms of reality within which Indigenous peoples now find themselves?

Let us imagine this sort of supersession argument in the minds of Canadian jurists as they think of the history of Crown-Indigenous relations. They may very well imagine that the dispossession of Indigenous peoples of their traditional territories, the oppression of Indigenous peoples under overtly colonial law and policy, and attempts to destroy Indigenous modes of creating and transmitting knowledge that amount to cultural genocide were clearly historically unjust activities of the state (fully assisted by its courts). However, they may also place all these events firmly in the past, and now imagine Indigenous peoples are – through changing and changed "morally relevant" circumstances – citizens of a liberal democracy, subject to good governance and falling within a system that promotes liberty and equality. The "tide of history" has washed over Indigenous peoples, and what was unjust does not now require redress.

However, there are significant complications in this seemingly straightforward argument that render it highly suspect – so suspect that it should be set aside, at best left as a parallel to the arguments presented by Indigenous collectives. First is the unjust historical activities of the Crown (and its supportive courts). There was a strong voice throughout the dark colonial era that ignored or dismissed the notions that dispossession, oppression, and cultural genocide were unjust. One can certainly locate countervailing voices (many of which, naturally, were the voices of Indigenous peoples). But clearly the dismissive voice within the power centres of the state was dominant, as it carried the day for generations.

161 Mabo and Others v Queensland (No. 2) (1992) HCA 23.

162 The general nature of these criticisms is laid out in Gordon Christie, "The Supersession of Indigenous Understandings of Justice and Morals" (forthcoming).

One might dismiss this fact, resting one's arguments about justice and injustice on what is *today* considered to be the forms these measures take on. But this, then, needs to be carefully explored, as the normative notions at play in (for example) Waldron's work are remarkably narrow. Unsurprisingly, they reflect unreflective acceptance of Western notions of justice and fairness, of theories of political morality that emerge from centuries of the growth of arguments about the reasons for the state, about state-citizen relations, and about the nature of human nature. Much of the discussion in chapter 6, exploring current thought on liberalism and liberal positivism, highlights the narrow origins and equally narrow debates that these theories of political morality and the law exhibit.

As damning as these points are, the core shortcoming of supersession arguments lies elsewhere. What are the "morally relevant" changing circumstances in any argument of supersession of historic injustice? More to the point, *who* determines what they might be? Not surprisingly, in Waldron's examples, discussion of moral relevance tracks the same narrowness we see with his treatment of justice and injustice. Those changing circumstances that warrant reappraisal of injustice are those that trigger concerns held by liberal theorists.

Returning to the point at which we slid into this short aside, we had noted the Crown (and its courts) seem to operate within a world structured upon the presumption that Indigenous peoples are already contained within the liberal state as citizens, while many Indigenous people (and entire communities) hold to the independence of Indigenous legal and political authority. We considered the arguments the Crown (and its courts) could appeal to in giving life to their presumptions but now note that the most common argument rests on the notion that non-Indigenous theories of morals and political morality should supply the required normative premises. Why should Indigenous peoples accept these normative underpinnings of the supersession arguments? Because their lives and capacities for meaning-generation are captured within the liberal state!

These last few words on the nature of the puzzles that animate Canadian jurisprudence on Aboriginal rights were meant to highlight the general Indigenous perspective that generates so many of these mysteries. Rather than begin our analysis of this jurisprudence with the presumption it requires only an internal form of critique (that, for example, the liberalism that we will see in chapters 6 and 7 that this area of law exhibits is not fully realized, that the current law fails to adequately protect Indigenous individuals as free and equal in Canadian society) we begin with the sense that Canadian law sits alongside separate and independent Indigenous legal and political authorities, with Indigenous communities continuing to exercise their capacities to determine what *law* might mean, indeed what *justice* and *fairness* might mean, and what *reconciliation* might require.

In the next chapter we look more closely into how one might respond to the law so far described. We first turn to the sorts of evaluations we find as general observers consider the nature of Aboriginal rights. Towards the end of this investigation we introduce theoretical accounts, to record some of the variance we encounter in reasoned efforts to make sense of Aboriginal rights. All this collects into a mass of problems we need to address if we hope to make sense of Aboriginal rights. The next chapter ends with a detailed examination into how I propose to undertake this exercise.

3 Differing Understandings and the Way Forward

Understandings and Evaluations

We begin with a point made earlier, that from one perspective Aboriginal law can seem progressive, while from another it can seem oppressive. Consider, in that regard, two of the most common – and opposed – general views on the history and nature of Canadian Aboriginal law.

On one side, some see in the general history of the relationship between the Canadian state and Indigenous peoples primarily a tale of dispossession, alienation, cultural (and physical) genocide, desecration, fraud, and racism.[1] On the other side, we find those who – while quite often acknowledging the same events in history – see in this relationship a story of progress, the rise of civilization (in political, economic, and social terms), and efforts to work towards a just and equitable relationship between Aboriginal and non-Aboriginal societies.

---

1 See e.g. Taiaiake Alfred, *Peace, Power, Righteousness: An Indigenous Manifesto* (Don Mills, ON: Oxford University Press, 1999) [Alfred, *Peace, Power, Righteousness*]; Taiaiake Alfred, *Wasáse: Indigenous Pathways of Action and Freedom* (Peterborough, ON: Broadview Press, 2005); Glen Sean Coulthard, *Red Skin, White Mask: Rejecting the Colonial Politics of Recognition* (Minneapolis: University of Minnesota Press, 2014); Howard Adams, *Prison of Grass: Canada From a Native Point of View* (Saskatoon, SK: Fifth House Publishing, 1989).

In its executive report, the Truth and Reconciliation Commission referred to the effect of the residential school system as "cultural genocide." See Truth and Reconciliation Commission of Canada, *Honouring the Truth, Reconciling for the Future: Summary of the Final Report of the Truth and Reconciliation Commission of Canada* (2015), online: <http://www.chaireconditionautochtone.fss.ulaval.ca/documents/pdf/Honouring-the-truth-reconciling-for-the-future.pdf> at 1:

> For over a century, the central goals of Canada's Aboriginal policy were to eliminate Aboriginal governments; ignore Aboriginal rights; terminate the Treaties; and, through a process of assimilation, cause Aboriginal peoples to cease to exist as distinct legal, social, cultural, religious, and racial entities in Canada. The establishment and operation of residential schools were a central element of this policy, which can best be described as "cultural genocide."

When we narrow focus within this relationship to the role Canadian law has played over the last 150 years, different understandings are just as starkly opposed, if more subtly structured. My experience has been that when educated about the role this institution played in the Canadian–Aboriginal relationship until the middle of the twentieth century, Canadians of all backgrounds often change their views significantly on the nature of Canadian law – from thinking of it as a benign or positive institution to seeing it as *at best* benign in *some* instances. In the earlier overtly colonial era, Canadian law (and policy) was clearly designed to facilitate (and justify) the dispossession – and indeed elimination – of Indigenous peoples. While (seemingly) acceptable to some at that time, in our time these practices seem, to most, to be unfortunate and even genocidal.[2]

Matters become more difficult when attention is focused on events past the mid-point of the past century. Many (even some within the larger Aboriginal community) see developments within Canadian law and policy over the last fifty years in a mostly positive light,[3] while significant numbers (especially within Aboriginal communities),[4] while acknowledging that some developments could be seen as positive, hold that the law has been generally regressive and/or oppressive right through this period, up to present times.[5]

Arguably, this is not just about how history *looks* to varied parties, but how parties *understand* what went on and is going on. If it were only the former, one explanation could be that bias has crept in, as claims to "understanding" in

---

2 *Ibid.*

3 See e.g. Thomas Isaac, "Balancing Rights: The Supreme Court of Canada, *R. v. Sparrow*, and the Future of Aboriginal Rights" (1993) 13 Can J Native Stud 199; Calvin Helin, *Dances with Dependency: Out of Poverty through Self-Reliance* (Woodland Hills, CA: Ravencrest, 2008).

4 See e.g. D'Arcy Vermette, "Dizzying Dialogue: Canadian Courts and the Continuing Justification of the Dispossession of Aboriginal Peoples" (2011) 29 Windsor YB Access Just 243 [Vermette, "Dizzying Dialogue"]; D'Arcy Vermette, "Colonialism and the Suppression of Aboriginal Voice" (2009) 40 Ottawa L Rev 225; D'Arcy Vermette, "Colonialism and the Process of Defining Aboriginal People" (2008) 31 Dal LJ 211; Patricia Monture-Angus, *Journeying Forward: Dreaming First Nations' Independence* (Halifax: Fernwood, 1999). A look into the archives of Aboriginal newspapers offers a glimpse into fairly common sentiments in "Indian Country." See e.g. *Windspeaker*, online: <ammsa.com/category/article-origin/windspeaker>. I should be clear, however, that I undertook no survey – careful or not – in forming impressions conveyed over the last few paragraphs of the text. Much of this should be taken as that – impressions formed from numerous conversations, often at conferences on Aboriginal legal-political issues in Canada held over the last few decades.

5 Of course there are also others – likely representing a significant number of Canadians – who see in Aboriginal law misguided developments, as they understand there to be no need for "special rights" or other legal instruments. See e.g. Thomas Flanagan, *First Nations? Second Thoughts* (Montreal & Kingston: McGill-Queen's University Press, 2000); Frances Widdowson & Albert Howard, *Disrobing the Aboriginal Industry: The Deception behind Indigenous Cultural Preservation* (Montreal & Kingston: McGill-Queen's University Press, 2008) [Widdowson & Howard].

this regard are seen to be coloured by perception. To the extent, however, that the divergence is about understandings of what has been going on within the world built through and around the jurisprudence, these differences in position are more interesting and more problematic. Here we come face-to-face with the possibility that perspectives (broadly construed) play an important role in accounting for divergence in understanding (and not merely perception).

While some of this divergence of position is likely the result of historical misinformation (or lack of information), a significant extent seems to be the result of the imposition of layers of interpretation laid on events and "facts." One might argue that contemporary facts – such as they exist, on a physical or non-interpretive level – can be removed from serious contestation. For example, we could set out a survey detailing laws and regulations passed, agreements ratified, measures taken to implement agreements reached, and so on. We could further track numbers over recent decades reflecting how many (or what percentage of) Aboriginal people have access to clean drinking water, how many have indoor plumbing, how many have access to an educational experience of such-and-such nature, how many are incarcerated, what the levels of employment might be, what the rates are in communities of suicides (or attempts), or how many have access to a health system that provides such-and-such a level of care, and so forth.[6] These numbers and events, however, (a) have *meaning* only in the context of set views about what count as indicators of a meaningful life, on both individual and community and collective levels, and (b) can be seen only as expressing something essential or defining within a framework of analysis that sees and understands the "problem" with Aboriginal peoples in this way. This is to say that "facts" pointed to are contestable – not so much as "facts" (though that is so to some extent),[7] but as *relevant and interpreted facts.*

---

6 Governments of Canada have collected data on the "well-being" of Aboriginal populations for over a century. Large collections of data can be found in different government sites. For a tracking of many indicators, see e.g. Statistics Canada, "Aboriginal Peoples: Key Indicators" (2019), online: <www150.statcan.gc.ca/n1/en/subjects/aboriginal_peoples>. For other large datasets and collections of reports, see Crown-Indigenous Relations and Northern Affairs Canada, "The Reporting Guide" (2019), online: <aadnc-aandc.gc.ca/eng/1385559716700/1385559777677>; Employment and Social Development Canada, "Reports and Publications" (2018), online: <canada.ca/en/employment-social-development/corporate/reports.html>; Health Canada, "Reports and Publications – First Nations and Inuit Health" (2018), online: <canada.ca/en/indigenous-services-canada/services/first-nations-inuit-health/reports-publications.html>; Council of Ministers of Education, Canada, "Publications," online: <cmec.ca/9/Publications/index.html?searchCat=1>; Canada, Department of Justice, "Indigenous Peoples" (2018), online: <justice.gc.ca/eng/rp-pr/aj-ja/index.html>. Non-profit groups and Aboriginal organizations also conduct research on related topics. See e.g. Canadian Council on Social Development, online: <ccsd.ca>; First Nations Information Governance Centre, online: <fnigc.ca>.

7 This is because, to reiterate something suggested in a previous paragraph, it is hard to conceive of facts that are non-interpretive. Deciding which matters to explore, how these

To see this point more clearly, consider how these "facts" are put to use. Some people place primary emphasis on just such indicators, to measure the ability of the law to assist in finding or building an appropriate place for Aboriginal peoples in Canada in terms of how these sorts of numbers change.[8] Others, however, see these numbers as important indicators, but (a) question the historical and political forces that result in despair,[9] and (b) question whether then *other concerns* might be at least as pressing. To what extent, one might ask, have particular historical policies of the Canadian state led to problems faced by Aboriginal communities and individuals? More pointedly, how, precisely, are these problems to be *understood*?

A complex set of interconnections links such questions, a set that when laid out reveals the need to pay close heed to the sorts of Indigenous perspectives earlier described. The focus on social and economic indicators excludes other considerations that, from the point of view of those subject to generations of colonial law and policy, are at least equally pressing.

From a general Indigenous perspective, the story of times before the heavy hand of colonialism was laid upon Indigenous communities is that of collective self-determined existences.[10] Before the advent of the colonial era the many and varied Indigenous peoples living across what is now Canada generated and lived through their own forms of social reality, each Indigenous social formation regulating lives of individuals, families, clans (in some cases), and the larger community, and regulating interaction with neighbouring communities.

---

matters will be explored, how the data will be presented, etc., all conspire to make it hard to imagine such things exist as "pure" facts.

8 See e.g. Flanagan, *supra* note 5; Widdowson & Howard, *supra* note 5; Thomas Isaac, *Aboriginal Law: Commentary and Analysis*, 5th ed (Toronto: Carswell, 2016) [Isaac, *Aboriginal Law*]. Complicating matters is the fact that over the last few decades these numbers either have not improved or (in the case of over-incarceration, for example) even become worse. For those who put great weight on such indicators, a clear lesson can still be gleaned from all this – it was a mistake to "grant" "special rights" to Aboriginal peoples. The better approach to the physical, social, and economic straits Aboriginal peoples find themselves in would be to finish the program of full assimilation. Flanagan, for example, would have remote reserves recognized as economically unfeasible, with the result being a final push to have the citizens of these communities move south to cities and towns (where, with the right focus on education and training – coupled with a proper Protestant work ethic – jobs, and fulfilling lives as wage-earners and consumers, await).

9 That is, these observers argue that the primary reason for the dire economic and social straits of Aboriginal communities and individuals lies in laws and policies of the Canadian state – laws, and policies that to a significant degree are not all in the past. Without such historical and political context firmly in mind, those in this camp allege, focus on such indicators will tend towards solutions that do not address the most pressing causes of the challenges faced.

10 This is not to romanticize this pre-contact period. I recall a conversation with elders a few years ago about how *hard* life was in their childhoods (when contact in the far north was a very recent phenomenon).

Those who measure progress and assess Aboriginal law by social and economic indicators pick out only certain strands of the historical narrative on Crown-Indigenous relations, which veer away from Indigenous perspectives on not just historical events, but on what it means to be human in distinct social settings. The world within which such observers live is circumscribed by a sense of Indigenous peoples being *already absorbed* into the body politic of Canadian society (of there being *only* "Aboriginal peoples *of* Canada"). A strand of the historical narrative at the core of Indigenous perspectives is that of the Crown's usurpation of de facto control over collective self-determined existences.

So which historical and political forces account for social, political, and economic situations within which Aboriginal peoples live, and what considerations – other than those tied to directly addressing these dire social and economic situations – are most pressing from an Indigenous perspective?

I noted earlier that some argue that rights under section 35 simply should not exist. Some of their arguments focus on these social and economic problems, their central argument being that Aboriginal (and treaty) rights cannot address these matters (and they get in the way of implementing programs of assimilation that would raise levels of indicators, with Aboriginal peoples in Canada coming to enjoy levels of education, health, employment, and so forth, comparable to the average Canadian).[11] Those who accept the existence of Aboriginal (and treaty) rights, and furthermore see them moving Canadian society towards "reconciliation" and a just world, seem to disagree fundamentally with assimilationists. But they, too, often appeal to these very same social and economic indicators, and in doing so reveal an underlying world view that coincides with assimilationists and conflicts with that of many Indigenous peoples.

While no one denies the importance of raising standards of living of Aboriginal peoples, from an Indigenous perspective there is *also* the loss of the ability to exercise collective means of self-determination. While some put this in terms of identity – to what extent can Aboriginal peoples maintain their identities as Cree/Nēhilawē, or Inuit, or Innu? – this is fundamentally a matter of self-determination. To what extent are Indigenous peoples able to chart their collective futures, caring for *themselves and their territories* through visions they carry forward from shared histories and world views? At the core of this power of self-determination for any Indigenous collective is the ability to continue to generate one's own sense of social reality, then live through meaning that one gives to the social world one constructs.

11 See e.g. Flanagan, *supra* note 5; Widdowson & Howard, *supra* note 5; Gordon Gibson, *A New Look at Canadian Indian Policy: Respect the Collective – Promote the Individual* (Vancouver: Fraser Institute, 2009).

Academic Understandings

When exploring the base level of social life we find ourselves engaging with the notion of perspective. We want to explore the nature of Aboriginal law and to consider whether its contemporary form is progressive or not and receive diametrically opposed views. Yet we cannot see why one perspective should be privileged, nor pin down a way of thinking about how to measure such a matter. One might begin to suspect that this all indeed comes down to perspective, with one's understanding of Aboriginal law tied to one's perspectival position in and on the world. The observer seems to engage in an interpretive enterprise that – depending on individual perspective – determines that the lives and situations of Aboriginal peoples in Canada improve through the development of Aboriginal rights or determines that Aboriginal peoples continue to be denied those matters essential to their self-defined interests.

This suggests we spend time with the notion of perspective to address this sort of problem, moving towards an adequate understanding of Aboriginal law. Does paying attention to perspective hold out hope in addressing puzzles noted above? One troubling possibility is that focusing on how differing perspectives function to interpret and evaluate Aboriginal law simply reinforces the notion that at some fundamental level of moral sensibility (or political morality) people fundamentally disagree, and that nothing can be done to effect convergence.[12] Similarly, it might be that starting from the fact of divergent perspectives leads nowhere other than a view of "communities of meaning," the notion that social-linguistic communities generate and live within distinct "normative universes."[13] Differing understandings of Aboriginal law would be ultimately explained, then, as nothing more than the product of different interpretations of the world, emanating from distinct normative realms. From within one such world Aboriginal law appears to be liberal and progressive, while from within another it appears colonial and oppressive.[14]

Legal positivism suggests a possible route forward. We might consider approaching Aboriginal law in a purely descriptive manner, to study the law in a way that seemingly puts aside evaluative (or other forms of normative) assessment. Following such an approach we would presumably arrive at an understanding of the nature of Aboriginal law as nothing more than a system of valid rules, tests, and procedures we can catalogue and describe.

12 See J David Velleman, *Foundations for Moral Relativism* (Cambridge, UK: Open Book, 2013).

13 See e.g. Robert Cover, "Nomos and Narrative" in Martha Minow, Michael Ryan & Austin Sarat, eds, *Narrative, Violence, and the Law: The Essays of Robert Cover* (Ann Arbor: University of Michigan Press, 1992) 95 [Cover, "Nomos and Narrative"].

14 An ethical non-cognitivist (or expressivist) might sum this up by pointing out that no more can be said about this matter than that one side says "hurrah" while the other proclaims "boo." See e.g. AJ Ayer, *Language, Truth, and Logic* (London: Gollancz, 1936).

There are several reasons to think this path is not promising. First, at best this seems to forestall the problems with which we hope to grapple. The positivist approach tightens the concept of law to the point where evaluative enterprises are (purportedly) removed from the scope of "legal" analysis, but this does not remove evaluative enterprises from the scene. They reappear. They are just removed from what is "properly" termed legal analysis – they return, that is, as moral or political concerns.[15] I am not interested in an analysis of Aboriginal law that stops short of *making sense* of the law, fully and richly. Whether this entails including within legal analysis evaluative measures or adding such evaluative concerns on top of "proper" legal analysis is not a central or pressing concern for me.[16]

Second, recall that I earlier pried apart concerns with bias from questions about perspectives. "Perspectival" concerns arguably infect not just evaluative mechanisms but also attempts to understand what has happened and is going on.

Nevertheless, something about the positivist approach suggests a way forward – perhaps we should not be concerned so much with how people *react* to the experience of living in relation to Aboriginal law, and instead focus on *analyses* of Aboriginal law. While positivism seems – at least on its own – unlikely to settle questions about the nature and merit of Aboriginal law, we might expect it would be more likely in the realm of critical reflection that we find movement towards resolution of such puzzles.

Differing Theoretical Perspectives

However, focus on analyses of Aboriginal law only generates further reasons to spend time in looking into challenging theoretical and philosophical matters. First, when we consider the efforts of *others* to make sense of the law – and more specifically, Aboriginal law – we notice further layers of seemingly fundamental

15 This is so in two ways. The way pointed to in this section should be obvious: once the work of detailing "the law" according to positivist analysis is carried out, the work of evaluating this law remains. The second way is pursued later in this text. I argue later (particularly in chapter 6) that positivism itself is arguably a sociocultural construct, that its vision of law expresses nothing more than a particular "perspective." This argument is, however, difficult to effectively summarize at this point, though I begin to sketch out its grounding in the next section.

16 Debate about this question about the borders of "the law" will be reintroduced in a later chapter and will prove fruitful in advancing the development of the particular methodological approach adopted in this work. It will also be argued that while the business of providing "purely descriptive" accounts is possible, this is so only when understood properly (and so carried out properly). A descriptive account, on naturalist groundings, must detail how *normative beliefs* inform the structure of the social system, which is to recognize that what is under examination is a social reality built through the manipulation and use of sociolinguistic tools and structures.

disagreement.[17] Furthermore, as we shall see when we step back to think of the place of the theoretician in this picture, questions arise about the positions of parties involved in such theoretical efforts.

On the one side we find numerous legal academics who expend considerable time and energy to explicate the nature of the jurisprudence carrying out "doctrinal analysis." Here we find, for example, works by Sebastien Grammond, Thomas Isaac, Peter Hogg, Brian Slattery, Dwight Newman, Kerry Wilkins, and Kent McNeil.[18] Some of these same academics also swell the ranks of those who find great promise in the recent development of Aboriginal law, seeing it exemplifying the common law as it "works itself pure by principles drawn from the fountain of justice."[19] Here we find again, for instance, Slattery, Grammond, Newman, and Isaac, joined by Mark Walters, John Borrows, Patrick Macklem, and Paul McHugh.[20]

---

17 Lange notes a similar form of fundamental disagreement about differing interpretations of colonial history. She notes, "On one hand, this history is presented as unjust appropriation and domination; on the other hand, it is cast as a civilizing or (more recently) a liberalizing or developmental process": Lynda Lange, "Dialogue, History, and Power: The Role of Truth" in Sandra Tomsons & Lorraine Mayer, eds, *Philosophy and Aboriginal Rights: Critical Dialogues* (Don Mills, ON: Oxford University Press, 2013) at 369.

18 Sebastien Grammond, *Terms of Coexistence: Indigenous Peoples and Canadian Law* (Toronto: Carswell, 2013); Isaac, *Aboriginal Law*, *supra* note 8; Peter Hogg, "The Constitutional Basis of Aboriginal Rights" in Maria Morellato, ed, *Aboriginal Law Since Delgamuukw* (Aurora: Canada Law Book, 2009) 3; Brian Slattery, "Understanding Aboriginal Rights" (1987) 66 Can Bar Rev 727; Brian Slattery, "The Legal Basis of Aboriginal Title" in Frank Cassidy, ed, *Aboriginal Title in British Columbia: Delgamuukw v. The Queen* (Fernie: Oolichan Books, 1992) 113; Brian Slattery, "Making Sense of Aboriginal and Treaty Rights" (2000) 79 Can Bar Rev 196 [Slattery, "Making Sense of Aboriginal and Treaty Rights"]; Brian Slattery, "The Metamorphosis of Aboriginal Title" (2006) 85 Can Bar Rev 255; Dwight Newman, *Revisiting the Duty to Consult Aboriginal Peoples* (Saskatoon: Purich Publishing, 2014); Kent McNeil, *Emerging Justice? Essays on Indigenous Rights in Canada and Australia* (Saskatoon: Native Law Centre, 2001). For the most complete and clear piece of doctrinal analysis, see especially Kerry Wilkins, *Essentials of Canadian Aboriginal Law* (Toronto: Carswell, 2018). While I include Wilkin's text in this quick survey, note I would not actually place Wilkins into a camp of doctrinal analysts, as he notes in the *Preface* to this work that he was under clear instructions to simply "describe the law accurately." Elsewhere Wilkins is clear in his criticisms. A similar point could be made about the work of Kent McNeil. Slattery's work, on the other hand, has a very specific doctrinal flavour, explored in an upcoming section.

19 Walters refers to this famous quote from Lord Mansfield in several pieces. See e.g. Mark D Walters, "Histories of Colonialism, Legality, and Aboriginality" (2007) 57 UTLJ 819 at 829; Mark D Walters, "The Morality of Aboriginal Law" (2006) 31 Queen's LJ 470.

20 *Ibid*; John Borrows, *Recovering Canada: The Resurgence of Indigenous Law* (Toronto: University of Toronto Press, 2002); John Borrows, *Canada's Indigenous Constitution* (Toronto: University of Toronto Press, 2010); Patrick Macklem, *Indigenous Difference and the Constitution of* Canada (Toronto: University of Toronto Press, 2001) [Macklem, *Indigenous Difference*]; Paul McHugh, *Aboriginal Societies and the Common Law: A History of Sovereignty, Status, and Self-Determination* (Oxford: Oxford University Press, 2004); Patrick

On the other side we come across the camp of sceptics and critics, those who deeply question the ability of Canadian law to effect justice for Indigenous peoples. Sceptical concerns emanate from two widely opposed camps – first, those who go beyond sceptical concerns to find efforts in the jurisprudence to continue generations-old colonial law and policy, and second, those who find in Aboriginal law a barrier to the "proper" goal of fully assimilating Indigenous peoples into the general social-political milieu. In the former camp we find, for instance, Taiaiake Alfred, Patricia Monture-Angus, James Youngblood (Sakej) Henderson, D'Arcy Vermette, Larry Chartrand, Peter Russell, Grace Woo, and Michael Asch,[21] while in the latter we can identify Tom Flanagan, Frances Widdowson, Albert Howard, and Gordon Gibson.[22]

Finding these further layers of fundamental disagreement heightens the frustration and distress that come from seeing how people disagree widely in general about Aboriginal law. We here witness a parallel divergence, though on two levels. When we look at this literature we witness not only divergent opinions on the nature and merit of Aboriginal law, but also divergent

---

Macklem & Douglas Sanderson, eds, *From Recognition to Reconciliation: Essays on the Constitutional Entrenchment of Aboriginal and Treaty Rights* (Toronto: University of Toronto Press, 2016) [Macklem & Sanderson]. See especially *ibid* at 17–203.

It is not an easy or definitive matter putting scholars into the categories I use in this section – John Borrows, for example, seems at times to be arguing in a highly critical fashion, challenging the very core of constitutional law and the common law as it relates to Aboriginal peoples in Canada. See e.g. John Borrows, "Sovereignty's Alchemy: An Analysis of *Delgamuukw v. British Columbia*" (1999) 37 Osgoode Hall LJ 537. But on the whole his message – in relation to Canadian law – seems fairly positive, as though it is just a matter of Canadian law (and jurists) failing to see what is required according to the very principles buried within it (such as adherence to the rule of law). Likewise, while I place Larry Chartrand in the more critical camp, his work also at times suggests he may well believe the Canadian system is not built around irremediable colonial mechanisms and principles, but rather has within it the necessary components from within which justice (appropriate to Aboriginal peoples) might flourish. See note 21.

21 Alfred, *Peace, Power, Righteousness*, *supra* note 1; Monture-Angus, *supra* note 4; James Youngblood (Sakej) Henderson, *First Nations Jurisprudence and Aboriginal Rights: Defining the Just Society* (Saskatoon, SK: Native Law Centre, 2006); James Youngblood (Sakej) Henderson, "Postcolonial Indigenous Legal Consciousness" (Spring 2002) Indigenous LJ 1; Vermette, "Dizzying Dialogue," *supra* note 4; Larry Chartrand, "The Aboriginal Peoples' Movement and Its Critics" in Joseph E Magnet & Dwight A Dorey, eds, *Aboriginal Rights Litigation* (Markham, ON: Butterworths, 2003) 453; Peter Russell, *Recognizing Aboriginal Title: The Mabo Case and Indigenous Resistance to English-Settler Colonialism* (Toronto: University of Toronto Press, 2005); Grace Li Xiu Woo, *Ghost Dancing with Colonialism: Decolonization and Indigenous Rights at the Supreme Court of Canada* (Vancouver: UBC Press, 2011); Michael Asch, *Home and Native Land: Aboriginal Rights and the Canadian Constitution* (Toronto: Methuen, 1984); Michael Asch, *On Being Here to Stay: Treaties and Aboriginal Rights in Canada* (Toronto: University of Toronto Press, 2014).

22 Flanagan, *supra* note 5; Widdowson & Howard, *supra* note 5; Gibson, *supra* note 11.

(and seemingly incommensurable) points of view about the way one should *approach* the project of theorizing the nature of Aboriginal law.[23]

How do these scholars arrive at their interpretations of the nature of Canadian Aboriginal law? Flanagan (and Widdowson, and Gibson) might be categorized as a classical liberal, focused almost entirely on the notion of the individual and the need to structure society so that *only* individual rights and interests carry weight and are protected.[24] Flanagan's interpretation, given the fact that over the last few centuries colonialism has shifted almost all power, wealth, and land to non-Aboriginal society, is powerfully conservative, arguing forcefully for the status quo (achieved through a final push for complete assimilation).

Brian Slattery, on the other hand, provides both "taxonomies" for Aboriginal rights (which lie on top of what the courts have said about the nature of Aboriginal rights a system of classification meant to capture hidden forms of structure and content) and critiques based on "principles of justice." His view is of the Supreme Court exploring new territory, coming upon a landscape touched on only in years past, a land it slowly maps out.[25] To the extent the

---

23 *Cf.* Monture-Angus, *supra* note 4; Flanagan, *supra* note 5. *Cf.* Mary Ellen Turpel, "Aboriginal Peoples and the Canadian Charter: Interpretive Monopolies, Cultural Differences" (1989–90) 1989 Can Hum Rts YB 3; Newman, *Revisiting the Duty to Consult, supra* note 18; Slattery, "Making Sense of Aboriginal and Treaty Rights," *supra* note 18. I briefly contrast the approaches of Flanagan, Slattery, and Monture-Angus in the next few paragraphs of the text.

Such comparisons, of course, do not fall along simple Aboriginal/non-Aboriginal lines (defined either ethnographically or politically), as many Aboriginal scholars have mixed cultural and intellectual backgrounds, just as many non-Aboriginal scholars provide interpretations or understandings that align fairly well with those proffered by Aboriginal commentators (Michael Asch, for example, has consistently provided interpretations that align fairly closely with those offered by Monture-Angus or Sakej Henderson).

24 Flanagan accepts that his work could lead to him being labelled "either conservative or libertarian, if that means 'classical liberal'": Flanagan, *supra* note 5 at 8. Over the next few paragraphs he lays out a vision easily pulled out of classical liberalism, when tied to Hayekian economic theory.

25 Slattery begins with this remarkable set of images in "Making Sense of Aboriginal and Treaty Rights," *supra* note 18 at 197:

> Over the past thirty years, the Supreme Court of Canada has begun remapping the neglected territory of aboriginal and treaty rights. It has done so piecemeal, in a series of important decisions.... When it started, the Court had little to go on. The results of previous forays into this territory had been uncertain at best and misleading at worst. The leading authority ... was replete with dubious assumptions and obscure terminology. In effect, the Supreme Court inherited a sketch map of shadowy coasts and fabulous isles, with monsters at every turn.
>
> Let it be said that the Supreme Court has fared well in its initial ventures. Little-known areas have been brought to light and apocryphal seas dispelled. We now know broadly what is *terra firma* and what is not, and the monsters have been largely tamed or banished to the decorative margins. Nevertheless, the first fruits of the Court's labours amount to a series of explorer's charts, enlightening

landscape is improperly recognized, he steps in to provide appropriate guidance. Many mainstream legal academics working in this field seem to function along similar lines – they provide occasional criticism grounded on amorphous principles of justice. In effect they imagine the Supreme Court is following – or trying to follow – guideposts that set out how the jurisprudence should develop (for it to reflect principles of justice and fairness).[26]

Patricia Monture-Angus, on the other hand, approaches the analysis of Aboriginal law from the perspective of a Mohawk woman. The Mohawk never ceded their lands, authority, and intellectual traditions to the Crown, and so her analysis naturally begins from a point external to the Canadian system, questioning at a fundamental level how this foreign system could presume legitimacy in its application to those forcefully pulled into its orbit. This analysis works outward from an initial point within a Mohawk world, a world that carries within itself a separate vocabulary, separate sets of understandings, and separate normative visions. From this perspective Monture-Angus came to see that "law contains no answers but is in fact a very large and very real part of the problem Aboriginal people continue to face. Law is one of the instruments through which colonialism continues to flow."[27]

Her approach, beginning from within the Mohawk world of ideas, principles, and values, is not "to displace the western or liberal theory of rights with an Aboriginal theory of rights," as to do so would be to risk capture within the underlying Western discourse.[28] Rather, in relation to the Canadian approach to Aboriginal rights all she can meaningfully contribute is realization "that the theory is excluding my voice."[29] Behind this is forceful articulation of the basic

---

so far as they go, but covering different areas, drawn in varying projections, and sometimes bearing an uncertain relation to one another. We lack a reliable *mappamundi*. The purpose of this paper is to attempt such a map – one that surveys the subject as a whole and displays the various parts in their proper dimensions and inter-relationships.

26 Macklem's *Indigenous Difference* is founded on one central pillar, the principle of equality. As "equality" itself does not tell us "which similarities or differences might be relevant to the justice of any given distribution," Macklem's text spells out the sorts of Indigenous difference that should be understood to ground appropriate considerations, leading to a sense of equality that can guide law and policy. Insofar as his analysis goes far beyond cultural difference to explore matters of territory and sovereignty, his analysis is critical (given that cultural difference seems to be the primary – arguably the only – form of difference accorded weight by the Supreme Court). While this appeal to equality as the fundamental organizing principle clearly puts Macklem in the modern liberal camp, the notion that the law could adopt a broader vision of what differences should be taken into account to ground an appropriate approach to the question of equality signals what sort of essentially positive view he takes of Canadian law. See Macklem, *Indigenous Difference*, *supra* note 20 at 29.

27 Monture-Angus, *supra* note 4 at 9.

28 *Ibid* at 55.

29 *Ibid* at 55–6.

position, that work must be undertaken *from within* Indigenous communities in rebuilding relationships (work that goes to the heart of self-determination), where part of this includes reminding "ourselves that our experience and understanding are equally legitimate and encompass complete authority."[30] This work – beginning from within a separate world of understanding and authority – leads to a very different view of the nature of Canadian law as it applies to Indigenous peoples.

Monture-Angus clearly presents herself working from a situated perspective. Flanagan and Slattery do not do so. This latter fact is of considerable interest in the context of this study. Do scholars like Flanagan and Slattery occupy a point of view that is really not a point of view? Let us conclude this introductory discussion of diverging positions on Aboriginal law by digging just a little more deeply into possible roles played by perspective.

Theoretical Accounts and "Perspectives"

While there are interesting parallels and overlaps between this situation (of opposed theoretical interpretations) and the one outlined earlier in relation to general views on Aboriginal law, on at least one count there is substantial dissimilarity. Earlier we considered the role perspective might play in how a party might understand Aboriginal law, with the focus on how this field of law might strike someone living "within" the Canadian system.[31] The possibility of divergence in understanding was postulated as being substantially the product of differing moral and political sensibilities (themselves possibly tied to the nature of the moral evaluator as living in one normative world rather than another). Here, however, we are thinking of parties one might reasonably presume aim to rise above such matters as moral or political or ideological groundings. Theoreticians are well aware of concerns that moral groundings might influence, bias, or contaminate studies, and so one might reasonably expect they would strive to examine the world around in ways that – to the extent possible – these concerns are addressed.[32] That is, it would seem one way to distinguish activity on the level of theorizing from activity on a primary level of understanding and evaluation is that on this "higher" level one can expect that serious questions of methodology arise and are addressed.

30 *Ibid* at 56.

31 The term "within" poses some difficulties here, as one can describe Aboriginal peoples (and individuals) as living within Canadian law, but also arguably describe many such political communities (and their members) as living (at least to some degree) outside this system.

32 Leiter tackles this matter in his discussion of Dworkin's interpretive, non-Archimedean approach to legal theory. See Brian Leiter, "Objectivity, Morality, and Adjudication" in Brian Leiter, *Naturalizing Jurisprudence: Essays on American Legal Realism and Naturalism in Legal Philosophy* (Oxford: Oxford University Press, 2007) 225 [Leiter, *Naturalizing Jurisprudence*].

In fact, however, we see little to no work of that sort in the literature. Theoreticians from the main camps do not engage each other, arguing about which approach to the analysis of law might be objectively better.[33] Focusing on the bulk of analysis, one could reasonably distil the two most prominent camps to these positions: the mainstream liberal camp begins with a given framework (what I term "liberal positivism" in the rest of this text)[34] from within which they occasionally try to accommodate the Indigenous perspective, while those challenging the "givenness" of this liberal framework (a group I loosely amalgamate and place into the field of "critical theory" in the rest of this work) see this way of understanding and dealing with the "Aboriginal problem" itself responsible for primary challenges Indigenous communities have experienced and continue to experience.[35] Arguably, the two talk past each other.

Meanwhile, weaving in and around these two camps, but often situating themselves on the margins or even outside them both, we find Indigenous scholars. Indigenous understandings can on occasion be located *outside* this apparent dichotomy, by those who see or intuit that these two mainstream camps share essential features (both being forms of discourse that do not address the fundamental problem from an Indigenous perspective, that of the oppressive imposition of a foreign system upon Indigenous worlds). What is one to say – hoping to make sense of Aboriginal rights – in light of this lack of theoretical engagement on questions of methodology?

Further, reflecting on this a bit more, we can see it might be that the *place* of the theoretician is also a point of concern. To see how this might be so, consider one instantiation of larger struggles between different forms of theorizing.

33 It might appear Dwight Newman is working on this level, as, building on Charles Taylor's work, he attempts to advance a theory of cross-cultural dialogue. See e.g. Dwight Newman, "You Still Know Nothin' 'Bout Me: Toward Cross-Cultural Theorizing of Aboriginal Rights" (2007) 52 McGill LJ 725. But this, too, is presented not as a way to address divergence in theoretical understandings and approaches, but as an articulation of one particular theoretical understanding and approach. Arguably, it attempts to address the lower level of divergence, as it is crafted as a way to bring together those who express what are posited as divergent moral or normative views. But why would this approach be appropriate as a way of understanding what is happening in the jurisprudence? And how does it provide a *better* theory of the nature of Aboriginal law?

34 I lump many into this camp of "liberal positivists," knowing that a fair number might have to be pushed and twisted to actually fit under this label. Those who might otherwise seem to be in the camp of natural law theorists (Walters, for example) seem to adopt key elements of liberal positivism (as I have defined this field) for the purposes of this analysis – that is, they almost uniformly accept the givenness of Canadian law as law, and see liberal principles lying at its foundations. They rarely, then, see any need for Canadian law to reach outside itself for guidance – all that might be necessary to achieve justice and fairness lies within the system and needs only to be properly instantiated.

35 Here I focus on "critical" theories. Whether these overlap with Indigenous theories – and to what degree – is left unexplored at this point.

Consider how one might think the two main camps, pigeonholed above, align with objectivist and subjectivist models. The liberal positivist, one might well posit, sees himself presenting an objectivist model, as he can rest his model on a picture of law that treats legality as determined by social facts: whether a purported law is "law," he would contend, depends on whether (in the Canadian system, for example) it has been developed either legislatively or jurisprudentially in an appropriate fashion.[36] It is not someone's or some group's opinion, or subjective evaluation, that fixes whether any given rule or precept is law – it is something determinable on an "objective" level.[37] The critical theorist, on the other hand, would seem to disagree with the larger picture assumed true by the positivist, as she argues that what makes a thing "law" is usually determined by the actions of people in power, by some subjectively determined aspect of our social world. The critical theorist does not attempt to locate any fixed objective standard by which to measure "law," as her model posits only the interplay of subjectively determined webs of power and language.

But it is also arguable the liberal positivist *thinks* of his position as "objectively" grounded *because* of his being deeply embedded within a specific social reality – so deeply embedded he cannot see the environment within which he exists. With a liberal world all around, with an existence marked by unreflective development within this liberal world, the liberal positivist presents a theory of law that unreflectively *presents* itself as "objective," while arguably all the while it sits as just one expression of a subjectively determined world. That is, while the liberal positivist can connect his model to a form of objectivity (in that one can non-subjectively determine within this system whether x is law or not), the fact is the system itself may well be simply an expression of a sociocultural perspective on human nature and human affairs. The system, that is, may be subjectively grounded. We might well ask, then, what the liberal theorist is *doing* as he presents this purportedly objective account of the law.

The critical theorist, on the other hand, looks at this liberal world from a point outside it and is quite likely alienated from this social reality. She presents a position she may herself believe to be "subjectively" grounded, as she understands her position is based – to some extent – on her experience as an outsider, as a person with an experience made sensible as the result of her lived experience as a person not enfolded within (or at least not bamboozled by) the liberal world. To what extent is this theorist, one might wonder, projecting

36 HLA Hart, *The Concept of Law*, 2nd ed (Oxford: Clarendon Press, 1994); Joseph Raz, *The Authority of Law: Essays on Law and Morality* (Oxford: Oxford University Press, 1979); Scott Shapiro, "The Hart-Dworkin Debate: A Short Guide for the Perplexed" (2007), online: <ssrn.com/abstract=968657>.

37 In particular, the Hartian positivist would argue that what determines the legality of a rule or test is its being determined to be such by appropriate legal officials, according to the operative rule of recognition.

her alienation and frustration onto the phenomena she purportedly studies? To what extent, one might wonder, does she *in fact* (that is, objectively speaking) exist within a socioculturally determined system of meaning, one a third-party observer could explore and describe?

The first point to take away from this digression is that we cannot just accept the position of the liberal positivist (that his theory of law is in some acceptable and relevant sense "objective"). Neither can we simply accept, however, that the unreflective position of the critical theorist is the sole remaining alternative (that law is unfixed, that its nature is entirely subjectively determined). What we *should* accept is a second takeaway and a suggestion. The second takeaway is that the *place* of the theorist is something to be cognizant of, that concerns arise around what the theorist might be trying to present as *either* objective or purely political. The suggestion, on the other hand, is that one may be able to place *all* this (the presentation of theories by socioculturally grounded theorists) in a picture of a world of varied sociocultural senses of meaning. This suggestion is explored in the next section of this chapter and is a key element in the exercise in methodological naturalism carried out in the second half of this text.

What are the import and implications of this look into differing theoretical perspectives? The general objective in this text might have seemed clear to begin with – to provide a rich description of Aboriginal law explaining the nature of a body of jurisprudence. But when we pay attention to the dynamic between theorist, subject matter, and sociocultural setting we see this project becomes tangled with difficult matters, including potential complications in the nature of truth, reality, and knowledge.[38]

As we try to make sense of Aboriginal law we come to realize and acknowledge that this activity is itself an interesting (and arguably unavoidable) subject of study. My intent in later chapters is to explore the extent to which one can construct two distinct "sensible" models of Aboriginal law through the very different lenses of liberal positivism and critical (postcolonial) theory. The reader might suspect, at this early point, that the outcome of such an exercise is a stalemate between two opposed theoretical positions, one holding that Aboriginal law emerges as a vehicle for the promotion of liberal values of equality and liberty, the other that Aboriginal law continues to develop in line with an underlying unbroken fundamental thread of colonialism. If that suspicion were to bear out, what would this suggest for how one might try generally approaching this entire enterprise?

---

38 Furthermore, the theoretician, one might argue, is not only embedded as an individual within a particular culturally determined *world*, but as a researcher is also embedded within a culturally determined social *activity*. That is, one might argue that just as the *person* is culturally grounded, so too is the *activity* with which the person engages (whether it be scholarly or not).

This kind of concern, coupled with the argument that the theoretician is an element of the story to be included in analysis (set out in chapters 4 and 5, devoted to theory and method), drove my quest to find a place from which to begin analysis that at least promised to make it difficult to argue that subjective research-perspectives and normative universes indelibly taint any attempts to analyse Aboriginal law. I take seriously arguments about ideological or political taint, the outcome being that I develop an approach to the study of Aboriginal law I feel meets these arguments head-on. The approach itself has been touched on several times – the relevant aspect introduced at this point concerns theorists and their works, as all this is included in the set of things to be explained within a naturalist model. Whether it succeeds or not is left to the reader to consider.

TWO LENSES THROUGH WHICH TO MAKE SENSE: LIBERAL POSITIVISM AND CRITICAL (POSTCOLONIAL) THEORY

Before launching into a richer discussion of the approach adopted in this work, let me say a few words about the two theories explored in the second half of this text. Legal theories make up a large field, which strikes the reasonable observer as bereft of general form and structure. I narrow my study to two forms of legal theory.[39] Two points should be made about what might look like a narrow focus – first, the focus is actually not particularly narrow, as my intent is to construct what amount to two fairly large tents within which exist quite a large number of theoretical sub-varieties, and second, with the large umbrella-theories in place, it is possible to adequately explore the full range of important questions to be opened up in attempting to make sense of Aboriginal rights. Here I say a bit about how choices were made and how the large tents are constructed.

First, I choose to look at two theories that – regardless of their apparent disparity – share a common underlying point. These two theories accept the point that the law (in the field of Aboriginal law) is essentially doing as it is meant to do, as is intended. On one side we see liberal positivists, those who argue that – to a large extent – Canadian law is doing as it should in incorporating Aboriginal rights into the legal landscape as rights, and as rights that fit within and promote a liberal democratic framework. On the other side we encounter critical (postcolonial) theorists, those who argue that Aboriginal

39 It should also be noted that narrowing the field of study and contestation to that of legal theory is not mandated in any way. One could engage in a similar study while focusing primarily on political (or sociological, or economic) theory. Indeed, what I explore as "legal theory" in the second half of this text is often what others might (understandably) take to be political and social theory, applied to the situation of the law in this context. I consider this an exploration into legal theory, because my intent is to see the extent to which one can theorize about the law, where the original presumption is that the law can be the focused subject of theoretical analysis.

law is continuing to function as designed and intended, to further the colonial agenda of the Canadian state.

Second, I choose these theories because the one generally strives to exemplify the positivist approach in the field of human and moral sciences,[40] the other the interpretivist (or anti-positivist) approach. The first takes objects of study in the human/social system as things that can be adequately described and explained, the second as things that can only be "understood" (as things that have "meaning," that are to be examined and studied non-scientifically, through processes of interpretation).[41]

The largest tent holds liberal positivists. In this grouping I include most contemporary legal scholars working in the field of Aboriginal law. The position is positivist in its beginning, with the presumption that key matters about the nature of law are settled in this domestic setting – whether a purported law is a law is settled *within* the practices of Canadian law, and whether the Canadian legal system is a legal system is not a question seriously considered. The latter sort of question might arise for some Canadian scholars (those with natural law leanings) when thinking of *other* systems (the Nazi and apartheid legal systems being paradigmatic problem-cases), but there appear to be no mainstream theorists who seriously contemplate such matters in relation to Canadian law.[42] Even if the overtly colonial era were the subject of examination, while the Canadian legal scholar will likely decry the treatment of Aboriginal/Indigenous nations and peoples, the overwhelmingly predominant position is that Canadian law at that time was still law (as odious as it might have been in this one regard – after all, the reasoning seems to go, it then flowed from proper groundings, and it functioned appropriately in most other arenas [in, for example, the formation and sanctioning of perfectly valid contracts]).

That a common theory that attempts to describe Aboriginal law in Canada might have liberal content should not be surprising. Further, the marriage of liberal theory and positivist approaches to the nature of law is not difficult to imagine, and indeed we find many theorists who seem to put the two together. Inclusive positivists see no problem with including in the socially sanctioned criteria for law that it accord with certain moral or political moral principles, while exclusive positivists need never concern themselves with the content of law (as it is irrelevant for them to the question of whether law is law). And so it is that the liberal positivist is simply the theorist who imagines that positivistically valid law in Canada is built by importing liberal principles and values.

40 This is not the positivist approach in legal theory, though there are some connections between the two. The positivist approach in the social sciences traces back to seminal works by Comte and Durkheim.

41 See chapters 4, 5.

42 See e.g. Macklem & Sanderson, *supra* note 20.

Critical (postcolonial) theory is a more subtle and complex beast. While postcolonial discourse is not uncommon in the academy, it is found most often emanating from departments in the humanities. Meanwhile, the umbrella of "critical theory" (as I am using this expression) includes a number of legal theories or movements, all of which, however, generally do not have much to say about the nature of Aboriginal law. Critical race theory is an import from the United States (arising out of critical reflection on the nature of racism and the law, originally in the context of examinations of the law's treatment of black Americans), and it takes some serious intellectual gymnastics to twist it around so it says something meaningful about Aboriginal law.[43] Likewise, critical legal studies and critical legal pluralism, while fascinating on their own, are removed from most concerns that come up in discussions about the imposition of the Canadian legal system onto the lives and understandings of separate and independent Indigenous collectives.[44] The intersection of critical theory and postcolonial theory used in this text focuses our attention on an interpretivist strain of legal analysis (the critical theory component) that itself is focused on the history of the relationship between the Crown and Indigenous/Aboriginal peoples (the postcolonial component).

While the choice of these two broad forms of theoretical analysis leaves aside others who comment on Aboriginal law, it provides sufficient range to both (a) accommodate and address puzzles I described earlier around disparate understandings, assessments, and approaches to "making sense," and (b) demonstrate key points about how one might try to understand Aboriginal law. The interplay of theories under examination, puzzles infecting analysis, and the need to make sense of the field of legal phenomena lead to the picture presented.

I leave aside, then, those who see in Aboriginal law an aberration – that is, those who argue that Aboriginal rights simply should not exist (and that Aboriginal peoples – as distinct peoples – should not receive any sort of state support).[45] I also do not consider those who see in Aboriginal law a completely foreign and alien structure, one that should simply be ignored.[46]

The former commentator is not synchronized with Canadian law as it has developed – the fact is that this field, for reasons explored in this work, *has*

43 On the analysis of racism and the law in Canada, see Carol Aylward, *Canadian Critical Race Theory: Racism and the Law* (Halifax: Fernwood, 1998).

44 A Marxist/neo-Marxist thread running through much of critical legal studies shifts focus to class-based struggles that do not clearly intersect with colonialism and imperialism, while a focus on the law-generating subject, isolated from her sociocultural setting, renders much of critical legal pluralism difficult to use in this context. Thoughts on these limitations emerge in the last chapter, in the discussion of critical (postcolonial) studies.

45 See e.g. Flanagan, *supra* note 5.

46 In some ways, in some instances, this is what Taiaiake Alfred suggests. See Alfred, *Peace, Power, Righteousness*, *supra* note 1.

developed, and in a certain fashion. A theorist arguing that this should all be immediately and simply undone will not be particularly helpful as we struggle to understand what we see before us. Likewise, the scholar who advocates avoidance of any recognition or acknowledgment of Aboriginal law is unlikely to help in our quest to understand the nature of this creation (or, for that matter, what to do about the thing created). I can see the point of this latter position much more clearly than I can that of the person who argues Aboriginal peoples should be completely absorbed into the Canadian body politic,[47] but in the context of this quest – for an understanding of Aboriginal law, as a robust field within Canadian law – it is likewise of little immediate assistance.[48]

Puzzles must be temporarily put to the side so we can focus on the nature and depth of problems in theoretical perspectives and begin to wonder how they might be resolved. I argue in subsequent chapters that while one might try to locate reasons for the divergence in theoretical perspectives in a number of places, at some point it must be accepted (in a very particular manner) that varied theoretical understandings stand on their own, and that a particular form of legal-theoretic pluralism is a real possibility that must be accounted for in any sensible account of Aboriginal law. This form of legal-theoretic pluralism treats the existence of multiple and divergent legal theories as a fact in the world and attempts to see how this fact intersects with what we witness in Canadian jurisprudence. How I travel from here to there is, however, not a simple matter, as traversing the terrain of theoretical perspectives and of what divergence in this realm implies and how this divergence is to be managed is a bumpy ride.

Trying to make sense of this phenomenon – the existence of divergent theoretical understandings of seemingly one class of phenomena – is never far removed from main threads of analysis in this work. This matter of divergent

---

47 To be frank, I am quite sympathetic to this position as a matter of principle, that of self-determination.

48 It would be a mistake to see this as just apparent disinterest on my part about accounts that press for either absolute assimilation or absolute separation. The real difficulty in assessing such accounts through my frame of analysis lies in their both beginning from points separated from the "reality" of the situation. We have "facts" before us about the existence and nature of jurisprudence on Aboriginal rights (though we are always cognizant that "facts" are slippery creatures). These facts – concerning this legal phenomenon and implications and consequences – lead into puzzles. Neither of such accounts connects well to either the facts or the puzzles.

Of course, either of these positions could be adopted as the result of reasoned reflection on the nature of Aboriginal rights. Indeed, I support those who conclude Aboriginal law should be seen as a foreign intrusion (possibly to be ignored, dependent on the particular circumstances of the Indigenous community looking at the matter) *after* careful analysis of the history and nature of Crown-Indigenous relations. This text could be read as one path leading along this journey, the attempt being to make the journey "objectively" available to all, no matter their starting point.

theoretical models drives the push towards a methodological approach I argue permits a satisfactory accounting of Aboriginal law. It is essential we try to understand how alternate and opposed understandings are possible, preferably in a way that points us towards ways we can indeed come to objectively understand what Aboriginal law is all about.[49]

The Suggested Path Forward: A Naturalist Approach

With a sense in hand of both what I hope to arrive at through my analysis of an aspect of Canadian law, and key challenges that arise to arriving at this objective, we end this stage-setting chapter with a more detailed discussion of the nature of the approach to analysing Aboriginal rights. I introduce the nuts and bolts of a form of a naturalist approach, showing how methodological naturalism works when the naturalist explores both what the law might be in any given situation and how theories purportedly "make sense" of Aboriginal law. I present initial arguments to show the necessity for (or at the very least the preferability of) the particular approach used in the argumentative sections of this text, and some points on how this approach is expected to work in this context. Two related implications of this approach are explored later (in chapter 5), when our gaze turns to questions and concerns that arise about meaning and normativity.[50]

One route into introducing this naturalist approach is through puzzles outlined earlier. The attractiveness of the approach comes from reflection on the nature of challenges posed in making sense of Aboriginal law – in particular, puzzles we face in seeing that entirely different understandings and assessments of Aboriginal law are both possible and arguably reasonable. These different understandings and assessments arise not only in the context of attempts to describe the nature of Aboriginal law but also in relation to theories about Aboriginal law. There is wide variance in understandings at multiple levels,

49 Along the way we will have to grapple with the implications these problems pose for our attempts to make sense. Consider, for example, the possibility that the very "truth" of the matter is radically unsettled (this would be a real possibility under interpretivist approaches – a strong form of interpretivism rests upon an anti-realist foundation, both metaphysically and epistemologically). Given this seemingly radical instability, it may be that the term "truth" itself is unsettled and in need of investigation. Is there a single "sense" to be made of Aboriginal law, or rather do we encounter a field of contestation, with different investigators constructing different notions of "truth," using them to generate irreducibly different understandings of Aboriginal law? What does this imply – at least in this context – about cross-cultural communication?

50 First, there is the matter of the need to place theorizing (and in particular legal theorizing) into the naturalist framework, which requires simply treating legal theories as phenomena in the observable world. Second, there is the matter of ensuring that (to the extent possible) no a priori assumptions are entered into (regarding what objects of study may exist, or what processes of study may be best, and so on).

including between models purporting to emerge out of both "descriptive" and normative or interpretive projects. Put simply, the approach in this text centres on taking not just the law, but also various attempts at describing and theorizing Aboriginal law as material susceptible to empirical investigation.

Care must be taken in understanding what is involved in my saying, in this context, that empirical investigation can lead the way. Some empiricists conflate or intimately connect their position with forms of materialism or physicalism,[51] while others see themselves closely tied to strong forms of scientism.[52] I avoid being tied down to these narrower formulations, the empirical investigation with which I intend to engage being best covered under a broad and open understanding of naturalism – it is best fit under what is commonly termed *methodological naturalism.*

The approach is naturalistic in that it begins with the working assumption that what must be investigated consists essentially of natural phenomena. There are two sides to this starting point. On the one side, I explore possibilities in taking the law, its place in the world, and attempts at making sense of it, as all constituting natural phenomena (as all making up parts of the natural world).[53]

---

51 Taking these terms to be interchangeable (recognizing some strive to find distinctions between them), physicalists argue both that all is physical (or material) and that all statements about the world are synonymous with statements about physical (or material) objects. Empiricism, on the other hand, is at heart a thesis about the grounding for knowledge, holding that all knowledge begins from experience. While the former theory is metaphysical in focus, the latter is epistemological – but empiricists can take as an implication of their basic thesis the claim that all knowledge is about physical (or material) objects that exist in the observable realm. Neither of these positions (or their converses) is taken (or explored) in this text – I take methodological naturalism as not requiring a stance either way on whether or not (a) all knowledge is grounded in experience, or (b) all that "is" is physical (or material). For good accounts of the terms used, debates entered into, and arguments for and against positions drawn in regards to most discussions in this section of the text, see Edward N Zalta, ed, *Stanford Encyclopedia of Philosophy*, online: <plato.stanford.edu>. Entries on naturalism and scientific realism are good starting points for study.

52 This would be the view that any and all meaningful questions can be answered by the methods of science. My general position in developing an approach to the study of law that can be fruitful and insightful is to avoid adherence to positions that are stronger than necessary. I can accept that most knowledge we possess comes by the scientific method – that does not require that I accept, however, the strong claim that only the scientific method advances us to knowledge. In this text I focus on a method that parallels that of the scientific method broadly construed (and advocate the use of the methods of science – broadly construed – in developing knowledge of our social worlds), but I do not think I need to – and am not motivated to – commit to the strong claim. Further, that there is no clearly defined singular "scientific method" does not pose a problem, as I do not rest my approach on any such chimera.

53 We could begin, crudely, by identifying those things we take to be elements of the natural world as those we perceive. We quickly run into problems, however, with things like electrons and forces. At an early point, then, this ascription of "naturalness" ties to the scientific picture

On the flip side, I begin with the assumption that it would be best to undertake this investigation without any reliance upon, focus on, or connection with non-natural or supernatural elements, principles, processes, entities, or ideals (as far as this is possible).[54] It is in this latter sense that the naturalist asserts "philosophical theorizing should be continuous with empirical inquiry in the sciences."[55] It is *methodological* (and not ontological or material) in that the focus is on a way to approach the world and its study, without prior presumptions being made about what there is or what approaches to study are "right."

One can identify from the last few centuries numerous schools of thought (and scholars) holding a "naturalist outlook." That is, these parties saw value in appealing to methods employed in the study of the natural world in addressing all manner of inquiry, looking at all manner of phenomena. So, for example, we see positivists emerge in the social sciences in the nineteenth century, ostensibly making use of methods of empirical science in studying humans along various dimensions.[56] As Leiter notes,

> The 1920s and 1930s marked the heyday of "positivism," in philosophy and the social sciences: natural science was viewed as the paradigm of all genuine knowledge, and any discipline – from philosophy to sociology – which wanted to attain epistemic respectability had to emulate its methods, i.e. had to be "naturalized."[57]

Naturalism had, however, seemingly tied itself to a vision of the world that could not be justified – it seemed to have put its eggs into a basket that depended on science in fact being *shown* to be the vehicle for knowledge production it purported to be.

---

prevalent at the time. As Quine put it, "Our acceptance of an ontology is, I think, similar in principle to our acceptance of a scientific theory.... Our ontology is determined once we have fixed upon the over-all conceptual scheme which is to accommodate science in the broadest sense": WV Quine, *From a Logical Point of View: Nine Logico-Philosophical Essays*, 2nd ed (Cambridge, MA: Harvard University Press, 1980) at 16–17. For a discussion of Quine's approach in the early chapters and for an eventual argument for a more robust and sophisticated approach to the general natural thesis, see Jack Ritchie, *Understanding Naturalism* (Stocksfield, UK: Acumen Press, 2008).

Many years after Quine's statement, we are fortunate to have general agreement that mental states function within our current best scientific models – these mental states play key roles in the analysis to come in this text.

54 Here I mean that I may unwittingly engage in analysis resting on, or connected with, beliefs or propositions that refer to such non-natural phenomena.

55 Brian Leiter, "Rethinking Legal Realism: Toward a Naturalized Jurisprudence" in Leiter, *Naturalizing Jurisprudence*, *supra* note 32 at 34 [Leiter, "Rethinking Legal Realism"].

56 See e.g. Émile Durkheim, *The Rules of Sociological Method*, ed by George Catlin, translated by Sarah Solovay & John Mueller, 8th ed (New York: Free Press, 1938).

57 Leiter, "Rethinking Legal Realism," *supra* note 55 at 57–8.

There were several seismic developments in the middle of the twentieth century in our understanding of what we take to be the production of knowledge. By the midpoint of the century a sense of futility and a measure of fatigue characterized centuries-long efforts to demonstrate the grounding of the scientific enterprise. Over the next few decades, new ways of thinking of the process of theorizing arose – even paradigmatic examples of "knowledge production" in the sciences were charged with reflecting interests and predilections of researchers and not progress towards truth about a mind-independent reality.

During the same period, however, we see emerge seeds of a contemporary understanding of a mature program of naturalization, as the failure of grand efforts to ground scientific knowledge opened our eyes to the need to rethink such projects. By the late twentieth century naturalism had regained its feet, and over the last few decades we see it emerge again as a respectable way to understand how knowledge should be understood – in particular, it points to how we should work towards knowledge-production. Key to this re-emergence has been an understanding that we must subject *knowledge-production itself* to the acid-bath of naturalization. And so, while it was that in the middle of the twentieth century the general intellectual mood of much of the academy signalled a move away from an interest in the project of naturalization, over the last few decades developments in the philosophy of science led to renewed interest in and commitment to just such a program.

Renewal of interest is yet, however, minimal in the field of legal analysis (Leiter being a force out in front, pushing for revival of interest in naturalizing jurisprudence). Against the backdrop of this shift in the intellectual winds, I argue that in the context of the phenomena under examination in this work a naturalist commitment emerges not just as a matter of possible interest but as the approach to "making sense" that is most promising and fruitful.

What marks contemporary forms of naturalism (from earlier movements evincing a "naturalist outlook") is recognition that not only should inquiries into phenomena make use of tools and methods of the sciences but that theorizing itself should be understood from within a vision of the world built up by natural inquiry into our place in the natural world. In the context of a discussion of developments in the philosophy of science in the late twentieth and early twenty-first century, Godfrey-Smith points to the collapse of faith in a "logical analysis" model of the scientific enterprise and the emergence (in its place) of a naturalist model. Godfrey-Smith characterizes this mature naturalist model as "the idea that philosophy can *use* results from the sciences to help answer philosophical questions and can do this *even in the philosophy of science itself*."[58] This characterization fits with insights gleaned from the collapse

58 Peter Godfrey-Smith, *Theory and Reality: An Introduction to the Philosophy of Science* (Chicago: University of Chicago Press, 2003) at 149–50 [emphasis in original].

of the foundationalist projects that had so magnificently failed to ground the scientific enterprise.

The background to upheavals of the twentieth century lies in the longstanding notion that intellectual inquiry can and should play a role – from a position *outside* science – in making sense of the scientific enterprise. In particular, over the last few centuries philosophers took on the task of showing how scientific truths could be *justified* (in a very particular sense). As this exercise broke down in the twentieth century, some philosophers came to see that the problem was with the framing of the exercise – that is, with the model of an intellectual enterprise *outside* that of science purporting to have the tools to analyse science, and to answer (what were taken to be) fundamental questions about science itself.[59] Once aware of this framing, naturalists reframed the task of making philosophical sense of science, moving it to a project that must take place *within* the scientific enterprise.

How does this discussion translate into how to think about how to study law (and legal theory)? The key is that one has to see that what unsettled attempts at studying science was the realization that science is essentially a human endeavour and that human endeavours all take place within the natural world. Imposing on the scientific endeavour requirements that it be shown to lead inexorably to truth and knowledge was understood to be a misguided, fruitless, and unnecessary exercise. An alternative was to turn to the *practice of science* for standards to be applicable to its own understanding and assessment. Likewise, we can appreciate that study of law is both (a) a study of a field of phenomena essentially human, and (b) itself (the study that is) a field of phenomena in the human world. With these appreciations in mind we can look to standards of assessment that emerge in our understanding of the human-natural world to make sense of both law and theories about law.

The contemporary naturalist approach in the philosophy of science spells out into acknowledgement that all the questions about processes within science are themselves questions that must be framed and answered within the natural world (the world that science itself studies). Do scientific theories work towards truth and knowledge? These matters must be explored as questions about a human project (that of scientific study) with terms then that must have meaning within this human-natural world.

The naturalist approach in the field of legal theory, then, spells out into acknowledgment that all the questions about processes within the study of law are themselves questions that must be framed and answered within the natural world (the world that science itself studies). Can theories of law work towards truth and knowledge? These matters must be explored as questions about a

59 See e.g. Ritchie, *supra* note 53.

human project (that of study of a human construct, legal systems) with terms then that must have meaning within this human-natural world.

Essentially the same characterization of naturalism can be arrived at by working from the assumption that the mind exists in a mind-independent world (rather than that the world exists "in" the mind). This might seem a radically different thing to hold, but, as I understand what these two mutually exclusive options mean, turning to the mind-in-world option captures the same thought as that expressed in the idea that one might begin study exclusively with natural objects (as opposed to allowing in non-natural entities). The difference lies in the starting point. In putting matters this alternate way, I begin with the presumption that a realist metaphysics should be adopted. From there, joined at the hip so to speak, we find the presumption of a naturalist epistemology.

We begin with the presumption that the world exists around us, and that the human mind *arose within* this larger natural setting. Mental states, then, are approached (at least initially) as elements of the natural world, as things we can study as we might electrons, trees, and the weather. Insofar as mental states include such things as representations, beliefs, attitudes, dispositions, intentions, models, and theories, we see them all then as elements of a natural world. To the extent mental states seem to contain or reach out to non-natural entities, we wait to see whether our study of the natural world requires that we countenance containing within our best explanations such seemingly odd entities. We begin with the presumption that the mind is but a thing within the natural world unless driven to see it – or what it purports to connect to – as more.

This captures the sort of naturalistic commitment with which this project is carried out. I find promise in undertaking the study of law with this structure for several reasons. First, all through this work is woven the argument that a primary source of confusion encountered in the nature and merit of law (and Aboriginal law in particular) is the intertwining of so much discourse within and around law with terms and concepts that seem to lead us out to realms removed from science, reason, and nature. In those realms, hope diminishes not just for agreement or consensus, but for understanding and explanation. Limiting our analysis to the natural world can seem like a reasonable response to this negative conclusion. Second, this allows us to bring the matter of "perspectives" not only into focus, but in such a way as to account for the divergences we note. Third, there is the result of this work, what I take to be (and I hope the reader takes to be) fruitful outcomes that flow from beginning with naturalist groundings.

It might be suspected that taking a naturalistic approach places me in the (legal) positivist camp, arguing against the interpretivists, as (a) interpretivists seem to invite in, as they develop their accounts of analyses of the law, understandings that do not necessarily tie to natural phenomena, and (b) interpretivists are prone to placing "the world" – at least the sensible or knowable world – "in" the mind. But I am equal opportunity and find similar fault with the positivist account under investigation. Earlier I noted the positivist/critical divide does not map smoothly onto an objectivist/subjectivist division, the problem being that arguably the positivist can be seen as advancing a subjectively grounded account.[60] As well, the positivist account, I argue in later sections,[61] tends to slip into bringing into play non-natural phenomena, and can – without suitable caution – slip into thinking of the sensible/knowable world as dependent solely on the workings of the mind. One outcome of this criticism of both such kinds of accounts is that *both* are approached as best seen as phenomena in the natural world. Both liberal positivism and critical theories are treated as essentially sociolinguistic constructs – and so both are thereby subject to the form of analysis applied in this text.

One attraction of the approach here advocated is that it does not ignore or dismiss all the discourse built up within and around various theories and models of law – rather, it strives to place all this into the only sort of naturalist setting it can be reasonably fit within, that of the functioning of language in our social worlds. While terms and concepts may seem to point towards or refer to problematic realms, we can treat these terms and concepts naturalistically, as elements within sociolinguistic environments.

The approach is labelled "*methodological*" to highlight two related facts: (1) that no a priori ontological or epistemological *commitments* are being made one way or another about the make-up of the world and its constituent parts,[62] and (2) that *method* itself is understood to fall within the natural world. An *assumption* is made about what should be investigated and *assumptions* are made about how to proceed, but none of this is meant to preclude, for example, the possibility that a wide range of types of entities may have some independent existence, removed from any possibility of naturalistic explanation (or that there may in fact be, for example, some reason to trust in strong forms of conceptual analysis). Nor does this approach preclude the possibility that as a *result* of the investigation some apparently non-natural or supernatural entities, processes, or ideals may be required as elements of a "best" explanation or model, or indeed that there may be elements of our existence best categorized as non-natural. If any such entities or realms are required, however, my starting

60 See "Theoretical Accounts and 'Perspectives'" in chapter 3.

61 See e.g. "Theorizing about the Law: Perspectives and Social Construction" in chapter 5.

62 This matter of commitments is a bit tricky, as later I will set out what I take to be some fundamental commitments I must make in order to ground analysis that follows. Key is understanding that within the form of naturalism I deploy there are no a priori commitments made in the sense of axioms that serve in some absolute sense to fix what follows, but there are a posteriori commitments made – specifically in the position that the human arises within a mind-independent natural world – commitments that are themselves presumptions (non-absolute, or provisional).

assumption is that this can be known only *after* investigation has determined it to be so. One corollary to this approach is that while all these points about non-natural entities are left possible, I hold that the evolution of science and reason only functions or ranges over the natural, so trying to rationally explain the phenomena in question will presumably keep us within the confines of science (broadly understood).

This essentially methodological foundation flows from a cautious mentality I think must underscore the approach taken in this exercise in "making sense" – any and all "transcendental"[63] beliefs (a term I designate crudely as pointing to those beliefs intersecting in some manner with the non-natural or supernatural) must be considered in a very particular fashion for it to be possible that *sense* can be made of Aboriginal law. While it might appear I begin with a strong transcendental claim (that the mind arises within the natural world), I present this, however, not as an a priori truth but as a presumption, one on which to lightly ground explanation. If we accept mind-in-world, we then work *this* way, we see mental phenomena *this* way, we restrict our analyses *these* ways, etc.

One can think of this work as something of an experiment, conducted on the hypothesis that such an approach to the explanation of Aboriginal law can be fruitful – in particular that it can largely dissolve and/or avoid puzzles noted, potentially leading to some degree of convergence upon answers to both "What is the nature of Aboriginal law?" and "How is legal thought to make any real headway in the analysis of such a complex social institution?" A hypothesis is formulated: that it is possible to achieve acceptable explanations for and understandings of Aboriginal law through an approach that places the law itself, our experiential understandings and assessments of the law, and our attempts on a second level to make sense of the law, all firmly within the world of observable, natural phenomena. I then proceed to work with this hypothesis: the approach of the methodological naturalist (a) unpacks the law and varied understandings and assessments of the law, and attempts to place these understandings and assessments into sensible models, and (b) takes the material thereby revealed as something itself to be modelled on the assumption that all this material can be approached as natural constituents of a natural world.

---

63 The term is enclosed in quotation marks to denote its contested nature and the uncertainty I feel in demarcating a clear boundary in this instance. I mean not to avoid all metaphysically loaded beliefs (whatever that would mean), but to begin study with caution in relation to those beliefs, which seem to already contain reference to terms or concepts *carrying with them* purported insights into the nature of reality or our access to it. Of course the approach I am taking is completely underscored by a particular set of metaphysical beliefs, as this is unavoidable. I try to restrict these beliefs to assumptions and presumptions and try to remain aware of that status for these beliefs. On the notion that all theorists' positions seem unavoidably metaphysical, see Michael S Moore, "The Interpretive Turn in Modern Theory: A Turn for the Worse?" (1989) 41 Stan L Rev 871.

This may sound like a complex and technical enterprise, but it is actually accomplished in a relatively straightforward manner. There are three aspects of this approach to note: (1) it eschews unreflective acceptance of non-natural entities, (2) it avoids processes of investigation that do not (at least) parallel those of the sciences, and (3) it adopts a very particular position vis-à-vis matters of meaning and normativity. Let me say a few words about the first two, leaving an extended discussion of the third until the point we grapple with those notions in the social/moral realm (and specifically in relation to legal theories).[64] At a few points in the present discussion we will touch on overlaps between these three aspects of the approach.

Mention of non-natural or supernatural entities is accepted into modelling developed, but only insofar as these entities or processes are taken to be the subjects or objects of linguistic instruments, allowing for the role they play in this social-linguistic context. That is, mention of these things is entirely permissible within the models, but their intentional objects are not engaged with in the analysis.[65]

So, for example, mention of "free will" is not excluded in the context of discussion of a particular model, description, or theory, though the overall exercise remains agnostic on the nature and existence of such a potentially "transcendental" (i.e., non-natural) creature.[66] Some of the models we

---

64 See "The Social Construction of Aboriginal Rights" in chapter 5.

65 By "intentional object" is meant that potentially existing entity, that thing about which a reference may be made in a sentence or proposition (directly or obliquely). There is nothing improper, for example, in including analysis of *belief* in a "perfect island," but analysis would not reach out to engage with the purported object of this belief, the alleged "perfect island." As with most of the subjects touched on in this chapter, there is substantial debate about all sorts of matters that connect to the bare idea of "intentional objects." I do not think, however, that I need engage with these debates for the purpose of this study. I choose to refer to objects left aside under this approach as intentional rather than representational, as use of the latter too quickly suggests problems (i.e. "what" is being *represented*? A "perfect island"?). I hope to avoid getting entangled in Brentano's problems with my choice of language. People may *intend* to refer to all sorts of things, and our focus in this work can be on just the use of expressions purportedly meant to accomplish this task of reaching out to something. For a taste of the controversies around the notion of intentional objects, see Tim Crane, "Intentional Objects" (2001) 14 Ratio 298.

66 Here I mean to pick out a strong sense of the term "free will," referring to some human attribute that removes us from the natural world, understood as a world causally determined. In the overview of the articles that make up their collection on current debates in the area of free will, Paul Russell & Oisin Deery, eds, *The Philosophy of Free Will: Essential Readings from the Contemporary Debates* (Oxford: Oxford University Press, 2013) note at page 2 that in the early Modern period,

> when the concepts and categories of natural science were extended to include human thought and action, viewed as part of the seamless natural order of things, sceptical problems were generated relating to our self-image as free and responsible beings.... The thesis of determinism has traditionally

explore have trouble removing themselves from claims that presuppose the existence of a fairly robust form of free will. This is not problematic, insofar as these claims are approached as being nothing beyond this. We approach them as nothing more than statements or exclamations, deductions or presumptions, as being one or another sort of linguistic instrument going into the make-up of part of the world we inhabit (that is, as existing in the mind of the language user, expressed in a natural language, heard by some recipients, understood [to some degree] by those listeners, perhaps acted upon as a result, etc.).[67] In this particular case we might note a certain understanding of the law intersecting to some degree with acceptance of this notion of free will, and so *acceptance* within the model (and the role that plays in our social-legal world) may come to be of interest in this sort of study. That someone (or some group) *believes* (explicitly or implicitly) in the existence of a robust form of free will (and more particularly *how* this *belief* might function in the world) can be the subject of empirical interest and inquiry. Whether such a thing denoted *exists* in the world writ large (something that would enjoy some form of existence outside or independent of the representational realm) is left – initially at least – to the side.[68]

Let me trace this out just a bit further, hinting at problems we will encounter and tackle once discussion turns to issues of meaning and normativity. Cleaving to the model of mind-in-world, such things as notions, ideas, and concepts develop that form cores of meaning within the structured realities of varied social collectives. Some of these implicate the presumption of value in certain aspects of the world. For example, we see in the contemporary liberal world presumption of value in the possession by the individual of a robust form of free will, this capacity allowing for such things as a form of responsibility for chosen actions. Now, to the extent thoughts about some such possession of such an alleged property is woven into matters of normativity and meaning within the methodological naturalism at play in this work, we strive to constrain discussion so that the focus is on beliefs, attitudes, and other mental states. That is, difficult problems about meaning and normativity are tamed in this discourse,

---

been broadly interpreted as the claim that everything that happens in the world ... is subject to causal laws.... [I]t has been widely accepted that causation involves necessitation of effects by antecedent causal conditions. It follows from this that insofar as human action is caused it is thereby necessitated by causal antecedents in such a way that the action must follow, given the antecedent conditions. These assumptions are, according to some philosophers, *incompatible* with human freedom and moral responsibility.

67 For a general discussion of the transmission of culture, see e.g. Christophe Boesch, "Culture in Evolution: Toward an Integration of Chimpanzee and Human Cultures" in Melissa Brown, ed, *Explaining Culture Scientifically* (Seattle: University of Washington Press, 2008) 37.

68 Bearing in mind, again, that this thing denoted may be found to have some definite existence in our world, but only as the *outcome* of our naturalistic investigations.

the focus falling solely on how forms of meaning and normativity function within varied structured social realities.

On a different point (that this approach avoids processes of investigation that do not parallel those of the sciences), there are certainly numerous other methods that researchers can use to work towards insight about phenomena. It might seem I privilege an approach, and in a sense I do – but this is a cautious privileging in line with both the methods and outcomes of science. More importantly, the approach falls in line with underlying assumptions that animate the methods of science – beliefs in a mind-independent world, in our being embedded in this world, and in our ability to model this world (in what I later label a "common sense" approach or model). This cautious privileging, furthermore, is done for reasons. Cognizant of challenges faced by attempts to provide foundations for knowledge and knowledge production, a naturalistic approach makes sense of how knowledge is actually understood and produced, explaining how the methods of science further our insights into the natural world. The approach taken to legal analysis in this text does not simply adopt the methods of science (I do not try to be a scientist in this work, whatever that would look like in studying an area of domestic law!) – rather, it adopts that stance towards the world that itself makes sense of the scientific enterprise. One aspect of that larger understanding of our place in relation to the world of phenomena is an understanding that should the objective be to explain the nature of certain observable phenomena (even legal phenomena) efforts are likely wasted if attempts are made to make sense of this phenomena through deployment of non-natural processes.

To reiterate, the approach I develop and articulate comes out of reflection on the nature of challenges posed in making sense of Aboriginal law, and in particular those centred on the existence of disparate and seemingly incommensurable understandings and assessments of its nature. There is wide variance in understandings at multiple levels, including between models purporting to emerge out of both "descriptive" and normative or interpretive projects. My approach can be summed up fairly simply: it asks us to explore all attempts to link the bare substance of Aboriginal law with normative, interpretive, and theoretical matters as themselves elements of processes in our natural world susceptible to empirical investigation.

This introduction to the form of naturalism put to work in making sense of Aboriginal rights concludes with discussions about how it relates to the work of two scholars involved in developing theories moving in the same general direction. First, I situate my project in relation to Brian Leiter's ground-breaking work on "naturalizing jurisprudence." As I do so I show how our work – while similar in spirit – focuses on very different legal phenomena. This leads into discussion of John Searle, a scholar who writes little on the law but much about how a naturalist understanding of the construction of social reality can be put together. My focus is on a socially constructed system of law (Canadian law on Aboriginal rights), and later analysis is focused on how the fact sociolinguistic tools can generate aspects of social reality can be put to use in thinking of how Canadian courts attempt to pull Indigenous communities into the fold of Canadian law. While Searle provides a very useful springboard for thinking about how social realities are constructed in a natural world through sociolinguistic instruments, my discussion of his work focuses on a key shortcoming in his analyses – his inattention to the question of how one sociolinguistic community might go about attempting to overcome the meaning-generating capacity of other sociolinguistic communities (so that the first community might be able to construct a social reality that "captures" members of other communities within it). As will be made clear, Leiter and Searle suffer from the same basic failing in relation to the project I undertake in this work, that of myopia.

Leiter: "Naturalized Jurisprudence"

Leiter's work has been focused principally on resurrecting and revitalizing the legacy of American legal realism, with a key aspect of his project being a demonstration that many of the proponents of this early realist movement were advancing arguments that presaged later advances in understanding how to properly think about naturalism, advances for the most part initiated by Quine a few decades after the legal realist's juridical star had faded. As with the earlier realists, Leiter's focus is on adjudication – and principally in relation to "hard cases." The general thrust of his most general argument is captured in a short passage: "Theory of adjudication is concerned *not* with the relationship between 'evidence' and 'scientific theory,' but rather with the justificatory relationship between 'legal reasons' (the input, as it were) and judicial decision (the output)."[69] Quine had argued that the relationship between "evidence" and "scientific theory" was not such that one could *justify* the latter on the basis of the former. This essentially anti-foundationalist argument led to a specific naturalist conclusion Quine reached, put by Leiter in this form:

> For any pair of relata that might stand in a *justificatory* relation – e.g. evidence and theory, reasons and belief [etc.] – if no normative account of the relation is possible, then the only theoretically fruitful account is the descriptive/explanatory account given by the relevant science of that domain.[70]

The core argument in Leiter's *Naturalizing Jurisprudence* is one by analogy. If no normative account of the relationship between legal input and judicial output is

---

69 Leiter, "Rethinking Legal Realism," *supra* note 55 at 39 [emphasis in original].
70 *Ibid* at 37 [emphasis in original].

possible (which is what Leiter tirelessly strives to show American legal realists had demonstrated in the first third of the twentieth century), then the only theoretically fruitful account is the descriptive/explanatory account given by the science applicable to the legal phenomena under investigation.

Leiter's work was quite helpful in shaping my thinking leading into the work presented in this text. The assistance, however, has been primarily on a fairly general level and is often just motivational (that is, it helps immensely to see that at least one voice in the legal academy speaks to larger intellectual developments engaging the broader academic world in the last few generations). Let me say a bit about why the substance of Leiter's work has been of little assistance, and a bit about what I think might be problematic about arguments made and positions taken by Leiter. This last part of the discussion is not particularly germane to the analysis conducted in this work (and is gone over, though in different form, in the next chapter) and so is left mercifully short. What is important is that I indicate the distance that separates our respective projects.

Leiter's work is focused on "theory of adjudication." We do not differ sharply in that respect – I also examine how judges arrive at the outcomes they reach. We have to look at more than past rules and precedent, as the law judges create in the Crown-Aboriginal context is held to be largely sui generis, as section 35 jurisprudence is ostensibly meant to arise anew, not being overly fettered with or constrained by pre–section 35 common law.[71] This pushes us back to such things as principle – clearly judges were not going to begin their work in "interpreting" section 35 in the early 1990s without some frame within which to make sense of how to flesh out what this section means and how it functions. Legal/moral principles would be what one *expects* they would work with and within.

The naturalist-realist would demand, however, that we examine the situation in all its complexity to see how judgments are *actually* arrived at. Regardless of how judges *say* they arrive at outcomes (or what armchair commentators might pipe in with), how do outcomes *actually* emerge? This, too, is the very sort of question I ask in this work, and so on this general level Leiter and I are on the same page.

But Leiter explores – and seemingly expects legal theorists following his lead to explore – a relatively uncomplicated world of adjudication. This comparatively simple world is that of the relatively self-contained polity: we see before

71 McHugh's look at the history of the development of section 35 jurisprudence reveals some of the tension that developed through the early decades, as the courts hoped the content of section 35 would be worked out through negotiations, but eventually had to face up to the task left to them. In light of that task (and following the lead provided by early Aboriginal law scholars – especially Slattery and McNeil), the Court did in fact turn to common law reasoning and common law tools – particularly notions within property law. See Paul McHugh, "A Common Law Biography of Section 35" in Macklem & Sanderson, *supra* note 20 at 137.

us (1) courts of a nation, together with (2) citizens (and other "persons") with interests and claims, and we explore how *these* courts resolve disputes that arise between *these* parties (and between the state and parties). A key matter to examine is the movement from a time just before a judgment is made to that time at which the judgment itself occurs – given all that exists at that earlier time, how is this judgment made? The legal realist (now relabelled the naturalist) would challenge the "legal model," which would have us unreflectively believe that the mass of *legal materials* at the moment before the judgment is made, along with the tools of *legal reasoning*, account for – can "justify" – the outcome reached. Running counter to this, the naturalist suggests we can come to see how the movement is made only if we focus on providing descriptive/explanatory models, those that the tools and outcomes of contemporary science can help us work towards (as science is that mode we have of developing explanations of the natural world).

The last part of this account, again, is not something I fight against – indeed, I search for means by which just such descriptive/explanatory accounts can be built and tested. The shortcoming of Leiter's work (besides the fact he does not himself actually do much work in providing descriptive/explanatory models) lies in the narrow focus he casts on situations he thinks to explore. I am looking at a situation in which the court system of one meaning-generating community is being imposed upon the worlds and lives of peoples possessed of their own separate and independent legal and political orders (and the meaning-generating systems that must underlie those orders).

With a different situation to focus upon I also, inevitably, must think of other types of natural forces that might account for judgments reached. Leiter (unavoidably, one might suggest) focuses on the individual judge, only entertaining a broader focus when considering ideological systems (of beliefs) that might generally animate groups of judges. This makes sense in the context of the narrower focus within which he works (where at most we can divide up the single given social world into political camps of varying sensibility, all *within* one given polity), but it is an inadequate starting point for my project. Individual agency is kept in focus, but all Canadian judges as a whole may be capable of being put into one sociocultural-linguistic group. Political/ideological divisions emerge *within* this group (and ideological leanings might not be particularly interesting as forces that account for how judges decide outcomes in the context of adjudicating on Indigenous issues before them).

With naturalist sensibilities the two of us are, then, gazing at different sorts of phenomena. This alone suffices to explain my reluctance to spend much time trying to put his work to use in my analyses. There is also the fact (again) that Leiter does not himself do much work along naturalist lines – his endeavours have been primarily to explicate the nature of naturalism as understood in the early years of the twenty-first century and show how this approach to legal analysis is the means by which serious scholars of the law should be trying to explain legal phenomena (like adjudication).

There are also, however, a few areas in which I could quibble with his work, some of which I would like to touch upon. As I noted earlier, none of this (insofar as it engages Leiter's work) seriously affects the analysis carried out in this work, and so the reader should feel free to advance to the next section, wherein a potentially useful approach to the construction of social reality – along a naturalist line – is introduced. What may be of interest is that in questioning Leiter's focus I sharpen my own focus, a point that should become clear again in the next two chapters.

Leiter is as much a realist (in the sense of scientific realism) as he is a naturalist, though his efforts tend to go primarily into explaining and defending an updated understanding of naturalism. As a realist he holds, then, that a naturalist program should be wedded to an understanding of the goals of knowledge-production – to arrive at models of mind-independent reality. While we can never know directly (or by means of some a priori reasoning) that our models do in fact represent this mind-independent reality, we have good reason to believe the approaches adopted under the fold of the scientific method work us towards better and better theories.

Parallels Leiter draws are between (a) the insights of the early American legal realists, and (b) Quine's work in showing how and why Enlightenment projects attempting to justify scientific knowledge run into problems. The latter problems are also placed up against a larger picture of where we fit in the world and how we can productively work to generate knowledge. As a realist, one presumes there is some "thing" there, some entity we can term "mind-independent reality." This thing serves as the ultimate check on our theories and models. Struggles over the last few generations around "justification" have been with the growing awareness we cannot *logically* demonstrate that our knowledge is grounded in our evidence. The naturalist move past this struggle does not throw out the notion our scientific theories should still be measured against a mind-independent "way things are," but just the notion that it is necessary to try to justify scientific theories in aprioristic ways proposed up to the middle of the twentieth century. In the latter part of the twentieth century, justifying scientific theories became a game played according to rules themselves set from within the natural world (acknowledging we are just parts of that world, looking back at itself, so to speak).

But what is the corresponding "thing" a legal realist is presuming as that *given* against which justification should be measured when imagining "legal knowledge"?

The natural law theorist has little trouble on this sort of point – the corresponding "thing" just need be "how the law should be." We can take any pre-existing mass of material (whether it be just legal material or the full mix of legal and non-legal material) and measure the outcome that results when a decision is made in light of that material against the outcome that *should* result. Indeed, we can say generally that if a theorist posits a world in which one can say there is an outcome that *should* occur, we can then complete the analogy (to Quine's general naturalist argument), as we can point out that we do not have any way to show that the pre-existing material justifies *this* outcome (the outcome we *should* see).

What to do, though, if one also questions the notion that there is a "way things should be" (when that is somehow independent of what anyone happens to believe or value)? What then functions as the measure against which one sets up actual decisions made?

There are two responses available to the naturalist. One is to drop any interest in working towards any such thing. Quine, in his earlier writings, seemed to be of a mind to do just this in the field of epistemology. Rather than try to work out how certain ways of forming beliefs could still be understood to be "better" than other ways of forming beliefs, the hard-nosed naturalist should be focused just on examining how beliefs are in fact formed.[72] One set of recordings, for example, could be of processes that lead towards representations of things represented (the naturalist has both sides of the ledger to work with, as she eschews any talk of some mysterious transcendental "way things are" – she can track the scientist as he examines how perceptual apparatuses [including the brain] work with incoming data [say, down the optic nerve], leading to visual representations [in "the mind"]). Serious talk of deep justification would fall by the wayside. Is person *x justified* in believing *y*? Only if we water down "justification," the hard-nosed naturalist asserts, is there sense to such a question.

At places Leiter seems to be suggesting the legal naturalist (and so the serious legal theorist) be satisfied with such an outcome. The important matter – the practically important matter – is that we have a sense of what the judicial outcome will be in any particular situation. This is what the lawyer (and her client) wants, and it would be what is provided in a "pure" descriptive/explanatory account. Talk of what the outcome "should have been" is essentially deemed senseless.

I have not parsed Leiter carefully enough to say whether he commits fully to such a response. Certainly, I would say, one need not be satisfied – as a naturalist – with this outcome. A second sensible response is available. The question (which I have not examined carefully enough to posit a serious answer to) is whether Leiter would take this second path.

The legal naturalist could agree there is no given or human-independent "way things are" that corresponds to the scientific realist presumption of a

---

72 See e.g. Ritchie, *supra* note 53 at 43–8.

mind-independent reality, but yet simply posit sets of beliefs and values that we set out as measures by which to weigh judicial outcomes. This may seem, of course, very different from what we are trying to analogize to – we are not presuming there is an independent "way things are," but rather imagining that we can *set out* sets of values to function as that by which we can measure judicial outcomes. This preserves some sense to the notion of "justification" – we can look at the mass of pre-existing material and the result of the judicial action and say whether it seems the result is as it should be – but this is not at all the sort of justification with which the natural law theorist (for example) is consumed.

Nevertheless we have, down this path, a perfectly naturalist way of thinking about how laws and legal systems function in the human-natural world. The "pre-given," then, would be *constructed* (so we cannot say it is "human-independent"), but it is constructed by legal-political communities. We posit communities constructing legal meaning, setting out sets of beliefs and values that then serve as vessels within which legal affairs take place. We posit something like the "nomoi" imagined by Robert Cover, but posited as natural phenomena in the world.[73]

What the naturalist misses if he fails to (or refuses to) go down this path is the sense of politics this then injects into not just matters of adjudication, but theories of law. The argument I develop in the middle chapters of this text is meant to tackle this matter, as I attempt to show that the response of the naturalist should be – must be – to embrace this part of the larger story, positing all *that* as "mechanical" matters that take place in the human-natural world. As I noted earlier, the form of naturalism I deploy in this text marries the sociocultural to the political, though all is placed into the observable world.

Doing so is made easier with the sorts of analyses of social construction we see in Searle's work, as he begins to build out a sense of how sociolinguistic instruments that humans pick up and use are tools generating meaning and forming social reality (including, of course, things like legal systems and all their components – particularly things like obligations, powers, responsibilities, and other instruments capable of generating social bonds and empowerments). We end this discussion of naturalism, then, with a brief overview of his work on the social construction of reality.

Searle: Naturalist Analysis of Sociolinguistic Instruments

A useful tool in this naturalist-study is provided by one contemporary form of analysis around how linguistic instruments function in our social world. In his *Making the Social World*, John Searle has set out an account of how we can

73 Cover, *Nomos and Narrative*, *supra* note 13.

do certain things and accomplish certain ends by way of various speech acts.[74] In the context of the present discussion, Searle's work provides a constructive starting point for grappling with causal interrelations between (a) jurisprudence (and here I mean the law as manifest in systems of statements and propositions), (b) legal theorizing (again referring here to the products of theorizing as manifestations in language and discourse), and (c) actions and reactions in the world. All these phenomena are observable – all can be the subject of "empirical" study. Searle, in a nutshell, points to how linguistic instruments can play interesting roles in creating, maintaining, strengthening, and dissolving forms and structures that make up our social reality (that social world we all inhabit, itself – for each of us – a heterogeneous mix of varied and overlapping social sub-worlds).

In the case of what Searle terms "institutional facts" – facts that exist and function within our structured social realities – we come across (Searle maintains) an institutional reality built out of the functioning of sociolinguistic instruments.[75] Searle argues that particular kinds of speech acts function in this reality to both constitute and maintain forms and structures of the reality itself.[76] The institutional fact, for example, that the Musqueam enjoy an Aboriginal right to fish for food and ceremonial purposes within Canadian law rests on the existence of an institution (Canadian municipal law, here narrowed

---

74 John Searle, *Making the Social World: The Structure of Human Civilization* (Oxford: Oxford University Press, 2010). One thing this approach allows me to do is sidestep what might otherwise come in as pressing debates. I do not have any need, for example, to engage with deep debates over the relationships between free will, determinism, and moral responsibility. I recall coming upon the compatibilist picture when first reading Hume as an undergraduate and being struck by the concurrence of elegance and obfuscation. Under the approach adopted in this text I need not sink deep into these sorts of matters. The kind of discussion I do need to enter – one that floats, as it were, above these debates – appears at the end of chapter 5.

75 Others use this term to refer to a category of facts deemed "non-natural." I am not using this term in that fashion. For a prolonged discussion of various uses, and more particularly, abuses, of the notion of social construction in modern academia, see Ian Hacking, *The Social Construction of What?* (Cambridge, MA: Harvard University Press, 1999).

76 Searle, *supra* note 74 at 16. Searle argues, for example,

> The human mind is able to create systems of symbolic representations. We can use those systems to perform meaningful speech acts.... Because of the nature of meaning itself, there are... only five possible types of illocutionary speech acts.... Of these types, the Declaration is peculiar in that it creates the very reality that it represents.... Once you see the power of the Declaration to create an institutional reality, a reality of governments, universities, marriages, private property, money, and all the rest of it, you can see that social reality has a formal structure as simple and elegant as the structure of the language used to create it.

Much of the rest of his text is an unpacking of this schema, with a "gap" (or perceived gap) between the reasons for our decisions and actions and our actual decisions and actions making sense of the institutional structures we actually happen to enjoy (the reader, at the end of my work, might sense that I would put scare quotes around "we" in this last sentence).

in focus down to Aboriginal law) created through the operations of a complex set of speech acts. The larger institution has no existence independent of these sorts of acts – it is only through collective acceptance or recognition of certain rules expressed through these kinds of linguistic acts that something like an institution comes into being.[77] Constitutive rules (establishing, in this situation, the basic existence of both the institution of Canadian law and the field of Aboriginal law) make possible statements that then function to make it possible that such a particular right (of the Musqueam to fish for food and ceremonial purposes) could exist.

As with our discussion of Leiter, I propose to sketch out those aspects of Searle's extended argument that I can use as a springboard for subsequent discussions of what might be going on within the development of Aboriginal law. Much of the scaffolding of Searle's work is helpful, but, as with Leiter, there is a narrowness of focus at play that ultimately limits its usefulness. As well, Searle presents something of an apology for liberal thought in *Making the Social World*, though the work is not presented as such – oddly, Searle seems fairly oblivious to the possibility that he is thinking and working within a constructed social reality and that this might seriously limit what he might productively say about politics and power.[78] This requires that we pay careful attention to the core of Searle's work, as there comes a point at which he unreflectively advances past an attempt to explain how social reality is made to a project of articulating how *his* particular social reality is structured.

Two sociolinguistic instruments – Declarations and status functions – play central roles in the theory Searle has developed over the last few decades. The theory is meant to fit with two key features of the *one* natural world we inhabit, presented as sets of basic facts, "the atomic theory of matter and the evolutionary theory of biology."[79] We can read out of these initial premises the fact his work is avowedly both naturalist and realist in orientation.

His central thesis is quite strong: that *all* aspects of the social worlds we inhabit can be explained by reference to these two types of sociolinguistic instruments. Declarations – statements that are such that by their very utterance reality is changed to fit their content – and status functions – the imposition on physically instantiated parties of forms of status – are means by which collectives can generate meaning and forms of social reality. To sketch out Searle's "grand"

77 Here, as a point of interest, is where it would seem Searle's account could use some work. While loosely speaking it seems right to say that "collective acceptance" is a condition for the emergence of a new structure in a social world, what this "acceptance" was is underdeveloped in Searle's account.

78 John Searle, "Human Rights" in Searle, *supra* note 74 at 174. By the time he enters his discussion of negative and positive rights Searle is clearly ensconced in a specific world-construction, which he is helping to support and expand. See especially *ibid* at 184–98.

79 *Ibid* at 4.

theory, let me work through how these two instruments are understood to function in making the social world. An overview is contained in "Status Functions as Created by Declarations," an early section of *Making the Social World*.[80]

AN OVERVIEW: DECLARATIONS AND STATUS FUNCTIONS

One particularly interesting kind of speech act – what Searle terms "Declarations" – functions to "change reality to match the propositional content of the speech act ... [where interestingly] we succeed in so doing because we represent the reality as being so changed."[81] Good examples of Declarations are certain performative utterances – where someone, for example, makes a promise or issues an order. In *saying* "I promise to repay you," I *make it the fact* that, within the social world we inhabit (which importantly includes the institution of promising), a certain kind of reality now exists *as a result of the utterance* (namely that I now fall under a promise, within the institution of promising, entailing, *inter alia*, that you now have certain legitimate expectations).

Declarations, in turn, are linked to status functions. Earlier Searle had noted that

> humans have the capacity to impose functions on objects and people where the objects and the people cannot perform the functions solely in virtue of their physical structure. The performance of the function requires that there be a collectively recognized status that the person or object has, and it is only in virtue of that status that the person or object can perform the function in question.[82]

So, for example, Sally may be the associate dean of the Faculty of Law, and functions tied to this status-position, "associate dean" (functions made available to Sally by virtue of her having been accorded this status), are such that they can be performed only because of the status a social grouping has generated (that it collectively recognizes). Members of the law school community (including university administration) recognize a certain set of "deontic powers" that accompany this status (that is, a certain set of obligations, powers, rights, entitlements, responsibilities, and so on, that flow from and are connected to the holding of this status by an individual). With recognition of these deontic powers, the associate dean (not the person but the office) comes into existence as a component of a form of social reality. Sally, for example, has the collectively accepted power to determine who teaches what courses in the upcoming year. Thinking generally about status functions not only gives us a window into the

80 *Ibid* at 11–15.
81 *Ibid* at 11–12.
82 *Ibid* at 7.

nature of aspects of our social reality, but also lets us begin to see how social reality itself is created and maintained.

Searle's strong claim is that "all of human institutional reality is created and maintained in existence by (representations that have the same logical form as) SF [status function] Declarations."[83] Assuming the soundness of this picture, Searle is pointing out how the content of certain kinds of sociolinguistic performances can create aspects of social reality, collectively accounting for social reality itself. Simple forms of Declarations generate particular aspects of reality – the promise itself, for example, makes a certain kind of reality come into existence, one marked by a certain set of rights and obligations.

These simple instances themselves are possible and make sense only within larger constructed institutions – in this case a promise is made possible and understandable only in the context of the institution of promising, itself created through other speech acts. And then other forms of speech acts (with the same logical structure as Declarations) generate such things as status functions, which generate social structures wherein relationship-possibilities are expanded (pieces of paper can come to function as money, an individual can come to stand as chief justice of the Supreme Court, two individuals can be understood to be legally married, etc.).

At the heart of creation of social institutions lie constitutive rules – a Declaration exists that sets out that a status function exists, a statement of the form "*X* counts as *Y* in *C*." So, for example, one can understand the generation of aspects of Aboriginal law within this framework: "Traditions, customs, or practices integral to the cultures of Aboriginal peoples count as Aboriginal rights should conditions *C* be met." Of course, this is predicated on the prior existence of larger institutions within which we might find such a specific constitutive rule – in particular, this is embedded within the larger social reality constituting the Canadian legal system.

COLLECTIVE ACCEPTANCE, FREE WILL, AND DESIRE-INDEPENDENT REASONS FOR ACTION

Three additional aspects of this account of the creation of social reality need to enter our discussion, two that Searle argues serve as necessary conditions for the making of forms of social reality, the third an apparent attribute or consequence of the picture drawn.

First, as we noted in our overview, status functions operate only to generate forms of social reality under certain general conditions, one of which we noted – that of collective acceptance or recognition of the status imposed. It is not enough that I declare on my own that certain moves constitute checkmate in the game of chess – it must be generally accepted, as a condition of playing the

83 *Ibid* at 13.

game of chess, that these certain moves will count as checkmate. This notion of collective acceptance (put most frequently as "collective recognition" in Searle's later work, to avoid the suggestion that *agreement* with the rule established is required) is vitally important in the analysis to come in the last few chapters of this text, and so it is explored more fully in an upcoming section.

A second general condition is not so easily discerned, and its discussion in *Making the Social World* is muddled around the edges. Searle argues that a condition for the generation of social reality is the presence of a subjective experience of a form of free will:

> [W]e have a special kind of consciousness ... where we choose one thing but we have a sense that we could have chosen something else. In such cases we sense a *causal gap* between the reasons for our decisions and actions and the actual decisions and actions.[84]

Searle is careful (usually) to be clear that he is not arguing that the fact we create forms of social reality means we possess strong forms of free will. For the most part he is careful to point out that what we need to presuppose is the existence of a *sense* of free will.

Further – and here we arrive at the third component of this theory germane to the task of trying to explain the nature of Aboriginal rights – the presence of this sense of free will serves to explain why we develop social reality as we do, as status functions work to generate *desire-independent reasons for action*:

> [I]f I recognize that I have made a promise, then I have a desire-independent reason for keeping the promise; and it is no good to say to that, "Yes, but it is only because you want to keep your promises." I do indeed want to keep my promises, but the desire to keep my promises comes from the nature of promising rather than the nature of promising coming from the desire to keep them.[85]

We do not experience ourselves in the world functioning as automatons – rather, we sense that we make choices and that there is a causal gap between how we actually decide and act and those possible reasons for our decisions and actions. Status functions, in their generating deontic powers like obligations, rights, powers, responsibilities, and so forth, create a social world we inhabit in which possibilities are (apparently) opened up to us, as we are provided with *reasons* for acting one way rather than another. Do I actually accept, for example, that I have an obligation at this moment to keep this promise? Or do

84 *Ibid* at 133 [emphasis in original].

85 *Ibid* at 131. This passage occurs in the context of Searle's answer to those who follow Hume's argument that "reason is and ought to be the slave of the passions": *ibid* at 130.

I decide, for some other reason, that I will not keep this particular promise? The promise, in these calculations, provides a desire-independent reason for acting, one that I may ultimately (seemingly) *choose* not to act by.

SHORTCOMINGS IN SEARLE'S ACCOUNT

Searle's most detailed examination of what collective recognition means and entails takes place in a section following an extended discussion of the nature of collective intentionality. Intentionality refers to the "directness or aboutness" of mental states. I can say, "I am *afraid that* x will win the election," or "I *believe that* there is a single natural world," or "I *intend* to type these words." In each case a mental state is *directed towards* or *is about* a thought or action. Searle spends considerable time extending what is generally understood to be a notion applicable to individual thoughts and actions to "collective" matters, defending in particular the notion that there is sense in such statements as "We believe that *x* ...," or "We intend to do *y*" – sense that does not require this be reduced to a mass of statements of individual intent (as if saying, "We intend to do *x*" can only mean "I intend to do *x*" *and* "Bob intends to do *x*," etc.). When you and I say, "We intend to play a game of chess," we can understand this to mean that there are presumptions in each of our minds that the other is cooperating, so I understand you have the same goal in mind (of playing this game) and you understand as well that I have this goal in mind. In this way it can make sense to speak of "collective intentionality" that functions to move our individual bodies, all in something of a dance of cooperation.

Now, importantly, Searle is careful to note that on institutional levels it is not necessary, in order to make sense of this, that any one person involved in some large-scale collective matter *know* what everyone else in this collective endeavour is doing (as in the case for the simple example of a game of chess).[86] There must be a belief in the background – namely, the belief that others in the endeavour share the common aim of the enterprise, and that that animates their actions – but no one need know what is happening in the minds of all the others. Likewise, it is sufficient to see that each person's actions are caused by his or her own internal mental states.

All of this carries collective intentionality, it would seem, into the territory of cooperation. But with the notion of "collective recognition," that notion that plays a central role in his account of how human societies construct social reality, cooperation is not a necessary element. Within an institution there may be many activities that require cooperative action (so, for example, those *making use* of the institution of marriage will have to act cooperatively to do so), but on the level of the creation of the institution of marriage itself, there is no requirement that the collective cooperate in its creation and maintenance.

86 *Ibid* at 54.

So what is required on this institution-creating level? Searle unpacks this with the example of the institution of money:

> [P]articipants ... take the existence and validity of money for granted. They simply recognize it. Of what does the collective recognition consist? It does not seem to me that it requires *cooperation*. Rather, what it requires is that each participant accepts the existence and validity of money in the belief that there is mutual acceptance on the part of the others.... [C]ollective recognition can be constituted by the fact that each person recognizes money and there is mutual knowledge among the participants that they all recognize money.[87]

It is hard to find fault with the notion that institutions owe their existence to some form of collective intentionality, where that does not require cooperation but rather a weaker form of collective recognition. It is also hard to disagree with the idea that this does not require any sense of approval or agreement. Dissatisfaction with the model sketched may come as much from the difficulty in precisely spelling out what may well be a family of types of events as with problems that emerge from within the theory. But on certain fronts – especially in relation to the project undertaken in this work – there are clear shortcomings.

Consider the notion of the *collective* that recognizes within itself the existence and validity of some institutional structure or entity. The nature of such collectives is not directly investigated as a thing in need of explication in Searle's account, but even in the unproblematic world he is exploring – focused on *given*, defined societies – one has to wonder about the boundaries of any particular group. The closest he comes to thinking about the sorts of problems that could come up is in his look into such matters as approval, disapproval, acquiescence, and acceptance.

Why, he asks, do we – individual participants living within social realities – seemingly accept (or at least acquiesce in) the functioning of certain institutional structures? Few of us would ever have played any role in the creation of a large-scale feature of our shared social reality (like, say, a system for the enforcement of our criminal laws, or the criminal law itself), and we simply find ourselves living in a mass of layered and overlapping social systems, many of which, if we reflected on matters, we might disagree with.

One answer to such matters is just to note that systems we live within are simply there, and we have little choice but to live and act accordingly. Searle also notes in passing the roles that apathy, ignorance about the nature and workings of these systems, and the agency-bolstering effects of political

---

87 *Ibid* at 58 [emphasis in original].

activism can play in accounting for our general acquiescence to life within surrounding social realities.[88]

But what of situations in which a given group, with its given built social systems, wishes to reach out and pull into itself other meaning-generating, social-reality-constructing collectives?

It is entirely fair to pull back from criticizing Searle for his lack of attention to this point – he has in mind the task of articulating a theory that takes as its subject matter existing forms of social reality emergent out of given collectives. But for our purposes we have to press on, past his bare account. Searle's theory does provide springboards for discussion, since we find in his exploration of power hints about how to think about what happens in the interface of meaning-generating collectives. How can we speak – sticking to the framework of his account of the making of social reality within a naturalist and realist setting – of collective *A* coming to see its social reality be that generated initially within the generating structures of another collective, collective *B*?

The immediate answer has to be that collective *A* comes to "collectively recognize" the form of social reality initially generated by collective *B*. While collective *A* does not have to approve of this form of social reality, it would seem to be necessary that each participant – the members of collective *A* – accept (at least weakly) the existence and validity of this institutional structure or entity.

Such an immediate response, however, generates new questions. Is it reasonable to suppose this must occur on the level of "participants"? Must not collective *A itself* (and not the collection of individuals who make up collective *A*) come to accept the existence and validity of this institutional structure? But what would it mean for such to be the case? Alternatively, is it possible that the only sensible mechanism is that over time, as more and more members of collective *A* begin to think of the world through this new form of reality, collective *A* comes to be pulled into the world created by collective *B*? What, furthermore, are we to make of the notion of "validity" at play in this context? What would it be for collective *A* to accept the *validity* of a form of social reality generated by collective *B*?

One consideration that seems to complicate the picture is the sense that we have to pay attention to the totality of forms of social reality separately enveloping collectives *A* and *B*. That is, while it is tempting to focus on isolated aspects of the social reality created by collective *B* (say its institution of money) and imagine how such isolated bits and pieces might be individually carried over to the social world built by collective *A* (so that eventually collective *A* comes

88 Searle explores the question "How do we get away with it?" by which he means, How do we manage to create aspects of the social world using just words? See *ibid* at 106–8. Searle also devotes a chapter to broader questions around how the social world is created and maintained. See John Searle, "Power: Deontic, Background, Political, and Other" in *ibid* at 145.

to accept the existence and validity of any such particular institution), what we tend to face are two worlds of layered and overlapping institutional complexes, where each bit and piece, on micro and macro levels, is interconnected with numerous other bits and pieces. Meaning, one might argue, is not embedded in isolated bits and pieces, but spread out diffusely throughout the totality. There may well be some forms of social reality that can move about relatively freely between collectives (whereby we mean to say that collective *A* could relatively easily come to accept a new (to it) form of social reality – it can accommodate it relatively easily within its existing network of institutions), but there will also certainly be many aspects of social reality built by collective *B* that will not easily be taken up by *A*. There will be forms of reality that can be taken only into the world of *A* (so *A* becomes more tightly pulled into collective *B*) with great effort and with fundamental transformations to *A*'s self-understandings.

This last thought brings us to a larger concern – to what extent might we witness, with attempts by one collective to have its forms of social reality infect (and thereby envelop) the social worlds of another collective, the subsuming of the one world by the other? These are the sorts of larger concerns we need to keep track of as we look at how Canadian courts create legal rules and tests for such constructed legal instruments as Aboriginal rights.

With such questions and concerns in mind, there is one other matter we can pull out of Searle's account that can aid in our quest to think clearly about what seems to be the imposition of Aboriginal law on the lives and worlds of Indigenous peoples. We might ask, *How* exactly could collective *B* go about attempting to have its forms of social reality "taken up" by collective *A* (so *A* is effectively pulled closer into being essentially a part of *B*)? What are the techniques and tools available to collective *B* should it wish to accomplish this sort of task in the natural world?

In the context of a different discussion Searle suggests tools available for such attempts. Coercion, of course, is one such tool, especially when coupled with destructive forces. That is, force could be applied to collective *A*, breaking up its systems of meaning-generation and transmission, and replacing them with forms of built social reality emergent out of collective *B*. There are also, however, "softer" means available. Recall that what collective *B* requires is recognition by collective *A* of the existence and validity of its forms of social reality. As Searle notes in his discussion of power,[89] this can be attempted by getting collective *A* to think there are no other viable options. Similarly, collective *B* could attempt to get collective *A* to come to think exclusively in terms of the institutional forms through which it wishes collective *A* would see the world (so collective *A* does not even think in terms of options). The fact is that in the

89 *Ibid* at 145–52.

world around us the thoughts and actions of individuals (and hence the groups they might constitute) can be manipulated and subverted.

So, while Searle's naturalist account of the making of social reality does not focus on the very sorts of concerns that animate the writing of this text, significant elements of his account provide tools and guidance in our quest to make sense of Aboriginal rights. We can see in broad strokes how institutional reality is a constructed, complex thing, and we can begin to think clearly about how forms of social reality are made, transmitted, and (potentially) imposed. We end this look into Searle's work with a few words about how to think about the things we can create with sociolinguistic instruments.

THINGS NOT CREATED THROUGH SPEECH ACTS

Declarations, as we noted above, play a special role in institutional reality in Searle's model – indeed, they create "the very reality that [they] represent."[90] Note, though, that nowhere within Searle's larger model of how aspects of social reality can be created does he suggest that either representations of "non-naturalistic" entities or the intentional objects of such representations might somehow come into being simply by the operation of sociolinguistic instruments. That is, as much as the content of a belief might include a representation of, or point towards, a supernatural, transcendent, or a-natural being, such a being – the thing represented, not the representation – does not thereby magically come into existence. In Searle's account, things created – like institutions, with attendant roles, themselves carrying along deontic components like obligations, privileges, powers, and rights – are not themselves non-naturalistic. While we create them (through linguistic means), they themselves arise out of and become new aspects of the natural world. Searle speaks of our creating large parts of our social world, but these created aspects never advance past aspects of our larger world defining the naturalized borders of our larger reality. They are, essentially, institutional structures around and components of a newly created set of relationships. I, for example, may place myself into a new set of obligations, should I promise to you (within the institution of promising) that I will repay the debt I owe you.

Searle's account, then, is focused on how new aspects of our social world can come into existence. On the flipside, within the world of methodological naturalism within which this text operates is the matter of what we do *not* thereby let slip into our world of natural objects and properties. For example, what of a speech act – or set of speech acts – that expresses the notion that a particular fundamental (non-derivative) "good" should guide the development of the law in some field? Let us suppose that, absent human

90 Searle, *supra* note 74 at 16.

conceptualizations of such, the natural world does not contain *intrinsic* goods.[91] Does the intrinsically valuable good *spoken of* (where the speech act is entwined within the proper sort of social activity) thereby come into existence (does the intent generate a thing in the world, some entity corresponding to this representation of an intrinsic good)?[92] It should be clear that in making the social world in the ways sketched out under Searle's account, no such acts of creation are imagined.

The cautious approach adopted in this text allows not just that people exist in the world, but that relationships between these people – which define the core of their social reality – enjoy a form of existence. These varied relationships can determine how one acts, and newly generated forms of relationships (around things like promises or orders) can affect how one thinks about how to act. These entities all fit comfortably within a naturalist model of reality and existence.[93] It is interesting to note that humans can create forms of reality through sociolinguistic activity, but this reality (as it is imagined in the account deployed in this text) is not non-naturalistic in any troubling sense. We can "see" this reality all around us – in the form of such institutions as marriage, chess, hockey, and the law.

One has to be, within such an approach, particularly cautious when working with such notions as intrinsic value or "good in itself." Consider the ideal of liberty, lying at the heart of liberal doctrine. This concept does not simply capture the notion of being free from external constraint (or that of being in a position to pursue one's own interests) but carries along with it in certain dominant strands of liberal philosophy the sense of ultimate and fundamental value. In these systems of belief, liberty is not just a "thing" (or situation) to

---

91 Here I do not concern myself with whether one understands the notion of an intrinsic good as referring to a "final end" (versus an instrumental end) or something with value in virtue of intrinsic, non-relational properties (versus those things with value in virtue of extrinsic, relational properties). Debate around these very sorts of matters illustrate the advantage in avoiding efforts to make sense of accounts that contain such terms (when the project of making sense entails working within a world in which it is presumed the terms might refer to properties or things independent of representations).

92 An alternative might be that such goods are non-natural entities. Arguably, beginning with such a position does not launch a theory about the good that persuades the world that a non-natural account makes sense. The response to Moore's high-water non-naturalist ethical theory seemed to be movement towards non-cognitive (emotivist) ethical theories. See GE Moore, *Principia Ethica* (Cambridge, UK: Cambridge University Press, 1903).

93 As Ritchie notes in discussing "qualia" (a term used to denote the subjective experience of a phenomenon, such as the experience of the colour red), "[I]f you call yourself a methodological naturalist ... you can be more relaxed. There is nothing wrong in principle with positing new entities in science": Ritchie, *supra* note 53 at 142. As we noted in our brief discussion of Quine, a naturalist of his stripe allows for commitment to entities when they fit the currently established scientific paradigm concerning that field of study. See *supra* note 53.

describe in the world, but an *ideal*,[94] an end to be pursued in itself. Individuals can certainly believe many things that involve this ideal – they can believe in the ideal itself, they can believe that certain rules should be drafted to uphold the ideal – indeed, they might believe that all social institutions should be constructed to maximize the presence of this thing as a structuring element in the lives of the citizens of a state. But in having such beliefs, even in holding such-and-such belief at the core of one's life and existence, the ideal *itself* (as reflecting a property of inherent goodness or value) does not become part of our world.[95]

There are ways, of course, to generate some reasonable sense of such a "thing itself" existing in the world. We could, for example, translate any statement that seemed to imply some sort of Platonic existence into some other statement (or set of statements) that reduce this to natural phenomena. Alternatively, one could deny that in speaking of "liberty" the intent is to point to some ideal property (of which forms of liberty in our world are but shadows), instead holding that the term refers only to actual instantiations of a property in actual situations in the world (inviting a form of nominalism to resolve the matter). Or one could appeal to a form of conceptualism, arguing that the supposedly universal term enjoys an existence in the world, but only in the minds of people employing this concept. All these techniques, however, do one thing – they defuse the possibility of a non-natural thing existing in the world, replacing the referent of the term with some other thing or set of things that can fit naturally with what we can observe and study. These techniques allow us to turn away from the threat that an ideal may be thought to somehow link up to a transcendent or Platonic realm, and allow us to keep the (now non-threatening) language.

A form of conceptualism is most often turned to in this study when we come up against linguistic expressions that seem to refer to entities that might be themselves non-natural (or super-natural). Treating these expressions in this context as doing no more than indicating concepts bounded by the limits of thought permits a broad and workable understanding and acceptance of what we might mean by such things as ideals. This is not a strong form of conceptualism, as it does not assert that such terms must be understood as performing *no more* than this function – I leave open the possibility such terms might actually refer in some mysterious way to mind-independent non-natural properties or things, but I advocate in this study avoiding forms of analysis or discourse that either begin with the presumption of such powers of referral or that invest time

94 One could perhaps more properly say it has the property of being an ideal, and this property has to be handled with care.

95 Once again, this is not to say such a thing could not exist, only that it does not come into existence just in our saying or believing certain things (which, of course, would also be paradoxical, given what we are saying this thing is!). Should "liberty" exist as an "inherent good," it would have to do so independently of one coming to think of it as so – and this mysterious thing then needs to be *found* to exist.

and energy into the exploration of such possibilities. The former conflict with the methodological naturalism at play here, while the latter, I argue, prevents us from arriving at the best explanations possible for what we observe in the natural world around us. These other sorts of exploration, I argue, are invariably diverting, and they divert from what should be the focus when one wants to *make sense* of the phenomena of the emergence of Aboriginal law, and of attempts by theorists to make sense of Aboriginal law.[96]

The form of naturalism at play in this work does not begin with a priori assertions regarding what may or may not exist as "natural" objects or processes – rather, we let our best science of the day (where we understand what counts as "science" itself to be a product of our current understanding)[97] guide us on the nature of nature. Psychological or mental states fit within current scientific study as reputable subjects,[98] and so we (at least for the moment) countenance their presence within naturalistic accounts.

Following this general approach allows us to see the law itself (in this regard, as it generates Aboriginal law as a sub-subject) as essentially comprising forms of sociolinguistic instrument and the forms of social reality these instruments generate and make possible. We can explore all these instruments and their natural products, asking how they intersect with each other, how they influence our social reality, how they make certain things happen (or not happen), how they influence the actions of individuals and groups, and how they

96 One might be tempted to think this kind of conceptualist approach is best used as well for such things as principles or rules, or such similar instruments as may potentially denote or contain abstract terms, but the concern is not with abstract concepts, but with the possibility one could imagine that simply by denoting a certain kind of term (and having acceptance within a linguistic community of the meaning of this term) a non-natural entity could come into being (or be successfully referred to), such that we were required to grapple with the meaning of this term in debates that make use of it. We might otherwise imagine, in looking at how to make sense of Aboriginal rights, that we would need to engage with debates on the *merits* of liberalism and its core constituent principles.

An abstract concept (or instrument containing the abstract concept) need not pose any serious challenge in the context of the study as framed – here we aim only to carry out an examination into the role this concept may play in social interactions (examining, for example, the impact a concept might have on how individuals and groups think and act) to see what form of existence it may have in the social realm.

97 This allows us to sidestep some of the controversies some see dogging naturalism, that, for example, it is too closely aligned with aggressive forms of scientism, or too closely tied to the particular theory of science of the day. For a discussion of variant forms of naturalized philosophy of science, see e.g. Jack Ritchie, "Naturalized Philosophy of Science" in Ritchie, *supra* note 53 at 74.

98 This follows Searle and others in distancing their forms of naturalism from the more behaviourist-centred variant apparent in Quine. Desires, intentions, attitudes – all these and more can be considered "natural" to the degree they play meaningful roles in contemporary scientific discourse.

intersect (as systems) with each other. When I turn in later chapters to explain how liberal positivism and critical (postcolonial) theory might make sense of Aboriginal rights, it will be such matters that are up for dissection and debate.

With this approach we are able on a first-order level to see different understandings and assessments of Aboriginal law in relation to each other. We have a common setting within which we can wonder about causal relationships, about how forces and influences function, and about what all this might mean to those who are placed in relation to the law and these understandings of it. This permits, as well, consideration of second-order understandings and assessments. We can ponder the place of theories in this common social setting. We can see theorists are also presenting sets of statements and propositions, about many and varied matters. We take all these claims to be – at least initially for the purposes of our study – nothing more than sociolinguistic instruments.

Within this approach, references to non-natural entities or processes within collections or systems of statements are neither ignored nor eliminated, but those that might appear troubling (those potentially meant to refer to some non-natural or super-natural things or things) are treated (as a *methodological* matter, not *substantively*) as nothing more than ideas or concepts. That is, such attempts at reference are treated as elements of statements or ideas about which we reserve any thought about their actually referring to some thing to which they purport to refer. Avoiding the inclination to wrestle with referents not only frees us from difficult discussions – much more importantly, it allows us to explore the role of theories that use or contain these attempts-at-referring in our complex social reality.

Pulling Threads Together

We have seen where the jurisprudence lies several decades into the twenty-first century. We have woven into our introduction of this jurisprudence key puzzles that arise, highlighting when appreciation of a puzzle is enhanced by paying attention to Indigenous perspectives. We noted at the end of this discussion that efforts to theorize Aboriginal rights do not address key puzzles – in fact, theoretical accounts add to the sense of puzzlement, as theorists say conflicting things about Aboriginal rights and offer no way past this conflict towards an acceptable sensible account of Aboriginal rights.

With this situation laid out before us, in the last section the nature of the approach to this set of problems worked with in this text was introduced in more depth. Before applying this to the task of making sense of Aboriginal rights, time is spent in the next chapter to ground this approach in a richer discussion of theorizing, and of problems about theorizing that inform the development of larger intellectual traditions of the last century or so. Following that, discussion moves to legal theorizing, and focus narrows to concerns that arise around meaning and normativity. Can meaning and normativity be accommodated within an approach centred on methodological naturalism, and if so, how? Those matters resolved, we are then prepared to move into an analysis of the ability of theories about the law to make sense of Aboriginal rights in the latter chapters.

Besides connecting this work to the larger world of debate and controversy about the role of theory in the modern academy, the intermediate discussion introduces us to "critical" concerns – those arguments and positions about the business of theorizing that rose to prominence (especially in the social sciences and legal analysis) in the latter half of the twentieth century. When we turn to applying methodological naturalism not just to the jurisprudence and its puzzles, but also to attempts to explain the development of the law, we will be looking at two representative contemporary theories, liberal positivism and critical (postcolonial) theory, where the second stands in for the panoply of critical theories. Critical theoretical concerns, however, infect both theoretical accounts, since these concerns call into question the ability of "mainstream" legal theory to objectively or non-ideologically explain the nature of legal phenomena. Besides grounding and defending the use of methodological naturalism in this work, the next two chapters give us a glimpse into how critical analyses entered the general discourse, and what is entailed in that development.

4 Remarks on Theorizing and Method

Earlier we introduced a range of puzzles connected to making sense of Aboriginal law. One set emerged from within the jurisprudence, as elements of Aboriginal law were presented as striking the observer – particularly from an Indigenous perspective – as puzzling. This led into another set – puzzles tied to divergent views of members of society, people who can, seemingly reasonably, think of Aboriginal law as being either progressive or regressive. I speculated that one could take this as signalling no more than diverse (and possibly incommensurable) moral, political, or normative sensibilities, perspectives, or ideologies. Should this speculation be born out, the task of otherwise pursuing a resolution – trying to work out a settled understanding of Aboriginal law – might begin to seem futile, as conceivably the whole matter could come down to a standoff between sensibilities, perspectives, or ideologies.

One might presume critical and reflective exploration into *how* to make sense of Aboriginal law would be more fruitful, if we left behind observations and intuitions and moved into what theorists make of this field. What would legal theorists, *critically reflecting* on the nature of Aboriginal law, say about its nature (and evaluation)? Presumably legal theorists would attempt to speak from positions adjusted for the possibility of bias or distortion – we might expect that legal theories flow from digging below superficial and potentially biased understandings to a level of mechanisms and forces that could accurately *explain* the phenomena making up this field of law.

Unfortunately, as we noted in the last chapter, our exploration runs into another layer of puzzlement. Theories about Aboriginal law do not lead us away from simple stalemates on perspectives, but rather reveal (at least initially) yet more instances of fundamental divergence. One might expect explanations for phenomena to converge at some point, as theorists (struggling to overcome bias and distortion) work towards common explanatory ground. Unfortunately, however, we do not see common ground between those we might have thought were trying to make sense of Aboriginal law.[1]

Given this lack of theoretical convergence, it is somewhat surprising that, should we scan the literature, we find no attempts to identify an approach to the study of Aboriginal law that might address this problem – indeed, we witness another layer of disagreement, as theorists approach the study of Aboriginal law with differing methodologies.[2]

This confusion accounts for the search in this text for a way to make sense of Aboriginal law that might hold promise of moving us around stalemates and divergences. This quest for a suitable approach builds through this chapter and the next, bits and pieces of the resolution to these puzzles being gathered and put together over the course of several kinds of discussions. The end of this journey into the heart of legal theorizing is realization that such theories have to account for both meaning and normativity. These two features of human social activity generate challenges that must be addressed if explanatory models are to be possible. The adoption of methodological naturalism is a plausible means by which these features can be accommodated in explanatory models. In a later discussion, the ability of methodological naturalism to similarly manage puzzles that arise from conflicting legal theoretic accounts of Aboriginal law is developed and explored.

First, we work through some thoughts about theorizing. The intent is to begin to flesh out the nature of the approach taken herein while simultaneously explaining why this approach seems best suited to the task (given the sorts of puzzles introduced earlier). As the discussion progresses, the focus narrows, first to theorizing about human activity at the end of this chapter, and then in the next chapter to theorizing about the law. That is, in exploring the relationship between law and theory, I begin with questions about the nature of theory and the activity of theorizing, eventually narrowing focus to difficult questions swirling around the use of theories to explain human and social activity, ending with a few words about how this makes the application of theoretical models to the law challenging. I follow this up with a walk to roughly the same point from a different vector, beginning with remarks about the nature of law

---

1 A postmodern legal theorist might argue, however, that this divergence of theoretical positions is not problematic, but rather just the product of the realization that there is no possibility of "grand theory," some theoretical account that could provide a set of fundamental (and justifiable) truths about the phenomena under study. See e.g. Gary Minda, *Postmodern Legal Movements: Law and Jurisprudence at Century's End* (New York: New York University Press, 1996). I explore a general "critical" perspective on legal affairs in chapter 8, in applying naturalistic analysis to critical (postcolonial) theory and its ability to make sense of Aboriginal law jurisprudence.

2 For a discussion of several representative theorists, see e.g. "Differing Theoretical Perspectives" in chapter 3.

to arrive at further (complementary) insights into the nature of legal theory. As all these discussions progress, the theoretical and methodological approach adopted and employed in the latter chapters of this text is elaborated upon and defended. The hope is that this multi-pronged discussion illuminates and supports the approach I adopt, advocate, and work through.

We begin with theorizing in general because the general critical/interpretivist position reaches back that far, challenging what is (taken to be) assumed to work in the study of the natural world. I look at what is generally argued to be wrapped up in the business of theorizing about the natural world, about general challenges to this account developed over the last few generations of scholarly activity, and then develop means by which one can sensibly meet challenges posed. My intent is to build on these means through this chapter and the next, showing how more focused challenges (to theorizing in the social realm and to legal theorizing most particularly) can be similarly addressed.

This excursion into legal theory begins, then, with some initial thoughts about theorizing and a first stab at presenting some of the merits of following the approach taken in this study.

Initial Remarks on Theorizing in General

A starting point for this investigation is a presupposition fairly characterized as "common sense": the notion that in theorizing a researcher is trying to make sense of or explain some phenomena.[3] While leery of continuing to use the moniker "common sense" as I expound on this initial presumption, I nevertheless push ahead. Given the overwhelmingly powerful argument that is the success of scientific endeavours in describing the natural world, I continue to label "common sense" the sense that understands speculation and testing as the appropriate means to explore and explain phenomena in general.

Within this realm of common sense, proposing that some theory is more or less *correct* is connected to a claim that statements and claims contained

3 Of course, in some sense I am prejudicing matters in labelling this "common sense." I attempt to frame a very general articulation of a form of theorizing aligned with a modest form of scientific realism, a form that rests on a picture of the world as *given*, *independent* of thought of it, with theorizing being that process by which we think about this concept-independent world in a systematic fashion, trying to capture in language the form and structure this world possesses. Much of the history of debates in a number of fields over the last half century or so has to do with challenges to this "common sense" model, all revolving around the notion that in theorizing – even in the scientific realm – nature (or the world) is generated. See e.g. Peter Godfrey-Smith, *Theory and Reality: An Introduction to the Philosophy of Science* (Chicago: University of Chicago Press, 2003) at 173–89. On the notion that even scientific facts might be generated as social constructions, see Bruno Latour & Steve Woolgar, *Laboratory Life: The Social Construction of Scientific Facts* (Beverly Hills, CA: Sage Publications, 1979).

in the constructed theoretical structure substantially explain the nature of the phenomena thereby modelled.[4] Within this vision of theorizing, a theory is typically measured and evaluated (is deemed "good" or not) along two scalars, accuracy and richness. A very good theory would be both extensive in its ambitions and accurate in its modelling of the range of phenomena it attempts to explain.[5]

"Accuracy" in this account needs a bit more unpacking, and in doing that we begin to run into complications in this "common sense model" of theorizing (CSM). One might suppose the focus invited by accuracy is on the "fit" between models developed under the theory and the phenomena thereby modelled. One could then unpack this notion of fit so it connected with the idea that as one gained a better grasp of models, one's abilities to work with the phenomena would be heightened. A particular model might be mathematical – say, a series of mathematical formulae, expressing relationships between components of the world being modelled – and understanding the nature of the mathematical formulae would likely increase one's ability to manipulate those components.

Would this, however, provide a satisfactory *explanation* of the phenomena modelled? Do we hope for more than "accuracy," where by that we mean nothing more than "fit" with data? Do we also mean to capture the notion that the theory advanced provides an *explanation* for the mechanisms modelled? Marks on paper (or bits in the machine) provide an explanation, one might suggest, when they do *more* than capture in formulae the "how" of dynamic phenomena. We want, with an explanation, some account of the "why" that explains what we have captured with our formulae. This "fit" would (a) assist in our desire to be able to work with the world (i.e., our concern with accuracy would track with our success in interacting with the world around, allowing us, for example, to develop the ability to send people to the moon), and (b) provide *insight* into the way things are, independent of how we think about things.

4 See e.g. Godfrey-Smith, *supra* note 3 at 190–201. Godfrey-Smith tracks debates about the notion of explanation through the twentieth century, ultimately arriving at his own position on the matter, that a few different forms of "explanation" are operative in science, though he argues that generally "explanatory inference is a matter of devising and comparing hypotheses about hidden structures that might be responsible for data": *ibid* at 199.

5 A theory could conceivably, however, be exemplary should it perfectly explain a smaller, localized phenomenon. All things considered, however, it would be a better theory if it could link up this explanation to explanations of other, related, phenomena. Kitcher notes, for example, that one factor (among several) that underscored Galileo's arguments for heliocentrism was its ability to simultaneously explain more of the physical world – its intertwining, as it were, with other observed phenomena. The unified account of the motions of bodies was slowly worked out to be better than the traditional Aristotelean model it eventually replaced. See Phillip Kitcher, *The Advancement of Science: Science Without Legend, Objectivity without Illusions* (Oxford: Oxford University Press, 1993) at 205–11.

We might be tempted to say, then, that under the common sense understanding of theorizing, the best theory provides the best *explanatory* model, where that model describes what we observe in a way that answers our questions about *reasons* for things happening as we have captured them. In the case of Aboriginal law, for example, the best theory would provide the best explanation for how the law in this area works, how it has developed, and *why it is the way it is.*[6] Such an explanation would *also* provide means by which something substantial and meaningful could be said in predicting such matters as how actors within this field will act or how the law will continue to develop.

A Common Illustration of the Progress of Explanations

Let us first pause to illustrate how one hopes theorizing about some phenomena progresses, gradually adding to our general understanding of the world around us. Consider the motions of the planets around the sun, a common topic in such excursions.[7]

For thousands of years motions of planetary bodies were noted by people around the world, as planetary bodies stand out vividly in the skies, given their unusual tracks in relation to the relatively fixed stars. Stories about attempts to explain the motion of these bodies often begin with early debates in the Western world between proponents of geocentric and heliocentric models.[8] With gradual acceptance of the heliocentric model through the end of the sixteenth century and (especially) the first half of the seventeenth century (at least amongst a small body of European astronomers), matters were still far from resolved, as the earliest Copernican (heliocentric) models used circles for orbits (making use of epicycles, circles on circles, to manage the fit between model and data), much as had been the case with the Ptolemaic (geocentric) system

---

6 Even within the ambit of the project of "making sense," one can argue that divergence in both method and outcome will be an unavoidable fact. The theorist, this argument would go, must make judgments about what things are relevant, what facts are important (or trivial), how one goes about deciding what terms like "relevance" will mean, and so forth. See e.g. Paul Feyerabend, *Against Method: Outline of an Anarchistic Theory of Knowledge* (Atlantic Highlands, NJ: Humanities Press, 1975).

7 See e.g. Thomas Kuhn, The Copernican Revolution: Planetary Astronomy in the Development of Western Thought (Cambridge, MA: Harvard University Press, 1957) [Kuhn, Copernican Revolution].

8 This is to isolate one strand of the story – essentially the same story could be put in terms of the struggle between geostatic and geo-kinetic models, between models that had the Earth motionless (and at the centre of the universe) and the Earth moving (as the third planet around the Sun). For a good discussion in this form, see Maurice Finocchiaro, "Criticism, Reasoning, and Judgment in Science (1995)" in Maurice Finocchiaro, *Arguments about Arguments: Systematic, Critical, and Historical Essays in Logical Theory* (Cambridge, UK: Cambridge University Press, 2005) 409.

it was meant to challenge and replace.[9] While Copernican models made – on the whole – better predictions than Ptolemaic,[10] on other accounts they did not seem satisfactory (in that, for example, obviously this general model had the planets revolve around the sun, an odd business, given both some of the theological understandings of that time [and place] and the fact that this entailed earth's motion both around the sun and on its axis, neither actions being, however, immediately observable).[11]

Making use of Brahe's comprehensive collections of meticulously gathered observational data, in the early 1600s Kepler spent years attempting to arrive at simpler, more elegant, and more accurate models describing the motions of the planets. His three laws replaced circular orbits with elliptical movements (placing the sun at one of the focal points for these figures) and described (a) a relationship between the distance of a planet from its sun and the time it takes to complete an orbit, and (b) a relationship between the time a planet sweeps along a certain extent of its orbit and the area contained in the figure describing the amount of the ellipse thereby swept out.

As clearly progressive as Kepler's account might be, it went only some way to providing the sort of *explanation* we might consider full and comprehensive. The first two movements in this account – from a geocentric to heliocentric model, and from a heliocentric account based on circular movements to one based on elliptical movements – were essentially movements from mathematical model to mathematical model. While Kepler's model provides a mathematical model better fit with the observational data (making for much better predictive capacity), it does not tell us much about *why* the planets move the way they do.[12] The one model comes to be accepted as better than the other,

---

9 An epicycle – a circle inscribed on a circle – allowed models to account for the occasional retrograde motion of the planets, as well as changes in apparent distances from different planets to the Earth.

10 That is, with the developments provided by Galileo – in the first few decades of the "war" (to use Kitcher's metaphor), just after the publication of Copernicus's *De Revolutionibus* – the geo-centric models could hold their own in the face of helio-centric accounts. See Nicolai Copernici, *De Revolutionibus*, (1543), online: <loc.gov/item/46031925>.

11 The Copernican model also did not provide a particularly close fit between the mathematical models themselves and the observational data. While making use of epicycles closed this gap, it did not eliminate it (just as these devices had not with other models). Being more useful (in making better predictions) was its major attraction, a point made in trying to "sell" it as an instrumental theory in an unauthorized preface to Copernicus's text by Osiander.

12 Kepler published *Astronomia Nova* in 1609, setting out two of the three laws of planetary motion (the third was discovered a decade later). He did postulate some sort of "magnetic" force that held the Moon to the Earth and the Earth to the Sun, but this was not developed into any sort of serious explanation for the motions of the planets he detailed in his work. See Johannes Kepler, *Astronomia Nova*, (1609), online: <e-rara.ch/doi/10.3931/e-rara-558>.

but we lack an explanation that fleshes out *why* the picture described by the equations is the way it is.

While Galileo went some way along the path to providing such an account, it was not until Newton (through the combination of his law of gravity and his laws of motion), that we began to have some idea about *why* the planets move as they do. While Kepler's equations fit the observational data quite well, only with Newton's work do we begin to understand what the *forces* might be that account for the motions we witness.

Our attention at this point shifts, then, to the development of ever better *explanations* for the motions witnessed. We did not really have any more than a set of equations with Kepler's model – they were after all equations *about* motion, a thing we observe in the world. The motion modelled, however, itself needed explanation – *why* do the planets move the way they do? Newton's equations are about forces that can account for the motion modelled in Kepler's equations. Newton's laws provided an explanation for the models developed.

But now what are the "forces" that Newton's equations model? While Newton's picture provides a mechanism *explaining* the motion we observe (a system that nicely subsumes Kepler's laws), the mechanism itself was left in a fairly mysterious form.

Einstein was particularly concerned with the fact that gravity, in the Newtonian system, could seemingly act *instantaneously* across great distances, a problem occasionally expressed as an instance of "spooky" action at a distance.[13] With his own account – having gravity be the effect of the mass of an object in the generation of curves in non-Euclidean space – this spookiness is eliminated, and a *much richer account* is presented.[14] This theory not only gives us a much better sense of *why* planets move as they do, but also makes predictions that can be tested,[15] the theory itself being susceptible to non-verification by such

13 Einstein's later concern with "spooky action at a distance" concerned a quantum phenomenon, the entanglement of particles – a problem that still concerns physicists. For an overview, see Brian Greene, *The Elegant Universe: Superstrings, Hidden Dimensions, and the Quest for the Ultimate Theory* (New York: WW Norton, 1999) at 56.

14 For example, inertial mass and gravitational mass are found to be equivalent. Tying together what might otherwise have appeared to be disparate physical phenomena is often a factor in building support for one particular theory over another.

15 Weinberg argues that making sense of the then-known (and troubling) precession of Mercury's orbit – essentially a "retrodiction" – was at least as significant (or at least should have been as significant to reasonable scientists) in gathering favour for Einstein's theory as the prediction of the bending of light by the mass of the Sun. See Steven Weinberg, *Dreams of a Final Theory: The Scientist's Search for the Ultimate Laws of Nature* (New York: Pantheon Books, 1992) at 96–7. Greene also points out that there are reasons to believe, looking back at events, that a sceptical observer could have questioned Eddington's experiment and its reported results. See Greene, *supra* note 13 at 78.

means.[16] With such subsequent observations as those of the bending of starlight as it passed by the edge of the sun (the light being affected by the great mass of this object, its "bending" of space),[17] this theory gradually gained ascendency, coming to be seen as the *better* theory (providing the better *explanation*).[18]

A Common Sense Model (CSM)

What do we glean from this look into how a "common sense" model is supposed to function, a model of how one generates explanations that includes the notion of working towards progressively better explanations? An important, central feature of this account is its resting upon the notion there is *a way things are* (independent of how we might *think* about these things). We assume there is a matter to be uncovered – something to be discovered – about the movement of the planets (and not some account that does not answer to, or attempt to relate to, this way things are). One account is accepted as *better* than another in accord with the sense that this better account gets us closer to an understanding about the nature of this independently existing realm of phenomena (closer, that is, than the less-than-better account).[19] Furthermore, we see as an explanation that what we expect in more accepted accounts are those that more fully answer questions about *why* things are the way they are. While it is better than no account to have one that gives us what seems to be good information about how one sort of event or phenomenon will follow another, what we hope to arrive at is an account that goes some way to explaining what it is in the initial situation that results in the latter situation. Finally, what we also see in this example of how the common sense approach is supposed to function is the emergence of acceptance of an element of the natural world that had not been present in our accounts. We do not immediately (and do not directly) perceive "gravity." It enters the picture as a postulated force in Newton's theories, and over time takes up a place as a "thing" required for our best explanations of

16 For a number of reasons, verification or confirmation is not commonly held to be the process by which theories are – provisionally – validated. As a matter of logic, for example, a process of confirmation would be an instance of affirming the consequent, a common fallacy. One cannot infer the truth of a claim by means of the truth of a consequence of that statement (though one can infer the falsity of a claim by means of determining the falsity of a consequence, which indicates that disconfirmation better captures the means by which scientific statements are validated).

17 Again, it is best to see this as the theory passing a test of non-verification, with more such successes in not being defeated seen as the slow accretion of validity.

18 This is not the end of this tale of exploration, as attention is now focused on working out how gravity fits with the standard model in physics and in particular with quantum mechanics.

19 We shy away, of course, from the notion of "best" explanations, as contemporary models of common sense theorizing do not hold to such incautious aims. We get into reasons for this in a bit more detail in upcoming sections. See Godfrey-Smith, *supra* note 3.

what science tells us about objects with mass and how they interact. In the twentieth century it is shown to be not a force at all (as we intuitively think of such matters), but rather a feature of warped space-time. We cannot fully articulate what we accept to be – at the present moment – our best account of the motions and interactions between bodies (of mass) without this feature of space-time, and it becomes then an element within our conception of the natural world (though not as a "force," but as space-time curvature).

General Challenges to a CSM: "Knowledge" and "Progress"

We now complicate matters by introducing some of the reasons this picture of explanatory modelling seems to run into difficulties (at least in some contexts). Ultimately I hope this discussion persuades the reader of the virtues of adopting a particular sense of "explanation,"[20] one that both accommodates the notion of context-dependency (the notion that some phenomena – for example, the law and theories about the law – may depend for their very being on the sociolinguistic context in which they appear) and allows for the inclusion of normative-evaluative concepts as things that can be explained as part of the natural world. The general argument is that this helps open the door to an understanding of theorizing in the context of legal analysis that gets us beyond the apparent dead end indicated by the puzzles detailed earlier.

Challenges to this CSM come in several forms. In latter sections of this chapter and in the next chapter, I look at problems that arise if we entertain either (a) the notion that the world is not homogenous as a subject of inquiry (that what can be studied is composed of at least two kinds, the natural and the human [or moral]), or (b) the more focused notion that the law itself is a special (autonomous) field, one not amenable to "scientific" analysis. In this section I begin with a distinct and highly generalized sort of problem for the CSM, the focus being on features of this model of theorizing.

Let us begin with general features we arrive at if we abstract away from the account of common sense theorizing earlier provided. We suggested the account

---

20 The notion of explanation advanced in this study is put forward provisionally and restricted to the question of making sense of Aboriginal law (for reasons detailed in this and subsequent sections). For an extended discussion of explanation in the context of a naturalist program, see Godfrey-Smith, *supra* note 3. Here I provisionally accept (with modifications) his position on "explanation" as it fits the general program in this text. I take it as possible, and in some cases as plausible, that some of our normative-evaluative concepts are conceptual-scheme-dependent – that they are based, that is, on localized sociolinguistic practices. And so we can ask of legal theorizing what would be a notion of explanation that accords with practice – but, I also insist (for reasons that become apparent in the next few sections) on bearing in mind the placement of legal theorizing *into the world.* The notion of explanation we end up engaging with in this work is, then, naturalistic and – in some cases – context-based.

presupposes a way things are, independent of what we (or anyone) might take them to be. So, for example, it did not matter to the business of providing better explanations of the motions of the planets that particular scholars along the way had their own peculiar ways of thinking about the phenomena, the data, the concepts used, or the theories developed. Tied to this is the presumption that the better explanation does a better job of according with, and better job explicating the nature of, the way things are. Finally, to make the point explicit, one might suggest the measure of "better" here is in relation to this fit between the theory and the ways things are. The Einsteinian account is understood to be better because it better accords with, and better explains the deeper nature of, the way things are (better than the Newtonian account, and far better and richer than the earlier model afforded by the basic Copernican system).[21]

But how do we *know* the Einsteinian account better accords with the way things are? A line of challenges to the CSM in its most general form begins with questions such as this. First, one might ask about the standard to be reached for us to *know* of this alleged progression to the better Einsteinian account. Second, one might ask about the nature of this alleged "way things are," a state the CSM seems to presuppose as the fixed ground for all our assessments of models and theories. These two questions can be linked together: Is this "way things are" truly mind-independent? If so, how could we *ever know* that any proposed theory accords with the way things are?

Much of the debate on such matters is restricted to philosophy, and in particular the philosophy of science. We need not engage with core elements of various debates that consumed the energies of so many Western thinkers over the last few centuries – a sketch of some of the early history of intellectual struggles in these matters will suffice to launch us into key arguments developed through the length of the twentieth century. Fortunately, as well, questions tackled through these key arguments do not need to be definitively resolved – this is certainly not the place to attempt to do so! – as the purpose in delving into these matters is just to lay out reasons in support of the contention that a naturalist approach to the study of law can be meaningful and fruitful.

This CSM is not simply the scientific method described loosely. Rather, the scientific method developed over the last five centuries as a way to approach the study of the world that corresponds to this more general sense around the business of theorizing.[22] The scientific method (a) accords with the ontological picture offered (of the world existing as a concept-independent realm, its nature and

21 We also noted how a theoretical entity could come to be accepted as a constituent of the natural world when deemed essential to the production of an explanation of natural phenomena. This will be an important point developed in later discussions.

22 Whether this convergence was principally coincidental or directed is of little concern in the context of this project.

properties providing a check on what anyone might think of it), (b) aims to provide accounts that fit this picture of the mind and the world, and (c) fits with the evaluative regime postulated. Our short narrative on the move from a geocentric model to a heliocentric model began in times when at best a proto-sense of a "method" was emerging and concluded in the twentieth century, when not only was the scientific method firmly established, but also debated and contested.[23]

Progress within the narrative provided seems obvious and so one might expect the notion of *progress* is incontestable – the Einsteinian theory is vastly richer than the earlier models and has been confirmed so often that no scientist would question it as it stands (recognizing that a new theory may *supplant* it, especially one that quantizes gravity, that demonstrates how it fits with quantum mechanics).[24] Likewise, the *truth* of the Einsteinian model seems immune to serious challenge, especially if we focus on particular, narrow aspects – that, for example, space-time topology accounts for the motion of massive objects in relation to each other.[25] There are several arguments, however, that force us to think carefully about the nature of these assertions. Return to questions posed just a few paragraphs ago – how do we *know* the Einsteinian model is *true*, and that it is *better* than previous models?

GENERAL CHALLENGE: THEORIZING AS A HUMAN-INTERPRETIVE ENTERPRISE

It would not be unusual now to turn to a discussion of Kuhnian paradigms, and of Kuhn's analysis of shifts in scientific understanding between such paradigms as the Ptolemaic and Copernican models of the nature and movements of bodies in the solar system (or between Newtonian and Einsteinian models of gravity).[26] Kuhn explored the scientific enterprise as a social phenomenon and

23 Debates continue, but battle-lines were clearly drawn in the middle of the twentieth century, in struggles between verificationists and disconfirmationists. For verificationists, see e.g. Rudolf Carnap, *Logical Foundations of Probability* (Chicago: University of Chicago Press, 1950); Carl Hempel, *Aspects of Scientific Explanation and Other Essays in the Philosophy of Science* (New York: Free Press, 1965). For disconfirmationists, see e.g. Karl Popper, *The Logic of Scientific Discovery* (New York: Basic Books, 1959); Imre Lakatos, "Falsification and the Methodology of Scientific Research Programmes" in Imre Lakatos & Alan Musgrave, eds, *Criticism and the Growth of Knowledge* (Cambridge, UK: Cambridge University Press, 1970) 91. In rejecting Popper's solution to concerns raised by logical empiricism, Popper's student, Paul Feyerabend, charted one possible radical path out towards the sort of epistemological relativism explored later in this chapter. See Feyerabend, *supra* note 6.

24 For a discussion of string theory, see e.g. Greene, *supra* note 13.

25 This was most recently confirmed (in the fall of 2015) with the strong likelihood of detection of gravity waves with the LIGO detector. See *LIGO*, online: <ligo.caltech.edu>.

26 Kuhn's classic text makes much of the particular shift in models of planetary motion. See Thomas Kuhn, *The Structure of Scientific Revolutions* (Chicago: University of Chicago Press, 1962) [Kuhn, *Structure of Scientific Revolutions*]. This is not surprising, given the focus of his earlier work. See Kuhn, *Copernican Revolution*, *supra* note 7.

seemed to show that scientists exist within worlds of meaning tied to times, places, and practices. As accumulations of problems within a given paradigm emerge, pressure builds up, eventually leading (sometimes) to ruptures in the very framework within which particular meanings are embedded (ruptures to the "paradigm" itself). With such an event we witness a "scientific revolution," resulting in the emergence of a new paradigm. In comparing two paradigms, we would be thinking, then, of two systems or models (of planetary motion, for example, or of gravity), each relatively isolated from the other, *each model existing within its own larger system of meaning.*[27]

This notion of isolation within a paradigm makes it difficult to fathom understanding that bridges models and seems to render any form of universal evaluation meaningless. But this jumps into a way of thinking of an understanding of theorizing that is better seen as a *consequence* of challenging the CSM rather than constituting an argument against it. Kuhnian studies seem to demonstrate important matters in the *sociology* of knowledge (how humans – as scientists – are trained within systems of meaning, and how difficult it then is for them to move into new terrains, dominated by entirely different ways of thinking of fundamental matters). Do these studies actually indicate that different fundamental theories cannot be evaluated along such scalars as "progress" and "truth"?[28] How do we arrive, independently, at the plausibility of the Kuhnian account as a way of thinking about knowledge per se?

Arguments can be generally divided into those negative in tone and those positive in tone. We begin with a look into some of the negative reasons for questioning "progress" and "truth."

Negative Arguments Moving Us Away from the CSM. On the negative side are arguments about the failure of projects meant to demonstrate the soundness of knowledge of the world. The Cartesian project initiated in the early seventeenth century launched efforts undertaken over subsequent centuries to provide foundations for knowledge (foundations thought to be necessary). The grand aim was consistent – to use such tools as reason, logic, and immediate experience to demonstrate the solid foundations upon which knowledge rests

27 Note how this seems to implant theorizing into the world in a way that renders it context-dependent (where the context is the specific life-world of the researcher, determined principally by her immersion in specific paradigms).

28 Kuhn found the reception of his seminal work, *Structure of Scientific Revolutions*, *supra* note 26, troubling. John Horgan notes Kuhn told him, "If I had my choice of having written the book or not having written it, I would choose to have written it. But there have certainly been aspects involving considerable upset about the response to it": Godfrey-Smith, *supra* note 3 at 87, citing John Horgan, *The End of Science: Facing the Limits of Knowledge in the Twilight of the Scientific Age* (Reading, MA: Addison-Wesley, 1996).

(particularly scientific knowledge). Logical positivists (and their progeny, logical empiricists) undertook the last grand effort in this regard through the first half of the twentieth century.[29] Details of their strenuous efforts are not important to us – only that they failed spectacularly.

In the wake of this latest failure (as it unfolded over several decades), some began to wonder at the *sense* of the grand project itself.[30] What were prospects for success when the aim was to devise a priori structures that then purportedly sufficed to (somehow) establish the ultimate validity of scientific knowledge? Why, for example, would philosophically determined standards be thought to be proper measures of the success of science (or knowledge production in general)? Why would the practices of science be properly measurable from a stance *outside* science (and, indeed, outside what we might suspect are the boundaries of the natural world)?[31]

Challenging the sense in such a vision of ultimate validation, Quine arrived at a more palatable prospect – that of leaving the business of assessing "success" of scientific endeavours to processes *within* the practice of science itself. We arrive at a call for the naturalization of epistemology (that is to say, to have the very meaning of "knowledge" in the scientific realm be determined from within the scientific realm, removed from all "metaphysical" projects). Rather than suppose non-natural (i.e., a priori or metaphysically established) criteria might have any sensible role in evaluating the practices and products of science (and knowledge production generally), we might assume such things as "evaluative standards" are themselves properly the product of a self-contained system of meaning.

The reader may have noticed I began with a quest for an argument meant to challenge the CSM of theorizing and arrived ultimately at support for the notion that the production of scientific knowledge should be assessed naturalistically, by standards that emerge from our study of the natural world (through the scientific method). Let us step back for a moment to appreciate the argument for the naturalistic assessment of scientific knowledge. The CSM seems to come with notions of progress and truth that cannot be sensibly maintained in light of the failure of core Enlightenment projects.[32] What was the problem

29 Again, for representative figures, see Hempel, *supra* note 23; Carnap, *supra* note 23.

30 We touched on this earlier when naturalism was introduced. See "The Suggested Path Forward" in chapter 3.

31 See e.g. Jack Ritchie, "Naturalized Philosophy of Science" in *Understanding Naturalism* (Stocksfield: Acumen, 2008) 74 [Ritchie, *Understanding Naturalism*].

32 One reason I focus on a "common sense model" (instead of just discussing the scientific method) is that it is not at all clear that within science we find scientists preoccupied with thoughts about the larger matters caught by and articulated within the CSM. Scientists work within processes made meaningful within their respective fields – whether what they produce is meant to model a mind-independent world, for example, is not likely much of a concern for them.

with these notions of progress and truth? They imported two elements (the argument goes) that make forms of validation sought actually impossible.

On the one hand, the notion of the "ways things are" can generate problems, since if this "way things are" is truly separate from our experiences, thoughts, and representations of things, we can never hope to establish the absolute veracity or accuracy of our linguistically formed worlds. We would have to imagine we could somehow "step outside our thoughts" in order to determine that they correspond to the way things are. On the other hand, a specific notion of "knowledge" – importing criteria of certainty and infallibility – can create problems. With such impossibly high standards, once again it can seem we could never hope to establish an absolutely solid foundation upon which to rest our knowledge of the world.[33]

We quickly noted these arguments in passing and then moved on to the solution provided by Quine. The arguments themselves attribute the failure of the epistemological program – to provide solid foundations for all knowledge – to poorly formed understandings of what we should attempt to seek and of the tools by which we could hope to attain these goals. While Quine's solution will be explored a bit later,[34] at this point we should carefully unpack what conclusions we arrive at with these anti-foundationalist arguments.

We should appreciate that they are directed towards firmly establishing anti-foundationalism in epistemology. A key conclusion commonly drawn from these arguments is that there are no absolutely objective or neutral means by which we could ever hope to assess the truth (meaning or value) of any given piece of scientific knowledge (as all possible standards of assessment are now properly seen as internal to social practices – as essentially *historical* and *cultural*). Indeed, *now* one should be able to see some sense in adopting the relativist approaches to knowledge production that many took from Kuhn's work.

However, does acknowledging the strength of anti-foundationalist arguments mean we *inevitably* arrive at this sort of conclusion? Do arguments for anti-foundationalism inevitably lead to such corollaries (that, for example, there really is no possibility of maintaining anything like a strong form of meaning attached to the notion of "progress" in knowledge)? Do we lose all possibility of vesting "progress" and "truth" with sense (sense that allows for some connection to meaningful forms of objectivity or neutrality)?

---

33 The Humean problem of induction proved most troublesome in this regard – no matter the number of instances of what we take to be a scientific law at play (a law developed *inductively*, through observation of such consistency in events over time), we can never *know* that the next time we see the antecedent event the subsequent event will *necessarily* follow.

34 Quine's approach obviously has some appeal in the context of the experiment in this text, as we see whether a form of naturalism could aid in "making sense" of Aboriginal law.

Recall why I enter into such seemingly arcane debates and discussions. We now see how, through the twentieth century, some theorists came to denounce the idea of theorizing as leading to *explanations* of phenomena. An "interpretive turn" was advocated by many, argued to be the only reasonable alternative now that ahistorical, acultural knowledge was deemed nonsensical. All "knowledge" comes to be understood to depend on what a community of thinkers decides it will take as counting as knowledge, with all communities being both temporally and culturally bound.[35] To theorize, then, is really just *to make sense of one's own sociocultural practices*, to work within a given historical and cultural form of meaning. To explore the nature of Aboriginal law would be to interpret cultural forms of knowledge (where some such forms may emerge from the position of Canadian society and other forms from the societies of Indigenous peoples).

I do not dismiss projects that constitute attempts to understand cultural forms of knowledge, but rather aim to (a) question the inevitability of finding that is *all* there is and ever could be to theorizing, and (b) suggest we explore carefully the sort of solution proposed by Quine. In particular, the position advanced here is that context-dependent activities – i.e., coming up with sociolinguistically determined models for "explanations" and "theorizing" – can themselves be seen as elements of the natural world, and so studied naturalistically. But before going more deeply into this, let us step back into the thread of arguments introduced earlier, to take a quick look at the more positive arguments meant to drive us away from the CSM.

Positive Arguments Moving Us Away from the CSM. The specific positive argument I discuss rests on the notion of the under-determination of theory. By this is meant the idea that either (a) with any given theory, if it should seem to run into a problem, there is always the opportunity to question either the theory *or* the source of the problem,[36] or (b) that for any given explanation for a given set of phenomena, there are always other (equally plausible) explanations available. These two scenarios capture two senses of the notion of "under-determination" – on the one hand, a theory *on its own* may under-determine what to do if problems are presented for the theory, and, on the other hand, the *evidence* for any given theory will always under-determine the acceptance

35 This is to us a broad sense of "culture," encompassing, for example, the culture of contemporary quantum physicists.

36 Indeed, arguments developed in this regard suggest it would always be possible to question such things as logic or reason themselves, as nothing in these forms of thinking dictate their unwavering adoption. Quine's holism is meant to capture this notion, of the possible mutability of, for example, even our axioms or processes of logic.

of *that* theory (since there will always be other theories that can equally well fit with, and explain, the given evidence).

To see how this is supposed to function, working with the first understanding of under-determination, take a slice of the way things are, and then imagine an explanation for this apparent slice of reality (the explanation provided by some theory). Now imagine that some problem arises for the explanation in relation to this slice of the way things are – perhaps an experiment is carried out, with the theory predicting outcome *x*, but instead some entirely different outcome, *y*, manifests. We can never be sure that what we need to do in this sort of situation is (a) fix up the theory, (b) question the experimental result, or (c) question some other (set of) auxiliary theories or assumptions. The *problem itself* does not seem to determine any path forward – we could, in principle, do any number of different things to deal with the challenge posed. Second, and equally problematic, consider, hypothetically, what seems to be a good explanatory model for some mass of observations – the second form of under-determination holds there are a multitude of equally "good" explanatory models available for this mass of data. How are we justified in singling out the one we cling to as *better than* these others?

These arguments – presented and defended since at least the work of Duhem in the early twentieth century – challenge key elements of the CSM.[37] They function much the way the negative arguments do – they show that assumptions embedded in the CSM seem unsupported. It is not sensible to suppose it is a simple matter of a "way things are" and of human efforts to provide better and better explanations for the way things are (where better explanations "better fit" with the way things are). Strong forms of the under-determination argument now add a premise – that there is no way to specify (reasonably or determinatively) a means by which one can in the one case choose between different explanations that fit with the evidence, or in the other case decide whether to adjust the theory or challenge the new evidence. Something *other than* the notion that a new theory better explained new observational data (and so *required* its adoption) explains the move, for example, from one scientific model to another.

The upshot of both negative and positive arguments against adopting the CSM is that many theorists from the middle of the twentieth century on found an attractive alternate way to imagine what happens when we theorize about "the world." Alternate "interpretivist" models have been around since ancient times,[38]

---

37 Pierre Duhem, *The Aim and Structure of Physical Theory*, translated by Philip Wiener (Princeton, NJ: Princeton University Press, 1954).

38 With twists and turns one could, for example, argue the position of Parmenides was "interpretivist", insofar as he argued that man is the measure of all things.

but gained widespread modern respectability only in the wake of these recent intellectual challenges.

In the last section I began to sketch out how a naturalist response can address these concerns, with remarks about how negative arguments can be tamed through realization that anti-foundationalism in epistemological matters need not drive us into an anti-realist (interpretivist) world. As with the negative arguments, we are not driven to interpretivist conclusions by concerns with such matters as under-determination. At most these concerns highlight matters we need to seriously consider in thinking through how we should function – existing as we do in the natural world – if we wish to develop better and better models of the way things are. Once again, so long as we begin with the presumption that not only is there a mind-independent world to explore, but that an aspect of that world is the fact of human efforts at making sense of phenomena (that is, if we naturalize – at least provisionally – all aspects of epistemology and metaphysics), we can defuse the supposed deep implications of under-determination. Under-determination is supposed to push us to see the essential irrationality of believing we can ever *know* one theory or model is better than another, or that we are working towards better accounts, since for any given theory there are always equally good alternates. But what we see with under-determination is simply how difficult it is to work out in the world (*of which we are a part*, as theorizing-animals) what normative-evaluative standards we should adopt by which to measure progress.

As with the negative arguments, good comes from thinking through the nature of concerns that arise, as we are helped along by concerns about under-determination to see that we cannot *know* (if by "know" we mean to be certain) that a theory we move to is absolutely better than a rival we might contemplate. But this is a far cry from thinking we cannot rationally choose evaluative criteria that seem to work well (while, again, we cannot "know" this absolutely to be the case).[39]

Before extending this exploration into how a naturalist approach to the question of theorizing functions in addressing this interpretive turn more directly, let me introduce a second main challenge to the CSM. This challenge builds on the first, as we wonder what it might mean for the activity of theorizing to think it is a mistake to imagine one is ever really building models of "the way things

39 With the word "know" being either italicized or bracketed throughout the last few paragraphs, the signal was sent that part of the business of naturalizing epistemology is redefining what the term might mean. Since all notions of "knowing" seem to carry with them a core element of justification (which brings along with it concerns over normativity), clearly this is no small task (should we want this to work within an entirely naturalized model). See Ritchie, *Understanding Naturalism*, *supra* note 31.

are" when attempting to theorize. As a side benefit, in articulating this challenge we flesh out what a deep interpretive turn might look like. We are then in position to discuss more fully how a naturalist response to these challenges to the CSM functions, and to assess its strength and efficacy.

GENERAL CHALLENGE: THEORIZING AS A HUMAN-NORMATIVE ENTERPRISE

The last section ended with the use of normative language – I argued we can normally think we *should* employ certain evaluative tools, and that we *should* think we can move from weaker to stronger, poorer to better, theoretical accounts of mind-independent reality. Let me take a slightly different track, using a variant of some of the arguments used by interpretivists to see if there still might be something to the notion that we cannot explain mind-independent phenomena.

If we suggest theorists stick to the CSM, we seem to be saying that in the presence of other choices the theorist *should* choose to work on projects aimed at producing accurate representations of the way some phenomenon has developed, how the phenomenon functions, and why it operates the way it does. But are there indeed other acceptable choices? If there are – if we are *prescribing* a course of action for theorists – then we seem required to take seriously the notion that the very act of theorizing is – in some sense – a *normative* enterprise. Further, if we accept the implied conclusion that it is a *mistake* to think the aim of developing "correct" models is the only acceptable objective, we arrive at a stronger conclusion, that scholars should understand all their efforts as essentially aimed at potentially different and equally legitimate objectives.

What other forms of evaluative measure might be applied to (or within) theories?[40] Besides "correctness" – measured or evaluated by things like production of testable predictions – in accord with what other means might a legal theorist undertake, guide, and measure her work?

"Utility" could be introduced as an evaluative term. While utility and correctness can be linked on a general level of description (one might, for example, think to measure the *correctness* of a theoretical account by how *useful* the model turns out to be),[41] a more fine-grained notion of utility aids in imagining other

---

40 Norms establish standards of conduct or action. To say here that in some sense it would seem the act of theorizing can be seen as embedded in a normative universe – that the act can itself be seen as embodying a normative project – is to hold that there are options open within and about the general enterprise of theorizing. How is one to go about the activity of theorizing? If it would appear there is choice, and it would make sense for someone to argue that one *should* act in a certain manner (and criticize those who deviate) according to a certain standard of conduct, we can contemplate the possibility that it is normative.

41 A strong tradition within American philosophy has argued for such a conclusion since before the turn of the nineteenth century. More recently Rorty championed a version of this, as a neo-pragmatist approach. See Richard Rorty, *Philosophy and the Mirror of Nature* (Princeton, NJ: Princeton University Press, 1981).

sorts of models of the theoretical enterprise. The door thereby swings open to any number of alternative models of modelling – we might imagine, for example, legal scholars trying to "make sense" of Aboriginal law through the production of accounts that generate and maintain useful patterns of power distribution in society. Or we could imagine theorists producing accounts and explanations of Aboriginal law that strategically advance the interests of Aboriginal or non-Aboriginal communities.[42] Given any sort of (set of) ends, a theory might be assessed against its ability to move matters towards those ends.[43]

Why would anyone think it *appropriate* to conduct research with these sorts of vision behind it? How could a researcher *not* be primarily and fundamentally concerned with making sense in the "common sense" way described above? Besides the arguments we canvassed that challenge the view of progress and truth seemingly embedded in the CSM, we can also note a second general set of challenges to this model, those emanating from such fields as "science studies."[44]

This amorphous body of study, principally a branch of sociological studies, argues (on ostensibly empirical grounds) that theorists do not, *in fact*, work in the ways philosophers of science seem to presume they do (namely, within processes that aim to construct models of "the way things are").[45] These sociologists of knowledge argue that when one examines the activities of theorists and researchers, one finds they act in (not surprisingly) human fashion: they all develop hypotheses, conduct research, gather observations, and the like, but in ways that fit *not* with some rational system of objective knowledge production, but with a-rational sets of systems of "knowledge production."[46] Knowledge

42 For work on the strategic deployment of rights-talk and rights-action, see e.g. MW McCann, *Rights at Work: Pay Equity Reform and the Politics of Legal Mobilization* (Chicago: University of Chicago Press, 1994).

43 This line of thought connects to an earlier discussion, as we can see that thinking the measure of a theoretical enterprise is essentially utility best makes sense within an anti-realist understanding of our place in relation to the world. See "Suggested Path Forward" in chapter 3.

44 I borrow the expression from Sokal. See Alan Sokal, "Science Studies: Less Than Meets the Eye" in Alan Sokal, *Beyond the Hoax: Science, Philosophy and Culture* (Oxford: Oxford University Press, 2008) 115 [Sokal, *Beyond the Hoax*]. See especially *ibid* at 118 [emphasis in original]: "[O]ver the past three decades there has emerged a new and more radical breed of critique, which aims at the scientific *method* itself. Even more surprisingly, it is claimed that the long-accepted *content* of the natural sciences ... is contaminated by bourgeois and/or sexist and/or Eurocentric prejudices."

45 These sociologists seem, for the most part, to be those who took to heart the more radical path suggested by Kuhn's ground-breaking work.

46 Some feminist epistemologists, for example, argue scientists work within sexist and/or gendered frameworks (and that there are equally valid feminist frameworks, out of which would issue a distinct form of science), some post-structuralists and anti-imperialists that science is built on processes advancing imperialist objectives, and some multiculturalists that science is essentially Eurocentric. For extensive coverage of the various groups that can be pulled under the general umbrella, see Sokal, *Beyond the Hoax*, *supra* note 44.

production is revealed to be not the production of objective knowledge of the way things are, but rather the generation of pronouncements, all of which serve other purposes, all of which emanate from particular perspectives.

Transposing this to legal theorizing, the underlying point to the strong claim (that the researcher should not mistakenly think one can provide a correct account of some concept-independent phenomenon) is that one simply cannot make sense of the law by deploying the "common sense" methodology described earlier. There is no way, such an argument suggests, to engage in the sort of work a scientist might *think* she is engaged with, as this is a mistaken view of how the human intellect can and does make sense of phenomena.

There are two sides, then, to this form of challenge. On the one hand, the science studies group argues there is no privileged way to "do science" – different groups will have different ways of thinking of science, of developing a scientific method, and of developing therewith the content of science. On the other hand, they argue the picture advanced by the mainstream world of science (articulated principally by philosophers of science) is *mistaken* (as it presents what it claims to be *the* right way to do science, arriving at "right" answers to questions about the nature of the world).

And so we have introduced two possible general challenges to the CSM, which we will encounter more forcefully when we explore what some legal theorists say – or can say – about Aboriginal law. The one was presented as a direct challenge to the purported truth of certain theories of epistemology (theories said not to have any actual basis in how research in the real world is carried out), the second as a challenge to the notion there might be some privileged method within which scientists should fit their work (so they can advance towards knowledge of the world). They closely connect, however, as they run side-by-side to lead many to think that with a lack of any sense of privilege (of statements, or processes, or theories) an interpretive turn is appropriate – working with "knowledge" is understood to be a matter of self-consciously working within a given interpretive community, attuned to the meanings this community gives to such notions as method, or "privileged" statements, or outcomes of knowledge production.

With these general challenges in mind, let us now turn back to how I propose to begin directly meeting concerns they raise, as I work towards introducing challenges in the realm of legal theorizing, and then meeting those challenges using essentially the same tools and arguments.

Meeting Challenges to a CSM: Methodological Naturalism

I would like to suggest, and then spend a few words trying to defend, the idea that a particular sort of naturalist response to the sorts of general challenges so far noted can, in the very least, preserve the plausibility of the CSM. The step

I focus on is that between (a) challenges to the foundationalist vision (which animated so much of the Enlightenment project around knowledge production), and (b) conclusions made about the impossibility of representing concept-independent reality in explanatory models. A move has been made to push the (now) widely accepted position on matters in epistemological inquiry (anti-foundationalism) into positions on the nature of a world independent of mind and our ability to think about, or theorize about, this world (non-representationalism). However, if we begin with the notion that there are no privileged belief-statements or belief-producing mechanisms (that could found our beliefs in science, the world, etc.), are we (in essence) trapped in our thoughts, and must we accept that attempts to theorize about the world are really not capable of being evaluated as "correct" (as moving towards better models of the nature of a mind-independent world)? Must we forsake all sense of "explanations," replacing them with "understandings"? In another way of putting this, can we accept that we all exist (with our theories and methods, and forms of meaning) within and are defined by times and places, and yet find a way to defend the CSM?

We noted in passing one powerful articulation of arguments about the impossibility of Enlightenment-inspired epistemology, found in the works of Quine. We noted that he leads us to the conclusion about the impossibility of there being – in the realm of thought and belief – sense to the notion of a privileged foundation for knowledge. He still manages, however, to locate support for something akin to the CSM, resting it on the simple fact that science is immensely successful.[47] Not only is Einstein's explanation for the motion of the planets better than Newton's, in the sense that it provides a richer account (one that fits a broader range of observational data, and so forth), but it is a part of a scientific world view that *simply works* (in so many ways).[48]

I agree with the general thrust of Quine's arguments – that foundationalism should be discarded, as the very project itself rests on untenable and unacceptable premises – but want to suggest that one key support for the sense of this project came as well from certain aspects of the "problem" faced by scientists and philosophers *as set out by Descartes*. This is the split between the mind and the material

47 See e.g. WV Quine, "Two Dogmas of Empiricism" (1951) 60 Phil Rev 23 at 43: "I espouse a more thorough pragmatism [than that of Carnap, et al]. Each man is given a scientific heritage plus a continuing barrage of sensory stimulation; and the considerations which guide him in warping his scientific heritage to fit his continuing sensory promptings are, where rational, pragmatic."

48 I earlier noted in passing the distance that I hope to maintain between my adoption of a form of methodological naturalism (for the purposes of trying to come to a defensible understanding of Aboriginal law) and more egregious forms of scientism (that assert, for example, that the methods of science are the only methods capable of leading to truth and knowledge). The project in this text has next to nothing to say about the question of the ultimate status of science as a means to the production of knowledge *simpliciter* (i.e., whether it is the *sole* cause).

world, with the mind said to be better known (immediately known, and immune to the most devastating arguments of the sceptic) and our knowledge of the material world said to be in need of reasoned support.[49] Not only have we had a different starting point available in the West since (at least) the time of Darwin, but this starting point is a vision of the mind and the material world more in line with some Indigenous perspectives.[50] This is a simple view of the mind in the world.

Over the last few centuries a scientific understanding of the human (and the human mind) has developed – that of the human as a social animal, endowed with a powerful wet-computer, occupying a multitude of environmental niches, existing in a natural world.[51] A particularly interesting characteristic of this animal (besides relative hairlessness and bipedalism) is the possession of a complex mind, capable of using signs and symbols, language and culture, social institutions and social capacities. At a base level this creature does something many others can do – its organic computing device can take in sensory data and make sense of it, generating internal representations of what accounts for the incoming data. It can also think about these internal representations, wondering about their relationship to the things represented (that is, to the "outside" material responsible for the sense data).[52] It might even begin to explore this relationship (as this relationship exists *within* the natural world, as both the animal and the material providing sense data exist in the same natural realm). This creature can even marvel at how rich a representation is achieved from such a paucity of actual sense input.[53]

---

49 René Descartes, *Meditations on First Philosophy*, translated by John Cottingham (Cambridge, UK: Cambridge University Press, 1996).

50 In many Indigenous communities elders are revered, not simply as a matter of respecting the elderly but as recognition of the wisdom that comes from experience, and long reflection on experience. In this frame the world around is just there, to be lived in and experienced, humans being but one animal making sense of how the world works so as to better provide for families and communities. The world around us is not seen as known through social constructions, but known through experience of a given reality, one we inhabit with many other plants, animals, birds, and fish.

51 For arguments about this, see e.g. Hilary Kornblith, *Knowledge and Its Place in Nature* (Oxford: Oxford University Press, 2002).

52 "Outside" here indicates a very particular use of the term – with the intent being to distance it from Cartesian dualism. The "outside" here is just physically the exterior source of data processed on the "inside" (within the structures of the brain, within consciousness presumed to be part of the natural world).

53 Quine, for example, remarked at the gap between the two, noting that our rich mental image of the world around emerges out of nothing more, at the sensory level, than such things as photons hitting receptors. See WV Quine, *Theories and Things* (Cambridge, MA: Harvard University Press, 1981) (noting that "the epistemological question is ... a question within science: the question how we human animals can have managed to arrive at science from such limited information" at 72).

We presume (at least in this text) the natural world to be ontologically primary. The human mind – with which we are reasonably well acquainted – can be tracked through its emergence and development *within* the natural world, existing today as a physiologically based instrument of a certain primate. We are safe in presuming other primates, many other animals, and who knows what else, are likewise possessed of mental capacities and abilities.[54] Representations and models emerge within an aspect of the natural world, as those mental-symbolic mechanisms residing in and attached to our brains are put to use in better understanding and explaining the very world these brains inhabit, to which they are intimately connected as just one component amongst many. The nature of this world, interestingly, is apparently explicable to beings such as us – at least to a significant degree.[55] There may be bounds to our ability to model all that makes up the natural world. If there are definite bounds, we are not yet entirely certain where they lie: Will we be able to explore more than the four dimensions we clearly inhabit (assuming the notion of extra dimensions attached to some models holds up)? Will we reach back "past" the Big Bang (assuming time was not generated in that singular event)? Can we hope to detect what might lie beyond the light cone dictated by our position in space-time and the speed of light, etc.?

Within our salvaged CSM we willingly forsake all stake in "truth" and "progress" when these notions are vested with meanings connected to the socio-culturally bound visions of Descartes (and like-minded European thinkers of the Enlightenment). We do not, however, thereby forsake *all* sense of truth and progress. We can still maintain a theory or model to be true when its articulation of what it represents as being or happening in the world captures what exists or happens in the world.[56] How we *know* a given model is true is not a simple matter, but a modest sense of progress assists.[57] We do not imagine that we can step completely outside our mentally formed models to see how

---

54 For a collation of some of the relevant research in the field of cognitive ethology on various animal species, see Hilary Kornblith, "Knowledge as Natural Phenomenon" in Kornblith, *supra* note 51 at 28.

55 I am fine with the ideas that (a) we may perceive the world through a filter of some sort (conceptually speaking), and (b) we may never arrive at anything like a complete or fairly accurate set of representational models of concept-independent reality.

56 Christopher Norris has been engaged for many years in an ongoing struggle against the forces of anti-realism. See Christopher Norris, *Truth Matters: Realism, Anti-Realism and Response Dependence* (Edinburgh: Edinburgh University Press, 2002); Christopher Norris, *On Truth and Meaning: Language, Logic, and the Grounds of Belief* (London: Continuum International Publishing, 2006). He traces many of the anti-realist's arguments to such things as vestiges of Humean scepticism and over-valuing of "Kripkenstein," the marriage of later Wittgensteinian thought with radical scepticism about rule-following that emerges from Kripke's work.

57 I admit I am drawn to Kitcher's account of rationality in the scientific process. See Kitcher, *supra* note 5.

they align with "the world in itself" that they purport to model, but we can nevertheless be reasonably assured of one model being better than another (on the basis, for example, of practical success, of fit under a principle of parsimony, of success in meeting attempts at falsification, of connections to other likewise well-founded beliefs, and – perhaps – even of elegance and aesthetics). Einstein's account of gravity is better – both more accurate in its depiction and richer – than Newton's. Newton's depiction of the nature of gravity was really no more than what we glean from the equations, which did not tell us much about what the "force" might be, or what accounts for it in the natural world.

Generally speaking, then, challenges to the CSM considered to this point would be met by (a) accepting the position that Enlightenment notions of progress and truth should not be held, and (b) dismissing science-studies claims that it is a *mistake* to adopt the CSM. Enlightenment notions are replaced with salvaged naturalized concepts of progress and truth, concepts that allow us to continue to hold to the basic parameters of the CSM, while the CSM is itself argued to be acceptable because defensible adoption of this method simply requires attention be paid to those aspects of knowledge production *that work*, those that in this day and place we are warranted in believing do indeed lead to accounts of the way things are (independent of beliefs and attitudes).

The discussion in this section was not directed towards persuading the reader that sense can be made of theorizing about the natural world around us, since I hope most readers do not need to be persuaded.[58] The focus, rather, has been on discussing what we now better realize about just how this theorizing must be understood. We now turn to the social sciences (or the study of human activity more generally), for it is there that general challenges introduced in this introductory section really grow teeth. The next discussion serves as a stepping-stone, then, to the close examination of challenges to theorizing in the context of the law, and of Aboriginal law in particular.

Problems with Theorizing about Human Activity

General Remarks: Two Realms

Earlier I drew a simple connection between advancing a theory about the nature of Aboriginal law and the aim to make sense of this legal phenomenon – theories could be seen as attempts to "make sense" of the phenomenon by explaining what

58 Philosophers of science and some in the social sciences and humanities seem to be most concerned with these matters, on this most general level – interestingly, scientists themselves seem unconcerned (or, rather, some seem concerned with what they take to be the wrong-headedness of those who misunderstand the scientific enterprise and the production of knowledge). See e.g. Sokal, *Beyond the Hoax, supra* note 44. This frustration was the impetus for his original hoax and his writing the book about it.

is observed. We also noted, however, that it is not clear that theories in general serve this sort of function. We explored questions about how theories might work in this common sense manner, questions that led us into wondering whether theories are actually capable of providing explanations of mind-independent phenomena. This led into a strange land, one touched on in the Introduction, as we there entertained the concern that our coming to the task of analysis of Aboriginal law primed with our own interpretive and normative presumptions and positions might itself account for what we end up saying.

At the end of the last section I advanced a suggestion about how to think of the human in the world, a starting point for inquiry that maintains plausibility in the vision of the theorist capable of explaining concept-independent phenomena. The most general sorts of challenges were met, not in the sense they were defeated or dissolved but rather in the sense that we could reasonably understand the CSM to be defensible, just in terms of what is going on with the activity of theorizing.

This entire discussion, however, was cast at a high level, because it was about the theorist-in-general and the world-in-general. There are other challenges to the CSM when we delve into particular aspects of the world that might be the subject of exploration. Over the next few sections we explore the business of theorizing about the law. The first discussion works from questions about theorizing that take stock of an apparent divide in the world between the material and the moral, between the natural and the human. The second, in the next chapter, works from questions about the purported special nature of the law itself, ostensibly as an institution in the world understandable only as vested with "meaning" and attached to ineliminable forms of normativity. The intent in both discussions is not just to raise and then meet more particularized challenges to the CSM, but also to set out in more detail (and with more support) the naturalized approach to the study of law followed in the rest of the text.

It is essential that we grapple with perspectives, and in doing so with a form of methodological naturalism we accept fully some implications noted in the last few sections. There are two key implications: first, that the criteria for development of models of representation emerge in the natural world (and so should reflect this fact and be seen to be empirically determined); and second, that some normative matters to be explored – specifically the emergence of normative concepts and meaning in the legal arena, both in law and theorizing about the law – must be placed in the natural world in a way that allows for their study, noting that forms of normativity emergent in these social realms are all constructed.

Theorizing in the Scientific Realm (1): The "Hard Sciences"

The paradigm for theorizing is what we see in the scientific realm. The best models for such theorization are in the "hard" sciences (physics, chemistry, and associated domains). The key is not found in the content of theories in these areas, but in methods employed. The "scientific method" is usually pointed to as – or in our day and age, *presumed* to be – the paragon of theorizing.

Unfortunately, there is no clear (or at least relatively complete) consensus on the nature of the scientific method. Commonly, scientific theories aim to produce scientific laws – equations that set out relationships in strict, universal terms.[59] The Newtonian law of universal gravitation, for example, ranges over all objects with mass, specifying the mechanics of an attractive force that acts on such objects, each centre of mass of an object in the universe attracting each other centre with a force directly proportional to the product of their masses and inversely proportional to the square of the distance between them. The method of arriving at such laws is typically said to consist in the initial framing of a hypothesis, the testing of the hypothesis, and the gradual confirmation (or more potentially abrupt disconfirmation) of this hypothesis.[60] The hypothesis can be gradually converted to a theory or element of a theory, laying out laws, through repetitious testing and subsequent refinement.

At the end of a previous section we noted a central line of questioning about this picture of the activity of scientific reasoning, one focused on the under-determination of scientific theories. Other questions abound, several intimately tied to problems of under-determination. How does the scientist develop a hypothesis? What relationship should this hypothesis have to the world of scientific theory? To what extent or in what manner must a hypothesis be testable? Are there "pure" empirical observations to be made in testing the hypothesis (or are observations always "theory-laden," formed at least partly as a result of their being made within a pre-existing scientific framework)?[61] Is the progression from hypothesis to theory/law one of confirmation or of disconfirmation (is the scientific method grounded in confirmation or falsification)? Must a disconfirmation remove a hypothesis from serious consideration, or may it suggest that the larger scientific framework within which the hypothesis

59 Nancy Cartwright's work has forced philosophers and historians of science to rethink the role the most general laws play – her arguments point to the ever-present need to cast any such laws at the level of workable models in order for their application to the world around. Her main argument is that scientific theories – when cast on the level of general matters, detailing highly abstract law – are successful only in limited circumstances (where, recall, success is a key reason and argument for many who – especially realists – find science to be defensible). See Nancy Cartwright, *The Dappled World: A Study of the Boundaries of Science* (Cambridge, UK: Cambridge University Press, 1999). For a discussion of Cartwright's criticisms, see Ritchie, *Understanding Naturalism*, *supra* note 1 at 148–53.

60 See e.g. Godfrey-Smith, *supra* note 3. See especially *ibid* at 57–74. We touched on debates between verificationists and disconfirmationists (or falsificationists) in an earlier discussion. For our present purposes that debate is not relevant.

61 For a good discussion of this particular problem, see *ibid* at 155–62.

is set out needs rethinking (or that the process of making the observation was flawed)?[62] All these questions swirl around the scientific method, providing seemingly endless work for philosophers of science.[63]

As interesting and important as such questions might be, we need not get bogged down with them in this study. Rather, questions germane to analysis at this stage have to do with (a) the status of the products of scientific methodology, or more particularly with the relationship between certain aspects of the nature of the methodology and its products, and (b) whether there are things we encounter in the world around us not amenable to study within this sort of framework.

In the last section we looked at the first sort of question. There I attempted to build a sense of mind-independent reality and the human capacity to model this reality that kept true to the CSM of theorizing while acceding to anti-foundationalist arguments. The question could have been put so: are we better justified in assuming (or holding) that science functions within a realist or an anti-realist framework? That is, do the products of scientific endeavours attempt to, and manage to, *reach out* to describe, model, and explain a reality independent of the mind, or is all the work (all the theorizing, observing, confirming/falsifying, and products) such that this endeavour never advances past limits of the mind? If the latter were the case, the products of science would then not be *about* a mind-independent reality, but about what we think or believe, our thoughts and beliefs only *purporting* to be about this other unreachable realm. As we noted earlier, the slide from this to an interpretivist model of theorizing seems fairly quick and easy. The mind-in-the-world picture sketched was meant to support sense in a realist picture of the human in the world, supporting continued adherence to a CSM of theorizing.

Now we turn to the second concern, that some things in our world might not lend themselves to proper study with the scientific method. Things that some argue lie outside the reach of the scientific method vary wildly (supernatural entities, matters of Freudian psychoanalysis,[64] or elements of sociology provide some examples). It would appear there are two general sorts of conditions that can obtain, signalling barriers to the operation of the scientific method

62 This again is a problem of under-determination.

63 See e.g. Popper, *supra* note 23; Larry Laudan, *Progress and Its Problems: Toward a Theory of Scientific Growth* (Berkeley: University of California Press, 1977); Bas Van Fraassen, *The Scientific Image* (Oxford: Oxford University Press, 1980); Wesley Salmon, *Scientific Explanation and the Causal Structure of the World* (Princeton, NJ: Princeton University Press, 1984).

64 William James once said of the unconscious, the ground floor of Freudian analysis, that it becomes "the sovereign means for believing what one likes in psychology, and of turning what might become a science into a tumbling-ground for whimsies": William James, *The Principles of Psychology* (New York: Henry Holt & Company, 1890) at 163.

in relation to the human. On the one hand, there might be some capacity of humans – some attribute of their being – that removes their thoughts and actions from scientific study. On the other hand, there might be something about the inner world of human experience that makes it impervious to scientific study. Perhaps these two conditions are linked, and something possessed by the human accounts for the special nature of inner existence, the general result being that science cannot be deployed in making sense of human life (whether on the individual or collective level).

We begin with the thought that there may be an attribute of the human that removes this species from general scientific inquiry. In the modern context, one specific attribute raises this sort of concern – the will. A certain conception of the human will presents an entity or attribute that (by definition) seems removed from serious analysis through the tools and methods of science. A truly "free" will – one capable of acting one way in a given set of circumstances, *and any number of different ways with all those circumstances left intact* – cannot be analysed (ex hypothesis) in a way that brings it into the causally determined universe. If the natural world is delimited by notions of causality,[65] one might suggest this places the will in the realm of the non-natural (or supernatural).

The second sort of barrier is harder to pin down. MacArthur argues we are licenced to

> think that in addition to the aspect of nature that natural science reveals, there is a non-scientific (that is, scientifically irreducible) aspect including normative facts. The world we inhabit is not a bare physical-cum-biological world but a social and

---

65 See Philip Pettit, *A Theory of Freedom: From the Psychology to the Politics of Agency* (Oxford: Oxford University Press, 2001). Philip Pettit puts the matter this way, *ibid* at 9:

> [T]o explain how it can be that for anything that is freely done, the agent must have been capable of doing something else instead. Under the most radical interpretation this means that at the moment of choice it must have been possible for the agent, regardless of the causal regime and causal history of the world up to that point, to have done otherwise.... [T]his condition is in tension with a naturalistic picture of the universe: that is, with a picture of the universe under which every aspect of the world, including the freedom of agents, is fixed in place by the way the world is constituted, and the way it is organized by law, in the microphysical realm postulated in physics.

The situation would not necessarily indicate the action was uncaused – *ex hypothesi*, we are supposing a mental event caused a physical action. The problem is that the mental event – itself causally efficacious – is presented as (seemingly) uncaused. Whatever physical conditions preceding the mental exercise of the free will, we cannot say of them that they account for the decision reached as to what to do. The same set of preceding conditions could equally well have led to a distinct and different decision to act.

One might suggest, perhaps, that the entire set of preconditions establish a situation within which a range of possible thoughts and decisions are made possible, and a random moment leads to the decision reached (and action taken). But of course that is not what we seem to experience (usually), as we often feel after the fact what we decided to do was what we *wanted* to do (and not the product of a roll of the die around possible outcomes).

> cultural world involving human actions, languages, institutions, and various forms of art, architecture, and artefact.[66]

The social and cultural worlds he references seem all present in the natural world, but he goes on to note they are social and cultural, not because of their manifestations in the physical world, but because of their being vested with "meanings" and "significances":

> The significances, meanings, and values (ethical, social, aesthetic etc.) of such things are essential aspects of our experience of the world. When we discover such things as the meaning of an artwork or the significance of a gesture or the reasons expressed in someone's words, then it is as if we had discovered what was there anyway, regardless of whether we had discovered it or not.[67]

Furthermore, these meanings and significances, he argues, are there to be discovered. If I want to know the meaning of a piece of artwork, or the significance of a gesture, or the reasons expressed in someone's words, I search for them and assume they are present "out there" in the things to be explored. So here we are describing a form of reality (something not dependent on just my thoughts or projections). But he goes on to note, "Normative facts are not mere projections of subjective states; but nor are they understandable in complete independence of our responses. They are, as McDowell has put it, 'essentially within reach of human beings.'"[68]

This describes a realm of being made difficult – if not impossible – to study with the tools and methods of science. We are now to suppose that meanings, significances, and reasons are out there, in the thing to be discovered and explored, while we simultaneously acknowledge they are *understandable* only in light of *our* (human) responses to them. The meaning of the artwork is there to be discovered in the piece of art, but ultimately (when I articulate it) this meaning is essentially a product of *my understanding* of the artwork. Things such as "meanings" and "significances" and "reasons" are to be found then in the *interstices* between things vested with meaning and significance and the mind of the person seeking meanings and significances. Insofar as the existence of each human is found within social and cultural worlds, we find, then, a world – a reality – understandable only insofar as individual meanings, significances, and reasons are generated, all of which happens in an inner world of meaning. It would seem there is no such thing as "objectivity" in this realm, as

66 David MacArthur, "Naturalizing the Human or Humanizing Nature: Science, Nature and the Supernatural" (2004) 61 Erkenntnis 29 at 36.

67 *Ibid.*

68 For a discussion of McDowell's work, see *ibid.*

each packet of meaning (for example) is intimately connected to the individual seeking meaning or understanding.[69]

We come upon concerns, then, about the ability of science to grapple with such "things" as the free and creative will, or to reach sensibly into realms of being that are irreducibly subjective and private. Are these concerns plausible in relation to, say, theoretical physics? Can one reasonably argue that perhaps our best theories about gravity (a) range over objects and forces that cannot be placed into law-like models, and/or (b) express mere interpretations of data (reflecting an inner experience of the phenomena)? The aim in the last section was to reduce the strength of arguments that led some to such conclusions. The "hard sciences," it was suggested, can be meaningfully understood within a carefully constructed model of the common sense approach to knowledge production.[70]

Nevertheless, likely such concerns – both pressing and relevant – have their proper place. It would seem, indeed, to have some traction in relation to the social realm, as there we arguably encounter both (a) entities meaningfully accessible and understandable only as constituting elements of a mind-dependent reality, and (b) forces (i.e., the human will) incapable of simple placement in causal nexuses. Let us move away from our paragon, then, to consider the question of theorizing in the social realm. Let us move this discussion away from the hard sciences to disciplines that purport to study the social world.

Theorizing in the Scientific Realm (2): The Social Sciences

Several things complicate thinking about theorizing in the realm of the human. We have the suggestion that in and around the lives of humans – especially "from the inside" – there is a different realm of being, not susceptible to analysis in a materialistic or scientific – or even naturalist – manner. The strong form of this suggestion leads to the idea that on a physical level this special realm of being manifests in the presence of humans who somehow occupy a place in the natural world but who, as a special sort of being, cannot be studied materialistically or naturalistically. This suggestion can be pulled apart into two kinds of concerns. On the one hand, we have the notion that in some manner humans do not necessarily fall under causal laws (via the presence, for example,

---

69 Another way to argue for some inner world immune to scientific inquiry is to focus on the purportedly special nature of experience "from the inside." For a canvass of arguments around "qualia" (a term designating the "what-it-is-like dimensions of conscious experience"), see "Naturalism without Physicalism?" in Ritchie, *Understanding Naturalism*, *supra* note 31 at 134.

70 I hope to have made the case in the preceding section. One can also see how Quine and others responded to anti-foundationalist arguments. See e.g. Kitcher, *supra* note 5; Salmon, *supra* note 63.

of radically "free" will). This, on its own, might lead one to wonder how humans could ever be studied scientifically. On the other hand, we have the notion that the experience of humans "from the inside" is susceptible only to discussions of a particular sort (often expressed as "phenomenological"), such that *explanations* of human life are impossible (the only discourse available being that of "understandings").

Let us begin by refocusing on the notion of a free will. We can see how this apparent human capacity seems to pose problems, but then defuse some of them (in the context of this study), leaving us to focus attention on aspects of the social/moral realm that truly challenge the notion of the application of the CSM to the study of the law.

That the human will might be essentially "free" (in some meaningful sense of the term) seems to pose interesting problems for anthropologists, historians, sociologists, and all others working in "soft sciences." Imagining that human action can be directed by an "uncaused" causal force would not render impossible the task of systematically studying human action (or humanity itself), but any such study would be precluded from generating results guaranteeing law-like generalizations. In conducting research and generating or presenting results one would always be, at best, exploring contingent patterns and describing matters as being completely localized. After study and reflection, one could always conclude something like "The mental states of *x* at *t* caused *y*," but one could never conclude something like "With conditions *z*, *x* will necessarily act in such-and-such a manner." One could, for example, compose histories containing discernible patterns of behaviour and action, but such histories could not present accounts that could not have been otherwise.

What does this mean for the production of theory in the soft sciences? What would be the form of such a theory when directed towards a realm wherein laws are not possible? Such a theory would have to be directed at localized events and couched in localized terms, both temporally and spatially (and presumably in terms of both the content of the theory and the place of the theory in a specific society). A theory might describe some events, pattern of behaviour, movement in society, or kind of human activity – but such a description would always fall short of the possibility of elevation to high levels of generality or to universality.

This is all based, however, on the postulation of a strong form of free will. Of course a vast literature is consumed with debates about the existence of this alleged human capacity.[71] There are no (third party, independent) observations

71 For a gateway into this literature, see Pettit, *supra* note 65. Pettit discusses not just the modal concept of freedom (the notion that on a "metaphysical" level humans may be true agents), but implications of debates about this for matters of responsibility. For a canvass of contemporary debates, see Paul Russell & Oisin Deery, eds, *The Philosophy of Free Will: Essential Readings from the Contemporary Debates* (Oxford: Oxford University Press, 2013).

on which we can build a theory about this phenomenon, though much social research rests on a priori acceptance of some such capacity.

The approach advocated in this text, however, takes a cautious line on theoretical entities – we imagine study of the human using current tools and techniques of modern science, and hold that we will countenance (as *naturalistic*) theories of and about the human that, in deploying the best scientific methods available, contain reference only to entities *required* within the theories thereby developed.[72] Furthermore, we restrict the ambit of any such reference made within such a theory in such a way as to not countenance the appearance of any ontological commitment to something not required by the theory.

This touches on a key attribute of a naturalistic approach to such matters, one at its heart methodological. No a priori claims are made about or countenanced concerning what may or may not exist – assertions of existence are predicated on the development of the best scientific theory possible, at any particular time and place. What, then, of "free will"? Have we pushed it aside by fiat, letting it in our studies only if necessary to explain some observable phenomena? Do we not all imagine we directly, personally experience such a thing, at any given moment "freely" deciding to do something we suppose we could just as easily have decided – all conditions remaining the same – not to have done? The reply, again, is centred on caution – we do not dismiss the *possibility* of free will being part of the world around us, but we do not begin studies of humans-in-the-world with presumptions that such a capacity is part of explanations tendered or that it itself must be explained.

What then should a reputable "social science" look like? It need not be based on some reductionist model – it need not, that is, try to place the hard sciences at its base, only constructing its own theories when they can be erected on top of – indeed, out of – this hard base. The social realm is there before the researcher to explore, and perhaps elements of it, once full and rich theories are developed, are simply incapable of reduction into models built upon theories and

---

72 I am glossing over major challenges to this approach, permitted (I baldly assert) as I am not writing a treatise on methodological naturalism. Ritchie discusses problems in ontology under this approach. See Ritchie, *Understanding Naturalism*, *supra* note 31. At this point, for example, I have not spelled out any sort of manner by which we get the body of scientific tools and techniques off the ground simultaneously with a given body of "natural entities." It seems the vision is of the two somehow evolving at the same time. I leave this sort of problem up to others better capable. As an aside, research into how we do act when we think of ourselves exercising free will seem to indicate – at very early stages in such research – that our perception of freely acting lags behind the biological functions that, for example, raise my arm. For a discussion of some of this research, see Anthony Cashmore, "The Lucretian Swerve: The Biological Basis of Human Behavior and the Criminal Justice System" (2010) 107 Proc Nat Ac Sci 4499.

explanations of physics (or chemistry, or even biology).[73] There may indeed be, for example, irreducible emergent "things" within the social realm.[74] The key is simply to deploy what we currently understand to be the best methods of scientific inquiry, methods that do not *begin* with subjects of study we unreflectively or presumptively take to exist as "non-natural" elements of our world.

That leaves us still with the possibility that scientific inquiry into human life is not tenable because certain aspects of that life invoke "meaning" and "normativity." Would it not be a mistake to think we can meaningfully study the human as human-in-the-world if we presume that the human is simply (and no more than) a part of the natural world?

We explore this last challenge to the CSM when thinking of theorizing about the law, as it engages core debates that consumed legal theorists through much of the last century. What we have in hand is realization that a CSM of explanation-building remains sensible and operational, especially when we begin with the notion of the mind arising within a natural world, and consequently of theorizing emerging as a natural activity carried out by creatures trying to make sense of the world around them. As we turn to a focused look at law and legal theory, we shift attention to arguments that suggest the CSM cannot be used to make sense of legal phenomena, as they are infused with meaning and normativity, set as they are as constructs within sociocultural settings.

---

73 I must admit, for example, that I find it hard to see how some of the convoluted accounts of human activity emanating from evolutionary sociobiology will stand the test of time. Tracing all activity back to gene-transmission and propagation seems both implausible and unnecessary. See especially Edward Wilson, *Sociobiology: The New Synthesis* (Cambridge, MA: Harvard University Press, 1975).

74 Indeed, I make use of Searle's mature theory, which posits the construction of social reality creating new elements of the natural world, institutions, and institutional facts.

5 Problems with Theorizing about the Law

We turn now to an exploration of the nature of legal theory. We begin with a look into a traditional preoccupation within Western legal theory about what we can say about the nature of "the law," a step that leads into contested arguments, principles, and norms. This initial foray opens up dialogue about theory in an attempt to make sense of Aboriginal rights, with a springboard for a more expansive discussion being the matter under the microscope throughout this chapter – the relationship between theorizing and the law. We noted that challenges to a CSM of theorizing can arise on a very general level and on the level of social or human existence, and I hope to have begun to illustrate how more serious challenges arise around the purported scientific or naturalistic study of the human. Now we concentrate on challenges that attend the notion that a common sense approach to theorizing might be used to try to make sense of an aspect of the law, the law concerning Aboriginal rights.

As we progress through this discussion, we narrow serious challenges to those emerging from the fact that law carries meaning and is inextricably a normative matter, where these challenges are articulated in a discussion of the constructed nature of legal orders. The last few sections demonstrate the ability of methodological naturalism, carefully applied, to sidestep these challenges to theorizing about the law (specifically, when the focus of analysis is the sort of matter being investigated in this text, attempts by one social collective to construct law that will apply to the lives of peoples with separate, independent meaning-generating capacities).

General Remarks about the Nature of "Law"

I take an indirect approach to saying something substantive about the nature of the law. Eventually I say quite a bit about whether we should think of the law as a thing in the world constructed according to certain "objective" architectural plans, or as a thing constructed on the basis of a community's understanding of its values and its own moral and political sensibilities. The path to this later discussion is, however, somewhat winding, as we begin with a look into a paradigmatic example of a legal system, all in search of things we can begin to say about what makes something law-like rather than not.

We begin with a look into the law without fixating on the notion that it is essentially a social institution, entirely constructed. As we move along, we shift attention to its constructed status and what this may imply. The starting point is simply a concept. We speak of the law – we talk of *x* being the law or an element of the law, of a case standing for a legal proposition, and so on – and that suggests that behind legislative and judicial practice there is *meaning*, that jurists intend to project meaning through such statements. That is, much of the language of everyday discourse in legal communities (and broader society) rests on the notion there is such a thing as "law," a concept we hold that captures what it is for a particular rule to be law, a particular action of a legislative body to be legal, and so forth.[1]

One challenge at this early point lies in the fact that trying to describe the nature of the law seems to require initial theoretical or conceptual presumptions. This thing we might all feel we can identify – the law – is incapable of self-definition and does not simply rises up before us to declare what it is like. We might suspect that to say "this" and "that" go into the nature and existence of the law is to do nothing but pick out features of our collective social existence we seem licensed to say go into our conception for no discernible reason other than we intuit or feel this is so.[2] Likely there is no fixed thing attached to the term or concept, but only locally determined social phenomena. This, in turn, implies our concept of law might be socioculturally fixed – that there may be no such thing as *the* concept of law.

Let this initial suspicion rest for a moment. Caution in hand, let us begin with the *supposition* there *can* be some sort of reasonably well-defined answer to the question, "What is 'the law'?" to see where this leads. Let us further suppose the world is populated with legal systems or orders, structures that are "legal" insofar as they exhibit either (a) essential features associated with the law, or (b) share in common familial characteristics, such that we can say these

1 Given earlier discussions about the adoption of methodological naturalism, the reader may suspect where this discussion is going: the investigation is into the nature of this discourse as functioning sociolinguistic constructs (making use of the platform provided by Searle). See John Searle, *Making the Social World: The Structure of Human Civilization* (Oxford: Oxford University Press, 2010).

2 Leiter touches on this sort of matter. See Brian Leiter, "Naturalizing Jurisprudence: Three Approaches" University of Chicago Public Law & Legal Theory Working Paper No. 246 (2008), online: <chicagounbound.uchicago.edu/cgi/viewcontent.cgi?article=1200&context=public_law_and_legal_theory>.

systems belong to this "family."[3] We might further suppose, then, that if we wish to pin down precisely what the word "law" refers to, we might begin by laying out possible constituent matters going into a legal system.

One way into this would be to work from an example of a legal system, of the sort so clearly identified as making up a legal order or structure that no one seriously asks whether it is an example of such or not. We can then consider what seem to be key features of this system, hoping to arrive at a sense of what a social subsystem must encompass in order to be labelled a "legal system." In tandem with this process we introduce some concerns and inquiries proposed by legal scholars, using them to develop our understanding of what goes into the constitution of an order that generates and contains law. Besides providing us with some sense of the nature of the law, this bridges into the next section, a direct investigation into the nature of legal theory.

The system we begin with is that of a liberal democracy of the first world – the Canadian domestic or "municipal" legal order. If our concern were to provide a detailed articulation of the nature of this system, likely space (and patience) would quickly run short. This exercise is meant to do no more than provide a skeletal sense of core elements of this system – a few pronouncements about what seem to be key features. Bear in mind again that no conclusions are being formulated – this is just an initial exercise, meant to kick-start analysis of "law" and propel us into the world of legal theory.

We begin with the obvious, noting the Canadian system seems to have at its heart many rules, prescriptions, or codes commonly labelled "laws." These typically either forbid individuals or parties from engaging in certain kinds of behaviours (or actions), or impose obligations on individuals or parties. They may also confer powers or privileges to individuals or groups. They may also specify how relationships between parties are to be structured in order to be "legal" (i.e., in the formation of a contract), or they may spell out forms of retribution (as with systems of punishment in the criminal law context).

Furthermore, some of these rules specify how the larger legal-political system is generally structured, in relation to, for example, legislative, administrative, and judicial bodies. These structural rules (about larger matters) are supplemented with rules about how these bodies should properly function (though in many cases the rules merely indicate – or suggest through omission – degrees

3 These options, of course, presuppose particular approaches to the question of the nature of the law. The general assumption at play here is that the law is either a natural or functional kind, the sort of entity that admits of either "essential" features or a set of possible sufficient conditions (where some appropriate subset must be present for an instantiation to be present). Suggesting "the law" does not have an existence susceptible to this sort of analysis – that it does not have a nature such that it can be unpacked in some such manner – constitutes a primary challenge to this approach that enters the discussion in an upcoming section.

of discretionary power or matters of unwritten convention).[4] It should be noted these rules on structure and process-matters relating to legislative, executive, and judicial bodies encompass rules or conventions that spill out into abilities and capacities of these bodies to themselves generate, transform, or eliminate rules, codes, regulations, and prescriptions.

A path forward appears that we can follow as we begin to track the intersection of contemporary legal theory and this question about the nature of the law. We can begin paralleling H.L.A. Hart (from his seminal work *The Concept of Law*),[5] separating those *primary* rules directed towards regulation of action (broadly construed) between individual parties (broadly construed) from *secondary* rules that relate to the structuring and functioning of those bodies that play a role in the enactment, maintenance, and transformation of this mass of primary rules (following Hart's labelling convention).

As we noted above, the heavily prescriptive primary enactments take many forms and function in many ways. They seem clearly designed to order relations between individuals and between individuals and the state – simply put, they most often instruct citizens in how to act or generate conditions that affect how parties *may* act (where this encompasses not only simple prohibitions on actions but also [a] rules or principles setting out sorts of actions or behaviours deemed im/permissible, [b] rules or principles specifying actions or behaviours deemed laudatory or to encourage, and [c] rules that create structures around relationships – creating relationships themselves, as it were – which are thereby deemed legally permissible, laudatory, or necessary).[6]

Secondary rules, on the other hand, structure the ways by which these primary rules are managed and overseen: "[T]hey provide that human beings may by doing or saying certain things introduce new rules of the primary type, extinguish or modify old ones, or in various ways determine their incidence, or control their operations."[7] Hart identified three matters that plague mere collections of primary rules (if one can indeed imagine a social environment in which there are only primary rules that govern behaviour), problems that secondary rules exist to address. First, there would be uncertainty, as no procedure would settle such questions as what rules are actually to count as laws or how determinations are to be made about the precise scope of a given

4 Unwritten conventional rules were one focus of the Supreme Court of Canada's decision in *Reference re Secession of Quebec*, [1998] 2 SCR 217, 161 DLR (4th) 385.

5 HLA Hart, *The Concept of Law* (Oxford: Oxford University Press, 1961) [Hart, *Concept of Law*].

6 Note, again, Searle's work on the creation of social reality in his *Making the Social World*. See Searle, *supra* note 1.

7 Hart, *Concept of Law*, *supra* note 5 at 79. Again, it is interesting to note similarities between the language Hart here deploys and that used by Searle to describe how we structure institutions with linguistic tools.

rule.[8] Second, there would be a problem of stasis, as there would be "no means … of deliberately adapting the rules to changing circumstances, either by eliminating old rules or introducing new ones" (or of adopting modifications of obligations or duties under a rule to meet circumstances).[9] Finally, there would be lack of final and authoritative determinations on inevitable disputes about whether a rule really applies or not, a problem likely to exacerbate disputes.[10]

A "rule of recognition" would address the first concern (establishing within any given legal system a means by which it can always be determined whether a particular given primary rule is authoritative and binding), "rules of change" the second concern, and "rules of adjudication" the last. These rules would all have natures peculiar to the legal system they help structure, but in general outline or form we might expect to see them all present in any social environment containing something more than mere "pre-legal" structuring of human activity.[11]

Continuing to follow Hartian convention, let us refer to *all* the instruments being discussed to this point as "rules."[12] These rules have an existence marked out in complex ways both in relation to and within social institutions. This complex set of relationships between and within laws and the social institutions to which they connect can be separated into several forms.

First, these rules may actually generate certain social structures (as when, for example, rules themselves play central roles in establishing and/or maintaining social institutions, such as tax regimes). Furthermore, as constituting laws, many of these rules typically exist within and are usually inextricably connected to a network of systems of enforcement (the *Criminal Code*,[13] for example, being inextricably connected to the police forces of the state, the criminal component of the judicial system, and the penal system [and/or other systems of punishment]). Finally, the placement of primary rules within larger

---

8 *Ibid* at 90.

9 *Ibid* at 90–1.

10 *Ibid* at 91.

11 Of course, Hart argues we would see these in all systems that have advanced past the pre-legal.

12 This is less problematic than it might seem, as in the postscript to the 1992 edition of *The Concept of Law*, Hart argued (fairly persuasively) that he did not mean to exclude from his notion of a "rule" the notion of a "principle." See HLA Hart, "Postscript" in HLA Hart, *The Concept of Law*, 3rd ed (Oxford: Oxford University Press, 2012) 238. Attempting to deflate one of the arguments Dworkin levelled at his positivist picture, Hart argued that at most he had inadvertently left the impression that his notion of a rule would not accommodate that of a more general principle (which to him lay along a spectrum containing those instruments – rules – that provide more definitive outcomes in specific situations). See especially Ronald Dworkin, *Taking Rights Seriously* (Cambridge, MA: Harvard University Press, 1978) [Dworkin, *Taking Rights Seriously*]. Dworkin, of course, meant to invoke, with the language of principles, things with content substantially different from rules – in his view, principles *carry* normative content.

13 RSC 1985, c C-46.

sociopolitical structures may indicate attributes by which we recognize them as properly constituting "laws." As we noted above, the core rules of a liberal democracy will properly emerge from legislative or judicial bodies, and we regard them as acquiring a certain status by virtue of that genesis (for instance, this could lead to these laws being viewed as "legitimate,"[14] as having the right pedigree to be acknowledged as "proper" laws).[15]

Arguably, our process of abstracting features away from the Canadian domestic system that seem essential to its nature as a legal system seemed to track well how Hart's analysis led to his distinctive unpacking of the concept of law. One might suspect, however, that this is accidental or coincidental, for while Hart presents his attempt as providing a "descriptive sociology,"[16] he presents his methodological approach as conceptual analysis. That is, he proposes to unpack the concept of law, revealing individually necessary and jointly sufficient conditions that must obtain for this concept to be properly applied to objects in the world.[17] We, on the other hand, began with a concrete system in the world, wondering at what seemed to be key core features that define it as "legal."

One wonders, however, where Hart found the concept of law he then unpacks in his analysis. While conceptual analysis is still a tool commonly employed by Western (analytic) philosophers, some question its pretensions as a useful route into philosophical insight.[18] One challenge is directed at the *source* of the concepts – and at divisions and distinctions found within them through

14 "Legitimate" here is used in a fairly weak sense, denoting only that a judgment could be made that a rule properly grounded in the right kind of genesis is thereby legal (as opposed to not being legal). Here there is an elision with "legality." We discuss stronger forms of legitimacy in later sections.

15 Hart seemed to suggest in the first edition of *The Concept of Law* that primary rules must enjoy the right pedigree to be properly laws, but later – in the postscript, for example – his focus shifted to the requirement that primary rules be seen to be grounded in social facts (one instance of which might be social facts setting out a system for matters of pedigree). See *supra* note 5.

16 *Ibid* at v. Perhaps this is more properly characterized as the objective of the study, a way of describing what is meant to be the end product.

17 For example, Hart justifies time and energy spent examining the nature and interaction between primary and secondary rules by saying, "We accord this union of elements a central place because of their explanatory power in elucidating the concepts that constitute the framework of legal thought": *ibid* at 79.

18 See e.g. Jerry Fodor, "Water's Water Everywhere," review of *Kripke: Names, Necessity and Identity* by Christopher Hughes (2004) 26:20 *London Rev Books* 17, online: <lrb.co.uk/v26/n20/jerry-fodor/waters-water-everywhere>. As Fodor notes,

> Whereas it used to be said that philosophy is about, for example, Goodness or Existence or Reality or How the Mind Works ... it appears, in retrospect, that that was just a loose way of talking. Strictly speaking, philosophy consists (... or ought to consist largely) of the analysis of our concepts.... It's not the Good, the True or the Beautiful that a philosopher tries to understand, it's the corresponding concepts of "good" "beautiful" and "true."

analysis – the question being whether conceptual analysis rests uncomfortably on *intuitions* essentially removed from ultimate analysis.[19]

This challenge captures the notion that intuitions play a role ripe for contestation. It is a small step from concern about the source of intuitions to the notion that these intuitions can reasonably be seen only as coming out of the lived experience of the analyst – in this case, out of Hart's life within the United Kingdom in the twentieth century. As some have noted,[20] it is an interesting coincidence that the schema Hart details in unpacking *the* "concept of law" just happens to lie so close overtop the legal system with which he is intimately familiar, as if it were simply an abstraction away from what he knows by experience.[21] Then, of course, we must question the project we entered into – we began with a paradigmatic given legal system and purported to abstract

---

As Fodor goes on to note, such events as Quine's publication of "Two Dogmas of Empiricism" called into question this enterprise of conceptual analysis:

> Quine's ... conclusions [that there are no intelligible distinctions between conceptual truths and empirical truths or "matters of fact"] were patently germane to the agenda of analytical philosophy. If there are no [necessarily true] conceptual truths, there are no conceptual analyses either. If there are no conceptual analyses, analytic philosophers are in jeopardy of methodological unemployment.

See WV Quine, "Two Dogmas of Empiricism" (1951) 60 Phil Rev 23. See also Joseph Henrich, Steven Heine & Ara Norenzayan, "The Weirdest People in the World?" (2010) 33:2–3 Behav & Brain Sci 61. These experimentalists argue that while useful generalizations *can* be made about human nature, one should suspect research based on samples drawn primarily (or exclusively) from Western, educated, industrialized, rich, and democratic societies. These sub-populations, the researchers argue (on the basis of their own research), are odd outliers in many respects. Interestingly, intuitions serving as the basis for nearly the entirety of analytic legal philosophy emanate from just this sub-population (though accentuated and concentrated).

19 A more sophisticated approach has the investigator moving back and forth between "considered judgments" grounded in intuitions, aiming for moments of "reflective equilibrium." John Rawls's *A Theory of Justice* is built around such an approach. See John Rawls, *A Theory of Justice*, 2nd ed (Cambridge, MA: Belknap Press, 1999). This, however, does not seem to entirely defuse questions about the source of the intuitions (which still play a foundational role in the analysis). For an inquiry into the interplay between concepts and intuitions, see Hilary Kornblith, *Knowledge and Its Place in Nature* (Oxford: Oxford University Press, 2002) at 8–21.

20 See e.g. Margaret Davies, *Asking the Law Question*, 3rd ed (Sydney: Thomson Reuters, 2008).

21 Perhaps, however, we should be cautious in immediately questioning the efficacy of Hart's approach. Some scholars have noted that it makes sense to read *The Concept of Law* as built around a "modest" form of conceptual analysis, one that "restricts itself to drawing conclusions about what the *concept* is, illuminating the concept's underlying structure, and determining whether particular situations are covered by the concept ... this typically involves an exposition of the folk theory of the concept": Ian Farrell, "H.L.A. Hart and the Methodology of Jurisprudence," review of *A Life of H.L.A. Hart: The Nightmare and the Noble Dream* by Nicola Lacey (2006) 84:4 Texas L Rev 983 at 999 [emphasis in original]. Within this form of modest conceptual analysis, intuition, theory, and experience would be played back and forth, the outcome being a relatively well-grounded sense of what must be meant by the terms employed, which goes into the construction of the theory advanced. Note, though, that this would imply Hart was firmly culture-dependent and culture-centred.

general core features away from it. Have we not also just tied ourselves to a specific sociocultural context?

We are knocking at the door leading to questions about the place of culture and perspective in thinking about "the law." To make the shift to that sort of discussion, let us return to the basic model of a legal system we now have in hand, asking about its status as a social construction.

Theorizing about the Law: Perspectives and Social Construction

No one seriously questions the status of any given legal system as the product of the society in which it is embedded.[22] Positivist theories of law make something out of this notion of social construction, while those opposed to the positivist hegemony argue that while it is indisputable that any particular legal system is built by some specific society, to be properly designated a *legal system* it should satisfy certain requirements (typically put in terms of moral or political normativity).[23] In thinking about the particulars of how any given system of law might be built, we can explore the nature of these different (mainstream) theories about the law. The main objective, however, remains: to explore possible challenges to the CSM of building explanations of legal systems.

Each of us undeniably lives within a complex social reality, built out of and around a multitude of lesser social realms, one being that complex subset of reality we label "the legal world." It would be obtuse to challenge the notion of "social construction" of social institutions on a base level, as there can be no question actual "physical" instantiations of, say, legal systems are the products of social construction. Where matters begin to get complicated is when we ask about how this construction is understood to take place. How do legal

22 Regardless of how we and Hart progressed from a blank piece of paper to a developed model of the law, the end products seem to collapse into a remarkably similar picture, one reflecting key features of the legal realm within which we happen to live, with which we happen to be most familiar. This is not surprising in our case – we just abstracted away from the domestic Canadian system. It is only slightly more interesting in Hart's case, given we have few places to go to figure out where his intuitions might have come from. With marked similarities between the British and Canadian systems, it is not at all surprising we ended up with similar general accounts. This goes to support the suggestion that general understandings of the law are grounded in particular social existences.

23 The reader may have noted I propose to pursue examination (in later stages of this text) into a *particular* positivist position, which I term "liberal positivism." In terms of analysis of the law, this approach takes a decidedly positivist line (in that it is taken that a law is properly a law should certain social facts be satisfied – for example, that a properly accepted process, legislative or juristic, was followed). In terms of content of rules and principles adopted, it describes a system built to work towards a liberal democratic society. Whether a rule or principle is or is not "liberal" is not, however, a criterion for whether the rule or principle is a law or part of a legal system.

components of social reality come into being, presuming this happens within the natural world (ourselves being animals, possessed of certain attributes emergent from our specific evolutionary tale)? Must we understand, for example, that the legal world *must* be built according to a particular set of architectural plans, or is the important consideration that it be built out of – and so encompass – particular moral or political values and principles? Or are there no constraints of any sort on the construction process?

If we deny the notion of any and all construction requirements, we arrive at strong forms of social constructivism. Strong forms would have the law be *nothing more* than a social construction, in the sense that at all levels we imagine that both the form and content of built institutions are provided by the society in which the institution arises. A strong form of constructivism would assert that *nothing but* what is originally present in any given society is required in order for that society to construct a fully functioning legal system.[24] One might think a line between positivists and natural law theorists could be easily drawn at this point, but distinguishing between these camps of theorists using such tools requires careful unpacking. Once done, critical theorists can then be slotted into the picture drawn.

Positivists of the Hartian variety see a specific legal system as "legal" if it is built according to essentially structural requirements, with the structure containing elements that are themselves *reason-giving* (with rules, that is, that are followed "from the inside," that function independent of personal or subjective reasons or desires). A functioning legal system, under this model, is analogous in some ways to an ongoing game, one overseen by officials applying the rules, with authority over player rules and the power to alter these rules if need be. This game would be played by real players (and not automatons, which might be simply obeying algorithms provided), and rules of the game would give them reasons to act in certain ways rather than in others.[25] For Hart the key structural element in legal systems is found not in the split between primary and secondary rules but rather in the obligation for the set of secondary rules to spell out (for legal officials) how any given primary rule is authoritatively determined to be part of the law or not (what Hart labels the "rule of recognition"). With this rule in place, generating obligations for legal officials, a *legal* system exists.

24 Here I leave open the question of whether the tools that Searle identified as sufficient to build all forms of social reality – declarations and status functions – are truly sufficient. See Searle, *supra* note 1. This matter, as interesting and important as it may be in larger analyses, is not pressing in the present context.

25 Some put the requirement as such that determinations of the legality of any item be based on social facts. See e.g. Joseph Raz, *The Authority of Law: Essays on Law and Morality* (Oxford: Oxford University Press, 1979) [Raz, *The Authority of Law*]. It cannot, of course, be just that an item is labelled a social fact (which would be one sort of fact), but that some processes account for an item's being determined to be legal, which is to say some structural feature of a system (constituting a process matter) makes it so.

Natural law theorists, on the other hand, are a bit harder to pin down. Some heed the classic refrain that an unjust law is no law at all.[26] This can apply not just to particular laws but to legal systems as a whole – a natural law theorist may see a particular legal system as being such *only* if the system accords with essential requirements of morality or political morality.[27] A more modest form of natural law theory, however, holds that moral considerations are primary when *judging* the law, but questions the ontological status of a law (or a legal system) only in extreme cases.[28] Moral requirements then seem to be key evaluative tools, available to guide legal reform, with moral failure usually spelling out into need for criticism and activism.

Whether these requirements question the status of law as law or principally guide our development of "good law," natural law theorists hold that these requirements are objectively determinable (at least theoretically) and objectively "good" or absolute. Further, these measures are such that even natural law theorists who see moral codes being used principally to distinguish "good" from "bad" law accept that a serious ontological question arises when faced with a claimed legal system that is judged under these codes to be clearly evil. At some extreme point natural law theorists tend to rally together and question whether it is possible to say a truly evil system is *in fact* a legal system. A society, they generally tend to argue, might construct a social system in accord with what positivists argue are architectural or structural requirements, but with content falling far too short of moral/political requirements (as Fuller argued in relation to the Nazi regime from the mid-1930s to its destruction at the end of the Second World War).[29] Any who label an *essentially* "wicked" social system a *legal* system, natural law theorists generally maintain, are simply mistaken in their denotation.[30]

---

26 Aquinas seemed to hold to this point. See Thomas Aquinas, *The Summa Theologica*, online: <http://www.documentacatholicaomnia.eu/03d/1225-1274,_Thomas_Aquinas,_Summa_Theologiae_%5B1%5D,_EN.pdf>. See also Brian Bix, *Jurisprudence: Theory and Context*, 2nd ed (London: Sweet & Maxwell, 1999) at 61–6.

27 For the rest of this discussion I slide together non-religious and religious forms of natural law theory. In saying that natural law theorists see law as having to be built according to requirements of morality or political morality, I hope to include those who then also see the source of moral pronouncements (indeed, what provides the source of the authoritativeness of moral pronouncements) as being some religious realm.

28 See e.g. John Finnis, *Natural Law and Natural Rights* (Oxford: Clarendon Press, 1980); Lon Fuller, *The Morality of Law* (New Haven, CT: Yale University Press, 1969) [Fuller, *Morality of Law*].

29 See *ibid*; Lon Fuller, "Positivism and Fidelity to Law: A Reply to Professor Hart" (1958) 71:4 Harv L Rev 630 [Fuller, "Positivism and Fidelity to Law"].

30 One should note these two contrasting positions are clearly not prescriptive (though of course they can be put to prescriptive use). They both attempt to answer a non-prescriptive question – "what is required for a built social system to be properly labelled a legal system?" – and arrive at quite different answers.

Beginning with a common unassailable position – that all legal systems are social constructs – we can now begin to see how some might argue that the law cannot be "made sense of" via the CSM. Let us first focus on natural law theorists, as this point leaps out in relation to their theoretic position, and it provides an opportunity to place critical theorists in the mix.

Natural law theory locates a measure for law outside any identifiable legal (or social) system. For the general natural law theorist, this measure, as we just noted, not only serves a normative role but also plays an ontological role – a system that utterly fails to meet certain moral or political requirements can be argued to not constitute a legal system at all.[31] Where do we look in the natural world, however, for this measure? What experiments can we conduct to determine whether a particular social system satisfies these requirements? What empirically verifiable and reproducible observations can we expect to make as we examine the fit between a given system and these requirements? What predictions flow from the purported success of a given system when it is found to be "legal"? These "outside" measures, predicated on the existence of moral or political noumena,[32] point us away from the possibility of study through the application of the CSM. Natural law theory posits a realm removed from naturalistic inquiries, a realm outside the natural world.[33]

The critical theorist, on the other hand, eschews the possibility of any such transcendent or objective moral realm (or – what amounts to the same outcome – denies any access to such a postulated realm). Indeed, finding no sense in the notion of "objective knowledge" itself (seeing all knowledge as essentially subjective, tied to the practices of any given community of meaning), strong forms of critical theory eschew any talk of either transcendent or fixed notions or concepts.[34] Understanding legal systems to be *nothing but* constructs of individual societies, they understand such systems to be

31 Walters, for example, argues that Canadian law as it applies to Aboriginal peoples is not law at all, as it fails to meet substantive requirements of mutual acceptance and respect. See Mark D Walters, "The Morality of Aboriginal Law" (2006) 31 Queen's LJ 470.

32 I consciously use this expression according to one of its meanings, "noumenon," denoting an unknowable object, the existence of which is not capable of proof.

33 I am here discounting the small camps of moral realists and moral naturalists. See e.g. David Copp, *Morality in a Natural World: Selected Essays in Metaethics* (Cambridge, UK: Cambridge University Press, 2007). I do not think the realists, in particular, present a coherent picture of the nature of moral matters, and their marginal status would seem to support this suspicion. For a detailed discussion of moral realism, see e.g. Geoffrey Sayre-McCord, *Essays on Moral Realism* (Ithaca, NY: Cornell University Press, 1988). As should be clear from other sections of this text, the fact of moral disagreement weighs most heavily as I ponder the capacity to see how moral facts could exist in a natural world.

34 I am most interested in strong forms in this text. When I examine the ability of postcolonial theory to explain Aboriginal law, I focus on the post-structuralist thread woven through some versions of postcolonialism.

determined by the meanings created by and through members of each such particular society. Adopting an essentially anti-realist position vis-à-vis the moral realm, they localize (and historicize) not just the construction process itself, but also the generation of meaning.[35] The study, then, of any identifiable legal system itself is particularized, and we seem to lose the ability to say anything objective about "the law" (or any abstract legal phenomena). Indeed, the act of theorizing itself is localized (and historicized) as the critical theorist sees all activity as essentially subjective.[36] Again, the application of the CSM becomes – at best – highly problematic.[37]

Let us turn then to positivist theories of the law. As noted earlier, the paradigmatic twentieth-century articulation provides a model of a legal system remarkably aligned with key constitutive features of the Canadian domestic system – whose primary constitutive feature, according to Hart, is a rule of recognition. Hart, arguably, advanced his position as a response to concerns about theorizing we touched earlier. If law is essentially culturally determined, we seem to arrive at an impasse when comparing legal systems, or even in determining what is law within a single system. However, with law essentially constituted by *form* and *structure* (and not content), we seem removed from concerns about fundamental disagreement over values and principles, and we seem to keep our gaze focused on things in the world we can study naturalistically (via the CSM).[38]

However, we must continue to note sociocultural grounding, and so, naturally enough, we probe the archetypal positivist account further, asking about the *degree* to which systems of rules are social constructs. This further question about the degree or depth of construction need not be about the content of rules and rule-systems, but can be about such matters as questioning whether for a social system to be a legal system it *must be* – at its core – a matter of rules at all. To what extent is Hart's *concept* of law itself a construct?

---

35 In a later discussion I suggest that some critical theorists (I focus on the postcolonial theorist as illustrative) adopt this anti-realist position more broadly, as they generally question such notions as truth (as correspondence with forms of external reality) and knowledge (as objective).

36 There is no apparent bottom to the well of critique. James Boyle, for example, works towards articulation (as best as possible, given his radical thesis) of an argument that even "reason" is not a fixed notion, but rather a label for historically/culturally contingent ways of thinking, assessing, etc. See James Boyle, "The Politics of Reason: Critical Legal Theory and Local Social Thought" (1985) 133:4 U Pa L Rev 685.

37 I qualify the point in this sentence, for my developed position is that some kernel of critical insight can be put to use in forming an appropriate CSM of the study of legal systems.

38 In an upcoming discussion I explore aspects of Hart's positivism that do not accord well with the naturalist project (his means by which his analysis is grounded – conceptual analysis – arguably relies on a-naturalistic a priori assumptions, and his efforts to explain legal normativity seem to bring up mysteries best addressed a-naturalistically).

One common contemporary response – that there are more ways to think of the law than are captured within the world of centralized rule-based systems – is neither new nor all that radical. Anthropologists have been recording the legal traditions (or systems or orders) of diverse peoples around the world for the last century. Indeed, a powerful account of the non-centralized system making up the Cheyenne legal world was gathered and articulated by Llewellyn and Hoebel in the 1930s, while Malinowski's 1926 classic *Crime and Custom in Savage Society* did much the same for the Trobriand Islanders of Papua New Guinea.[39] Much of the growth in interest in legal pluralism over the last few decades seems connected to greater understanding and appreciation of the ways groups in diverse social settings regulate their affairs in ways that seem as law-like as what we witness within dominant highly centralized nation states. At the heart of legal pluralism is the claim there are many different types of legal systems besides the centralized system epitomized by our Canadian model.[40]

This marks an interesting shift in what one could reasonably consider to have been to this point a rather myopic "analysis" of the law. Recall we began with what we presumed to be (for this exercise) a paradigmatic instance of a

---

39 Karl Llewellyn & E Adamson Hoebel, *The Cheyenne Way* (Norman: University of Oklahoma Press, 1941); Bronislaw Malinowski, *Crime and Custom in Savage Society* (New York: Harcourt, Brace & Co, 1926), online: <archive.org/details/crimecustominsav00mali>.

40 As much as legal pluralism might seem to align with positions being slowly developed in this chapter, I do not press on to focus on this sort of theory (at this point) for two reasons.

First, a theory of law is not clearly forthcoming from the pluralist camp. See e.g. Brian Tamanaha, "The Folly of the 'Social Scientific' Concept of Legal Pluralism" (1993) 20:2 J L & Soc 192. It has been pointed out on numerous occasions by numerous theorists that the legal pluralist position seems to rest on acceptance of many types of social systems into the pantheon of "the legal," with no clear justification for this rapid expansion of scope of the concept. I work towards a legal pluralist model, but only once I develop a picture of meaning-generating communities that accounts for not just the generation of different *sorts* of legal systems, but different *concepts* of what might constitute legal systems.

Second, the utility of legal pluralist scholarship is unclear in the context of interactions between different Indigenous systems and that of the nation state. We here explore attempts by the one system to enjoy a monopoly in matters of fundamental authority (where we come to see that one primary concern is with control over meaning-generation in relation to notions of "law"). To go into analysis as undertaken by theories of legal pluralism (and of more general theories within the larger field of socio-legal analysis) is to already make the first major step (arguably the crucial step) to envisioning *a* social setting within which exist multiple legal orders or systems. Such a vision, however, advances us beyond key areas of inquiry – we are asking, for example, *how* it is that one system can attempt to subsume all others (so there can be envisioned *a* social setting, and not multiple social setting*s*).

The important point for our current discussion is simply that it is widely acknowledged that within any given geographical setting there may indeed be multiple "legal orders" or legal traditions – within the borders of a nation state like Canada, for example, there may be different *kinds* of "law," the dominant positivist-defined system only one of many that function to order the lives of citizens.

legal system – the domestic Canadian system – and we developed a sense of what might be key features informing our understanding of legal systems in general. We noted an interesting parallel between the picture we developed and a Hartian/positivist model of "the law," though the suggestion we made at that point was that this might just reflect the fact that Hart likely engaged in a similar sort of exercise (though he claimed to be – and indeed may have thought he was – conducting an exercise in conceptual analysis). We can now reopen our analysis by returning to this presumption and calling it into question.

We are left at *that* juncture, however, with a troubling set of possibilities. There might be no such thing as "the law," but rather just many labels used by different groups, and vain attempts by some to organize a "family" out of resemblances pulled out of the amorphous set. Alternatively, perhaps an actual family exists, though how we understand the nature of such a thing then needs to be explored and explained. Do we indeed inevitably arrive at this juncture? Might even the Hartian/positivist model itself sit firmly in a particular sociocultural setting?

The Possibility of Non-Rule-Centred Legal Systems

Let us draw up an account of how a non-rule-centred model might come to pass and what it might look like. We can then better appreciate just how culturally grounded a Hartian (and Canadian) model of "the law" might be. Imagine a people who, over many generations, conclude that centralization of power is too dangerous and inevitably allows for structures ripe for exploitation and domination. This community chooses, rather, to ensure, as best possible, that all its members are habituated in the qualities of thinking and acting best suited for ensuring both the stability of this society and the flourishing of its members and families.[41] Much energy is placed, then, in bringing up "good humans," individuals who know, without having to think about it, that – for example – sharing amongst community members is vitally important (and right), that honesty in interactions with others facilitates productive forms of interacting, and so forth.

Imagine this community vests a great amount of energy and expertise in carefully nurturing and sculpting its youth such that on reaching adulthood they emerge as responsible sovereign individuals. That is, each adult member of this community immediately and reflexively first thinks of herself or himself as living according to responsibilities that must be met (to family, clan, and people), and then according to whatever pursuits he or she builds on top of

41 I use the term "chooses" here advisedly – I do not mean to suggest that members of a society require or create a mechanism by which they can collectively decide to generate institutions or structures of one form or another – rather, I just mean to suggest that over time a society will move in a certain direction rather than another, where what accounts for directions chosen can be thoughts and values passing through the minds of many members of the society.

that.[42] There is no centralized power to fix, apply, and enforce normative standards, as such a centralized power structure has been effectively avoided in this model. Rules meant to dictate from *outside* the self (that would typically have issued from such centralized authority) are minimized to the extent possible (they are arguably absent – as deemed unnecessary – in all but crises).[43] Ways of living bind all together, but they do so by existing as webs of common belief and value *within* each individual. On the level of community stability, it is reasonably expected community members will act appropriately, and so tension between individuals is minimized (and such tension as does inevitably arise is managed – except in extreme situations – through common agreement arising out of common understandings of how people should be).

The suggestion here – coupled with questions raised about the role of intuitions in Hart's program carried out under conceptual analysis – is that what we might take to be key constitutive features of "the law" are in fact just those elements considered essential for their being put – at a fundamental level – *into* the reality constructed. Rather than reflect some Platonic essence of "law-hood," these elements – including the apparent need for a rule of recognition to generate and maintain system stability in this centralized structure – reflect choices made in particular sociocultural settings.[44] Other sociocultural groupings may generate not just different sets of rules, but indeed non-rule-centred structures.

What follows from the possibility that the positivist concept of law reflects a form of deep constructivism? We can begin to see that purportedly pure descriptive models of the law that this theory offers are at best *descriptions of systems built*, and so we begin to ponder the possibility that such models are sensible only within (and *from* within) the sociocultural milieu out which any identifiable rule-centred system emerges.

This seems to force positivism into one or another of the other two camps. Rather than locate a middle ground between (a) the fixed/transcendental grounding of natural law theory, and (b) the unfixed/creative/subjective field of critical theory, the positivist seems to have to either (i) argue that structural requirements are themselves transcendentally mandated (that for some mysterious reason for a society to create a legal order it *must* follow certain architectural plans), or (ii) accept that any positivist account is itself entirely socioculturally grounded (e.g., in a Canadian or British setting). Following either of these paths seem to lead, however, to problems with studying the law naturalistically.

---

42 There would not be, of course, complete success in this project – that becomes fodder for stories and lessons, told and retold to the young as part of the maturation process.

43 It would be a mistake to think rules are still present, but just function "internally." This social collective has made ways of acting habitual. The picture drawn is much closer to what one might see in virtue-theory models.

44 Again, one has to be careful with what "choices" means in this context.

Social Construction and Aboriginal Rights within Canadian Law

Let us step back for a moment to see how this talk of social construction affects making sense of Aboriginal rights. Consider a key constitutive rule within Aboriginal law, one that dictates how Canadian law identifies (and thereby creates) Aboriginal rights. The Supreme Court has specified that an Aboriginal right is a practice, tradition, or custom integral to the distinctive culture of the Aboriginal community claiming the right ("integral" at the time of contact with Europeans).[45] The right being claimed today – and so the practice, custom, or tradition "integral to the distinctive culture" – must enjoy continuity with the ancestral practice.

This functions as an attempt to generate an aspect of the social reality within which we find the Crown, Canadian society, and Indigenous peoples situated. Imagine an Aboriginal community holding an established right to fish for food and ceremonial purposes: besides making acceptable in Canadian law the pursuit of this activity by members of this community, the attempt – through a sociolinguistic tool that has meaning within a larger social setting – is to generate obligations on the Crown in relation to these activities. Just as making a promise generates obligations on the promise-maker to the party to whom the promise is directed (all within and premised on an institution of promising),[46] finding an Aboriginal right in any given situation generates obligations for the Crown in relation to the Aboriginal rights-holder – all within a legal institution, that of the regime of "rights" in both the common law and constitutional law in Canada.[47]

Hart's positivist model would assuredly have no problem locating law in this account on both general and more particular levels. We noted earlier how well the account of the law he deployed parallels the account we derived by thinking about key skeletal features of general Canadian law, and we are safe in presuming a properly functioning regime of secondary rules that indicates a fully and properly functioning legal system. Not only, then, would we find obligations being generated in this tale of the identification of an Aboriginal right, but we can presume legal officials approach the rules of the system they work within – like the rule of recognition – "from the inside."

It is not clear, however, whether a natural law theorist would find legal obligations fall on the Crown. While some natural law theorists might find that

45 *R v Van der Peet*, [1996] 2 SCR 507, 137 DLR (4th) 289 at para 46.

46 Expectations, naturally, are generated as well, but even "legitimate" expectations generated when a promise is embedded in a legal context are not accorded the same stature in Canadian law. Here I am making use of elements of Searle's work on the construction of social reality, discussed earlier. See Searle, *supra* note 1.

47 Generally, the obligation is to "recognize and affirm" the right in question – what this means "on the ground" depends on other aspects of the law of Aboriginal rights. Of course, establishing such a right leads to legally sanctioned activities; obligations on the Crown parallel powers enjoyed by the Aboriginal community and its members.

Aboriginal law advances the ideals of liberalism (finding, then, that Aboriginal law at the very least meets demands of a particular political morality) and is therefore law, other natural law theorists might argue Aboriginal law is a continuation of colonialism, that it is thereby an essential component of a wicked system, and so that it is not law at all.[48] Indeed, it is just this sort of debate – arguably endless and futile – that underscores the sort of divergence of legal theorizing about Aboriginal law noted in the opening chapters.

Critical theorists, on the other hand, argue there are no *objective* means by which to assess whether Aboriginal law is "law" and whether the possession of an Aboriginal right means that *objectively* speaking the Crown is then under legal obligations. In seeing all meaning emanating from and confined to socio-historical settings,[49] they could locate an expression of "truth" in the claims of the first set of natural law theorists, but only when truth is understood to reside wholly within the sociocultural world presently inhabited by people with those views about liberalism. Similarly, critical theorists could look at the claims of the second set of natural law theorists and see those also expressing "truth," when truth again is wholly a resident of a sociocultural world, this time one that encompasses people with beliefs in the continuation of colonial law as an underlying base for contemporary jurisprudence. Seeing no valid outside transcendent measure by which one could reasonably choose between these two expressions of socioculturally grounded "truths,"[50] the critical theorist comes to see these matters devolving to a base level of power and politics. The critical theorist is not focused on saying there is just lack of agreement on whether what we might take to be an aspect of Aboriginal law is actually "law," but rather on pointing out that there is no possible sense to the idea that there is a means by which we could "objectively" determine such a thing one way or another.[51]

At first glance it would seem the CSM offers little assistance in choosing between natural law and critical perspectives, as it would seem equally challenged by these two different (and opposed) views of the law itself. One rests on

48 See e.g. Walters, *supra* note 31.

49 As with the discussion of critical (postcolonial) theory in the last chapter of this text, I am here focused on the post-structuralist wing of critical theory (and not other wings, such as those dominated by different iterations of Marxism).

50 It is not that such an outside measure is difficult to detect or pin down, but that such outside measures come to be seen as non-existent and, ultimately, as meaningless.

51 The critical theorist also similarly challenges positions taken by the positivist. For example, Hart holds that the legality of such a thing as a claim about the existence of an Aboriginal right can be traced back such that we eventually arrive at a set of social facts that ground legality itself (which then settle whether this specific legal fact obtains). While the critical theorist can accept that a society can determine that certain "facts" can settle questions of legality, she, again, embeds this entire matter in a sea of power and politics. Others, the critical theorist would argue, can have different ideas not just about what count as specific relevant facts, but about whether in all cases social facts ground matters of legality.

the notion of some transcendent or a-natural realm that both accounts for and justifies the existence of law and legal obligations (a normative realm that can be neither observed nor studied from a naturalist frame). The other vision of law rests on the notion that all law is freely and "subjectively" created, that any legal construct we see is nothing but the product of a free and creative society (a vision of the world-in-mind that seems to make representational models of truth and knowledge meaningless).

Complicating matters, note as well that we also raised concerns about what might have otherwise seemed to be the solid positivist alternative. Positivism seemed to allow us a means by which we could continue to cling to the CSM, as it seemed – on its surface at least – reasonably well aligned with naturalist thought. We noted several times that Hart seemed alive to the advantages of a naturalist approach. We can see this manifest as well in his invocation of (and attempt to explain) legal normativity, as being seemingly the result of – and so explicable entirely in terms of – social rules, themselves understandable in terms of acceptances of rules and corresponding convergences in behaviour.[52]

We also noted, however, that the model of law-as-rules can fall into and be challenged by the larger and deeper sense of law as construct. The supposedly solid structural grounding of the positivist vision of law can be shaken, as we are required to take seriously the notion that this vision is itself the product of a sociocultural setting. If we could reasonably take the concept of law to refer to some object in a Platonic realm (inhabited, we might also imagine, by the perfect forms of Justice and the Good), we might reasonably suppose this vision could be solidly grounded, though of course then positivism would be in the same camp already occupied by natural law theory. Alternatively, the positivist could accept that his concept of law is parochial, that behind it lies *nothing but* a sociocultural community and its history of social development. But then, of course, positivism runs the risk of falling into the camp of the critical theorist, where the "truth" of its vision is entirely local and historical (and, especially in this context, *sociocultural*).

Given the existence in this context of other (Indigenous) socioculturally grounded visions of "the law" and what it might mean, the theorist cannot simply accept the positivist's account, or simply presume it functions to make sense of Aboriginal rights. This is a problem not just for positivist theorists, but for the business of theorizing about the law concerning Aboriginal rights.

To return to our narrower focus on positivist analyses of law, placed in the context of mainstream modes of analysis, a core problem with the study of law

52 It should be noted, however, that when one digs more deeply into Hart's (and other positivists') attempts at explaining legal normativity, things become quite murky. For a discussion of Hart's attempts at explaining legal normativity, see e.g. Ruth Gavison, ed, *Issues in Contemporary Legal Philosophy: The Influence of H.L.A. Hart* (Oxford: Clarendon Press, 1987). See especially Gerald J Postema, "The Normativity of Law" in *ibid* at 81; Neil MacCormick, "Comment" in *ibid* at 114; David Lyons, "Comment" in *ibid* at 126.

is that theorists seem to come down to a forced "choice" between two visions, neither of which connects well with the possibility of study by a naturalist, common sense approach. We find either a sense of the law as governed and dictated by a realm "above" or beyond the senses, or a sense of the law as essentially fluid and inherently subjectively grounded.

If it seems we might tend to slip into strong constructivism, does this reach over to call into question the CSM? How can we hope to naturalistically study mind-independent legal phenomena if the phenomena to be studied are in fact entirely mind-dependent, arising out of the very construction of meaning by social groups? Are we forced to seriously consider weak constructivism as our sole alternative, trying to work out how law is fixed and determined by other elements? What if these other elements are themselves non-natural? Are we then forced to consider the possibility it is simply misguided to think we can naturalistically explore the law and legal systems?

Actually, we are only halfway to seeing all the problems posed by the constructed nature of law and legal systems. At this juncture we seem to see only two possibilities – weak and strong constructivism. This suggests that an unavoidable choice now lies before us: we can choose to approach the law as either (a) weakly constructed (and then have to account for outside, potentially *non-natural* elements or processes that determine or fix the nature of law), or (b) strongly constructed (and then have to account for the law arising mysteriously [some seemingly non-natural mental/human capacities responsible for the possibility of our making these social realities out of whole cloth] and settle for nothing more than socioculturally fixed *understandings* of law).

But the choice does not exist in this form, as if we (or positivism for that matter) must choose between these options and no others. We can respond to these challenges by placing into the natural world not just systems of law, but *sociocultural worlds that build systems of law*, that give them meaning. To see this possibility and how methodological naturalism works us out of what might have seemed to be a no-win situation, we need to press on a bit further. We need to complete the second half of this expedition into problems that the social construction of legal institutions and concepts of law suggests for the CSM. After examining and responding to challenges posed by notions of meaning and normativity, we can return to this discussion, at that point dissolving these concerns with the constructed nature of the law.

The Social Construction of Aboriginal Rights: Meaning and Normativity

The second half of this expedition begins with a look into how modern legal theory attempts to grapple with difficult questions posed by meaning and normativity – I track how core aspects of this struggle unfold and then argue that problems posed for the CSM ultimately rest on starting points for inquiry we need not adopt. In pulling together threads in the concluding section of this chapter, we will also see how this treatment of this specific problem points the way to removal of the apparent forced choice we noted above (between thinking there must be some transcendent and fixed means by which to settle "what is law" or holding that all "law" is socioculturally dependent, including *concepts* of law).

Let us go back for a few moments to our original enterprise, that of talking about the nature of "the law," to review our insight into the paradigmatic/concrete system under investigation, that of Canadian domestic law. We arrived at a positivist picture of the law as a two-tiered mass of rules, principles, and codes, embedded within and intertwined with various social institutions. Bearing in mind we now see this is arguably a sociocultural instantiation of what "the law" *may* look like, do we imagine this system can be adequately explored and explained as *nothing more than* elaborated rules, principles, and codes? Or do we need to include, in some fashion or other, links to the larger social reality within which they exist? Indeed, and crucially, no matter what form we might imagine law might take (accepting, that is, the possibility that the *concept* of law itself might be a social construct), do we need to reach past the elements of the law so conceived to explain the social reality within which this understanding and its related systems are embedded?

We can use this question, posed in the narrower context, as a point of departure, to engage with threads of mainstream legal theoretic discourse while introducing further serious challenges to the CSM of explanation-generation. We find in particular several matters that generate questions within mainstream legal analysis about the scope and function of "the law" in its relations to larger social structures within which law arises. Within mainstream discourse we find debates about whether we must acknowledge within analyses (a) those elements of the larger social reality that some suggest give law "meaning,"[53] (b) the role interpretation plays (some argue) in making sense of either an entire legal system or components thereof,[54] and/or (c) questions that arise about normative aspects of rules and rule-following.[55] In talking about the law (and then going on to talk about Aboriginal law) *must* we discuss interpretation, normativity, and meaning? If so, how?

53 This constitutes, for example, one of the major components of the famous Hart-Fuller debates of the mid-twentieth century. The core of the debate is captured in a paper and a response to it in the Harvard Law Review and is woven through larger texts. See HLA Hart, "Positivism and the Separation of Law and Morals" (1958) 71:4 Harv L Rev 593 [Hart, "Positivism and the Separation of Law and Morals"]; Fuller, "Positivism and Fidelity to Law," *supra* note 29. Hart, *Concept of Law*, *supra* note 5; Fuller, *Morality of Law*, *supra* note 28.

54 See e.g. Ronald Dworkin, *A Matter of Principle* (Cambridge, MA: Harvard University Press, 1985) [Dworkin, *A Matter of Principle*]; Ronald Dworkin, *Law's Empire* (Cambridge, MA: Harvard University Press, 1988) [Dworkin, *Law's Empire*]; Ronald Dworkin, *Justice for Hedgehogs* (Cambridge MA: Harvard University Press, 2011).

55 See e.g. Gavison, *supra* note 52.

Questions like these seem central not just to twentieth-century legal theoretic debates but to all serious discussions of law, meaning, and morals. This is so, but only if we expand upon the view of these matters as they come up within mainstream legal discourse. I propose to follow aspects of mainstream theoretic debates about these issues, but to illustrate how certain ground-level assumptions buried at the heart of mainstream theory inexorably lead us into a second thicket of problems attending the project of explaining legal phenomena via the CSM. The larger project involves resolving challenges posed by this second thicket of problems, arguing that we end up in this thicket only because we are enveloped from the start in *framing* provided by mainstream theoretic concepts and concerns. Once we realize that not just "the law," but also concepts deeply embedded within and theories of the law are themselves deeply socially constructed and determined – with all this transpiring *within* a natural-social world – can we then comfortably deal with the purported deep challenges in ways that give us a sense that naturalist explanations of legal phenomena are entirely possible and helpful.

Beyond the Question of Disciplinary Boundaries

Hart had no truck with the notion that rules (even the rule of recognition) might contain moral or political *content* (a rule of recognition for a system, for example, could be that a rule is properly a law only to the extent that it reflects certain prescribed moral principles or values).[56] To what extent, however, does this inclusive positivist picture – allowing for a role to be played by moral and political content of rules – tell us about how any particular functioning legal system either (a) *emerged* and *developed* in the world, or (b) actually *works* in the world?

Hart's model would not tell us much on the level of legal analysis about how a system under study comes into or functions in the world, beyond the points that (a) "proper" laws generate legal possibilities and obligations, and (b) legal officials, functioning under rules of change, can respond to social changes to add, delete, or modify primary rules.[57] Raz's extension of the positivist picture adds a bit more

56 This lies at the heart of the contemporary distinction between inclusive and exclusive positivism. Most positivists maintain that the boundary between themselves and non-positivist theories in relation to the question about how law and morals are related is set out by the core positivist principle on this point, that there is no *necessary connection* between law and morals (while any specific legal system might have some sort of "moral content" requirement for its rule of recognition, this would be a contingent matter).

57 The only strict requirement for any particular system's being legal (within the Hartian model) is that legal officials within that system find themselves legally obligated to recognize that system's rule of recognition "from the inside." Coleman notes this weakens the notion that Hart's positivist picture can be simply framed as "law as rules." The rule of recognition came to play

to the dynamic model of a legal system working in the world – generated rules function as *authoritative* pronouncements to citizens, giving them reasons to act that circumvent the need to do their own subjective, personal evaluations in any given situation – but while legal rules may be meant to function this way we gain no further insight into why specific rules may be generated within a society.[58]

Where does all this put us, though, in our quest to *make sense* of Aboriginal law? The positivist can accept that the content of legal rules, when they are properly formed, *may* come from liberal principles, she can explain the application of these rules to Indigenous peoples, and she can understand that legal obligations on the Crown come out of the doctrine of Aboriginal rights. Positivists, however, do not label certain investigations going beyond this point as "legal" – those investigations, for example, that might look more deeply into *how* things came to be and *why* things work the way they do in this "legal" field. For example, inquiries into *purposes* that actors might have in mind that motivate their work in building the Canadian system the way it has been built during the last few decades would not, in the positivist model, fall under "legal analysis."[59] For example, Hart would not see further or deeper analyses of these principles as a *legal* matter – it largely falls to moral or political scientists/philosophers/researchers to carry out these forms of analysis.[60]

In the context of the analysis in this text, attention does not linger on a sort of disciplinary-boundary dispute – my focus is on making sense of Aboriginal rights, not on marking out domains for legal versus moral or political analysis. The only pressing concern posed by the common boundary-dispute for this inquiry is that it seems that one prime motivator for drawing such lines has been to isolate legal discourse from the vagaries of moral and political discourse. For the purposes, then, of making full sense of Aboriginal rights, the fact we are told once we step past positivistically defined borders of "the law" we immediately face seemingly intractable confusion and discord just reframes one key concern that animates this exercise in methodological naturalism.

---

in Hart's mature picture the key role of determining the validity of laws, making it sensible to say that any particular law need not be a rule (so long as it was affirmed as law by legal officials who treat the rule of recognition appropriately). See Jules Coleman, "Rules and Social Facts" (1991) 14:3 Harv JL & Pub Pol'y 703.

58 Joseph Raz, *Ethics in the Public Domain: Essays in the Morality of Law and Politics* (Oxford: Oxford University Press, 1996). See especially "Authority, Law and Morality" in *ibid* at 210; Raz, *Authority of Law*, *supra* note 25.

59 That is, liberal positivism would not advance beyond analysis that simply pointed to the presence of liberal values and principles infusing principles used as blueprints for particular rules and tests developed. This is, in a sense, the conclusion reached at the end of chapters 6 and 7, those chapters that look into the ability of liberal positivism to explain the nature of Aboriginal law.

60 Hart, Positivism and the Separation of Law and Morals, supra note 50.

So let us put this boundary-dispute issue to one side. The question here is whether in trying to make sense in as rich and defensible a manner as possible, one must examine not just the bare content of rules (and their structural connections) but also the ways these rules may be interlaced with societal matters. One can press on with the sorts of questions that seemingly bring into the picture such things as purposes: *why* do the rules emerge in the form they have? To turn this back to the matter of social construction, what are parties attempting to achieve – what are they attempting to build – with the systems they construct?[61] Here is where the second set of problems begin to emerge for the CSM. It takes a bit for work, however, before we really arrive face-to-face with serious problems.

At first glance it might seem the CSM would struggle with the notion of purposes and other societally determined matters, things one can imagine need to be explored in working towards a rich understanding of Aboriginal law. Some theorists (like Fuller) argue it is essential we treat a legal system as a construct in a very particular sense, that we focus attention on the law's nature as an artifice built to *achieve* or further some (set of) *social purpose(s)*.[62] Do we need to see the law *imbued* with purpose, as reflecting sets of purposes held by those who craft and manage the system?[63] Would the requirement we see the law imbued with purpose entail that law receives an essential component – its meaning – in connection to its purposes, so that to know something basic

61 Several words of caution are appropriate here. First, it may well be that much of the construction we are thinking of in this general discussion – the building, maintaining, and strengthening of social institutions – could happen with little conscious planning. It may be that much of what we witness comes about as a result of a vast number of day-to-day acts carried out by a vast number of differently situated actors, with few acts the product of conscious attention to the larger construction projects being imagined. Second, we need not limit ourselves to conscious planning and acting, as it may well be that other forces account for what we witness (for example, the sorts of "historical forces" with which Hegel and Marx played around). Our project, however, is focused on the construction of the jurisprudence concerning Aboriginal rights, and it is entirely reasonable to begin this focused study with the presumption that there are relatively few actors wielding potentially enormous influence (and that they are not hard to identify), acting in discrete and consciously determined ways. The query here is why they might decide to act as they do.

62 See e.g. Fuller, *Morality of Law*, *supra* note 28.

63 Interestingly, Searle's view of social reality as constructed, but in line with naturalist thought, encompasses as well the notion that law is imbued with purpose. The law would be constructed as an artificial kind, and so for some end (much as a screwdriver is not a "natural" entity insofar as it exists as a screwdriver in order to put in screws). As Fletcher notes, this means that on Searle's account the law is "ontologically subjective" (which is to say, the nature of any particular law or legal system depends on what has been – subjectively – put into it): George Fletcher, "Law" in Barry Smith, ed, *John Searle* (Cambridge, UK: Cambridge University Press, 2003) 85 at 94.

about any identifiable legal system is to know it must be interpreted in light of that system's particular purposes?[64]

But the CSM need not get hung up on difficult matters posed by the possibility that sociopolitical purposes help to determine how legal institutions are designed and built. That is, one can approach "purposes" naturalistically without any serious concerns arising, treating purposes as contents of beliefs held, as mental objects that may direct planning and action.

In turning attention to such matters, however, other concerns come into focus. Fortunately, some of these further matters need not be particularly problematic. For example, earlier we discussed human capacities that might seem to pose problems for a common sense approach to the study of the law (such as a radically free will),[65] but we also noted that beginning with mind-in-the-world has us start with such seemingly mysterious forces or entities *put to one side*, only to be brought into our analysis if *required* for a good explanation of what we observe and test.

We are now, however, gazing more deeply into legal analysis. In this context, other objects come into view. We noted in bringing in but then moving past questions the role purposes could play in the construction of the law that one might argue that the *meaning* of a law comes ultimately from the purpose(s) for which it has been built. Indeed, legal structures marked by *meaning* and *normativity* are generally understood to make up aspects of social worlds. The second set of problems for the CSM revolve around these aspects of the "inner world" of human existence, an inner world postulated as a *constitutive source of being* for legal structures. On the one hand, meaning and normativity intertwine with subjective forms of experiences often understood – or, rather, presumed – to have no *necessary* or structural causal law-like relations either between themselves or with the social world with which they intersect. Alternatively, meaning and normativity bring us into contact with "higher" forms of existence, inaccessible to the normal senses.

64 Positivists (like Hart) oppose the notion that law can be understood only in light of purposes it serves, arguing instead that we can be content – in doing legal analysis – in producing nothing more than a detailed exposition of the nature of the rules and tests that make up any given legal field. Interpreting these rules in light of particular social purposes to which the system under study might be connected would be to engage in extra-legal analysis.

65 The larger concern at this point comes from attachment to the notion of constructed self-understandings of the element of free will (and free play). Not only is it the case, this argument goes, that meaning emerges within the mind (as a product of interplay within language, between members of a society), but it can do so in a completely creative and free manner. There would be no possibility, then, of knowing enough about *how* a given society at one point in time means *x* by *y* such that one could determine or predict that at a later point that society would come to mean *x*' by *y*'. Causal networks between systems of beliefs do not exist, this argument goes, and so trying to generally model (and so explain) human-social systems and behaviours is not just currently impractical, but impossible.

Meaning and Interpretation

The problem with *meaning* is that it is argued to be a matter that arises in the interstices between (a) what we witness in the world and (b) those self/society understandings that imbue world practices and world structures with sense. By "self/society understandings" I refer to the fact that what one thinks of oneself and what a society has as its self-image (and hence its image of selves within itself) are mutually constitutive. That is, a sense of self cannot arise in isolation from the existence of the self in a social setting, and so one's sense of self is unavoidably the product of *this* existence in *this* social setting.[66] Meanwhile, any understanding of what constitutes a society (or what a society "thinks" of the nature of those who might make it up) likewise cannot exist in isolation, but must come from thoughts of *individuals* making up this social grouping. The two work back and forth, senses of self and society shifting as selves shift how they think of themselves and how society is thought of – hence the notion of mutual-constitution, though all the thinking, of course, takes place in the minds of individuals.

The problem with *normativity*, meanwhile, is that the law is argued to provide an actor with a reason for acting, a reason that (a) does not rest on that actor's subjective feelings, evaluations, or calculations, and (b) (arguably) functions to *justify* both actions and criticisms. As Hart so famously put it, a properly constituted law does not merely oblige an actor to act, but generates an obligation.[67] Let us take these two general concerns in order, along the way fleshing out why it is these sorts of concerns pose the deepest challenges to the common sense approach to generating explanations of legal phenomena.

MEANING

We are fundamentally wondering how to *make sense of* Aboriginal law, where one could reframe this as a quest into the *meaning* of Aboriginal law. What do we mean by "meaning" here? We can avoid weighty and technical debates about meaning,[68] as the question before us is simply whether we miss an important

---

66 See Charles Taylor, *Hegel* (Cambridge, UK: Cambridge University Press, 1975). Taylor argues at pages 380–1 that:

> We can think that the individual is what he is in abstraction from his community only if we are thinking of him qua organism. But when we think of a human being, we do not simply mean a living organism, but a being who can think, feel, decide, be moved, respond, enter into relations with others; and all this implies a language.... But now a language, and the related set of distinctions underlying our experience and interpretation, is something that can only grow in and be sustained by a community. In that sense, what we are as human beings, we are only in a cultural community.

67 See *Concept of Law*, *supra* note 5, at 80.

68 See e.g. Scott Soames, *What Is Meaning*? (Princeton, NJ: Princeton University Press, 2010); Jack Ritchie, *Understanding Naturalism* (Stocksfield, UK: Acumen Press, 2008).

dimension to our understanding of Aboriginal law if we fail to try to see "what it means" (particularly in this context, embedded as the law is within a larger social reality). Let me expand on two ways meaning can seem to complicate the notion of naturalistically examining legal matters, the first focused on "inner" or subjective aspects of meaning and the role meaning seems to play in the construction of social systems, and the second on the link between meaning and interpretation, which arises once one considers how people are to make sense of a socially constructed system.

In thinking of constructed socio-legal systems, we have questions about the nature of meaning that connect to it being essentially an "internal" matter (internal to the human mind, on an individual level, and the human collective, on a sociolinguistic level). One might argue, for example, that there is a synergistic interplay between the self and society, both centred on and generating self/society understandings, a synergy that *imbues with meaning* those sets of rules we might identify as constituting elements of legal systems.[69] In being built, a system is put together by *individuals* who make up a *group*, the self/society dyad building according to understandings concerning what the dyad takes to be valuable and meaningful. Given that the thing built reflects this purposeful under-layer, one essentially interlaced with "subjective" meanings,[70] we seem forced to acknowledge one can understand the nature of the system only through study of what the system *means* to the society it exists within (and more properly, to those individuals who make up this society).

Let us take as our first example the proposition that within Aboriginal law in Canada if certain conditions are met in certain situations the Crown has obligations to accommodate merely asserted Aboriginal rights. What is being expressed in this proposition? Is there a *fact* of the matter this is about? Must one decompose the proposition into its constitutive elements (and analyse them) in order to arrive at the proper understanding of what it means? Might these elements themselves gain their meaning in the context of the larger whole? Further, does the meaning of this proposition ineluctably arise in the space between the bare rule(s) and such things as the purposes society vests in the rule(s) established, which are mere manifestations of those forces within that elements of society take to be worthy of pursuing? Can we tackle these questions as earlier suggested – as all capable of being repackaged in terms of beliefs held?

69 See e.g. Fuller, *Morality of Law*, *supra* note 28. Fuller argued that law exists in order that human conduct may be *guided* by rules. This purpose in mind, an "inner morality" for any legal system then presents itself as necessary, for the guidance of rules can occur only when certain conditions are met.

70 "Inter-subjective" might seem the better term in this context, but since all inter-subjective meaning exists *in* subjects, we can use this more individual-centred term.

Meaning as Deeply Subjective. Weighty debates about meaning hinted at earlier threaten to intrude at this point, as we wonder what we could possibly mean by the "sense" or understanding of the legal proposition. Fortunately, our focus moves us away from such deep waters – we are exploring the notion that *whatever "meaning" amounts to*, some assert it arises in the space between the world and a group of meaning-generating people, so this thing we try to grasp must be found in some sense *within* the thoughts of the group that has generated a certain kind of meaning in this context. The argument would be, essentially, that the meaning of a proposition in the legal context carries with it something of the party expressing it, an in-eliminable component. In our discussion of truth in the natural sciences, we noted that in that context the role of the theorist (and her community) can be minimized to the point that it plays no significant role in determining the meaning of scientific claims. Ultimately, the meaning of a scientific claim can be measured against the way things are and not the perspective brought to the scientific enterprise by the scholar. With legal propositions and legal analysis, things are not so clear – rather, propositions emerge out of such things as decisions made, as judges (or legislators) weigh many matters before determining the framework to apply to disputes before them, and analysis typically does not shy away from interacting with legal propositions with further masses of decision-making (built around parallel matters of weighing multiple factors and values).

This in mind, we begin to sense some of the central philosophical problems that "meaning" generates (about whether, for example, the sense that must be attributed to a proposition exceeds whatever references may be made by terms within the proposition), but we also begin to see that these philosophical quagmires need not detain us, as our central concern at this juncture is just with the purportedly deep subjectivity that meaning indicates. Our concern is with the notion that an independent observer can never hope to locate some sort of "true" meaning of a legal proposition, if this is meant to indicate meaning expressed in a language *removed* from the sociocultural setting of the proposition and the system it arises within.

This specification of one central concern in hand, we can move towards showing this is a manageable problem, resolvable within a naturalist approach to the study of law and legal theory. Thinking of deep subjectivity leads us, however, into other related concerns with meaning, those that bring into the picture the notion of meaning-generating communities.

Meaning as Socially Constructed. Consider a second illustrative example: in *Mitchell v Minister of National Revenue*, Binnie J held that whatever Indigenous sovereignty might have amounted to before the assertion of Crown sovereignty, it now exists solely as an element *within* Crown sovereignty – the "merged sovereignty" model of Indigenous sovereignty.[71] Here we clearly witness the relevant problematic aspect of "meaning" in the situation under examination – the meaning of "Indigenous sovereignty" is seemingly being generated, and by a sociocultural community. Let us here designate this stipulated or generated meaning, coming back to its nature later when we unpack what is going on in more detail.

The key point to note at this juncture is that Indigenous collectives may (and many indeed do) disagree with this stipulated meaning, suggesting not just that Canadian law may *seem* distinctly different in nature, depending on one's perspective, but – should we accept that meaning is socially constructed – that Canadian law may in fact *be* different, depending on the perspective occupied. We seem left faced with some difficult questions. Is there a definite meaning of the expression "Indigenous sovereignty" (as it appears within Canadian law) that could settle contestation witnessed? While different collectives might see different things in this expression, is there nevertheless a right or correct understanding?

We might hope to find a parallel to what we earlier observed to be a defensible naturalist position in understanding how the natural sciences function. While anti-foundationalist arguments have carried the day in the academy with good reason, we drove a wedge between that and the anti-representationalism some then tried to move everyone towards. We can make sense, then, of the notion that what grounds truth-claims in the sciences is "the way things are" (where the practices of science determine what "truth" means in this context). What, however, could play an analogous role in the context of legal propositions?

Are there facts of the world that can determine (or at least be used to measure) the meaning of an expression such as "Indigenous sovereignty"? While the Supreme Court seems to concretize the meaning by *specifying* what the term can refer to in the world occupied by both Indigenous and non-Indigenous societies, do they do so by simply recording "the way things are"? Could we measure the success of theories containing this expression by the extent to which they too capture the way things are? Would it be a mistake in meaning, for example, for an Indigenous collective to dispute the meaning attributed to this term by the Canadian court?

Two matters complicate this attempt to parallel truth and meaning as they function in the natural sciences. First, an Indigenous collective can indeed dispute any set of facts Canadian courts can try to point to, in order to pin down the meaning of the expression. Before the intrusion of the Crown, Indigenous "sovereignty" would have been whatever an independent Indigenous collective believed it to be (with meaning fleshed out in how they acted).[72] We now find

71 *Mitchell v MNR*, 2001 SCC 33 at paras 129–35.

72 It is challenging, of course, to work with the term "sovereignty" in this context, given its loaded sets of meaning within the world of Western legal and political philosophy. I here just indicate that when conceptualized at a high enough level – as indicating the power of

the expression arising in the intersection of asserted Crown sovereignty and the continued lives of Indigenous collectives. Certainly many facts have changed – some radically – but has this removed from the scene the meaning-generating mechanisms of Indigenous collectives? Are we now in a world wherein they cannot meaningfully determine (at least partially) what Indigenous sovereignty means? Can a Canadian court simply stipulate what this means? Is this not an attempt to create reality by saying it is so?

There seems to be only a single path towards concrete meaning, and it is not a path down which naturalist analysis can travel. A jurist might hold that meaning is not created out of whole cloth (subjectively), but on the basis of constraints imposed by a theory of human nature (or some similar-functioning theory of morals or political morality). "Indigenous sovereignty," such an account might hold, has its meaning fixed by a deeper account of that end to which the law is meant to be built and measured. In chapters 6 and 7 this sort of path is explored – here we need only note the ground contemplated is itself fixed and determinate only if we assume it is "transcendent." A jurist might hold she is expressing a meaning of Indigenous sovereignty determined by what *must* be put into the world according to liberal doctrine. Liberal doctrine, however, concretizes the meaning of this expression fully (in some *objective* fashion) only if it is the *right* theory about how *all* societies *must* be organized. We would have to imagine there are universal truths about how human societies *must* be organized, a matter that runs into real problems with naturalist accounts.

We now have the elements necessary to spell out what the problems are for meaning in this context. We need to acknowledge we have components of the world created by meaning-generating collectives. Can we find anything like determinative meaning in this context? We might search for some transcendent grounding, but while this might lead to interesting discussions, it seems ultimately futile, especially if we want to *explain* what we witness (and note that once we enter such discussions we move away from the natural world, debating the nature of things removed from what we can reasonably sense). The only alternative, however, seems to be full immersion in a world dominated by forms of subjectivity. Meaning would be nothing else, it seems, than what collectives make, with matters of explanation seemingly removed from the table once again.

---

a community to have a fundamental say in what happens in relation to lands and waters to which it is connected, and in relation to what both the society and the people who make it up think and do – what the Crown might stipulate will be distinct (in its coming from the Crown) from what meaning-generating Indigenous communities would have in mind. Alfred has clearly pressed some of the serious problems that arise when attention is not paid to these matters. See Taiaiake Alfred, *Peace, Power, Righteousness: An Indigenous Manifesto* (Don Mills, ON: Oxford University Press, 1999).

Once we posit meaning-generating collectives, we can, however, also see the false choice this way of understanding the world puts to us. Meaning-generating communities arise in the natural world (the mind-in-world assumption), and this puts matters before us that we can study and attempt to explain. The present study offers a clear matter for serious naturalist exploration – we need not attempt to settle "deep" matters of meaning, since what we witness and wish to explain is one meaning-generating collective attempting to generate social reality, an attempt it is directing towards the lives and futures of other meaning-generating collectives. We can examine what "Indigenous sovereignty" means from within the dominant meaning-generating community (which is relying on its courts to generate meaning for this expression), and we can examine what this term might mean for numerous, varied Indigenous collectives. Our attention is focused ultimately on key legal matters before us – the attempt of Canadian courts to have the meaning it stipulates reach out and remove not just Indigenous concepts, but the very capacities Indigenous communities have enjoyed for countless generations to generate concepts and meanings.

INTERPRETATION

Unfortunately, however, this path forward is not free of obstacles. While concerns about meaning in this context can be defused within the appropriate naturalist approach to the study of law and perspectives, concerns about interpretation and processes of interpreting seem to persist. We can make a quick appeal to our discussion of meaning to put aside one sense in which interpretation seems problematic, but the matter of *our* place in all this – as researchers seemingly unavoidably involved in interpretation – requires careful attention in order to be resolved.

The central problem in this context is not with questions about "local" interpretation (how we know, for example, what the extension of a term like "vehicle" might be) but with questions that come up about the role of interpretation itself (wondering, for example, what role interpretation generally plays in making sense of phenomena). Parallel with what we noted with meaning, some argue there is an irreducibly subjective element to the process of interpreting social matters. Things expressed in and through language – things that emerge in the world as signs and sounds, visible in the natural world – are said to point to deeper things – meanings – that lie behind them. Interpretation is then posited as an essential process that moves one towards meaning – "meanings" do not arise of themselves when one is faced with some aspect of the social world, but (as the result, in part, of their being buried within subjectively determined worlds) must be accessed through interpretation. These interpretive processes – inherently emanating themselves from within sociolinguistic worlds – then add a layer of subjectivity to what was already argued to be irreducibly subjective.

We can see how this might function in the realm of legal analysis in tracing Dworkin's "interpretive turn." After decades working within a fairly middle-of-the-road approach to legal theorizing, in the 1980s Dworkin shifted to a position that took *all* legal decisions to be products of interpretation, accepting that an essentially human element infects adjudication.[73] He went on to argue, however, that this did not preclude an ideal adjudicator from finding the "right answer," though this answer would not come from some outside source, but from the mass of previous legal materials, properly approached.[74] The key to Dworkin's rescue of a measure of objectivity was his claim that the interpretive process – to function as it should – must cleave to such principles as integrity. In effect, Dworkin's response to the threat of bias and perspective – something he clearly took seriously – was to simply accept the fact there is no transcendent realm that the adjudicator, *as an interpreter*, can be trying to access, a realm that might provide the right or true answer.[75] Deciding on the basis of what the interpretive community would ideally accept is his substitute. Dworkin came to accept, then, that the jurist works entirely within a sociocultural setting. All adjudicative processes are seen as interpretive practices, which use principles and materials drawn from the sociocultural world the jurist inhabits.

In the Canadian context, of course, this means accepting that the jurist works within a liberal sociocultural context. While this picture has room within it for the fact of other sociocultural worlds (within which, for example, live Mohawk, or Innu, etc.), and the fact of world overlap, each of these other perspectives is usually understood to be (or presumed to be) concomitantly buried within the dominant setting. This invites a political dimension into the analysis of law, though to the extent any particular theorist is deeply or completely immersed in his larger sociocultural setting, this political dimension may not be visible in his writings.

We see here a parallel with a concern raised earlier, that this challenges the notion that a global explanation for the nature of Aboriginal rights might be possible. If the law itself is *entirely* interpretive in this manner – so that what the law is at any point is actually a function of the interpretive stance of the jurist deciding on its nature – it would seem that an understanding or explanation that would make sense to anyone, no matter her sociocultural perspective, is chimerical.

73 Dworkin, *Matter of Principle, supra* note 54; Dworkin, *Law's Empire, supra* note 54.

74 Dworkin's "interpretive turn" was arguably more of an underlying shift in theoretical emphasis, as he had laid out an aspect of this vision of the adjudicative process in the 1970s. For his discussion of "Hercules," the ideal jurist, see e.g. Ronald Dworkin, "Hard Cases" in Dworkin, *Taking Rights Seriously, supra* note 12 at 81.

75 Of course, to the extent the mass of materials the adjudicator works with contains reference to moral principles, and to the extent the interpretative process lying at the heart of the law requires deployment of determined or fixed current understandings of justice and fairness, there is a sense in which interpretation is constrained "from the outside."

This sort of general concern can be quickly defused, making use of arguments introduced earlier. Consider again the rule from *Van der Peet*: for a claim to constitute an Aboriginal right, it must be a practice, tradition, or custom integral to the distinctive culture of the Aboriginal community claiming the right (integral at the time of contact with Europeans). In the last section we saw that a central concern with meaning is that it might seem that we are faced with an unpalatable choice: either the meaning of this rule is meaning *to x* and depends on the place of *x* in a complex social system of meaning, or meaning is somehow grounded in a manner that can lead to the determination of something fixed and objective (where this grounding inevitably reaches out to non-natural realms). We noted, however, that placing the entire situation in the natural world – seeing meaning-generating collectives arising within this one world – can defuse these concerns about meaning, particularly as they arise in the narrower context of our present study. Within the form of methodological naturalism being developed, we can acknowledge that meaning is a product of sociocultural collectives, but understand that sociocultural collectives (generating meaning) are themselves aspects of the natural world. This placement of meaning-generating communities *in* the natural world then likewise defuses this first layer of concern introduced when our focus shifts to interpretation and interpretive practices.

Again, all such practices can be understood to be local and historical, but emergent within a larger natural world inhabited by meaning-generating communities. One thing any meaning-generating community allows for is a milieu of interpretive activity and interpretive products. We can accept, for example, that the most salient forms of meaning that any party can generate (and other parties grasp) is what is generated through intersubjective agreement. We then leave to the side (under the methodological naturalist approach) the possibility that such meanings are (somehow) potentially linked to "deeper" transcendent meanings.

INTERPRETATION AND THE PLACE OF LEGAL THEORISTS

A second level of concern, however, remains to be addressed. We still have to wonder about the location of ourselves – *legal theorists attempting to make sense of Aboriginal law* – in this entire process, presuming we each inhabit a sociocultural world through which we perspectivally make sense of legal phenomena. It would seem *we* either (a) struggle to say what any particular rule "really" means, or (b) give up the struggle, having to acknowledge that, given *our* place within a social setting, when we try to arrive at an understanding of the meaning of any rule, we generate yet another set of meanings, as *we* interpret what we see from *our* socioculturally determined vantage point.[76] Clearly, then, the

76 Note, again, how this is (yet another) retelling of central challenges I attempt to meet in this text.

apparent problem of our place in this web of interpretation adds a wrinkle, as we seemingly come to the task with our own meaning/interpretive baggage.

How can we not begin with the truism that we, too, inhabit sociocultural settings? Do we not unavoidably come to the study of law with either our own allegiances to transcendent/a-natural objects by which we impose order on what we see, and/or a set of subjectively established values and principles through which we add a new layer of creative interpretation?

Within sociocultural settings within which we function as researchers, there seem to be three possible roles we could play in "studying" the law: (1) we *support* the construction of law we witness (perhaps unwittingly for the most part), as we naturally fit into the social world constructed – *our world*, as it were; (2) we do not support (and possibly *attack*) the legal world we see constructed, as it conflicts with our distinct and separate sets of ideologically or culturally fixed meanings and ideals, meanings, and ideals we ardently believe to be right or "true"; or (3) we acknowledge all is nothing but power and politics, accepting there are no fixed legal concepts with inherent meanings.

Again, however, the unique nature of the investigation in this text intrudes at this point. These three possible roles can all be situated *within* a picture of a larger social world. That is, we can readily slip into thinking of a *given* social world and a researcher investigating that social world, a dynamic within which we then allow for the three possibilities: support of the construction taking place, critique of the process, or (possibly) acknowledgement that both positions simply reflect a struggle over discourse that is entirely political. But, given the investigation undertaken in this text, *this given social world is not being presumed.*

We begin, rather, with a *question* about the status of Canadian law in relation to facts of Indigenous self-determination. If we unreflectively suppose legal theorizing begins from a position presuming a single social world (encompassing within it both Canadian society and Aboriginal peoples), we thereby remove from the scene the possibility of a deep layer of Indigenous self-determination. For countless generations, Indigenous communities and polities have enjoyed the ability to make meaning, to construct social realities. We have to entertain the possibility that multiple meaning-generating communities inhabit the world of legal phenomena that we explore.

From this vantage point we note once again the three possible positions we earlier detailed that we might come to inhabit as researchers, but now all three take on very different nuances. We begin with positions that a scholar might take as inhabiting the social world within which Canadian law is a constructed component, the three we earlier described. However, we can also now think of positions that a scholar might take when reflecting on the fact that Canadian society constructs Canadian law as expressive of meanings it generates. Such a scholar might be an Indigenous legal theorist, or she might be someone inhabiting the world built up by and around meanings generated by Canadian society but capable of putting her usual place in this built-world to one side in order to conduct the sort of analysis required by the situation before her. This scholar could still wind up accepting the imposition of Canadian law on Indigenous peoples,[77] or she might strongly critique the legal system that attempts to destroy Indigenous meaning-generating capacities from the point of view of other understandings of "law" and authority, or she might decide what is before her is no more than the inevitable struggle that marks the field of politics (though this would not be understood to be domestic politics but something at least quasi-international).

All this leads us to wonder whether we might be trapped in a model of the world that has all that *we* can say generally about the nature of Aboriginal law be itself nothing but an interpretation. Furthermore, we might wonder whether we might have to accede that such interpretations are neither *privileged* (accepting, that is, that no single interpretation can be said to be "true," though it may be "better" than some other criteria), nor *intrinsically better* (accepting, that is, that at best it may be said to be better by local measure). These concerns bring to the fore concerns about the relationship between the interpreter and the thing interpreted, which in turn invites concerns about power and knowledge.[78]

How might one address such concerns along a naturalist line? We can begin by looking at how Leiter responds to Dworkin's interpretive turn. While a careful look at Leiter's arguments uncovers shortcomings, it also opens the door to a richer naturalist response.

Leiter argues that it is possible to do legal analysis without losing sight of an acceptable form of "objectivity."[79] In contesting Dworkin's adjudicative model,[80]

---

77 Many Indigenous scholars come to the business of legal analysis firmly embedded in an education in Canadian law and politics, and one might suspect this plays a role in their either unreflectively accepting the "fact" of Crown dominance or submitting to its power. Some may come, as well, from communities that have self-consciously accepted submersion in the Canadian system, or that over time have come to see themselves as simply parts of the larger Canadian world.

78 The way these questions have been posed might suggest to the reader a rough link to the emergence of American legal realism in the first half of the nineteenth century, and then the use to which some legal realists' insights were put by the Critical Legal Studies movement in the 1970s and 1980s. It should be born in mind, though, that critical legal scholars are not, by and large, updated legal realists. In particular, their respective views on indeterminacy are quite far apart (though both schools put substantial weight behind the notion that some aspect of the law is indeterminate).

79 See Dworkin, *Law's Empire*, *supra* note 54; Brian Leiter, *Naturalizing Jurisprudence: Essays on American Legal Realism and Naturalism in Legal Philosophy* (Oxford: Oxford University Press, 2007) [Leiter, *Naturalizing Jurisprudence*]. Note that in today's intellectual milieu, intersubjectivity is usually understood to be a good proxy for older senses of objectivity. The question would be whether, given the same data, observational instruments, and methodological approach, observers in other social settings or with other social backgrounds would arrive at the same results as the original researcher.

80 This was touched on in the previous section, in the text accompanying notes 74–5.

Leiter finds fault with the notion that it must be "interpretation all the way down" – he disagrees, that is, with the notion that one cannot escape one's embeddedness in normative and interpretive worlds.[81] Distinguishing between epistemic and moral norms does all the heavy work, in his eyes. Once one sees that (a) one can agree that it is difficult to disengage from *moral* matters, but (b) in modelling phenomena one relies on *epistemic* norms and values (such as "evidentiary adequacy ... simplicity, minimum mutilation of well-established theoretical frameworks and methods ... [and] explanatory consilience"),[82] the way is clear to study of the law that allows for a workable form of objectivity.

Does this approach address Dworkin's shortcomings? And what exactly are these shortcomings? That is, in what way is Dworkin's approach unacceptably "subjective"? None of Dworkin's arguments are presented as the intrusion of his subjective point of view – rather, Dworkin argues, via his interpretive turn, judgments are not determined by such things as facts and modes of legal reasoning. Facts, in this view, are products of interpretation, and modes of legal reasoning depend on those engaged in adjudication. While one could explore this all the way down to an idiosyncratic/personal level (as some American legal realists did), Dworkin seems content to locate a measure of non-objectivity in the fact that social groups (i.e. judges) agree on how they will arrive at constructed facts and on ways of settling legal disputes. Is Dworkin engaged with the idea that it might be interpretation all the way down to the legal theoretic level?

As interesting as these matters may be, more interesting and pertinent for our purposes are questions that seem to plague Leiter's approach and that pull us back into the concern we were focused on when we got into this look into the Dworkin-Leiter debate: is *Leiter's* approach also not unavoidably subjective, expressing no more than the sociocultural world *he* inhabits? I have no objection to Leiter making the sorts of moves he attempts, but I begin my swing to a way of thinking of these matters that fits more fully within the fold of methodological naturalism by noting that it is *open* to the naturalist to accept (if need be) that *it is indeed* "interpretation all the way down" *within* a sociocultural world, and that we all live "trapped," as it were, in worlds of socioculturally constructed meaning. All this can be accommodated, I have been arguing throughout the second half of this chapter, if we accept that the mind exists within the world, and that collections of minds – i.e., sociocultural collectives – can generate meaning.

Leiter is focused on a "theory of adjudication" in his analysis, and in that context he argues we need not accede to the notion that it is interpretation all

81 See Brian Leiter, "Objectivity, Morality, and Adjudication" in Leiter, *Naturalizing Jurisprudence*, *supra* note 79 at 225.

82 Brian Leiter, "Beyond the Hart/Dworkin Debate: The Methodology Problem in Jurisprudence" in Leiter, *Naturalizing Jurisprudence*, *supra* note 79 at 168.

the way down, so long as we focus on certain epistemic norms, avoiding focus on other normative commitments. But matters of interpretation come up in the context of legal analysis that require us to be cautious about a wider range of normative and interpretive matters. The legal theorist is engaged in more than merely semantic exercises – Leiter's position may adequately address problems with exercises of that sort, but the legal theorist exists *within* a sociocultural setting that plays a fundamental role in generating meaning around such terms as "law," "obligation," and "sovereignty."

The legal researcher, then, cannot avoid entrapment in a spiral of subjectivity without heeding her own existence within a world of legal meanings. Should she engage in an interpretive project, attempting to make sense of legal phenomena, she must acknowledge she is embedded in a social setting that provides meanings for key legal terms. To consider the meaning of legal phenomena outside her own social compass, she has to correct for the possibility her interpretive exercises will be unreflectively coloured by this personal grounding in a meaning-generating collective.

Still, does this suffice? If the goal is to completely remove the thought that the researcher comes to the task embedded in a specific form of social reality, or correlatively to assert she is armed with objectively fixed epistemic norms that provide a guarantee of interpretive certainty, the answer is no. However, neither of these sorts of goals parallels the aim in this work, with analysis herein operating under the umbrella of methodological naturalism. The goal of identifying epistemic mechanisms that ultimately *ground* meaning and interpretation was *always* unachievable, the alternative not being acceptance of a spiral of subjectivity but calibration of meaning that fits with how we, as knowing creatures, work within the natural world.

A set of commitments have been made and must be acknowledged. I commit to a way things are (a mind-independent natural world), to the emergence of the human mind and human collectivities in this natural world, to our ability to explore how collectivities construct forms of social reality, and to our ability to explore legal phenomena (including theories of law) as aspects of the natural world. Work carried out in chapters 6 to 7 is meant to adhere to these acknowledged commitments. Support can be added to the sense and promise of this approach by examining our second concern with the notion that we can explore Aboriginal law via methodological naturalism, that questions of normativity preclude the possibility of naturalistic explanations.

Normativity

It is accepted in modern legal theory that law has a normative aspect. In saying a legal system is essentially composed of various sorts of rules, thought turns to ways subjects can be said to *follow* rules. To the extent that since the mid-twentieth century legal theorists fell into line behind Hart's attacks on legal realists (discounting what Hart took to be sceptical arguments about the efficacy of rules in legal matters),[83] we witness solidification of thinking about the law as fundamentally a source of norms guiding behaviour. Law is presumed to be essentially made up of rules that constitute ways by which certain forms of action are made possible and promoted and other forms prohibited or placed under disapproval. Parties' actions are guided, channelled, or controlled by these rules (and the institutions that generate and apply them), with one function being that rules provide evaluative measures tied to norms that rules contain.

While an individual may follow a rule out of threat of sanction, or more directly through simple coercion, legal scholars have generally accepted that the more interesting fact is that those subject to the law can (and do seem to) follow rules from an "internal" perspective.[84] Central to Hart's theory, for example, is the position that legal officials, those who work with secondary rules (thereby "controlling" primary rules) follow these secondary rules "from the inside."[85]

From this perspective, following a rule is understood to entail that the rule-follower *acknowledge* that the rule provides a *reason for action*.[86] That is, the subject finds herself under an *obligation* to obey the law, coming to see she has a reason provided by the rule itself (existing independent from both external, physically grounded reasons, those coming from fear of sanction and the like, and internal desire-grounded "reasons"). This is not to say the subject needs to "accept" the obligation – one can understand one has an obligation to pay taxes and yet avoid doing so, thereby not accepting this obligation (that is, while the subject "accepts" the obligation in one sense of the term – acknowledgment of its existence and apparent reason-giving attributes – she does not "accept" the obligation in another sense – she chooses to disregard the obligation and acts against it).

---

83 Hart's key arguments can be found in chapter 7 ("Formalism and Rule-Scepticism") of the *Concept of Law*, *supra* note 5. Academics have noted (a) that most legal realists were not rule-sceptics in the forms that Hart attacked, and (b) that knocking down these straw-skeptics does not justify the lessons Hart pulls from his analysis. See e.g. Brian Leiter, "American Legal Realism" in Martin Golding & William Edmundson, eds, *The Blackwell Guide to the Philosophy of Law and Legal Theory* (Oxford: Blackwell Publishing, 2005) 50.

84 Focusing attention on this aspect of the law (in trying to move analysis away from "command" theories, such as those presented by Hobbes and Austin) was another key contribution of Hart's *Concept of Law*.

85 Key to the normativity of this picture is that the *rules, in a sense*, "control" the officials.

86 Hart makes much of this "internal perspective" in *The Concept of Law* (introduced originally in the text to move the discussion beyond the "command theory" of positivism propounded by Austin in *The Province of Jurisprudence Determined*. See Hart, *Concept of Law*, *supra* note 5; John Austin, *The Province of Jurisprudence Determined* (Cambridge, UK: Cambridge University Press, 1995).

Furthermore, the point is often pressed that the essential matter is not that the agent comes to *believe* that the rule provides a reason (as if she just *thinks* the rule provides a reason to act, that she *thinks* it would justify her action), but that the rule does indeed provide a reason – the legal rule *itself justifies* her action, as (all else being unproblematic) following the rule is the *right* thing to do.

This invites two forms of challenge to the CSM. On the one hand, there is concern that in following a rule "from the inside," a form of legal normativity arises that cannot be explained without introducing the language of justification. When does the rule provide a reason for acting? It seems natural to suppose this is when an agent would be justified in acting in accord with its dictates. In such a situation purely explanatory (descriptive) analyses will not be complete, as justification itself is an essentially normative matter.[87] When we explore the matter of being given a reason to act, will we not have to wonder about *when* the reason provided is such that we are justified in acting in accord with its dictates? But no degree of naturalist exploration, the argument goes, can ever tell us more than that the rule *tells us* we should do *x* (or not do *x*, or some other matter) – this, however, will not enlighten us about whether we are *justified* in doing *x* (or not *x*, or whatever).[88]

On the other hand, there is concern that the notion of legal normativity is itself muddled and incomplete, that what has to actually transpire is that the citizen be *morally* bound by the legal rule. This, in turn, requires that, again, the rule be justified, that it provide a moral reason for acting (which, again, makes the notion of purely explanatory accounts suspect, as they struggle to work with these questions of justification). As these are complex issues, let us unpack this matter a bit more.

The notion that rule-following (in the legal context) has an irreducibly normative aspect splits into two mainstream camps hinted at above. To what extent does such reason for action intersect with moral considerations? Is this inescapably a moral obligation one faces, or might the law provide its own form or

87 Following Hart's lead on this, we might say that to follow rule y is to say A is given a reason to act by y. To say this is to place the matter outside A's subjective evaluations of the situation or of the weight of the norm. The rule tells A he should act a certain way, and in doing so as a rule approached "from the inside," A is faced with a justified belief in y's nature as presenting an obligation to act.

88 This is, in a modified form, a central criticism faced by Quine's argument about naturalizing epistemology. Critics argue that while it might be all well and good to explore the relationship between input and output in the natural system that is the human sensory-representational apparatus, the questions we want epistemology to focus on have to do with when we arrive at the "right" outputs – those we are *justified* in believing (as, for example, true or known). It is interesting to note hints of a Humean argument at this point as well – Hume would argue reason cannot step in here to distinguish between those forces that truly motivate our actions (our desires), as reason cannot judge between them.

kind of reason, one divorced from moral considerations? In what way does the rule provide a norm?[89]

Mainstream legal theories generally accept this articulation of the overall problem of normativity, and then struggle to address challenges posed by the normative aspect of the law. Natural law theorists link normativity to the presence of "higher" law, human laws *justifiably binding* when in accord with moral and/or political requirements.[90] Critical theorists argue that communities *construct* senses of normativity, with different communities potentially building up different belief systems around (a) what it is to be bound by an edict, principle, or value, and (b) what these edicts, principles, or values might be. Positivism, on the other hand, simply struggles with normativity.[91] Hart identified a form of legal normativity in the world (noting that we observe in the world that the state law–citizen relationship does not function analogously to what operates between the gunman and hostage, that the citizen can legitimately feel state law generates

---

89 What of matters of legitimacy? It would seem questions of legality can be settled *within* a system of rules (provided there are rules that determine what counts as a rule – that is, provided we are imagining the sort of system-structure we developed earlier in our abstraction away from the municipal Canadian order, with secondary rules managing primary rules). But legitimacy (at least in stronger senses) seems as well to be tied to larger questions of moral or political evaluation.

While questions of legitimacy can pose pressing problems when directed towards the following of a primary rule (by a citizen subject to the law), the whole matter becomes particularly troublesome when we consider the situation of a legal official working with secondary rules. Is the legal official *bound* to follow a secondary rule if she deems the system to be, in some larger sense, illegitimate? What binds legal officials to higher-order rules with which they work? In what way does a rule of recognition generate a reason for action for an official occupying a role from which she is expected to apply the rule? Can this reason for action be overridden by serious questions of legitimacy? Would it be appropriate that at times an official applying the dictates of Aboriginal law assess the bindingness on herself and see she is in fact not under an obligation to apply this specific rule, in this situation? As all these questions run parallel to those we might entertain in wondering about the place of normativity in making sense of rules, we can subsume any discussion of legitimacy within this other, larger discussion.

90 Some modern forms of natural law theory try to place this justificatory function into the "natural" realm, for example by arguing one is justified in acting according to the law's dictates when the law accords with some fundamental theory of human nature. These accounts, however, then face the "naturalistic fallacy" – how can any fact(s) about the natural world ever serve to make it so that *x* is right? It may well be that it is a fact of human nature that we achieve more individually if we construct a cooperative system within which we act, but how could such a fact show it is right to construct such a system? While the naturalistic fallacy carries its own weight, one could also note that others could point to other aspects of our nature – as competitive and selfish – to seemingly "ground" other systems.

91 Hans Kelsen, for example, built much of his positivist picture in response to the perceived challenge of working out how the law is in fact normative. His solution was to work backward to an ultimate ground for the normativity of any particular law, a ground located in the *grundnorm*. See Hans Kelsen, *Pure Theory of Law*, translated by Max Knight (Berkeley: University of California Press, 1967). Of course, this just packs all the mystery into a singularity.

obligations in relation to his actions). Hart struggled within his descriptive sociology, however, to *explain* how this form of normativity should be unpacked (given that he wished to show it is *not* a matter simply of a citizen *thinking* she is bound by the law, but rather that the rule does provide a reason for acting).[92]

To what extent might this be a problem that carries sense only within the horizons of a specific world of constructed meaning? To explore this possibility, let us hypothesize that in the Judeo-Christian-dominated Western world there will be generally unrecognized or unacknowledged *presumptions* made within this larger meaning-enclosed world about *agency*, tying such a notion inexplicably to the notion of a free will, such that imagining "following a rule" is naturally thought to be a matter not only of *believing* one is bound by the rule, but of having it *be* that the rule really gives to the agent a mind-independent reason for acting.

Then theorists working and writing in the tradition of the West (that is, within a broadly determined conceptual/normative world of locally constructed meaning) will inevitably come up against very challenging matters. Hart, for example, wants to hold that legal rules *give* reasons for acting, in that a legal rule (properly followed from the inside) will operate on the citizen independent of his or her particular desires or beliefs. The citizen may believe in many matters, may desire many things, but the rule that is law acts independent of all these mental states and motivators.

Now, should the theorist think it is necessary not just that the citizen *thinks* she is given a mind-independent rule (that motivates her), but that the rule *really* is an independent "thing" of some sort that actually does come to the citizen, possessing the attribute of being truly mind-independent (of containing some "force" that should call on the actor), the whole business becomes very difficult and mysterious.

Mysteries do not end here, however, as the theorist operating within a Western framework will most likely have her thoughts on this further confused with notions of "choice" and "free will." In the Judeo-Christian Western tradition, what tends to amplify problems is the fact that the theorist will tend to see the citizen finding in the inner world a gap between what exists at any moment in her thoughts and what she has in mind when she adds to it the understanding she is now faced with a reason for acting. This gap, recall, is what Searle identifies as the manifestation of a *sense* of free will.[93] The citizen feels she is faced

92 An attempt to provide an account through analogy with rules in game-playing fails. Players want to play an organized game, and so rules can sensibly be understood from that point on providing reasons for acting (that can sensibly also be used in justifiably critiquing actions of players when they fall outside or seemingly bend the rules). To say the law is game-like in this way (to underscore some sense in this context to rule-following and rule-bindingness) would be to *begin* with pragmatic interest in "playing a game" (structuring society along rule-centred axes).

93 Recall this presents some problems in Searle's account of the construction of social reality. See Searle, *supra* note 1. See *supra* "Searle: Naturalist Analysis of Socio-Linguistic Instruments" in chapter 3.

with a choice, and a rule in law exists as something that may or may not lead to action that the rule demands.

All this, however, is a discussion predicated on our working within the conceptual/normative universe that we began by presupposing.[94] Is there actually a gap that requires explanation? Or is this nothing more than a perceived matter, one interpreted *within* this conceptual/normative world as something that "*must*" be embedded in any normative-theoretical structure developed? Note how it comes up in Hart's (and Searle's) conceptual world, with the presumption that the citizen could have acted otherwise with this reason to act in her mind. This, after all, is the essence of choice. If agents were – at a deep level – automatons (if elements she considers in making a choice are actually such that when all are present in just this constellation, with these weights, this outcome will follow, this "choice" will have been made – so theoretically an observer privy to the input and relevant mental-algorithms would be able to predict the outcome accurately) then radical free will would be a chimera.

A priori notions of "justification" are the source of problems here, just as a priori notions of "truth" and "progress" were the source of challenges in the mid-twentieth century in the philosophy of the natural sciences. We can follow the lead of those who naturalized epistemology and put strong notions of "justification" to one side (perhaps even labelling these "examples of socioculturally developed aspects of Western legal and political theory"), and leave questions of justification in this context to what can be meaningfully said from a naturalist point of view. We do not entirely discard strong forms of justification, as methodological naturalism allows that we might later need to return to these notions if required by our best model of how the natural world functions, a world inhabited by meaning-generating communities. In the meantime, we allow *talk* of strong forms of justification into our analysis, but only in the context of our study of how Western legal and political thought – the product of specific meaning-generating communities – has developed and functions within the reality these communities have generated and continue to try to expand and strengthen.

In dissipating concerns with meaning, I argued the way forward is to cleave closely to the form of methodological naturalism experimented with in this text – that is, to avoid a priori assumptions about possible objects of study or processes of investigation, and to begin, rather, with the picture of the mind developing within the natural world (carrying along with it sociolinguistic capacities and the social forms and realities this makes possible). This means not just thinking that meaning-generating collectives can give meaning to specific understandings of identifiable legal rules and norms, but coming to think of meaning-generating communities (in the context of the construction of "law")

94 The fact this may indeed roughly present an accurate description of the Judeo-Christian Western world of meaning is not the most important departure point in this discussion.

building *entire systems of meaning*. That is, we can see meaning-generating communities generating worlds of meaning, locally constructed. We can imagine the possibility that sociocultural communities develop systems of belief that constitute entire worlds of meaning. We can then work with these imaginings as grounding elements of hypotheses, looking to see how such constructed systems of social reality function within the natural world. With all this arising in the natural world through the activities of language-deploying sociocultural units, this is all subject to naturalistic analysis.

Pulling Threads Together

With this response, concerns about normativity are not addressed explicitly. Rather, the tactic is to direct attention to the picture of the mind arising within the world. A part of this picture describes sociocultural collectives generating meaning. As part of that, we also posit these collectives developing local systems of belief about what constitutes "normativity." We need not go down the rabbit hole of trying to work out how certain questions about normativity must be addressed when faced with concerns about normativity that arise only as a result of the sociocultural groundings of a specific sociocultural collective. The purported problems with normativity for the CSM are of this variety.

And so we see that methodological naturalism provides a reasonable way to understand how explanations of legal phenomena are possible. More importantly, this discussion demonstrates how one can build a defence of such explanations in the context of examinations of Aboriginal law, examinations that inevitably bring into the mix perspectives (those sets of meanings that arise within, and as a result of, sociocultural settings). We end this chapter by returning to our discussion of the social construction of legal institutions and the law, transposing responses to problems with normativity and meaning into where we left this earlier discussion, so they may also defuse challenges we seem to face when we note that Aboriginal law is constructed.

At the point we broke off discussion of challenges posed by the social construction of the law and theories of law, we were faced apparently with a forced choice between approaching the law as strongly constructed, in which case we struggle to naturalistically explain how particular constructions of law arise, or as weakly constructed, in which case we struggle to explain what requirements for construction exist and why they might be necessary. Under the spectre of strong constructivism we seem to have to accept that societies freely create legal systems and institutions out of whole cloth, in localized and historicized ways that preclude the ability to say anything that connects to aspects of the world that might account for what we observe. Meanwhile, alternatively, under the spectre of weak constructivism we seem to have to imagine there are necessary conditions that account for the development of law, with this modal argument seeming to quickly slip into postulation of transcendental groundings (such matters as "truths" of political morality).

But it is important we note that conditions creating this seeming conundrum appear and function in the natural world. That is, this is a constructed conundrum, one that arises within a socially constructed environment. We can well imagine, for example, a social world within which law is *conceived of* as strongly socially constructed, so members of this society – even its jurists – see themselves unconstrained when it comes to the task of generating legal rules, structure, and roles. Likewise, we can well imagine a social world in which law is *conceived of* as weakly constructed, so members of this society – even its jurists – see themselves constrained by external, transcendentally grounded conditions for construction. We can examine these sorts of situations, ones in which particular meaning-generating communities have developed sets of large-scale meanings.

Of course, these are two imaginary worlds, and in the world in front of us we find both those who think of legal systems as all strongly constructed, and those who think of legal systems as all weakly constructed.

All through this we – researchers noting these possible collective acts of meaning-generation – acknowledge that we too occupy sociocultural settings. Nevertheless, this position – one of self-aware self-reflexivity – is one we can occupy while committed to a world of explanation we believe (provisionally) allows for a defensible measure of objectivity.

How does all this work? Spelling this out in some detail both reinforces points already made and pulls things together, so we are then ready to progress into our analysis of the ability of liberal positivism to explain the nature of Aboriginal law.

This all pivots upon the point that law, normativity, and meaning can all be products of social construction in varying ways. With all three understood to result (at least provisionally) from acts of social construction, we are led to imagine social settings in which construction projects are possible and ongoing. We begin, that is, with meaning-generating social collectives. We also note, as we spin upon this pivot point, that not only are we seeing specific legal systems and their components as the products of meaning-generation, but that we must be ready to see that some theories of law themselves arise – and are given meaning – only within social worlds. We remain alive to the possibility, that is, that some theories or models of social construction are themselves socially constructed.

We allow for the possibility that a social collective is not restricted to such matters as the generation of its own interpretations of a legal order, or "the law," or events linked to the law, but that social collectives generally can generate meaning in the social arena *about* such things as "law," "sovereignty," and the like. This was essentially how we came to defuse concerns about meaning and normativity in the last few sections, and now we see that it can accomplish the same end with concerns that the law itself is socially constructed. We wish to examine various forms of social reality given this starting point, and so we examine whether actors in any given social setting, going about constructing law, believe in (and act on belief in) the free construction of all things law-related, or believe in (and act on belief in) the notion that for *x* to be law[95] certain independent constraints must be met. Concerns we noted about the ability of naturalist approaches to function in properly studying the law dissolve at this point, as the fact is we – researchers trying to make sense of the sort of phenomena under study in this work – do not need to decide between these two.

We are interested in the functioning of one social collective as it goes about building its social reality, attempting as it does so to pull into itself the independent social worlds of Indigenous peoples (thereby destroying these social realities, *as independent*). What we see, along either path laid out on the level of theory of law, is loss of Indigenous self-determination. With allegiance to a vision of transcendent norms comes some constructed moral/political-moral theory or other consuming the lives of Indigenous communities, removing chances for Indigenous visions to continue to animate Indigenous ways of living writ large. Alternatively, in a world where social realities are all free-built, we find Indigenous communities lose out to the power and ruthlessness of non-Indigenous forms of law and sovereignty. But, again, these are not paths either Indigenous scholars or those simply interested in understanding what is happening in the world around need step onto.

The choice these theoretical standpoints present is not just false (as if we *must* choose one or the other), it is dangerous (at least for Indigenous scholars and their communities). If we think we *must* choose (and so make a choice*) we thereby enter a socially constructed world*, that of non-Indigenous making, one with centuries of non-Indigenous intellectual history accounting for the point we reach in today's world of law and legal theory.

These two theories are two sets of beliefs about social construction, both of which function in the world (as beliefs held by actors) to assist in construction. But the construction of a specific social reality presupposes a given social world, and this is precisely what we do not want to presuppose in this situation. And so we treat these two theoretical standpoints as interesting data for inclusion into our study of what is going on in the world around us, as one social collective seems intent on having its systems of meanings, its understandings of normativity, its ways of interpreting events, history, and law, and its theories of law simply enfold Indigenous worlds of meanings, normativity, history, interpretation, and legal theorizing.

We are now prepared to look at Canadian law on Aboriginal rights, understanding this to be the product of a social collective, putting to one side engagement with the contents of social realities this collective hopes to expand out over the lives of Indigenous peoples.

95 Where *x* might be either a legal system or an element of a given system.

6 Liberal Positivism and Aboriginal Rights

We now turn to the question of the ability of liberal thought to make sense of Aboriginal rights. The model explored is that of "liberal positivism," a blending of positivist understandings of how law is generated and its legality determined, and liberal thought about what ought to go into the content of laws and the structure of legal systems. The process of investigating this is relatively straightforward: we presume that liberal positivism is being put forward as an explanatory model for what we see in the jurisprudence and test as a hypothesis that it is a good model. To do this in accord with the CSM of explanatory modelling there are, however, very specific constraints imposed on how we proceed.

The primary requirement is that we cleave closely to the sense of "good" appropriate to a form of objective analysis. This entails not engaging with liberal thought from *within* the world of normativity it generates, just as it requires we not engage *from* the stance of our own field of normativity. We are not inquiring about the merit of liberalism (either from within or outside the normative world circumscribed by liberal thought) and are not asking about whether Aboriginal law *should* be constructed the way it has been. The investigation is into the construction of law, and the question is the extent to which the holding of liberal principles and values explains the construction process and its outcomes.

This on its own suggests how this form of investigation differs substantially from what one might expect from standard legal analysis. It is important to flesh this out, showing more fully the nature of the analysis conducted, clearly articulating differences with other forms, and setting out conditions within which this analysis is carried out. The first section of this chapter sets all this out, building on results from the last two chapters. That complete, we then spend some time getting an appropriate picture of liberal thought as it may animate the work of jurists in Canada in the late twentieth and early twenty-first centuries. The next two chapters then test the hypothesis, with chapter 8 closing with some thoughts about key implications of our findings, taking into account the role legal theorists often play in the development of Canadian law concerning Aboriginal rights.

Methodological Naturalism in the Context of Analysis of Legal Construction

Key Elements of Naturalist Analysis

Over the last few chapters I have done my best to show that methodological naturalism (a) can meet challenges commonly thrown up against the notion that a reasonable form of objectivity is possible in relation to the production of knowledge, even when the focus of study is the law, and (b) is particularly well-suited to attempts at making sense of the role perspectives play in both the generation of law and in the business of theorizing the construction of legal systems. I noted above one distinct standpoint of this approach, that it eschews engagement with normative worlds of morals and political morality, and I return to this shortly. Let us first note other equally important features that mark the nature of this approach to legal analysis.

Methodological naturalism embraces an avowed a posteriori approach to the development of explanatory models. We avoid, then, the general use of a priori concepts and processes, and that includes avoidance of strong appeals to intuitions and to "transcendent" objects of concepts employed.[1] This means how we *talk* about a liberal universe accounting for jurisprudence is constrained. Within the naturalist model, we eschew talk that uncritically invites in realms that seem to transcend the natural world, those that are strongly unobservable and that are thereby potentially non-testable.[2]

---

1 I am here targeting strong forms of conceptual analysis, a common tool historically used by analytic legal philosophers. It is not uncommon now, however, for some legal philosophers to appeal to intuitions in a softer manner. For an argument that Hart was ahead of his time, and that his blending of conceptual analysis and descriptive sociology led to a weak form of conceptual analysis, where intuitions were introduced but then subject to revision as necessary, see Veronica Rodriguez-Blanco, "A Defence of Hart's Semantics as Nonambitious Conceptual Analysis" (2003) 9:2 Legal Theory 99. Standard forms of conceptual analysis, on the other hand, appeal to intuitions as measures of the truth of explanations tendered. This is to make use of an a priori mode of analysis.

2 By "strongly unobservable" I mean to link observation with testability – of course we do not observe with our unaided senses much of what now makes up the commonplaces of our contemporary scientific picture of the world, such things as quarks and fields. I do not follow Van Fraassen in adopting an attitude of ontological scepticism about entities "observed" on the basis of inference, but do, as a naturalist, have some sense of realms completely removed from the possibility of observation and inference – these I would label the strongly unobservable. See Bas Van Fraassen, *Scientific Representation: Paradoxes of Perspective* (Oxford: Clarendon Press, 2008).

From a naturalist perspective we begin, for example, with the notion that a universe exists of posited *ideas* and *principles*, but initially, at least, we want to restrict its ontology to beliefs (and such) in the minds of individuals, or locate such an ontology in shared space between individuals, in a carefully delimited collective space. This is to begin, for example, with the notion that judges and other legal actors may *believe in* (or otherwise hold beliefs about) liberal principles. On this basis, we then investigate the extent to which these actors develop legal instruments and thereby potentially assist in crafting entire legal institutions while making use of these liberal ideas and principles.

How, then, do we work with held beliefs, especially when we want to see how pieces of the world around us function and interact, and we want to have the ability to address issues of normativity and meaning? Our search is principally for causal relations, with an examination into the extent to which rules and principles found in the jurisprudence on Aboriginal rights could be said to not just evince liberal underpinnings, but to be accounted for by this underpinning. That is, there is a depth to our explorations that must be appreciated. One might suppose that if we simply see that the jurisprudence evinces liberal underpinnings, we should be able to argue that the law can be explained on liberal grounds. To the question "Why is rule *x* the way it is?" one could respond "Because it reflects liberal principles *y* and *z*." But we want to be able to plausibly argue that the relationship is more than coincidental. Locating a conceptual connection between elements of the jurisprudence and certain liberal principles would not suffice, for we hope to be able to see that the liberal universe – within which these principles have substance and meaning – *accounts for* (a) the way legislators and jurists understand a situation before them, and (b) how they respond (with a construction built within this universe, manifesting in the presence of principles and rules reflecting liberal thought). These are the sorts of causal relations we hope to elucidate as we examine the hypothesis that liberal thought can explain the jurisprudence.[3]

The natural way to imagine ideas and principles of liberalism structuring Aboriginal law would be to assume they purposely function to structure Aboriginal law – that Aboriginal law has been built, and continues to be built,

---

The test is testability – say, in terms of falsification. This is not to suggest I propose to actually test propositions advanced, but just that the approach taken here allows in theoretical entities only if their existence is in some way testable. This does not require they be amenable to laboratory experiments, but that there be some conceivable means by which we could ascertain they are either (a) natural constituents of the world, or (b) required for the best explanation of what we reasonably take to be the natural constituents of the world.

3 It should be borne in mind that there are also limits to the depths to which this analysis in search of causal connections aspires. I do not, for example, try to get right into the minds of legal actors. The search, for example, is not for explanations of the form "X held beliefs a, b, and c, and thereby arrived at the development of rule z."

upon or through the use of these ideas and principles.[4] We assume, for the purposes of this sort of inquiry, that at least one *purpose* of the law is to develop a liberal democratic structure that both governs Aboriginal-Canadian relations and regulates and structures the lives of Aboriginal peoples in Canada.[5] That is, we understand that beliefs can have a form of directionality to them, that, for example, where we suppose legal actors hold beliefs in liberal ideas and principles, we imagine they can hold them for reasons, primary of which for our purposes (given our hypothesis, that liberal thought can explain the development of the law concerning Aboriginal rights) is that these actors can have certain purposes in mind.[6]

As we noted in the last chapter (when defusing concerns raised with the limits of legal analysis), we can easily accommodate purposes in naturalist analysis. We position them within and attached to beliefs: we focus on the fact of the holding of certain beliefs, here that the law should be built to further certain ends, where the ends themselves are captured in other sets of held beliefs. We can naturally *expect*, then, to see a trajectory in development of the law following a path towards these goals. Furthermore, we should be able to safely begin with the assumption that the path we trace points us towards future developments.

We imagine then what might be described as a quasi-teleological model of law – background ideals set out an understanding of the ideal state to which law and society are understood to strive (through actions of appropriate actors). This is not, however, posited in some mindless structural sense, but rather is initially taken to be the result of *people* – in appropriate positions – *thinking* about the value they might see in these ideals and for that sort of reason forming rules (and institutions) around them. This suggests we analyse the law so construed in an appropriate manner, accommodating this model of purposeful construction. To do so we posit, in essence, a loose system of liberal principles and

4 While we loosely talk of liberal democratic principles in ways that suggest they constitute "forces" that act in and through society, coming to account for the rules, principles, and tests we see within Aboriginal law, keeping within the bounds of naturalistic inquiry, we must take this to be shorthand for something like "certain actors, vested with certain capacities, as the result of various constitutive sociolinguistic instruments, *believe* in certain liberal ideals, these beliefs functioning to guide the development of further sociolinguistic instruments (which, from the facts around their roles in society, can come to constitute law)."

5 This structure would also, of course, regulate the lives of non-Aboriginal peoples in Canada, as they must fit into the matrix of rules and principles constituting Aboriginal law, even if indirectly.

6 I do not search for presentist-conscious purposefulness. Rather, it is sufficient that we uncover that construction follows paths determined by a sense of purpose. In particular, then, what I hope to capture are situations in which living in a liberal world of sense places the jurist in a context in which she naturally thinks of problems put before her in terms of liberal ideals, principles, and mechanisms.

ideals, those we argue that contemporary jurists might plausibly hold, tracking the role they might play in explaining the development and ongoing dynamics of Aboriginal law.[7]

This captures a key element of our naturalist commitments in this exercise in legal analysis. There are two other general elements to bear in mind. First, we return to a key point touched on earlier: we remove ourselves from moral engagement. This involves our making commitments to not make our own moral-normative commitments and to avoid assessing and evaluating those normative elements of what we explore as we unpack efforts at social construction. Put more simply, debate over the *merit* of liberal thought is avoided. The aim is to see the extent to which a plausible explanation of Aboriginal rights can be built out of or from liberal theory, taken as a set of *beliefs about* (or dispositions or attitudes about) liberal principles and ideals. The fact that I come to this sort of project with my own normative and evaluative principles is acknowledged, but in conducting this study with this awareness in hand, and with normative matters restricted to the epistemic realm, the thought is that Aboriginal law can be made sense of (and that indeed better and better explanations can be forthcoming).[8]

Finally, our target is an arena of social construction, the Canadian legal system, where we are aware of the potential that perspectives may play in the generation of both structure and content of this socially constructed institution. Here I take "perspectives" to mean those webs of beliefs constructed by social collectives by which and through which meaning is both generated and deployed. A meaning-generating collective both generates meaning and makes use of its systems of meaning to make sense of what is built. So, while we explore in this chapter and the next the ability of liberal positivism to explain Canadian law on Aboriginal rights, we are paying attention simultaneously to the way a liberal mindset may assist in the generation of legal meaning and the way this way of structuring social worlds may then delimit sense that can be made of what is constructed.

---

7 Articulated this way, it might seem we should undertake two studies, one fundamentally static (a snapshot of the reflection of liberal principles in jurisprudence, a study we might suppose to be descriptive), and a second fundamentally dynamic (a study into the pull liberal ideals have on the development of law, one we might more naturally suppose touches on or implicates normative matters). I do not, however, accept this bifurcated characterization, as (a) the descriptive account can aim to capture change over time, *describing* how beliefs in normative claims can drive legal actors to develop the law in certain directions, while similarly (b) normative aspects can be cast in essentially descriptive terms. I begin with the notion that liberal principles (*in themselves*) do not have causal efficacy (in the sense gravity accounts for the motion of planets). This captures a key aspect (and key attractor) of the naturalistic approach taken. Much of the section on normativity focuses on making and defending these points.

8 That is, the focus is only on asking what generates good explanations, and the testing of these matters against epistemic norms.

Framing Our Naturalist Analysis

With this summary of how the exercise in analysis must be understood, we now need to set out key background conditions within which the actions of the Supreme Court have taken place over the last few decades. We begin with a skeletal understanding of historical interactions between British and Canadian Crowns and separate, independent Indigenous collectives. This is not the understanding of this history held by the Court as it goes about its work, but an understanding of interacting meaning-generating communities appropriate to our naturalist stance on the nature of legal systems and their development within the social worlds of collectives. That is, we construct a loose and tentative picture of the history of the interactions between the institutions of Canadian society and the institutions of Indigenous collectives, where in both cases what counts as "institutions" is itself left to the meaning-generations of the social collectives in question. We adopt a bird's-eye view of human collectives, seeing them as dynamic aspects of the observable world around us, as sources of forms of social reality where these forms of reality are generated by (and arise within) the meaning-generating capacity each collective enjoys.

While we note centuries of colonial activities by the Crown, we must reserve judgment about what this has generated in the world. That is, we leave entirely open a picture that begins with the existence of meaning-generating Indigenous collectives at pre-contact and presume these capacities for meaning-generation persist through the early era of contact, through the assertion of Crown sovereignty, through the darkest periods of overt colonialism, up through the post–Second World War era of apparent rapprochement, to the constitutionalization of Aboriginal and treaty rights, up to today, with the jurisprudence we currently witness. Meaning-generating capacities of Indigenous social collectives, I hold, sit at the core of Indigenous self-determination *however it is understood* (where the articulation of self-determination depends, indeed, on the meaning each separate Indigenous collective might give to such matters).

Why is this particular presumption made? Why not begin with the existence of Crown sovereignty and of Aboriginal peoples living under this authority and within the world of meaning that Canadian society generates in order to define parameters of sense within which Aboriginal communities would understand their social realities? One reason should be clear: this alternate picture, one that presumes the absolute nature of Crown sovereignty, places us firmly in a world the Crown has been *trying to create* for many generations. Assuming it now exists as a starting point for analysis is to make a presumption at least as unfounded as that with which we begin.[9]

9 It is arguably more unfounded, as one has to wonder why the Court would be doing what we chronicle if in fact Indigenous meaning-generating capacities and authorities were already removed from the Canadian landscape.

The second related reason is that the meaning-generating capacity of a collective is a very difficult attribute to eliminate. Recall our discussion in chapter 3 of Searle's thoughts on how a new aspect of a social reality is brought into being.[10] His thoughts are too targeted and narrowly focused to be of much help in our quest, given our look into interactions *between* meaning-generating systems, but they can be quite suggestive. Key is the notion of "acceptance" or collective recognition. In the context of the interaction of meaning-generating systems, where we are wondering at how one system, *A*, might be eliminated and replaced by a second, *B*, it is not just that the ideas or "truths" of *B* need to be (somehow) adopted by *A*, but rather that the meaning-generating capacity of *A* must be overcome (or subsumed within) the meaning-generating capacity of *B*. The meaning-generating *capacity* of *A* must itself be eliminated. We are imagining, then, either the destruction of *A* as a people, or the voluntary release by *A* of both its *ability* and its *authority* to construct new forms of social reality. Over the course of several centuries, numerous overtly colonial practices of the Canadian state were directed towards the destruction of the ability of Indigenous collectives to exercise their meaning-generating capacities, but (a) it is at least arguable they did not fully succeed, and, more importantly, (b) it is not clear at all that the *authority* to continue to construct meaning Indigenous collectives enjoyed has been seriously undermined.

Naturalist Analysis in Complex Social Worlds: An Aside

We should also note before we begin that the social worlds we inhabit and that we hope to explore are messy and chaotic. Before we jump into thinking about the grounding for liberal thought, it would be good to lay out a few concerns along these lines – concerns we will not directly touch on in the ensuing analysis, but that should be borne in mind.

There are numerous ways we could imagine the real world complicating any simple analysis from "rule *x*" back to "liberal principles *y* and *z*."[11] We must

---

10 See *supra* "Shortcomings in Searle's Account" in "Searle: Naturalist Analysis of Sociolinguistic Instruments" in chapter 3.

11 One could note, for example, that even if we were to restrict ourselves to activity within one social world, say a hypothetical social world of a bounded liberal democracy, within this society one could likely identify a set of rules that arguably reflect core liberal principles, yet it would also be very likely that other rules exist "imperfectly," necessitated at a point along the development of this liberal democracy as this society slowly works itself towards what is envisioned as an ideal liberal state. Any such imperfect rule, then, would not necessarily or simply instantiate liberal principles, but it could be understood as having its nature as a necessary tool advancing this society towards a more perfect liberal form. Furthermore, there is also the shifting understanding of what the ideal end state might look like – we will see in our upcoming overview of liberal thought how visions of how the ideal liberal state should be structured

pay attention, for example, to forces and structures that oppose liberal development.[12] These sorts of forces (those, for example, covered under such broad umbrellas as conservatism, nationalism, or traditionalism)[13] can either work directly against the development of an ideal liberal state, or work to modify or alter what would be thought to be the ideal model of the ideal liberal state. Social worlds, to put it succinctly, are very messy places, and in any specific liberal society there will almost certainly be countervailing or tangentially tracking political, social, economic, and ideological forces pulling and twisting at efforts to instantiate liberal principles in legal rules or systems.

Even just to suppose, then, that we can track principles as they reveal themselves in legal rules, codes, and such (describing how the law develops) is to acknowledge a project far from simple in execution. But we also need to bear in mind that what we are exploring is the interaction of one social world with many, varied, other social realities. In particular, it will be argued that what we witness is the meaning-generating capacity of one sociocultural community being put to use (through the development of jurisprudence) in an attempt to envelop the sociocultural worlds of other distinct meaning-generating peoples. While we will not delve deeply into regions below this level of analysis, we can certainly note implications, that further explorations would have to turn to considerations of how principles and ideas fit into the rough-and-tumble world of law and politics. Once we see how the jurisprudence concerning Aboriginal rights makes sense as the outcome of efforts to destroy the last, core vestiges of Indigenous self-determination, questions naturally follow, such as *why* elements within Canadian society push towards this outcome. Why is it an ongoing

---

have shifted and how internal disagreements manifest. Such complexities and subtleties should be expected in actual social worlds explored naturalistically, as they reflect (amongst other things) the "real world" of politics, ideology, historical struggle, and development.

12 We must bear in mind, again, that by "forces" are meant such things as motivating beliefs held by actors in position to affect how society is structured. We do not countenance unreflective talk of mysterious social forces that might exist outside the minds and actions of individuals living in societies.

13 Complications arise when we attempt to contrast liberalism (in Canada) with other political ideologies. For example, as Ducharme and Constant note, first, conservatism historically shared core values with liberal thought, and second, in contemporary Canada we can see a thread within conservative thought that sees the liberal order (now firmly established in Canadian society) as that which is to be conserved. See "Introduction: A Project of Rule Called Canada: The Liberal Order Framework and Historical Practice" in Jean-Francois Constant & Michel Ducharme, eds, *Liberalism and Hegemony: Debating the Canadian Liberal Revolution* (Toronto: University of Toronto Press, 2009) 3 [Constant & Ducharme]. One can make sense of Flanagan's work by keeping in mind both this historical grounding in shared values (as Flanagan is, for example, deeply concerned with the protection of property interests) and this more recent historical development. See Thomas Flanagan, *First Nations? Second Thoughts* (Montreal & Kingston: McGill-Queen's University Press, 2000).

objective of the courts of Canada to finish the colonial project of the state? But delving into such matters is for the next stage of this work, a subsequent volume.

Back, then, to tasks at hand. The nature of the work in this chapter and the next has been laid out, key aspects of the setting for this work have been noted, and now we just need to have a solid grasp of the liberal world of ideas and principles that we might reasonably expect judges of the Supreme Court to have in mind as they go about developing jurisprudence on Aboriginal rights. This in hand, we can then turn to elements of Canadian law to discern the extent to which these principles and ideas arise to explain the nature of the law being studied. Equally importantly, in doing so we also explore the universe of meaning within which these principles exist (again, inextricably connected to the fact that these principles and ideas are held by legal actors within sets of beliefs).

General Remarks on the Nature of Liberal Theory

We begin our investigation with some general remarks on liberal theory, first noting that liberal theory is most often seen nestled in the field of political theory (or political philosophy).[14] It is not directly and naturally a theory of or about the law, though it is not difficult to discern the kinds of things it might fairly naturally say about this social institution. Regardless, our focus is only partially directed towards what liberal *theory* might say about Canadian law (where a liberal theorist might attempt to explain law itself), as our more focused (connected) objective is to explore how liberal *thought* enters the law (where the liberal theorist is accounting for the *content* of a particular legal system). Our primary objective is to develop a sense of what it is reasonable to expect judges of the Supreme Court of Canada have in mind as they go about constructing the law concerning Aboriginal rights. Given these objectives, we are able to put debates about the nature of the law itself principally to one side in the present discussion, assuming such matters are fairly settled in the minds of jurists functioning within the domestic system, as we assume they understand law-is-law so long as it arises through proper social processes (this, recall, is the "positivist" side of our liberal positivist model).

---

14 Rawls (at least in his later writings) considered the variant of liberal theory he was concerned with to be essentially "political" (as opposed to comprehensive, which would be to encompass a position applicable across time and culture). I attempt to skirt debates about the detailed inner workings of his theorizing, but do pause to note that underpinning these later thoughts of how liberal democracies should be structured (given commitments emergent within modern liberal societies) lies his own particular Kantian view of human flourishing. Still, as Rawls's thought matured, he came to appreciate that the political doctrine of liberalism could be fully legitimated only from within any one party's comprehensive view. See John Rawls, *Political Liberalism* (New York: Columbia University Press, 1996) [Rawls, *Political Liberalism*].

At the core of liberal doctrine we find adherence to two principles, liberty and equality.[15] How these are understood, how they interrelate, and how the ensuing system builds into a vision of how society should be structured are all contentious matters, resulting in varied understandings of liberalism itself. Bearing in mind discussions about these matters lead to *internal* debates, before looking at them we spend time looking at the *kinds* of liberal theory that can be produced and what this has to say about what we might expect Supreme Court judges could reasonably believe about liberalism. Particularities of liberal doctrine emerge within internal discussions and debates, but much can be ascertained if we first focus on the general contours of theories loosely accorded liberal status. Indeed, as we progress through this discussion I advance the thesis that there are commonalities underlying the panoply of liberal theories, commonalities seen from this more abstract level. Of course, this greatly assists our project, as we can safely assume jurists have these commonalities in mind (though they may not articulate them).

We begin, then, with thoughts about the nature of possible theories of liberalism and about how I intend to work with them. My approach is idiosyncratic, as I take them to be essentially constellations of interrelated beliefs. This approach to the nature of these theories affects how I work with them.

The Nature of Theories of Liberalism

In "What Is Liberalism?," Duncan Bell tracked varied ways of thinking of liberalism through the last few centuries, noting, "The history of liberalism ... is a history of constant reinvention."[16] Bell argues for continued attention to historical context in making sense of language that arises to give meaning to liberalism, showing how historical settings play a dominant role in delimiting specific understandings of the concept. In particular, he notes that since the time liberalism rose to prominence in the contemporary world – in the context of an ideological struggle with communist alternatives in the middle of the twentieth century – we see the term come to "denote virtually all non-totalitarian forms of politics as well as a partisan political perspective within societies."[17]

I pull together what I take to be several dominant contemporary threads of understanding, plucked from the works of a range of contemporary political philosophers. My endgame is the generation of a general sense of what

15 Some liberal theoretic accounts form around a triad: liberty, equality, and property. I choose to work property into the mix with liberty and equality. For the three-element approach, see e.g. CB MacPherson, *The Life and Times of Liberal Democracy* (Oxford: Oxford University Press, 1977).

16 Duncan Bell, "What Is Liberalism?" (2016) 42:6 Political Theory 682 at 705.

17 *Ibid.*

liberalism might look like in the minds of Supreme Court judges at the end of the twentieth century and the beginning of the twenty-first, one that advances beyond the notion that it simply denotes non-authoritarian forms of politics. This does not mean, however, that my aim is the synthesis of a settled theoretic meaning for liberalism in the early twenty-first century. Besides the fact that this is impossible, theories of liberalism substantially diverge.

Fortunately, this pattern of divergence does not create significant difficulties for the core project in this work. Recall that our general aim is to determine what we might reasonably expect Canadian judges to have in mind concerning the principles of liberalism as they go about (purportedly) injecting them into the law regulating the lives of Aboriginal peoples. This narrow project in mind, divergences and debates within liberal theory can be put to use, as they assist in delineating key matters that arise *within* the larger theoretical field, marking the development of thought through this period of time. We need not get tangled up in the bushes, since we engage in this not to settle debates, but to get a sense of what legal actors might be thinking when considering how to add to a social institution within a liberal democracy.

Some divergences arise from different approaches taken by theorists (sometimes the result of different disciplinary groundings), where these approaches differ not just in methodology but in what questions are being asked and what types of account are being sought. Other divergences arise from disagreement – numerous debates rage about key matters within theorizing about liberalism. Crowder helpfully provides a matrix of four possible types of liberal theory, revolving around two axes – a universalist/particularist axis and a perfectionist/neutralist axis.[18] While Crowder puts his typology to use showing ways theorists can work to *justify* liberalism, the schema also identifies ideal-types of liberal theory. Universalists argue that "liberal principles and institutions are rationally and ethically superior to all alternatives regardless of time and place," while particularists hold that "liberalism is to be justified not universally but only within particular historical and cultural conditions."[19] Meanwhile, perfectionist accounts hold that liberalism provides "a substantive conception of the good life involving the privileging of certain characteristic values and virtues rather than others," while a neutralist "presents liberalism not as a substantial conception of the good life in competition with others but as a purely instrumental political settlement which avoids judgements about the good in order to accommodate several such conceptions."[20]

There are other axes one could introduce to complicate the business of categorizing types of liberal theory, but most would almost certainly not

18 George Crowder, *Liberalism and Value Pluralism* (London: Continuum, 2002).

19 *Ibid* at 26.

20 *Ibid* at 27.

advance our inquiry into the nature of liberal theory writ large.[21] Let me introduce one, however, that assists in our efforts to take seriously the constructed nature of both the law and legal theory, a task that invites discussions about perspectives. We could place varied liberal theories along a line from those that emerge from *within* the normative world marked out by liberalism to those that adopt perches *outside* this normative universe.

On the one end of this spectrum we find theorists who accept (or at least acquiesce in) the general normative features of the social reality they inhabit. Within this world, delineated by various sets of conceptual parameters, the theorist can argue about how liberal thought should be modelled, what principles or values should be accentuated, what should be weakened or discarded, how the social reality about him should be shifted, etc. Note, though, that within the latitude for theorizing we can locate some fundamental commonalities, those general animating features of a liberal mindset this theorist lives through. In the world constructed around him, meaning is given shape through these deeper structures, concerning what counts as a person, a society, a state, a proper relationship between person and society and person and state, and what counts as appropriate social structures and institutions.

A theorist closer to the other end of the spectrum, modelling liberal thought from a stance outside that of liberal normative worlds, can be working from one of two general positions (which can overlap in one researcher). First, she could be someone who has lived her life in a social world constructed according to liberal precepts and beliefs, but who has on reflection come to adopt a set of normative positions at some remove from that defined by the set of delineating conceptual parameters set out by liberal thought. She questions these

21 One might, for example, suggest Crowder's typology is incomplete in that it does not consider how liberal accounts can be either principally descriptive or prescriptive. The fact that Crowder pays little attention to this distinction is understandable, however, given that his analysis is directed solely towards what we could label "prescriptive" theories (and that his personal project in *Liberalism and Value Pluralism* is to produce a particular value-pluralist case for liberalism, which is a narrow *justificatory* program). Descriptive accounts aim to lay out how liberal principles and values appear and function in the world, while prescriptive accounts aim to illuminate how collectives should reform their societies and social institutions so as to work towards ideal liberal structures. But beyond thinking of Crowder's interests, there are reasons not to bring in this additional complication. Besides the fact that the third axis I do introduce cuts across and intersects with this distinction, adding this distinction would make classification murkier than one might suppose. The fact is the divide between universalist and particularist accounts already hints strongly at the presence of a prescriptive/descriptive distinction. Universalist accounts will be strongly prescriptive, while particularist accounts suggest a model that either aims to be descriptive or is weakly normative. Murkiness comes from the fact that while the weak normative element suggested ("our society *should* be built along *these* liberal lines, given our history and culture and the commitments to values and principles this implies") does not rest on claims about how all societies should structure themselves, it does nevertheless invite normative concerns into ongoing theorizing.

precepts or starting points that liberal theory must presuppose. The second sort of theorist adopting a stance outside the liberal normative universe is attempting to distance herself from entanglement in normative worlds of political or moral construction. She aims to adopt a perspective from which she can hope to more objectively describe what she witnesses in the world.

We bring in these matters of positioning and perspectives in this context for several reasons (all of which were introduced in the last chapter). It is not a matter of acknowledging that some argue knowledge is perspectival, as that position, if taken to its global extreme, is being challenged within the naturalist approach adopted in this text. Rather, the presumption at play in this work is that humans in social collectives create meaning as they go about creating forms of social reality. This approach encompasses an attempt to pull apart two forms of theorizing, allowing for the possibility that one can adopt a stance from which one can reasonably expect to objectively theorize about varied forms of constructed social reality, while simultaneously accepting that one thing that can be modelled is in fact the creation of theory (about such things as law, politics, and morals) from within constructed social worlds.

To bring this down closer to the world of people and institutions, this means that we are entering this examination into how to model liberal thought while thinking of two key matters: that liberalism can be a source of insight for legal and political actors as they go about creating, maintaining, and enhancing social institutions, and that liberal theory (models of liberal thought) can itself play a role in these ongoing matters of social construction. Some forms of liberal theory, then, begin deep inside a world structured by liberal thought, and while they may seem to be going about the business of describing the nature of liberalism, they – as themselves products built within specific social worlds of meaning – can participate in the ongoing construction and maintenance of meaning.

The addition of this third axis is not helpful in the detailed work of the next few sections, as all the theorizing we will be exploring comes from those who work from positions within liberal normative worlds. Its import comes from the realization that the theory of liberal thought we are constructing in this exercise is being built from that other position, from outside normative worlds built according to liberal principles, meanings, and values.

Regardless of how one could go about creating a taxonomy of liberal theories from within the sea of liberal thought, my mission in this work is to try to occupy a vantage point removed from this sea, one from which the various theories are explored simply to get a sense of how a project of building an institution within a liberal democracy might be thought through. And so, to the extent that I am trying to paint a picture of liberalism, I am principally interested in building up a descriptive account (at least of how judges might think through problems using sets of beliefs in liberal principles, values, and ideals). In this narrow context my aim is to make sense of liberal theories and how they might function in the natural world around us, rather than to develop a settled liberal theory from within the liberal universe as defined by conceptual parameters presumed within worlds that arise from liberal thought (the sub-project at this point in the analysis is a type of meta-theoretic endeavour).[22]

One clear benefit to this approach is that it allows us to avoid significant theoretical entanglement, since we need not debate about whether "purely" descriptive accounts are possible, or about whether better theories of liberalism are universalist or particularist, perfectionist or neutralist. We are examining types of liberal theory from a naturalist perspective.

Let us focus then on the two axes introduced in Crowder's taxonomy, beginning with the separation of universalist from particularist theories (the neutralist/perfectionist divide is examined later in the context of our exploration of current debates concerning diversity and pluralism). A few words about the nature of this division can illustrate how such high-level divergences help us work out what it is reasonable to expect judges of the high court of a contemporary liberal democracy might deploy as they go about constructing a field of law. The key is a search for commonalities, those background shared structures within which this division makes sense. One commonality underlying this divergence is the concept of the person (and the role it plays in the fundamental liberal project, that of determining how society should be structured). I propose to use this notion of a concept of the person as a pivot point around which the bulk of the rest of the discussion will spin.

Once this initial illustration of the presence of a common belief in the priority of the person in the liberal project is behind us, we can examine specific notions of liberty and equality, noting divisions within liberal thought that arise at that level (internal to the theory). Once again, commonalities will be identified, once again the dual focus will be on how they connect to the fundamental project of determining how society should be structured, and how this speaks to what we can reasonably expect judges to be thinking about when building the law up around Aboriginal rights. We conclude with a look into a debate that engages directly with the sorts of concerns with which these judges, I suggest, are deeply concerned: the ongoing debate about how difference, particularly *cultural* difference, is to be accommodated within a liberal democracy.

---

22 Note, though, that this is a different sort of descriptive exercise from the sort introduced a few paragraphs ago in the liberal theory context. On one level, the projects would be similar (in that liberal theory presenting a descriptive picture will also carefully try to avoid debating the merits of liberal principles and values), but on another level they will be quite distinct (as the liberal theorist would be trying to describe *from within* a world structured by liberal thought how liberal principles and values manifest in his social world). The weakly normative aspect of the liberal theorist's project will inevitably seep into his world, while I attempt, amongst other things, to study *this* sort of activity in the world. That is, I will also explore how the liberal theorist can play a role in the construction of social reality. See "Liberal Theory and Liberal Theorists in the Natural World" in chapter 7.

The Universalist/Particularist Divide and Rawls on a Conception of the Person

The universalist/particularist division lays out two approaches to developing a full-fledged liberal theory – one approach attempts a "global" view (a theory that would set out how societies in general should be structured), while the other attempts to explain how *given* liberal democratic societies are, or should be, structured. The two are obviously related, but the second is more modest in its ambitions, fitting the fact that it aims only to spell out how existing commitments would ideally flesh out into the best structure possible (that is, *given* an existing liberal democracy, given its own conceptions about fundamental matters to which such a society and its citizens would seem to be committed, what would be the best guiding principles for the construction of political and legal institutions within this society?).[23]

In *Justice as Fairness: A Restatement*, Rawls set out to clarify how his earlier *A Theory of Justice* should be understood in relation to this latter project.[24] The later Rawls deliberately circumscribed his account, arguing only that *within* the modern liberal democracy he inhabited were certain given commitments present, commitments he could then parlay into a theory of liberalism appropriate to this socio-historical, cultural setting. In the public political culture of the liberal democracy he inhabits, Rawls notes that the concept of a person as free and equal has come to play a central role, a socio-historical fact that grounds a particularist account of liberal theory.

One clear virtue of Rawls's later particularist approach, and one reason he adopts this less ambitious approach in this later work, is that it avoids leading immediately into deep metaphysical issues. It would seem the project can be carried to fruition without anyone having to wonder about whether people *really* do have (biologically or metaphysically) attributes attributed to them within the commitments made by members of the given society.

Links to global accounts of liberalism are not, however, entirely severed in this particularist account, as socio-historical, culturally based conceptions that

23 This is how the later Rawls advanced a "political conception," as he turned his attention to how a given society – the one he inhabited – thought of liberal ideals, and what this meant for how they could best justify acceptable shared principles of justice. This distinction, again, Crowder sets out as between universalist and particularist models of liberalism. See Crowder, *supra* note 18 at 26:

> [L]iberals might argue on "universalist" grounds, claiming that liberal principles and institutions are rationally and ethically superior to all alternatives regardless of time or place.... Alternatively,... liberals might make a more qualified, "particularist" claim, namely that liberalism is to be justified ... only within particular historical and cultural conditions.

24 John Rawls, *Justice as Fairness: A Restatement* (Cambridge, MA: Belknap Press, 2001). One could argue about the extent to which the *Restatement* is indeed a restatement and not a redoing, but I do not need to get into that matter.

inform the inquiry (the "fundamental ideas" Rawls grounds his account on) can themselves be examined on more general (ahistorical/acultural) levels. While it is certainly true subsequent theorists can follow Rawls's path, each positioning her study self-consciously within an existing liberal democracy, finding herself there as the result of historical contingencies, theorists are still free to ask about whether societies *in general* should be structured in accord with the account generated in this more localized/historicized study. Should *Indigenous peoples*, for example, generally think of "persons" in the normative/political fashion found at the heart of life within a given modern liberal democracy?

It might seem that particularist accounts, and their means of avoiding metaphysical problems, would find favour in our present work. Would it not be attractive, for example, to simply assume that judges of Canada's Supreme Court self-consciously operate within a socio-historical, cultural framework built up around a concept of the person similar to the one we find in Rawls's narrowed account? We could imagine jurists in Canada simply *thinking* of "persons" in a specific (liberal) form. We could examine the ability of liberal doctrine to explain Aboriginal law, bearing in mind that Canadian judges work within a constitutional democracy, understanding then that it is natural to imagine these judges work with intuitions about personhood similar to those grounding Rawls's (and other liberal theorists') account.

We do not, however, arrive at the proper level of naturalist analysis if we follow Rawls's adoption of a particularist approach. Rawls can be understood to be making a tactical move, where the challenge is to decide which is likely to be more fruitful, the universalist or particularist approach. The tension is between these two approaches, and while it might seem the particularist approach eschews metaphysical matters, it actually reflects a choice made *within* a metaphysical debate. Liberal theorists face this choice – to try to construct a theory that reaches out to (and ultimately is aligned with) universalist understandings of morals and political morality, or to limit theory construction to those that avoid universalist pretensions. *Our* focus, recall, is not on such debates but on what lies underneath them, linking them into one type of activity in the world. We, that is, are looking at either sort of theory as simply the manifestation of one set of beliefs rather than another.

We need not be concerned, that is, with whether it is better or not for liberal theory to aim at universal or particularized truth. We are simply interested in the fact that there are different approaches within the larger field of liberal theorizing, where some theorists believe they can satisfactorily construct universally applicable theories, while others see problems in reaching for this level of abstraction and so limit themselves to simply exploring the nature of the liberal democracy within which they find themselves. Our focus is two-fold and directed elsewhere – might we expect judges of the Supreme Court to aim at and work within universalist or particularist theories of liberalism, and might we find it would have an impact on what they build in the context of Aboriginal law if they *believed* one thing rather than another?

This leads us up, then, to the cusp of looking into Rawls's conception of the person. Noting this is one liberal theorist's attempt to articulate a core belief that accounts for much of the rest of the liberal conception of the world (and, specifically, of the business of going about constructing social institutions), we need to see what it contains and entails, and how it functions in the world around us. And so we look into how Rawls presents a "political conception" of the person, embedding this in an overview of his project of articulating "an acceptable philosophical and moral basis for democratic institutions."[25] Providing this basis, Rawls argues, allows him to "address the question of how the claims of liberty and equality are to be understood."[26]

The starting point for his inquiry into a philosophical and moral account of the basis of a liberal democratic society is the "public political culture" of such a society (the one he happens to inhabit), out of which he elicits three fundamental ideas: "the idea of society as a fair system of social cooperation over time," "the idea of citizens ... as free and equal persons," and "the idea of a well-ordered society."[27] Rawls's general aim is to produce a theory of justice, and more particularly to describe principles of justice falling out of such a theory, where these principles – reflecting claims of liberty and equality – provide an acceptable basis for the construction of liberal democratic institutions.

The beginning point of this larger project is this "public political culture" and the three fundamental ideas he pulls out of this culture.[28] Our concern is narrower, principally with the "idea of citizens ... as free and equal persons."[29] We aim to carve off from Rawls's larger project this notion that underlying the overarching liberal project is a vision or conception of the person (and of her relationship to others and to the state and its institutions).

While I am loath to over-complicate what is already a complex theoretical construct, the fact is that we face two "conceptions of the person." On the one hand, we have the "idea of citizens ... as free and equal persons,"[30] while on the other hand, we have the notion of the person lying behind or underneath the theoretical machinations that take place within Rawls's work. Let me say a few words about the first, the political conception of the person, and then turn to how this conception functions within a liberal theorist's work, where this work itself rests on a notion of what it is to be a specific sort of being in the world.

---

25 *Ibid* at 5.
26 *Ibid.*
27 *Ibid.*
28 *Ibid.*
29 *Ibid.*
30 *Ibid.*

It is important for our purposes to bear in mind that the first form is a *conception* of the person, and indeed in this particularist account of liberalism, this is a political conception. To say this is a political conception is to place it into a very particular frame. The claim is not that citizens are, in any biological or metaphysical sense, truly "free and equal." Rather, Rawls is building up a sense of how "persons" are *conceived of within* a liberal democracy. This conception exists as both the product of a historical process and as an ideal (at least partly) driving this process. That is, over generations of working towards the construction of a liberal democracy, this concept of the person has begun to crystallize, as institutions emerge that reflect societies' thinking of their citizens in this manner, while this building process is continually unfolding, its nature developing as the ideal of the person as free and equal is gradually incorporated into new and improved societal structures.

The second conception is hidden in plain sight in Rawls's work. We can divine what such a vision or conception might be when we consider that Rawls describes the general project as being to explore what the reasonable person would be "ready to propose, or to acknowledge when proposed by others, [in terms of] the principles needed to specify what can be seen by all as fair terms of cooperation";[31] these would be the principles of justice sought after. Just behind this notion of proposing fair terms of cooperation lies a specific vision of the person, of that being who is concerned to *reason* her way to what might be expected to be acknowledged to be fair terms of cooperation with all others in society. In this view of the social world, the person is *primary*, epistemically, morally, and conceptually (though she physically exists – in that we are contemplating a given democratic society working towards a theory of justice to guide its activities – already embedded in a social setting).

Fortunately, we do not need to grapple with complexities and debates that arise when we try to sort out how all this fits together and is supposed to function.[32] We need only keep our attention focused on this pivot point, the concept of the

---

31 *Ibid* at 6–7.

32 These conceptions seem closely linked, as the reasoning self that works her way to the principles of justice appropriate to a liberal democracy is placed in that privileged position (as the arbiter of how societies and social institutions should be structured) due to her being conceived of as inherently valuable, as essentially free. Paying attention to their respective functions in the social world reveals, however, clear distinctions. The "political" conception is fundamentally a conception – that is, while its content is important, so too is the fact that what we are focused on is that within a liberal democracy a certain *concept* of what it is to be a citizen has emerged, and this concept plays a role in the structuring of social institutions. The rational/reasoning self, on the other hand, while also a conception as used in this theoretical business, is just that – a useful theoretical tool to help articulate and justify a set of principles of justice. The liberal theorist can see herself in both concepts, but in different ways. When deploying the "theoretical conception," she sees herself as this sort of being, channelling her inner reasoning/rational self in doing theoretical work.

person as free and equal, and as essentially primary (as an individuated, reasoning being). Whether a specific liberal theory be universalist or particularist, neutralist or perfectionist, underscoring the theory will be this concept, positioned such that society is seen properly built to answer to this free and equal being.

We now move on to the second stage of discussion of the nature of liberalism. Bearing in mind that the concept of the person lies at the base of the essential project (working out how the institutions of society are to the conceived of, created, and/or reformed), we can now look at what this conception might entail internally.

Liberty and Equality

The rise of classical liberalism in the West is often located in the unsettled period of the demise of absolute monarchical rule, feudalism, and mercantilism (the pre-modern structures of governance, and social and economic ordering), and the related rise in the nineteenth and into the first half of the twentieth centuries of modern "classical" institutions of formal democratic governance, legally defined rights regimes and (laissez-faire) capitalism. A common explanation for the rise of "new" forms of liberal thought in the second half of the twentieth century is that they were necessitated by challenges and crises generated by free-for-all attitudes marking liberalism's earlier stages of development.[33] Laissez-faire capitalism was subject to wild economic swings marked by low periods of intense economic deprivation, while the practice of speaking of liberty, but only for those "more equal" (providing empty promises of formal equality for everyone else), fed waves of resentment and struggle.[34]

Through all these developments, however, run threads of liberty and equality. One reading of this historical tale asks us to see it all as a coming-to-terms of the implications of taking seriously what it means to hold and entrench these values at the foundations of society (both locally and globally). What would it mean in a *full and rich sense* to treat individuals as free, not just in a completely

---

Interestingly, the fact that the theoretical work goes on this way reveals a slippery path to a universalist model, as much as the theorist might argue he is developing a particularist model. While a later-Rawlsian could say he is willing to acknowledge that other societies can and will develop other "conceptions of the person" in the political sense – since his model of theorizing presupposes the pre-existence of this rational/reasoning self – a universalist underpinning seems to peek out from around the edges. This is the sort of argument generated in the last section of this discussion, in the analysis of debates over pluralism.

33 See e.g. Alan Ryan, *The Making of Modern Liberalism* (Princeton, NJ: Princeton University Press, 2012). The instability seemingly built into the structures created (partly) through classical liberal architectural principles is accompanied by strong challenges from other ideologies. Greater concern over the welfare of the citizen played a major role in deflating the attractiveness of these alternatives.

34 See e.g. *ibid*; Constant & Ducharme, *supra* note 13.

formal sense but substantively? What would it mean in a *full and rich sense* to treat all humans as substantively equal?[35]

DIFFERENT CONCEPTS OF LIBERTY

We begin our look into the content of liberal theories with the notion of liberty, or freedom.[36] This is strongly linked to a liberal focus on individualism, the common theoretical position being that the freedom of the individual is a fundamental good in the world.[37]

How we characterize and understand this notion of a "fundamental good" and its relationship to the individual is problematic, but as with many problems one might otherwise have to deal with, this is not a matter with which we need to engage. Under a naturalist approach such confounding problems are effectively put to one side, a point made clear if we pause for a moment to consider how liberal theory would attempt to achieve the end of demonstrating how it is grounded in a picture of the individual capable of supporting a normative edifice. One way to ground theories of liberalism would be to place this focus on the individual on metaphysical grounds, and one way to achieve this grounding would be to assert a special status, to claim the human is metaphysically distinct from all else in the natural world. One might argue, for example, that a person is able to act outside causal webs that otherwise determine events in the natural world.[38] Alternatively, one could try

---

35 See e.g. *ibid.*

36 One could begin with equality, but (avoiding disputes over which is primary) I approach the matter with equivocation – I do not think it matters for my sketch whether liberty or equality is primary, or how these two must interact. Notably, some theorists see an irresolvable tension between the two; for example, given a narrow sense of what liberty amounts to – for example, as nothing but a protected sphere of non-interference in action – one can then see efforts to achieve substantive equality undercutting liberty. Some theorists, indeed, go so far as to argue that the fundamental individualism of freedom conflicts with any projects of equalization. We need not even introduce such notions, since Canadian jurists do not inhabit a world of ideas that intersects with these marginal "liberal" theories.

37 This touches on the core division between perfectionist and neutralist liberal accounts – if liberalism holds that objective value is found in aspects of individuality (e.g., autonomy or rationality) it presents a perfectionist model, as this privileges a set of conceptions of the good life (those that accord with this value), while neutralist accounts cleave to the notion that no privileged values could inform particular models of the good life.

38 Of course, a vast literature grapples with the many philosophical opportunities presented by the intersection of different notions of free will and determinism. Compatibilists attempt to show how a form of free will is compatible with determinism, while incompatibilists argue that the sort of free will we intuit and that is required for moral responsibility requires we be removed, to some extent and in some fashion, from causal webs that might otherwise seem to determine our actions. For a collection of essays canvassing many of the contemporary debates around these points, see Paul Russell & Oisin Deery, eds, *The Philosophy of Free Will: Essential Readings from the Contemporary Debates* (Oxford: Oxford University Press, 2013).

to avoid these challenging metaphysical claims, grounding theories of liberalism, for example, on nothing more than developed notions of the person, arguing that liberalism is intimately connected only to *beliefs* in attributes of personhood.

As with similar situations we encountered in the last few sections, this could, however, be said to be itself a metaphysical debate, one with which we need not engage. On one side is the position that the individual is *indeed* primary, morally, epistemically, and conceptually. On the other side is the claim that liberalism need rest only on commitments to *beliefs* in this concept of the person. We are in a position that allows us to step back from this debate, being concerned only to note the commonality, a grounding of liberalism in the primacy of the individual (whether this be argued for or presumed, whether seen as something inherent in the moral fabric of the universe or merely held).

Let us move on, then, to arguments and debates under the liberal umbrella. We encounter a core debate within the liberal community when we ask whether the freedom prized should be understood principally as (a) lack of external constraint (principally freedom from coercion or control by the state),[39] or (b) freedom to act from a self-directed or self-legislating will. The former – "negative freedom" – is understood as entailing the *protection* of a certain sphere around the individual *from* external threat of coercion or control, while the latter – "positive freedom" – is generally understood as that *power* to act from one's self-directed will (and can call for the creation of structural elements of society necessary to facilitate the enhancement of this power).

We can see a thread of this debate spinning out from Isaiah Berlin's defence of negative liberty.[40] Focus on and concern with positive freedom, Berlin argued, can easily introduce a slide into authoritarianism. The notion of positive freedom rests ultimately on a division between differing levels of the self, the one level (tied to theories of self-fulfilment or self-expression) being taken by some to be more "authentic" and important than the other level (tied to simple action protected from outside interference). And on the basis of this division, Berlin argued, people can be said to be *mistaken* about what they believe freedom "really" entails, and forces can be deployed (under the veil of "legitimate" state action to promote "freedom") to corral individuals into ways of living claimed to be more in accord with *proper* ways of exercising freedom.

39 On some accounts of the philosophical origins of liberalism, much is made of the choice of those inhabiting a hypothetical original state of nature to release some of their power to a central authority so that such things as attacks and threats from others can be avoided or minimized (see, for example, various forms of social contract accounts, particularly those of a Hobbesian bent). The state, on such accounts, has then a fundamental purpose or function in protecting each individual from violence by or intrusion from all others.

40 Isaiah Berlin, *Two Concepts of Liberty* (Oxford: Oxford University Press, 1958) [Berlin, *Two Concepts of Liberty*].

The fact is Berlin's concerns – rooted as they were in semi-hysteria over a now long-faded "Red Menace," and strongly resisted by a line of subsequent liberal theorists – have been washed over in the early twenty-first century. Positive liberty is now commonly cast as "autonomy,"[41] and its links to pre-Enlightenment notions of self-fulfilment and Enlightenment notions of personal choice and responsibility have coalesced into what is now taken to be a concept of personhood providing the primary motive for the protection and promotion of freedom, the need to enhance each person's capacity to exercise her reasoning and rational self, to own her choices, and to be seen and held to be responsible for her choices.[42]

We see this in Galston's recasting of the positive-negative divide as one between "autonomy" and "diversity."[43] In this recasting autonomy and diversity are ideals, the ideal of autonomy in tension with an interest in tolerating diverse sub-cultures within a single sociopolitical system (where perceived value in diversity leads to toleration, even of subcultures that are potentially illiberal). "Diversity," in Galston's formulation, corresponds crudely with negative liberty, marking a thread of liberal thought that emerged out of the history of the Reformation, as European states sought to manage conflict between different communities of religious believers by foregrounding toleration. To advance interests in societal stability in the face of seemingly intractable conflict between religious sects, a liberal political order was affirmed, one centred on the toleration of forms of living even when they might advance within themselves illiberal modes of thinking and being. Autonomy, on the other hand, corresponds in this account to positive liberty and emerged out of a different thread of history – Enlightenment concerns with the rational, reflective, and critical self, that being both capable of standing up to authority and tradition, and properly to be placed in situations wherein attributes of autonomy could be protected and enhanced.

We will return to this way of casting this basic divide between ways of theorizing within liberalism when we conclude the discussion, with a look at a lively contemporary debate concerning the need to properly account for pluralism within liberal societies. There we can grapple with the fact that tolerance for diverse subcultures seems to imply that spheres of non-interference are erected around sociocultural communities and not simply individuals.

---

41 See e.g. William Galston, Liberal Pluralism: The Implications of Value Pluralism for Political Theory and Practice (Cambridge, UK: Cambridge University Press, 2002) [Galston, Liberal Pluralism]; Will Kymlicka, Liberalism, Community and Culture (Oxford: Oxford University Press, 1989) [Kymlicka, Liberalism, Community and Culture]; Andrea Baumeister, Liberalism and the "Politics of Difference" (Edinburgh: Edinburgh University Press, 2000).

42 See e.g. Philip Pettit, *A Theory of Freedom: From the Psychology to the Politics of Agency* (Oxford: Oxford University Press, 2001).

43 Galston, *Liberal Pluralism, supra* note 41.

For the moment, we pause to make two points. First, we reinforce a key element we can take away from this sort of debate: the fact that while liberal theorists disagree *within* the theory, they adhere to a common ground of understanding, that the individual is primary and that society (properly) exists to enhance freedoms enjoyed by individuals (and must be built in accord with this vision). It is important to bear in mind that on a general level, seemingly radical divergences we happen upon fade into the background, and a common way of thinking of the world emerges. We are expected to accept the position that individuals (and their life-plans) are primary, and "society" is secondary (with society including all matters connected to interpersonal relations, but also linked to the functions of a centralized governing structure, understood to need a reason to be, and thought of as at best a tool to promote or enhance the lives of the only beings with value, individual citizens or subjects).

Second, we can begin to weave in thoughts about one aim in this discussion, namely to articulate a sense of what one might reasonably expect judges of the Supreme Court of Canada believe as (we presume for the sake of our investigation) they go about infusing liberal doctrine into the law concerning Aboriginal rights.

Here we note that when we consider fine-grained characterizations of negative and positive freedom, they tend to play out into different emphases once we contemplate how liberal society should be properly structured.[44] Those who favour the promotion of negative freedom will tend to focus on limited government, a free market economy, and the enhancement of private property regimes,[45] while those who focus attention on positive freedom will tend to favour enhancing conditions that promote the development of the individual (for example, education, free speech, rights of association), welfare and/or redistributive programs (to ensure optimal conditions for the development of each individual), and "responsible" government.

---

44 Alan Ryan's text, *The Making of Modern Liberalism*, is linked for the most part to the particular American narrative. It highlight tensions pervading the history of liberalism in that historical-cultural context. One such tension percolating into the political-legal arena is this distinction between negative and positive freedom, a distinction that marked Isaiah Berlin's work. See Ryan, *supra* note 33. See also Berlin, *Two Concepts of Liberty*, *supra* note 40; Isaiah Berlin, "Two Concepts of Liberty" in Isaiah Berlin, *Four Essays on Liberty* (Oxford: Oxford University Press, 1969) 118.

45 What fundamentally distinguish liberalism from libertarianism are respective views on government. For the most part, libertarians see government as an unnecessary evil, to be minimized in the lives of free individuals. Liberals, on the other hand, treat governmental power and authority with caution, but can see value in the instruments and capacities of governmental structures. Not too surprisingly (given several fairly obvious reasons I leave to the reader), one can see from the fact the Supreme Court of Canada never questions the very being of the Canadian state (at least in this way!), it is clearly not of a libertarian mindset.

DIFFERENT UNDERSTANDINGS OF EQUALITY

Intersecting with these different notions of liberty are different understandings of "equality." Early (proto-liberal) accounts made much of what was argued to be the fact that human existence is marked by (roughly) equal abilities between individuals. Lack of substantive differences in strength, intelligence, and other innate characteristics of individuals reveal our (rough) equality, which requires equal treatment of citizens within social-political structures we might choose to adopt.[46] Over time these arguments were supplanted by those focused on the notion of equal worth, emphasis shifting to the sense that each individual is equally deserving of equal concern for his or her well-being. Together these sorts of arguments undercut traditional structures, which tended to rest on and to support divisions between classes or groupings of people.

Equality is a concept that marks an essentially relational matter – how are distinct (and potentially quite different) individuals to be approached within a liberal democratic state? There are three areas to consider when thinking of a body of individuals: initial starting positions, processes (for distribution of such things as resources, opportunities, and positions), and outcomes. Few egalitarians (and especially those firmly in the liberal universe) are attracted to positions that call for equality of outcomes. A grounding consideration, that of the need to treat persons as equals, is not seen as leading to a call to ensure decisions and actions of individuals lead to (roughly) equal outcomes. Normatively important characteristics of persons are accounted for in allowing individuals to *make choices*, which (a) leaves aside the question of what it is that individuals might seek to obtain, and (b) leads inevitably to "winners" and "losers."

While attention continues to be paid to "starting" positions, debate from roughly the mid-twentieth century on has focused principally on the question of whether liberal doctrine requires that each person be able to access (roughly) equal resources and opportunities (whether in "initial" positions or, more pressingly, as goods distributed through state intervention). The state needs to treat persons as equals, and in doing so it both creates social structures and institutions that determine how resources and opportunities are conceived of and distributed, and sets up processes and institutions for settling problems and disputes that might arise around such distributions. Freedom and equality come together in the fact that freedom, many have come to acknowledge, can be empty and meaningless without attention to disparities between differently situated individuals in access to resources and opportunities.

We find in the narrower legal context that an earlier focus on "formal equality" (focused, for example, on the imperative that all be equal *under the law* – that is, that the law apply equally to all subjects) was joined (and in some

46 See e.g. Thomas Hobbes, *Leviathan* (1651), online: <gutenberg.org/files/3207/3207-h/3207-h.htm>.

jurisdictions arguably superseded by) the notion of "substantive equality."[47] This latter form of equality focuses not so much on process for the sake of process but on process that takes account of the matter of distribution of access to resources and opportunities. Liberal theorists enamoured with a notion of substantive equality argue that individuals should expect more from their social institutions than mere equality of treatment – they should be able to expect that society will, to some reasonable degree, work towards ensuring that all *are* actually as equal as can reasonably be expected (in access to resources, or to opportunities, or the like) as each person sets out deciding how to live his or her life.

Liberty and Equality Intertwined

Within the business of building society (particularly its governing structures), we see there is no simple intersection between one understanding of liberty and some corresponding understanding of equality.[48] But it should be obvious that those who favour the notion of positive liberty or autonomy will tend to be sympathetic to the notion of substantive equality (just as those who lean towards the promotion of negative liberty will tend to favour formal equality, all else being equal).[49]

Consider the question of redistribution of resources or opportunities – matters called for if substantive equality is a goal. The advocate of negative freedom will tend to find this activity questionable, given that (a) decisions on how to redistribute and actual redistribution would fall to the state, and (b) for *x*

47 Through the last few decades of the twentieth century, the law in Canada on discrimination (under, for example, section 15 of the *Charter of Rights and Freedoms*) moved towards a model falling under the broad notion of substantive equality. See *Canadian Charter of Rights and Freedoms*, Part I of the *Constitution Act, 1982*, being Schedule B to the *Canada Act 1982* (UK), c 11. Interestingly, one of the most prominent recent decisions dealing with section 15 of the *Charter* arose in a dispute between Aboriginal and non-Aboriginal fishers on the West Coast. See *R v Kapp*, 2008 SCC 41. The Supreme Court there reaffirmed its commitment to an approach that focuses on substantive (as opposed to formal) equality – but also noted its earlier turn in *Andrews v Law Society of British Columbia*, [1989] 1 SCR 143, 56 DLR (4th) 1, to the notion that "human dignity" should inform discrimination-analysis had been unfortunate, in that such a notion did not seem well-suited to the development of a legal test.

48 Indeed, many argue the fundamental tension in liberal theory is between the different directions in which liberty and equality can pull a society. For example, in John Gray's examination of Isaiah Berlin's work on liberalism, Gray notes liberty and equality are not only in tension, but also express fundamental liberal values, generate instability within liberal theory, and in particular render incoherent forms of liberal universalism. See John Gray, *Isaiah Berlin* (New York: Harper Collins, 1995).

49 Just to consider one possible connection between these two visions, those who tend to favour negative freedom will tend to favour limited government, and that would align these people with the camp favouring formal equality, which would be expected to require less positive action by the state.

to be available for redistribution to *A*, this might very well necessitate *taking* from *B*. The proponent of negative freedom need not be opposed to any and all redistribution, but calculations of justifiable processes will be complex and will require careful balancing of costs to the liberty of individuals at the hands of the state (capable of being cast as "coercion" or control) against the possible gains to individuals (seen by some in this camp as normally suspect and always minimal at best).[50] The advocate of autonomy, on the other hand, will tend to welcome such matters (when carried out appropriately), asking how society could be better structured to best ensure that all individuals are treated substantively the same – that they all enjoy roughly the same opportunities for personal growth and flourishing – as self-legislating individuals.[51]

Again, it is essential to note one can locate common ground behind all these debates about value accorded the individual. In the early twenty-first century we see this commonly expressed as according prime value to the ability of the individual to live as she prefers and to have the ability to reflect on how she might wish to live (to be free to live according to her wishes, and free to reflect on her choices about how to live, in order to alter her future path should she consider this change in life-plans preferable).[52]

In the liberal picture, this articulation reflects valuation of reason and will at the level of the individual, two attributes that tend (in the early twenty-first century) to coalesce around the notions of choice and personal responsibility. The individual's capacity to *consider and determine* what values she might live by is prized, as is her *ability to act* on her decisions on how to live, and these together give sense to (a) what it is to hold the individual *accountable* for her actions (and outcomes), and relatedly, (b) the core normative character of the person, cast as the ability to develop and hold a conception of the good and to act responsibly as a result.

The form of reason commonly upheld is, arguably, not merely instrumental – that is, the liberal theorist does not find value in reason simply in its capacity to determine how best to work towards goals. Instead, reason is understood to

---

50 For the classic text in this regard, see especially Robert Nozick, *Anarchy, State, and Utopia* (New York: Basic Books, 1974). This moves us over to the libertarian wing of liberal thought.

51 See e.g. John Rawls, *A Theory of Justice* (Cambridge, MA: Belknap Press, 1971) [Rawls, *Theory of Justice*]; Ronald Dworkin, *Taking Rights Seriously* (Cambridge, MA: Harvard University Press, 1978); Ronald Dworkin, *Sovereign Virtue: The Theory and Practice of Equality* (Cambridge, MA: Harvard University Press, 2000).

52 We see this liberal position at the core, for example, of Kymlicka's articulation of liberal philosophy. See Kymlicka, *Liberalism, Community and Culture*, *supra* note 41. Ryan notes that this view – which he sees emerging from Mill's articulation of "modern liberalism" – runs into problems within the broader world of liberal thought. It has, he argues, "at best a minority appeal," it promises "a degree of personal fulfillment that the welfare state cannot deliver," and (building on this) there is a "grave risk of disillusionment ... as a result of its failure when it [modern liberalism] overextends itself": Ryan, *supra* note 33 at 26.

encompass a critical or reflective capacity. One might wonder, however, why it might be normatively important that the individual be critically reflective.

A theory of the normative self is embedded in this picture. To act normatively (within this account) is to follow a choice made, a choice connected to one's conception of the good. While historically in the West how to think, what to value, and how to live were strongly circumscribed by various levels of authority, the rise of liberalism coincided with – some would argue it is defined by – challenges to these authorities and their pronouncements. The normative theory that emerges is that of the freedom of the individual to decide *on her own* what she values, how she will act, and how she will live her life. Again, it is not deemed sufficient that the person be free to choose to act in accord with her understanding of what is valuable and good, but that she be the author of this account of what is valuable and good. The person must be free to reflect on these values and ideals she lives by, and free to adjust them as she sees fit.

One might try to cast this element of critical reflection in sceptical terms, arguing that the liberal model connects to a sceptical attitude about knowledge of the good (for if there were a sense that "the good" can be known and identified, it would not seem to be so important to value the ability of each individual to search for what is good and right).[53] Historically, as the Western world shook off the shackles of traditional thought and authoritarian control, this may have been a powerful animating consideration, the focus being on the need for the individual to question all values and belief systems ordained from on high and to search on her own for answers to questions about the right and the good.

In contemporary liberal thought, however, the notion that we need to create conditions conducive to the free search for elusive truths seems restricted principally to matters of politics and other forms of social decision-making. Downgrading the role of scepticism about the good and right also tracks a shift in thinking about the centrality of the person, and in particular the notion that liberty is essentially and entirely concerned with personal choice and personal responsibility. This would be, amongst other things, to place value on "ownership" of knowledge and on having this knowledge come to one outside the possible taint of ideological imposition or control. This signals an ongoing rise in concern about identity (which will be the focus of our discussion in the next section, where we explore the intersection of liberalism and pluralism).[54]

---

53 Kymlicka discusses this interpretation – which he argues is a misinterpretation – as developed in Jaggar and Unger's works. See Alison Jaggar, *Feminist Politics and Human Nature* (Totowa, NJ: Rowman & Littlefield, 1983); Roberto Unger, *Knowledge and Politics* (New York: Free Press, 1984). See Kymlicka, *Liberalism, Community and Culture*, *supra* note 41 at 17–18. Kymlicka notes that the Millian articulation of modern liberalism entails individual freedom to pursue the good, which is, at least in principle, knowable.

54 One could still frame all this in the language of scepticism, though it would be a narrow use of this language. One would be saying it is important within liberal thought that each

It might seem difficult in the early twenty-first century to see how any underpinning of scepticism could fit below or behind a liberal position built upon the notion of negative freedom, but one need only wonder at what might motivate the contemporary "negative-freedom" liberal thinker in valuing the protection of a sphere around the individual. It cannot be simply an interest in protecting established beliefs, traditions, and ways of life, as this is what characterizes conservative doctrine. The conservative values the continuation of established ways. A liberal (of any stripe) is not directly opposed to the continuation of established ways, but this is on the understanding that the individual is free to *choose* her status vis-à-vis this way of life or tradition. For example, the liberal theorist tends to find considerable value in the ability of each individual to be free to opt out – or "escape" – if she freely decides not to live within a particular social milieu, or under a particular cultural code or tenet.

It cannot be just state structures, then, that the liberal (of any stripe) is concerned about as a threat to the individual – otherwise the liberal position (whether defined upon negative freedom or not) would slip into conservative territory. Indeed, when we turn to look at current efforts to link liberalism with forms of pluralism, we will see that in contemporary liberal thought attention becomes fixed on external factors understood to limit the expression of liberty, even within the negative-freedom model. We will see that within a contemporary liberal society, sub-societies that potentially limit the exercise of autonomy will themselves be subject to limitation. This matter is left for a more complete examination in our concluding discussion of the relationship between pluralism and liberalism.

All this points to the contemporary proponent of negative freedom valuing a certain kind of critically reflective attitude, one adopted by the individual.[55]

individual begin the journey to self-fulfilment without preconceived or imposed notions of the good and right – that he or she be uncertain (on this "personal" and subjective level) about what they encompass and/or entail.

55 We might extend this picture for the liberal (of any stripe), analogizing the status of the individual to that acknowledged to fall upon the status of the sovereign in pre-modern times, in the European setting. The sovereign (besides said in the medieval era, by some, to rule by divine right) was understood to enjoy a form of absolute rule (in some cases conceptually tied to his ruling by divine right). For example, Bodin's *Les Six Livres de la République* ascribes a form of absolute authority to the sovereign. See Jean Bodin, *Les Six Livres de la République*, (1576), online: <gallica.bnf.fr/ark:/12148/btv1b86268103/f13.image>. As Mario Turchetti points out in his discussion of Bodin, this, though, is more a theory of sovereignty than an expression of "absolutism," as Bodin believed that the sovereign, while answerable only to God, being so answerable was subject to natural and divine law. See Mario Turchetti, "Jean Bodin" in *Stanford Encyclopedia of Philosophy* (2005), Edward N Zalta, ed, online: <plato.stanford.edu/entries/bodin/#4>. The modern individual in a liberal setting is positioned as properly "sovereign" over her own personal Queen-dom, accorded the fundamental right to decide on her own what she will value, what she will believe, and how she will live.

This attitude being attached to this vision of the free self – seen as the ultimate arbiter of value, and so necessarily armed with a natural unwillingness to unreflectively accept beliefs and customs – we can expect that even many current articulations of negative freedom slip into considerations that speak as well of concerns with autonomy, with the exercise of "self-legislation."

Liberalism and Pluralism

By the mid-twentieth century, primary focus had begun to shift from concern with traditional, authoritarian structures to acknowledgment of the existence of "reasonable pluralism" or, more recently, value pluralism. Now, in the early twenty-first century, the primary concern is not that we cannot know what the good life might be (so the state is not justified in dictating what the good life entails), but that the good life is itself variable. That is, a dominant position in liberal thought is now that there is a range of possible ways of living, each of which is as valid as the next.

We witness a shift from what had been predominantly a struggle between proponents of negative freedom and proponents of autonomy to envelopment of these concerns within a system built to protect and enhance autonomy. Nowhere is this more apparent than in the emergence over the last few decades of one of the most pressing debates within liberal theory, that of the proper way to accommodate "difference" within liberal societies. Arguably, the twenty-first century has seen a shift from attempts to tie liberalism to a *plurality of beliefs* (where the fundamental difficulty is in coming to know the truth about how to live when faced with a panoply of possible ways) to tension between this stance and what connects to a stronger "fact," that of a *plurality of value itself* (which suggests there is *no truth* about the way to properly live). This debate hones our understanding of the position of liberal thought in the contemporary Western world, particularly the presence of communities possessed of sets of values-held, and provides an opportunity to sum up what we might reasonably expect judges of the Supreme Court to believe as they inject liberal doctrine into the law concerning Aboriginal rights.

We close this overview of liberal thought in the early twenty-first century, then, with a look into this debate that swirls around the seeming tension between liberalism and pluralism. Once again, one aim is to show that the strain this generates arises within – or is contained within – liberal theory, while the ultimate objective remains fixed, to gain a sense of what we can reasonably expect judges of the Supreme Court of Canada believe as they construct the law concerning Aboriginal rights.

We work into this with a quick summary of our investigations to this point, noting roles played by the concept of the person in liberal theory and in our inquiries.[56] We then need to follow certain concerns raised about this concept as they evolve, eventually leading into contemporary interest in "diversity," "community," and "pluralism."

In the last few sections we explored tensions that arise within liberal theory as notions of liberty and equality are fleshed out. I argued that, first, we need not resolve debates on these internal matters, and, second, that we need only focus on sets of *beliefs held*, and in particular on commonalities that lie behind tensions we observe. We noted in this context that the concept of the person (as free and equal) can be seen resting below all liberal positions, and functions as a starting point for the liberal project, that of structuring sociopolitical institutions. As more substantive concepts of liberty (as autonomy) and equality (of resources) dominated thought in some Western liberal democracies (including, crucially, Canada) the concept of the person – as free and equal – continued to sit behind all developments, though particularities of how society should be built adjusted accordingly.

A different sort of debate emerged, however, in the latter half of the twentieth century, one that challenged the core of the liberal concept of the person. Over the last half-century, debate began to swirl around the conception of the self that inhabits and animates much of liberal theorizing over the last few centuries. The notion of the "atomistic" self – the individual conceived of as removed from his societal connections, able to exist and reason independent of what might otherwise seem to be entanglements in cultural and social webs – played a major role in forming and supporting powerful articulations of liberal theory. We noted earlier that in Rawls's work this concept of the person appears *both* as that concept held by members of society (of the free and equal person) and as describing the entity who reasons her way to principles of justice.[57] We noted that the first instantiation of the concept of the person (whether functioning as the concept of a metaphysical being or merely *belief* in a being possessed of freedom and held to be equal) underlies all liberal imaginings, while the second concept dances around the edges of liberal theorizing itself (accounting, it would seem, for how liberal models of society are built and justified).[58]

---

56 While our work in this section runs somewhat parallel to Bell's call for more focused time/place analysis, note we have looked at a fair sweep of time and place: the last half-century or so in the West.

57 We noted, for example, that within the development of principles of justice a key role is played in positioning the hypothetical agent behind a "veil of ignorance." See Rawls, *Theory of Justice*, *supra* note 51; Rawls, *Political Liberalism*, *supra* note 14.

58 Within Rawls's iconic justification of a liberal model of society, without knowing what status or position she might have in society, what class she might inhabit, what gender or race she might enjoy, the agent could best determine what fundamental principles would be both just and fair. Reduced to a thinking, calculating maximizer of self-interest, she could best choose how we would all agree to live together.

Does this vision of the *primacy* of the individual accord, however, with the nature of the human?[59] Through the last few decades of the twentieth century, challenges to this conception of the person came from several directions. Michael Sandel articulated a powerful challenge from a communitarian perspective (with parallel challenges emanating from other directions).[60] Communitarians argue the human is *essentially* a social animal, defined by its existence in relational webs.[61] A theory of justice (or political morality), this argument goes, would then have to rest on such a ground – to build upon a vision of the self radically removed from the core of our nature would be to develop a fundamentally mistaken theory.

Numerous liberal theorists rose to meet this sort of challenge. Kymlicka, for example, devoted time and energy to this matter in his earlier works, *Liberalism, Community and Culture* and *Multicultural Citizenship.*[62] His response boiled down to acceptance of the "metaphysical" claim (that the human is essentially a social animal),[63] but entrenchment around (1) the fundamental value placed on individual freedom, and (2) the impact it has on the need to *imagine* the self able to step back from social and cultural contexts (in order to critically reflect on their value and place in this individual's particular life). As Kymlicka notes,[64] the demand of the liberal is not that we conceive of the self as *ontologically* atomistic, but that we acknowledge (a) the self (as embedded as she may be in social and cultural webs) is *capable* of removing herself from *uncritical*

59 Note that one could think of this person as a conceptual construct, distancing Rawls from the notion that he was advancing anything like a "metaphysical" picture of the person. This fits neatly with his discussions in the *Restatement*, but less so (seemingly) with what goes on in the construction of the *Theory of Justice*. Again, however, nothing in my project hinges on such matters, and so I step around them.

60 This form of challenge came particularly from one form of feminist stance. See e.g. Catriona Mackenzie & Natalie Stoljar, eds, *Relational Autonomy: Feminist Perspectives on Autonomy, Agency, and the Social Self* (New York: Oxford University Press, 2000); Jaggar, supra note 53.

61 Michael Sandel, *Liberalism and the Limits of Justice* (Cambridge, UK: Cambridge University Press, 1982). A succinct argument making use of Hegel's philosophy can be found in Charles Taylor. See chapter 5, n 66, *supra*.

62 Kymlicka, *Liberalism, Community and Culture, supra* note 41. Will Kymlicka, *Multicultural Citizenship: A Liberal Theory of Minority Rights* (Oxford: Oxford University Press, 1995). See especially *ibid* at 91, where he challenges Sandel's argument to the effect that "some of our ends are 'constitutive' ends, in the sense that they define our sense of personal identity." Kymlicka argues that while "[i]t is not easy or enjoyable to revise one's deepest ends ... it is possible, and sometimes a regrettable necessity": *ibid.*

63 This is here not a biological, taxonomic claim, as it reaches past notions of what the animal *Homo sapiens* might have as species-characteristics to a claim about the *essential* identity of a kind of *normative* being.

64 *Multicultural Citizenship, supra* note 62 at 91–3; Kymlicka, *Liberalism, Community and Culture, supra* note 41 at 51–70.

adherence to given values and beliefs, and more importantly (b) that the self must do so – or be *able* to do so – to be free (which is a condition of being a *normative* being).

Note, though, that Kymlicka's response to the communitarian challenge is embedded in works with the words "community" and "multicultural." In their titles Kymlicka's work responds to the communitarian challenge while reflecting developments within liberal doctrine over the last few decades that are attached to a deep concern about diversity. Diversity is now commonly discussed in the context of what have come to be known as forms of pluralism and the "politics" of identity or difference.[65] As social science increasingly pressed results indicating that one's self-identity is unavoidably grounded in cultural and social foundations, defined in terms of community-established sets of beliefs and values, the stage was set for rethinking certain basic liberal positions. Acknowledging (as Kymlicka does) that the self exists in varied social and cultural contexts, and that, given these contexts, diversity of belief – and, more importantly, of *value* – must enter into and colour analysis, liberal theorists have struggled to work out how distinct *communities* of *belief* and *value* can be accommodated within the classic liberal framework.

This wave of interest in diversity and pluralism can be seen across a range of modern legal and political scholars. For example, while Kymlicka examined the place of Indigenous peoples in thinking through how liberal theory can accommodate culture and "multiculturalism," Macklem and Schouls carried out analyses of "Indigenous difference" in the context of liberal thought,[66]

65 Isaiah Berlin popularized the notion of value pluralism (that of the existence of varied incommensurable fundamental goods), but pitched at the level of the lives of individuals. See Isaiah Berlin, *Four Essays on Liberty* (Oxford: Oxford University Press, 1969). This notion plays a key conceptual role in the work of subsequent theorists.

Of more interest is the notion of value pluralism at the group level, sometimes referred to as political pluralism. See e.g. Galston, *Liberal Pluralism*, *supra* note 41; William Galston, *The Practice of Liberal Pluralism* (Cambridge, UK: Cambridge University Press, 2005); Baumeister, *supra* note 41.

66 Patrick Macklem, Indigenous Difference and the Constitution of Canada (Toronto: University of Toronto Press, 2001); Tim Schouls, Shifting Boundaries: Aboriginal Identity, Pluralist Theory, and the Politics of Self-Government (Vancouver: UBC Press, 2003). Schouls looks at two ways the struggles of Aboriginal peoples have come to be articulated – with the language of culture and with the language of nationhood – and traces how theorists and communities emphasize one or the other (and sometimes both). In placing this in the context of matters of identity, he argues, ultimately, that this under-describes the situation in need of analysis, as "this precludes from serious discussion the fundamental and prior question of how and under what terms Aboriginal persons adopt the attributes associated with culture and nation as the principal markers of their identities in the first place": *ibid* at 48. All of Schouls's analysis, however, presumes a location within a given liberal democratic state (and its "society").

while James Tully discussed how contemporary constitutionalism builds on certain liberal principles in advancing a form of "strange" constitutionalism (accommodating, amongst other things, the presence of Indigenous communities in Canada).[67]

The liberal theorist, however, can (and does) locate this discussion of diversity and pluralism entirely *within* the horizon of existing liberal states. The liberal theorist typically begins with the state as a *given*, its liberal pedigree assumed, discussion then focusing on how diversity and pluralism should be received and theorized. Theorists either (a) wonder at how liberal societies *already* accommodate plural centres of value (even on collective levels), or (more commonly) (b) expound on why and how deep liberal principles call for societal reform, so that arguments can be advanced on how an existing society (for example, Canadian society) might *better* accommodate such things as "Indigenous difference."[68] We might well imagine then that, in the development of Aboriginal law within the courts, we should expect to witness a concern in the liberal Canadian state to situate Indigenous collectives into the matrix of liberal systems to (a) accord proper attention to the individual, while (b) allowing for some accommodation of "Indigenous difference."

Our focus, however, requires that we reframe the discussion. I propose exploring more carefully the "*critical*" line (challenging the very concept of the person in liberal thought) in order to delve more deeply into how liberal theorists manage the borders of discourse, ensuring that their construction of social reality dominates all sub-discourses. Keeping to the central place of the concept of the person is important, but we place this concept in the context of discussion of the "fact of value pluralism." The fact is, value pluralists hold, we are faced with multifarious values: with values we face structuring how we organize our lives, individually and collectively, with no way-of-living structured by a collection of such values capable of being held to be better than any other.[69]

67 James Tully, *Strange Multiplicity: Constitutionalism in an Age of Diversity* (Cambridge, UK: Cambridge University Press, 1995).

68 Macklem, *supra* note 66; Duncan Ivison, *Postcolonial Liberalism* (Cambridge, UK: Cambridge University Press, 2002).

69 Recall that in contemporary debate in political theory, it is the fact that the self exists in and is in some sense defined by relational webs that generates problems for liberal theory, as the self becomes, in this picture, embedded within communities of belief and value. Any specific person finds herself living within a community defined, to a large extent, by the values this community expresses or manifests. Society, in turn, is composed of a large array of such value-defined communities. How is liberal theory – *itself* seemingly the expression of a set of values, *itself* seemingly put to use to structure a "community" (of communities) – to fit within this picture of value pluralism?

We can break this down into digestible bits. First, there is the core notion in value pluralism that values are *incommensurable* – that is, that the multifarious values that can order people's lives

> cannot be compared. Hence ... conflict amongst ultimate values cannot be resolved by an appeal to the relative worth of each value or by attempts to find an overarching value. Values cannot be reduced to "one value that serves as a common denominator to all the valuable ways of life."[70]

Second, there are the ways imagined that incommensurable values complicate how we think about how lives are lived. As we will see shortly, to dig more deeply into critical challenges to the liberal concept of the person it will help to have in mind a clear sense about how liberalism imagines incommensurable values manifest in the human-social world. The liberal mode of thinking of the world sees this happening in the world we inhabit at three levels.

First, at the level of persons, liberal theory presents a picture of *individuals* being faced with (that is, between themselves they can believe in and can hold) incommensurable values. Contemporary liberal thought does not see this at all as a challenge to the theory, but rather as a precondition for meaningful choice. The challenge we all confront (as moral beings) is to work out how to live our lives in the face of the open equally valid *ways of being* generated through free choice in values and sets of values.

Second, at a *first level of collective existence* (as individuals form immediate communities, along, for example, ethnic or religious lines) pluralism emerges in a different form in that lives of individuals may be (or, in some theorists' minds, must be) coordinated, where stability is often understood to rest on the establishment of a relatively fixed, accepted set of traditions. The problem here is that ways of living set out in traditional forms may stifle the flourishing of individuals, by making it unnecessarily difficult for individuals to experiment, or by preventing or impeding ways of living from being followed when they conflict with values that underscore traditional ways that the collective has chosen.

Third, at a *higher level of collective existence*, we find multiple collectives co-existing in one society (that is, for example, a number of ethnic or religious communities), each with their own ways of living as collectives set out in sets of values relatively fixed as traditional ways. Here we find pluralism arising as a *prime problem* addressed by contemporary liberal theorists, as here liberal theorists find any number of subsystems struggling to co-exist, what is described by some as states of multi-ethnicity or multi-nationalism, but that some argue also encompasses subgroups defined by gender, sexual identity, and other

70 Baumeister, *supra* note 41 at 178 citing Joseph Raz, "Multiculturalism: A Liberal Perspective" (1994) 41 Dissent 67 at 72.

identifiers.[71] Again, we find a common understanding that stability requires coordination, though here this must be achieved not just between individuals but between groups, and between groups and individuals.

Let me interject a point that will be pressed more fully later, when the full argument is developed. This third level is presented as if it encompassed, and fully and meaningfully described, the world we are exploring in this text. *From an Indigenous perspective*, however, *this is the contested point*, not just of fact (that we do not all inhabit a *common* social setting where conflict between groups and individuals holding different sets of values needs to be managed), but on the level of the *construction of social reality*. We need to press on to see this (and to finish our look into what we can reasonably expect Supreme Court judges are thinking as they build up the law on Aboriginal rights).[72]

We noted that Kymlicka responds to the communitarian challenge to the liberal notion of the primacy of the person by dividing concepts of the self into "metaphysical" and "normative" camps. Communitarian (and related) critiques are then argued to really be about the metaphysical self (said to be socially determined, not atomistic), and argued to leave untouched the normative concept of the self that liberal theory rests upon. But is there a deeper "critical" challenge to liberal theory buried in these questions about the nature of the self?

---

71 This, of course, is a contentious matter – many (especially those who look into these matters on the leading edge of science) distinguish between communities built around chosen sets of values and those that form around attributes born into.

72 There are two forms of value pluralism with which one could engage, forms that place "values" in different realms. On the one hand, some theorists make much of the fact that people *believe* in all sorts of values, and that people believe these values (that people can believe in) are incommensurable, while, on the other hand, other theorists hold that multiple incommensurable values *exist* (as pieces of the moral fabric of the universe). Both states of the world arguably lead to seemingly irresolvable conflict between individuals, between groups, and between individuals and groups.

In the text that follows I focus analysis on a world in which the fact people *hold* sets of *beliefs* about values and about their incommensurability is said to be an important feature of the social world, one that political (and legal) institutions must be built around. I focus on this strand not simply because it claims to reflect the state of the natural world (in which humans hold disparate sets of beliefs), but because it is the far weaker claim, more easily defended. Most importantly, it functions as a commonality between these two camps, whether or not values have the odd metaphysical existence some liberals attest to, what makes the act of society-building challenging (within the liberal mindset) is the fact that people *believe* that values have this nature. In the debate between liberal theorists who attempt to build liberal thought to mesh with the fact people hold different beliefs, and those who argue the key feature to be accommodated, is that different incommensurable sets of values actually exist, this then is the commonality, as those who struggle to accommodate a feature of the moral universe rest part of the problem on this indisputable fact, that different people *believe in* different values that structure their lives. That is, it is an outcome of their being existing incommensurable values, and the fact of personal choice, that different sets of beliefs in values exist.

With its focus principally on the second level of collective existence, liberalism must think through how the liberal project (of the construction of social institutions) unfolds. Two paths stretch ahead. On the one hand, liberalism can posit liberal values as *privileged* within this world of sets of incommensurable (sets of) values. That is, liberal theorists can hold that while the multi-ethnic (second level) situation poses particular challenges in societal structuring and governance, *one* set of *liberal* values specifies a form of life that *should* underscore both how a multi-ethnic society must be properly structured and how individuals must be understood and responded to. This is the "perfectionist" strand of liberal theory according to Crowder's terminology.[73]

Alternatively, liberalism can acknowledge that the multi-ethnic world of sets of incommensurable values encompasses *any and all* possible chosen sets of values, *including* those that might define a liberal set. That is, this *neutralist* position accepts that a liberal set of values is simply one possible (non-privileged) set of values amongst many. The liberal project, in such a view, is not morally demanded, but rather argued to be either (or more likely, both) simply that project already underway, or pragmatically the preferable project.

We can reintroduce Galston's retelling of the long-view history of the development of liberal thought, as it overlies well on this divide (when kept suitably general). A focus on *diversity*, arising from a history of concern with interference with religious ways of life by state authorities, throws a sceptical and wary cast on claims to the privileged status of liberal values, as this status can too easily motivate efforts to police the inner workings of subgroups.[74] "Autonomy" is the label for the contemporary manifestation of the second historical thread, tracking out of the Enlightenment, which posits and defends a specific theory of the normative, free self. This theory in hand, liberalism would indeed police the inner workings of ethnic and religious groups that make up larger society, as concern with the autonomy of individuals that make up *all* groups will – in some situations – supersede the operation of sets of values that inform the lives of subgroups.

Which of these ways of thinking of value pluralism is ascendant will have an effect on how liberty and equality act as architectural principles in the liberal building project. We live in a time and a place (Canada in the first decades of the twenty-first century) where common belief in the inherent value of autonomy tends to dictate how society is built and maintained. Just as Berlin's concerns with "positive liberty" have been essentially washed over since the mid-stages of the last century, autonomy, positive liberty's very close cousin, has come to

73 Crowder, *supra* note 18.

74 Galston, *Liberal Pluralism*, *supra* note 41 at 24–6. See also Baumeister, *supra* note 41.

sit as the underpinning of the dominant understanding of the nature of liberal thought in much of the Western world.[75] We see the Supreme Court of Canada, for example, interpret the *Charter* in terms of rights of citizens, not just to be free of unjustifiable state activity, but to be free to lead dignified, autonomous lives (within whatever ethnic sub-setting they happen to find themselves living).[76]

However, tension still marks this area of liberal theory, as debate continues about the best way to manage forms of value pluralism manifest in multi-ethnic societies. As debate continues, the ground on which the diversity side rests has shifted, as the diversity-neutralist link has come to be recast in contemporary Canada. Efforts to foster and maintain diversity have shifted from historical concern with "the political consequences of religious differences in the wake of divisions within Christendom"[77] (what Galston identifies as the Post-Reformation roots of liberal diversity) to focus on the tension between the possible imposition of state-sanctioned forms of living and ways of living that express deep attachments to *group-identities* (which account largely for how individuals think of themselves).[78] The neutralist strand now tends to challenge the perfectionist approach on the basis that perfectionists present ways of thinking of the self and the selves' relationships to others and to the state that threaten

---

75 The situation of the United States has always been hard to parse, and the current chaotic situation in that "liberal democracy" makes any attempt to make sense seems more akin to reading tea leaves.

76 In *Blencoe v British Columbia (Human Rights Commission)*, 2000 SCC 44, the Supreme Court held at para 49:

> The liberty interest protected by s. 7 of the *Charter* is no longer restricted to mere freedom from physical restraint. Members of this Court have found that "liberty" is engaged where state compulsions or prohibitions affect important and fundamental life choices. This applies for example where persons are compelled to appear at a particular time and place for fingerprinting (*Beare*, [1988] 2 S.C.R. 387); to produce documents or testify (*Thomson Newspapers Ltd. v. Canada (Director of Investigation and Research, Restrictive Trade Practices Commission)*, [1990] 1 S.C.R. 425); and not to loiter in particular areas (*R. v. Heywood*, [1994] 3 S.C.R. 761). In our free and democratic society, individuals are entitled to make decisions of fundamental importance free from state interference. In *B. (R.) v. Children's Aid Society of Metropolitan Toronto*, [1995] 1 S.C.R. 315, at para. 80, La Forest J., with whom L'Heureux Dubé, Gonthier and McLachlin JJ. agreed, emphasized that the liberty interest protected by s. 7 must be interpreted broadly and in accordance with the principles and values underlying the *Charter* as a whole and that it protects an individual's personal autonomy:
>
> [L]iberty does not mean mere freedom from physical restraint. In a free and democratic society, the individual must be left room for personal autonomy to live his or her own life and to make decisions that are of fundamental personal importance.

77 Galston, *Liberal Pluralism*, *supra* note 41 at 24–5.

78 See e.g. Baumeister, *supra* note 41 at 136–47 (where she explores Charles Taylor's reflections on a "politics of recognition") and part IV ("Value Pluralism and the 'Politics of Difference,'" 171–95) where she looks at how a post-Reformation thread of liberalism locates value in diversity itself. Caroline Dick examines the group-identity grounding of both Taylor's and Kymlicka's positions. See Caroline Dick, "'Culture and the Courts' Revisited: Group-Rights Scholarship and the Evolution of S. 35(1)" (2009) 42:4 Can J Pol Sci 957 at 962–7.

to subvert freely chosen ways of associational living, undermining forms of living that construct and define core aspects of the *identity* of individuals.[79]

We find ourselves back, then, to the business of challenging the liberal theory of the self, what I earlier labelled deep criticism, though now we can see how adept liberal theorists can be in subverting even such seemingly deep challenges. The difficulty was that something about the constitutive make-up of humans is lost when the starting point is that of the individuated, isolated free and equal person, the argument being that normative (liberal) theories built on this impoverished concept of the person must be viewed with scepticism. It might seem that the emergence of a new strong defence of diversity that grounds itself in *group forms of living*, tying these to matters of *identity*, could itself *radically* challenge how liberal democracies think of the place of diverse peoples within one liberal state, but of course what we actually witness in this regard is an instance of the ability of liberal theory to tame deep, critical challenges. The moral of this account for our purposes, however, is that it is important, as always, not to be become lost *within* liberal theory.

We noted in this retelling of the strands of evolution of liberal thought over the last few decades a tale that shows the remarkable ability of liberal thought to tame challenges, principally through control over forms of discourse employed. While the critical challenge is to what seemed to be the very underpinning of the liberal world view – the concept of the person as individuated, and as free and equal – we can see now that a strand within liberal theory has responded by essentially encompassing this challenge, pulling it into the liberal domain. The neutralist essentially agrees with the *deep* communitarian challenge (agreeing that it is not just a mistake to think the metaphysical self is atomistic, but that it is mistaken to think the normative self as well must be conceived of in an individuated sense), but does so by (a) holding that there is *no* set right way of living, but then still (b) holding to the sense in the larger liberal project.

In this form yet again we come upon tension *within* liberal theory that rests upon distinct, background commonalities, here quite visible if we think of the primacy of the person, specifically in the role this notion plays in *theorizing* about self-state relations (what I earlier labelled the second instance of the appearance of the concept of the person in liberal thought). As important as the concept of the person as free and equal is to the inner workings of liberal theory, the second instance of the concept (of the being theorizing about self-society relations and

79 Galston puts this in the form of a paradox that can emerge too easily in modern liberal democracies. See Galston, *Liberal Pluralism*, *supra* note 41 at 20:

> If we insist that each civil association mirror the principles of the overarching political community, then meaningful differences among associations all but disappear; constitutional uniformity crushes social pluralism. If ... our moral world contains plural and conflicting values, then the overzealous enforcement of general public principles runs the risk of interfering with morally legitimate individual and associational practices.

about how to properly build societal structures) is just as important. Here we see it backgrounding the neutralist position (which is willing to weaken the liberal attachment to the normative concept of the person as free and equal).

We earlier noted these two "concepts of the person" within Rawls's development of his variant of liberal theory. While focus on the first instance of the use of this concept pulls us *inside* liberal theory, when attention shifts to the second instance – that of the person as rational, reasoning, and isolated – we can pull back and clearly see the umbrella of liberal theory as a whole. When we focus on the first instance, the primacy of the person in the "nut and bolts" of the construction of social institutions is clear, but equally clear, when we shift attention to the second instance, is how the concept of the individuated, reasoning being is primary in the construction of *theories* of political morality and political philosophy.

Do we thereby cede the battleground of theorizing about self-society relations and about ways of building society and social institutions if we unreflectively slip into this manner of conceiving of the person engaged in theorizing about such matters? An advantage in keeping our focus on the second instance of a concept of the person is that this opens the door to wonderment at the nature of this concept and of the role it then plays in theorizing: is the concept a social construct, implying that so too are resulting theories of political morality and political philosophy? If so, then while how Supreme Court judges think through how to accommodate group differences will be affected by the respective weights they attribute to the value of diversity or the value of autonomy, all this resides within a *constructed world view* that *predetermines* a liberal approach to theorizing the entire business of social construction.

If we keep attention focused on both ways in which the concept of the individuated person functions within liberal thought, we can see that (a) within liberal theory the normative view of the person as free and equal can be weakened (as variants of liberal thought place greater weight on the need to tolerate ways of living), but also (b) still the larger project is upheld (of building societal structures using liberal architectural principles). The whole edifice of liberal thought may strike the reader as shaky (and perhaps internally inconsistent or even contradictory), but the intent in this work is not to articulate or defend a reasonable, global theory of liberalism. The primary goal has been to arrive at a place from which we can say something sensible about what we can expect Supreme Court judges in the early twenty-first century likely think as they go about constructing jurisprudence concerning Aboriginal rights.

Liberal Thought in the Construction of Jurisprudence on Aboriginal Rights

Though we looked at numerous divergences and debates beneath the larger liberal umbrella, we largely avoided entanglement in theoretical quagmires (as our focus was not on attempting to detail a settled, complete theoretical model) and we are not in the business of making normative assessments. We developed our picture by detailing commonalities underlying debates and fissures, and by suggesting how thought may waver between or amongst different responses to ongoing tensions.

We generally explored the structure of liberal thought by foregrounding the concept of the person – this was a way to get into discussing both broad parameters of the theory and finer details within, serving as it does (I argued) as a central unifying element, underlying different threads within the broad theory. We kept our eyes on two instances of the general concept: as a concept held by members of liberal democratic societies (that of the free and equal person), and as a concept playing a key role in how liberal theory itself is developed and articulated (as that imagined-being engaged in thinking through how she intersects with others and how society should be structured to best facilitate productive interactions, in light of her representative interests in such things as human flourishing, diversity, and general stability in society).

This double use played a key role in making sense of how liberal theory has worked over the last few decades to manage plurality and identity. We saw that concern in a liberal democracy such as Canada is no longer fundamentally with societal stability in the face of varied and potentially conflicting religious communities (though this remains *a* concern), but with matters of group identity. Increasingly, liberal thought has been taking seriously the notion that subgroups in society have a measure of moral authority, now seen due to the matter being essentially about sources of identity, not just metaphysically, but normatively. As some liberal theorists pull back from simple blanket assertions of universal truth about "right" ways of living based on sets of liberal values, the state seemingly vacillates between thinking it can and should ensure all individuals are treated as free and equal (no matter their particular embeddedness in sub-societies) and an ever-emerging and strengthening sense that it enjoys only a weak (theoretical) authority for dictating how individual lives are lived within any subgroup.

With this background tension at play, the basic problem, as defined and described by liberal theory, is that the state understands that it is in charge of societal institutions at the state or national level, *and* of working out how all components of society are treated as between themselves, and in relation to the power and authority of the central state. In the context of its self-understanding (that it is *properly* positioned to structure society), as the modern liberal state is pulled back and forth between two positions – liberal values as privileged versus diversity as a strong countervailing value in itself – it accedes to the notion that it should not simply assert that liberal ways of life *must* guide existence *within* subgroups.

As we earlier noted, one way for the state to respond is to attempt to restrict allegiance to the liberal "way of life" to larger society-wide structures, which is to say that liberal values should go only to the project of constructing the larger superstructural elements of society, and should not be imposed upon subgroups who play a role in structuring the lives of their members, a position that can be coupled with the neutralist stance through arguments grounded more in pragmaticism. This accepts the notion that local, potentially illiberal, normative orders might require protection from state interference (meaning, then, that a liberal society should *tolerate* local ways of living). This matter becomes very challenging, however, once it goes so far as to call on the state to struggle with what to do once it becomes clear some such local order is seriously restricting the liberty and equality interests of its members.[80]

This leaves a difficult threading-the-needle exercise to the state. In Canada, for example, as questions of group identity and value in diversity rise in currency, a countervailing movement pulls towards the perfectionist end of the liberal spectrum. As we noted earlier, we see matters of autonomy taken increasingly seriously in recent decades, indicating a movement towards taking positive liberty very seriously (and a parallel movement towards taking substantive equality very seriously). Naturally enough (*within liberal theory*) this tension manifests in the state weighing and balancing interests within and between subgroups (interests that ultimately *it* defines and assigns weights to).

We need to say more about this strategy, as it lies at the heart of what we can expect Supreme Court judges think as they go about building the jurisprudence tied to Aboriginal rights. We should begin by once again noting that nothing in this analysis requires either that we agree or disagree with what we uncover and articulate, or that we are called upon to attempt to adjudicate on the merits of positions drawn.

The general goal for the liberal state is simple to describe – to *manage* the problem by mediating the tension that arises when concerns with negative liberty and concerns for autonomy are both taken seriously. In the contemporary liberal state, value is accorded diversity itself – either through holding that culture and community are important sites within which *options for living are developed* and held out to individuals, a fact of the world *providing for meaningful choice* (the Kymlicka model), or through holding that subcultures *express choices made* (so to interfere with them is to go against a basic principle of liberalism). A problem then emerges, given the high esteem the ideal of autonomy is also accorded.

Turning to this task, the modern liberal state has forces, tools, and techniques to deploy: first, of course, is how it understands the setting, as it sees itself *authoritatively* applying its legal and political system to *all* who live within the geographic bounds of the nation state; second, it enjoys complete control over societal resources (no element within society is understood to enjoy either an inherent right to material resources [either at a base level, or generated as a result of interaction between members of society] or an absolute right to control resources to which it has obtained any form of ownership); and finally, it works

80 Dick presents this as a key shortcoming in the group-identity models developed by both Taylor and Kymlicka. See Dick, *supra* note 78 at 964, 966–7.

according to the larger vision of the liberal project, working with architectural principles that inform and guide that project.

The first two points setting the stage, so to speak, the liberal state understands that the look and function of the state at all levels is not completely rigid. Highest, superstructural levels are relatively fixed, as they are built in close accord with the fundamental liberal vision, provided by theorizing, which has at its core the individuated, reasoning being and which places value in ideals tied to the concept of the "free and equal person."[81] But below that the state must mediate tensions, and in doing so it will determine how to *think* of problems it faces, how to generate workable solutions, and how to implement them.

That is to say, the state will acknowledge the need to value diversity in light of a powerful contemporary concern with individual autonomy/positive liberty. This acknowledgment in hand, it gets to work, determining what all this means and how these meanings can be implemented in light of all relevant concerns. The starting point is that the larger project is clearly and unambiguously informed by liberal values and principles: the state is tasked with building societal structures to further liberty and equality for all. It acts within these institutions and structures to determine how societal resources are distributed. As was noted when discussing "equality," it does so in the modern Canadian context by acting to ensure substantial equality in access to resources and opportunities.

Consider, as an example of how it can mediate the tension it faces, the question of allocating resources for the education of the young. In recent decades, increasingly the pendulum has swung towards the position that groups should have not just equitable access to resources for educating their young, but to equitable degrees of decision-making authority over how these resources are to be deployed. But while the state increasingly demonstrates this approach to equality, it enjoys absolute control over the distribution of societal resources, and it also has in mind the value increasingly placed in autonomy. It will understandably be leery of a particular group's interest in educating its young (with much of the group's resources for doing so coming from the societal pool) if signals are that this group will be attempting to educate in ways that look coercive or manipulative. With control over all societal resources, the state can (within its sense of what is legitimate within a liberal democracy) withhold resources for any questionable educational enterprise.

Finally, we now turn to the analysis at hand. With this grasp of key elements of liberal thought we can expect jurists to have in mind, we are equipped to begin an exploration into the extent to which liberal thought might make

81 Even the neutralist places value in this concept of the person when envisioning how the state constructs societal structures. The difference with the perfectionist lies in the extent to which this vision of the person percolates down into considerations about how lower-level structures of society should be managed (or not) by the state.

sense of Aboriginal rights. To facilitate this discussion I introduce at various points along the way a fairly complex hypothetical situation, one that mirrors situations that have arisen with some frequency, looking at how a hypothetical Aboriginal polity, asserting a right to trade fish on an open market (on a commercial scale),[82] might work its way through the labyrinthine law of the state. Such an Aboriginal community, we further imagine, claims behind this right a capacity to regulate or manage activities in relation to the harvesting and use of fishery resources taken from its traditional territories. We can follow the asserted claim as it works its way through processes that structure the law around Aboriginal rights, while working out how this law reflects liberal principles.[83] Along the way we will reintroduce key puzzles articulated in our earlier examination of the jurisprudence.

This look into liberal doctrine proceeds in two stages. In the next chapter, our sketch of liberal thought in hand, we turn to an examination of roughly half the jurisprudence concerning Aboriginal rights, looking at the possibility that a specific form of liberal theory can make sense of tests for the existence, definition, and (possible) extinguishment of Aboriginal rights. As we move into chapter 8, analysis deepens, as we examine interactions between Crown power and Aboriginal rights, essentially looking at the place of Aboriginal rights in

82 A number of the high-profile cases in Aboriginal law over the last few decades involved similar claims: (a) The Musqueam argued in *R v Sparrow*, [1990] 1 SCR 1075, 70 DLR (4th) 385, for a right to fish, a right they conceived of (on this broad level) as encompassing rights to fish as they determined, to an extent they determined; (b) the Heiltsuk, in *Gladstone*, successfully argued for a right to trade herring spawn on kelp on a commercial scale (and by implication, given that they argued for a right that would not be limited by state regulation, a right to decide themselves the extent to which herring spawn on kelp was harvested); and (c) the Mi'kmaq, in *R v Marshall*, [1999] 3 SCR 456, 177 DLR (4th) 513, argued their right to trade eel included a right to regulate the harvesting of eel (and other produce of the sea).

Both the Lax Kw'alaams and Ahousaht First Nations attempted in the early stages of the twenty-first century to show rights not just to take life from the sea but to trade in produce thereby obtained. Only the Ahousaht were successful. See *Lax Kw'alaams Indian Band v Canada (AG)*, 2011 SCC 56; *Ahousaht Indian Band v Canada (AG)*, 2011 BCCA 237, leave to appeal to SCC refused, 34387 (29 March 2012). The "win" by the Ahousaht led, however, to another stretch in court, with a trial decision ostensibly on the issue of justification coming out only in 2018. See *Ahousaht Indian Band and Nation v Canada (AG)*, 2018 BCSC 633. The appeal of this decision to the British Columbia Court of Appeal is underway as of the completion of this text. The many complex matters captured in this latest court battle will likely be resolved only at the Supreme Court sometime in the 2020s.

83 In *Sparrow*, *supra* note 82, *Marshall*, *supra* note 82, and *Gladstone*, *supra* note 82, we find different sorts of cases involving different sorts of claims, with an interesting thread weaving them together – in each case the Indigenous community asserted that the activity in question (running afoul of Canadian law) could be legitimately regulated through its own legal structures and processes. For the most part, this side of the respective narratives was ignored in the Canadian court setting.

the Canadian landscape. There the form of liberal thought deemed most reasonable shifts somewhat (necessitated in order to make sense of how Aboriginal rights are placed in this landscape). In the context of the larger project of making sense of Aboriginal rights, we turn in this latter chapter to focus more directly on the possibility that liberal thought is *itself* a construct, asking why a legal system based on this construct would be imposed upon the lives and lands of Indigenous peoples. As we ponder what this might mean in relation to the larger project, we begin the transition to an analysis of the ability of elements of critical (postcolonial) theory to generate a *better* explanation for the nature of these rights.

7 Characterizing and Defining "Existing" Aboriginal Rights

In chapter 2, in our overview of Aboriginal law, we noted Aboriginal rights of an Aboriginal people are defined as those communally held rights constituting practices, traditions, and customs "integral to the distinctive culture" of that people at the time of contact with Europeans.[1] An Aboriginal community claiming a right, for example, to trade fish from the sea on a commercial scale would need to argue, then, that they aim to exercise today a right that in some sense is contiguous with a similar practice, tradition, or custom integral to their distinctive culture at the time of contact with Europeans.

How, though, do such rights conceptually fit into the legal landscape in Canada, which is dominated by liberal thought and doctrine? To what extent do they exhibit that thought and doctrine? How well can we "make sense" of such rights from within a liberal framework?

We begin our exploration into these matters with a set of presumptions: first, that Aboriginal law is constructed with certain purposes in mind (where we examine the possibility the law makes sense if we suppose a core purpose is to build a social world according to principles of justice appropriate to liberal thought); second, that in constructing jurisprudence the Supreme Court has understood it must consider historical interactions between the Crown (and Canadian society) and Indigenous peoples; and, third, that in engaging in this project the Court has felt it must both (a) determine what aspects of this history cannot be addressed if liberal thought is to guide a forward-looking construction project, and (b) arrive at a conception of those harms suffered by Indigenous peoples that can be remedied through the recognition and affirmation of Aboriginal rights.

These presumptions all emerge from consideration of what we can reasonably expect judges of the Supreme Court to have in mind as they go about building jurisprudence concerning section 35. To these we add a further foundational

1 *R v Van der Peet*, [1996] 2 SCR 507, 137 DLR (4th) 289 at para 46 [*Van der Peet*].

presumption, that Indigenous forms of meaning-generation persist (grounded in Indigenous self-determination as peoples), a presumption that forces analysis to account for a key fact of the encounters of Crown authority and Indigenous authorities. That is, we need to keep our attention focused on the construction project that is the building of jurisprudence concerning Aboriginal rights, *bearing in mind* that Aboriginal law expresses a specific form and body of meaning, one generated by one dominant and dominating legal and political authority.

The general plan is to work through the jurisprudence we laid out in chapter 2, beginning with a look at how Canadian law generally conceives of the nature of Aboriginal rights, turning to some specific details in a middle section, and then broadening our investigations towards the end of this chapter with a look at how Indigenous legal and political authority fares in this construction project. The intersection of Crown power and Aboriginal rights as laid out in the jurisprudence is explored more directly in the next chapter.

Characterization: Rights in a Liberal World

It should be no surprise that legal actors in this context work with liberal doctrine, as we are here interested in a particular legal system – the domestic Canadian system – embedded in a nation state long self-identified as a liberal democracy. To see the extent to which legal actors in Canada are immersed in a liberal universe, one need look only to the *Constitution Act, 1982* (containing key elements speaking to the nature of Canada as a liberal democratic state), and recent jurisprudence (solidifying the judiciary's understanding of its role in furthering the infusion of liberal principles into Canadian law).[2] Indeed, arguably Canada's history as a political entity is the story of the emergence of a specific form of liberal order.[3]

---

2 A look into the voluminous jurisprudence on the *Canadian Charter of Rights and Freedoms*, Part I of the *Constitution Act, 1982*, being Schedule B to the *Canada Act (1982)* (UK), c 11 [*Charter*], reveals the depths to which liberal principles have become entrenched within Canadian jurisprudence. Indeed, the Supreme Court has advised that the jurisprudence on rights and freedoms in the *Charter* should be noted by lower courts when faced with challenging matters outside the (fairly narrow) ambit or reach of the *Charter* itself (for example, in the context of tort actions). On the actions of investigating police officers, see e.g. *Doe v Metropolitan Toronto (Municipality) Commissioners of Police*, (1998) 39 OR (3d) 487, 160 DLR (4th) 697 (Ont Sup Ct). On the defence of fair comment in defamation actions, see e.g. *WIC Radio Ltd v Simpson* 2008 SCC 40.

3 See, in this regard, McKay "The Liberal Order Framework: A Prospectus for a Reconnaissance of Canadian History" (2000) 81(4) *Canadian Historical Review* 616, and a text that sprang from the call to arms McKay presented in that article (that Canada's community of historians consider the project of describing the specific ways a liberal world was built to encompass Canadian society): Jean-François Constant and Michel Ducharme, eds, *Liberalism and Hegemony: Debating the Canadian Liberal Revolution* (Toronto: University of Toronto Press, 2009).

We can begin to imagine how Aboriginal rights might make sense within a liberal framework if we focus on an initial difficulty Lamer CJ saw himself addressing in *Van der Peet* as he began to work out what became Canadian law's approach to Aboriginal rights. Recall these rights were said to exist as a means to (a) recognize that Aboriginal peoples were "here first," in organized societies, and (b) reflect the need for reconciliation between Aboriginal peoples and Crown sovereignty (a notion alternatively expressed – or reframed? – as reconciliation between Aboriginal peoples and non-Aboriginal society in Canada).[4]

Given these reasons for the constitutionalization of these rights, they are then determined to exist so as to protect the "Aboriginality" of Aboriginal peoples, the ability of Aboriginal peoples to live according to those practices, traditions, and customs that defined them as the people they were at the time of contact with Europeans (and that may continue to define them in the contemporary world). The acknowledgment of a continued ability to maintain Aboriginality as it manifests in the contemporary world is linked to a line of continuity between practices, traditions, and customs in the present day and those of the distant past.

Lamer CJ's difficulty in working out how Aboriginal rights were going to be initially conceptualized is set out in a section immediately preceding the articulation of this "integral to the distinctive culture" test. Lamer CJ noted that Aboriginal rights must be conceptualized as "rights," but *somehow* reflect the fact they are held by a *segment* of the Canadian population.[5] As being only held by a portion of the population, he noted, it is not easy (indeed he claims it is not possible) to fit them into liberal Enlightenment notions of rights – the "rights of man," to use the language of the Enlightenment.

Today one would more commonly speak of "human rights." The "rights of man" was not such an odd expression, however, when rights-talk first began to enter discourse of the Enlightenment. While the narrowness of the expression appears on its face, it would also have been overly broad at that time, if we (mistakenly) think it was meant in the first few centuries of the modern era to be taken literally (that is, as if it included non-Western European males – in particular, any male not "propertied" and from select areas of Western Europe).[6]

---

4 Reconciliation in the first sense appears in *R v Van der Peet*, *supra* note 1 at para 43, while in *Gladstone*, a decision released the same day in 1996, the Court said at paragraph 73,

> Aboriginal rights are a necessary part of the reconciliation of aboriginal societies with the broader political community of which they are part; limits placed on those rights are, where the objectives furthered by those limits are of sufficient importance to the broader community as a whole, equally a necessary part of that reconciliation.

5 *Van der Peet*, *supra* note 1 at paras 19–20.

6 Oddities around the expression are at least twofold. On the one hand, the expression *fit* historical circumstances in that on its face it excluded women, that subsequently half of humanity had to struggle for recognition as "human." On the other hand, however, on its face it would

One might attempt to pass by use of a term simultaneously overly narrow and overly broad as an unfortunate quirk of history, holding that while women and many non-European ethnocultural/racial groups were able to *exercise* human rights only after long struggles, in terms of the "true" extension of the expression they always *possessed* these rights. Given that such rights are understood to *inhere* in the holders,[7] the matter of recognition (while politically and socially important) could be understood to be theoretically secondary. All humans, contemporary theory behind such rights maintains, have always enjoyed such rights (though many may not have enjoyed the full exercise of these rights in all times and all places).

To return to Aboriginal rights, the existence of "rights" *held* in fact by only a portion of the population might seem, then, to create some real theoretical difficulties.[8] This characterization of "Aboriginal" rights as protecting Aboriginality seems to require rights that attach to groups *defined* on ethnocultural lines, rights that seem to be truly "special" in that they would define, inter alia, spheres of permissible action *not enjoyed by others* in the general population. Our hypothetical Aboriginal community, for example, is posited claiming something distinct from anything akin to a ramp making a building equally accessible – they are claiming rights that include a right to trade produce of the

---

also seem to have included (amongst others) African, Indigenous, and Asian men, populations around the world excluded for the most part from the extension of the term up to the middle of the twentieth century.

As but one example of the narrowness of the extension of rights, the federal right to vote in Canada was extended to status Indians only in 1960, and while the Inuit were enfranchised in 1950, ballot boxes were commonly made available in the far North only in the early 1960s. Again, a key distinction preventing most non-European males from fitting under the protection of the "rights of man" would have been their pagan nature and not merely some sort of racist ideology or beliefs (though it would be difficult to imagine racist beliefs did not have a significant place in all this).

7 Readers should note the apparent transcendent notions at play here. To say such rights "inhere in the person" is to employ language that can be, in a materialist model of the universe, quite mysterious. What can it mean to say such a thing? Is this to posit a property of the human (possessed of all humans)? At what point in the development of a physical human does it emerge – at conception? past the second trimester? at birth? at some point around puberty? One might imagine (or some might argue) it is a property supervening on other properties (rationality perhaps?). As with similar nodes of confusion we encounter in our analysis of law, we sidestep debates about such matters, leaving it *possible* that such odd properties exist in the human realm, but avoiding all attempts to explain Aboriginal law that require recourse to such entities (unless the best available naturalist account requires we accept such things into the panoply of objects of the natural world).

8 The reader might initially wonder about this supposed difficulty, as she turns to such things as the rights of the disabled, or the rights of gays, lesbians, and the transgendered. Note, however, that the dominant understanding of such rights is as necessary instruments in the struggle for *equal* recognition, as equally human, demanding the same treatment (requiring differential action in circumstances where to be treated the same as everyone else requires "special" treatment – say, for example, with the provision of ramps to ensure that all public buildings are equally accessible).

sea that others (primarily non-Aboriginals) in the area would likely *not* enjoy (at least not without authorization from Canadian governments – and in that case one would better say they would not so much hold a "right" as a privilege).

Shortly after the remark about the difficult nature of Aboriginal rights, Lamer CJ developed the general picture we are now exploring.[9] The first puzzle we face, then, is where this characterization – of rights protecting Aboriginality – came from. What accounts for the *sort* of right he details? How does it respond to the challenge he saw himself facing, that such rights would seem to have to be "special"?

Aboriginal Rights and the Protection of Culture in a Liberal World

We approach these questions by stepping back from the jurisprudence as found, asking what we reasonably imagine a jurist, faced with the situation laid out in *Van der Peet*, could have decided upon as an approach. To do so we need to acknowledge that by this time the generic jurist works in a world determined, to a degree, by *Sparrow*. In that earlier decision the Court had established a general framework for dealing with contemporary claims of Aboriginal peoples, placing them into the Canadian legal landscape. From *Sparrow* we know the Court decided that Crown sovereignty is unquestioned (and seemingly unquestionable), a point we see reflected in what is set out as a purpose behind section 35, the reconciliation of pre-existing Indigenous societies with Crown sovereignty.

This framework in mind, could a generic jurist in Lamer CJ's position have had in mind a process of reconciliation that rests on a vision of two sets of legal and political authorities having to reconcile their systems of authority over one geographic space? This question firmly in mind, consider a second: could someone in Lamer CJ's position have had such a broad process of reconciliation in mind as she approached the problem *from the perspective of liberal thought*?

The answer to the first question is yes, and setting out what models could look like that might emerge from this approach would be instructive. We quickly see, however, that when we unpack particulars of the jurisprudence, it is clear Lamer CJ was not operating from a point of view from which he could see the situation before him in this underdetermined manner. The answer to the second question is no, and one aim in this chapter is to show how, from the perspective of liberal thought, broad forms of reconciliation are not conceivable. The second aim is to illustrate how reasonable it is to believe Lamer CJ approaches the situation from the perspective of liberal thought (visible in how well the construction of the jurisprudence from the perspective of liberal thought *explains* what we see), and together demonstrating these two matters helps show the actual mechanics of what we witness in development of Canadian law on Aboriginal rights – continued movement towards the removal of Indigenous self-determination.

9 *Van der Peet*, *supra* note 1 at paras 27–46.

Let us focus on where the characterization comes from. There are two possibilities, if we note the purpose for Aboriginal rights lying in the confluence of the existence of organized Aboriginal societies and the need for reconciliation, and if we begin from the initial supposition that the Court is working within a liberal universe.

On the one hand, we can imagine Lamer CJ is thinking in a way that aligns (roughly at least) with the sort of approach to multiculturalism advanced by Kymlicka and others.[10] That is, he might imagine Aboriginal rights fundamentally exist to protect Aboriginal culture, where Aboriginal culture has value not in itself, but in something like it providing essential conditions for human flourishing (on an individual level), through the provision of a context of meaningful choice.[11] Kymlicka argues,

> In deciding how to lead our lives, we do not start *de novo*, but rather we examine "definite ideals and forms of life that have been developed and tested by

---

10 Will Kymlicka, *Liberalism, Community and Culture* (Oxford: Oxford University Press, 1989).

11 Off to the side, note that the culture-as-context approach – especially in how it acknowledges the force of being "here first" – fits well with differentiation within the expanded liberal notion of cultural rights. Kymlicka, for example, notes that a collectives' basic claim to protection of its core cultural ways can be stronger or weaker, depending on whether a threat comes to the collective or the collective comes to a threat. Minority communities formed out of immigration to a liberal state should enjoy some cultural protection (so they can continue – within this liberal setting – to provide a context for choice for the members of the community), but this would have to entail weaker rights and weaker protections than one would expect with Indigenous communities in similar settings. The immigrant body *came to* the threat (in a sense we can say they *chose* to locate themselves in this setting), while Indigenous populations are always "here first," with threats to their cultural well-being the product of colonial policies and events.

See e.g. Will Kymlicka, *Multicultural Citizenship: A Liberal Theory of Minority Rights* (Oxford: Oxford University Press, 1995) at 95–6, 100. In the earlier pages, Kymlicka discusses claims immigrant groups might have to *become* "national minorities" where "'nation' means a historical community, more or less institutionally complete, occupying a given territory or homeland, sharing a distinct language and culture," claims he argues a modern liberal state would not be unjust to deny, as "[a]fter all, most immigrants ... choose to leave their own culture": *ibid* at 95. On the latter page, on the other hand, he discusses national minorities (a category within which he locates most Indigenous communities in Canada), and the notion that it could be expected that they integrate into the dominant system, and holds that "the decision about whether to integrate must be up to the members of the minority themselves." While Kymlicka never makes clear the basis for this distinction, the contrast with immigrants – who can be understood to have chosen to have left behind their rooted cultures – must be central to this matter.

This suggests the possibility – within this way of thinking – of positing weaker rights for the Metis. I can imagine a liberal theorist – or jurist – seeing Metis forming themselves in a situation they know is dominated by, or soon to be dominated by, certain emerging Enlightenment values and principles.

> innumerable individuals, sometimes for generations."[12] The decision about how to lead our lives must ultimately be ours alone, but this decision is always a matter of selecting what we believe to be most valuable from the options available, selecting from a context of choice that provides us with different ways of life.[13]

The second possibility is that the Court might be responding to *harms* suffered by Aboriginal communities in the long history of relations with British and Canadian Crowns. As we look more carefully into this second path we see, though, that it intertwines with the first.

Down this second path we should note that what constitutes "harms" may depend upon perspective. That is, in certain situations differently placed individuals may come to very different conclusions about the impacts of certain actions. For example, imagine a situation in which one individual, from a people who think of ownership of objects entailing absolute control, has possession of a well-maintained, efficient axe, while another individual, from a society where immediate need trumps any ownership claim, takes the axe for use in making traps at a time when gathering food for his family is a pressing need. The first sees theft and demands some form of remedial justice, while the second sees in the circumstances an innocent and blameless act of necessary borrowing. In the context we are exploring, where Canadian courts are empowered to reflect on generations of Crown-Indigenous interactions, the possibility that sociocultural embeddedness accounts for perceptions of "harms" suffered needs to be borne in mind.

We ask, then, about the specific notion of "harm" operating in this context. It is arguable that for Lamer CJ to locate harms in the colonial narrative they must be translatable into damage inflicted upon the ability of Aboriginal individuals to enjoy sociocultural worlds constructed and maintained by their peoples (so that we can arrive at the sorts of rights defined in the rest of the judgment). What would these harms then be? Seeing the world from a liberal perspective, he would understand *harms befalling individuals, beings to be treated as free and equal.* Recall that at the ground floor of the liberal system of thought is the primacy of the person.

These individuals would have sociocultural structures they had *chosen* to build and live within. These structures were damaged through colonial law and policy, and (a) a corrective form of justice would require a response (looking back at this history), while (b) it would be necessary to ensure that future *choices made* would be protected (so, to the extent "historic" Aboriginal sociocultural practices continue, they should be accorded a measure of protection).[14]

---

12 Rawls, *A Theory of Justice*, at 563–4.

13 Liberalism, Community and Culture, supra note 10 at 164.

14 A third possibility is that some combination of these two concerns animated Lamer CJ's reasoning in this situation, though this does not require separate analysis, both because we can see their individual reach and because when we looked more deeply into the second sort

We find, then, two ways Lamer CJ might have thought of the problem the Court faced, where these two intertwine to construct an understanding of how jurists of a liberal democracy might respond to the need to recognize and affirm rights that come out of a historic interaction. This understanding (that "Aboriginality" should inform the generation of jurisprudence concerning Aboriginal rights) can itself be seen connected to two ways of thinking of the value of what must be protected: culture as context for choice or culture as choice expressed.

Differences between these two ways of thinking of value located in culture do not require our extensive examination, as both ground Aboriginal rights in the notion of cultural protection, where the focus of attention is on discrete practices emanating from a way of life shared by a community. This is the general path Lamer CJ laid out.[15]

That said, one can find affinities between the culture-as-context approach and a thread of liberalism that helps account for its gradual emergence through generations of the Enlightenment and that matured into a prominent branch of reasoning in support of a specific understanding of the link between modern liberal thought and multiculturalism. Recall that historians of ideas note that one animating force accounting for the rise of classical liberalism was its ability – in managing collectives within one liberal society – to generate peace and stability amongst conflicting religious sects.[16] Toleration was promoted as a virtue of a specific form of liberalism, one that welcomed diversity of point of views within one polity. As the twentieth century progressed, this view shifted, the focus being no longer merely upon managing diverse collective points of view but acknowledging that diverse points of view (expressive of the holding of incommensurable sets of values) is a *fact* of our larger social world that we need to accommodate (with liberalism being the best way we know to structure non-uniform societies).

---

of reason for finding value in Aboriginal cultures we noted its close alignment with the first. Under the first umbrella, we imagine Aboriginal culture being accorded a form of derivative or secondary value, according to its role in making possible contexts of choice, while under the second umbrella these cultures likewise are accorded secondary or derivative value, though here due to their having been (and presumptively, continuing to be) expressive of choices made. In both cases the key is that the individual is understood to be the only possible locus of value, with the search being for some way to locate some form of derivative value in culture.

15 It seems safe to assume Lamer CJ understood the need to protect Aboriginal culture tied to the fact that various Aboriginal cultures across Canada reflect ways of living "chosen" (in a sense) by those living within them. To the extent a way of life can be said to express the exercise of both reason and will, the liberal actor will see (derivative) value in that way of life. The alternate approach – one seeing value in any specific Aboriginal culture due to its role in providing a context of both choice and meaning for the people living within it – developed and began to mature only through the last few decades of the twentieth century. It seems best not to imagine it had gained enough traction by 1996 to serve for judges of the Supreme Court as the underpinning for liberal views on culture.

16 See especially *supra* "Liberalism and Pluralism" in chapter 6, n 69.

It should be noted as well that either approach dissolves concerns about these rights being "special." While Aboriginal peoples are found to enjoy rights only they hold (each communal body enjoying its own set of culturally defined rights), cultural rights per se are understood as naturally extending out of Enlightenment concerns with individual choice and development. These are not then, strictly speaking, "special" rights. The same sorts of rights *could* be held by any similarly situated collective – specific circumstances dictate the emergence of the need for a particular collective to have recognized rights that strengthen their ability to maintain and promote their ways of living.

Weight Accorded Culture in a Liberal World

What can we reasonably expect a jurist of the late twentieth and early twenty-first centuries to think of the value of culture, supposing as we do this jurist sees the world through the normative lens of liberal thought? Whether value is located on the basis that culture provides an individual living within its bounds with meaningful choices on what to believe and value, or on the basis that a cultural practice is a manifestation of choices made by a social collective over generations (where the individual may find herself making choices aligned with those that express group identity), or on the basis that both individuals and groups can come to value ends without any reason at the foundations (so we simply find ways of living that reflect value-sets structuring lives), the liberal jurist can see value in protecting specific cultural practices through connections to inherent value located in the individual.

If we imagine Lamer CJ found value in Aboriginal culture, how much *weight* can we expect he finds in this derivative value? That is, how much weight could one expect that the culture of a sub-society would be accorded within a normative world defined by and built in accord with liberal ideals and principles?

We noted in our look into liberal thought that, on a general level, weight will be strongly affected by how a core contemporary tension plays out, between the position that liberal values should be privileged (so the expectation is that sub-societies will be moved into being liberal-minded, presumably through liberal means) and the position that diversity has its own value (so that toleration of sub-societies is heightened, even when their internal mechanisms might be illiberal).

Before we move directly into that discussion, let us pause to note how we can reasonably expect tactics designed to move sub-societies into the larger liberal fold emerge by further exploring this question of weight to be accorded Aboriginal culture, noting its ties to this tension at play in modern liberal democracies. Begin by noting that even if diversity is accorded significant value, it will never be able to absolutely overwhelm concern with the potential illiberality of sub-societies. The only thing of value, again, is the individual, narrowed to his ability to determine his own life plans, to re-evaluate these plans as he sees fit, and to be able to pursue said plans.

With this in mind, one defining feature of liberalism, we noted earlier, is its deep concern about the possibly negative influence of tradition on the lives of (inherently free) individuals (cleaving it from forms of traditionalism or conservatism).[17] This is particularly so when the autonomy branch of liberal theory is engaged, but as we just noted, those principally concerned with diversity also struggle with the potential impact of tradition construed broadly.[18] While liberalism is not necessarily or simply opposed to the content of traditional practices, it is based on a vision of the self that demands traditional practices never absolutely constrain the ability of the individual to critically reflect on his or her sense of values and principles, a liberal society being one in which the individual can always, in the least, "escape" a tradition he or she has decided to move away from.

This notion of escape becomes one of collective transformation when transferred from the level of the individual to that of communities or peoples. On the group or collective level, liberalism demands a cultural-societal structure making it possible for groups of individuals to critically reflect on their collective values (and related practices), such that they can transform themselves should they decide to do so. To the extent a culturally defined society lacks such mechanisms, it must be possible (a) for individuals to escape, and (b) that culturally defined society can wither away (i.e., minimal state support should underpin its existence). To the extent, then, that current traditional practices of a subcollective may seem to be "illiberal," larger societal structures within which this collective exists (its political and legal setting) will be expected to both push and pull on the group (on both individual and group levels, creating incentives and disincentives), such that forces gently drive or lead the group (or bleed off individuals) into forms and ways of living aligned with liberal principles.

Let us now slide back into the discussion focused more directly on the measure of value to be accorded Aboriginal culture. We can readily appreciate and imagine that several sources of concern (tied to programs of response) animate Canadian judicial officials. In the contemporary setting we witness the Supreme Court beginning with the fact of the pre-existence of Aboriginal peoples, living in organized societies before the arrival of Europeans. This fact demands a liberal response, given that it represents a reality within which one would have to presume that, as a result of long histories within which

17 It should be noted, again, that avoiding "metaphysical" issues around freedom, Rawls notes we need focus only on how we think of the person when living within a liberal democracy. It is important, though, to wonder at how this conception held by those living with a liberal democracy is imposed upon – or meant to insinuate itself into – the lives of Indigenous peoples.

18 The liberal theorist falling closer to the diversity end of the spectrum of liberal thought will see prioritizing liberal values as the political imposition of "tradition" on people (though here on collectives and subgroups). See Andrea Baumeister, *Liberalism and the "Politics of Difference"* (Edinburgh: Edinburgh University Press, 2000) at 173–95.

Indigenous peoples *chose* to adopt these forms of individual and collective existence, both individual Indigenous persons and Indigenous collectives were living in certain ways.

The first level of response would be marked by respect and tolerance – to the extent Aboriginal peoples are living as they have *chosen*, these choices (playing out into ways of living) must be respected, and so these ways of living tolerated.

A second level of response, however, attends concern about the nature of the ways of living (and the degree to which a liberal mind – especially when aligned with concerns over autonomy – can agree with the notion they are "chosen"). Scepticism abounds around "traditional" ways, around the possibility that individual freedom and equality are hindered or constrained within such potentially stifling environments. Given that the liberal cannot easily (or consistently) countenance *forcing* individuals or groups to change their ways, mechanisms must be put in place within these Indigenous societies that "gently" encourage movement towards more liberal environments.[19] This transpires, however, through the exercise of Crown power, enabled through the development of these pushing/pulling mechanisms. In the next chapter we examine mechanisms arguably designed to push and pull, mechanisms developed within the jurisprudence, the argument being that their development helps explain some apparent peculiarities built into, and puzzles emerging out of, the world of Aboriginal rights in Canada.

We are not yet looking at the interplay of Crown power and Indigenous claims, and so we here re-enter our examination into the general characterization of Aboriginal rights. We first need to dig more deeply into the Court's approach to characterization, and with that in hand then shift focus in the next section to thoughts on how this all plays out when we think of how the jurisprudence has been crafted so parameters are erected around the nature of Aboriginal rights, the means of their definition being such that thought is constrained (and possibilities concerning Indigenous self-determination removed from consideration).

In the Court's only focused attempt to address issues seemingly in need of attention with the *Van der Peet* test – in their 2006 decision in *Sappier & Gray* – we find strong support for the notion that the Court developed jurisprudence thinking of Aboriginal cultural practices deserving of protection as a result of their expressing choices made.[20] Here, however, we focus on the way that the discussion in *Sappier & Gray* shows how the characterization of Aboriginal rights functions to narrow discourse in ways that remove from sight ways of thinking of Indigenous meaning-generation.

---

19 This discussion, of course, is focused on contemporary situations. From the early 1800s up to the middle of the twentieth century efforts to "liberalize" Indigenous societies were not so "respectful." Canada's legacy of residential schools can be thought of in this light.

20 *R v Sappier; R v Gray*, 2006 SCC 54 [*Sappier & Gray*].

Sappier & Gray *and Ways of Living*

First, some background. A decade after *Van der Peet* the Court took the opportunity presented in a specific fact situation to respond to criticisms that had developed about the "integral to the distinctive culture" test. Separate but similar sets of circumstances led to three individuals (two Maliseet and one Mi'kmaq) running afoul of New Brunswick's *Crown Lands and Forests Act*. The individuals had harvested trees on their respective First Nations territories, in Sappier and Polchies's case to (primarily) build a home and some furniture and in Gray's case to (primarily) construct some furniture. In the years since *Van der Peet* some had argued its test incorporated a naive and arguably ill-informed understanding of "culture,"[21] that what must be meant by both "integralness" and "distinctiveness" had not been clearly and definitively set out, and that the notion of acceptable evolution (of the nature of a practice, from pre-contact to modern times) was muddled (and unduly limiting).

For our purposes we need to track how the Court dealt with what it might mean for an accepted right to have been found to be both "integral" and "distinctive" to a community's culture. The Court held in *Sappier & Gray* that for a practice, tradition, or custom to be "integral" to a culture, there need not be found some singular "core" identity of the community to which the impugned activity is intimately connected.[22] Further, and relatedly, the Court chided lower courts for being occasionally obsessed with asking whether a people would be "fundamentally altered" should an impugned activity be removed (which had been suggested in *Van der Peet* as one way to ascertain whether an activity is "integral" to a people).[23] Finally, in determining whether an activity marks what is "distinctive" about a people, the Court reiterated that it did not mean "distinctive" in the sense of "distinct."[24] A community need not show the claimed right was tied to a practice, tradition, or custom peculiar only to them – indeed, in these two instances the Court was willing to find the use of wood for domestic purposes was "traditional," and something "distinctive" to both the Maliseet and Mi'kmaq. The process of determining this, the Court clarified, requires a judicial investigation into the "way of life" of the claimant group, the focus ultimately being on those practices, traditions, and customs tied to the particular *Aboriginal* way of life of the claimant community (pre-contact).[25] In

21 See e.g. RL Barsh & James Youngblood (Sakej) Henderson, "The Supreme Court's *Van der Peet* Trilogy: Naïve Imperialism and Ropes of Sand" (1997) 42 McGill LJ 993.

22 *Sappier & Gray*, *supra* note 20 at paras 40–1.

23 *Ibid* at para 41.

24 *Ibid* at para 45.

25 This must be accomplished, however, without the judge actively engaging in a "commission of inquiry" into the ways of life of the Aboriginal community. The presentation of the larger picture of culture is to be made by the community, so the pleadings can show how the claimed right fits into this cultural mosaic. The Court dismissed the "commission of inquiry" model. See *Lax Kw'alaams Indian Band v Canada (AG)*, 2011 SCC 56 [*Lax Kw'alaams*].

this case, the Court found, there were specific "Aboriginal" ways of using wood (that could, though, evolve into "modern" forms of use).

What model of "culture" (and of a people) is visible in how the Supreme Court clarified matters around "integralness" and "distinctiveness"? We are called upon to imagine an Aboriginal community engaged in a variety of *activities* pre-contact, some of which courts today could identify as "Aboriginal." This occurs through a court's examination of (or at least taking into account) the entire way of life of the claimant group and finding aspects that are identifiably "Aboriginal" – that is, aspects of the way of life of this people, the court can say looking back, that mark these people as essentially who they were *as "Aboriginal,"* before they began interacting with Europeans. Some of those activities lie at the heart of what makes these people who they traditionally were (as *Aboriginal* people), and these the Court holds deserve protection. As the Court notes in *Sappier & Gray*, "The object is to provide cultural security and continuity for the particular aboriginal society. This object gives context to the analysis."[26]

Imagine the Maliseet and Mi'kmaq living in their traditional territories before the sixteenth century. Onto this scene arrive European explorers and fishers, followed in the next century by Europeans settlers (and the Crown). It is held *today* that cultural security and protection are valued, and so what counts as "Aboriginal" culture at that point of contact, pulled up into contemporary settings, is said to deserve protection. This protection happens *today*, in some cases centuries after the fact (while in those distant times, and in most cases for many generations afterward, these traditional activities were under relentless assault by colonial law and policy). What can the value *today* be in relation to? The Court made clear in *Sappier & Gray* it is not veering from the position taken in *Van der Peet* on the things to be protected – they are still those *activities* that count as practices, traditions, and customs, now carried out in a modern context. The value must be connected to the *continuance* of "Aboriginality," on the ability of Aboriginal communities today to maintain activities that are said today to have marked who they were as Aboriginal peoples long ago.

In a liberal universe this can be value located only in activities *chosen* by people, even if culture-as-context is the underlying theory (as, again, the only thing of inherent value is the reasoning/will-exerting individual). The presumption would be that Aboriginal communities chose ways of living in the past, ways that reflect how they valued their place in the world (as they conceived of the world). These choices were made manifest in activities carried out, and so those activities invite protection. To the extent today that descendants of this community *continue* to engage in these practices, traditions, and

26 *Sappier & Gray*, *supra* note 20 at 33.

customs, Canadian law is willing to presume these ways of living are *still* valued by these people – in the sense, again, that they are *chosen* by these peoples.[27]

We shift now to a more focused examination into how the Supreme Court locates value in the cultures of Aboriginal peoples, our gaze falling on how the *Van der Peet* test rests on an approach to generally characterizing what Aboriginal claims consist in, that narrows down *how one can think* of social worlds we might inhabit. This opens up our analysis, as we can come to see how meaning is being constructed by the high court through the placement of conceptual parameters, channelling thought down certain defined pathways.

Parameters around Possible Conceptions

Going back and forth between the majority judgment in *Van der Peet* and the dissenting judgments of L'Heureux-Dubé J and McLachlin J illuminates the nature of some of these broad parameters, particularly when we contrast the set of remarks from *Van der Peet* with what the Supreme Court said more recently in *Sappier & Gray*.[28] We begin by setting out in general terms concerns expressed by L'Heureux-Dubé J and McLachlin J and then examine how these concerns make sense in light of the embedded nature of this judicial discussion, in the world of liberal thought.

In her dissent in *Van der Peet*, L'Heureux-Dubé J argued that Aboriginal rights should be separated from their exercise, suggesting that the conceptualization the majority works with is too narrow (too focused on activities) to really count as picking out what we commonly take to be rights. Aboriginal rights, she argued, "should be viewed as protecting ... the 'distinctive culture' of which aboriginal activities are manifestations."[29]

This, she suggested (without explicitly arguing), would better align Aboriginal rights with those "liberal enlightenment" rights protected in the *Charter of Rights and Freedoms*, as the *significance* of the activities would be protected, not the activities themselves. So, for example, while freedom of expression does not protect a catalogue of forms of speech but rather preserves "the fundamental purposes for which one may express oneself,"[30] so too should Aboriginal rights be understood not to protect a catalogue of activities, but something more

27 Note that this discussion of how this liberal underpinning is visible within *Van der Peet* and animates *Sappier & Gray* is not directed to defending either the use of the classic approach over the "culture-as-context" approach or vice-versa. The question of which deeper approach might have been put to use is not particularly important in the context of the analysis underway in this chapter.

28 *Sappier & Gray*, *supra* note 20.

29 *Van der Peet*, *supra* note 1 at para 157.

30 *Ibid* at para 158.

general and abstract, something tied to "the fundamental purposes for which aboriginal rights were entrenched."[31]

L'Heureux-Dubé J went on to characterize this as a "social" form of describing Aboriginal rights, the approach taken by Lambert J, at the level of the British Columbia Court of Appeal.[32] This would require considering claims in direct light of the purpose for their constitutionalization, which she characterized as recognition of the "historic occupation and use of ancestral lands by natives."[33] With this light shining on the proceedings, Aboriginal rights would be those "practices, traditions and customs which form the core of the lives of native people and which provide them with a way and means of living as an organized society,"[34] those that are "sufficiently significant and fundamental to the culture and social organization of a particular group of aboriginal people."[35]

L'Heureux-Dubé J believed the approach taken by the majority was driven by their adherence to a notion of "distinct culture" that favours a reading of "distinct" requiring comparison – in this context, primarily with European culture. As we noted above, under the majority's conceptualization those elements of Aboriginal cultures now protected as "rights" have to be demonstrated to be "distinct from" European culture, the result being that the "rights" so understood are but bits and pieces of culture – what L'Heureux-Dubé J terms "manifestations" of Aboriginal culture (those bits and pieces clearly non-European).[36] While the Court's comments in *Sappier & Gray* were meant to reaffirm the point that "distinctive" is not intended to indicate "distinct," it remains true that as an Aboriginal community moves towards adapting to or adopting "European" culture, it leaves behind protection under section 35.

In her dissent in *Van der Peet*, McLachlin J found the approach adopted by the majority (a) too broad (in possible range, allowing "trivial" matters to be constitutionally protected), (b) indeterminate (in that what narrows down "integral" are concepts like "distinctiveness," "specificity," and "centrality," all subject to subjective interpretations), and (c) too categorical (in that determinations are "all or nothing").[37] She agreed with L'Heureux-Dubé J that this approach focuses too narrowly on activities, when the attention should (at least on the level of definition) be on underlying broad rights. When such broad rights are understood and established, the *exercise* of these rights in particular circumstances would define the nature of a contemporary dispute. She would ask of our hypothetical Aboriginal community about the nature of broad,

31 *Ibid* at para 159.
32 *Ibid* at para 161.
33 *Ibid* at para 159.
34 *Ibid* at para 161.
35 *Ibid* at para 160 [emphasis omitted].
36 *Ibid* at paras 150–7.
37 *Ibid* at paras 256–8.

general rights they might enjoy, and then consider any contemporary legal dispute to be about how these rights might be exercised today.

To arrive at appropriate characterizations of broad, general Aboriginal rights McLachlin J advocated an approach that built on what had already been recognized and protected in the common law prior to the constitutionalization of Aboriginal rights in 1982. This "incremental and pragmatic" approach would build on the common law's doctrine of continuity in law over settled territory. This doctrine, she argued, would recognize the continued existence of pre-existing laws and customs of Indigenous peoples after settlement by British colonists.[38] Aboriginal rights, then, would be grounded in these recognized pre-existing laws and customs of the Aboriginal peoples of Canada.

Following this approach, Canadian law would ask about the laws and customs of our hypothetical Aboriginal polity, with the thought in mind that whatever these laws and customs are within this community, they ground the rights of the community today. The exercise of their Aboriginal rights would, then, hinge on how these rights play out in a contemporary setting.

Culture and Significance: Protection of Ways of Living and the Place of Indigenous Understandings

A decade after *Van der Peet*, in its comments on the "integral to the distinctive culture" test in *Sappier & Gray*, the Supreme Court noted that at trial "the respondents led most of their evidence about the importance of wood in Maliseet and Mi'kmaq cultures and the many uses to which it was put."[39] This was not a good strategy. Aboriginal rights, the Court notes, "are not generally founded upon the importance of a particular resource."[40] Rather, the Court held, "the jurisprudence of this Court establishes the central importance of the *actual practice* in founding a claim for an aboriginal right."[41]

---

38 McLachlin J notes, "As might be expected of such a long history [of the interface of Europeans and the common law with Aboriginal peoples], the principles by which the interface has been governed have not always been consistently applied": *ibid* at para 263. This seems to me – and I imagine to most who are aware of 150 years of oppressive colonial law and policy leading up to the middle of the twentieth century – to be a remarkably rosy retelling of the history of Canadian law and policy towards Aboriginal peoples, as if there were in fact some principles at play. When the exception is not the exception, it is hard to find principles from which the "exceptions" are supposed to stray.

39 *Sappier & Gray*, *supra* note 20 at para 21.

40 The Court in *Sappier & Gray* was concerned (amongst other things) with the possibility that Aboriginal rights might be found to be in relation to objects, which would transform them into property rights. They are all said to be rights to *use* things (at most – some Aboriginal rights are not connected to things or objects at all, as with language rights). See *Sappier & Gray*, *supra* note 20 at para 21.

41 *Ibid* [emphasis added].

On the one hand, this starkly illustrates one of the puzzles emerging from the test for Aboriginal rights, that these rights do not carry with them any form of property.[42] While the respondents argued about the importance of wood to them as Indigenous people, the test is focused solely on activities, not things in the world. The suspicion of the Court was that the Mi'kmaq and Maliseet were of the mind that they had Aboriginal rights *to* wood and wood products, which the Court notes cannot be the case, given the nature of these rights.

On the other hand, this also leads us into one of the debates between the majority and the dissents in *Van der Peet*, on what the purpose of section 35 should be seen to be and how this should play out in relation to the nature of the rights protected. L'Heureux-Dubé J had argued that more attention should be placed on the import or "significance" of the practices being protected. She had hoped this could shift focus to a broader, underlying stratum, where one could more sensibly position Aboriginal rights (in line with rights jurisprudence in other domains). Arguably, McLachlin J had something similar in mind (supporting her contention that the way Lamer CJ characterized Aboriginal rights they did not seem to be "rights" at all).

Thinking about this more carefully leads us into seeing how discourse has been moved away from realms within which richer forms of Indigenous self-determination might have been part of the discussion. Recall that L'Heureux-Dubé J argued Aboriginal rights should be seen protecting "the 'distinctive culture' of which aboriginal activities are manifestations."[43] She would have had it be that the significance or import of a specific activity would be found in its existence within a cultural matrix, value being attributed to the matrix itself. This cultural preservation would be what section 35 exists to further.[44] There seems no way, however, for a jurist occupying a liberal world to locate value directly in culture itself.[45]

Of interest for our discussion is the fact that the ensuing debate takes on a peculiar flavour, contained as it is now within narrow parameters. Once we see the narrowness in which the majority's approach fits debate, we then turn to the

42 The exception being Aboriginal title, discussed in an upcoming section.

43 *Ibid* at para 157.

44 Recall that Lambert J of the British Columbia Court of Appeal and L'Heureux-Dubé J (and arguably, though to a lesser extent, McLachlin J) dissenting at the Supreme Court level had focused on the purposive nature required in this context and developed a "social" description of Aboriginal rights that generated a vision of broad, underlying rights and protected the core of Aboriginal communities' cultures, as these peoples would understand that to be.

45 Arguably there is no actual serious disagreement here – L'Heureux-Dubé J might be seen placing indirect value in Aboriginal culture (perhaps seeing it as the source of value placed in choices made or as itself the product of choices made), the difference being only in that she sees more sense in protecting the cultural edifice itself rather than those activities that emerge from the matrix.

more open kinds of debates L'Heureux-Dubé J's approach would have made possible. From that we turn, finally, to how even L'Heureux-Dubé J's approach can be seen to be quite narrow, once we note the more expansive ways of thinking about how Aboriginal rights could have been conceptualized, were it not for the fact the jurists building these forms of social reality work from deep within a liberal-normative world.

In *Sappier & Gray* the question becomes one of which kinds of objects are to be examined for "import," with the question of who determines import addressed and resolved on an "objective" level. In the form that this debate takes, there are only two possible answers to the first matter, "*things* in the world acted upon," or "the *activities* themselves," while whether something holds a specific degree of "import" is seen as a matter that an impartial observer can determine (in this case, for this test, a trial judge).

We have a concrete case of how this works out before us in *Sappier & Gray*. A judge is going to have to determine whether a practice, custom, or tradition is an integral part of the distinctive culture of the claimant Indigenous communities, the Mi'kmaq and Maliseet. Here the question is about the practice of cutting down trees to obtain wood for building either home structures or furniture for personal use. The first part of the juridical debate is whether the focus is then on how important the *object* of the activity is to the Mi'kmaq and Maliseet (the wood), or on how important the *activity* itself is to them. The Court follows firmly in the footsteps of the majority in *Van der Peet*: the matter of import is one connected to the activity itself and not the kind of thing acted upon. The second matter is likewise determined in line with the test laid out in *Van der Peet* – this question of import of the activity is not determined by considering how significant the activity is *to the claimants* (though that can go into the mass of evidence the trial judge must consider): rather, the trial judge is expected to become someone capable of objectively determining – from a third-person perspective – what activities are of sufficient import (in the sense they are sufficiently "integral" to this people's culture). As the Court notes in reinforcing the approach taken in *Van der Peet*:

> The goal for courts is ... to determine how the claimed right relates to the pre-contact culture or way of life of an aboriginal society. This has been achieved by requiring aboriginal rights claimants to found their claim on a pre-contact practice which was integral to the distinctive culture of the particular aboriginal community. It is critically important that the Court be able to identify a *practice* that helps to define the distinctive way of life of the community as an aboriginal community. The importance of leading evidence about the pre-contact practice upon which the claimed right is based should not be understated.[46]

46 *Sappier & Gray*, *supra* note 20 at para 22 [emphasis in original].

It is highly instructive to now work out how this fits together. Imagine our hypothetical First Nation arguing that harvesting from the waters in their traditional territory, trading aspects of that harvest, and regulating both the harvesting and trading are and have been all practices, traditions, and customs integral to their distinctive culture. In making these arguments they argue about the "significance" to them of these activities, which Canadian law will translate into arguments that can go to showing the integral nature of the activities in question. It is essential we track, however, what "*significance*" can mean in the context of how it plays out within the *Van der Peet* test and what it might have meant if the jurisprudence on Aboriginal rights had taken different approaches to the matter of cultural protection.

Imagine you have a young child who on her birthday receives a letter from her favourite aunt containing 100 dollars. You know she has some ideas about how to spend the unexpected funds, but you feel it would be best if you were to make wise choices on her behalf, considering what you know (or at least believe) to be her preferences. You know, for example, that she likes to spend what monies she manages to accrue to purchase the latest games for her game console (so she can play online with her friends). You also know she very much enjoyed the outdoor-experience summer camp she went to last year. You consider the importance to her of these two options, placing it into the calculations *you do* (where, naturally, you colour matters by how you think the two activities will enhance her growth as a person). This, somewhat crudely, captures how the Supreme Court has constructed a process for making use of claimant's notions of "import" or "significance." How they make use of this in determining "integralness" goes beyond this, but when it comes to the matter of "significance," they allow that it is proper that lower courts pay heed to how much *value* Aboriginal claimants give to events, though they place in the hands of these lower courts the determination itself of the general question of whether something is indeed sufficiently of value (in this case to count as "integral" to the distinctive culture of the Aboriginal community).

We see a hint, however, of a potentially different approach to the notion of "significance" in L'Heureux-Dubé J's comments. Her preferred approach asks how an activity fits into a larger social structure (a way of living), where the larger structure is presumed to be the thing of value. In a sense, the activity gets its *meaning* ("significance") from its being a manifestation of the web of social structures we label a culture. This is all underdeveloped in L'Heureux-Dubé J's remarks (in, for example, how we might understand "culture" in this context), and of course also suffers from the fact that the majority dismisses this way of thinking of how to approach Aboriginal claims (tied, again, to how it is difficult, if not impossible, to locate value in culture itself within a liberal approach to social realities).

For our purposes the import of this is the suggestion that there are other, more significant ways "significance" might have entered into approaches to mediating settler-society/Indigenous interactions. The significance of a practice might be the *meaning* it is vested with as a result of its being carried out within a meaning-generating world, one that imbues actions and events with normative content. To see how thinking of significance this way might have played out in the context of efforts to work out how two kinds of meaning-generating worlds could co-exist, let us step back from the sequence of events the Supreme Court imbues with liberal meaning, exploring how this history – and the contemporary world it is meant to create – actually exists in a world populated by multiple independent meaning-generating collectives.

We begin with the fact of the construction of social worlds – constructed normative worlds lived in – where existence within such worlds gives meaning to actions of individuals, families, and peoples, where each large-scale collective can generate complex patterns that total a form of social reality. At the core of the existences of multiple Indigenous worlds we find overlapping and intricate systems of thought. These systems go into structuring how people *understand* their lives (how they *ought* to act – "normalized" normative senses of what is correct and incorrect behaviour), and how they *understand* their interactions with others, with neighbouring peoples, non-humans, the lands, waters, and the rest of the natural world. These understandings, in turn, depend on understandings of what it is to be human and to be embedded in a larger natural world (as a member of a family, community, and larger collective, as related to other inhabitants of traditional territories and as related to the rest of the natural world).

We earlier sketched out something similar in relation to settler society in Canada. Putting to one side ongoing tensions between grounding visions and the history of struggles between these visions, by the late twentieth and early twenty-first centuries we can focus on a dominant understanding at play at the foundations of meaning-generation in Canadian society, an understanding that accounts for built social realities: that of the free and equal person and the need to structure social institutions in order to maximize opportunities for individuals to flourish. This is a complex system of thought meant to inform how people should (and do) understand their lives, and their interactions with other individuals, with neighbouring peoples, and with the non-human natural world.

As an example of how this plays out, consider once again the use of the dominant system to inform the building of social institutions in Canada – such as the law – when this complex guides how those building new aspects of the social world view *harms* to which the law can respond. We see Lamer CJ looking back at historical interactions between the Crown and pre-existing Indigenous peoples and struggling to frame how these encounters will be given sense within a liberal world. Does Lamer CJ see interactions between two worlds of meaning, such that different understandings of what it is to be human, etc., are set off against each other? Or does he choose to function entirely within the normative world he inhabits, using meaning generated within this world to impart meaning onto events of the past, out of this reconstruction then crafting a liberal-specific legal structure? "Harms," along this second pathway, come to be understood exclusively in terms of impediments to free and equal persons, and to the creation, maintenance, and strengthening of structures that facilitate the flourishing of said individuals.

There are other views of this history of interactions. From the perspectives of Indigenous peoples, by the middle of the nineteenth and into to the early twentieth century interactions on a physical level had devolved, as generations of lives came to be marked by oppression and dispossession. On a societal level these interactions came to be marked principally by attempts by the state and settler-society to remove the meaning-generating and meaning-transmission capacities of Indigenous communities. While this can be cast as attacks on "culture," it involved much, much more than what is conceived of – and conceivable – within the liberal world.

Governments and courts of settler society did not act just to prevent Indigenous peoples from engaging in discrete "cultural" activities – though, of course, this was and continues to be an overwhelmingly common phenomenon. These governments and courts did not act just to undercut cultures themselves – though, again, this was an all-too-common phenomenon.[47] To see what the jurisprudence keeps our attention away from, we need to step back, to appreciate fully the fact of the settler society and its dominant ways of thinking of – and building – forms of social reality up against a multitude of Indigenous societies and their rich and varied ways of thinking of – and building – their forms of social reality.

These Indigenous forms are not simply *culture* the way this term has been used by *both* the majority and dissents in *Van der Peet*. These forms set out how distinct peoples *think* of the world around them and their places in it. Just as a liberal mode of thought generates sets of architectural plans for how to build social institutions, like the law, Indigenous modes of thought provide foundational plans for the sorts of social institutions that make sense within the social realities they generate.

Most importantly, as we think of the question of building up a legal framework in response to the history of Crown-Indigenous interactions, Indigenous forms of social reality do not give sense and meaning just to discrete *actions* of individuals or to their relationships to each other within a closed group – they also give meaning to how an Indigenous society thinks about its relationships to territory and to all the lives and spirits that share that territory.

47 Arguably, contemporary child welfare regimes and the current criminal justice system continue on patterns of activities of the Crown that still further this objective of undercutting Indigenous cultures whole-cloth.

What, then, can we make of the structure the Court begins to build in *Sparrow* and fleshes out in *Van der Peet* and later cases? The Court begins with several overlapping assumptions (out of which it can choose which serves its purpose in any given scenario): first is the common assumption Indigenous forms of reality (as foundations of normative orderings) are simply not there, that all is already encompassed within a single societal vision dominated by liberalism; second is the assumption Indigenous forms of reality are inefficacious when imagined to reach out past the membership of the Indigenous community (that is, that the state is the sole source of a nationwide grounding normative vision); third is the assumption that Indigenous forms of social reality are in the present world essentially just cultural artefacts (of the sort protected by section 35); and fourth is the assumption that to the extent substantive Indigenous forms of social reality persist and are understood to function to structure *all* of an Indigenous community's understandings of how to live in the world in relation to its territories, the function of the Court in a liberal democracy is to move Indigenous peoples away from such understandings.

We see all four assumptions at play when we carefully consider the nature of the narrow debates with which we see the Court engage. The fourth is most interesting, as it moves us towards asking why the sentiment captured might be so – why might it be a function of the law (according to the self-understanding of a liberal court) that Indigenous communities' understandings of how to live in the world be removed from the landscape.

Recall our discussion of where we find liberal thought in the early twenty-first century. A key tension is between diversity and autonomy, a recent translation and transformation of an older debate between negative freedom and positive freedom. As the Court struggles to work out how to protect diversity (specifically when it emerges as the manifestation of lifeways of *subgroups* within a multicultural liberal democracy), it simultaneously places more and more weight on the notion of autonomy, on the notion that there is a *sort* of freedom that each citizen should be equally free to enjoy. The contemporary Canadian legal system is tasked with ensuring all citizens are seen as, and can see themselves as, free and equal persons, a task intertwined with the mission of building the social institution that is the law so that this unified system is built, maintained, and strengthened in order to function to allow each such person to have equal opportunities and resources to pursue his or her chosen way of living.

Independent Indigenous meaning-generating communities challenge this vision on levels of both form and content. On the level of form, note that Indigenous meaning-generating communities exist not as subgroups within a given liberal social world but as independent worlds built on independent foundations of social construction. To the degree Indigenous communities may continue to know this is so, to live within these independent worlds of social reality, Canadian legal authorities must work to make this no longer the case.

Aboriginal law – specifically the field of Aboriginal rights – must be built in such a fashion as to move Indigenous communities away from these modes of thinking and towards acquiescence in existence within a single social reality, dominated by liberal thought. Narrowness of debates within the case law make sense just in light of this.

On the level of content, note once again that Indigenous communities are multifarious, but also note they are all "illiberal" in at least one common way. The liberal world begins with the human, and the liberal-minded human thinking of the nature of herself and of her place in the world is consumed with thinking of the only thing of value, the rational and free human. Indigenous communities, however, likewise begin with understandings of the human and the place of the human in the natural world, but with very different understandings of what it is to be human that do not limit value to human life and human existence. Whereas within the liberal universe non-human components of the world around (other life, the water or air, the landscape, ecosystems, etc.) can have value only in the sense that some humans value these (otherwise valueless) things, within Indigenous forms of social reality the free and equal person exists embedded within vast webs of pre-existing relationships. Social realities that Indigenous peoples construct will be content-wise, then, of an order different from that manifest in a liberal-defined universe. Once again, a legal system tasked with overseeing interactions between a liberal order and a multitude of Indigenous orders will function to remove these competitors from the landscape. The act of removal is accomplished – as it is in relation to matters of form – by focusing all attention on other matters, namely, how aspects of "culture" can be accommodated within a realm of rights-discourse. Aboriginal rights jurisprudence makes sense as the product of such efforts.

Rights and Law: Indigenous Law and Indigenous Understandings

We turn now to a second debate about the nature of Aboriginal rights contained in the back-and-forth between dissents and the majority in *Van der Peet,* adding in remarks from *Sappier & Gray.* Again, the aim is to look into this debate to see what might otherwise have been richer ways of thinking of such rights in the modern setting. While one might think these are other options the jurists simply failed to see, options they could not see, or options they refused to see, the result is the same – resulting discourse is narrow and constrained. I argue that alternatives avoided are plausibly understood to be options not visible from a liberal perspective. We witness acts of attempted meaning-generation, as Canadian courts attempt to fix how all parties (including those with their own meaning-generating capacities) come to think of the history of Crown-Indigenous interactions, the nature of "harms" suffered at the feet of Crown law and policy, and of what paths forward are possible within Canadian law.

In the last section we took note of how the Court in *Sappier & Gray* removed one layer of richness the jurisprudence might have otherwise enjoyed, what would have been present had Aboriginal rights come to be seen as necessarily comprising a broad underlying stratum, below the level of activities (practices, traditions, or customs), at a level of generality at which it would have made sense to inquire about the significance or purpose lying behind the rights claimed.[48] We turn now to an aspect of McLachlin J's discourse, beginning with another layer of richness that we might imagine Aboriginal rights jurisprudence could have otherwise enjoyed, one connected to this notion of a broad stratum underlying activities. As we dig further we will again uncover deeper layers of richness the Court as a whole seems unwilling (or unprepared) to entertain.

Recall McLachlin J suggested that a source of the content of Aboriginal rights might be their nature as manifest in "*organized societies*" predating the arrival of Europeans (and settler societies). Aboriginal rights, that is, might derive their content from the existence of *rights* and *responsibilities* in Indigenous communities *prior* to their falling under Crown sovereignty. The imperial doctrine of continuity would (presumably) be invoked, allowing a sense or form of these rights to survive into the new world.[49]

McLachlin J, however, went on to place this notion in a larger structure, thereby taming the rights that might otherwise have arisen.[50] She would have had it be that while their *content* might be traced back to Indigenous laws and legal orders, the current status of Aboriginal rights would depend on how they might be brought up into and function within the common law. Just as historically the common law would have had the resources to recognize the continued existence of Indigenous rights and obligations, so too would it now take upon itself the task of placing these pre-existing legal structures into the (post-1982) common law world. Their *source* might be said to lie in worlds predating the

48 Given that both dissenting judges saw this purpose to be cultural protection, it is not clear how far this form of reconceptualization would have gone in changing or strengthening jurisprudence concerning Aboriginal rights. If arguments developed in this chapter are given credence, it is unlikely that the jurisprudence would have been altered significantly (as the central liberal-minded concern – that protection of culture [defined narrowly] be understood as the purpose behind section 35 – holds in either case).

49 *Van der Peet, supra* note 1 at paras 263–75. Interestingly, it is L'Heureux-Dubé J who mentions the doctrine of continuity (within imperial law). See *ibid*, L'Heureux-Dubé J, dissenting at paras 173–4. For a detailed analysis of the imperial doctrine of continuity, see Mark D Walters, "The 'Golden Thread' of Continuity: Aboriginal Customs at Common Law and under the *Constitution Act, 1982*" (1999) 44 McGill LJ 711.

50 *Van der Peet, supra* note 1 at paras 285–321.

Crown, but their *natures* would depend on how the common law takes them up into itself.[51] In fact, the extent to which it had already done so (comprising the extent of common law Aboriginal rights, those already recognized before 1982) would largely define the extent to which we could now suppose rights would be recognized and affirmed within the new constitutional structure.

But why are Indigenous legal orders *themselves* not carried up into Canada's constitutional order (bypassing the era of common law Aboriginal rights)?[52] This introduces a rich third layer avoided and sets us along a path that brings us face-to-face with other possibilities seemingly ignored or avoided. As we work our way along this path we find clearly illuminated how the Court operates within a liberal sensibility and how it removes Indigenous self-determination from Canadian legal discourse. We need to begin, however, by stepping back a bit, thinking first of the larger gaps visible in how the Court approaches the question of the status of Indigenous law and legal orders.

There are essentially two intertwined aspects of the larger story around Aboriginal rights we might imagine either ignored or denied. First, there is something we touched on in the last section: we have encountered nothing so far within the jurisprudence that directly acknowledges (let alone directly attempts to address) *fundamental harms* wrought by colonization itself. Second is an interlinked point, that specifying "harms" can be a normatively charged enterprise. That is, the Court fails to entertain the possibility that its immersion in a liberal world *determines* how it comes to understand and identify harms in historic (continuing into contemporary) Crown-Indigenous relations.

Earlier we noted Lamer CJ – operating within a liberal normative world – is constrained in his ability to conceive of "harms," restricting them to negative effects on the abilities of individuals to flourish as reasoning, will-exerting

---

51 *Ibid* at paras 260–80. This has to be read out of her discussion in these paragraphs. She begins her "empirical-historic" approach with an examination into what Aboriginal rights have been recognized in the past, and finds deployment (though very spotty!) of the doctrine of continuity. Aboriginal laws and customs, that is, have been pulled up into the common law over the last 150 years and more. But the Indigenous laws recognized within the common law in this manner – even when now recognized under section 35 – magically lose their status as "laws." Rather, all that exists now in the common law are customary rights, which allow, for example, the Stó:lō to claim a right to fish for a "moderate livelihood": *ibid* at para 279.

52 Some scholars point out that certain Indigenous legal principles and processes were deployed within the common law (as, for example, when custom adoption was recognized in *Casimel v Insurance Corporation of British Columbia* (1993) 106 DLR (4th) 720 (BCCA) [*Casimel*]). See e.g. Walters, *supra* note 49.

However, (a) the few examples that exist do not show the common law paying particular attention to the doctrine of continuity, and (b) it is arguable whether these examples show what is being discussed, the inclusion of Indigenous legal orders into Canadian law (showing, as they do, no more than that in the context of a particular common law dispute a particular practice or principle was noted and used).

persons. There are, however, two sorts of harms – clearly identifiable within Indigenous perspectives – that mark Crown-Indigenous relations and yet are not addressed by section 35 jurisprudence. On the one hand, there is a harm wrought in the transition itself from pre-colonial to colonial eras, while on the other hand there are vast ranges of harms wrought within the colonial era, as colonial laws, policies, and activities devastated Indigenous collectives.

In the brief historical narrative provided earlier in this text, a "magical" transition was noted, *from* periods of European-Indigenous interaction marked by quasi-international relations *to* the colonial era. In this transition a fundamental shift took place, as the British (and Canadian) Crowns sought to undercut the ability of Indigenous collectives to chart their own futures. As fundamental as such a shift is, it goes virtually unmentioned as a harm within Canadian jurisprudence.[53]

Within the overtly colonial era (from roughly the 1840s right up to – at least – 1982) the British (and then Canadian) state engaged in numerous activities that directly devastated Indigenous communities and individuals. Peoples were removed from territories, Indigenous economies were destroyed, families were torn asunder, and Indigenous forms of social construction and understanding fell under constant and relentless attack, in ways that go far beyond "physical" attacks on the lives of individuals and families. None of that, as well, is directly addressed in the doctrine of Aboriginal rights.

Let us focus on pre-existing Indigenous legal orders, those systems of laws McLachlin J suggests might inform Aboriginal rights under section 35. We noted that while McLachlin J considered the possibility Aboriginal rights might be *sourced* in pre-existing Indigenous law, she did not consider the notion that *pre-existing systems themselves* might be pulled up into the current legal landscape. Such a move, of course, would require more than the transmission of rules, principles, and the like into a new legal context – it would

53 That the judiciary avoids even the possibility of acknowledging fundamental harms of colonization does not, of course, go unnoticed by commentators, and in recent jurisprudence we can begin to see hints of unease with this judicial stance. Yet the fact remains that jurisprudence on Aboriginal rights is founded on the notion that in the Crown's act of asserting sovereignty, Indigenous self-determination was fatally undercut. This is evident in the nature of extinguishment (discussed in the next section – both possible forms), but also informs the doctrine of Aboriginal rights itself. In avoiding a discussion of the appearance within the Canadian legal and political system of Indigenous power and authority the assertion of Crown sovereignty is truly fundamental.

The one (and only) crack in this facade appeared in *Haida Nation v British Columbia (Minister of Forests)*, (2004) 3 SCR 511 [*Haida Nation*], wherein McLachlin CJ characterized (or re-characterized) the elements in the picture needing reconciliation (at least in the early treaty-making era) as two forms of sovereignty. We find "Treaties serve to reconcile pre-existing Aboriginal sovereignty with assumed Crown sovereignty": *ibid* at para 20. The hint (helped by the tense of the word "serve") is that this sense also informs the current treaty-making process.

require consideration of fully functioning *systems*, with all the machinery (and meaning-generation and authority) they enfold and from which they emerge.[54]

Of interest is the fact that it is not seen as problematic that the initiation of the colonial era begins with the presumption that Indigenous legal orders and their authoritative pronouncements bear no impact on how the state comes to manage the entire territory that becomes Canada. The fundamental transition marked at this point is *not understood* to constitute a harm that might need redress. Exploring the fact that fundamental colonial impacts on the lives of Indigenous peoples are not understood, from one perspective, to constitute harms to be remedied provides a route into the construction of an account of a liberal understanding of Aboriginal rights that seems the most sensible possible.

We begin by disentangling points of view of Canadian government officials and jurists in earlier generations – when it was common to either believe or assume that Indigenous law was "primitive" or non-existent – from what we are concerned with, the point of view of contemporary jurists working out what to think about the transition to the colonial era. Given that contemporary jurists no longer seem to believe Indigenous law did not really exist in any substantial form,[55] do they either believe or assume Indigenous law at that time was so primitive as to not warrant further consideration?

We are approaching this question from the perspective of a liberal jurist, focusing initially on the question of whether an identifiable harm arose as large areas of what became Canada fell under Crown sovereignty, as Indigenous legal orders came to be pushed aside. We can begin with a troubling point, that today's liberal jurist will understand Indigenous peoples to have all had illiberal legal orders at contact and potentially up to the present day.

This is not an unreasonable position for the liberal jurist to adopt. We noted earlier that Indigenous peoples do not begin building forms of social reality with the presumption that the rational/will-endowed human is the sole entity

---

54 Of course, an attempt could be made within Canadian law to work out how "whole" legal orders are pulled up into contemporary constitutional law in a manner that leaves relatively intact the fundamental authority of the Crown. One such attempt could involve carving off Indigenous systems from their founding authority, pulling up into Canadian constitutional law only the rules and principles embedded in systems at contact (as much as those could be identified, as much as they might exist). Arguably, this impoverished vision is emerging today, both in Aboriginal and non-Aboriginal circles. A second option could be to imagine Indigenous authority continued to exist (though deeply buried) and can now be resurrected as a component of the Crown. Binnie J suggested just this sort of conceptualization of matters in his concurring judgment in *Mitchell v MNR*, 2001 SCC 33 *MNR*, citing as one source for this notion the *Report of the Royal Commission on Aboriginal Peoples* (Ottawa: Minister of Supply and Services, 1996).

55 It should be noted, however, it is not clear just how deep this new belief lies, as all we really witness in the jurisprudence are remarks that *suggest* today's Canadian jurists now believe Indigenous peoples possessed their own legal orders before the Crown asserted sovereignty.

of value in the moral universe, that entity that *gives* value to other otherwise valueless components of the world (like animals, plants, water, landforms, etc.). We also noted that from this alternate starting point projects of building social institutions do not proceed as if the principal aim should be ensuring the creation of conditions within which individual humans can maximally flourish.

That Indigenous legal orders through the colonial era would be – indeed, should be – deemed illiberal is not to say today's liberal jurist would simply dismiss their relevance in the context of determining the nature of contemporary Aboriginal rights. The key query is narrowed down: taking their illiberality into account, *could* Indigenous legal orders have been pulled into the common law (much as a multitude of legal orders were pulled together in the early formation of the *common* law in England)? If this was possible, and given that overwhelmingly this pulling up into the common law did not happen, did a harm arise that today requires remediation (in pursuit of reconciliation)?

Approaching this project from within a liberal normative world we see, however, severe limitations emerge that curtail how deeply Indigenous legal orders can be conceived of as potential guides to the construction of jurisprudence on Aboriginal rights. Paralleling our discussion in the last section, we can note that Indigenous legal orders challenge the liberal order manifest in Canadian law on levels of both form and content.

In relation to form, the Canadian legal order rests on the presumption of a unitary system, overseeing (as a superstructural component of Canadian society) how *all* interests of members of society are managed. To the extent independent, separate Indigenous legal orders claim fundamental authority over a wide range of matters – over key aspects of the lives of their membership, but also over the territories to which they bear sacred responsibilities – they cannot be worked into the Canadian system.

On the level of content, recall general comments in the last section. At contact (and for many, up to contemporary times) Indigenous legal orders functioned (and function) not just in terms of having different sets of rules and principles (though they often do have them), but as differently grounded normative systems. Different sets of meanings were (and are) attached to what we might generically label "law," "governance," "rights," "responsibilities," and so forth. These different structures and differently grounded systems cannot be accommodated easily within the one, unitary Canadian legal order.

We conclude this examination into conceptual limits generated through the construction of a specific form of liberal legal order with some thoughts about the *extent* to which the contemporary Canadian system *might* be able to accommodate Indigenous law. While today's jurist is unlikely to mimic those of yesteryear, when a finding that an Indigenous law or custom is "barbaric" or "contrary to the law of God" could break the chain of continuity presumed in imperial law, nevertheless there are "moral" and political limits contemplated.

In *Thomas v Norris*, for example, the British Columbia Supreme Court found that the practice of "spirit dancing" (a traditional Coast Salish dance, in which an initiate, if all goes well, is expected to find and sing his or her song), should it be found to be protected under section 35 as an Aboriginal right, would not suffice to overcome civil claims of assault, battery, and false imprisonment.[56] The court found that the plaintiff's rights to autonomy and dignity have the power to overwhelm any community rights that might exist, tied to traditional practices.[57] There are also "political" limits, as when Binnie J (writing a concurring judgment) noted in *Mitchell v Minister of National Revenue* that claims to Aboriginal rights that conflict with the exercise of Crown sovereignty would not lead to rights that exist in the modern world.[58]

Both sorts of limits restricting the extent to which Indigenous law might be capable of being pulled into the common law reflect the nature of the characterization of Aboriginal rights mapped out over the last few sections. We can see more clearly where lines have been drawn by working our way from elements of Indigenous legal orders that could be pulled into the Canadian system up to elements that clearly pose challenges for Canadian law, to those that are clearly removed from any prospect for their being accommodated within the liberal legal order.

At a low, concrete level we find discrete, narrow holdings emanating from Indigenous law that can be accommodated within the Canadian system. Two examples of this phenomenon populate most discussions of the presence of Indigenous law within the common law: *Connolly v Woolrich* and *Casimel v ICBC*.[59] In the first decision, from Monk J of the Quebec Superior Court in 1867, the doctrine of continuity was invoked, and the marriage practices of the Cree were found to continue past the assertion of Crown sovereignty (such that the son of a deceased French-Canadian trader could claim some of the estate from the trader's marriage to his Cree mother, regardless of the fact the trader also had a second wife back in Montreal). In the second decision, from the British Columbia Court of Appeal in 1993, a customary adoption of the Carrier was

56 *Thomas v Norris*, [1992] 2 CNLR 139, 31 ACWS (3d) 558.

57 Hood J noted, "If spirit dancing includes criminal conduct as an integral part of it, it could not be said to be an aboriginal right which survived the introduction of English law into the colonies": *ibid* at para 89. Hood J went on, however, to hold that (for the purposes of this case) the conduct of the defendants (in seizing and holding the plaintiff in a Coast Salish bighouse in order to initiate him into spirit dancing) was not criminal – instead, the focus fell on "civil wrongs": *ibid* at paras 89–90. Hood J went on to find that "most importantly, it seems to me that the protection of the plaintiff's civil rights is a more than adequate and valid objective served by the application of the common law of tort to the defendants' activities": *ibid* at para 99. In particular, the plaintiff's right to withhold consent was violated (in contrast to the situation before the court, dealing with a Coast Salish practice wherein it is sufficient that a close family member give consent).

58 *Mitchell v MNR*, *supra* note 54 at paras 129–35.

59 *Connolly v Woolrich* (1867), 11 LCJ 197, 17 RJRQ 75 [*Connolly*]; *Casimel*, *supra* note 51.

recognized, the grandparents of a deceased individual being found to be adoptive parents entitled to death benefits. In both cases it is arguable that it is not that Cree or Carrier law itself is incorporated into the common law, but that outcomes from the application of those two systems – a marriage in one, an adoption in the other – are found acceptable as outcomes within the common law. Further, we should note the "moral" limits noted above might have arisen, which would preclude the practices being accommodated within the common law.

At the next two levels we find not specific outcomes pulled into specific common law determinations, but rather that the *rules* and *principles* that inform outcomes are considered by common law authorities. It is arguable that both *Connolly* and *Casimel* are examples of this transpiring, as one could read these decisions generously as holding either the *rules* from Cree law and Carrier law are pulled into the common law (that the Cree ceremony between William Connolly and Suzanne Pas-de-nom is recognized as establishing marriage within the common law, and that the adoption practice of the Carrier functions within the common law to establish parentage) or the *principles* function as principles do in the common law (so Cree law and Carrier law supply principles that work to help resolve problems when rules are insufficient). While one would presume this imagines carrying up into the common law something significant about Indigenous legal orders, we still are not in a space where Indigenous law itself is being elevated into the common law.

Even so, with this last possibility we began to find ourselves in a grey area, where we would need more to go by to see that Canadian jurists were comfortable pulling Indigenous law into the common law. As we move further up the ladder we encounter much stronger suspicions: can we imagine a Canadian court accepting into the common law a fully functioning Indigenous legal system, one that emerges out of the life-world of an Indigenous community, a social reality that supplies meanings that inform laws making up the legal order? We might think this is possible on the condition that either (a) the Indigenous legal order was fundamentally liberal in its design, construction, and functioning, or (b) that the Indigenous legal order was fully overseen by a dominating central state system. In either case, however, we find ourselves conceiving of a world inhabited by one social realm, that of the liberal state, the only difference between the two being whether the Indigenous subsystem functions as a component of a third order of government or as something always under the control of the central state.

Finally, we arrive at the possibility of parallel, independent Indigenous legal orders, imagining the common law accepting its position as just one source of authoritative law amongst many others. Note this is never contemplated within the case law of Canadian courts. The one hint that this exists in the imagination of the high court was its comment in *Haida Nation* that "[t]reaties serve to reconcile pre-existing Aboriginal sovereignty with assumed Crown sovereignty."[60] The existence of functioning Indigenous legal orders is a fact of the landscape of territories now encompassed within the limits of Canada, but the state does not accept that these other legal orders are grounded in independent Indigenous self-determination.[61] More will be said about this conundrum in the next chapter, as we look into how the jurisprudence tackles the question of the place of Aboriginal rights in relation to Crown power.

We now dive into details under the characterization of Aboriginal rights, zeroing in on the test for establishing an Aboriginal right. We begin with the determination of the definition of a claimed right (in many cases this is a key stage, as how a specific Aboriginal community's claim is defined within litigation often essentially predetermines the outcome) and proceed to work our way through the test. As we do so we return to our example of a complex set of claims, those advanced by the hypothetical Aboriginal community asserting rights to gather from their traditional waters, to trade some of this harvest on a commercial scale, and a right behind these claims to regulate harvesting and trading activities. This enables us to witness the many and varied ways an Aboriginal community can find that the promise of its Aboriginal rights is shuttered and dim. Many of the puzzles we detailed earlier re-enter the story.

Working within the Characterization: Establishing an Aboriginal Right

Recall our hypothetical Aboriginal community would have to argue that each practice it hopes to engage in today is linked to a "practice, tradition, or custom" integral to its distinctive culture at the time of its early encounters with Europeans (placing this community in the western half of Canada, that date would likely be set sometime in the late eighteenth century into the middle of the nineteenth century).[62]

Tied into questions about the existence of each claimed right are questions about how to go about defining a right. While the Aboriginal community would have an opportunity to argue this point before a Canadian court, the power to

60 *Haida Nation*, *supra* note 53 at para 20.

61 See *Kunst'aa Guu – Kunst'aayah Reconciliation Protocol*, 2009, online: <haidanation.ca/wp-content/uploads/2017/03/Kunstaa-guu_Kunstaayah_Agreement.pdf>. While the province allowed this protocol to be developed, note that in the preamble it does not accept the Haida's ultimate authority over Haida Gwaii.

62 In *Tsilhqot'in Nation v British Columbia*, 2007 BCSC 1700, for example, Vickers J found the Tshilhqot'in (with traditional territory in south-central British Columbia) made contact with Europeans in 1793, as Alexander Mackenzie made his way to the Pacific. Note that this is the trial-level decision in *Tsilhqot'in Nation v British Columbia*, 2014 SCC 44, the current leading case on Aboriginal title.

decide how each claim should be properly understood and articulated is held by judicial authorities.

In *Van der Peet* the Court noted that while Aboriginal rights should be approached in a generous and liberal fashion, a particular claimed right should be defined in a fairly narrow manner. This happens in a number of ways, one of which is tied to state regulation.[63] In that context the Court went on to hold that to properly identify the nature of an Aboriginal claim,

> a court should consider such factors as the nature of the action which the applicant is claiming was done pursuant to an aboriginal right, the nature of the governmental regulation, statute or action being impugned, and the practice, custom or tradition being relied upon to establish the right.[64]

In *Van der Peet* itself this matter of definition was contentious,[65] as the claimed right could be reasonably parsed along several lines: (a) dividing "barter" or "trade" in fish (for other goods) from "commercial trade" (the exchange of fish for money), and (b) separating out trade tied to provision of sustenance, from trade tied to the making of a moderate livelihood, from trade that is essentially unlimited. While members of the British Columbia Court of Appeal characterized Mrs Van der Peet's claim as that of an Aboriginal right to sell fish on a commercial scale, Lamer CJ felt the appropriate definition was of a claimed right to "exchange fish for money or for other goods."[66]

Much of the outcome of *Van der Peet* hung on this question as it intersected with the requirement of "integralness," as the evidence tendered did not well support the claim that it was an *integral* aspect of the distinctive culture of the Stó:lō people (at contact with Europeans) that they traded fish for money or

---

63 Supreme Court remarks on this matter have taken place mostly in the context of the use of claimed Aboriginal rights to meet quasi-criminal charges (in relation to, for example, hunting or fishing outside regulated seasons, or running afoul of other specific regulations). *R v Sparrow*, [1990] 1 SCR 1075, 70 DLR (4th) 385 [*Sparrow*], *Gladstone*, *supra* note 4, and *Van der Peet*, *supra* note 1, were all fishing cases. *R v Morris*, 2006 SCC 59 is an example of the many hunting cases brought before the courts.

64 *Van der Peet*, *supra* note 1 at para 53.

65 The question of characterization is relatively unsettled, as the method for doing so spelled out in *Van der Peet* is in terms of the interaction between (a) the relationship between the current activities being carried out and the traditions, practices, and customs in the past relied upon to ground the claimed right, and (b) the government regulation concerning which the current activities have run afoul. See *Van der Peet*, *supra* note 1 at para 53. If we are asking simply about a hypothetical claimed right, it is difficult to see how to properly characterize the claim without any government regulation in the mix. Regardless, one might argue that, given the looseness around this process for characterization, much here is in the hands of the discretion of the judiciary.

66 *Van der Peet*, *supra* note 1 at para 76 [emphasis omitted].

for other goods. The key stumbling block was the central attribute of being "integral." As the Court went about unpacking that concept, it held that an activity cannot be "incidental" or unimportant if it is to be integral to a distinctive culture.[67] In the case at hand, the Court held that the evidence indicated that, at best, trading in fish was incidental to aspects of the Stó:lō culture that might be characterized as integral to that culture.

Beyond how each claimed right is defined, there is the general matter, then, of how a defined right is established, the requirements all connected to whether the impugned activity today is suitably contiguous with a practice, tradition, or custom integral to the distinctive culture of the community in question at contact with Europeans. Our hypothetical Aboriginal community, then, would have to hope that how each of their claims was defined would turn out to be such that they could then muster the sort of evidence necessary to fulfil requirements for establishing each right.[68]

It is interesting to note that the Aboriginal community could not be settled in its own mind on what it would actually be arguing for as it went into the Canadian legal arena.[69] Particularly striking is the fact that the Aboriginal community (forced to go to court to try to establish an Aboriginal right to engage in what it takes to be a traditional activity) would find that the story it wishes to tell is under the control of the court at the very first stage. While they can attempt to describe what the activity in question means to them, ultimately this too must fit within understandings generated and controlled by Canadian judicial authorities, working within a liberal normative universe.

Establishing and Defining: Sense within a Liberal World

There are numerous other factors the Court tied into the question of the definition and establishment of the claimed right. Any claim is understood to be narrowed down to the activity in question (so no other activities or practices

67 McLachlin J, dissenting, took issue with the way that "integrality" was open to subjectively driven interpretation. There would always be a need, she observed, to narrow down which aspects of culture were sufficiently important to receive constitutional protection, and the use of such a notion as "non-incidentality" would allow only an unacceptable amount of judicial discretion into such determinations. Her position on these questions is discussed below.

68 This can be accomplished, with great expense of time and resources, given the right set of conditions. See *Gladstone*, *supra* note 4; *Ahousaht Indian Band and Nation v Canada (AG)*, 2011 BCCA 237, leave to appeal to SCC refused, 34387 (29 March 2012) [*Ahousaht*].

69 The way around this has been to argue for as wide a panoply of rights as possible, forcing the trial court to decide how it will characterize each claimed right, and to determine whether each can be tied to a practice, tradition, or custom integral to the distinctive culture of the nation making the claim at contact with Europeans. See e.g. *Lax Kw'alaams*, *supra* note 25; *Ahousaht*, *supra* note 68.

can be said to "piggyback" on the established right).[70] As well, should a right claimed be successfully established, it is understood to apply only to the Aboriginal people who succeed in having it recognized in Canadian law – while their immediate Aboriginal neighbours may entirely share language, history, culture, and traditions, for them to enjoy a similar right they too would need to spend the significant time and resources necessary to establish this right in court (or through negotiations).[71] Further, when we move to the edges of the question of definition, we encounter the issue of the relationship between Aboriginality and European culture and influence. The Supreme Court in *Van der Peet* made clear that in looking at a contemporary claimed right, a court must be careful to inquire into whether the Aboriginal practice (or the integral nature of the practice) arose as a result of European influence:

> European arrival and influence cannot be used to deprive an aboriginal group of an otherwise valid claim to an aboriginal right. On the other hand, where the practice, custom or tradition arose solely as a response to European influences then that practice, custom or tradition will not meet the standard for recognition of an aboriginal right.[72]

We should take note of this point about time and resources. All these factors play into the creation of very heavy burdens on any Aboriginal community claiming an Aboriginal right. Vast amounts of time, energy, and resources are required to move from a merely asserted right to an established right. As noted in the overview earlier in this text, Aboriginal communities are by and large the poorest in Canada. They often live today in small and remote communities, removed from economic and social opportunities. The burden of establishing their constitutionally protected rights falls squarely on their shoulders, and with rules requiring they show each right separately and independently

---

70 Lamer CJ states in *Van der Peet, supra* note 1 at paragraph 70:

> In identifying those practices, customs and traditions that constitute the aboriginal rights recognized and affirmed by s. 35(1), a court must ensure that the practice, custom or tradition relied upon in a particular case is independently significant to the aboriginal community claiming the right. The practice, custom or tradition cannot exist simply as an incident to another practice, custom or tradition but must rather be itself of integral significance to the aboriginal society.

Interestingly, this runs counter to jurisprudence on treaty rights, where the Court held it only makes sense to say, for example, that if a treaty nation has a right to hunt in a certain area, it must also have the "incidental" right to travel to that area with hunting implements to hunt. See e.g. *Simon v The Queen*, [1985] 2 SCR 387, 24 DLR (4th) 390; *R v Badger*, [1996] 1 SCR 771, 133 DLR (4th) 324.

71 "[T]he existence of an aboriginal right will depend entirely on the traditions, customs and practices of the particular aboriginal community claiming the right": *Van der Peet, supra* note 1 at para 69 [emphasis in original].

72 *Ibid* at para 73.

(with a test that demands evidence reaching back generations, usually accessible and collectible only with the aid of experts in history and anthropology), the time and resources demanded of such communities is enormous and out of all proportion to their economic means. Why is this so? Why are struggles of those affected by centuries of colonial law and policy placed almost entirely on the shoulders of those who are harmed by it?[73]

But let us keep our attention focused on conceptual puzzles generated by this jurisprudence, here the mystery being why undue "European influence" should pose a fatal threat to a claimed Aboriginal right. One clue to unravelling this puzzle can be found in thinking of how the Court treats culture in this context. If we read "European influence" as a proxy for "European culture" we come upon a vision of the meeting of disparate, unique cultures – as quite different ways of living and being in the world. On the one hand, we can note how this functions to narrow the range of possible Aboriginal rights claims (to those that are "non-European" in some fundamental manner mysteriously tied to the evolution of practices). On the other hand, we can note how this approach to distancing Aboriginal rights from European culture intersects with notions of choice.

If we step back from the day-to-day details of historic interaction, we can imagine the Court contemplates a picture of Aboriginal people living close to and intersecting with new colonies and their settler-populations (and then the new nation state), from early encounters up to the overtly colonial era. Throughout this stretch of time, but particularly through the period of colonization and settlement, some of these people – individually, but in doing so in larger numbers, *collectively* as well – occasionally *choosing* to adopt European ways. In doing so, the Court holds, these individuals, and the collectives they comprise, *choose* to move away from their Aboriginal roots, and so leave behind traditions that might have engendered some limited measure of respect and tolerance. Cultural anthropologists point out this is what cultures do – cultures respond to their environments in many ways, including adopting and adapting practices from other cultures they encounter, in order to meet new and evolving needs. Doing so in the context of European settlement translates in this

73 During the writing of this text, in the years after the election of a new Liberal government, a federal legislative initiative was underway to implement a new "Recognition and Implementation of Indigenous Rights" framework. In the fall of 2018, in the face of significant resistance from various sectors – including Indigenous leadership unhappy with the way this initiative was, for the most part, unilaterally rolled out – the introduction of legislation was delayed until after the next federal election (in the fall of 2019). Why, one might wonder, would rights "recognized and affirmed" in section 35 require then (more than thirty years after this act of recognition) a further act of recognition? While this text does not explore these political machinations, they eerily parallel the sorts of movements we are detailing within the jurisprudence, as we go about showing how the Supreme Court attempts to have Indigenous peoples more fully accept a place with a world determined by liberal norms and values.

legal setting, the Court seems to be saying, into the *choice* to move away from "traditional ways" (that get treated in one manner) and toward modern ways (life entirely embedded in a liberal setting, treated with in other ways, centred on other notions of equality).

We noted earlier that the sense behind all this is that Aboriginal culture is understood by Canadian judicial authorities to be *of a whole illiberal.* While particular cultural practices may be manifestations of choice, they are not (so this picture goes) embedded in suitable contexts (that is, the sociocultural contexts within which these choices might have been and continue to be made are not structured properly). We can expect from the judiciary, then, not just weak protection of "Aboriginality" as manifest through particular cultural expressions (as these particular cultural activities lack inherent value in the liberal world), but also distrust of "Aboriginality" manifest in cultures made up out of whole cloth (as liberal understandings of these alternate cultural worlds will most likely not see them providing the right conditions for individuals to be able to exercise liberty, the supreme value in the world). This suspicion, in turn, provides an explanation for the factors concerning the test for which we noted puzzles emerge.

Extinguishment of a Right

Should it show a right could be established, an Aboriginal community must be able to meet arguments to the effect that this practice, tradition, or custom had not been extinguished in the period from the assumption of Crown sovereignty up to the time these rights were constitutionally protected within the *Constitution Act, 1982.*[74] In *Sparrow* the Supreme Court found this reflects the language of section 35, in particular the inclusion of the modifier "existing" to Aboriginal and treaty rights.[75] All this is predicated on the presumption of an ability enjoyed by the Crown during this historical period (in its legislative capacity) to act unilaterally under a model of parliamentary supremacy. In *Sparrow* the Supreme Court determined that extinguishment is demonstrated by legislative activity evincing a "clear and plain intent" to eliminate the right in question.[76] For example, mere regulation of a fishery (even to the point of making it impossible for an Aboriginal community to fish for a period of time) would almost certainly not suffice.[77]

74 Since this would be a point raised by a government of Canada (or inheritors of earlier colonial status, such as the province of British Columbia), the onus is not on the Aboriginal community to show lack of extinguishment, but merely to meet arguments raised by the Crown.

75 *Sparrow*, *supra* note 63 at 1091.

76 *Ibid* at 1099.

77 *Ibid* at 1099.

Given the strictness of the test for extinguishment, we are reasonably safe in assuming a "live" claim in motion relative to a number of the positions advanced in our hypothetical case (where we assume we are past the exceedingly difficult stage of establishing the right under the *Van der Peet* test). It should be noted, however, that a separate form of "extinguishment" may undercut some sorts of claims. In *Mitchell v Minister of National Revenue,* the majority of the Supreme Court dealt with a Mohawk claim involving the transport of goods from their communities in upper New York state across to their communities in southern Ontario by finding that there was no "north-south" inter-community trading at the time of contact as an "integral" aspect of Mohawk culture.[78] Writing a concurring judgment Binnie J, however, suggested this sort of claim might *also* fail as a result of "sovereign incompatibility," the notion that some Aboriginal claims simply cannot survive transition into the context of a world falling under Canadian sovereignty.[79] The establishment of the Canadian sovereign state would, for example, necessarily encompass the establishment of absolute authority over national borders, eliminating any Aboriginal claim that involved any sort of challenge to these borders. A certain set of "Aboriginal rights" – those "incompatible" with Crown sovereignty – would never arise within the Canadian legal arena, as they would be those otherwise determined to conflict with the existence of Canadian sovereignty.

Note the impact of "sovereign incompatibility" on prospects for the background claim of our hypothetical Aboriginal claimant. This First Nation also wishes to assert the "right" to manage and regulate both the taking of resources from the sea in their traditional territories and trade in these resources. Would such claims be compatible with the exercise of Crown sovereignty? We return to such matters more directly later, as we progress towards positions taken, and arguments mustered in their support, concerning the place of Aboriginal rights in relation to Crown power. We also touch on this matter in the next section, as we wrap up how the characterization and definitional stages of the Court's jurisprudence has affected the likelihood of Indigenous self-determination playing a role in contemporary Canada.

Gathered together, these points about the characterization, definition, and possible extinguishment of claimed rights indicate some support for a type of argument meant to show that one particular liberal vision has informed jurisprudence on Aboriginal rights. One can plausibly read off (a) the manner

78 *Mitchell v MNR, supra* note 54.

79 *Ibid* at 111–73. Binnie J, writing only for two members of the Court, wrote a concurring judgment. His conclusion and supporting arguments do not, therefore, clearly reflect the position of the Court. It is interesting to wonder, however, how far from his line the Court strays when it begins all Aboriginal rights jurisprudence with the notion that the sovereignty of the Crown cannot be questioned.

by which Aboriginal rights are to be identified, (b) ways they are narrowed through forms of extinguishment, and (c) concerns around their intersection with European influence, that the judiciary sees Aboriginal rights as expressive of choice about cultural setting, and resting on suspect traditional ways.[80] Seeing them treated as suspect (within a liberal mindset) would *explain* these narrowing tactics, which are means by which Aboriginal peoples are gently persuaded to move into "modern" circumstances and structures.

The Inability of Liberal Theory to Account for Loss of Indigenous Self-Determination

We conclude this look into the integral-to-the-distinctive-culture test with thoughts on how far off the page matters of Indigenous self-determination have been pushed. Let us return for a spell to the discussion of the dialogue between the majority and the two dissenting judges in *Van der Peet*, placed in relation to more recent remarks from *Sappier & Gray*. We noted McLachlin J suggested an alternate source for the content of Aboriginal rights, namely their nature as elements within the legal orders of Indigenous peoples as these were before the Crown asserted sovereignty. McLachlin J agreed with L'Heureux-Dubé J that Aboriginal rights should be cast in terms that have them exist as broad, underlying rights (finding that in the way the majority had framed them, they were more on the order of manifestations of rights, and not rights themselves). We stepped back from this discussion to see that the two sides engage in a narrow form of "debate" within which Aboriginal rights are capable only of having a very particular liberal-defined existence.

Whether such rights are "piecemeal" or not, whether they are understood to protect the significance of activities or not, they cannot respond to the loss of the ability of Indigenous peoples to direct their own collective futures, as this vision of a collective determining its own future according to its own meaning-generating collective "self" cannot be accommodated within contemporary liberal thought. Whether culture is placed into the liberal picture as having derivative value in that it reflects the choices of individuals, or as having derivative value insofar as it provides contexts of choice (within which individuals access meaning), the result will be a focus on "culture" that strips it of any connection to collective power.

What we run up into in the jurisprudence is what can be characterized as an inability and/or unwillingness of liberal doctrine to analyse fundamental harms attendant on one polity taking over another. Only insofar as *individuals* within

80 That is, that they are "traditional" in a pejorative sense, which is to read these ways as potentially constraining in relation to individual freedom.

the colonized polity *valued* the form of political existence they had created and maintained (that is, only to the extent one could say a collective *chose* the political organization manifest in activities and practices of social organization) could some understanding of the sort of fundamental harm we are considering be present within the liberal world view. A liberal society might tolerate the existence of a subsystem that was chosen by individuals making up a group, but it would simultaneously strive to have the individuals move away from this political structure out of concern with both its very existence (as a separate source of authority) and its content (as potentially illiberal and threatening to the autonomy of the polity's members). Of course, the overarching liberal society would feel compelled to use liberal-sanctioned means in attempts to undercut this other collective's authority, just as it would sanction the existence of this collective only to the degree it would see doing so in concert with reasons supplied by liberal thought.

It bears repeating that, within a liberal world, *chosen* political forms are ultimately acceptable only if they themselves have a liberal structure. Indeed, even should a sub-collective be entirely liberal-minded and structured in accord with liberal doctrine, control is still withheld by the larger liberal state, as an Indigenous collective operating under a chosen liberal governance structure would now be an Aboriginal community living fully within the larger, assumed liberal order. Overseeing this community's governance structures would be the state and its overarching legal order. The liberal-minded Aboriginal community could never find itself in the position of final decision-maker, especially in relation to its territory (that is, the liberal state understands it must step in, as there are, in relation to this territory within Canada, sets of distinct interests – of non-Aboriginal Canadians and of other Aboriginal groups, to name two – that must be weighed and balanced against each other).

Generally, then, this way of understanding the harm of political takeover works to essentially fit it within the sort of conceptualization of harm earlier contemplated (a kind of general harm fit within liberal parameters, as a harm colonization wrought on the ability of Aboriginal individuals to enjoy those *elements* of *culture* they lived within and through pre-colonization). Within the all-encompassing master plan for construction of a social reality encompassing Indigenous peoples, how an Indigenous polity governed (and governs) itself can be understood only to have been fundamentally a "cultural" matter, such that being colonized is the loss of a component of one's cultural existence. Any argument about the need to reinstate or reinvigorate Indigenous forms of governance would be cast, then, in terms of either a value possessed by that cultural component (a value *for*, essentially, the individuals making up the Aboriginal collective), or in terms of the harm wrought in the dissolution of this cultural component (in Canada, in the denial of Indigenous sovereignty and the imposition of heavy-handed federal systems of control). To the degree the liberal theorist (let alone the liberal jurist) is unwilling to step back from her life within this all-encompassing environment, which supplies all the tools and products of meaning-generation, she simply cannot conceive of the harm wrought when viewed from Indigenous perspectives.

In the next chapter we turn more directly to this question of "Indigenous governance" and how to make sense of its place within the framework of Aboriginal rights (within a liberal framework). We begin with further analysis focused on the jurisprudence on Aboriginal rights (looking at how Canadian courts have located these rights in relation to Crown power). This stage of analysis allows us to continue with the line of argumentation under development over the last few pages, as we find ourselves better and better equipped to show how an explanation of Aboriginal rights within a liberal universe *makes sense* of these rights in a way that reveals how the construction of social institutions functions in our modern setting. The use of liberal theory in furthering this project is illustrated by unpacking literature that is representative of Aboriginal rights scholars. This then leads the way into discussions of elements of postcolonial theory, as these elements align well with the general unfolding of legal theory as this takes place in this text.

8 The Place of Aboriginal Rights in Canada

Justifying Infringement of Aboriginal Rights

Should a claim to an Aboriginal right work its way through the *Van der Peet* test and be found to have survived the possibility of extinguishment, Aboriginal law turns to the question of how this right fits into the contemporary Canadian legal landscape. Starting points for analysis are two matters the Supreme Court places at the core of all that follows: the overarching presence of Crown sovereignty and the non-absolute nature of Aboriginal rights. "New rules" expounded in *Sparrow* do not challenge the existence of the sovereignty of the Crown,[1] but rather spell out how it is tempered, as the law steps in to fetter what had previously been absolute federal power with forms of legal responsibility.[2] These forms of responsibility dictate how (non-absolute) Aboriginal rights can be legally regulated, their fit within Canada worked out in what the Court describes as a just manner.

What, though, of Indigenous perspectives on these affairs? From an Indigenous viewpoint, Crown sovereignty has never been "unquestioned."[3]

---

1 In *R v Sparrow*, [1990] 1 SCR 1075, 70 DLR (4th) 385 at 1106, the Supreme Court quoted with approval from an article by Noel Lyon: "Section 35 calls for a just settlement for aboriginal peoples. It renounces the old rules of the game under which the Crown established courts of law and denied those courts the authority to question sovereign claims made by the Crown." See Noel Lyon, "An Essay on Constitutional Interpretation" (1988) 26 Osgoode Hall LJ 95.

What the "new rules" that replace renounced old rules might be has always been a matter of contention. Chapters in the first section of Macklem and Sanderson's text on reconciliation in the context of section 35 jurisprudence all tackle this question of the status of Crown sovereignty, but none do so in any manner that points towards acceptance of the meaning-generating capacity and authority of varied Indigenous collectives. See Patrick Macklem & Douglas Sanderson, eds, *From Recognition to Reconciliation: Essays on the Constitutional Entrenchment of Aboriginal and Treaty Rights* (Toronto: University of Toronto Press, 2016) 17–134 [Macklem & Sanderson].

2 *Ibid* at 1109.

3 While there are certainly Indigenous individuals – and even, seemingly, Indigenous communities – who do not question the "unquestioned" assertion of Crown sovereignty, the

From an Indigenous standpoint, new rules propounded are sorely inadequate, as federal power remains firmly in place, controlling the lives and futures of Indigenous communities. The fact that Canadian law now tempers the previously unfettered power of the Crown is little consolation when (a) the law put to use in this context centres on fiduciary doctrine, which arises from nothing more than acknowledgment of the *power* the Crown asserts over the legal and practical interests of Aboriginal peoples, (b) Canadian courts – divorced from Indigenous forms of law and authority – make all fundamental decisions regarding not just how this doctrine will apply but even what it means, and (c) all this finds no place for Indigenous systems of legal and political authority, where this authority is intimately connected to Indigenous powers to generate independent legal and political meaning. We need to work our way through the "new rules," bearing in mind deep puzzles that emerge from Indigenous perspectives on the jurisprudence.

Crown Sovereignty and Indigenous Self-Determination: "New Rules"

With unquestioned Crown sovereignty and the legal regulation of Aboriginal rights in place, the framework from *Sparrow* then applies to structure the new interaction between Crown power and Indigenous peoples, spelling out how the Crown can attempt to justify infringement of an established right. Should the Crown be able to show that a sufficiently compelling and substantial objective lies behind its actions, and should it be able to show it acted under this objective in a manner that befits its role as fiduciary, it can be said to have acted according to the dictates of the law.[4]

How can it be, however, that the response to the history of colonial law and policy begins with simple acknowledgment of fiduciary obligations and the conditions that make it possible to find fiduciary relationships? Should the law not be structured to *remove* conditions that make it possible to understand the Crown–Aboriginal relationship in this manner? How can the entire apparatus of law rest on acknowledgment of the power of the state? Why (once again) is all this determined – both at the level of establishment of legal framework and of application to a particular situation – by *courts* of *Canada*, by the judicial arm

---

perspective I speak of has been and continues to be commonly espoused. See e.g. *Kunst'aa Guu – Kunst'aayah Reconciliation Protocol*, 2009, online: <www.haidanation.ca/wp-content/uploads/2017/03/Kunstaa-guu_Kunstaayah_Agreement.pdf>; *Declaration of Dene Nationhood Passed at the Second Joint Assembly of the Indian Brotherhood of the Northwest Territories, at Fort Simpson*, 1975, online: <http://www.canadahistory.com/sections/documents/native/Dene%20Declaration.html>. For the process and outcome of an independent environmental impact assessment conducted by the Secwepemc concerning a proposed mine on their traditional territory, see Stk'emlúpsemc te Secwépemc Nation, "Honouring Our Sacred Connection to Pípsell," n.d., online: <https://stkemlups.ca/files/2013/11/2017-03-ssnajaxdecisionsummary_0.pdf>.

4 *Sparrow, supra* note 1 at 1110–19.

of that legal-political apparatus responsible for the usurpation of Indigenous legal and political authority?

The Court went on in *Gladstone* to find that if the right at issue is defined (by a Canadian court) as not having an internal limit (a situation that the Court found posed the threat of exclusivity, potentially affecting others with valid interests at stake), the *Sparrow* framework must be modified.[5] The range of sufficiently compelling and substantial objectives is substantially broadened, and what it means to act as a proper fiduciary is substantially weakened. This modified approach, the Court went on to hold in *Delgamuukw*, would apply as well to claims to Aboriginal title.[6]

With the collapse in *Tsilhqot'in Nation* of any meaningful distinction between the exercise of federal versus provincial power in relation to Aboriginal rights, all key general features of the landscape become relatively clear – in the sense that those relatively weak protections for constitutionally recognized and affirmed Aboriginal rights developed since *Sparrow* have now been spread out so that a single entity – "the Crown" – enjoys relatively unlimited power to justifiably infringe on what rights are found (by Canadian courts) to exist.[7]

Consider, as well, hints about the direction the jurisprudence is tending towards found in *Mikisew Cree 2018*.[8] Since the *Haida Nation* trilogy came out in 2004–05, a momentous shift has occurred in how the energies of Aboriginal communities are channelled into specific forms of legal challenge (as communities expend vast amounts of time and resources challenging Crown consultation processes).[9] We see, in *Mikisew Cree 2018*, in broad form, what this movement would look like should it continue to sweep over the legal landscape. *Sparrow* set out a framework for analysis of Crown action in relation to *existing* Aboriginal rights, one that created conditions on the exercise of Crown power, namely that this exercise be justifiable. With *Haida Nation*, however, we see a shift to a new focus on *claimed* rights (though purportedly the rights

5 *Gladstone* at paras 54–84.

6 *Delgamuukw v British Columbia (AG)* [1997] 3 SCR 1010, 153 DLR (4th) 193 at paras 165–69 [*Delgamuukw*].

7 *Tsilhqot'in Nation*, at paras 117–53. It should be noted that while *Tsilhqot'in Nation* was focused on Aboriginal title, a week after this decision was handed down the Supreme Court used its remarks on interjurisdictional immunity to support its conclusion in *Grassy Narrows First Nation v Ontario (MNR)*, 2014 SCC 48, that treaty rights are equally subject to both federal and provincial "taking up" power. Clearly its weakening of borders between federal and provincial Crown power was meant to be far-reaching.

8 *Mikisew Cree First Nation v Canada* (Governor General in Council), 2018 SCC 40 [*Mikisew Cree 2018*].

9 *Haida Nation v British Columbia*, (2004) 3 SCR 511; *Taku River Tlingit First Nation v British Columbia* (Project Assessment Director), (2004) 3 SCR 550; and *Mikisew Cree First Nation v Canada* (Minister of Canadian Heritage), (2005) 3 SCR 388 [*Mikisew Cree 2005*].

themselves were "recognized and affirmed" in section 35). When an Aboriginal community advances merely asserted rights, the only recourse is to seek to have one's concerns adequately considered as the Crown goes about making its decisions. With this shift, focus on infringement of rights has weakened, as time and energy now go into seeking "meaningful" consultation. With *Mikisew Cree 2018* we see another nudge in this direction, as talk turns to the possibility the honour of the Crown may on its own generate obligations on the Crown, obligations Aboriginal communities would like to trigger (when interference with their rights amounts to "adverse affects" and not necessarily infringement). Note, however, how this pushes notions of independent Indigenous law and authority further into the background, as once again Crown decision-making remains relatively unscathed should this expansion to the power of the doctrine of the honour of the Crown be upheld.

Why would the fact that an Aboriginal right has the potential to affect others' interests have led to such a powerful response? Why would the possibility of friction not lead naturally to calls for negotiation and compromise rather than a court-determined structure that dramatically undercuts the ability of Aboriginal communities to work out how their interests might fit with those of non-Aboriginals? Why, with both the *Gladstone* framework and the new focus on "merely asserted" rights, is there no notice given of the fact of the *prior presence* of Indigenous polities, of the fact that this should place the onus on the Crown to validate its initial usurpation? Why are Indigenous forms of authority and law not accepted as providing means by which frictions around land and resource use might be resolved?

Liberal positivism can explain many of the apparent peculiarities we find when looking into the jurisprudence dealing with how Aboriginal rights (and Indigenous communities) fit into the Canadian landscape. It helps to begin by differentiating between rules and tests that make sense within a liberal framework and those aspects of the liberal framework itself that might go into providing an explanation. That is, besides liberal-structural rules and tests, there are also certain conditions we can label structural that must be satisfied should a liberal system be able to be applied to Indigenous peoples, conditions that then function to explain much of what we see develop in *Sparrow*, *Gladstone*, *Delgamuukw*, *Haida Nation*, and *Tsilhqot'in Nation*. We begin by considering how these required structures function to explain certain aspects of what we see in the jurisprudence.

Limits Generated by Structural Features of a Liberal World

The primary necessary structural feature is simple – for a liberal system to apply to Aboriginal peoples these peoples must be *within* the system. The liberal democratic structure in Canada is predicated on the unity of the system – on its being, that is, *a system that applies to all.*[10] The only clear sign the Court gives this condition any conscious thought is in its invocation of the sovereignty of the Crown. This sovereignty is understood (within the nation-state model presumed in this contemporary setting) to be unitary – all matters within the territorial extent of the nation state are presumed to be under the sovereign authority of this *one* source of law (and politics).

We are asking about the structural features that must be there for the liberal system to apply to Indigenous peoples. Being a system is one – all Indigenous peoples need to be under the unitary system. The logic here must be, however, carefully unpacked. We are not saying it is just a brute fact that in a liberal world a hegemonic system will encompass all potentially competing systems of authority (and, in the Crown-Indigenous context, meaning-generating capacities tied to independent Indigenous orders). There *is* a brute fact here, namely the repeated and continuous attempt to apply the one system of Canadian law to all Indigenous peoples. It is not, though, a fact of hegemony but rather the fact of attempts to achieve hegemony that explains why we see what we do: that is, the puzzles we encounter from an Indigenous perspective are resolved if we understand the Canadian system *feels a need* to have itself apply to all within the geographic extent of Canada. Hence, the repeated and continuous attempts to make this so. Indeed, and quite interestingly, one key attempt to make this so is to *assume* it has *always been* and is *now* the case. Many of the peculiarities we note are explained if we keep this in mind.

The positivist side of the liberal positivist coin also explains this presumption visible in how the Court approaches the issue of how Aboriginal rights and peoples will be fit into the Canadian landscape. The positivist locates sources of the validity of law not in any moral or normative realm, but in social practices.[11] The dominant Hartian picture is of a specific key (secondary) rule that (in being followed by legal officials) determines what definitively counts as law. One can readily see that this picture of sources establishing validity of law within a system also contains this presumption – a *system* functions to determine law, presumptively a system applying to all that falls within the society in question.[12]

Intimately connected to the presumption of a single system (ruled over by a sole sovereign authority) is the presumption that Indigenous authority can survive in the contemporary Canadian landscape only as an element *within*

10 James Tully, "The Historical Formation of Modern Constitutionalism: The Empire of Uniformity" in James Tully, *Strange Multiplicity: Constitutionalism in an Age of Diversity* (Cambridge, UK: Cambridge University Press, 1995) 58 (detailing much of the history around the development of this way of thinking of the modern constitutional state).

11 These are social practices, which positivists argue (amongst themselves) may or may not include reference to and adoption of principles of morality and/or political morality.

12 We could, indeed, arguably fold this into common invocations in liberal democracies about the sacrosanct nature of the rule of law. That exercise is left to another day.

this structure.[13] We touched on this in our discussion in the last chapter of how Canadian courts seem to be approaching the question of the role Indigenous law might play in informing the doctrine of Aboriginal rights, and we return to this point towards the end of this chapter, when we turn to attempts to resolve puzzles about Indigenous governance. Here we note that questions of what happened to Indigenous systems of authority and law within *Sparrow*, *Gladstone*, *Delgamuukw*, and *Tsilhqot'in Nation* begin to clear up once we realize that a legal system charged with determining how conditions can be generated that maximize the opportunities individuals have to pursue their individual interests will have no place for alternate forms of independent law and authority.

All this, however, could equally well be said about many possible sets of architectural principles that Canadian law could have been built around. More interestingly, much of the *content* of key Supreme Court decisions – and many of the puzzles about this content – can be explained through appreciation of the application of liberal principles.

Limits Imposed as Liberal Thought Guides Construction

The ability of liberal thought to explain the content of the decisions is best shown by focusing on one of the pivots around which this area of Canadian law moves. The shift from *Sparrow* to *Gladstone*/*Delgamuukw* is stark. Looking at this shift in some detail lets us see in equally sharp detail how Canadian law deploys liberal thought to build its approach to placing Aboriginal rights into the Canadian landscape.

Both central components of the *Sparrow* approach – examining Crown objectives and how the Crown acts under its objectives – are altered when a right is defined as having no internal limit. The Court in *Gladstone* began its explanation for the need to modify the framework with thoughts of what it meant to find significance in the distinction between rights with and rights without internal limits:

> The significance ... relates to the position taken in [*Sparrow*] that, subject to the limits of conservation, aboriginal rights holders must be given priority in the fishery. In a situation where the aboriginal right is internally limited, so that it is clear when that right has been satisfied and other users can be allowed to participate in the fishery, the notion of priority, as articulated in *Sparrow*, makes sense. In that situation it is understandable that in an exceptional year, when conservation concerns are severe, it will be possible for aboriginal rights holders to be alone allowed to participate in the fishery, while in more ordinary years other users will

13 Binnie J asserted this is already so in his concurring judgment in *Mitchell v MNR*, 2001 SCC 33.

> be allowed to participate in the fishery after the aboriginal rights to fish for food, social and ceremonial purposes have been met.
>
> Where the aboriginal right has no internal limitation, however ... the notion of priority, as articulated in *Sparrow*, would mean that where an aboriginal right is recognized and affirmed that right would become an exclusive one.
>
> ...
>
> The basic insight of *Sparrow* – that aboriginal rights holders have priority in the fishery – is a valid and important one; however, the articulation in that case of what priority means, and its suggestion that it can mean exclusivity under certain limited circumstances, must be refined to take into account the varying circumstances which arise when the aboriginal right in question has no internal limitations.[14]

There is remarkably little further elaboration on what drove the Court to find the need to modify the *Sparrow* approach to the question of prioritization of Aboriginal interests when allocating resource access. The next few paragraphs make essentially the same point, though on different grounds. The Court notes that all members of Canadian society enjoy a long-established common law right to fish in tidal waters, and finds that it must be possible for the government of Canada to make decisions respecting the two sets of interests (finding that it cannot have been the intent in recognizing and affirming Aboriginal rights that the rights of others were thereby extinguished). Tellingly, the Court also notes that there will be instances across Canada where different Aboriginal communities will have rights to fish that conflict with one another – a situation again in which, the Court argues, it must be possible for the Crown to make decisions about resource allocation between sets of interests.[15]

We begin our exegesis, then, by noting the significance that the Court identifies is quite simple – when an Aboriginal right has no internal limit, it thereby enters a realm whereby it simply *must be* considered against the interests of others in Canadian society. The "argument" the Court appears to muster is equally simple – it was not thinking in *Sparrow* of rights that might have the potential of seriously affecting others' interests, and so it cannot be understood to have meant in that earlier case to speak to such eventualities. The actual argument seems to be that now, faced with such a situation, the Court *cannot think* of any alternative other than that the Crown be seen as having the ability to decide between sets of interests (where the Aboriginal rights at issue become essentially, then, just one set of interests to be weighed and balanced in the mix). Out of this issues language about how, in meeting its fiduciary obligations under a sufficiently compelling and substantial objective, the Crown must be expected only to "respect" the existence of Aboriginal rights at stake.

---

14 *Gladstone, supra* note 5 at paras 58–9, 61.

15 *Ibid* at 67–8.

The Court then went on to examine the matter of what objectives might be considered sufficiently compelling and substantial in this sort of situation.

> This limited focus [in *Sparrow*] made sense ... because the net-length restriction at issue in that case was argued by the Crown to have been necessary as a conservation measure ... in this case, however, while some aspects of the government's regulatory scheme arguably relate to conservation ... other aspects of the government's regulatory scheme bear little or no relation to issues of conservation. Once the overall level of the herring catch has been established, and allocated to the different herring fisheries, it makes no difference in terms of conservation who is allowed to catch the fish.[16]

Yet again, we see the Court finds it impossible to think that once a situation like this arises it would not fall to the governments of Canada to work out how interests are weighed and balanced. Once the objective of conservation is addressed, the only question left of any import is who gets what cut of the distributed pie.

A truly startling aspect of the *Gladstone* decision lies in how the Court then goes on to detail how Canadian governments can conceptualize and bring about modes of distribution. It begins by importing an approach to the limitation of rights from the *Charter* context:

> Although the aboriginal rights recognized by s. 35(1) are ... fundamentally different from the rights in the *Charter*, the same basic principle – that the purposes underlying the rights must inform not only the definition of the rights but also the identification of those limits on the rights which are justifiable – applies equally to the justification analysis under s. 35(1).[17]

In some respects this is a focal point in the reasoning the Court presents in these important paragraphs, especially as we try to work out whether – and to what extent – it reasons through a liberal mindset. The puzzle we identified in chapter 2 at this point in our exegesis arises from the move the Court makes here, from (a) an approach to the limitation of rights protected under the *Charter of Rights and Freedoms* to (b) the adoption of a similar approach to the limitation of Aboriginal rights protected under section 35. The Court begins by noting these sets of rights are "fundamentally different," but then goes on nevertheless to find they should be open to limitation by government action under the same theory – that whatever accounts for their constitutional status can be brought in to justify their limitation.

---

16 *Ibid* at para 69 [emphasis in original].

17 *Ibid* at para 71.

Let us complete our look into how this unfolds before we turn to how this seems to show a deep attachment to liberal principles. The Court goes on to note purposes behind the constitutionalization of Aboriginal rights (articulated in *Van der Peet*) and how they affect questions of infringement:

> [Given purposes detailed in *Van der Peet*] the objectives which can be said to be compelling and substantial will be those directed at either the recognition of the prior occupation of North America by aboriginal peoples or – and at the level of justification it is this purpose which may well be most relevant – at the reconciliation of aboriginal prior occupation with the assertion of the sovereignty of the Crown.[18]

We find ourselves back at an earlier discussion, about puzzles wrapped up in the development of a theory of reconciliation, and its role in the development of Canadian law as it applies to Aboriginal peoples. Here we simply note that this facilitates the Court's finding that the Crown can act under any number of different (and exceedingly broad) mandates when potentially infringing upon Aboriginal rights, so long as it can argue the objectives it pursues are directed towards the reconciliation of "Aboriginal prior occupation" with its continuing sovereign authority:

> Because ... distinctive aboriginal societies exist within, and are a part of, a broader social, political and economic community, over which the Crown is sovereign, there are circumstances in which, in order to pursue objectives of compelling and substantial importance to that community as a whole (taking into account the fact that aboriginal societies are a part of that community), some limitation of those rights will be justifiable. Aboriginal rights are a necessary part of the reconciliation of aboriginal societies with the broader political community of which they are part; limits placed on those rights are, where the objectives furthered by those limits are of sufficient importance to the broader community as a whole, equally a necessary part of that reconciliation.[19]

We noted above that a condition for the application of liberal doctrine is that Aboriginal peoples be conceived of as contained *within* Canadian society, subject to both the power and authority of the Crown and the dictates of the courts of the state. This shift in *Gladstone* becomes understandable (within liberal doctrine) if we focus on the question of *how* Aboriginal peoples are going to be conceived of as members of society, as elements within the system, to be worked on vis-à-vis such matters as resource allocation (noting, though, this leaves mysterious how

18 *Ibid* at para 72.
19 *Ibid* at para 73.

the embeddedness is understood to have already happened, when the jurisprudence seems to be aimed at the project of making it so!).

At the heart of the liberal vision dominant in contemporary Canada we find two forms of the freedom of individuals held supreme – the freedom to choose how to live one's life, and the freedom to pursue one's plans, once conceived. The second form of freedom generates particular challenges, as should each individual pursue her goals without regard for the interests of others, given limited resources, conflicts will inevitably arise.

Governments are imagined to exist (at least in part) to manage such challenges.[20] Regardless of whether the existence of governments is *justified* in this manner (some argue, for example, that our reason for surrendering a portion of our natural and unrestricted individual freedom is that in doing so to establish the state we make possible more varied and rich forms of freedom),[21] the fact remains that governments function to manage interpersonal conflicts (and to create and foster other conditions that make possible individual flourishing). The apologist notes that in a liberal setting a government will properly approach such a task with liberal principles of equity and fairness in mind.

Within this liberal setting, unacceptable ways of determining the distribution of resources and opportunities between individuals are not too difficult to identify – the state should not act arbitrarily, it should not (unreasonably) coerce individuals through the process, corruption is not to be tolerated, state officials should not (unreasonably) favour one party over others, and so forth. Determining the positive side of the equation is not so simple, as what it means to function "equitably" is open to contestation.

Nevertheless, all (liberal-minded) would agree that one acceptable function of the state is to manage matters that come up between individuals and groups of individuals (when, between the individuals, it may not be possible to attain resolution). Let us bring back into the discussion our hypothetical First Nation, imagining they have successfully demonstrated the existence of a right to fish to trade products of the sea on a commercial scale (leaving to one side for the moment their assertion of a right to regulate both the activity of fishing and

---

20 Connected to this primary purpose is a related matter – that a state-government can exist to generate conditions that make it possible for hitherto impossible or difficult projects to be pursued by individuals. So, for example, the private area of contract law facilitates the establishment of relationships that further the interests of the pre-existing parties.

21 Kymlicka notes that classical liberals strove to answer the question, in Will Kymlicka, *Contemporary Political Philosophy: An Introduction*, 2nd ed (Oxford: Oxford University Press, 2002) at 62:

> [H]ow people born free and equal can come to be governed. Their answer was roughly this: due to the uncertainties and scarcities of social life, individuals, without giving up their moral equality, would endorse ceding certain powers to the state, but only if the state used these powers in trust to protect individuals from those uncertainties and scarcities.

the activity of trading). This community, we noted several times above, could be understood (by courts of Canada) as existing only *within* the nation state, as falling under both state and judicial control. How, though, would its interests be conceived of and dealt with, given this base understanding?

Indications are clear in details provided in *Gladstone*. The first point of note appeared in the invocation of "reconciliation" not just to determine the nature of Aboriginal rights, but their limitations as well. This signals that Aboriginal rights will be measured and balanced "in the mix" with those of non-Aboriginal parties. How, though, will this be accomplished? Details emerge on close reading of a key paragraph in *Gladstone*:

> Questions relevant to the determination of whether the government has granted priority to aboriginal rights holders are those enumerated in *Sparrow* relating to consultation and compensation, as well as questions such as[:] whether the government has accommodated the exercise of the aboriginal right to participate in the fishery (through reduced licence fees, for example), whether the government's objectives in enacting a particular regulatory scheme reflect the need to take into account the priority of aboriginal rights holders, the extent of the participation in the fishery of aboriginal rights holders relative to their percentage of the population, how the government has accommodated different aboriginal rights in a particular fishery (food *versus* commercial rights, for example), how important the fishery is to the economic and material well-being of the band in question, and the criteria taken into account by the government in, for example, allocating commercial licences amongst different users.[22]

Indications are that Aboriginal rights (those that might intersect with interests of non-Aboriginal Canadians – or, indeed, with interests of neighbouring Aboriginal communities) are put into the mix with no real sense they are "special." It would appear the Crown is expected to show "respect" for these rights by essentially weighing them under normal understandings of equity and fairness. These Aboriginal interests are not to be treated arbitrarily, they are not to be ignored (in favour of the interests of others), and they are not to be weighed unfavourably (in respect of the interests of others). When, for example, the question comes up of how the fishing interests of our hypothetical community are to be weighed and balanced against the interests of others in society, the Crown is expected to consider their presence in the area in terms of such metrics as their percentage of the population.

What we witness, when we consider how all this is expected to play out, is a response to the fact that over the history of colonial law and policy in Canada, Aboriginal peoples were often (from a liberal point of view) unfairly treated.

---

22 *Gladstone*, *supra* note 5 at para 64.

That is, their interests as people (as collections of individuals making up segments of the overall population) were often degraded, ignored, or sacrificed for the interests of others. Aboriginal rights enter the landscape today (now constitutionally protected) to address or correct *that* set of wrongs. Aboriginal rights emerge as essentially ameliorative, requiring that the Crown ensure the interests of Aboriginal peoples (as collections of individuals) are *now* treated as one would expect within a liberal society.

The liberal apologist might ask at this point what it would have looked like for Aboriginal rights to be accorded some sort of "special" status (when the question of their placement into the modern Canadian landscape came up). How *should* a Canadian court have dealt with our hypothetical community and its claims around rights to trade products of the sea on a commercial scale? What would it mean to do something *other* than count up the population of this community and put that into the mix when determining what is fair in the matter of the allocation of a finite, regional resource?

It is important to re-interject the point that the aim in this analysis is not to criticize the application of liberalism to the question of how Aboriginal interests should be dealt with in the modern setting. We are not working towards the presentation of an alternate world, built around an alternate moral or ideological vision.[23] The aim is simply to try to explain what we witness, to *make sense* of Aboriginal law. The key point in this context is that it seems evident the Supreme Court ultimately deals with Aboriginal rights in an entirely liberal fashion, as constituting ordinary claims of individuals (who happen to live in distinct sociocultural worlds, who happen to have been discriminated against through a long period of colonialism). An important corollary of this point provides one possible response to the apologist – perhaps it should not be liberal doctrine, liberal institutions, and the liberal state (that directly inherited overt colonial aftermaths) that determine how Indigenous peoples (and the history of Crown-Indigenous relations) should be conceptualized, should we wish to imagine possible responses to colonialism.

What complicates matters when viewed in this manner is the fact that Indigenous peoples can claim not just the power to decide how their shares of resources are to be used, not even just how all shares connected to their territories are to be distributed and used, but how we go about thinking about "shares," "distribution," and "use." That is, it is not just a matter of tweaking linguistic terms (moving, say, from images like cutting up a pie to images of sharing the pie as whole), but about how the world itself is approached by collectively determined modes of understanding. For countless generations Indigenous communities have generated understandings of how to live infused with the sense the world and its components are as alive as humans. Such understandings challenge the liberal world at its foundations, as they represent not simply

23 This partially describes a future project, branching off from this endeavour.

ways of thinking that it may be difficult to tolerate when informing the lives of sub-societies within a multicultural liberal state, but foundations of different ways of thinking how social realities – *where the liberal universe is itself understood to be no more than one possible form of social reality* – can be constructed.

Stepping Back: Forming Beliefs around Existence in a Liberal World

All along we have been looking at what amounts to the construction of social reality. Some involved in the construction may think they are supplied with elements of architectural plans from somewhere without, from a moral or noumenal realm. Regardless of these *beliefs*, what we *observe* is a world within which certain parties assume a position from within which they can – and do – build aspects of social worlds around, and from which they can – and do – attempt to build other aspects. These actions and attempts are designed alike to channel behaviours into acceptable paths and away from unacceptable paths, by the introduction of products of sociolinguistic tools such as new understandings of obligation, duty, power, authority, right, responsibility, and freedom.

For example, within the social world we have been examining, attempts are made to have Aboriginal peoples come to believe that the authoritatively acceptable path to resolution of historic grievances is by the deployment of Aboriginal rights. The Supreme Court has helped bring this about, and in light of the associated need to "make it so" it thereby goes on to try to bring about a sense in the Crown that there are *legal* restrictions on what used to be considered fairly unlimited forms of power enjoyed by both federal and provincial governments.[24] Without the sense that the rule of law now effectively limits previously unlimited state power (vis-à-vis Aboriginal interests), Aboriginal peoples would have little reason to think Aboriginal rights will serve their long-term interests.

One thing not explored in this work is the extent of the judiciary's success in getting the Crown to *accept* this aspect of the new social "reality" it is attempting to build (in the sense that the reality is not fully formed until the Crown accepts it has these legal obligations).[25] Also not directly discussed to this point is a similar matter, the extent to which Indigenous communities, in *resisting* having to think the way the Court constructs "reality," interfere with the Court's machinations becoming reality.[26]

---

24 Acting appropriately, in their proper federal or provincial spheres of jurisdictional authority (though concern over division of powers is now considerably lessened in the Crown-Aboriginal context, post-*Tsilhqot'in Nation*, *supra* note 7).

25 Arguably, legal obligations seem to have this peculiar nature when tied to the Crown. See Gordon Christie, "'Obligations,' Decolonization and Indigenous Rights to Governance" (2014) 27 Can JL & Jur 259 (where I attempted to make this sort of point).

26 This notion of Indigenous resistance to ways of thinking is discussed, if somewhat obliquely, in the last section of this chapter and much of the next.

If we think in terms of long-term goals that seem just visible behind the recently developed jurisprudence – and in doing so also think of the world from the perspective of liberalism – we can also see other aspects of the reality the Court seems to be trying to bring about. In the above picture sketched out, Aboriginal peoples are led to believe Aboriginal rights will function in the modern Canadian context, as the Crown will accede to the notion its power is tempered by legal responsibilities. Connected to the proper functioning of this model is installation in the minds of Aboriginal peoples and communities of the *belief* they fully live within a liberal universe (that is, as normative beings). Let us explore this – considering ways Canadian law works to try to instil this belief – as doing so adds to the strength of the general explanatory force we find lying within liberal thought.

THE PUSH/PULL OF THE LAW OF ABORIGINAL RIGHTS

We begin with a sense of the current status of Aboriginal communities across Canada. Generally speaking, as noted earlier, Aboriginal communities are the poorest of the poor in Canada, and Aboriginal populations suffer from the sorts of social problems observed in the poorest segments of populations around the globe. While there is substantial variance between Aboriginal communities, much of this inter-Aboriginal variance is also of note in calling for explanation.[27] The key matter on which to focus (as we turn to what we might see just behind the veneer of the jurisprudence) is *continuing* social and economic deprivation of most communities.

Generations after federal and provincial governments began to wake up to the need to address inequities in the relative positions of Aboriginal versus non-Aboriginal populations and decades after the constitutionalization of Aboriginal and treaty rights,[28] most Aboriginal communities (especially those further away from the belt of cities and towns hugging the Canadian-U.S. border) remain as mired in poverty and senses of hopelessness as they have been since the midpoint of the twentieth century (and in some cases as far back as Confederation). This fact is particularly remarkable when we also note that Canadian law and policy – overtly colonial through much of the first hundred years after Confederation – was largely responsible for the generation and continuation of these conditions of deprivation (right up to the latter stages of the twentieth century). For over a century, systems of law and policy developed and implemented by Canadian governments went so far as to often prevent Aboriginal

27 Interestingly, as well, there are other noticeable patterns of variance, as, for example, urban Aboriginal populations generally enjoy socio-economic levels significantly above those of land-based Aboriginal communities.

28 It is commonplace to point to the aftermath of the Second World War as the birthplace of this awakening.

peoples from pursuing traditional modes of living, their backstop to sliding into absolute economic despair.[29]

With that history in mind, with the fact of *continuing* deprivation and despair *to this day*, what are we to make of the jurisprudence in *Sparrow*, *Van der Peet*, *Gladstone*, *Delgamuukw*, and *Tsilhqot'in Nation*? On the one hand, we have every sign the federal government is not particularly interested in working with Aboriginal communities in order to help them persist as "traditional" communities living in their traditional territories as many of them have (more or less) for hundreds – if not thousands – of years.[30] On the other hand, we see in current Canadian law forces and mechanisms that can be fairly described as incentives and disincentives – "pulls" meant to *attract* Aboriginal communities away from traditional ways of living towards life more fully ensconced in the liberal (capitalist/consumerist) world, and "pushes" meant to *drive* Aboriginal

---

29 Interestingly, in many contexts across Canada we see early government policy being to ensure traditional ways of living were maintained, not just as this was promised in the large numbered treaties across much of the heart of the country, but for the simple reason that this allowed Aboriginal communities to remain self-sufficient (and so not much of a burden on government services and coffers). With pressure from non-Aboriginal settlers, miners, and other resource-extractors came increasingly restrictive policies, eventually making it difficult for Aboriginal people even just to hunt or fish for food for families. Some of the history of this is presented in *Jack et al v The Queen*, [1980] 1 SCR 294, 100 DLR (3d) 193. At page 306, we find the Court accepting the testimony of an anthropologist, Barbara Lane, concerning government regulation of Indian fishing in the colonial era of British Columbia:

> [T]he policy was one of encouraging the Indians to fish not only to provide food for themselves so that they wouldn't be a burden on the public purse but also to supply the resident non-Indian population with fish and also turning back a moment to the Hudson's Bay Period, the Hudson's Bay relied very heavily upon the Indian Fisherman to supply and provision all of the forts throughout what is now the Province of British Columbia and that cured salmon was the food staple provision for all the forts and this was procured from Indian Fishermen who harvested and in some cases cured the resources.

As the decades pass, legislation becomes increasingly draconian, until fishing of any sort becomes extremely difficult, if not impossible, for most Aboriginal peoples in British Columbia. For a look at the development of policy in the 1800s, see *ibid* at 306–11. For an examination of a longer timeframe for the province, see Doug Harris, *Fish, Law, and Colonialism: The Legal Capture of Salmon in British Columbia* (Toronto: University of Toronto Press, 2001).

30 At the time of this writing a liberal government has replaced a conservative government that enjoyed power for most of the past decade. While the shift in political attitude towards Aboriginal peoples has been quite noticeable, it should also be noted that few of the stated policy objectives of the new progressive government have anything to say about the notion that Indigenous peoples have their own meaning-generating systems that range over vast traditional territories. The closest the government has veered in that direction is in its claim that it will work towards integrating the United Nations *Declaration on the Rights of Indigenous Peoples* into the domestic framework. See *United Nations Declaration on the Rights of Indigenous Peoples*, UNGAOR, 61st Sess, Supp No 49, UN Doc A/RES/61/295 (13 September 2007) [UNDRIP]. While UNDRIP articulates a strong form of Indigenous self-determination, whether we see this political promise bear fruit, and whether we see it done in a way that cleaves to a strong form of Indigenous self-determination, are matters to be seen.

communities in the same direction. With our eyes focused on the jurisprudence, let us detail some of these pushes and pulls, making connections to explanations in liberal thought for these forces and mechanisms.

First, of course, are matters already noted, now put in the context of this model. On the topic of "pushes" we earlier noted that (a) Aboriginal rights are defined "culturally," in ways that make them narrow and exceedingly hard to establish and deploy, (b) Aboriginal interests in land are either minimized or, when established as property rights, seem divorced from matters of jurisdictional authority, and (c) while when connected closely to non-economically threatening activity, Aboriginal rights receive fairly substantial protection from Crown interference, when they do potentially threaten others' economic interests they are, practically speaking, not protected *at all* (as their protection amounts to no more than what might be expected if "Aboriginal rights" were not at issue).

On the topic of "pulls" or incentives, we can note several matters only touched on so far. First, we can mention the fact that protections Aboriginal peoples do manage to enjoy in asserting their Aboriginal rights are less when these rights are *merely asserted*.[31] To receive full protection (such as it is), Aboriginal communities must consider going beyond mere assertion of their constitutionally protected rights, one option being to go through the expensive and time-consuming process of having rights proven and established in court.[32]

While this is a powerful incentive, driving many Indigenous communities to think seriously of engaging in battles in Canadian courts, I do not focus attention on it other than to note the obvious, that this goes to show that Aboriginal rights themselves tend to provide little assistance to Aboriginal communities

---

31 This has to be put carefully, as we are here (as in most of the rest of this text), considering how Indigenous communities try to establish legal claims in Canadian courts (or in negotiations with the Crown). Claims asserted in this context are likely fully established (in a different form) in Indigenous legal systems. These issues were covered in *Haida Nation*, *supra* note 8. For a discussion of *Haida Nation*, see *supra* "The Honour of the Crown" in chapter 2.

32 The law on such matters was set in a trilogy of important Supreme Court of Canada decisions in 2004 and 2005. In *Haida Nation*, *supra* note 9, the Court built up a new regime on duties to consult and accommodate, as it dealt with what had become a pattern of provincial Crown behaviour in British Columbia in relation to rights claimed but not yet proven – the Crown was seen as "running roughshod" over such interests, its argument being that it had no obligations in relation to interests only asserted (interestingly, fiduciary doctrine played a key role in the Crown's argument, as it felt there were no suitably definite or specific legal or practical interests to which it could hold fiduciary obligations). While the Court responded with obligations resting on the "honour of the Crown" (circumventing limitations of fiduciary doctrine), it should be noted that the spectrum of consultation was found, in this context, not to reach to a requirement to achieve an agreement on contemplated Crown action. Two aspects of this new area of jurisprudence are, then, most troubling: (a) Aboriginal communities with asserted but not yet proven interests have no legal right beyond a call on the Crown to listen (meaningfully) to this concerns, and (b) to advance beyond this minimal (indeed, seemingly merely procedural) interest an Aboriginal community must expend the energy necessary to establish their rights in Canadian law.

until they are established in Canadian law (through litigation or negotiation). This itself is an interesting (indeed, puzzling) matter, as it suggests to Indigenous communities that interests they *know* they possess (if only because they have possessed these interests since "time immemorial"!) are of little value in the current Canadian landscape until they have been translated into something quite distinct and then made concrete *within* the Canadian system of law.

What this sort of situation points to are similar such situations wherein rights may be inadequate (especially economically speaking) without further action. For example, in *Delgamuukw*, in talking of established Aboriginal title,[33] the Court noted that not all uses to which a community might want to put its title-lands would fit under the concept of Aboriginal title. An "inherent limit" apparently exists,[34] which precludes the use of title lands in ways that run counter to ways in which the community was able to show its connections to its lands at the time of the assertion of Crown sovereignty.[35] The Court went on to note, however, that the solution to this (most likely economic) conundrum was simple – this community need only surrender its title-interests to the Crown, so these lands can then be put to the planned use.[36]

This alternative – this "solution" – is an instance of the common solution to all such problems: to *negotiate* to arrive at a modern agreement or treaty that sets out the nature of the sought-after rights.[37] Just as the Aboriginal

33 Noting, once again, that title has been established so far once in the entire country, in 2014 in *Tsilhqot'in Nation, supra* note 7.

34 *Delgamuukw, supra* note 6 at para 111. *Tsilhqot'in Nation, supra* note 7, reaffirms the presence of the inherent limit, but seems to use the notion as it appeared in *Delgamuukw* to suggest a major shift in legal restrictions around Crown action. The Court held at paragraph 86 that the Crown, as well, must bear the inherent limit in mind:

> [T]he Crown's fiduciary duty means that the government must act in a way that respects the fact that Aboriginal title is a group interest that inheres in present and future generations. The beneficial interest in the land held by the Aboriginal group vests communally in the title-holding group. This means that incursions on Aboriginal title cannot be justified if they would substantially deprive future generations of the benefit of the land.

35 An example commonly provided would be that of an Aboriginal community interested in building a shopping mall on lands they established title over by showing its use as a hunting ground.

36 *Delgamuukw, supra* note 6 at para 131.

37 Indeed, the Supreme Court often works on generating incentives on the Crown to likewise negotiate arrangements. In *Tsilhqot'in Nation, supra* note 7, the Court expanded the "inherent limit" such that it also applied to decisions about land-use the Crown might contemplate. The Crown, in thinking about infringing upon Aboriginal title, must also, apparently, imagine its plans limited to those that would not infringe upon the ability of future generations of Aboriginal titleholders to make use of their title lands. At paragraph 86, they held that "incursions on Aboriginal title cannot be justified if they would substantially deprive future generations of the benefit of the land." Of course, the implication (once again) is that a negotiated "release" of these rights would clear the way to full use of the lands in question.

title-holder can substitute its inadequate legal tool for others better suited to its contemporary needs, any Aboriginal community can attempt to negotiate its way out of the narrow options provided by Aboriginal rights. Large-scale modern treaties, for example, now cover the entire far north (agreements that were, it must be noted, much easier to negotiate north of the sixtieth parallel, in the absence of provincial governments and in areas where Aboriginal populations make up substantial – in places dominant – proportions of the general population).

Such modern agreements, however, do not promise what one might initially suppose – they have turned out to be very difficult to negotiate south of the sixtieth parallel, their content in the southern context is quite limited, they can be unilaterally justifiably infringed upon (a startling proposition when one notes they are – for the most part – constitutionally protected agreements),[38] and their implementation by modern Canadian governments has been fraught with disappointment.[39]

Nevertheless, leaving aside for the moment these sorts of problems with modern agreements, we see in the general lay of the land that *incentives* are provided Aboriginal communities to leave behind their inadequately functioning Aboriginal rights, to move completely into the "modern" world. The Aboriginal rights a community may hold are (most likely) going to be almost entirely economically inert in the modern capitalist setting, and given the *continuing* economic deprivation most Aboriginal communities exist under, the incentives to *choose* to leave behind "traditional" ways are powerful.[40]

38 In *R v Badger*, [1996] 1 SCR 771, 133 DLR (4th) 324, the Supreme Court found that treaties were subject to the same framework and tests for infringement as had been developed for Aboriginal rights within *Sparrow*. As modern treaties also provide treaty rights under section 35, they are also subject to Crown action that can be justified under this framework.

39 See e.g. *Nunavut Tunngavik Inc v Canada (AG)*, 2014 NUCA 2. This Court of Appeal decision provides a window into the larger litigation, concerning numerous allegations of failure by the Crown to implement the Nunavut Land Claim Agreement. In May 2015, negotiations undertaken in light of this ruling resulted in a settlement. See *Moving Forward in Nunavut: An Agreement Relating to Settlement of Litigation and Certain Implementation Matters* (5 March 2015), online: <tunngavik.com/files/2015/05/FINAL-SETTLEMENT-AGREEMENT-PROOF.pdf>. While a clear victory for the Inuit of Nunavut, the decade-long struggle to have provisions of the original agreement implemented shows the challenge facing Indigenous peoples with modern agreements. Groups with modern agreements work together in facing such challenges within a Land Claims Coalition. See *Land Claims Agreements Coalition*, online: <www.landclaimscoalition.ca>.

40 Since the turn of the twenty-first century we have seen Aboriginal communities reach many "impact benefit agreements," essentially agreeing to industrial activities and developments that affect their interests in exchange for a variety of "benefits" (including such things as training and employment, subcontracting on aspects of the project, and promises on environmental management and clean-up).

HAVING INDIVIDUALS AND GROUPS SEE AND ACT AS EMBEDDED SUBUNITS

The roles that "choice" plays in this slowly unfolding drama are vitally important. Consider, once again, the hypothetical First Nation. We noted in chapter 6 that liberalism does not find value in culture per se, but can locate derivative or secondary value in culture's role in either (a) providing a context of choice, and/or (b) being the product of choice. Assuming the First Nation had met requirements for establishing a right to trade products of the sea on a commercial scale, we can understand liberal thought finding value in this aspect of culture insofar as both (a) at the time of contact with Europeans this practice, tradition, or custom was an integral part of their distinctive culture – an aspect "*chosen*" – and (b) this practice continues today to be an integral part of their continuing Aboriginal culture insofar as it *continues* to be *chosen*.

The first mention of being "chosen" in this last sentence is in scare quotes, as it is not at all settled what form of "choice" is being invoked. When we passed through a similar discussion in chapter 6 we noted that liberal theory could find value in culture insofar as it exhibits choices made – the First Nation fighting for recognition of a right to trade fish on a commercial scale would be arguing (within the liberal universe) that at the time of contact with Europeans its cultural life revolved around such "choices" its people had made to engage in trading (on a scale or in a form that today corresponds with commercial trading). Seeing a particular cultural artefact manifesting choices made by individuals would be what triggers recognition and acceptance in the liberal world, holding up the sense in that world view of saying such cultural artefacts could be considered "rights." The challenge in pinning down exactly what it means to speak of "choices" in this context is that it would actually not be possible to point to *particular choices* made by particular *individuals* – rather, an *assumption* is made about the presence of countless "choices" made by many members of this society over many years – generations in fact. The presumption (based on appropriate evidence) would be that over generations this community evolved (through successive series of such choices) such as to come to be *defined* as a trading culture, so an objective observer would fairly say this feature of this community's way of living is integral to their distinctive culture.

"Choice" in the modern context is the focus of our inquiry, and we do not run into the same problems in coming to an understanding of how this is conceptualized within the contemporary liberal universe. In fact, it is in seeing that the members of an Aboriginal collective are *assumed* to be in positions from which they are free to choose to continue to live according to their traditional ways that we see how pushes and pulls are expected to work.

A common position underlying understandings of choice is that collectives do not make choices (that is, as if a collective possessed some sort of "collective mind"). Within the general liberal universe it is understood that groups of individuals can make decisions that bind that group, but choices reflected in those decisions are still understood to be ultimately choices made by individuals who make up that group. Fortunately, though, we can leave aside questions some might raise about sense in the notion of decisions made *by* a collective (as opposed to decisions made by members of a collective), as our focus is on how Canadian governments and courts *think* of the situation of members of Aboriginal collectives in the context of the modern liberal state. In this context the *operating presumption* is that individuals – "persons" – *should* be free to choose how to live. The contemporary Aboriginal person, living within an Aboriginal cultural setting, is expected, then, to be *able* to choose to live through this cultural setting – or, more importantly, to be *able* to choose *not* to live through traditional cultural norms, to choose rather to adopt both ways of thinking and forms of action that bespeak a liberal frame. It is fascinating that in just coming to *see* herself this way the Aboriginal person finds herself slipping over to a liberal frame of mind (as the community itself then also inches closer to being liberal-embedded).

We can now appreciate why – and fully acknowledge the impact of the fact that – Canadian law is highly sceptical of the value (to the individual) of Aboriginal culture. Recalling our earlier discussion of the basic parameters of liberal thought, this scepticism comes about both (a) because Aboriginal cultures (as wholes) are understood to be traditional (in the liberal sense of this term, as forms of living antithetical to the liberal ideal), and (b) because within these cultures (as a result of their assumed illiberality) individual choices are constrained, so that any manifestation of the general culture is itself suspect (as not "really" chosen). And so the objective of pushes and pulls is to transform the collective from the inside out, shifting the entire collective, individual decision by individual decision, away from adherence to traditional ways towards acceptance of life lived entirely within the liberal setting. To restate the important underlying point, it is not the individual decisions themselves that affect this shift, but rather the fact that in *seeing oneself* as being the sort of person to properly make such decisions (and the community *seeing itself* as being properly a place within which such individual decisions are proper and primary) the society one is in becomes liberal-minded. This is the form of construction of social reality most important in the modern work of "liberalizing" Indigenous communities.

There are a few subtle points contained in this discussion, points essential to understanding how best to make sense of Aboriginal law from within a liberal world. With that in mind, let me unpack this idea that both the liberal construction of Aboriginal rights and their subsequent placement in the Canadian legal and political landscape are meant to transform Indigenous individuals and communities. This provides an opportunity to repackage this discussion in a way that may help illuminate some of the subtleties and help build up the sense that liberalism explains much of what we see in contemporary Aboriginal law.

Consider again the hypothetical First Nation. Its status as a collective is of great interest here, as its heritage as a collective reaches back generations to a past in which, as a "traditional" society, it was clearly illiberal. To say this is not to deny the existence (and indeed the importance) in those earlier times of ideals of freedom and equality for individuals living within this society, but to point rather to different conceptions of the individual on a more fundamental level, of the individual's relationships to natural and social worlds, and of the nature of the collective to which the individual belongs.[41]

The liberal world begins with a normative vision of the individual – recall our earlier discussion of the communitarian challenge and responses by contemporary liberal theorists.[42] The contemporary liberal vision posits essential properties of the individual, around which revolve entire theories of moral and political normativity. The core vision has the individual possess abilities both to step back from his or her values to examine and re-examine them, and to be able to then pursue new goals and plans based on new valuations of the good (as now accepted by this person). These are senses of freedom commonly held to be inherently valuable – indeed, the only real good we can *know* in the world (within the perfectionist strand of liberal thought). *This normative vision of the individual then accounts for the model of the appropriate structuring of the collective.* At a superstructural level, the collective should allow all individuals to exercise these forms of freedom equally well (and, in some forms of liberalism, such as to maximize opportunities for individuals to come to and work towards personal senses of value and good).

Back, then, to the hypothetical First Nation collective. We assume it had not been structured with a liberal architectural plan in mind many generations ago. Canadian courts will approach this situation, then, from a very particular liberal point of view. Insofar as an Aboriginal people continue to live within a cultural setting based on "traditional" ways, we can *expect* institutions within the larger liberal setting within which this is assumed to happen (a) to be wary of the influence this has on the ability of those living in this community to enjoy the freedoms that underscore their inherent value (as persons, as understood from the liberal point of view), and (b) thereby to exhibit tolerance of these cultural practices that is limited at best.

41 I trust the reader has seen this point, but it bears repeating and reinforcing in this note. In saying an Indigenous society may be illiberal, one is not suggesting that in such a sociocultural setting such things as freedom and equality are somehow devalued or considered unimportant. Rather, what this means is that the society under discussion is understood to be built upon a different vision of the individual-collective dyad. Liberalism is not a theory restricted to beliefs about the value of the individual, but primarily a theory about what this means in the context of the construction of society around this vision of the individual. All indigenous societies (as far as I am aware) were built (and most continue to be built) upon different theories of the relationship between the free individual and the society within which these individuals are embedded.

42 See *supra* "Rawls on the Liberal Conception of the Person" in chapter 6.

With Aboriginal rights constitutionally protected, one might expect tolerance to extend to attempts to find ways Aboriginal nations might fit within the larger liberal context without attacks on the core of their being. What we seem to observe, however, when we gaze out over the entire structure of Aboriginal law, is a remarkably thin shell of tolerance, lying over apparent attempts at liberalizing Aboriginal communities. It is on these attempts at liberalization that we must focus attention, trying to illuminate subtleties in how "choice" is meant to play out in the contemporary Canadian landscape around Aboriginal communities and their rights.

We noted above how incentives and disincentives within the regime of Aboriginal law aim to get Aboriginal individuals and communities to choose to move *away* from their traditional ways of living and *towards* "modern" (capitalist/consumerist) forms. In a sense this is all quite mechanical – what we are trying to elucidate here, on the other hand, is a process that runs parallel to (indeed, is wrapped up with) these mechanical efforts. For these pushes and pulls to fully *work* within a liberal setting, Indigenous individuals and communities exposed to them need to come to understand themselves through the liberal (normative) vision outlined earlier.

As the hypothetical First Nation is faced with these pushes and pulls, members within feel the forces meant to move them fully within the liberal fold. On the one hand, they face the simple fact this all transpires within a larger liberal setting – they find themselves living within a liberal democracy, this particular situation being predicated (from within this liberal world) on the notion that they (as a collection of *individuals*) are *presumed* to be free to decide to continue to choose to follow traditional practices or free to give way to the pressures that Canadian law generates, to accept alternate pathways. On the other hand, then, we see how this all shows attempts to construct a form of social reality within which these individuals and their community can be constructively *formed*.

The most important part about this situation for those trying to understand what is happening (in this *naturalist* mode of explanation) is that the only material fact we witness is the presence of a normative system that makes a *presumption* about the status of a collective of Aboriginal individuals. This presumption is *actualized* only if Indigenous individuals and communities facing such situations do in fact come to understand themselves in ways presumed by the larger system, based upon this liberal normative vision. We witness, then, a wonderfully clear attempt at the construction of a particular sort of social reality.

THE CHALLENGE OF PRE-EXISTING INDIGENOUS SOCIETIES: SEPARATE MEANING-GENERATING COLLECTIVES

While I cast the form of scepticism behind what we witness as directed towards the possibility of "illiberal" forms of Indigenous culture, I think one should be careful to probe a bit deeper, to see if this makes sense as being that part of the liberal response to the presence of pre-existing Aboriginal societies that best makes sense of the liberal construction of Aboriginal law. Arguably, being "illiberal" does not appear to be the most important characteristic of Indigenous societies viewed as suspect.

Return to our hypothetical First Nation. Imagine this nation exists as a relatively bounded and discrete subunit within the larger Canadian liberal democracy. Questions would then arise about how it would – as a unit unto itself – fit into the Canadian legal and political landscape. Imagine further – as part of a thought experiment – that, taken on its own (removed from any thought about its existence within Canada), it actually functions today as a liberal society. That is, as part of this experiment, imagine that viewed in isolation it functions in a way that individuals *understand* themselves as persons in the liberal sense, with the First Nation governance structure *understood* to have as its proper role the creation of conditions that best ensure the flourishing of individual members *as persons*, with distinct normative characteristics (of freedom and equality).

Now, place this community back into its current setting, as a relatively discrete and bounded subunit of the larger Canadian liberal democracy. The question still remains: how would this larger body accommodate the existence of this subunit? If we stick to the notion that the subunit is a distinct society – in the sense it can be conceived of as having its own membership and governance structure – whether that governance structure is modelled on liberal principles would likely not affect the most important aspects of the scene we would witness. Arguably, Canadian courts would still characterize the Canadian state as the proper sole over-arching sovereign, such that this First Nation would have to fit within this over-arching power structure. Furthermore, arguably Canadian courts would be incapable of seeing any other role for themselves than to work out how – under liberal principles – this can be can be brought about.

How would Canadian law approach this subunit, structured and governed under a liberal self-conception? Again, we see the impact of requirements for being dealt with in a liberal (positivist) framework – a *single system* of law and authority must be presumed, within which the interests of this First Nation must fit in order to avoid unjustly affecting the interests of other groups and individuals. The structures we see presented in *Sparrow*, *Gladstone*, *Delgamuukw*, and *Tsilhqot'in Nation* would still "make sense" within this imagined liberal world (even when the First Nation, as a subunit, is itself entirely liberal).

There must, of course, be some adjustment to ways of thinking of the situation – suspicions cast on the First Nation, for example, would be tempered. But this is at best an impotent tempering of suspicion. An observer might argue – fairly convincingly – that the larger liberal body should be able to allow power to be placed in the hands of this First Nation in relation to how resources and opportunities might be generated amongst, and then allocated or distributed to, individuals. With liberal principles structuring decision-making institutions in this community, it is hard to see what might prevent devolution of power in this manner. But what of *Aboriginal rights*? This First Nation has shown it has an Aboriginal right to trade products of its fishing endeavours on a commercial scale. Might we not expect this community – liberal-minded as it is – *capable* of making decisions about resource allocation in relation to this activity, having this power fall within the ambit of its constitutionally protected rights?

The larger Canadian state would, however, remain "suspicious," though in a different form. Both the state and its courts would presume this community would not be in a position to properly approach the interests of *others* (other Aboriginal communities or non-Aboriginal individuals and groups), as the governance and decision-making abilities of this First Nations community *reach out only to its membership*. Without having these other interests *properly* within its purview, it would not be seen as the system that should be making decisions regarding these other interests when questions arise about Aboriginal rights lacking internal limits. While this community may be liberal within itself, it finds itself entirely within the larger legal and political community, and it is *that* community that properly (within a liberal positivist model) makes decisions necessitated by this kind of situation. The placement of Aboriginal rights makes sense, then, when viewed from a liberal mindset, as the need, most generally, is for a way to manage Aboriginal interests so they properly function within one unified liberal society.

The explanation for Aboriginal law provided over the last few chapters provides an answer to this question: given the ambitions and goals operative within a liberal world, given the initial starting conditions after Aboriginal rights were recognized and affirmed in the Canadian constitution, and given core principles structuring thought and action within the liberal universe, how do we expect Aboriginal rights to have been constructed? I approached this question from the endpoint backward – given the construction we witness, how might we account for it? Can we reconstruct the thinking and actions that would have gone into the construction, given the starting points? To the extent the explanation makes sense, we can say we have made sense of Aboriginal rights – an explanation for this presence and form has been provided.

We are on the cusp of being in a position to summarize, to see the extent to which Aboriginal law can be explained through liberal positivism. It might seem one last matter requires direct investigation before we move into providing this summary – the treatment of Indigenous governance within Canadian jurisprudence. Putting together the pieces developed over the last two chapters into one collapsed narrative shows how this one last piece of Indigenous power and authority does not fit well. The act of laying out the explanation provided by liberal positivism for the development and nature of Aboriginal rights offers an opening to the discussion of the next stage of analysis, as we turn to thinking about evaluating the *adequacy* of the explanation we now have before us. Tying these threads together points us towards those matters within Aboriginal law – particularly from an Indigenous perspective – that simply cannot be *adequately* explained in the manner so far witnessed.

A Liberal Positivist Explanation of Aboriginal Rights and the Place of Indigenous Self-Determination

We noted that the nature of Aboriginal rights – as narrowly defined (tied to cultural activities), as partially constructed in relation to non-Aboriginal Canadians' interests and governmental power, and as subject to a wide range of sanctioned infringement (where often the government need only "respect" the priority expressed in these rights) – makes sense when seen in the context of the placement of Aboriginal interests in a liberal setting. Canadian courts – courts of a liberal democracy – have constructed legal instruments and placed them into a socio-legal framework, such that they both (a) make sense in a liberal world and (b) help generate a reality within which Aboriginal peoples feel pushed and pulled towards leaving behind whatever elements of non-liberal reality they continue to possess and live within, where the key power they retain is the capacity to generate separate, independent meaning.

What exactly is this non-liberal reality Indigenous peoples possess? How is this reality the product of a past that persists up to this contemporary setting? Furthermore, to what extent do liberal institutions actually pay attention to the past that grounds this reality (and to its evolution into the present) as they seem to attempt to build a social environment in which it is anticipated Aboriginal peoples will come to be *fully* citizens of a liberal democracy? Let us once again pass through some key developments in the history of Crown-Indigenous relations, this time with a clear focus on roles Canadian law and policy played in generating conditions (or realities) within which Indigenous peoples have had to live. We can consider, then, the extent to which liberal institutions pay attention to key elements of this history.

From the mid-nineteenth century up to just past the midpoint of the twentieth century, Canadian law and policy was overtly colonial. This is not an evaluative assessment but an observation. Most of the territories occupied by Indigenous peoples were taken, sometimes in quasi-consensual arrangements, often in murky arrangements, and in places like British Columbia, the Maritimes, Quebec, and the far north (for the most part), through simple takings (with little or no concern with the interests thereby stripped away). Indigenous communities were placed on small plots of (usually) economically marginal land, and the lives of Aboriginal peoples (now legally defined) became tightly controlled by government bodies in faraway centres.[43]

These *overt* forms of colonialism – underscored by racist beliefs running counter to basic liberal principles – began to fade after the Second World War. By the 1970s it was clear new laws and policies were required. What we seem to witness with development of the modern law around Aboriginal rights, however, is arguably a continuation of efforts directed towards the same ends, though now to be achieved in more subtle – indeed, seemingly masked – fashion. What do we witness in this unfolding series of events? Can we tie what we *actually* witness to what we *seem* to witness?

We begin once again where we must – by acknowledging the presence for hundreds of years (in some cases, thousands of years) of many, varied Indigenous communities living in territories that effectively blanket what has become modern-day Canada. Over the course of many generations these communities not only formed their own sorts of collectives, but did so through the development of their own normative models of individuality and community, forms and models that – whatever else they may be – certainly were not liberal on the superstructural level. As the overt period of colonialism progressed, we see clear efforts to undercut or eliminate these foundational structures, those that make possible and that generate sociocultural meaning.

At the core of this naturalist telling I acknowledge that humans are a species of hominoid possessed of sociolinguistic tools by which they can generate rich cultural forms, and thereby generate forms of social reality. Indigenous collectives have each built up and inhabited particular forms of social reality, within which particular understandings of such things as "responsibility," "legitimacy," "duty," "obligation," and "right" are formed and modified over time.[44] Through

43 While only "Indians" were directly mentioned in the drafting of Canada's original Constitution (making possible the creation of "status Indians" under *Indian Act*, RSC 1985, c I–5, provisions), in doing so those left outside the clear purview of section 91(24) of the *Constitution Act, 1867* (UK), 30 & 31 Vict, c 3, reprinted in RSC 1985, App II, No 5, were also (indirectly) legally placed within the Canadian legal and political landscape. In an early decision of the Supreme Court, the legal status of Inuit was settled, while only recently were definitive moves towards doing the same for the Metis and non-status Indians concluded. See *Reference as to whether "Indians" includes in s 91 (24) of the BNA Act includes Eskimo in habitants of the Province of Quebec*, [1939] SCR 104, 2 DLR 417; *Daniels v Canada (Indian Affairs and Northern Development)*, 2016 SCC 12. Unfortunately, in *Daniels*, as was noted in the overview of Indigenous peoples in chapter 1 (and particularly the "Metis" section), the Supreme Court upheld much of the reasoning of the trial judge (accepting that self-definition without necessarily nation-grounding may suffice in certain circumstances), separating tests for being Metis for the purposes of legislative jurisdiction (under section 91(24)) from tests for being Metis for the purposes of exercising rights under section 35.

44 These terms are all in scare quotes, as it is not at all clear (and indeed seems quite unlikely) that they have close cognates in Indigenous systems of meaning. One project to try

the long period of overt colonialism, alongside acts of physical dispossession, both the *expressions* of these underlying systems of meaning-generation and the mechanisms responsible for these expressions were under constant and (often) brutal attack. Indigenous systems of governance and law were subject not just to denial and maltreatment, but often to legal censure. Let me mention just one such attack, one that might strike the observer as directed towards "religious" or spiritual activities: in 1884 amendments to the *Indian Act* outlawed "Indian festivals" and "dances."[45] These ceremonial events, however, were (and continue to be) far more than "festivals" and "dances" – they were also social, economic, and political events, where laws were recited, histories recollected, identities strengthened, decisions made, and political allegiances forged and strengthened.[46] This ban lasted until further amendments to the *Indian Act* were made in 1951.

Some of the attacks were more obviously directed towards underlying systems and subsystems of meaning-generation, the residential school policy offering a most obvious and clear example.[47] As collectives, each Indigenous community has its own way of forming social reality within which its members not just live,

---

to avoid (or to engage in very carefully) is that of beginning with the meanings of these terms in Euro-Canadian frames and then searching for similar concepts or expressions in particular Indigenous communities. For discussions on these vitally important concerns, see Taiaiake Alfred, *Peace, Power, Righteousness: An Indigenous Manifesto* (Don Mills, ON: Oxford University Press, 1999); Patricia Monture-Angus, *Journeying Forward: Dreaming First Nations' Independence* (Halifax: Fernwood, 1999).

45 *An Act Further to Amend "The Indian Act, 1880,"* SC 1882, c 27, s 3:

> Every Indian or other person who engages in or assists in celebrating the Indian festival known as the "Potlach" or in the Indian dance known as the "Tamanawas" is guilty of a misdemeanor, and shall be liable to imprisonment ... and any Indian or other person who encourages ... an Indian or Indians to get up such a festival or dance, or to celebrate the same ... is guilty of a like offence[.]

46 See e.g. Robin Fisher, *Contact and Conflict: Indian-European Relations in British Columbia, 1774–1890* (Vancouver: University of British Columbia Press, 1977). In discussing the effects of the ban of the potlatch in 1884 amendments to the *Indian Act*, Fisher notes at pages 207–8: "It would have been degrading and economically disastrous for many chiefs to stop potlatching while they still owed obligations.... But most of all the ceremony was fundamental to the social organization of the coast Indians[.]"

See Arthur Ray, "It Is a Strict Law That Bids Us Dance" in Arthur Ray, *I Have Lived Here since the World Began: An Illustrated History of Canada's Native People* (Toronto: Key Porter Books, 1996) 222 (writing of the ban that extended initially to both the potlach and the Tamanawas). For a more extensive detailing of the ban, see Christopher Bracken, *The Potlatch Papers: A Colonial Case History* (Chicago: University of Chicago Press, 1997). Bracken goes through many of the multiple forms of this social institution amongst coast peoples, showing how meaningless it was to ban something simply labelled "potlatch."

47 See Truth and Reconciliation Commission of Canada, Honouring the Truth, Reconciling for the Future: Summary of the Final Report of the Truth and Reconciliation Commission of Canada (2015), online: <http://www.chaireconditionautochtone.fss.ulaval.ca/documents/pdf/Honouring-the-truth-reconciling-for-the-future.pdf>.

but come to think of what it is to be and to live together. Residential schooling – removing children from their families through their formative years – was meant to destroy these systems of meaning-generation and transmission, to destroy "the Indian" in the Indian.[48] Not only were residential schools meant to eliminate knowledge – they were designed to destroy the *sources* of knowledge in family and community life, and the means of *transmitting* knowledge through those social units.

New laws and policies of the modern era fail, however, to respond to earlier colonial events directed towards the destruction of sources and manifestations of meaning-generation. Indeed, in a key respect modern laws and policies must (given a liberal understanding of the world) continue on with the same goals and objectives that informed previous Crown actions. As much as earlier overt actions to destroy Indigenous systems of meaning-generation may have conflicted with liberal principles, this conflict can be understood in the modern liberal mind only as being due entirely to their basis in racist beliefs, not in the goals towards which they advanced. A liberal society *requires* (a) a population understood to be entirely contained within a unitary system of law and governance, and (b) citizens who understand themselves to be members of a liberal society. In the modern anti-racist liberal world, attempts to fulfil these two conditions that emanate from racist beliefs will not be acceptable, but *fulfilling these two conditions will still be essentially required.* Clearly, efforts that advanced towards those requirements in the overt colonial period, while they might be censured today for their racist motivations, are not capable of being considered "wrong" or harmful. They can only be seen in the liberal mind as necessary.

This is what it means to say that the modern system of law built up around Aboriginal rights fails to respond to earlier efforts at destroying Indigenous systems of meaning-generation: indeed, it *cannot* respond, as there is no way within the modern liberal-judicial mindset to make sense of *wrongs* or *harms* in those earlier actions (other than that they were based on racist beliefs). The actions themselves are to be neither challenged nor undone. Indeed, to the extent earlier overt activities failed to achieve goals deemed necessary, they must be carried on, though now without racist beliefs animating them, and in ways that more clearly accord with liberal principle.

For the most part, in this text questions about the place of Indigenous authority and governance in the modern Canadian landscape have been raised and

48 The notion of removing the Indian from the child is often lifted from various quotes by Duncan Campbell Scott, then superintendent of Indian Affairs. In 1920 he wrote, cited in JR Miller, *Skyscrapers Hide the Heavens: A History of Indian-White Relations in Canada*, 3rd ed (Toronto: University of Toronto Press, 2000) at 281–2: "I want to get rid of the Indian problem.... That has been the whole purpose of Indian education and advancement since the earliest times.... Our object is to continue until there is not a single Indian in Canada that has not been absorbed into the body politic."

then addressed only indirectly. We touched on the treatment of Indigenous law at several places, but principally noted just that that treatment within Canadian law was skewed. When we occasionally observed that a Canadian court acknowledges "Indigenous law" as a source of Aboriginal rights, we noted as well, though more in passing, that a legal system is not captured as a *legal system* if it is conceived of as simply a set of laws (or rules or principles). An Indigenous *legal system* would be thought of as such when understood to emanate from a meaning-generating collective, from a polity with the authority to determine its own understandings of "law," "governance," and (even) "authority."

Earlier we asked why in foundational cases – in *Sparrow*, *Van der Peet*, *Gladstone*, *Delgamuukw*, and *Tsilhqot'in Nation* – the Supreme Court failed to acknowledge the existence of Indigenous sovereignty. Much earlier, in our first overview of Aboriginal law, when we introduced key puzzles (especially those tied to Indigenous perspectives), we noted that a central puzzle is this failure to acknowledge the power and authority of Indigenous legal-political bodies. Is the usurpation of power and authority a central, defining harm of colonialism? How can the entire edifice of Aboriginal law completely ignore this aspect of the history of Crown-Indigenous relations? We have arrived at a point when an explanation – from within liberal sensibilities – can be provided, *but one that only heightens puzzlement from an Indigenous perspective.*

Liberal Theory and Liberal Theorists in the Natural World

What, then, are we to make of the fact that puzzles remain? Over the last two chapters we explored a set of rules and principles that constitute the contemporary domestic law on Aboriginal rights, and we have seen that – should we suppose this area of law was provided with its form and content in order to accord with a liberal vision of human nature and how society should be structured within a single state – we arrive at a reasonably rich explanation for what we observe. If aspects of this law appear puzzling or troubling to Indigenous peoples and their allies, should this then not be a matter of debate in the realm of norms and justification? Is it not at this point a matter principally about whether the Supreme Court has been *justified* in using liberal principles in constructing the law concerning Aboriginal rights?

A question running parallel to this last query – its flip side, if you will – is critical to seeing where all this analysis has actually led: are the puzzles – particularly those that remain deeply troubling – on a level that engages with what we observe in the natural world? What we witness around us, and what we observe stretching back historically, is the meaning-generating capacity of the state and its courts set up against the separate and independent meaning-generating capacities of numerous and varied Indigenous collectives. If we leave to one side normatively charged questions about the liberal world and its belief structures, we witness such things as the Supreme Court attempting to build a system of rules on liberal principles that encompasses the lives, futures, and systems of meaning-generation of all Indigenous peoples.

When we turn the question around in this way – when we focus on the matter of *explaining* what we *observe* in the world, if we avoid entanglement with normative matters, if we stay *outside* not just the normative system of the liberal world, but our own (whatever that might be) and those of Indigenous collectives, if we focus our gaze on what we can see happening in the natural world – two mutually reinforcing conclusions can be reached. First, a negative conclusion: we do not travel down paths that eventually lead to claims that "this should not be so." Rather, our investigation is into whether we arrive at as full an explanation as is possible if we cleave to beliefs held and actions undertaken by various actors. When we keep our minds focused on what we are attempting to do – to make sense of, to explain the nature of, Aboriginal rights – we arrive at our positive conclusion: we arguably witness a power-dominant meaning-generating collective attempting to achieve a central objective, the final removal of all competing meaning-generating systems, while other (Indigenous) meaning-generating collectives experience the effects of these actions of the dominant system. A third conclusion we can reach emerges from consideration of what liberal theory is doing in "theorizing," and it is to this analysis we now turn.

We shift our focus in this way by first returning to the query that animates the last two chapters: does liberal theory provide a reasonably *full* explanatory account (within a naturalized view of the law and theorizing)? The answer is no, as we can appreciate that the liberal construction project functions, and makes complete sense, only *within* a world already bounded by liberal thought. This point is vividly illustrated if we take a look into the work of liberal scholars who write on the nature of Aboriginal rights. As we will see, rather than grapple with the task of explaining what the Supreme Court is doing and why, they principally act as facilitators and coaches. The "game" is that of working out a relationship between Aboriginal peoples and the Crown (and so, as well, non-Aboriginal society), and liberal theorists all assume that a set of rules for this game *already exist*, that how this game will be "*properly*" played is set, and so how it should unfold is *predetermined*.

One key aim in this work has been to design and implement an approach to legal theorizing that avoids engagement with particular normative worlds established through sociocultural-linguistic instruments. There can be a place for such engagement – but only on the condition those debating *already co-exist* within one general system of belief (which can be as amorphous in its conditions for establishment as a belief of each participant that they are all members of one collective, whether it be clan, tribe, society or nation). In such a setting, members of the defined group can productively debate what *should* be done, how society *should* be conceived of, and how it *should* be organized.

But that is *not* what we have before us in the situation under examination in this text. Should an Indigenous collective try to engage with those of a liberal mindset about (for example) whether the Supreme Court is *justified* in its efforts to domesticate Indigenous collectives from within the common discourse concerning "justification," it would be in danger of losing its struggle for self-determination. In the natural world within which exist numerous and varied collectives capable of generating their own meanings, we find independent sets of beliefs into what is "right" and "good." Indigenous peoples must be careful in arguing with the state and its agents that they not cede their authority to stamp their sets of beliefs about norms as authoritative (especially when those norms regulate how they live in relation to their territories).

Slattery and Macklem and the State of Aboriginal Rights Literature

And so, as we turn to a look into how the works of liberal scholars function, the aim is not to engage with the content of normative beliefs and assumptions. The aim is to lay bare these beliefs and assumptions and to suggest how they assist the state in burying the meaning-generating capacity of Indigenous peoples. It bears stressing once again: the analysis that follows is not meant to show something is *wrong* with what we witness, but simply to explain what is happening in the world around us.

SLATTERY, GENERATIVE RIGHTS, AND INTER-SOCIETAL LAW

In "The Generative Structure of Aboriginal Rights," Brian Slattery argues that while in the years since *Van der Peet* came down the Supreme Court has been moving towards a better ("generative") account of the nature of Aboriginal rights, this new focus on Aboriginal rights as generative (as opposed to purely "historical") will still not do all the work necessary in the modern context.[49] A proper theory of Aboriginal rights would go further, building on two sets of principles, those of recognition (tied to the historical grounding of these rights), and those focused on reconciliation (tied to the need to find the place of these rights in relation to non-Aboriginal interests). It would be only with rights designed with these two sets of principles in mind, Slattery argues, that Aboriginal rights can be properly situated in the modern world.

Slattery approaches the task of unpacking the jurisprudence in a manner we see informing the work of nearly all contemporary mainstream legal scholars

49 Brian Slattery, "The Generative Structure of Aboriginal Rights" in Macklem & Sanderson, *supra* note 1, 100 [Slattery, "Generative Structure"].

writing in this field.[50] Indeed, his work shows most clearly what this common approach amounts to. We begin, then, with a look into his *method* for "making sense" of Aboriginal rights, showing the schema of an approach that bears little resemblance to the CSM underscoring theorizing about phenomena we explored in the middle chapters of this text. As we then track how this method unfolds in this article, we can begin to appreciate the nature of Slattery's "theorizing" or "making sense" of Aboriginal rights. We then turn to one other prominent scholar working in this field, Patrick Macklem, to illustrate how this common approach to legal analysis animates so much of the literature.[51]

Slattery's approach rests on the notion that the law dealing with section 35 has been in flux over the last few decades, and that as the years pass it advances gradually towards having content better in accord with some (fairly amorphous) notions of what it should look like. His general argument also requires that we imagine some impending leap over the remaining chasm, the result being transformation into doctrine that resolves long-standing challenges. What exactly are these challenges? Who decides what the challenges are? How will this imagined leap forward address these challenges? Where in all this are meaning-generating Indigenous legal and political collectives?

There are two sets of answers to these questions: those we can develop should we work *within* the conceptual/normative world Slattery cohabits with the state and its courts, and those we can develop should we attempt to make sense of Aboriginal rights from the vantage point of a general naturalist/realist (that is, a vantage point that stands *outside* and takes into view the various conceptual/

---

50 For a recent arrival in the field of study (if only for its name!), see especially Jamie Dickson, *The Honour and Dishonour of the Crown: Making Sense of Aboriginal Law in Canada* (Saskatoon, SK: Purich Publishing, 2015). In this book-length treatment of Supreme Court jurisprudence we find a general argument that Canadian law finds itself in a transition era, the old framework (based on both conventional and unconventional fiduciary obligations) being replaced with the new, where "Aboriginal law ... functions primarily if not exclusively to regulate against the mischief of Crown dishonour in circumstances involving Aboriginal and/or treaty rights": *ibid* at 144. This new era will come complete with greater "doctrinal clarity and functionality," allowing for the development of cleaner approaches to remedial matters (which will be potentially more meaningful for Aboriginal parties): *ibid* at 133, 141–3. Suggestions are made about how we get from here to there (for example, having parties *see* the lack of doctrinal clarity and the inability of the old framework to advance Aboriginal interests) and larger matters are to be properly understood to be the subject matter of different arenas – with, for example, reconciliation (and the matter of "Aboriginal sovereignty") to be worked out politically between leaders of Canada's government and Aboriginal leaders. All this analysis takes place deeply embedded within a liberal sensibility, something I leave the reader to see, should she take up Dickson's text after noting how I make and support this sort of claim in relation to Slattery and Macklem's work. The form of Dickson's "making sense" is then laid bare.

51 Patrick Macklem, "Indigenous Peoples and the Ethos of Legal Pluralism in Canada" in Macklem & Sanderson, *supra* note 1, 17 [Macklem, "Indigenous Peoples"].

normative worlds at play in this situation before us, a situation marked by struggles between meaning-generating communities).

The divide between the two sets opens clearly when we think about "who gets to decide" on key legal issues. This matter is not seriously questioned by most Aboriginal law jurists, and Slattery is no exception – it is assumed that Canadian courts (and/or legislative bodies) enjoy this power. This aligns the contemporary scholar with the position of both the state and its courts and moves us into a shared conceptual/normative world of discourse.

From within this world, what is/are the challenge(s)? Again, the answer is relatively common amongst most contemporary legal scholars – to work out a just and fair resolution to harms incurred (harms that arose principally as a result of *mistakes* made). What are these harms? Here we come face-to-face with the liberal positivist world, and our unpacking of scholars' arguments intersects with arguments canvassed in the last two chapters. "Who gets to decide" turns out to have been the decisive matter, since assuming Canadian courts and legislature rightfully enjoy this power lands us in one and only one conceptual/normative universe. While these scholars often remark about the unfortunate loss of Indigenous lands and the stripping of legal authority over those lands, only the former survives as a possibly recognized harm, while the latter is never more than mentioned in passing as a sort of harm that *might* need to be addressed, *though in a radically weakened form*. Further, even in relation to loss of lands and livelihoods, the harm is conceptually minimized to the extent that proper responses fit within some variant on a need for "equitable distribution of *x*," a characterization of matters found across nearly all contemporary legal scholars and in full accord with what the Supreme Court purports to be ultimately concerned about – more equitable distribution *within a given society*, all overseen by Canadian law.

Slattery's articulation of the nature of reconciliation envisions legal instruments guiding courts towards the task of calculating how rights protected under section 35 could exist in a modern context, a context in which they run up into valid, innocent interests of "third parties" (which presumably includes not just interests of non-Aboriginal people but of their economic structures, including such things as extractive industries):

> Reconciliation is a complex and multifaceted objective.... In focusing (necessarily) on the rights of Aboriginal groups, the doctrine has difficulty taking proper account of the competing interests of third parties and indeed the body politic as a whole.... [I]t does not provide an adequate basis for determining how ... limited resources should be shared with other user groups.[52]

52 Slattery, "Generative Structure," *supra* note 49 at 128.

How would a system designed to more equitably distribute resources address the harms identified and defined? With harms restricted to inequitable distributions of lands and resources, there is only one conceivable way to address issues – to press Canadian courts (and have them press Canadian governments) to better balance all the interests at stake.

What happens to Indigenous self-determination in this form of analysis? Or to Indigenous meaning-generating communities, encompassing and informing Indigenous forms of legal and political authority? Early in his academic career Slattery made much of the notion of "inter-societal law."[53] An early pillar of his position was the view that Aboriginal law emerged in the space between European and Indigenous societies. What came of this structure, manifest in the first few centuries of contact, when Indigenous and non-Indigenous societies regulated their interacting and sometimes overlapping lives through inter-societal law? As we wonder what role this form of law might play in Slattery's view of the contemporary situation, we can begin to bring into our analysis the naturalist/realist perspective, as puzzles emerge that can be brought into sharp relief only by our stepping *outside* the normative universe this scholar would otherwise have us *all* live and think within.

"Inter-societal law" is as the title suggests – law that develops out of interactions between societies, and that exists in a space between these societies. A good example of this is the matter of protocol and treaty negotiations in the first few centuries of contact in eastern North America, as British representatives *listened* to Indigenous understandings of what such negotiations meant and how they could lead to particular sorts of relationships, which led to protocol followed and particular forms of agreements reached, where this protocol and these agreements existed in an intersocietal space. Aboriginal rights in Slattery's theory, however, bear no relation to what we might imagine would reflect forms of inter-societal law, even though early in this article Slattery continued to connect Aboriginal rights to inter-societal law.

One way to make sense of this is to imagine Slattery has moved away from a focus on substantive inter-societal law. Another would be to carefully parse how inter-societal law always functioned in his analyses. Let us examine this latter possibility, as showing how it is a plausible reading illustrates an aspect of the common pattern of "theorizing" about Aboriginal law we see animating the works of nearly all Aboriginal law scholars.

Mentions of forms of inter-societal law throughout Slattery's corpus need to be carefully unpacked (as is the case with mention of "legal pluralism" and "Indigenous sovereignty" in the works of other mainstream legal scholars).

53 See e.g. Brian Slattery, "Understanding Aboriginal Rights" (1987) 66 Can Bar Rev 727; Brian Slattery, "Making Sense of Aboriginal and Treaty Rights" (2000) 79 Can Bar Rev 196.

Slattery has often spoken, and continues to speak, of Aboriginal rights being *grounded* in forms of inter-societal law at play in early relations between the Crown and Indigenous peoples, but this is *not* to say Aboriginal rights exist *today* as outcomes of the application of inter-societal law in contemporary settings. If there had been "Aboriginal rights" in the seventeenth and eighteenth centuries, one could then have argued they existed as key elements of a form of inter-societal law, working in some complex inter-societal space alongside "British-Canadian" rights. But Slattery argues all Aboriginal rights should be seen arising at the assertion of Crown sovereignty (the "critical date" he argues courts should focus on),[54] and *as features of Canadian law* by definition they *cannot* be themselves a key element in a strong form of inter-societal law.

Parsing a passage from "Generative Rights" lays bare the odd way that "inter-societal law" functions in Slattery's analysis. In a subsection, "The Identity of Rights," we find Slattery digging into what appears as the key shortcoming of contemporary jurisprudence, the failure to clearly distinguish within the *Van der Peet* test between the larger body of "integral" practices and those worthy of constitutional protection as Aboriginal rights:

> The reason why such practices as eating, joking and gambling fail to qualify as Aboriginal rights is not because they are not integral features of Aboriginal societies (they may well be) but because they do not rise to the level of constitutional significance. How do we know that? The answer, in part, lies in the historical relations between Aboriginal societies and the Crown and the principles that underpin those relations – what we have called intersocietal law. There is little evidence that intersocietal law ever supported a right to sleep or joke, but much that attests to a right to gain a livelihood.[55]

Much of Slattery's analysis echoes comments made by McLachlin J in her dissent in *Van der Peet*. There she noted shortcomings in Lamer CJ's formulation of the test for Aboriginal rights, where her criticisms principally questioned the juridical nuts and bolts of a test that seemed so poorly thought through.[56] Slattery finds that the *mistake* in the early Aboriginal rights jurisprudence is a failing at this initial stage in fully thinking through what such a test had to accomplish, the result being these very shortcomings. In particular, the test failed to take rights it recognized in their historical/descriptive dimension and, by paying attention to the normative dimension, place them into the modern legal landscape. This latter matter would be forward-looking (the "generative" part of this model) and focuses attention on what Slattery identifies as the odd

54 Slattery, "Generative Rights," *supra* note 49 at 121–7.

55 *Ibid* at 116.

56 *R v Van der Peet*, [1996] 2 SCR 507, 137 DLR (4th) 289 at paras 224–59.

feature of Lamer's test, namely that insufficient attention was paid to the need for identified rights to have proper "constitutional significance."

We need to pause here, however, to carefully unpack some of the moves being made. We might see both McLachlin's trenchant critique and Slattery's call for refinement of the test as explanations of a mistake made in the majority's reasoning. But this mistake itself (a) *occurs only within* a normative framework (as much as Slattery might think the court was fixated on the historical/descriptive dimension), and (b) *makes sense only within* this normative world. The mistake, one must see, is simply in finer details in how *interests* Aboriginal peoples could claim in the modern world might manifest properly as rights.

We noted earlier how there is no sense or room whatsoever in McLachlin's criticism that Indigenous legal and political authority might persist into the modern world – indeed, it would seem such authority was washed away at the point the Crown became sovereign. This is clear when we note that the larger picture is of rights emerging within an existent liberal democratic state – the task set the court, and the task it left partially unfulfilled, was that of working out the nature of the rights within one set legal order.

But what of academic critique? Now properly primed, let us turn to the matter of "constitutional significance." Who determines what is constitutionally significant? In Slattery's analysis it is principally the court, with guidance he provides. By digging into what the court had already put in place (the "integral to the distinctive culture test") Slattery can discern a pattern, one that unfolds as a model of generic rights, that all emerge at the assertion of Crown sovereignty, that focus principally on matters of cultural integrity. Rather than say Indigenous self-determination is removed from the world, it would be better to say that within this approach it was never there as a serious consideration once the Crown asserted sovereignty. What formerly existed as "inter-societal law" that emerged in the space between two separate legal and political authorities is now conceived of as "inter-societal law" that exists between two "societies" (Indigenous and non-Indigenous), all within one legal and political authority (that of the Crown and its courts). Through a hidden elision, strong forms of inter-societal law (which seem to function to provide an air of acknowledgment of Indigenous law) are replaced with radically weaker forms of "inter-societal law." The entire discussion from this point on then functions to support the Court's attempts to subvert Indigenous forms of legal and political authority. A single normative universe is presumed, within which alternate forms of understanding are absent, and nothing like what one might suppose a naturalist analysis would look like is either visible or contemplated.

MACKLEM AND AN ETHOS OF LEGAL PLURALISM

To see how this general approach to explaining the nature of the jurisprudence is fairly ubiquitous across contemporary mainstream legal scholars, let us turn to what might otherwise seem to be "progressive" analysis, in this example a recent piece that seems to be arguing about the need to rethink Crown-Indigenous relations in line with legal pluralist analysis.

As we unpack Patrick Macklem's "Indigenous Peoples and the Ethos of Legal Pluralism,"[57] we encounter the same general approach we witnessed in Slattery's work. We are asked to acknowledge that Aboriginal rights have their source in some situation in the past (when a reasonable form of interaction between the Crown and Indigenous peoples was subverted), we are to imagine contemporary jurisprudence is fluid and dynamic, working its way towards a better way of dealing with the claims of Aboriginal communities, we are expected to come to see remaining barriers and how they can be overcome, and so we are led to expect that Aboriginal rights jurisprudence is close to reaching a point where a just and fair world is constructed through and around Aboriginal rights.

Macklem attempts to build on a look into the rise and fall of legal pluralism in early Crown-Indigenous relations, beginning from the observation that a form of legal pluralism marked the nature of legal authority in early Canadian history. The "ethos of legal pluralism" was "immanent"[58] in early encounters between the British Crown and Indigenous peoples, but this gave way in the overtly colonial era, an era of denial of Indigenous authority that persisted until (at least) the latter half of the twentieth century. Macklem sees value in the form of legal pluralism that he argues marked those "early encounters" – at that time it was commonly acknowledged that *multiple sources of legal authority co-existed in one geographic territory*.[59] He also sees signs of movement back to this sort of relational dynamic.

Before jumping to those signs of movement, note it is important to constantly ask about (a) the sort of legal pluralism he imagines might "re-emerge" in contemporary Canada (and how this looks in comparison to the earlier form), and (b) how he thinks we can get back to (some measure) of this pluralist model. Macklem speaks of a contemporary jurisprudential move afoot to "interpret treaties in a manner consistent with Indigenous understandings."[60] This interpretive process would take place within a world that acknowledged Crown-Indigenous treaties are "constitutional accords," documents that "articulate basic terms and conditions of social coexistence and make possible the exercise of constitutional authority."[61] In several ways, however, imagining

57 Macklem, "Indigenous Peoples," *supra* note 51.

58 *Ibid* at 21.

59 Macklem argues that "the legal pluralism relevant ... to all rich accounts of Indigenous-settler relations ... is one where the sources of legal validity themselves are plural." This he characterizes as "constitutional pluralism, where there exists a plurality of constitutional orders within and, conceivably, across state boundaries": *ibid* at 18–19.

60 *Ibid* at 27.

61 *Ibid* at 28.

treaties interpreted in this manner is not at all to engage in a thought process that mirrors what marked early encounters.

Consider first the nature of the immanent legal pluralism Macklem imagines could come inform contemporary treaty interpretation, and then turn to Macklem's position on how we get to this new imagined world. This in hand, we can then wonder what led up to this current situation, wherein new modes of treaty interpretation all must unfold within the legal-normative world of the state and its courts. Taking a look at his "explanations" for why the earlier form withered away assists in seeing how a centred liberal positivist position guides his thought, and what this then says about how this "theorizing" functions in the world around us.

Of primary import in understanding the (re-)emergent "legal pluralism" that Macklem describes is the fact that this contemporary interpretive activity would *all* transpire *within* Canadian law. The reader might have anticipated Macklem was going to suggest treaties come to be interpreted today in some "interpretive space" *between* meaning-generating collectives, but as we saw in our discussion of Slattery's work, all such invocations of contemporary "inter-societal law" have this odd flavour – a law that one might think the author is suggesting might exist in the interstices or zones between two peoples is in today's world actually a law formed entirely within the legal system of the state. This naturally invites us to consider a further question: how can the sort of legal pluralism that structured earlier relations re-emerge *within* the law of the nation state?

Besides wondering why the argument would not be that the law needs to move towards an in-between interpretive space, we can note that interpreting treaties in the "new" manner envisioned by Macklem is not at all what one would expect in a legal pluralist world defined as marked by multiple sources of legal authority. Where is Indigenous legal authority in this matter of interpretation? The only way to begin to move towards an ethos of legal pluralism would be to imagine acknowledgment of separate meaning-generating communities, and to wonder how the state could co-exist with these other meaning-generating authorities.

Answers to these questions emerge if we focus on Macklem's account of how we find ourselves in the world we inhabit. We can see in this account a glaring gap, no account being taken of the key move from multiple legal and political authorities to a world dominated by Crown sovereignty. All the events Macklem sets out as responsible for how we arrived at the current jurisprudential situation – involving forces both "internal" and "external" to Crown law and policy, such things as the Crown and its courts acting in response to settler pressure and so furthering settlement and resource exploitation and the generation of settler wealth – took place and continue to take place *within* the Canadian legal-normative universe (that is, within the sphere of *assumed* Crown sovereignty). These are all events that took place once the Crown had asserted sovereignty over Indigenous peoples and their lands and waters. The "ethos of legal pluralism" that he describes early in his paper, on the other hand, is that of *strong* legal pluralism, of the sort captured, for example, in the Haudenosaunee's articulation of the Crown-Confederacy relationship in the two-row wampum.

The two-row wampum captures a model of the relationship between Dutch/ British authorities and the Haudenosaunee, the two rows of parallel beads representing two vessels travelling down a shared river, side-by-side, each vessel independent and self-guiding.[62] How do we slide from this earlier form of relationship to one where troubling events to be concerned about all take place *within* the one vessel? It must be that an assumption is made that the relationship had broken down, with the occupants of the one vessel simply asserting and exercising control over the other. The contemporary move back to an "ethos of legal pluralism" is presented, however, not in response to *this* key event, the *breakdown*, but as the emergence of a form of weak legal pluralism, with the one set of legal and political authorities now purportedly struggling to find a "fair" and "just" place within the one over-arching system of the state and its courts.

As with our discussion of Slattery's work, we need to carefully unpack moves Macklem has us slide through as we go from a form of strong legal pluralism, to "mistakes made," to the beckoning new world of weak legal pluralism. As with our earlier discussion, we enter this matter by asking about the nature of these "mistakes" made. Their very nature is determined by the normative universe within which they are conceptually embedded. In this case we see mistakes that centre (reading back through time, from emerging weak legal pluralism to events in the overtly colonial era) on a failure of the Crown and its legal officials to treat treaties as constitutional accords and Aboriginal title as that Canadian legal instrument meant to provide adequate protection from Crown (and settler) taking.

But the nature and sense of such mistakes presumes a setting in which the legal and political authority of Indigenous peoples is *already lost*, submerged within the overarching power of Crown sovereignty. One can make sense of these mistakes only from within a given, set normative universe. Macklem attempts to explain the fact these mistakes were made, but apart from some explanations that simply spin in circles,[63] the core explanation is that "reality" intruded. The Crown and its courts acted in their own interests (to further settlement, the unfettered exploitation of resources, and the generation of settler wealth), and Indigenous legal and political authority became not something removed, but something best understood not to ever have been contemplated.

62 The nature of the agreement is set out in Oren Lyons, "Indian Self-Government in the Haudenosaunee Constitution" (1986) 55 Nordic J Int'l L 117, at 119.

63 For example, Macklem argues that "legal pluralism did not take root in Canada in part because the Crown began to negotiate treaties for reasons antithetical to pluralism's promise" [Macklem, "Indigenous Peoples," *supra* note 51 at 23].

As with Slattery's "explanation" of mistakes the Court made in articulating the nature of Aboriginal rights *in Van der Peet*, the real problem here is that this explanation leads inexorably to resolution of the "error" that itself makes sense only within a given, set normative universe. We find ourselves at a call for further movement towards a world defined by weak legal pluralism, where Indigenous legal and political authority exists solely as an instrument defined by the Canadian state and its courts. We might find that at some future point Canadian law comes to accept treaties as constitutional accords (though frankly there is little sign the high court thinks this is something they need to consider, especially as this would drastically interfere with the jurisprudence they have developed concerning the "justifiable" infringement of treaty rights). We might also at some future point determine that Aboriginal title adequately protects Aboriginal land interests (which may be possible post-*Delgamuukw*, though the law concerning "justifiable infringement" is unlikely to be adjusted in this context as well). These sorts of eventualities, however, situate Aboriginal interests *inside* the legal regime of the state, governed by its courts, and fully embedded within the normative universe this both builds and inhabits. Where is strong legal pluralism in this picture?

As with Slattery's work, the pressing questions have to do with the nature of the "theorizing" we witness in Macklem's work. Is he attempting to explain the operations of the courts of Canada? Or is he functioning entirely within the normative world these very same courts are trying to inject under the lives of Indigenous collectives, as the one meaning-generating community tries to subvert the meaning-generating capacities of dozens of other collectives? Is he a facilitator or a scholar?

Functional Outcomes of the Work of the Liberal Legal Theorist

What do we witness in the development of the jurisprudence concerning Aboriginal rights if we restrict ourselves to what can explore in the world we think and act within? As we unpacked the case law, focusing on exploring puzzles embedded within, we found the Supreme Court is attempting to subvert whatever remnants of alternate meaning-generating capacity may have survived the oppression and repression visited upon Indigenous nations through the overt colonial period. We see Canadian law constructing a regime out of materials and processes provided by liberal doctrine so as to push/pull Indigenous peoples away from existence within and through separate meaning-generating communities to life lived entirely within a single liberal democratic state. Motives of judges arguably come from beliefs held as agents of the liberal democratic state, just as their understandings of "harms" they can address and the responses they can possibly conceive of to these harms come from that existence deeply embedded within the liberal world.

The liberal legal theorist, to the extent she is aware this is the backdrop to her work, takes this, in some way, as how it should be. The theorist either does not accept that her entire world is narrowly circumscribed by a specific conceptual/normative discourse, or she accepts this is the "right" way for the Crown-Indigenous narrative to unfold.[64] Either way, attention does not linger on the assertion of Crown sovereignty and what this entails for the survival of Indigenous meaning-generating capacity. Rather, attention turns to explicating "harms" the Court identifies, responses the Court holds out as "just" and "fair," and how a full appreciation of these matters can lead to a completed jurisprudential project.

It is entirely possible that from within a conceptual/normative world delimited by liberal thought the theorist fails to see how limited her horizon might be. We need not imagine, that is, that the theorist gives thought to how she might be *actively* allying with the state and its courts to work towards a world devoid of Indigenous meaning-generating capacity. The liberal legal theorist, after all, is herself to a significant degree the product of the meaning-generating system she finds herself living within, and she may not be able to leap out (or see the possibility of leaping out) of the water to see she has been totally immersed throughout her life in a specific medium of thought and action.[65]

That aside, there is a second, equally likely path the liberal legal theorist travels. The theorist may think it *best* that Indigenous peoples find themselves enclosed within the liberal democratic state, thinking (perhaps with minimal reflection) that this form of state presents a *good* political structure, and that Indigenous peoples should see themselves having come out of the colonial nightmare with what is essentially a *fair* quid pro quo – the exchange of independence for the acquisition of "civilization."[66]

This is, however, a normative judgment, one that then entirely frames the rest of the analysis. We see, then, that legal scholars largely either ignore

---

64 On the first branch of this we imagine the theorist does not see "Indigenous legal and political authority" as such, since to the extent she turns her mind to how Indigenous collectives organize their understandings of how to live in the world, she does not see this ever rising to the level of sophistication evinced by Western systems and required for serious consideration. On the second branch, she accepts Indigenous legal and political authority may meet minimal requirements to be considered systems of social and legal structuring, but feels Western liberal systems are clearly preferable for all concerned.

65 This is a difficult notion to hold to, as any contemporary theorist working in this field is well aware of the works of scholars like Patricia Monture-Angus, Taiaiake Alfred, and Mary Ellen Turpel-Lafond – works all of which clearly explicate the deeper nature of harms befalling Indigenous peoples. "It is precisely this form of thought [the 'unquestioned absorption of the colonial mentality'] that precipitates the dominant ideological monopoly, which results in the oppression of Aboriginal peoples": Monture-Angus, *supra* note 44 at 52.

66 For the discussion of such an argument, see Jeremy Waldron, "Supersession and Sovereignty" (2006) New York University Public Law and Legal Theory Working Papers, Paper 406.

fundamental facts or begin with normative judgments (and most combine these moves). The fact is that Indigenous collectives have been and continue to be meaning-generating communities, and the aim of domestic law in Canada has been and continues to be to replace their capacities with an existence entirely within a sphere of normativity centred on liberal thought.

There is no relationship, then, between the scholarship of scholars like Slattery and Macklem and what one would expect if the goal were to explain the nature of Aboriginal law. The law of "Aboriginal rights," as the product of attempts to create legal doctrine, comes out of minds of the judges of the high court. We would expect that an attempt to explain this body of law would involve exploration of what the jurisprudence does in the world, what it attempts to do, how it got to be what it is, what its implications are, and what situations in the world it might be moving us towards. One could imagine Slattery and Macklem aim at some of these matters, but only if we further imagine their work begins with the presumption that theorizing about the law is built on a platform of normative grounding (and fact-denial).

We just noted how Slattery and Macklem's accounts of where the doctrine comes from are mixes of apologies (for mistakes and errors made both early in the overt-colonial era and more recently as early jurisprudence was being developed) and normativity (with predetermined notions of what it was attempting to do, with "harms" to be addressed identifiable as such only through an assumed normative lens). We can likewise note that their accounts of where the law is going and where it should go are all tied to particular normative groundings, those shared by the Crown and its courts.

A different set of answers to these questions comes from beginning from a point outside the normative world built and inhabited by the dominant meaning-generating community. From this vantage point the phenomenon to be explained is principally that of attempts by this meaning-generating community to have its world undercut and then absorb Indigenous communities and their meaning-generating capacities and powers. From this vantage point an assumption would not be made that officials and jurists from the dominant meaning-generating community are properly placed to not only decide what the legal rules and tests would be to determine Aboriginal rights, but to also determine what "law," "rights," and "obligations" mean. To place the dominant system in position to determine these matters begins with the assumption that the undercutting and absorption are complete and behind us.

9 Postcolonial Theory and Aboriginal Law

Over the last half-century, vigorous challenges to the hegemony of empire emerged from the writings of third-world intellectuals. With the decolonization of "salt water" colonies after the Second World War came opportunities to reflect upon and rethink the history of colonialism, in a time many came to label the "colonial aftermath." This rethinking took a very particular form in the 1970s and 1980s, as many of these postcolonial thinkers turned their thoughts to the lingering effects of colonialism. In large areas of the world now removed from the direct oversight of colonial powers, many of the conditions and symptoms marking colonial existence seemed to persist – an effect some attribute to neoliberalism and globalization, others to the continuance (indeed an intensification) of capitalist modernity, and yet others to the persistence of forms of colonialism itself (now in forms tied more to economic and intellectual controls).[1]

This last movement in postcolonial theorizing – fuelled by the writings of Said and Spivak (in particular) – focuses on means by which colonial powers transformed Indigenous ways of knowing.[2] European forms of discourse had been

1 On the first point, see e.g. Isabel Altamirano-Jiménez, Indigenous Encounters with Neoliberalism: Place, Women, and the Environment in Canada and Mexico (Vancouver: UBC Press, 2013). On the second, see e.g. Ranajit Guha, Dominance without Hegemony: History and Power in Colonial India (Cambridge, MA: Harvard University Press, 1997). On the last, see e.g. Achille Mbembe, On the Postcolony (Berkeley: University of California Press, 2001). Naturally enough, most scholars shift between and amongst these forms of explanation.

2 See Edward Said, *Orientalism* (New York: Pantheon Books, 1978); Edward Said, *Culture and Imperialism* (New York: Vintage Books, 1993); Gayatri Chakravorty Spivak, "Can the Subaltern Speak?" in Cary Nelson & Lawrence Grossberg, eds, *Marxism and the Interpretation of Culture* (Champaign: University of Illinois Press, 1988) 271. Insofar as this implicates the "psychoanalytic" strand of postcolonial studies, we should note as well the foundational works of Mahatma Gandhi, Franz Fanon, and Ashis Nandy. See e.g. Louis Fischer, ed, *The Essential Gandhi: An Anthology of His Writings on His Life, Work, and Ideas* (New York: Vintage Books, 1962); Frantz Fanon, *Black Skin, White Masks* (New York: Grove Press, 1952); Ashis Nandy, *The Intimate Enemy: Loss and Recovery of Self under Colonialism* (Oxford: Oxford University Press, 1983).

deployed over many generations (a discourse, for example, of "the Orient"), gradually infecting the minds of the colonized. Colonized from within, colonial operations persist in contemporary times through actions voluntarily undertaken – *chosen* – by those very people freed of the overt colonial yoke.

Might there be value in thinking about the development of Aboriginal law in Canada from the perspective of postcolonial theory? We explore this question in this chapter, though by the time we get into the heart of the analysis, we find postcolonial theory (to continue to be useful) has been transformed in fundamental ways. Why this must be so is the springboard for discussion at the end of this chapter and leads us into our concluding remarks in the next and last part of the text.

The Roots of Postcolonial Theory

As can well be imagined from the introductory remarks, postcolonial theory is generally understood to have two roots – Marxism and post-structuralism. I focus on its post-structuralist underpinnings, returning to its Marxist connections later. Some point out tensions that arise between these two lead-in theories, noting that (a) Marxists can be dismissive of post-structuralists' versions of postcolonial theory on the basis that they fail to fully appreciate that colonialism is but a historical instance of the larger story of the rise of capitalist modernity,[3] and that (b) non-Marxist postcolonial theorists challenge Marxism for failing to study and fully appreciate connections between knowledge and power (that these theorists argue largely account for the troubled existence of those living in the colonial aftermath). When we return to Marxist threads underlying postcolonial theory, I will endeavour to defuse these tensions (though not in a way that would likely satisfy either camp!).

Post-structuralist underpinnings of contemporary postcolonial theory are captured well in Leela Gandhi's overview of postcolonial theory in *Postcolonial Theory*.[4] She notes the impact of such theorists as Foucault and Derrida on founding figures in modern postcolonial theory, and in particular on Said and Spivak.[5] The emergence of postcolonial theory as a major theoretic force in the second half of the twentieth century coincided with the emergence of a powerful set of critiques of the West from within the West, the foremost being directed

---

3 See e.g. Benita Parry, *Postcolonial Studies: A Materialist Critique* (London: Routledge, 2004) at 4:

> The abandonment of historical and social explanation was soon apparent in the work of those postcolonial critics who disengaged colonialism from historical capitalism and re-presented it for study as a cultural event. Consequently an air-borne will to power was privileged over calculated compulsions, "discursive violence" took precedence over the practices of a violent system, and the intrinsically antagonistic colonial encounter was reconfigured as one of dialogue, complicity and transculturation.

4 Leela Gandhi, *Postcolonial Theory: A Critical Introduction* (St Leonards: Allen & Unwin, 1998) [Gandhi, *Postcolonial Theory*].

5 *Ibid* at 25–7, 52–6.

towards Western epistemology (and championed by Foucault and Derrida). Notions of "universalism" and "rationality," these critiques attest, reached out from the works of Descartes,[6] became central elements in the reconfiguration of the burgeoning Enlightenment project, and framed the ensuing movement towards modernity. These core concepts, post-structuralist postcolonial theorists argue, continue to animate Western theories of knowledge production, and over the last few centuries they have facilitated the development of a colonial mentality that secures the complete dispossession of the colonized.[7]

Colonialism itself, besides encompassing the physical dispossession of lands and resources, evolved into a program of the infiltration of minds and thoughts. This infiltration is facilitated by a particular valorization of the human, by a theory of the "mature" human as someone (typically male) possessed of a particular form of rationality. This form of rationality sits at the core of a definition of the universal form of human nature, one that licenses – amongst other things – the proselytization of this vision to all yet-immature communities of humans around the globe.

The roots of all this are found in Descartes, in his conception of the human in relation to the world. From the point of view of the rational theorizer (the only real "point of view" in the world within the Cartesian system, apart from that of God), the world around initially appears unordered and chaotic, but it soon falls before the power of the human intellect. The mind, as the postcolonial thesis goes in describing this arc of development and progress, does not *record* order discovered in the world (an impossible task, given the infinite nature of the world and the finite nature of the representational mind). Rather, order is *generated* through theory, and through such *constructed* models the human begins the business of taming nature.[8] Along the way those other humans – those yet clinging to immature modes of existence, not yet fully rational – must also be tamed and taught (for their own good).

The post-structuralist postcolonial theorist kicks aside this story of the maturation of humankind through the Enlightenment and of the ensuing rise of modernity, arguing it is nothing but a fable, itself a form of "knowledge" constructed in

---

6 Gandhi notes, *ibid* at 34–5, that "Cartesian philosophy produces three revolutionary variants on the notion of the Self and its relationship to knowledge and thereby to the external world ... the notions of the self-defining subject of consciousness; the allknowing subject of consciousness; and ... the formally empowered subject of consciousness."

7 Ashis Nandy argues that in the second stage of colonialism (after physical conquest and dispossession has more or less run its course) focus turns to the conquest of minds, to the use of "universal truths" to buttress the West's hegemony over the other. See Nandy, *supra* note 2.

8 Gandhi, *Postcolonial Theory*, *supra* note 4 at 34–7. Gandhi cites Michel Foucault, *The Order of Things: An Archaeology of the Human Sciences* (New York: Pantheon Books, 1970) at 75–6, at page 36: "[The Cartesian mathematical method of modelling nature is] an exhaustive ordering of the world as though methods, concepts, types of analysis, and finally men themselves, had all been displaced at the behest of a fundamental network defining the implicit and inevitable unity of knowledge[.]"

pursuit or furtherance of power. Within the story itself lie further constructed narratives, labelled "truths," but true only within limited spheres, within worlds built around constructed notions of truth and knowledge. Universalisms contained in the general story - of the *true* nature of humankind, of the one *true* means to maturity, of the one *true* structure of knowledge - are all challenged, laid bare as products of particular times and places, indeed of one historically and culturally grounded epoch in Western history, that of "modernity." Indeed, it is this very particular narrative that seeks to hold up a myth of universal history, one that happens to capture in its sweeping universalism all non-Western peoples.

How would all this work to make sense of the development of Aboriginal rights in Canada? With our look in hand into the underpinning of this field of law in liberal democratic thought, we can put together a snapshot of how this form of postcolonial theory comes to view and understand the machinations of Canadian courts over the last few decades.

Applying Postcolonial Theory to Aboriginal Rights

We noted that liberal theory holds out a universal normative vision of the human, and that this vision encompasses a very particular view of the relationship between the human and the properly constituted state. The postcolonial theorist sees in the development of these forms of thought in the formation of law not only measures meant to consolidate physical forms of colonialism, but also efforts to colonize the minds, thoughts, and actions of Indigenous peoples.

In the Court's unquestioned acceptance of Crown sovereignty in *Sparrow*, we see parameters put up around what is sensible or conceivable within Canadian law. *Indigenous* peoples are shown ways of thinking of their existence (as *Aboriginal* peoples within Canada, with Aboriginal rights as defined by Canadian courts) - ways of thinking that solidify a power structure imposed upon them over preceding generations. The rights defined in *Van der Peet* fit with the universal liberal vision of "humankind" and "society," and for Aboriginal peoples to make use of these tools to improve their economic and social status in contemporary times they must come to see themselves - to accept their constructed nature - *within* these conceptual frames. With the decision in *Gladstone* the power of the state is reaffirmed, in terms that entirely tame the claims of Aboriginal peoples within a structure that avowedly has but one fundamental goal, that of "economic development." The dispossession of land - lands that make up territories of Indigenous peoples, lands over which they exercised and attempt to continue to exercise fundamental responsibilities - is furthered in *Delgamuukw* and *Tsilhqot'in Nation*, as Aboriginal peoples are pulled tightly into the title system, encouraged to think of themselves as landholders *within* the modern capitalist economy.

We noted in our discussion of the ability of liberal positivism to explain away or dissolve puzzles that emerge in the development of the particulars within

Aboriginal law that, while from within a liberal world much can be "made sense of," key puzzles remain. Central to the puzzles are their connection to Indigenous perspectives, and central to all is the denial of Indigenous peoples' sovereignty (defined in this context as the capacity of diverse Indigenous collectives to generate their own understandings of such things as "rights," "responsibilities," "law," the "self," and its relationship to the collective). Addressing this last, central puzzle is not a task attempted by liberal theory – its response is nothing more than a re-invocation of Crown sovereignty.

Within postcolonial theory, we find an explanation not just for what we see when we consider how efficacious liberal positivism is (as a model explaining developments) but for its failures. The postcolonial theorist argues it is understandable that liberalism accounts for so much of what we see develop in Aboriginal law over the last few decades, as this system of thought is that of the colonizer, and it functions as one should expect it would. It exhibits all the hallmarks of a product of modernity – its simply assumed universalism, its focus on utilitarian modes of decision-making, and its facilitation of the construction and expansion of power (power localized in nodes, in the hands of those who write the rules – legislators and courts – and those who benefit from the rules written – capitalists and exploitive industries). That Indigenous sovereignty is not even denied but rather simply ignored is what is to be expected when the situation is viewed through a postcolonial lens – the definition of Indigenous sovereignty articulated in this study is that of "the other," that mass of other meaning-generating systems that can challenge not just the base, physical power of empire, but its deployment of "knowledge."

Postcolonial theory calls our attention to the central need from within the liberal world to ignore and deny the other. This refusal to acknowledge other meaning-generating systems is not just set in the past, when colonial authorities acted as though the colonized were not organized in societies – were not capable of being conceived of as entirely "sovereign" in their own territories – but present today as well, as the Canadian state and its courts deny the status of the colonized as potential sources of other "knowledges," other systems of constructing thought. The most puzzling of the untouched puzzles is opened up and deftly explained (though not "solved") – postcolonial theory explains, in rich form, *why* we see what we see. Going beyond detailing the *how* of Aboriginal law – how the rules develop the way they do within a liberal setting – postcolonial theory sets out arguments about the forces and mechanisms that lie behind this construction of legal "knowledge." Canadian law on Aboriginal rights is re-constructed as the latest in ongoing efforts to colonize Indigenous peoples from within, to control their thoughts and minds and eradicate the power of other meanings and understandings.

Postcolonial theory can provide an explanation for a larger set of phenomena, an explanation that seems to do a good job of not just describing what we might see in a mechanical fashion, but of explaining why we see what we do. But is it a *good* explanation? Perhaps more importantly, does it provide a *better* explanation than that provided by liberal theory?

Postcolonial Theory as Providing a Better Explanation

We should begin by noting we need not couch these questions in normative-evaluative terms. That is, it is not necessary that we try to grapple with whether explanations provided by postcolonial theory are *better* in that they better accord with particular normative ways of thinking of the world, and of relations between Aboriginal and non-Aboriginal peoples in Canada (or, more perspicuously, between Indigenous peoples and non-Aboriginal peoples in what is today Canada). That is, one might think the real task here is to see how well the postcolonial theoretic account meshes with what we think the *right* kind of relationship should have been, and should be. To enter into debates on a normative level is to get pulled into potentially endless discussions about base-level values, principles, and ideals, most of which seem to inevitably reach out into transcendent realms of norms and values. Supposing that different meaning-generating communities develop distinct languages and attendant meanings around these very sorts of things, not only do we find ourselves in potentially fruitless debates, but we find ourselves wrapped up in essentially political struggles. But not only can we meaningfully grapple with the two sorts of theoretical accounts in non-normative fashion, but this is *appropriate* (when carried out within the naturalist approach advocated in this text). To see how this is so, let us walk through the various alternatives around evaluation.

Evaluating Postcolonial Theory

Leaving aside grand debate within some postulated "pure" normative realm (one rising above any particular normative account, one that is somehow understood to be the "right" account of normative matters), how might we otherwise assess the value or worth of postcolonial analyses of Aboriginal law? Perhaps we might turn to evaluative measures, as these are constructed *within* the theories themselves (or the larger systems of meaning within which each is embedded). Let us begin by thinking about the evaluation of an account of Aboriginal law from within liberal theory.

EVALUATION WITHIN LIBERAL THEORY

We noted earlier that from within liberal theory many past events are assessed in very particular fashion. What counts as a "harm" or wrong is dependent on principles emerging from within liberalism itself. So, for example, the taking of land without compensation can be considered a harm to be addressed, as would be unreasonable interference with the ability of an Aboriginal community to continue to *choose* how to live, and to live accordingly. But note then that on the flip side of both these harms are *acceptable* events (that do not constitute events causing "harm") – the taking of land in the sense of the enclosure of Indigenous claims within an overarching sovereignty of the Crown (with its attendant underlying Crown title), and efforts to non-coercively pull Indigenous peoples into thinking of the world in a way that fits within the larger liberal understanding (as individuals, as citizens, and ultimately as consumers).

The upshot is that it is deemed good *within* the liberal world to attempt – in non-coercive fashion – to change base-level understandings (the world views) of Indigenous peoples, to slide them into thinking of themselves as liberals must, within parameters setting out what it means to see oneself-in-the-world socially (and indeed metaphysically and epistemically) as the mythical liberal individual. Consider the contemporary response to the exceedingly troubling residential school chapter in Canada's history. The consensus within the liberal world is that government policy and the educational system this generated was bad, in that it was excessively coercive. But note that discussion of the end sought is muted – indeed, up to a point, it seems the end sought should be lauded (who could disagree with the goals of education?).[9] Note, then, there is correspondingly no acknowledgment that it might be conceivable to work towards restoration of pre-residential school existences, to work towards the restoration of separate, strong, meaning-generating Indigenous systems. Rather, coercion is acknowledged, and the state apologizes and commends processes of "healing," while efforts continue unchecked to press ahead with programs of intellectual assimilation.

We can see that from within liberal thought the development of Aboriginal law could be evaluated only in a similar manner. There is no development within this legal sphere that could possibly make sense of the notion of "rights" or claims that might speak to the taking of (and so the return of) Indigenous sovereignty (in the sense of independent and discrete systems of meaning-generation, tied to territories, outside and alongside systems of the state).[10] We see, then, that ultimately evaluations made from within the liberal world are intimately tied to universally "accepted" systems of liberal values and principles. While not actually universally accepted, within the liberal world there is no other sense possible than that of the absolute need to accept these deep truths about human nature and the proper structuring of society.

---

9 Even the recommendations of the Truth and Reconciliation Commission often turn to a focus on particular forms of education, ones that can easily pull people and communities into the modern capitalist/consumer world of resource-exploitation. See Truth and Reconciliation Commission of Canada, online: <http://nctr.ca/reports.php>.

10 It is difficult to imagine how one could even use the language of rights to get across the sought-after notion – rights being always contained within a given legal system.

Within liberal theory there is no particular difficulty in seeing Aboriginal law as a construct, and indeed we have considered an account of this construction that liberal theorists themselves should not find at all troubling (as it simply chronicled how well Aboriginal rights do fit with liberal philosophy). The key evaluative point concerns the *good* that liberal theorists would find in all the developments - Aboriginal rights *should* be narrowly defined, they *should* be hard to access and activate, they *should* be constructed so as to push/pull Aboriginal peoples into the modern economy as landholders and contractually defined partners in economic development (all according to proportionately established claims), and any conceivable challenge to centralized liberal authority *should* not be just denied, but ignored (as essentially inconceivable).

EVALUATION WITHIN POSTCOLONIAL THEORY

Let us turn, then, to the apparent alternative, to an evaluation of the account of postcolonial theory from within the world of meaning established by (and around) this theory. First and foremost we need to appreciate that postcolonial theory (at least on the post-structuralist side) does not purport to provide anything like an *explanation* as we earlier set out such a thing to be (when discussing the common sense model of theorizing). Rather, postcolonial theorists can only go so far as to claim they can illuminate how "truth" is constructed within different historical and cultural settings. The notion of "truth" itself is construed to be a living and dynamic thing, existing only in distinct form in particular times and places, always emerging from within a particular community of meaning.

The account of Aboriginal law developed through the application of postcolonial theory could be no more than (from within postcolonial theory) a reflection of the cultural grounding of the theorist, in her community setting. To the extent there is a good fit between the account of Aboriginal law and the systems of meaning within which she herself locates meaning, it can be a "good" account. There are, for the post-structuralist, nothing but interpretations, all of which are at most constrained by interpretive limits, with scalars being along such measures as "fit" and "life-affirmation" (good interpretations perhaps according well with former chapters in the narrative being constructed, or strengthening social structures underpinning a society, bad interpretations failing to accord with past conversational tropes or interfering with the flourishing of ways of living, or the over-man).[11]

---

11 This suggests, of course, that Dworkin's "interpretive turn" might parallel (or align with) post-structuralist accounts. His Herculean judge, for example, reaches the "right decision" on the basis of careful assessment of what the "best fit" would be with the judicial narratives constructed to that point (and with principles embodied in those narratives, themselves expressive of a particular legal environment, of a particular social setting). See e.g. Ronald Dworkin, *Law's Empire* (Cambridge, MA: Harvard University Press, 1988).

CROSS-SYSTEM EVALUATION

But what, then, of the remaining cross-system evaluation, of the assessment of the liberal account from the vantage point of postcolonial theory? We saw that from the perspective of liberal theory the postcolonial account is dismissible, as it needlessly questions and works against all that is "good" and "right" in the contemporary world, the submersion of all individuals in one large cosmopolitan liberal society. Postcolonial theory itself reaches its own peculiar conclusions, as it *can* see in liberal accounts the "good" as seen from within the liberal world. Unlike the liberal, the postcolonial theorist can see that the "good" can be context-dependent, and hence entirely variable. Postcolonial theorists can (and would) decry attempts to submerge "other knowledges" through the tools and techniques of Aboriginal law, but at best this is a call from within *its* system of meaning and evaluation. Nothing it says about how the world should be can function, within its theoretic confines, as a direct attack on what liberals themselves see as the good and the right, as any such attack would be misplaced within the postcolonial world. All is at most a struggle between systems of meaning – so, while postcolonial theorists can decry the violence of the struggle, liberal theorists see no harm in the submersion of "other knowledges" in the one best social structure, and ultimately the postcolonial theorist cannot say that her denunciation is "right" and the liberal submersion of the other is "wrong" (in some objective sense).

All said and done, however, postcolonial theory can *work* well for Indigenous peoples, as it speaks to their experience in not having a distinct voice recognized in the modern state about knowledge itself – the notion that each Indigenous community has its own constructed social world is upheld, and indeed is central to postcolonial analysis. But what are the costs that come with this form of analysis?

The Colonization of Indigenous Peoples by Postcolonial Theory

Everything comes down, in the postcolonial way of seeing the world, to questions of power and politics. The schism between postcolonial materialists and postcolonial culturalists (earlier cast as a division between Marxist and post-structuralist threads woven into the theory) can be pushed aside, as the common

---

Here we note a founding figure in many post-structuralist accounts, Friedrich Nietzsche. In *Beyond Good and Evil: Prelude to a Philosophy of the Future* (New York: Dover Publications, 1997), for example, he connects "truth" with life-affirmation at page 4:

> The question is, how far an opinion is life-furthering, life-preserving, species-preserving, perhaps species-rearing, and we are fundamentally inclined to maintain that the falsest opinions (to which the synthetic judgments a priori belong), are the most indispensable to us, that without a recognition of logical fictions, without a comparison of reality with the purely IMAGINED world of the absolute and immutable, without a constant counterfeiting of the world by means of numbers, mȃn could not live – that the renunciation of false opinions would be a renunciation of life, a negation of life. TO RECOGNIZE UNTRUTH AS A CONDITION OF LIFE; that is certainly to impugn the traditional ideas of value in a dangerous manner, and a philosophy which ventures to do so, has thereby alone placed itself beyond good and evil.

picture presented by this theory is of base political struggle, of a kind Indigenous peoples have little or no hope of "winning" (where, of course, the post-structuralist would go so far as to point out that "winning" can have very different meanings and connotations within different cultural and historic settings).

Are Indigenous peoples themselves (and not just Indigenous academics, who can find themselves vested in the academy)[12] open to the possibility of being colonized by Western cultural history? Recall the discussion of the common sense model and challenges launched by interpretivist alternatives: alternatives did not emerge from some Indigenous sense of the shortcomings of the common sense (or naturalist) perspective, but from centuries-old debates about the Cartesian model of the rational theorizer. This, note, is a vision that itself comes directly from a very particular theological history, as scholastics struggled to address shortcomings in the Aristotelian-centred picture of reality, one so clearly knocked down at the knees by Galileo and others. Interpretivist challenges attacked certain core presumptions of the modernist epistemic framework, knocking away foundationalist underpinnings and replacing Enlightenment models with non-representational models of truth and knowledge.

In the twentieth century, these challenges found strength and support in post-structuralist writings, with all these movements directed towards a general challenge to the idea of Knowledge itself (the capital *K* denoting both the possibility of one having the capacity to hold a belief known to be certainly true, and the beliefs thereby held as Known). It is not just that what constitutes knowledge (the concept, not any particular piece of knowledge) is seen as inherently culture and history dependent, but that post-structuralist/interpretivist models wash away any meaningful sense of progress in knowledge acquisition.[13]

Consider the implications. Begin with the imagination of a historicized theory of knowledge acquisition, one that, for example, requires that we believe we do not, in fact, ever have an opportunity to say we "truly know" *x* is true. Within such historicized models of knowledge the most we can ever say is that in our particular cultural and historical setting this is what we take to

12 See e.g. Vidya Kumar, "A *Proleptic* Approach to Postcolonial Legal Studies? A Brief Look at the Relationship between Legal Theory and Intellectual History" 2003:2 L, Social Justice & Global Development J, online: <warwick.ac.uk/fac/soc/law/elj/lgd/2003_2/kumar/>. Kumar asks, "Do postcolonial legal theorists have personal stake in the conceptualisation of [postcolonial legal theory] they advance, or a responsibility to investigate the possibility that they do?": *ibid* at 3.1.2.

He goes on to argue that "the intellectual must interrogate his/her own political commitments, and not allow their perspective to be embedded in 'relations of domination'": *ibid* at 3.2.

13 Homi Bhabha, for example, in speaking of the "many forms of political writing," in thinking of a "leaflet involved in the organization of a strike" or a "speculative article on the theory of ideology," argues that all such writings are "forms of discourse and to that extent they produce rather than reflect their objects of reference": Homi Bhabha, *The Location of Culture* (London: Routledge, 2004) at 32.

be "known." So, for example, we might want to talk about Einstein's model of gravity and its implications for explaining the motions of the planets. To deny knowledge in this post-structuralist/interpretivist manner is to deny that we can say what we "know" today is a better approximation to the Truth (defined as a complete and accurate representation of the way things are), or better in some objective sense, than what we (roughly the same cultural community) might have thought to be known before. So, deploying this model of knowledge and knowledge acquisition, we must be careful to say that our sense that Einstein's model is true does not, in fact, mean or imply that this model is in any meaningful sense *better*, as a model purportedly about the way things are, than other models taken to be "true" in other cultural-historical settings – which is what we would have to say, then, about this model in relation to the heliocentric model of planetary motion commonly held to be "true" centuries earlier.

Back to the question posed a few paragraphs earlier – how does this fit with Indigenous conceptions of knowledge and knowledge acquisition? We noted the attractiveness of the postcolonial understanding, but also questioned the costs that come with jumping wholeheartedly into postcolonial theory. The first concern raised – ironically – is the possibility of intellectual colonization. Is postcolonialism itself a foreign intrusion into Indigenous ways of thinking and being?

Before directly delving into this concern, let us consider other related matters that arise. Certain threads of response to all the concerns noted will weave their way through the rest of this section, the aim being to build towards a sensible reworking of the insights of postcolonial theory.

One might suggest, for example, that postcolonial theory truly speaks only to the lives and concerns of those living in the aftermath of colonialism, those from the decolonized third world. The vast bulk of its oeuvre comes from Southeast Asian writers – those from the subcontinent – or from African scholars. Writings in this field from Indigenous scholars – particularly from the Americas – are few and far between.

Connected to the earlier concern noted is wonder about the utility of postcolonial theory for Indigenous peoples. Linda Smith, for example, wonders at the faddishness of postcolonial theory, about its seeming attractiveness not to Indigenous peoples, but to privileged academics (many of whom are non-Indigenous), individuals looking for a boost to their academic careers:

> There is also, amongst indigenous academics, the sneaking suspicion that the fashion of post-colonialism has become a strategy for reinscribing or reauthorizing the privileges of non-indigenous academics because the field of "post-colonial" discourse has been defined in ways which can still leave out indigenous peoples, our ways of knowing and our current concerns.[14]

14 Linda Tuhiwai Smith, *Decolonizing Methodologies: Research and Indigenous Peoples*, 2nd ed (London: Zed Books, 2012) at 65.

Smith's criticisms centre on the notion that research dealing with Indigenous peoples is best conducted (indeed, is *properly* conducted) when designed, carried out, and interpreted by Indigenous scholars. Only then can one hope to see in the knowledge generated the voices of Indigenous peoples, those for whom and about whom the research is supposed to be conducted.

While this sort of focus fits with one of the themes of this text (insofar as the notion of Indigenous voices within research speaks as well to the notion of meaning-generating systems), my response to these sorts of concerns is to question their strength without investigation into the nature of theorizing on both abstract and concrete levels.

There are two levels to this concern with the status of postcolonial theory: one is that it is *possible* this theory could be put to use in the ways described by Smith (to "re-inscribe privilege"), and the other concern is that *in fact* it might be being put to such uses (the "sneaking suspicion"). We can really know these might be the case only if we look into the nature of theorizing, and in particular to the supposed ability to use a theory in this manner. My suggestion – developed extensively in earlier chapters, both on a meta-theoretic and practical level – is that *any* particular theory (a) is capable of being put to varied use within and by a meaning-generating system, and (b) should be investigated to see if that is so, in any given situation.

One outcome of the long investigation into the ability of liberal positivism to explain legal phenomena associated with the development of Aboriginal rights was to see that this particular theory does not function primarily to "explain" Aboriginal rights (in the sense that one might have thought it functions to simply accurately represent what is present independently). Rather, the liberal positivist – the theorist or jurist – was shown to be an active agent within a meaning-generating system, a system attempting to impose a form of social reality upon recalcitrant, alternate, Indigenous systems of meaning and meaning-generation.

This analysis, however, did not rest on the position that any and all attempts to arrive at an accurate model of legal phenomena must be seen in the same fashion. The larger vision of theorizing adopted in this text – one aligned with the common sense model, though carefully modulated to meet challenges presented by anti-foundationalist arguments about epistemological matters – allows for finding that certain particular theories do not function to explain independent phenomena but in fact function to build – or attempt to build – certain aspects of social reality, with other ends in mind. It preserves, however, the common-sense notion of theorizing, allowing that on the other hand *some* theories could in fact have as their objective or aim the project of making sense of independent phenomena. So, while it might well be that postcolonial theory does not indeed function to make sense of independent phenomena, to know this is the case requires an investigation into how it actually functions in relation to social reality. Can it function to explain what we witness in the world, or is it functioning to make certain things so? Perhaps it functions to do no more than build intricate systems of meaning, accessible only to an elite intellectual class, creating the conditions necessary to build and sustain an academic subfield within Western disciplines.

This brings us back to the doorstep of larger concerns about the use of postcolonial theory in attempts to make sense of Aboriginal rights. Is there sense to the notion that postcolonial theory is itself a form of Trojan horse, attempting to colonize the minds and actions of Indigenous peoples?

Not too surprisingly, the answer to this query takes us into a number of discussions about theory, theorizing, and identity. A short answer to the question of colonization is that postcolonial theory can indeed perform nothing other than this sort of function, if we simply stand this up as the contrast to the common-sense model, that of explaining independently existing legal phenomena. If we take "colonizing" to involve nothing more than the interjection of outside perspectives on meaning-generating communities (a model we would have to accept under postcolonial theory, since it disavows the possibility of a theory merely representing reality), then what else can postcolonial theory be doing in this context? At its post-structuralist core, postcolonial theory disavows any possibility of theorizing in any representational mode – all theory (including, of course, postcolonial theory) is said to be expressive of cultural-historical collectives, as they work to impose meaning upon the world.

This is clearly too quick an answer. We need then a more nuanced approach to "colonization"! What we seem to lack is the added definitional element of seeing any particular *colonizing* theory being used to *subvert* the self-understandings of Indigenous peoples, the sort of operation we witness in the development and functioning of the regime of Aboriginal law in Canada. Can we say of postcolonial theory that it attempts to colonize the minds and actions of Indigenous peoples in this manner?

With liberal positivism the key element in the colonization process is the attempt to *impose* upon Indigenous peoples a "universal truth," the normative model of the self-in-society (that then serves to provide architectural principles for the structuring of society itself, its courts, its divisions, its centralization of power and decision-making, and so on). We see in contemporary jurisprudence dealing with Aboriginal rights carefully crafted discourse that attempts to build up a form of social reality within which self-determining Indigenous peoples are encouraged to "choose" to become Aboriginal peoples, peoples with Aboriginal rights within the one liberal state.[15] Can we say something similar happens in relation to the advancement of postcolonial theory?

It is possible, but our focus must shift from normative models of the self-in-society to normative models of knowledge and knowledge acquisition.

15 By the very act of choosing, Indigenous peoples risk placing one foot squarely in the liberal world.

We would be saying – in an argument paralleling that for liberal positivism – that postcolonial theory functions principally to work towards having Indigenous peoples think of themselves within the fundamental epistemic-metaphysical frame of world-in-mind, as beings fundamentally constituted as minds, with the essential being and nature of worlds emerging out of the activity of minds (in contrast to other possible fundamental epistemic-metaphysical frames, such as mind-in-world, that begin with a pre-existing and independently existing world, within which emerges the human, a social animal with a highly developed mind and associated mental capacities). Would having Indigenous peoples come to frame all epistemic-metaphysical matters in alignment with a larger world-in-mind setting be an act of subversion of Indigenous self-understandings?

The short answer here is that it would depend on a number of factors, all of which require (for meaningful resolution) significant study. Given any particular Indigenous collective, what are its self-understandings and practices? What do these self-understandings and practices say about the adoption of perspectives that might not formerly have been at the core of the collective sense of what it is to be *x* (Nēhilawē, or Inuit, or ...)? In a few paragraphs I turn to the possibility that few if any Indigenous peoples would either (a) benefit from adopting the core framing perspective of post-structuralism, or (b) likely willingly adopt this fundamental way of thinking of themselves in relation to the world. Let me first, however, touch on other concerns some might raise at this juncture. As with so many of these discussions, this helps both build understanding of what is captured in the sort of methodological naturalism adopted and put to use in this text, and generate support for its adoption and use.

Some might suggest that imagining postcolonial theory could colonize Indigenous peoples in the way supposed is to make unfounded assumptions about the nature of identities and self-understandings of Indigenous peoples. It creates a model, this argument goes, that assumes (a) there are identifiable, discrete Indigenous perspectives at the heart of each identifiable, discrete Indigenous collective, and (b) postcolonial theory should be seen as an outside force, potentially harming the production and maintenance of identifiable and discrete Indigenous knowledges created out of these core identities. It would seem, amongst other matters, that essentialist underpinnings sneak into our discussions, as we now seem to be relying on the assumption that there are "authentic" core identities to each Indigenous collective, authenticity being potentially under attack from such culturally distinct forces as those mustered by postcolonial theory.

Besides inviting outmoded and unwanted ways of thinking of identity, the suggestion of colonization has to contend with alternate explanations for the intrusion of post-structuralist thinking in Indigenous settings – namely, that Indigenous peoples must be seen as changing over time, constantly modifying their systems of collective self-understandings in response to the many influences to which each community is exposed (which is as any cultural group would be expected to function).

The proper response to these concerns is to accept certain positions they push, but to temper them with placement of the entire situation within a naturalist frame (that asks about what we discover happening in the natural world within which we exist). The notion of cultural growth and development must be accepted – how could it not be? – but then in any particular case one must wonder at what *actually* takes place. One might wonder whether in any particular case an Indigenous collective has indeed grown "organically" by some such process as (a) the adoption of a cultural form it considers amenable to its self-understandings, or (b) a slide into ways of thinking that conceptually mesh with earlier forms of self-understanding.[16]

In the rich naturalist environment this study inhabits, we have the tools necessary to make these sorts of events sensible: within a naturalist understanding of cultures existing within a complex social milieu, meaning-generating communities are not conceived of as static, and nor are they essentialized (and nor, for that matter, are they conceived of as discrete and insular, in the sense that there might be sharp borders). We suppose, also, though, that each community and its attendant systems of meaning-generation would be open to study and reflection. What would be – *within a given Indigenous community* – *its* sense of cultural knowledge, cultural continuity, and cultural change? What does *it* see as acceptable and unacceptable forms of appropriation, modification, and growth? Only in having in hand some reasonable sense of these understandings for any given particular Indigenous community could we begin to discern whether for *that* community it makes sense to imagine that the adoption of the deep underpinning of post-structuralist postcolonial theory is "organic" (or, alternatively, whether postcolonial theory is attempting to slip under this Indigenous system of knowledge and knowledge generation a foreign and harmful way of fundamentally thinking of the world).

We must also, of course, allow for variance within any given cultural setting, for no Indigenous community today – no matter how tightly defined – is going to be culturally homogenous. But we still need to wonder at the notion of it being generally acceptable within an Indigenous collective to suppose *no* form of objective truth (no matter how carefully calibrated) is possible. Consider the explanation we developed in our discussion of the applicability of liberal thought to Aboriginal rights – could any Indigenous community wish to accept the idea that this "explanation" is nothing but the expression of cultural forms

16 There are likely innumerable mechanisms by which a cultural group can shift from its current set of self-understandings to some other collection. I present these two options to suggest both more intellectual and more practice-oriented modes.

by some community (purportedly whatever community – in its time and place – the researcher inhabits)?

Concerns remain about arguments about the potential for postcolonial theory to be understood to be colonizing Indigenous peoples, though the response to these concerns is the same – not to dismiss them, but rather to advocate study of meaning-generating systems within the natural world (to explore how theorizing can and does function in relation to Indigenous meaning-generating systems).

This emerges as the basic outcome of our look into the ability of postcolonial theory to aid in making sense of Aboriginal rights. This outcome, though, carries with it a fundamental alteration in the nature of postcolonial theory (insofar as it has post-structuralist roots). To see how we should treat its potential threat is to see how I propose we should think of all theorizing about social phenomena (such as the development of Aboriginal law).

Questions remaining about postcolonial theory bring this to the fore: *should* any Indigenous community adopt the post-structuralist perspective that lies under the mechanics presented by this theory? *Should* Indigenous peoples be swayed by the notion of world-in-mind, of "interpretation all the way down," of knowledge as essentially linked to power (and theorizing as fundamentally means by which power can be affected)? The reader knows I think not, and the arguments of this text all spin into one thread as I make the case for seeing postcolonial theory as offering a means by which a *good explanation* for the nature of Aboriginal rights can be provided, but only if the theory itself is severed from its post-structuralist roots.

Severing Postcolonial Theory from Its Post-Structuralist Roots

On a conceptual level this need for severance should be clear – when attached to its post-structuralist roots, postcolonial theory cannot (non-ironically) claim to ever provide an explanation for independently existing phenomena. But considerations go far beyond this point: we can also appreciate it would be a mistake – in an objective sense – for Indigenous peoples to see the sorts of explanations provided by postcolonial theory as necessarily linked to the denial of the possibility of explanations of the world around.

The first point to appreciate is that there is no reason for Indigenous peoples to follow postcolonial theory to its post-structuralist roots. That is, reasons one might advance for adopting a world-in-mind frame need not persuade Indigenous collectives. The path to the post-structuralist world began centuries before Europeans stumbled upon Turtle Island, born in arcane theological struggles around the relationship of man to a supernatural being (all this being posited within a particular (non-Indigenous) meaning-generating system). Within this system of meaning, man exists in some space between the supernatural and the natural, crafted by a supernatural being in its image.[17] By the time this debate about the nature of the human reached Descartes – a debate entirely divorced from observations or reflections about the natural world – the stage was set for a very particular construction of meaning around such things as knowledge, reason, the human mind, and the human "essence." As study of the natural world made incredible progress over the next few centuries, these supernatural speculations ran into more and deeper conflict or tension with developed explanatory models. As attempts to ground explanatory models in ways that fit the ancient supernaturally grounded metaphysics failed, one cultural response was to deny the possibility that the human could ever accurately model the natural world.

Here we can pull apart two strands of argument – one more directly embedded just in the notion of a cultural-historical stream, and one focused more directly on reason and argument. If we focus just on the long story itself, we see the cultural-historical stream is entirely non-Indigenous in origin, and continued on as a *particular* cultural-historical tale up to early stages of modernity. Indigenous peoples have their own meaning-generating systems, with histories reaching back untold generations, the origins of which do not posit a supernatural being as imagined within the Judeo-Christian tradition. The two streams have very different paths, up to those periods during which the non-Indigenous stream attempts to pull all alternate cultural-historical worlds into its flow.[18]

If we focus on *reasons* for shifts in meaning and thought, we do best to think of all as embedded within particular cultural streams. Reasons for movements *within* this non-Indigenous cultural-historical tale (reasons that explain why some in the Western academy now deny the ability of humans to accurately depict the natural world, particularly as it intersects with humans) make sense *within* this atmosphere of Western thought and ideology. The key question, of course, is whether these culturally embedded reasons should reach out to Indigenous meaning-systems, providing Indigenous communities and scholars with reason to likewise deny the possibility of accurately representing mind-independent reality. Note that not all reasons emerging within the Western intellectual milieu for a shift to post-structuralist positions track simple progression through the stages of the story – undoubtedly much also has to do with contemporary intellectual fashion, the desire to preserve a field of study entirely removed from (successes of) the sciences, and the like. These latter sorts of culturally determined reasons should not engage Indigenous communities and scholars, but neither should the dominant thread – it is entirely open to both Indigenous communities and scholars to reach within to their own long-established epistemological

---

17 Whenever we reach back to these medieval / early Enlightenment roots, it is always entirely appropriate to use the term "man."

18 See Vine Deloria, *God Is Red: A Native View of Religion* (Golden, CO: Fulcrum Publishing, 2003).

theories and positions, many of which (if not, indeed, all) likely intersect with neither notions of a "light of reason" that humans uniquely possess (that purportedly sets apart humankind from the natural world), nor the notion of a special inside-world, a world of the mind exceedingly superior to the world of experience and phenomena. Neither the fact of the story itself (with its twists and turns through the last few centuries), nor the reasons told within the story for shifts in fundamental thinking should engage the Indigenous scholar.

Reasons that Indigenous communities and scholars might *reject* adoption of post-structuralist threads running through postcolonial theory can themselves take two forms – those emergent from within particular Indigenous meaning-systems, and those common to Indigenous systems. Within any given Indigenous system, again, the question requires study and reflection – given what any particular Indigenous cultural world holds (or practises) around knowledge and knowledge acquisition, is there good reason to reject post-structuralist underpinnings of postcolonial theory? One could imagine the Indigenous scholar searching within her Indigenous community for positive arguments that could lead it to build within itself a sense of the human as essentially holding within it worlds of meaning (such that no theories or models could be said to be capable of reaching out to independent natural worlds, as the Indigenous community denies sense – within its world – for a notion of mind-in-world).

Leaving this to particular Indigenous communities to work out, let us turn then to possible reasons that might be common to many – if not all – Indigenous communities. While again one might strictly hold to the position that all these reasons emerge from communities of humans in the world (who, as beings in the world, can generate meaning through sociolinguistic practices), reasons can be common when they speak to the common place of Indigenous peoples vis-à-vis colonizing forces.

At the core of these common reasons is the flip side of the fact that the shift to post-structuralist underpinnings of theorizing in the West is intimately tied to a particular cultural-historical world (that of the West). The flip side, from Indigenous perspectives, is the realization that there are acceptable alternate ways to think of theorizing (even about social phenomena, such as the law). This was the import of much of the middle of this text, wherein a form of methodological naturalism was advanced as a plausible response to the reasonable anti-foundationalist arguments of the last century or so. Not only is a naturalist response a reasonable alternative within the non-Indigenous (Western) cultural setting, but it also speaks to Indigenous peoples.

It suggests we can speak *objectively* of the impact of liberalism on Indigenous peoples (via the operation of Aboriginal rights on the lives of otherwise self-determining Indigenous peoples). It suggests we can speak *objectively* of subjugated Indigenous knowledges (systems of meaning-generation being endemic to independent, self-determining peoples). It suggests we can speak *objectively* of provincializing non-Indigenous meaning-generating systems, holding them up in the light of (naturalized) reason as being put to use in attempts by one meaning-generating system to control the minds and lives of inhabitants of other meaning-generating systems.

These common reasons all turn, then, on accepting the value of certain insights of postcolonial theory, but only when shorn of its post-structuralist roots. One interesting outcome of this study into making sense of Aboriginal rights is that what might have seemed the more "hard-nosed" or empirically focused theory – liberal positivism – is shown to be not concerned principally with providing explanatory models, as it now is revealed as functioning – in the guise of liberal thought – as providing architectural plans for the creation of a system of meaning (for such things as legal rules, principles, and tests) designed to *subvert* the independent meaning-systems of Indigenous peoples, while what might have seemed to be the softer, more "critical" theory – postcolonialism – is shown to be the more empirically suited, the theory capable of providing the *objectively better explanation* for legal phenomena in the world.

Postcolonial Theory and Making Sense of Aboriginal Rights

We arrive, then, at an interesting endpoint in our study. We now see that in deploying a particular methodological approach – one that eschews a-natural phenomena, one that takes seriously sociolinguistic activities in the world (seeing such activity by collectives as something that must be examined carefully, as collectives are seen as meaning-generating centres, their aims sometimes being to damage or destroy other meaning-generating collectives), one that begins from the presumption that humans are simply part of the natural world, themselves open to naturalistic study – we can see how the development of Aboriginal law makes sense in light of liberal positivist theoretic frameworks, but makes *more sense* when we step back from this explanation to ask about the operations of these meaning-generating collectives. Some legal theories are best seen not as attempting to explain independent phenomena, but as attempting to generate forms of social reality. Other theories, once tamed within the naturalistic framework, are revealed as helpful tools in the development of truly explanatory models.

This leaves untouched vast realms open to further study. The aim in this text was to make sense of the development of Aboriginal rights as possible instruments within forms of legal and political discourse. We did not venture into questions that the explanations tendered now invite – just as Newton's explanation for the motion of the planets led to questions about *why* objects with mass would move the way they do, our explanation for the development of Aboriginal rights – that courts in Canada are attempting to liberalize Indigenous peoples, to destroy fundamental forms of Indigenous sovereignty – invite similar questions: *Why* do they act this way? *Why* do they seem driven to destroy other meaning-generating systems? What other forces are at play behind the models we now have of what is going on?

Conclusion

My primary intent in this concluding section is to suggest next steps, both in questions and research projects now capable of reasonably clear articulation, and in how work carried out in this text indicates that exploration of these questions might be undertaken. To present a few thoughts about next stages it would be helpful, though, to begin with a summary of where things stand at the conclusion of this look into how one should go about making sense of the jurisprudence on Aboriginal rights.

The historical oppression of Indigenous peoples in Canada – the imposition of oppressive policies, the dispossession of lands and resources, the suffering of individuals, families, and communities – was facilitated by Canadian law, backed by racist and colonial ideologies. With a sense of this history in mind, questions arise about recent events in Canadian law, as Aboriginal and treaty rights are "recognized and affirmed." The body of jurisprudence centred on recognition and affirmation has not addressed the colonial roots of Crown-Indigenous relations and is, for that reason alone, deeply troubling. Intertwined with the failure to address colonialism is the fact that many core elements of the jurisprudence are deeply puzzling, especially to Indigenous peoples.

One way to explain what we witness in the jurisprudence is to suggest that the deep discomfort I and others similarly situated feel is either the result of confusion about what is being put in place, or the product of ideological perspectives we bring to our attempts at understanding. In this text I attempted to lift veils of confusion that might seem to cloud what is actually transpiring in the jurisprudence, all the while paying serious attention to the presence of perspectives various parties may bring to the task of trying to make sense of Canadian law.

In the Introduction I wrote of my own journey in making sense of Canadian law on Aboriginal rights. One reason for presenting this as a personal journey was to introduce concerns about positionality and perspective, concerns I highlighted through the rest of the text, including in sections that grappled with matters of theorizing. At a point in my intellectual journey I had supposed – rather naively – that legal theory might shed some light on puzzles that populate the jurisprudence, but later it became clear that serious questions about perspectives intrude as well into the very business of theorizing. Widely divergent theories of the law seem to be grounded in sociocultural-historical positions occupied by differently situated scholars.

It was important, then, that the business of theorizing be explored in some depth, all with an eye to not just how Indigenous and non-Indigenous understandings of the law might colour analysis of Canadian jurisprudence, but also to how the position of the theorist carrying out analysis may need to be considered if some measure of objectivity is to be preserved. In the middle chapters, as we dug into how scholars go about explaining the nature of phenomena, we noted that on what seems to be deepest level of concerns there are questions about our ability to produce knowledge at all. At this foundational level we found arguments that bedevilled academic pursuits over the last century or so, arguments that percolate upward to infect theorizing about legal phenomena. My efforts to defuse these concerns centred on a newly resurgent approach to the study of phenomena, methodological naturalism.

While we saw that challenges to theories of the production of knowledge can be adequately addressed through the naturalization of epistemology, we also noted that debates that triggered these challenges emerged from a historical, localized set of intellectual traditions, those that unwisely attempted to imbue science with requirements of certainty and justification that could not be met. Besides value in seeing how contemporary naturalism provides a viable underpinning for modern accounts of the possibility of knowledge (providing an account of how best to go about searching for and deploying explanations of mind-independent phenomena), this exploration into key aspects of the larger intellectual milieu of the last century illustrated how naturalism functions when theorizing is itself under the microscope. Theories about the production of knowledge were themselves placed in the observable, testable world, subject to criteria of evaluation that emerge from our collective study of this one natural world. When we examined these theories in this manner, we saw how they emerged as expressions of meaning within sociocultural settings, and one way to understand the impact of the naturalization process is to come to see *all* theories as reflections of localized, historicized periods and peoples.

We applied this general approach to the business of theorizing about legal phenomena, and to theorizing specifically about Aboriginal law. Within this narrower context we now had multiple ways to understand how "perspectives" appear and function. Now, not only were we equipped to manage questions about Indigenous and non-Indigenous perspectives on Canadian law (as sociocultural expressions of differing understandings and evaluations), we were also now able to think about the role theorists and theories themselves play in the world about us, as we were able to meaningfully explore roles played by a theorist's understanding of her position and of the nature of the world. For example, a theorist working in a world partially structured upon notions of knowledge that demand its extension only include statements that are true in some absolute, grounded sense understands the world through specific sets of conceptual filters, ways of seeing that have much to say about what she considers sensible and understandable, just as theorists who see all knowledge to be entirely locally situated similarly build up a world of sense upon this sort of alternate central pillar. Perspectives that can arise and exist in these modes and on these levels are potentially limitless, but each is tied down to a meaning-generating community, a social unit that itself arises within the world about us.

For our purposes the key was in seeing that, likewise, we can now see how a theory about Canadian law on Aboriginal rights might emerge from and function within a world of meaning generated by a sociocultural collective. It is in this milieu of socially grounded perspectives that we find the world views of varied Indigenous communities, each community generating and living through its own social reality, constructed out of overlapping webs of meaning. It is also where we find the world view of Canadian society and its institutions, wrapped around a central pillar of liberal thought. The study in this text was into one subset of meanings generated by one social community, Canada, developed and expressed through one of its specific institutions, its judicial system. Our questions were about the nature of webs of meaning being spun, but rather than begin by placing ourselves and this analysis *into* the world marked by boundaries of sense cast by Canadian society and the Canadian state, we left open the presence of persisting, self-determining Indigenous collectives. Our examination, then, was into a certain set of phenomena in the world before us, as meanings expressed through the domestic Canadian legal system were generated to affect separate social worlds and realities built and inhabited by Indigenous peoples.

Work carried out in the context of this form of analysis led to very specific outcomes. Puzzles infecting the jurisprudence on Aboriginal rights were explained for the most part by the fact that this body of law has been built on a bedrock of liberal thought, judges of the Supreme Court building a new social structure out of architectural principles grounded in a liberal vision of how society should be ordered, with liberal ideals and values infusing the edifice then erected. But this form of explanation was strongly circumscribed. While the creation of such a structure would be entirely "natural" if it were being built as an aspect of an existing single liberal society, the explanation falters when we return to the fact that we are not examining a world in which we can just presume all individuals and communities are already embedded within one liberal society.

The key outcome of this study connects to the open-endedness of presumptions made about the world this structure is being built in, as we do not begin our analysis with the presumption that Indigenous peoples are already entirely subsumed within a single liberal world. When focus is kept on the history of Crown-Indigenous relations, when the existence of separate meaning-generating Indigenous communities is kept an open possibility (even after centuries of colonial activities), the nature of the jurisprudence is revealed in deeper form. Puzzles heretofore addressed are still explained, not in a way that explains them away, but in a form that heightens the confusion they engender. We see that liberal thought still accounts primarily for mechanisms, rules, and tests we encounter, not as aspects of a relatively benign building process that occurs within a given liberal society, but as aspects of a structure meant to remove Indigenous self-determination from the landscape, specifically in relation to Indigenous peoples' capacities to generate their own forms of social reality. We here note, as well, heightened puzzlement over the complete failure of the jurisprudence on Aboriginal rights to even engage with questions of Indigenous self-determination, the one key puzzle left untouched by the otherwise wide-ranging success of liberal thought to address the set of puzzles.

Besides just detailing how liberal thought can essentially explain the nature of the jurisprudence, we also looked into key implications of the activities and structures we were describing. For example, viewed from the perspective of a naturalist looking at the activities of meaning-generating communities, we can see the meaningfulness of understandings developed within these communities. Generally, those living *within* the liberal world of Canadian society do not find themselves in a position to question the meaningfulness of the liberal model of society they work within – the web of meanings built up around their lives is the very air they breathe. The flip side of this, of course, is that questions and concerns in Canada overwhelmingly arise about Indigenous perspectives. These are revealed in the naturalist model, however, as nothing more or less than parallel sets of understandings, providing sets of distinct views on the nature of Aboriginal law (grounded in distinct views on the nature of law itself).

How do we imagine advancing beyond this point, to engage in evaluative analyses of the situation we can now objectively describe? This matter was broached in the last chapter, as we explored the ability of critical postcolonial theory to explain the legal phenomena of Canadian law on Aboriginal rights, though there we focused on epistemic evaluation. Recall that one key argument of that section was that postcolonial theory provides a *better* explanation than liberal theory, as it can capture key aspects of the very model we developed in exploring a naturalist understanding of how liberal thought might account for the development of the jurisprudence, all while falling in line with the notion that what we witness is a struggle over meaning-generation. Besides, then, subsuming within it positive aspects of the explanation provided by liberal theory, it also addresses key puzzles that theory left not only untouched, but heightened. If our concern is with accuracy and truth, something along the lines of the model advanced by postcolonial theory is normatively *better* (where we are speaking of the deployment of epistemic norms, those committed to the production of knowledge of the world about us).

We are now in a position to begin presenting thoughts on next stages of analysis. There are actually quite a few matters up for consideration, but I want to focus on one particularly important horizon that now beckons along the way, making it clear how the form of analysis carried out in this work might be put to use in examining this area of study. I end with some thoughts about aspects of the business of theorizing that intersect with this horizon.

Recall that in broaching the topic of evaluation in the chapter on postcolonial theory the focus was fairly narrow, particularly when attention was not directed towards epistemic matters as defined within the naturalist mode. When the question of non-epistemic normative evaluation came up, I was concerned principally with attempts to measure the adequacy of one theoretical account from within the normative-evaluative criteria of another theoretical account. For example, from the space occupied by a grand theory such as liberalism, critical accounts are dismissible, both on theoretic and normative groundings. But from the space of critical theory, a theory like liberalism is just another form of discourse, an entirely constructed edifice that can be judged only from constructed worlds (there being no sense, for the post-structuralist, in any grounding evaluation). Aims in that extended discussion were, first, to show the shortcomings of postcolonial theory for Indigenous peoples and their struggles in the contemporary world (as it had no room for saying "this is the way things are"), and, second, to suggest that a form of postcolonial theory could be salvaged, one that dropped its post-structuralist roots and aligned itself better with the naturalist point of view being developed in this text.

Note, though, how this analysis progressed through this discussion – both liberal thought and postcolonial theory were placed *into* the natural world, seen as expressions of sociocultural communities functioning to build forms of social reality. Postcolonial theory was seen as potentially problematic for Indigenous peoples for two reasons: first, it expresses a point of view emergent from (and really sensible only within) a specific intellectual environment, one marked by a specific history and set of understandings, fundamentally non-Indigenous; and, second, it could well be a Trojan horse, siphoning off energies of resistance so necessary in the nature of struggles of today. Our look into evaluation and cross-evaluation were intended to make these points, as we saw how things in the world concerning such matters look when we take the naturalist point of view on theorizing that occurs within the larger landscape marked by separate meaning-generating communities.

Now we can return to questions of evaluation, given insights this study has provided. A researcher could simply throw up her hands and debate the treatment of Indigenous peoples by Canadian law from *within* webs of meaning constructed by Canada's courts (reflective of webs of meaning that infuse Canadian society). I have been laying the groundwork throughout this study, however, for a base level of caution in regard to that approach. Of course, Indigenous peoples are self-determining, and going in this direction could well be an instance of the exercise of this authority, so a researcher from a community adopting such a stance may have little choice in the matter (or have to be willing to be an internal dissenting voice). More likely, however, given the very long and tragic history of Crown oppression, taking this approach collectively would be a move forced upon an Indigenous community, or one seen as the only viable or sensible avenue open.

An alternative is naturalistic study into how systems of meaning change over time, how they self-evaluate, how they adapt to changing times, new insights, and new attitudes, and so forth. As part of our overview of liberal thought, we touched on changes within this universe of meaning evident over the last century or so. What brought about these changes? Can changes be directed or managed? Could contemporary liberalism be brought to a point where its adherents might respond to insights into Indigenous self-determination? Let me present some initial thoughts on these questions, based to a large extent on outcomes of the work of this text, and then spell out what these thoughts suggest about next stages of research.

It may well seem that while the direction liberal thought tacks may be shifted, the ship itself is fairly immune to radical change, and the general direction toward which the ships heads cannot be seriously altered. Responding adequately to Indigenous self-determination would be radical. We have seen that adequate accommodation (given what Indigenous self-determination implicates in terms of meaning-generation) presumes something other than a measure of accommodation *within* the liberally constructed universe of Canadian society as it is, for we have seen that independent socioculturally defined collectives are capable of being valued (and so fit into society) in only one of two ways, both of which still require a centralized, authoritative decision-making body, one that works within a world of liberal principles and values in order to determine how all aspects of society are integrated into one whole.

On the one hand, there seems to have been some movement in the latter half of the twentieth century towards a neutralist form of liberal thought that seems to permit a more tolerant stance towards potentially illiberal sub-societies (since, being neutral on the normative stance of liberal principles themselves, it would naturally not be strongly inclined to reach *into* the inner make-ups of these sub-societies, attacking, or undermining illiberal elements or aspects). On the other hand, there is the value we noted the Supreme Court finds in Indigenous subcultures, where these societies receive secondary value on the basis that they either provide contexts of choice or express choices made. This latter way of finding value in the existence of collectives fits within the perfectionist model of liberal thought and would most likely be less tolerant than the alternative of the presence of illiberal elements or aspects of these sub-societies (given its adherence to beliefs in the *correctness* of liberal principles and values, regardless of time and place). Note, however, that both approaches place sub-societies into one social setting, where decisions about how this one society is to be conceived of and managed are made according to liberal principles and ideals and by a centralized, authoritative body.

This limits what is conceivable in the continued presence of Indigenous self-determination (if it is to persist within a Canadian state). The limit, one can well see, places independent Indigenous meaning-generating societies outside what the Canadian state can currently accommodate. The strongest form of accommodation would most likely emerge from the neutralist position, but it would not permit Indigenous societies to generate their own understandings of such things as law and governance that have extensive scope (either geographically or in terms of populations). Such societies challenge the superstructure, one that claims to itself the sole authority to decide how Canada, as a whole, is to be conceived of and managed.

These preliminary thoughts call for more detailed exploration. First up would be simply the matter of determining if the destruction of Indigenous meaning-generating capacities is *required* in the liberal world of ideas with which Canadian society is built in accord. Second, if this so, would be working out why this might be so. We have seen that the best explanation for the jurisprudence we witness is that Canadian courts are attempting to remove Indigenous self-determination from the Canadian landscape, and, like a typical five-year-old, we can ask, "Why?"

One possible reason could be a finding related to the first question – perhaps Canadian courts are responding to a sense that there is simply no place within a liberal society for parallel meaning-generating societies. Other reasons, however, might be found to account for why we see what we do, and all this calls for naturalist analysis. It might well be, for example, that jurists raised in the atmosphere of a liberal society simply believe in the normative grounding of liberalism. Buttressing this view, they may also think the passage of time has swept over Indigenous peoples. This sweep-of-history position may have several sub-corollaries: that while the doctrine of discovery and other failed justificatory devices were racist and colonial when put to use, now, generations later, they are no longer what accounts for the current situation; that when put into contemporary scales, the "innocent" status of settlers outweighs the concerns of Indigenous peoples; that this weighing turns out this way primarily as a result of the gradual slipping away of Indigenous independence and distinctiveness; and that thoughts of rebuilding or revitalizing powerful forms of Indigenous self-determination are impractical and ill-advised.

Such possible reasons demand attention, but they also prejudge the current situation. They all, to one degree or another, rest on an assessment of the situation that privileges Crown sovereignty and the status of the liberal state. This assessment is suspect as well when it emanates from elements of this state, as the state seeks to justify why it might continue to attempt to remove Indigenous self-determination. The very fact that attempts at denial and removal lie at the heart of best explanations of the nature of contemporary Canadian jurisprudence indicates quite clearly the shakiness of prejudgment – in fact, the presence of any such arguments calls for further exploration, as the objective observer has to wonder *why* such beliefs might appear at all, driving a project that supposedly is already in the rear-view mirror.

This leads into the sort of study this work most strongly calls for – explorations, naturally, into what is really happening. We have seen clearly the sort of struggle Canadian courts are engaged in, and I have suggested some sets of beliefs to which judges may hold dear should they try to justify to themselves why they construct things the way they do. But are there other reasons that more likely account for what we see? Could it be that what drives courts is what has driven Canadian law and policy for many generations, the need to clear away opposition to unfettered access to Indigenous lands and resources?

Last words are on the subject of Indigenous perspectives – specifically, Indigenous theoretic perspectives. We are now decades into a modern Indigenous renaissance, as Indigenous scholars add their voices to analyses of law and society. Earlier generations spoke to harmful impacts of Canadian law and policy on their communities, but this was essentially shut down with the suppression of Indigenous resistance by the Crown in the 1920s. With post–Second World War shifts in Canadian law and policy, a resurgent Indigenous intellectual community reflected on changes, thought about what they might mean for their specific communities and for the collection of Indigenous communities stretching across Canada, and actively and effectively resisted attempts to finish the colonial project.

Throughout this modern era, however, attempts by the state to envelope all discourse in the language of liberalism have been unceasing. Have Indigenous scholarly efforts been sufficiently self-reflective? If arguments in this text bear up, if Indigenous legal scholars can begin to agree that Canadian courts have used and are continuing to use section 35 to remove the core of Indigenous self-determination once and for all, what should be the response? I noted above the challenging position some researchers may find themselves in, with their community welcoming opportunities to find accommodation within the single liberal state (and its capitalist economy). Different forms of acceptance or acquiescence may follow, with some Indigenous legal scholars working entirely within the normative universe of liberal thought. Some, of course, may not have noticed their acquiescence – we are, after all, generations into the latest efforts by the state and its courts to control all discourse, and this is certain to affect the abilities of Indigenous scholars, working within Western institutions, to note general features of the atmosphere they have been educated within.

When we turn our attention to the work of contemporary Indigenous legal scholars, we see these possibilities suggested. Work is called for: namely, examinations into how legal theories are being conceived of, what sorts of work they are expected to be put towards, what outcomes scholars are aiming for – all of which could be profitably explored as matters of the world around us, as phenomena and questions about phenomena that admit of naturalist analysis. That is, Indigenous legal scholars need to ponder how the work they are doing actually functions in the world, how it succeeds in describing what is actually going on, or serves other purposes. Is it possible, for example, that some work is not directed towards providing explanations, but towards building up forms of social reality? If so, which forms – those that reflect Indigenous or non-Indigenous systems of meaning?

A quick survey of work shows two broad, general camps of Indigenous scholars – those who work (consciously or not) within a normative world informed by liberal thought, and those who work to maintain grounded forms of Indigenous self-determination. As I noted above, one outcome of the work in this text is the realization that once an Indigenous community accepts or acquiesces a place within the one liberal society that is Canada, it has given up its ability to authoritatively generate its own universe of meaning. There is a line there, one that some may not see is the determinant between maintaining status as self-determining peoples and relinquishing (or losing) that status absolutely. What role does the work of any specific Indigenous scholar play in that situation, one that is most pressing at this point in the history of Crown-Indigenous relations as the state senses it is closing in on its objective of removing Indigenous self-determination?

Bibliography

Treaties and Agreements

Declaration of Dene Nationhood Passed at the Second Joint Assembly of the Indian Brotherhood of the Northwest Territories, at Fort Simpson, 1975, online: <www.canadahistory.com/sections/documents/native/Dene%20Declaration.html>.

James Bay and Northern Québec Agreement and Complementary Agreements, 1998, online: <epe.lac-bac.gc.ca/003/008/099/003008-disclaimer.html?orig=/100/200/301/inac-ainc/james_bay-e/jbnq_e.pdf>.

Kunst'aa Guu – Kunst'aayah Reconciliation Protocol, 2009, online: <haidanation.ca/wp-content/uploads/2017/03/Kunstaa-guu_Kunstaayah_Agreement.pdf>.

Land Claims Agreement between the Inuit of Labrador and Her Majesty the Queen in Right of Newfoundland and Labrador and Her Majesty the Queen in Right of Canada, 2005, online: <https://www.aadnc-aandc.gc.ca/eng/1293647179208/1293647660333>.

The Inuvialuit Final Agreement as Amended, 2005, online: <irc.inuvialuit.com/sites/default/files/Inuvialuit%20Final%20Agreement%202005.pdf>.

Moving Forward in Nunavut: An Agreement Relating to Settlement of Litigation and Certain Implementation Matters, 2005, online: <tunngavik.com/files/2015/05/FINAL-SETTLEMENT-AGREEMENT-PROOF.pdf>.

Nunavik Inuit Land Claims Agreement, 2006, online: <aadnc-aandc.gc.ca/DAM/DAM-INTER-HQ/STAGING/texte-text/ldc_ccl_fagr_nk_lca_1309284365020_eng.pdf>.

Treaty No. 8 Made June 21, 1899 and Adhesions, Reports, Etc., 1899, online: <canadiancrown.com/uploads/3/8/4/1/3841927/treaty_8.pdf>.

Statutes

An Act Further to Amend "The Indian Act, 1880," SC 1882, c 27.

An Act to Amend the Indian Act in Response to the Superior Court of Quebec decision Descheneaux c Canada (Procureur général), SC 2017, c 25.

Canadian Bill of Rights, SC 1960, c 44.

Canadian Charter of Rights and Freedoms, Part I of the *Constitution Act, 1982*, being Schedule B to the *Canada Act 1982* (UK), c 11.
Constitution Act, 1867 (UK), 30 & 31 Vict, c 3, reprinted in RSC 1985, App II, No 5.
Constitution Act, 1982, being Schedule B to the *Canada Act 1982* (UK), 1982, c 11.
Criminal Code, RSC 1985, c C-46.
First Nations Commercial and Industrial Development Act, SC 2005, c 53.
First Nations Elections Act, SC 2014, c 5.
First Nations Financial Transparency Act, SC 2013, c 7.
First Nations Fiscal Management Act, SC 2005, c 9.
First Nations Oil and Gas Moneys Management Act, SC 2005, c 48.
Gender Equity in Indian Registration Act, SC 2010, c 18.
George R, Proclamation, 7 October 1763 (3 Geo III), reprinted RSC 1985, App II, No 1.
Indian Act, RSC 1985, c I-5.
Manitoba Act, 1870 (UK), 33 Vict, c 3, reprinted in RSC 1985, App II, No 8.
Nunavut Act, SC 1993, c 28.

Cases

Ahousaht Indian Band and Nation v Canada (AG), 2018 BCSC 633.
Ahousaht Indian Band v Canada (AG), 2011 BCCA 237, leave to appeal to SCC refused, 34387 (29 March 2012).
Andrews v Law Society of British Columbia, [1989] 1 SCR 143, 56 DLR (4th) 1.
Blencoe v British Columbia (Human Rights Commission), 2000 SCC 44.
Calder v British Columbia (AG), [1973] SCR 313, 34 DLR (3d) 145.
Campbell v British Columbia (AG), 2001 BCSC 1400.
Canada (AG) v Lavell (1973), [1974] SCR 1349, 38 DLR (3d) 481.
Canada (Prime Minister) v Khadr, 2010 SCC 3.
Canadian Aero Service Ltd v O'Malley (1973), [1974] SCR 592, 40 DLR (3d) 371.
Casimel v Insurance Corporation of British Columbia (1993), 106 DLR (4th) 720, [1994] 2 CNLR 22 (BCCA).
Cherokee Nation v Georgia (1831) 30 US 1.
Connolly v Woolrich (1867), 11 LCJ 197, 17 RJRQ 75.
Daniels v Canada (Indian Affairs and Northern Development), 2016 SCC 12.
Daniels v Canada (Minister of Foreign Affairs and Northern Development), 2013 FC 6.
Daniels v Canada (Minister of Indian Affairs and Northern Development), 2014 FCA 101.
Delgamuukw v British Columbia (AG), [1997] 3 SCR 1010, 153 DLR (4th) 193.
Descheneaux v Canada (Procureur général), 2015 QCCS 3555.
Doe v Metropolitan Toronto (Municipality) Commissioners of Police, [1998] 39 OR (3d) 487, 160 DLR (4th) 697 (Ont Sup Ct).
Grassy Narrows First Nation v Ontario (MNR), 2014 SCC 48.

Guerin v The Queen, [1984] 2 SCR 335, 13 DLR (4th) 321.
Haida Nation v British Columbia (Minister of Forests), 2004 SCC 73.
Jack et al v The Queen, [1980] 1 SCR 294, 100 DLR (3d) 193.
Lac Minerals Ltd v International Corona Resources Ltd, [1989] 2 SCR 574, 61 DLR (4th) 14.
Lax Kw'alaams Indian Band v Canada (AG), 2011 SCC 56.
Mabo and Others v Queensland (No. 2) (1992) HCA 23.
Manitoba Metis Federation v Canada (AG), 2013 SCC 14.
Matson et al v Indian and Northern Affairs Canada, 2013 CHRT 13.
McIvor v Canada (Registrar of Indian and Northern Affairs), 2009 BCCA 153.
McIvor v Canada (Registrar of Indian and Northern Affairs), 2009 BCCA 153, leave to appeal to SCC refused, 33201 (5 November 2009).
Mikisew Cree First Nation v Canada (Governor General in Council), 2018 SCC 40.
Mikisew Cree First Nation v Canada (Minister of Canadian Heritage), 2005 SCC 69.
Mitchell v Minister of Natural Revenue 2001 SCC 33.
Norberg v Wynrib, [1992] 2 SCR 226, 92 DLR (4th) 449.
Nunavut Tunngavik Inc v Canada (AG), 2014 NUCA 2.
Nunavut Tunngavik Inc v Canada (AG), 2014 NUCJ 31.
Ontario v Dominion of Canada (1895), 25 SCR 434, 1895 CarswellNat 46.
Reference as to whether "Indians" includes in s 91 (24) of the BNA Act includes Eskimo inhabitants of the Province of Quebec, [1939] SCR 104, 2 DLR 417.
Reference re Secession of Quebec, [1998] 2 SCR 217, 161 DLR (4th) 385.
R v Adams, [1996] 3 SCR 101, 138 DLR (4th) 657.
R v Babin, 2013 NSSC 434.
R v Badger, [1996] 1 SCR 771, 133 DLR (4th) 324.
R v Castonguay, 2012 NBPC 19.
R v Côté, [1996] 3 SCR 139, 138 DLR (4th) 385.
R v Gladstone, [1996] 2 SCR 723, 137 DLR (4th) 648.
R v Hirsekorn, 2013 ABCA 242.
R v Horseman, [1990] 1 SCR 901, [1990] 4 WWR 97.
R v Kapp, 2008 SCC 41.
R v Marshall, [1999] 3 SCR 456, 177 DLR (4th) 513.
R v Marshall, [1999] 3 SCR 533, 179 DLR (4th) 193.
R v Marshall; R v Bernard, 2005 SCC 43.
R v Morris, 2006 SCC 59.
R v NTC Smokehouse, [1996] 2 SCR 672, 137 DLR (4th) 528.
R v Pamajewon, [1996] 2 SCR 821, 138 DLR (4th) 204.
R v Powley, 2003 SCC 43.
R v Sappier; R v Gray, 2006 SCC 54.
R v Simon, [1985] 2 SCR 387, 24 DLR (4th) 390.
R v Sioui, [1990] 1 SCR 1025, 70 DLR (4th) 427.
R v Sparrow, [1990] 1 SCR 1075, 70 DLR (4th) 385.

R v Taylor (1981), [1981] 3 CNLR 114, 34 OR (2d) 360.
R v Van der Peet, [1996] 2 SCR 507, 137 DLR (4th) 289.
R v Vautour, 2015 NBQB 94.
R v White (1964), 50 DLR (2d) 613, 52 WWR 193 (BCCA), aff'd [1965] SCR vi (note), 52 DLR (2d) 481.
Sandra Lovelace v Canada, Communication No R.6/24, UN Doc Supp No 40 (A/36/40) at 166 (1981).
Simon v The Queen, [1985] 2 SCR 387, 24 DLR (4th) 390.
St Catharine's Milling & Lumber Co v The Queen, [1887] 13 SCR 577, 14 AC 46 (JCPC).
Taku River Tlingit First Nation v British Columbia (Project Assessment Director), (2004) 3 SCR 550.
Thomas v Norris, [1992] 2 CNLR 139, 31 ACWS (3d) 558.
Tsilhqot'in Nation v British Columbia, 2007 BCSC 1700.
Tsilhqot'in Nation v British Columbia, 2014 SCC 44.
West Moberly First Nations v British Columbia (Chief Inspector of Mines), 2011 BCCA 247, leave to appeal to SCC refused, 34403 (23 August 2011).
WIC Radio Ltd v Simpson, 2008 SCC 40.

Articles

Asch, Michael. "The Judicial Conceptualization of Culture after *Delgamuukw* and *Van der Peet*" (2000) 5 Rev Const Stud 119.
Asch, Michael & Patrick Macklem. "Aboriginal Rights and Canadian Sovereignty: An Essay on *R. v. Sparrow*" (1991) 29 Alta L Rev 498.
Aupilaarjuk, Mariano. "Tirigusuusit and Maligait" in Jarich Oosten et al, eds, *Interviewing Inuit Elders: Perspectives on Traditional Law* (Iqaluit: Nunavut Arctic College, 1999).
Barsh, RL & James Youngblood (Sakej) Henderson. "The Supreme Court's *Van der Peet* Trilogy: Naïve Imperialism and Ropes of Sand" (1997) 42 McGill LJ 993.
Bell, Duncan. "What Is Liberalism?" (2016) 42:6 Political Theory 682 at 705.
Borrows, John. "Aboriginal Title in Tsilhqot'in v. British Columbia [2014] SCC 44" (Aug 2014) Maori L Rev, online: <maorilawreview.co.nz/2014/08/aboriginal-title-in-tsilhqotin-v-british-columbia-2014-scc-44/>.
– "Sovereignty's Alchemy: An Analysis of *Delgamuukw v. British Columbia*" (1999) 37 Osgoode Hall LJ 537.
Bowker, Andrea. "Sparrow's Promise: Aboriginal Rights in the B.C. Court of Appeal" (1995) 53 UT Fac L Rev 1.
Boyle, James. "The Politics of Reason: Critical Legal Theory and Local Social Thought" (1985) 133:4 U Pa L Rev 685.
Cashmore, Anthony. "The Lucretian Swerve: The Biological Basis of Human Behavior and the Criminal Justice System" (2010) 107 Proc Nat Ac Sci 4499.

Christie, Gordon. "'Obligations,' Decolonization and Indigenous Rights to Governance" (2014) 27:1 Can JL & Jur 259.

– "Who Makes Decisions over Aboriginal Title Lands?" (2015) 48 UBC L Rev 743.

Coleman, Jules. "Rules and Social Facts" (1991) 14:3 Harv JL & Pub Pol'y 703.

Crane, Tim. "Intentional Objects" (2001) 14 Ratio 298.

Dick, Caroline. "'Culture and the Courts' Revisited: Group-Rights Scholarship and the Evolution of S. 35(1)" (2009) 42:4 Can J Pol Sci 957.

Farrell, Ian. "H.L.A. Hart and the Methodology of Jurisprudence," review of *A Life of H.L.A. Hart: The Nightmare and the Noble Dream* by Nicola Lacey (2006) 84:4 Texas L Rev 983.

Fodor, Jerry. "Water's Water Everywhere," review of *Kripke: Names, Necessity and Identity* by Christopher Hughes (2004) 26:20 London Rev Books 17, online: <lrb.co.uk/v26/n20/jerry-fodor/waters-water-everywhere>.

Fuller, Lon. "Positivism and Fidelity to Law: A Reply to Professor Hart" (1958) 71:4 Harv L Rev 630.

Green, Joyce & Gina Starblanket. "Op-Ed: Recognition of Rights or Termination of Rights Framework?" APTN National News (2 Aug 2018), online: <aptnnews.ca/2018/08/02/op-ed-recognition-of-rights-or-termination-of-rights-framework/>.

Hart, HLA. "Positivism and the Separation of Law and Morals" (1958) 71:4 Harv L Rev 593.

Henderson, James Youngblood (Sakej). "Postcolonial Indigenous Legal Consciousness" (Spring 2002) Indigenous LJ 1.

Henrich, Joseph, Steven Heine & Ara Norenzayan. "The Weirdest People in the World?" (2010) 33:2–3 Behav & Brain Sci 61.

Isaac, Thomas. "Balancing Rights: The Supreme Court of Canada, *R. v. Sparrow*, and the Future of Aboriginal Rights" (1993) 13 Can J Native Stud 199.

Kumar, Vidya. "A *Proleptic* Approach to Postcolonial Legal Studies? A Brief Look at the Relationship between Legal Theory and Intellectual History" 2003:2 L, Social Justice & Global Development J, online: <warwick.ac.uk/fac/soc/law/elj/lgd/2003_2/kumar/>.

Leiter, Brian. "Naturalizing Jurisprudence: Three Approaches" University of Chicago Public Law & Legal Theory Working Paper No. 246 (2008), online: <chicagounbound.uchicago.edu/cgi/viewcontent.cgi?article=1200&context=public_law_and_legal_theory>.

Little Bear, Leroy. "A Concept of Native Title" (1982) 5 Can Legal Aid Bull 99.

Lyon, Noel. "An Essay on Constitutional Interpretation" (1988) 26 Osgoode Hall LJ 95.

Lyons, Oren. "Indian Self-Government in the Haudenosaunee Constitution" (1986) 55 Nordic J Int'l L 117.

MacArthur, David. "Naturalizing the Human or Humanizing Nature: Science, Nature and the Supernatural" (2004) 61 Erkenntnis 29.

McKay, Ian. "The Liberal Order Framework: A Prospectus for a Reconnaissance of Canadian History" (2000) 81(4) CHR 616.

McNeil, Kent. "The Vulnerability of Indigenous Land Rights in Australia and Canada" (2004) 42 Osgoode Hall LJ 271.
Moore, Michael S. "The Interpretive Turn in Modern Theory: A Turn for the Worse?" (1989) 41 Stan L Rev 871.
Murphy, Michael. "Prisons of Culture: Judicial Constructions of Indigenous Rights in Australia, Canada, and New Zealand" (2008) 87 Can Bar Rev 357.
Newman, Dwight. "You Still Know Nothin' 'Bout Me: Toward Cross-Cultural Theorizing of Aboriginal Rights" (2007) 52 McGill LJ 725.
Petersen, Nicole. "Aboriginal Title in Canada: The Standard of Occupation at Issue in William v. British Columbia" (2013), online: <papers.ssrn.com/sol3/papers.cfm?abstract_id=2394594>.
Quine, WV. "Two Dogmas of Empiricism" (1951) 60 Phil Rev 23.
Raz, Joseph. "Multiculturalism: A Liberal Perspective" (1994) 41 Dissent.
Ridge, Michael. "Moral Non-Naturalism," *Stanford Encyclopedia of Philosophy Archive* (Fall 2014), Edward N Zalta, ed, online: <plato.stanford.edu/archives/fall2014/entries/moral-non-naturalism>.
Rodriguez-Blanco, Veronica. "A Defence of Hart's Semantics as Nonambitious Conceptual Analysis" (2003) 9:2 Legal Theory 99.
Shapiro, Scott. "The Hart-Dworkin Debate: A Short Guide for the Perplexed" (2007), online: <ssrn.com/abstract=968657>.
Slattery, Brian. "Aboriginal Sovereignty and Imperial Claims" (1991) 29 Osgoode Hall LJ 681.
– "Making Sense of Aboriginal and Treaty Rights" (2000) 79 Can Bar Rev 196.
– "The Metamorphosis of Aboriginal Title" (2006) 85 Can Bar Rev 255.
– "Understanding Aboriginal Rights" (1987) 66 Can Bar Rev 727.
Stk'emlúpsemc te Secwépemc Nation. "Honouring Our Sacred Connection to Pípsell" (n.d.), online: <https://stkemlups.ca/files/2013/11/2017-03-ssnajaxdecisionsummary_0.pdf>.
Tamanaha, Brian. "The Folly of the 'Social Scientific' Concept of Legal Pluralism" (1993) 20:2 J L & Soc 192.
Turpel, Mary Ellen. "Aboriginal Peoples and the Canadian Charter: Interpretive Monopolies, Cultural Differences" (1989–90) 1989 Can Hum Rts YB 3.
Vermette, Darcy. "Colonialism and the Process of Defining Aboriginal People" (2008) 31 Dal LJ 211.
– "Colonialism and the Suppression of Aboriginal Voice" (2009) 40 Ottawa L Rev 225.
– "Dizzying Dialogue: Canadian Courts and the Continuing Justification of the Dispossession of Aboriginal Peoples" (2011) 29 Windsor YB Access Just 243.
Waldron, Jeremy. "Redressing Historic Injustice" (2002) 52 UTLJ 135.
– "Superseding Historic Injustice" (1992) 103(1) Ethics 4.
– "Supersession and Sovereignty" (2006) New York University Public Law and Legal Theory Working Papers, Paper 406.

Walters, Mark. "British Imperial Constitutional Law and Aboriginal Rights: A Comment on *Delgamuukw v. British Columbia*" (1992) 17 Queen's LJ 350.
– "The 'Golden Thread' of Continuity: Aboriginal Customs at Common Law and under the *Constitution Act, 1982*" (1999) 44 McGill LJ 711.
– "Histories of Colonialism, Legality, and Aboriginality" (2007) 57 UTLJ 819 at 829.
Walters, Mark D. "The Morality of Aboriginal Law" (2006) 31 Queen's LJ 470.

Texts

Adams, Howard. *Prison of Grass: Canada from a Native Point of View*. Saskatoon, SK: Fifth House, 1989.
Alfred, Taiaiake. *Peace, Power, Righteousness: An Indigenous Manifesto*. Don Mills, ON: Oxford University Press, 1999.
– *Wasáse: Indigenous Pathways of Action and Freedom*. Peterborough, ON: Broadview Press, 2005.
Altamirano-Jiménez, Isabel. *Indigenous Encounters with Neoliberalism: Place, Women, and the Environment in Canada and Mexico*. Vancouver: UBC Press, 2013.
Andersen, Chris. *"Métis": Race, Recognition, and the Struggle for Indigenous Peoplehood*. Vancouver: UBC Press, 2014.
Aquinas, Thomas. *The Summa Theologica*, online: <http://www.documentacatholicaomnia.eu/03d/1225-1274,_Thomas_Aquinas,_Summa_Theologiae_%5B1%5D,_EN.pdf>.
Asch, Michael, ed. *Aboriginal and Treaty Rights in Canada: Essays on Law, Equality, and Respect for Difference*. Vancouver: UBC Press, 1998.
– *Home and Native Land: Aboriginal Rights and the Canadian Constitution*. Toronto: Methuen, 1984.
– *On Being Here to Stay: Treaties and Aboriginal Rights in Canada*. Toronto: University of Toronto Press, 2014.
Austin, John. *The Province of Jurisprudence Determined*. Cambridge, UK: Cambridge University Press, 1995.
Ayer, AJ. *Language, Truth, and Logic*. London: Gollancz, 1936.
Aylward, Carol. *Canadian Critical Race Theory: Racism and the Law*. Halifax: Fernwood, 1998.
Bastien, Betty. *Blackfoot Ways of Knowing: The Worldview of the Siksikaitsitapi*. Calgary: University of Calgary Press, 2004.
Baumeister, Andrea. *Liberalism and the "Politics of Difference."* Edinburgh: Edinburgh University Press, 2000.
Berlin, Brent & Paul Kay. *Basic Color Terms: Their Universality and Evolution*. Berkeley: University of California Press, 1969.
Berlin, Isaiah. *Four Essays on Liberty*. Oxford: Oxford University Press, 1969.
– *Two Concepts of Liberty*. Oxford: Oxford University Press, 1958.
Bhabha, Homi. *The Location of Culture*. London: Routledge, 2004.

Bix, Brian. *Jurisprudence: Theory and Context*, 2nd ed. London: Sweet & Maxwell, 1999.

Bockstoce, John. *Whales, Ice, and Men: The History of Whaling in the Western Arctic*. Seattle: University of Washington Press, 1986.

Bodin, Jean. *Les Six Livres de la République* (1576), online: <gallica.bnf.fr/ark:/12148/btv1b86268103/f13.image>.

Borrows, John. *Canada's Indigenous Constitution*. Toronto: University of Toronto Press, 2010.

– *Recovering Canada: The Resurgence of Indigenous Law*. Toronto: University of Toronto Press, 2002.

Bracken, Christopher. *The Potlatch Papers: A Colonial Case History*. Chicago: University of Chicago Press, 1997.

Brown, Melissa, ed. *Explaining Culture Scientifically*. Seattle: University of Washington Press, 2008.

Cardinal, Harold. *The Unjust Society: The Tragedy of Canada's Indians*. Vancouver: Douglas & McIntyre, 1999.

Carnap, Rudolf. *Logical Foundations of Probability*. Chicago: University of Chicago Press, 1950.

Carroll, John B, ed. *Language, Thought, and Reality: Selected Writings of Benjamin Lee Whorf*. Cambridge, MA: MIT Press, 1956.

Cartwright, Nancy. *The Dappled World: A Study of the Boundaries of Science*. Cambridge, UK: Cambridge University Press, 1999.

Cassidy, Frank, ed. *Aboriginal Title in British Columbia: Delgamuukw v. The Queen*. Fernie, BC: Oolichan Books, 1992.

Césaire, Aimé. *Discourse on Colonialism*, translated by Joan Pinkham. New York: Monthly Review Press, 2001.

Constant, Jean-Francois & Michel Ducharme, eds. *Liberalism and Hegemony: Debating the Canadian Liberal Revolution*. Toronto: University of Toronto Press, 2009.

Copernici, Nicolai. *De Revolutionibus* (1543), online: <loc.gov/item/46031925>.

Copp, David. *Morality in a Natural World: Selected Essays in Metaethics*. Cambridge, UK: Cambridge University Press, 2007.

Coulthard, Glen Sean. *Red Skin, White Mask: Rejecting the Colonial Politics of Recognition*. Minneapolis: University of Minnesota Press, 2014.

Crowder, George. *Liberalism and Value Pluralism*. London: Continuum, 2002.

Davies, Margaret. *Asking the Law Question*, 3rd ed. Sydney: Thomson Reuters, 2008.

Deloria, Vine. *God Is Red: A Native View of Religion*. Golden, CO: Fulcrum, 2003.

Descartes, René. *Meditations on First Philosophy*, vol 2, translated by Elizabeth Haldane & GRT Ross. Cambridge, UK: Cambridge University Press, 1911.

Descartes, René. *Meditations on First Philosophy*, translated by John Cottingham. Cambridge, UK: Cambridge University Press, 1996.

Dickason, Olive & David McNab. *Canada's First Nations: A History of Founding Peoples from Earliest Times*, 4th ed. Don Mills, ON: Oxford University Press, 2009.

Dickson, Jamie. *The Honour and Dishonour of the Crown: Making Sense of Aboriginal Law in Canada*. Saskatoon: Purich, 2015.

Duhem, Pierre. *The Aim and Structure of Physical Theory*, translated by Philip Wiener. Princeton, NJ: Princeton University Press, 1954.

Durkheim, Émile. *The Rules of Sociological Method*, ed by George Catlin, translated by Sarah Solovay & John Mueller, 8th ed. New York: Free Press, 1938.

Dworkin, Ronald. *Justice for Hedgehogs*. Cambridge, MA: Harvard University Press, 2011.

– *Law's Empire*. Cambridge, MA: Harvard University Press, 1988.

– *A Matter of Principle*. Cambridge, MA: Harvard University Press, 1985.

– *Sovereign Virtue: The Theory and Practice of Equality*. Cambridge, MA: Harvard University Press, 2000.

– *Taking Rights Seriously*. Cambridge, MA: Harvard University Press, 1978.

Eber, Dorothy Harley. *When the Whalers Were Up North: Inuit Memories from the Eastern Arctic*. Montreal & Kingston: McGill-Queen's University Press, 1989.

Eisenberg, Avigail, ed. *Diversity and Equality: The Changing Framework of Freedom in Canada*. Vancouver: UBC Press, 2006.

Fanon, Frantz. *Black Skin, White Masks*. New York: Grove Press, 1952.

– *The Wretched of the Earth*. New York: Grove Press, 1963.

Feyerabend, Paul. *Against Method: Outline of an Anarchistic Theory of Knowledge*. Atlantic Highlands, NJ: Humanities Press, 1975.

Finnis, John. *Natural Law and Natural Rights*. Oxford: Clarendon Press, 1980.

Finocchiaro, Maurice. *Arguments about Arguments: Systematic, Critical, and Historical Essays in Logical Theory*. Cambridge, UK: Cambridge University Press, 2005.

Fischer, Louis, ed. *The Essential Gandhi: An Anthology of His Writings on His Life, Work, and Ideas*. New York: Vintage Books, 1962.

Fisher, Robin. *Contact and Conflict: Indian-European Relations in British Columbia, 1774–1890*. Vancouver: University of British Columbia Press, 1977.

Flanagan, Thomas. *First Nations? Second Thoughts*. Montreal & Kingston: McGill-Queen's University Press, 2000.

Foucault, Michel. *The Order of Things: An Archaeology of the Human Sciences*. New York: Pantheon Books, 1970.

Fuller, Lon. *The Morality of Law*. New Haven, CT: Yale University Press, 1969.

Galston, William. *Liberal Pluralism: The Implications of Value Pluralism for Political Theory and Practice*. Cambridge, UK: Cambridge University Press, 2002.

– *The Practice of Liberal Pluralism*. Cambridge, UK: Cambridge University Press, 2005.

Gandhi, Leela. *Postcolonial Theory: A Critical Introduction*. St Leonards: Allen & Unwin, 1998.

Gavison, Ruth, ed. *Issues in Contemporary Legal Philosophy: The Influence of H.L.A. Hart*. Oxford: Clarendon Press, 1987.

Geertz, Clifford. *Local Knowledge: Further Essays in Interpretive Anthropology*. New York: Basic Books, 1983.

Gibson, Gordon. *A New Look at Canadian Indian Policy: Respect the Collective – Promote the Individual.* Vancouver: Fraser Institute, 2009.

Godfrey-Smith, Peter. *Theory and Reality: An Introduction to the Philosophy of Science.* Chicago: University of Chicago Press, 2003.

Golding, Martin & William Edmundson, eds. *The Blackwell Guide to the Philosophy of Law and Legal Theory.* Oxford: Blackwell Publishing, 2005.

Goodman, Nelson. *Ways of Worldmaking.* Indianapolis: Hackett, 1978.

Grammond, Sebastien. *Terms of Coexistence: Indigenous Peoples and Canadian Law.* Toronto: Carswell, 2013.

Gray, John. *Isaiah Berlin.* New York: Harper Collins, 1995.

Greene, Brian. *The Elegant Universe: Superstrings, Hidden Dimensions, and the Quest for the Ultimate Theory.* New York: WW Norton, 1999.

Guha, Ranajit. *Dominance without Hegemony: History and Power in Colonial India.* Cambridge, MA: Harvard University Press, 1997.

Gumperz, John J & Stephen Levinson, eds. *Rethinking Linguistic Relativity: Studies in the Foundation of Language.* Cambridge, UK: Cambridge University Press, 1996.

Hacking, Ian. *The Social Construction of What?* Cambridge, MA: Harvard University Press, 1999.

Harris, Cole. *Making Native Space: Colonialism, Resistance, and Reserves in British Columbia.* Vancouver: UBC Press, 2002.

Harris, Doug. *Fish, Law, and Colonialism: The Legal Capture of Salmon in British Columbia.* Toronto: University of Toronto Press, 2001.

Hart, HLA. *The Concept of Law.* Oxford: Oxford University Press, 1961.

– *The Concept of Law*, 2nd ed. Oxford: Clarendon Press, 1994.

– *The Concept of Law*, 3rd ed. Oxford: Oxford University Press, 2012.

Helin, Calvin. *Dances with Dependency: Out of Poverty through Self-Reliance.* Woodland Hills, CA: Ravencrest, 2008.

Hempel, Carl. *Aspects of Scientific Explanation and Other Essays in the Philosophy of Science.* New York: Free Press, 1965.

Henderson, James Youngblood (Sakej). *First Nations Jurisprudence and Aboriginal Rights: Defining the Just Society.* Saskatoon, SK: Native Law Centre, 2006.

Hobbes, Thomas. *Leviathan* (1651), online: <gutenberg.org/files/3207/3207-h/3207-h.htm>.

Horgan, John. *The End of Science: Facing the Limits of Knowledge in the Twilight of the Scientific Age.* Reading, MA: Addison-Wesley, 1996.

Isaac, Thomas. *Aboriginal Law: Commentary and Analysis*, 4th ed. Saskatoon, SK: Purich, 2012).

– *Aboriginal Law: Commentary and Analysis*, 5th ed. Toronto: Carswell, 2016.

Ivison, Duncan. *Postcolonial Liberalism.* Cambridge, UK: Cambridge University Press, 2002.

Jaggar, Alison. *Feminist Politics and Human Nature.* Totowa, NJ: Rowman & Littlefield, 1983.

James, William. *The Principles of Psychology*. New York: Henry Holt & Company, 1890.

Kelsen, Hans. *Pure Theory of Law*, translated by Max Knight. Berkeley: University of California Press, 1967.

Kepler, Johannes. *Astronomia Nova* (1609), online: <e-rara.ch/doi/10.3931/e-rara-558>.

Kitcher, Phillip. *The Advancement of Science: Science without Legend, Objectivity without Illusions*. Oxford: Oxford University Press, 1993.

Kornblith, Hilary. *Knowledge and Its Place in Nature*. Oxford: Oxford University Press, 2002.

Kuhn, Thomas. *The Copernican Revolution: Planetary Astronomy in the Development of Western Thought*. Cambridge, MA: Harvard University Press, 1957.

– *The Structure of Scientific Revolutions*. Chicago: University of Chicago Press, 1962.

Kymlicka, Will. *Contemporary Political Philosophy: An Introduction*, 2nd ed. Oxford: Oxford University Press, 2002.

– *Liberalism, Community and Culture*. Oxford: Oxford University Press, 1989.

– *Multicultural Citizenship: A Liberal Theory of Minority Rights*. Oxford: Oxford University Press, 1995.

– *Multicultural Odysseys: Navigating the New International Politics of Diversity*. Oxford: Oxford University Press, 2007.

Kymlicka, Will & Bashir Bashir, eds. *The Politics of Reconciliation in Multicultural Societies*. Oxford: Oxford University Press, 2008.

Lakatos, Imre & Alan Musgrave, eds. *Criticism and the Growth of Knowledge*. Cambridge, UK: Cambridge University Press, 1970.

Latour, Bruno & Steve Woolgar. *Laboratory Life: The Social Construction of Scientific Facts*. Beverly Hills, CA: Sage Publications, 1979.

Laudan, Larry. *Progress and Its Problems: Toward a Theory of Scientific Growth*. Berkeley: University of California Press, 1977.

Leiter, Brian. *Naturalizing Jurisprudence: Essays on American Legal Realism and Naturalism in Legal Philosophy*. Oxford: Oxford University Press, 2007.

Lett, James. *Science, Reason, and Anthropology: The Principles of Rational Inquiry*. Lanham, MD: Rowman & Littlefield, 1997.

Llewellyn, Karl & E Adamson Hoebel. *The Cheyenne Way*. Norman: University of Oklahoma Press, 1941.

Mackenzie, Catriona & Natalie Stoljar, eds. *Relational Autonomy: Feminist Perspectives on Autonomy, Agency, and the Social Self*. New York: Oxford University Press, 2000.

Macklem, Patrick. *Indigenous Difference and the Constitution of Canada*. Toronto: University of Toronto Press, 2001.

Macklem, Patrick & Douglas Sanderson, eds. *From Recognition to Reconciliation: Essays on the Constitutional Entrenchment of Aboriginal and Treaty Rights*. Toronto: University of Toronto Press, 2016.

MacPherson, CB. *The Life and Times of Liberal Democracy*. Oxford: Oxford University Press, 1977.

Magnet, Joseph E & Dwight A Dorey, eds. *Aboriginal Rights Litigation*. Markham, ON: Butterworths, 2003.

Malinowski, Bronislaw. *Crime and Custom in Savage Society*. New York: Harcourt, Brace & Co, 1926), online: <archive.org/details/crimecustominsav00mali>.

Malotki, Ekkehart. *Hopi Time: A Linguistic Analysis of the Temporal Concepts in the Hopi Language*. Berlin: Mouton, 1983.

Manuel, Arthur & Ronald Derrickson. *Unsettling Canada: A National Wake-Up Call*. Toronto: Between the Lines, 2015.

Mbembe, Achille. *On the Postcolony*. Berkeley: University of California Press, 2001.

McCann, MW. *Rights at Work: Pay Equity Reform and the Politics of Legal Mobilization*. Chicago: University of Chicago Press, 1994.

McHugh, Paul. *Aboriginal Societies and the Common Law: A History of Sovereignty, Status, and Self-Determination*. Oxford: Oxford University Press, 2004.

McNeil, Kent. *Defining Aboriginal Title in the 90's: Has the Supreme Court Finally Got It Right?* Toronto: Robarts Centre for Canadian Studies, 1998.

– *Emerging Justice? Essays on Indigenous Rights in Canada and Australia*. Saskatoon, SK: Native Law Centre, 2001.

Mercredi, Ovide & Mary Ellen Turpel. *In the Rapids: Navigating the Future of First Nations*. Toronto: Penguin Books, 1994.

Miller, JR. *Compact, Contract, Covenant: Aboriginal Treaty-Making in Canada*. Toronto: University of Toronto Press, 2009.

– *Skyscrapers Hide the Heavens: A History of Indian-White Relations in Canada*, 3rd ed. Toronto: University of Toronto Press, 2000.

–, ed. *Sweet Promises: A Reader on Indian-White Relations in Canada*. Toronto: University of Toronto Press, 1991.

Minda, Gary. *Postmodern Legal Movements: Law and Jurisprudence at Century's End*. New York: New York University Press, 1996.

Minow, Martha, Michael Ryan & Austin Sarat, eds. *Narrative, Violence, and the Law: The Essays of Robert Cover*. Ann Arbor: University of Michigan Press, 1992.

Monture-Angus, Patricia. *Journeying Forward: Dreaming First Nations' Independence*. Halifax: Fernwood, 1999.

Moore, GE. *Principia Ethica*. Cambridge, UK: Cambridge University Press, 1903.

Moore, Kathleen Dean et al, eds. *How It Is: The Native American Philosophy of V.F. Cordova*. Tucson: University of Arizona Press, 2007.

Morellato, Maria, ed. *Aboriginal Law since Delgamuukw*. Aurora, ON: Canada Law Book, 2009.

Morris, Alexander. *The Treaties of Canada with the Indians of Manitoba and the North-West Territories, Including the Negotiations on Which They Were Based, and Other Information Relating Thereto*. Toronto: Belfords, Clarke & Co, 1880.

Nagel, Thomas. *The View from Nowhere*. Oxford: Oxford University Press, 1986.

Nandy, A. *The Intimate Enemy: Loss and Recovery of Self under Colonialism*. Oxford: Oxford University Press, 1983.

Newman, Dwight. *Revisiting the Duty to Consult Aboriginal Peoples*. Saskatoon, SK: Purich, 2014.

Nietzsche, Friedrich. *Beyond Good and Evil: Prelude to a Philosophy of the Future*. New York: Dover Publications, 1997.

Norris, Christopher. *On Truth and Meaning: Language, Logic, and the Grounds of Belief*. London: Continuum International, 2006.

– *Truth Matters: Realism, Anti-Realism and Response Dependence*. Edinburgh: Edinburgh University Press, 2002.

Nozick, Robert. *Anarchy, State, and Utopia*. New York: Basic Books, 1974.

Oosten, Jarich et al, eds. *Interviewing Inuit Elders*. Iqaluit: Nunavut Arctic College, 1999.

Parry, Benita. *Postcolonial Studies: A Materialist Critique*. London: Routledge, 2004.

Pettit, Philip. *A Theory of Freedom: From the Psychology to the Politics of Agency*. Oxford: Oxford University Press, 2001.

Pointing, Rick J, ed. *Arduous Journey: Canadian Indians and Decolonization*. Toronto: McClelland & Stewart, 1986.

Popper, Karl. *The Logic of Scientific Discovery*. New York: Basic Books, 1959.

Quine, WV. *From a Logical Point of View: Nine Logico-Philosophical Essays*, 2nd ed. Cambridge, MA: Harvard University Press, 1980.

– *Theories and Things*. Cambridge, MA: Harvard University Press, 1981.

Rawls, John. *Justice as Fairness: A Restatement*. Cambridge, MA: Belknap Press, 2001.

– *Political Liberalism*. New York: Columbia University Press, 1996.

– *A Theory of Justice*. Cambridge, MA: Belknap Press, 1971.

– *A Theory of Justice*, 2nd ed. Cambridge, MA: Belknap Press, 1999.

Ray, Arthur. *I Have Lived Here since the World Began: An Illustrated History of Canada's Native People*. Toronto: Key Porter Books, 1996.

Raz, Joseph. *The Authority of Law: Essays on Law and Morality*. Oxford: Oxford University Press, 1979.

– *Ethics in the Public Domain: Essays in the Morality of Law and Politics*. Oxford: Oxford University Press, 1996.

Reynolds, Jim. *Aboriginal Peoples and the Law: A Critical Introduction*. Vancouver: UBC Press, 2018.

Ritchie, Jack. *Understanding Naturalism*. Stocksfield, UK: Acumen Press, 2008.

Romanow, Roy, John Whyte & Howard Leeson. *Canada ... Notwithstanding: The Making of the Constitution 1976–1982*. Toronto: Carswell, 1984.

Rorty, Richard. *Philosophy and the Mirror of Nature*. Princeton, NJ: Princeton University Press, 1981.

Russell, Paul & Oisin Deery, eds. *The Philosophy of Free Will: Essential Readings from the Contemporary Debates*. Oxford: Oxford University Press, 2013.

Russell, Peter H. *Recognizing Aboriginal Title: The Mabo Case and Indigenous Resistance to English-Settler Colonialism*. Toronto: University of Toronto Press, 2005.

Ryan, Alan. *The Making of Modern Liberalism*. Princeton, NJ: Princeton University Press, 2012.

Said, Edward. *Culture and Imperialism*. New York: Vintage Books, 1993.
– *Orientalism*. New York: Pantheon Books, 1978.
Salmon, Wesley. *Scientific Explanation and the Causal Structure of the World*. Princeton, NJ: Princeton University Press, 1984.
Sandel, Michael. *Liberalism and the Limits of Justice*. Cambridge, UK: Cambridge University Press, 1982.
Sayre-McCord, Geoffrey. *Essays on Moral Realism*. Ithaca, NY: Cornell University Press, 1988.
Schouls, Tim. *Shifting Boundaries: Aboriginal Identity, Pluralist Theory, and the Politics of Self-Government*. Vancouver: UBC Press, 2003.
Searle, John. *Making the Social World: The Structure of Human Civilization*. Oxford: Oxford University Press, 2010.
Simpson, Audra. *Mohawk Interruptus: Political Life across the Borders of Settler States*. Durham, NC: Duke University Press, 2014.
Simpson, Bob et al, eds. *Taimani: At That Time*. Inuvik, NWT: Inuvialuit Regional Corporation, 2011, online: <issuu.com/itvg/docs/taimani>.
Simpson, Leanne Betasamosake. *Dancing on Our Turtle's Back: Stories of Nishnaabeg Re-Creation, Resurgence and a New Emergence*. Winnipeg: Arbeiter Ring Publishing, 2011.
Smith, Barry, ed. *John Searle*. Cambridge, UK: Cambridge University Press, 2003.
Smith, Linda Tuhiwai. *Decolonizing Methodologies: Research and Indigenous Peoples*. London: Zed Books, 2012.
Soames, Scott. *What Is Meaning?* Princeton, NJ: Princeton University Press, 2010.
Sokal, Alan. *Beyond the Hoax: Science, Philosophy and Culture*. Oxford: Oxford University Press, 2008.
Spivak, Gayatri Chakravorty. "Can the Subaltern Speak?" in Cary Nelson & Lawrence Grossberg, eds, *Marxism and the Interpretation of Culture*. Champaign: University of Illinois Press, 1988.
Taylor, Charles. *Hegel*. Cambridge, UK: Cambridge University Press, 1975.
Teillet, Jean. *Métis Law in Canada*. Vancouver: Pape Salter Teillet, 2013, online: <pstlaw.ca/publications.html>.
Tennant, Paul. *Aboriginal Peoples and Politics: The Indian Land Question in British Columbia, 1849–1989*. Vancouver: UBC Press, 1990.
Tomsons, Sandra & Lorraine Mayer, eds. *Philosophy and Aboriginal Rights: Critical Dialogues*. Don Mills, ON: Oxford University Press, 2013.
Treaty 7 Elders et al. *The True Spirit and Original Intent of Treaty 7*, ed by Walter Hildebrandt. Montreal & Kingston: McGill-Queen's University Press, 1996.
Tully, James. *Strange Multiplicity: Constitutionalism in an Age of Diversity*. Cambridge, UK: Cambridge University Press, 1995.
Unger, Roberto. *Knowledge and Politics*. New York: Free Press, 1984.
Van Fraassen, Bas. *The Scientific Image*. Oxford: Oxford University Press, 1980.
– *Scientific Representation: Paradoxes of Perspective*. Oxford: Clarendon Press, 2008.

Velleman, J David. *Foundations for Moral Relativism*. Cambridge, UK: Open Book, 2013.

Walkem, Ardith & Halie Bruce, eds. *Box of Treasures or Empty Box? Twenty Years of Section 35*. Penticton, BC: Theytus Press, 2003.

Weinberg, Steven. *Dreams of a Final Theory: The Scientist's Search for the Ultimate Laws of Nature*. New York: Pantheon Books, 1992.

Widdowson, Frances & Albert Howard. *Disrobing the Aboriginal Industry: The Deception behind Indigenous Cultural Preservation*. Montreal & Kingston: McGill-Queen's University Press, 2008.

Wilkins, Kerry, ed. *Advancing Aboriginal Claims: Visions/Strategies/Directions*. Saskatoon, SK: Purich, 2004.

Wilkins, Kerry. *Essentials of Canadian Aboriginal Law*. Toronto: Carswell, 2018.

Williamson, Pamela & John Roberts. *First Nations Peoples*, 2nd ed. Toronto: Edmond Montgomery Publications, 2004.

Wilson, Edward. *Sociobiology: The New Synthesis*. Cambridge, MA: Harvard University Press, 1975.

Woo, Grace Li Xiu. *Ghost Dancing with Colonialism: Decolonization and Indigenous Rights at the Supreme Court of Canada*. Vancouver: UBC Press, 2011.

Government Documents

Canada, Crown-Indigenous Relations and Northern Affairs Canada. "Treaties, Agreements and Negotiations" (2012), online: <rcaanc-cirnac.gc.ca/eng/1100100028568/1529354090684>.

– "The Government of Canada's Response to the Descheneaux Decision" (2016), online: <aadnc-aandc.gc.ca/eng/1467227680166/1467227697623>.

Canada, Department of Justice. "Indigenous Peoples" (2018), online: <justice.gc.ca/eng/rp-pr/aj-ja/index.html>.

Canada, Indian and Northern Affairs. *Statement of the Government of Canada on Indian Policy*. Ottawa: Department of Indian and Northern Affairs, 1969, online: <aadnc-aandc.gc.ca/DAM/DAM-INTER-HQ/STAGING/texte-text/cp1969_1100100010190_eng.pdf>.

Canada, Office of the Correctional Investigator. "Backgrounder: Aboriginal Offenders – A Critical Situation" (2013), online: <oci-bec.gc.ca/cnt/rpt/oth-aut/oth-aut20121022info-eng.aspx>.

Canada, Royal Commission on Aboriginal Peoples. *Report of the Royal Commission on Aboriginal Peoples*, vol 2. Ottawa: Minister of Supply and Services, 1996.

Council of Ministers of Education, Canada. "Publications," online: <cmec.ca/9/Publications/index.html?searchCat=1>.

Crown-Indigenous Relations and Northern Affairs Canada. "The Reporting Guide" (2019), online: <aadnc-aandc.gc.ca/eng/1385559716700/1385559777677>.

Employment and Social Development Canada. "Reports and Publications" (2018), online: <canada.ca/en/employment-social-development/corporate/reports.html>.

Health Canada. "Reports and Publications: First Nations and Inuit Health" (2018), online: <canada.ca/en/indigenous-services-canada/services/first-nations-inuit-health/reports-publications.html>.

Isaac, Thomas, Indigenous and Northern Affairs Canada. "A Matter of National and Constitutional Import: Report of the Minister's Special Representative on Reconciliation with Metis: Section 35 Metis Rights and the *Manitoba Metis Federation* Decision." Ottawa: Ministry of Indigenous and Northern Affairs, 2016, online: <publications.gc.ca/collections/collection_2016/aanc-inac/R5-123-2016-eng.pdf>.

Statistics Canada. "Aboriginal Peoples: Key Indicators" (2019), online: <www150.statcan.gc.ca/n1/en/subjects/aboriginal_peoples>.

– "Inuit in Canada: Selected Findings of the 2006 Census." Ottawa, Statistics Canada, 2008, online: <statcan.gc.ca/pub/11-008-x/2008002/article/10712-eng.htm>.

– "2006 Census: Aboriginal Peoples in Canada in 2006: Inuit, Métis and First Nations, 2006 Census: Findings." Ottawa: Statistics Canada, 2008, online: <www12.statcan.ca/census-recensement/2006/as-sa/97-558/index-eng.cfm?CFID=363213&CFTOKEN=81818789>.

Truth and Reconciliation Commission of Canada. *Honouring the Truth, Reconciling for the Future: Summary of the Final Report of the Truth and Reconciliation Commission of Canada* (2015), online: <http://www.chaireconditionautochtone.fss.ulaval.ca/documents/pdf/Honouring-the-truth-reconciling-for-the-future.pdf>.

Truth and Reconciliation Commission. "TRC Findings" (2015), online: https://nctr.ca/reports2.php.

Wilson-Raybould, Jodie. "Notes for an Address by the Honourable Jody Wilson-Raybould, PC, QC, MP, Minister of Justice and Attorney General of Canada" (speech, Niagara Falls, ON, 12 July 2016), online: <drive.google.com/file/d/0B_bPXJbq-wgWenpoa2NIRmgwT2NlWkx3enNSWXJELTFSSzc4/view>.

International Documents

International Covenant on Civil and Political Rights, 19 December 1966, 999 UNTS 171, Can TS 1976 No 47 (entered into force 23 March 1976).

UNGA. *United Nations Declaration on the Rights of Indigenous Peoples*, UNGAOR, 61st Sess, Supp No 49, UN Doc A/RES/61/295 (13 September 2007).

Other Documents

Barrera, Jorge. "Justice Minister Wilson-Raybould Tells AFN to Prepare for Future beyond the Indian Act," *APTN National News* (25 July 2017), online: <aptnnews.ca/2017/07/25/justice-minister-wilson-raybould-tells-afn-to-prepare-for-future-beyond-the-indian-act/>.

Canadian Council on Social Development, online: <ccsd.ca>.

First Nations Information Governance Centre, online: <fnigc.ca>.

Indigenous Bar Association. "Bill S-3 *An Act to Amend the Indian Act (Elimination of Sex-Based Inequities in Registration*" (24 April 2017), online: <indigenousbar.ca/pdf/ibc_bill_S-3.pdf> at 29.

Innu Nation, online: <innu.ca>.

Land Claims Agreements Coalition, online: <landclaimscoalition.ca>.

LIGO, online: <ligo.caltech.edu>.

"Lord Glenelg to Sir F.B. Head" (5 October 1836) in *Report on the Indians of Upper Canada by a Sub-Committee of the Aborigines Protection Society*. London: William Ball, Arnold, & Co, 1839, online: <eco.canadiana.ca/view/oocihm.35802/20?r=0&s=1>.

NunatuKavut: Our Ancient Land, online: <nunatukavut.ca/home>.

"Sir Francis Bond Head to Lord Glenelg" (20 August 1836) in *Report on the Indians of Upper Canada by a Sub-Committee of the Aborigines Protection Society*. London: William Ball, Arnold, & Co, 1839, online: <eco.canadiana.ca/view/oocihm.35802/19?r=0&s=1>.

Windspeaker, online: <ammsa.com/category/article-origin/windspeaker>.

Zalta, Edward N, ed. *Stanford Encyclopedia of Philosophy*, online: <plato.stanford.edu>.

Index

www.ingramcontent.com/pod-product-compliance
Lightning Source LLC
LaVergne TN
LVHW090759070826
844660LV00022B/1028
9781442628991